Economics and Personal Finance

Irvin B. Tucker
University of North Carolina
Charlotte

Joan S. Ryan
Clackamas Community College
Portland, Oregon

SOUTH-WESTERN
CENGAGE Learning

Australia • Brazil • Japan • Korea • Mexico • Singapore • Spain • United Kingdom • United States

SOUTH-WESTERN
CENGAGE Learning

Economics and Personal Finance
Irvin B. Tucker, Joan S. Ryan

Vice President of Editorial, Business: Jack W. Calhoun

Vice President/Editor-in-Chief: Karen Schmohe

Executive Editor: Eve Lewis

Senior Developmental Editor: Enid Nagel

Marketing Manager: Kara S. Bombelli

Senior Art Director: Michelle Kunkler

Senior Content Project Manager: Holly Henjum

Media Editor: Sally Nieman

Digital Project Manager: Lynn Vagg

Manufacturing Planner: Kevin Kluck

Rights Acquisition Specialist/Text and Image: Amber Hosea

Editorial Assistant: Anne Merrill

Production Service: Integra Software Services

Internal and Cover Designer: Grannan Design, Ltd.

Cover Images: © Songquan Deng/Shutterstock, © mrPliskin/iStockphoto; © jrroman/iStockphoto; © Masterfile

Library of Congress Control Number: 2012935634

ISBN-13: 978-1-133-56210-8
ISBN-10: 1-133-56210-8

South-Western
5191 Natorp Boulevard
Mason, OH 45040
USA

Cengage Learning products are represented in Canada by Nelson Education, Ltd.

For your course and learning solutions, visit **www.cengage.com/school**
Visit our company website at **www.cengage.com**

Printed in the United States of America
3 4 5 16 15

Reviewers

Andrew Canter
Business Instructor
Farmington High School
Farmington, Missouri

John Dawson
Business Department Chair
Hagerstown Jr. - Sr. High School
Hagerstown, Indiana

Traquel Dayley
Financial Literacy Consultant
Utah State Office of Education
Hurricane, Utah

Frank de Varona
Coordinator
Miami Coral Park Adult Education Center
Miami-Dade County Public Schools
Miami, Florida

David Dieterle
Director
Center for Economic Education
Walsh College
Novi, Michigan

Douglas Haskell
Associate Director
Economics Center for Education & Research
University of Cincinnati
Cincinnati, Ohio

Mark Helmsing
Department of Teacher Education
Michigan State University
East Lansing, Michigan

Martha Kleinfelter
Social Studies Teacher
Live Oaks Career Development Campus
Milford, Ohio

Mark Lyons
Business Department Teacher
East Aurora High School
Aurora, Illinois

Bob McKitrick
Social Studies Department Chair
Parkway North High School
St. Louis, Missouri

Phillip Santa-Maria
Social Studies Teacher
Christopher Columbus High School
Miami, Florida

Gregory Valentine
Director
Center for Economic Education in Southwest Indiana
University of Southern Indiana
Evansville, Indiana

Anthony Zambelli
Director
Center for Economic Education
Cuyamaca College
El Cajon, California

Brief Contents

Contents

About the Authors

Irvin B. Tucker, Ph.D. has more than 30 years of experience teaching introductory economics at the University of North Carolina Charlotte and the University of South Carolina. Dr. Tucker's work has received the Freedoms Foundation of Valley Forge Leavey Award honoring Excellence in Private Enterprise Education and the George Washington Honor Medal for Excellence in Economic Education.

Joan S. Ryan, Ph.D. has taught personal finance for more than 25 years. While teaching at Willamette High School in Eugene, Oregon, she developed the original personal finance course materials for publication. Dr. Ryan currently is a faculty member in the business department at Clackamas Community College, Portland, Oregon. She also teaches accounting at Portland State University and is a Certified Managerial Accountant.

Prepare to master Economics concepts and apply Personal Finance knowledge!

Learn how to live the American Dream with South-Western's *Economics and Personal Finance*. To culminate the Economics curriculum, in one semester, basic economic theories are introduced using practical applications that integrate personal finance concepts. Learn to develop a Free Market way of thinking using personal finance skills both today and tomorrow!

Economics and personal finance knowledge are applied using real-world simulated experiences to complete activities throughout the chapters for each **Unit Project**. Projects reinforce **21st Century Skills** such as:

- Learning and Innovation Skills
- Creativity and Innovation
- Critical Thinking and Problem Solving
- Communication and Collaboration

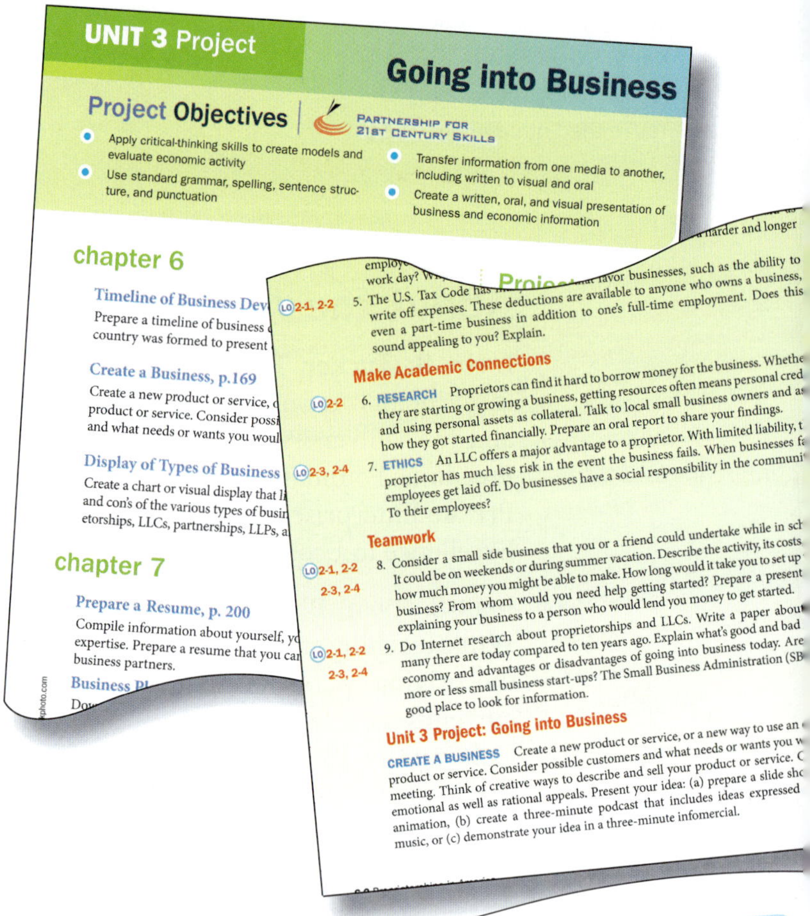

"You are to be congratulated for this new approach to organizing an economics program. I think your text will stand out because it is the most effective way to integrate personal finance by using examples that students can relate to."

~Economics Education Center Director

By reading and analyzing the **Real-World Focus** that opens each lesson, connections are made to help demonstrate why individuals, events, and ideas develop and interact in the world. **Work as a Team** questions help facilitate group discussions.

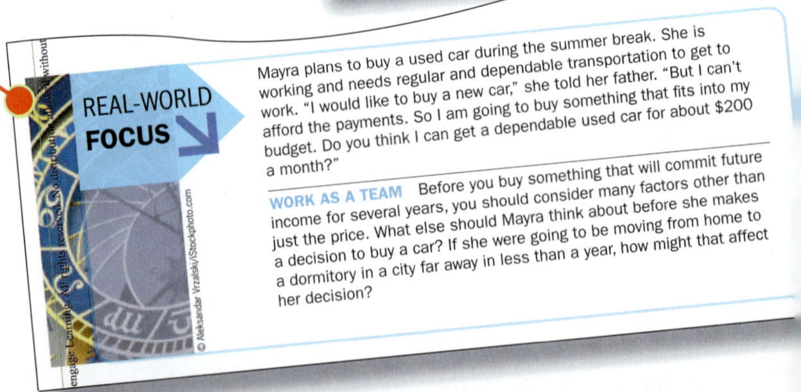

Connected Learning System

DO YOU THINK question provides motivation for learning the lesson.

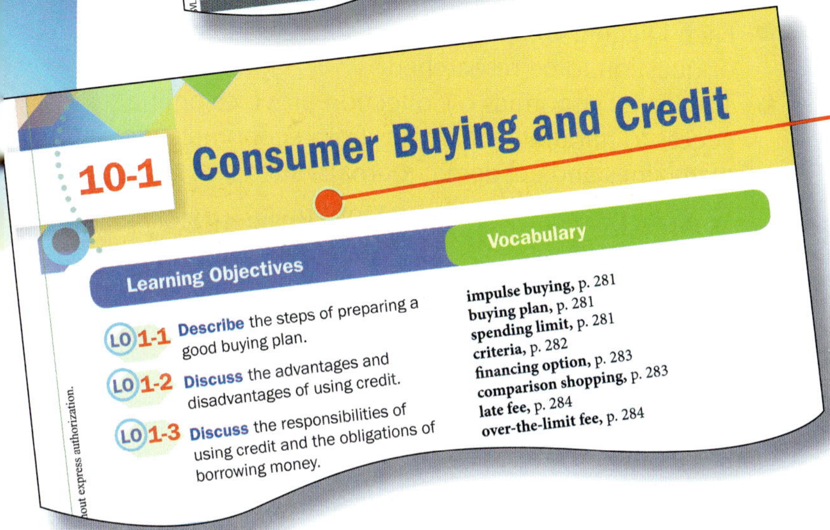

Labeling assessments with **learning objective** numbers ensures mastery.

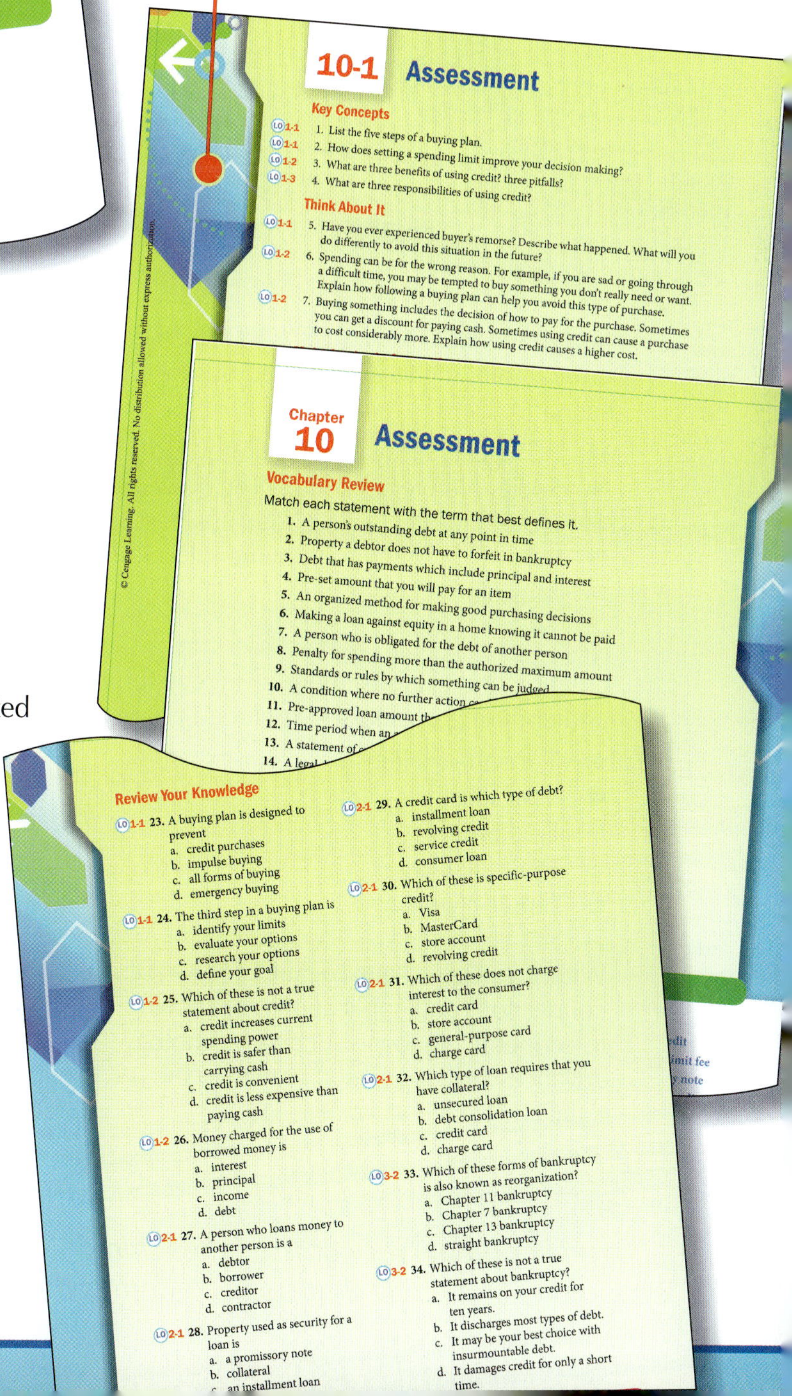

Formative Assessments appear at the end of every lesson and chapter, allowing frequent evaluation of student comprehension and progress.

Lesson Assessments include

- **Key Concepts** Reading comprehension exercises
- **Think About It** Critical-thinking applications
- **Make Academic Connections** Connects content across the curriculum
- **Teamwork** Collaborative learning opportunities
- **Unit Project** Activities to evaluate content presented in diverse formats and media to connect concepts across the unit

Chapter Assessments include

- **Vocabulary Review** Key vocabulary reinforcement for the chapter
- **Review Your Knowledge** Multiple-choice questions
- **Digging Deeper** Activities using the Gale Economics e-Collection
- **Think About It** Application questions
- **Make Academic Connections** Relates economics and personal finance concepts to other courses such as history, mathematics, social studies, and language arts.
- **Extend Your Learning** Higher-level questions

Engaging features throughout the chapters provide scenario/situation discussion opportunities related to real-world economics and business. These features are accompanied by critical-thinking questions to help increase engagement in learning.

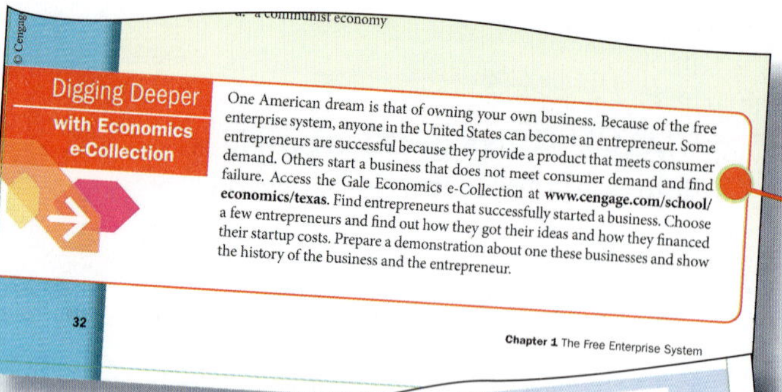

Digging Deeper activities link to an online economics database that allows further investigation of topics by accessing the Gale Economics e-Collection.

- Each Digging Deeper feature includes an activity or question to be researched.
- The Gale Economics e-Collection provides online access to hundreds of articles from economics-focused magazines and academic journals, such as:
  - *NewsUSA*
  - *Newsweek*
  - *USA Today* (Magazine)
  - *The Economist* (US)
  - NPR: Business Story of the Day
  - NPR: Economy
  - *New York Times Magazine*
- The database, which is updated daily, is a convenient method to access relevant information to help keep courses current.

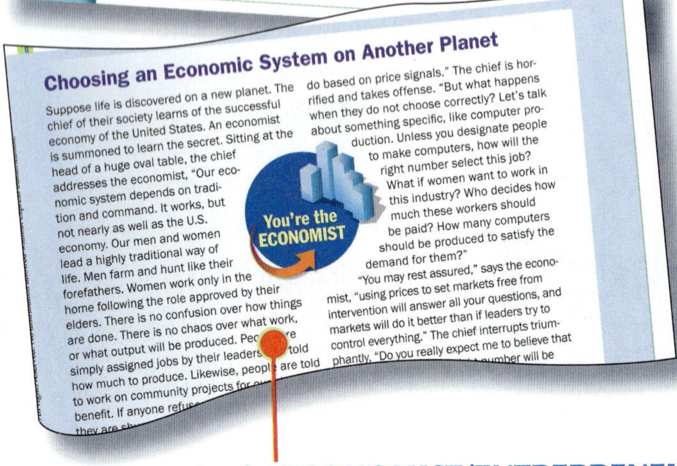

You're the ECONOMIST/ENTREPRENEUR incorporates critical thinking to a described business or economic scenario. Examples include:

- PC Prices. How Low Can They Go?
- Social Networking Sites: The New Advertising Game
- How Can You Protect Your Business Idea?
- What Kind of Unemployment Do Robot Musicians Cause?

MARKETS *in Action!* discusses the creation and establishment of successful, thriving, and enduring businesses. Included are real people, such as:

- T. Boone Pickens
- Vera Wang
- Fred Smith
- Walt Disney
- Oprah Winfrey

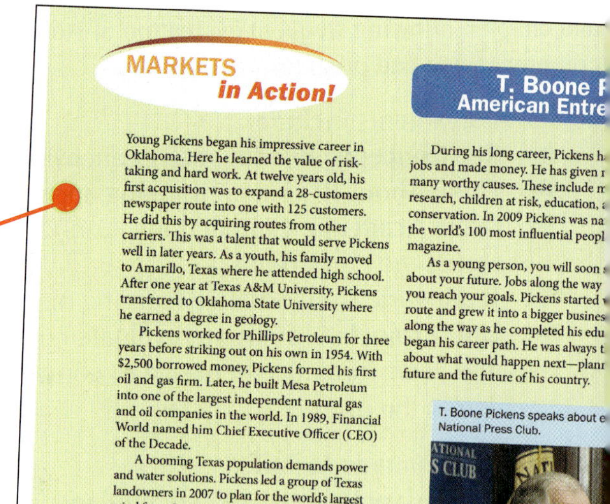

With **Investigate Your Local ECONOMY**, connections and applications are shown to economic concepts such as technology advances and population growth to the local environment.

"Unique content. Very timely in teaching economics. Anything that brings in things the kids understand is good."

~Economics Teacher

Covering Labor Needs

Math CONNECTION

You own a corner convenience market. Your store is open seven days a week, from 6 A.M. to 2 A.M. Each employee works a 6-hour shift. You recently had some employees quit and now you have 4 employees that can each work 5 days a week. Do you need to hire more people and, if so, for how many hours a week?

SOLUTION

Find the number of hours the store is open each week.

6 A.M. to 6 P.M. = 12 hours   6 P.M. to 2 A.M. = 8 hours

20 hours — number of hours open each day
× 7 — number of days open each week
140 hours — total number of hours of labor needed each week

Find the number of hours the employees can work each week.

6 hours — number of hours in a shift
× 5 — number of days worked each week
30 hours — total number of hours one employee works each week

30 hours — number of hours for one employee
× 4 — number of employees

Math **CONNECTION** reinforces math skills. Concepts are covered and practiced using economic scenarios, such as:

- Covering Labor Needs
- Extrapolating Data From a Graph
- Total Revenue
- Compute Unemployment Rate

> *"This brings in real-life math examples."*
>
> **~Economics Teacher**

What Is Bankruptcy Fraud?

ETHICS *in Action!*

When debtors try to hide assets so they cannot be used to pay off debts, this action is *bankruptcy fraud*, a serious crime. For example, if you put your valuables into storage or hide money in offshore bank accounts, this is considered an intentional act to hide assets. When people purposely run up debt with the intention of declaring bankruptcy, they can be accused of defrauding their creditors. In bankruptcy law, revolving or credit card debt must be at least three years old to be discharged without a repayment plan. One way people try to hide assets is by transferring ownership to another person. If discovered, the debtor can be denied bankruptcy protection. Bankruptcy laws are intended as a shield, to help consumers in hopeless situations.

Think Critically

1. Do you think there are people who abuse bankruptcy law? Why would they take such an action?
2. Do you think bankruptcy laws are a good thing to have, or should they be abolished? Why or why not?

(liquidated) and the money is used to repay as much debt as possible. Then all remaining debts (with some exceptions) are discharged.

2. **Chapter 11 bankruptcy** This is known as business reorganization. Businesses filing bankruptcy have the opportunity to retain assets and remain in operation after a plan for reorganization is filed and approved by the court.
3. **Chapter 13 bankruptcy** Also known as *individual debt adjustment*, this plan calls for individuals to enter a repayment plan. It is designed for debtors who have a source of income. Rather than liquidate assets, debtors follow a court-ordered plan to repay as much debt as reasonable over a three- to five-year period. Then remaining balances are discharged, again with exceptions.

Benefits of Bankruptcy

Sometimes bankruptcy is the best choice. For people who have reached their last resort, bankruptcy has several significant benefits:

ETHICS *in Action!* considers ethical scenarios, such as Natural Disasters and Monopoly Power, Are Late Payments Ethical?, What is Bankruptcy Fraud?, Truthful Applications.

Global View

Banco do Brasil (The Bank of Brazil)

The Bank of Brazil, founded in 1808, is the oldest active bank in Brazil, and one of the oldest financial institutions in the world. The bank is controlled by the Brazilian government. Its stock is traded at the Sao Paulo Stock Exchange and its management follows standard international banking practices.

Interest rates on loans vary to a great extent in Brazil. The Banco do Brasil is known for having high interest rates. The *Economist* "Survey of International Banking" (2006) reported that the average Brazilian interest rate on credit cards was an astounding 222%. As of June 1999, the standard interest rate in Brazil was 8.5% per month (102% per year).

Think Critically

1. Why do banks charge high interest rates on their credit cards?
2. What would it be like to pay more than 100% interest on borrowed money? How might your spending habits be affected?

Sources of Credit

A common type of credit available to consumers is service credit. *Service credit* is the ability to receive services and pay for them later. If you use electricity, water, sewer, cable, and utilities, you are using service credit. You may also receive service credit from doctors, dentists, and others. Some companies that offer service credit require you to pay a deposit before beginning your service, especially if you are a new customer. After a good payment record, the deposit is often refunded to you.

A *credit card* is a plastic card linked to a credit account ... can be used to make purchases. Using a credit card is a form of cons... available from banks and other financ... *cards*, you can make purchas... world. You can also...

Global View provides relevant information about business practices and the economies of other countries, such as China, Spain, Japan, and Brazil.

PROFILE

J. K. Rowling
Author

World-famous author of the Harry Potter series of books, J.K. Rowling (Joanne Rowling) was not born rich or affluent. Born in England in 1965, Rowling has won many awards and has sold more than 400 million copies of her books, which have now been made into movies that have grossed hundreds of millions of dollars each.

Rowling is famous for her "rags to riches" story. She was poor and living on welfare benefits when she took a train ride that gave her the inspiration to write her books. As an author, Rowling was self-employed and managed her own writing schedule. Within five years, she would become one of the richest billionaires in the world. Today she is a notable philanthropist, supporting charities such as One Parent Families, the Multiple Sclerosis Society of Great Britain, and Comic Relief.

Her first *Harry Potter* book was written under the name "Joanne Rowling," but her publisher required that she use initials rather than her full name, since her target audience was young boys. She has no middle name, so she chose the letter K as her middle initial, taken from her paternal grandmother, Kathleen Rowling.

In 1990, Rowling started writing her first *Harry Potter* book. She completed the book in 1995 on an old manual typewriter and was still living on state welfare support. She was unable to get credit or borrow money, but managed to squeak by with help from her family. Her book was submitted to twelve publishing houses, all of which rejected the manuscript. A year later she was given a small £1500 advance by Bloomsbury, a small publishing house in London, for the right to publish her first book. In June 1997, Bloomsbury published *Harry Potter and the Philosopher's Stone* initially printing only 1000 copies, of which 500 went to libraries. Today those copies have values from £16,000 to £25,000 each. In 1998, Scholastic, Inc. published the book in the U.S. under the title, *Harry Potter and the Sorcerer's Stone*. The rest is history.

THINK CRITICALLY

...activity and talent are often difficult to sell. It takes awhile for ... the product and buy it. Can you think of other ... rejected, but later became very

Biographies of actual business and economic leaders are provided in **PROFILE** summaries. Featured people include:

- Adam Smith
- Mark Zuckerberg
- Muhammad Yunus
- J.K. Rowling
- Bill Gates
- Mary Kay Ash
- Steve Jobs
- Mark Cuban

CENGAGENOW

Online Engagement with CengageNOW

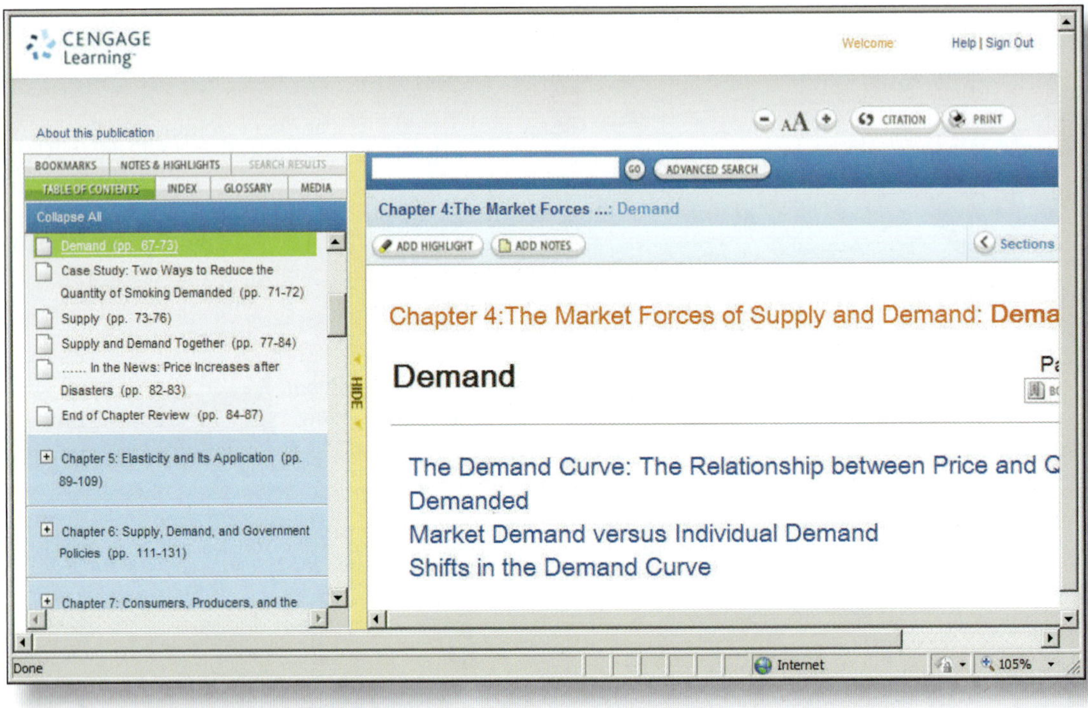

CengageNOW for *Economics and Personal Finance* offers:

- **Interactive eBook** With this enhanced eBook, students can highlight, take notes, and search the textbook easily and efficiently.
- **Auto-graded Homework**, including chapter and workbook activities.
- **Test Bank**, including **Exam***View*® and Chapter and Unit Tests.
- A **Personalized Study Plan** is a diagnostic tool with Pre-Test, Customized Study Plan, and Post-Test activities for each chapter, including:
  - Text Material
  - Learning Objectives
  - Ask the Expert Videos
  - PowerPoint® Slides
  - Crossword Puzzles
  - Flashcards
  - Net Bookmarks
  - Quizzing Games

Comprehensive Support for *Economics and Personal Finance*

Teacher's Wraparound Edition

ISBN: 9781133365372

The Teacher's Wraparound Edition includes instructional tools in the margin, including:

- Lesson Plans
- Answers
- Additional teaching suggestions for different learning styles and ability levels

Interactive eBook

An enhanced eBook that students can highlight, take notes, and search.

Workbook

ISBN: 9781133947608

Lesson review with objective questions and activities.

Chapter and Unit Tests

ISBN: 9781285060903

Printed chapter tests, unit tests, and a final exam.

Instructor's Resource CD (IRCD)

ISBN: 9781133593423

Ancillaries on the IRCD include:

- PDF of Teacher's Wraparound Edition
- Lesson Plans
- PowerPoint® Slides
- Teacher's Edition of Chapter and Unit Tests
- Teacher's Edition of Workbook
- Personal Finance Activities
- Activities and Project Masters
- Developing Reading, Writing, and Math Skills
- Developing Social Studies and Economic Measurement Skills
- Teaching Tools
  - Alternative Assessment
  - Block Scheduling
  - Business Math Activity Masters
  - Communications Masters
  - Distance Learning
  - Diversity
  - Ethics Activity Masters
  - International Business Activity Masters
  - Involving Families
  - Search for the Leader
  - Test Prep and Study Skills
  - Using Technology

Instructor's Resource Kit

ISBN: 9781133950479

Keep all of the teaching materials and solutions you need for your course in one handy location! This box includes:

- Instructor's Edition of the Workbook
- Instructor's Edition Chapter and Unit Tests
- Student Edition
- Instructor's Wraparound Edition
- Demo CD with samples from the Instructor's Resource CD, CengageNOW demo, and Spanish Guided Practice CD demo.

Exam*View*®

ISBN: 9781133593416

Assessment is a snap with this electronic testing software that allows you to edit and add questions, customize tests (scramble answers & questions), test online, and quickly evaluate professionally written tests.

Spanish Guided Practice CD

ISBN: 9781133947639

Chapter summaries and activities for English Language Learners.

COMPANION WEBSITE

www.cengage.com/school/economics/personalfinance

You and your students can access this free website to find a wealth of online learning tools, including:

- Crossword Puzzles
- Flashcards
- Net Bookmark
- Digging Deeper with Economics e-Collection

UNIT
1

Introduction to Economics

Chapter 1 The Free Market System
Chapter 2 Understand Decision Making

Unit 1 explains the foundation of the free market system. Chapter 1 sets the first three building blocks in place. These are the concepts of scarcity, choice, and resources. Here you will also learn about entrepreneurship. An additional building block for understanding free markets includes the advantages of free enterprise. You will learn the meaning of the goals of economic freedom, efficiency, and security. Other building blocks in the foundation are the basic types of economic systems. In Chapter 2, you will learn to apply the economist's toolkit. This involves applying graphs to economics.

Once you have mastered the concepts in Unit 1, you will be well prepared to continue expanding your knowledge of the free market system.

UNIT 1 Project

Free Markets

Project Objectives

PARTNERSHIP FOR 21ST CENTURY SKILLS

- Analyze the economic rights and responsibilities of individuals as consumers.
- Analyze the consequences of an economic decision made by an individual consumer.
- Use appropriate mathematical skills to interpret social studies information.
- Analyze information by sequencing, categorizing, identifying cause-and-effect relationships, comparing, contrasting, finding the main idea, summarizing, making generalizations and predictions, and drawing inferences and conclusions.

chapter 1

Showcase Free Markets in America, p. 12

Prepare a collage of pictures that describe what it is like to live in an economic system based on free markets.

Present Principles of Free Markets, p. 21

Create a PowerPoint presentation that lists and describes the principles of the free market system.

The Story of Economic Goals, p. 29

Write a poem, song lyrics, or a short story describing life in America based on the economic goals of people and businesses in free markets, and how those goals are met through the economic system.

chapter 2

Create a Model, p. 44

Draw a map of your home, including the driveway or other paths used to reach your front door, all exits, garages, and other features.

Analyze a Situation, p. 50

Prepare a quantitative and qualitative analysis for a given situation and present it.

Consider Possibilities, p. 57

You have just inherited $1,000. You have many choices including spending or saving the entire amount.

Project Wrap-up

Create a poster, newsletter, website, oral report, slide presentation, or video that explains the basic idea of economics—what it is, what questions are answered, what it means to you, and how you benefit from living within a free market system. Save a copy of all work completed to include in your economics portfolio.

alvarez/iStockphoto.com

chapter 1

The Free Market System

1-1 What Is a Free Market?

1-2 Principles and Goals of Free Markets

1-3 Types of Economic Systems

yienkeat/Shutterstock.com

MARKETS *in Action!*

T. Boone Pickens
American Entrepreneur

Young Pickens began his impressive career in Oklahoma. Here he learned the value of risk-taking and hard work. At twelve years old, his first acquisition was to expand a 28-customers newspaper route into one with 125 customers. He did this by acquiring routes from other carriers. This was a talent that would serve Pickens well in later years. As a youth, his family moved to Amarillo, Texas where he attended high school. After one year at Texas A&M University, Pickens transferred to Oklahoma State University where he earned a degree in geology.

Pickens worked for Phillips Petroleum for three years before striking out on his own in 1954. With $2,500 borrowed money, Pickens formed his first oil and gas firm. Later, he built Mesa Petroleum into one of the largest independent natural gas and oil companies in the world. In 1989, Financial World named him Chief Executive Officer (CEO) of the Decade.

A booming Texas population demands power and water solutions. Pickens led a group of Texas landowners in 2007 to plan for the world's largest wind farm. In recent years, Pickens has spent much time making the case for alternate energy solutions for America. These solutions include wind and natural gas. He is one of the foremost advocates of a comprehensive energy plan for America. And his online Pickens Plan Army encourages an outpouring of fresh ideas on energy policy. His second *New York Times* best seller is titled *The First Billion is the Hardest*. Pickens details what Americans must do to win back its energy independence.

During his long career, Pickens has created jobs and made money. He has given money to many worthy causes. These include medical research, children at risk, education, athletics, and conservation. In 2009 Pickens was named one of the world's 100 most influential people in *Time* magazine.

As a young person, you will soon start thinking about your future. Jobs along the way will help you reach your goals. Pickens started with a paper route and grew it into a bigger business. He learned along the way as he completed his education and began his career path. He was always thinking about what would happen next—planning for his future and the future of his country.

T. Boone Pickens speaks about energy at the National Press Club.

Think Critically

1. How do you think things will change and be different by the time you are working at your first career job?
2. What can you do along the way to be in the right place at the right time and thus be financially rewarded as you add value for your country?

1-1 What Is a Free Market?

Learning Objectives

LO 1-1 **Explain** the importance of free markets to consumers and businesses.

LO 1-2 **Identify** land, labor, and capital as scarce resources.

LO 1-3 **Explain** the differences between macroeconomics and microeconomics.

Vocabulary

- **market,** p. 7
- **free market,** p. 7
- **scarcity,** p. 7
- **resources,** p. 8
- **land,** p. 8
- **labor,** p. 8
- **entrepreneur,** p. 8
- **capital,** p. 9
- **economics,** p. 10
- **macroeconomics,** p. 10
- **microeconomics,** p. 10

© Aleksandar Vrzalski/ iStockphoto.com

REAL-WORLD FOCUS

Jamie has a part-time, after-school job where she makes money to buy things she wants and needs. She also does chores at home, and her parents give her a monthly allowance. Compared to many others, Jamie is able to buy more and save more, but she isn't able to satisfy all of her goals. She wants to earn and save more, but with school, activities, work, family, and friends, Jamie doesn't have any time left.

WORK AS A TEAM How would you describe Jamie's basic problem? What do you think she should do?

Vadim Ponomarenko/Shutterstock.com

In the telecommunications industry, large satellite dishes are aimed into space to transmit signals for various purposes.

DO YOU THINK a satellite dish, a resource used in the production of goods and services, is an example of land, labor, or capital? Why?

yienkeat/Shutterstock.com

LO 1-1 Importance of Free Markets

A **market** is any place or method used by buyers and sellers to exchange goods and services. A **free market** exists when consumers and businesses buy and sell products with a minimum of government restrictions. The free market system is also called the *free enterprise system*. In a free market system, individuals have the freedom to sell their labor. Businesses are free to be creative and sell their products to try to earn a profit. And consumers are free to buy or not buy. When people pursue their own interests, businesses produce a seemingly limitless selection of goods and services. When free markets exist both consumers and businesses benefit from exchange. Fans stand in line for Dallas Cowboys tickets because they will benefit from enjoying the game. The team also benefits. It makes a profit from ticket sales, and the Cowboys can afford to build a beautiful new stadium.

Ken Durden/Shutterstock.com

The football stadium for the Dallas Cowboys of the NFL is in Arlington, Texas.

The Problem of Scarcity

The free market system operates in a world where people face the problem of scarcity. **Scarcity** is the condition in which human wants are forever greater than the available supply of time, goods, and resources. Because of the vast number of human wants, it is impossible to satisfy every one of them. Pause for a moment to list some of your unsatisfied wants. Perhaps you would like a big home, or designer clothes. Or you may want clean air, better health care, shelter for the homeless, and more leisure time. There are always limits on the economy's ability to satisfy unlimited wants. Scarcity always exists because "you can't have it all."

Would the scarcity problem disappear if you were rich? In fact, wealth does not solve the problem. No matter how rich an individual is, there are still things that he or she might wish to have. Those things might include finer homes, faster planes, and larger yachts. Or they might want to travel to the moon. No matter how many possessions a person has, there will always be something else that he or she wants to have. Scarcity means all individuals, whether rich or poor, are dissatisfied with their material well-being. What is true for individuals also applies to society. Even the United States government cannot escape the problem of scarcity. The federal government never has enough money to buy sufficient goods and services to completely satisfy the desire to help the poor, educate all students, build highways, and fund every other program that could benefit Americans.

Scarcity is a fact of life throughout the world. In much of South America, Africa, and Asia, scarcity is often life threatening. In North America, Western Europe, and some parts of Asia, life is much less grueling. However, in these more developed countries, the problem of scarcity still exists. Individuals and countries never have all the goods and services that they wish.

CHECKPOINT

Why is scarcity an issue for everyone, including the wealthy?

LO 1-2 Scarce Resources and Production

Because of scarcity, no society has enough resources to produce everything it wants. **Resources** are the basic categories of inputs used to produce goods and services. Resources are also called *factors of production*. As shown in Figure 1-1, economists divide resources into three categories: land, labor, and capital.

Land

Land is any natural resource provided by nature and used in the production process. Land is anything natural found above or below the ground. Examples are forests, gold, diamonds, oil, coal, wind, and the sun. Farming, building factories, and constructing oil refineries would be impossible without land.

Labor

Another necessary resource is the people who produce goods and provide services. **Labor** is the mental and physical capacity of workers to produce goods and services. The services of farmers, assembly-line workers, lawyers, teachers, and economists are all labor. The labor resource is measured by the number of people available for work. It is also measured by the skills or quality of workers. Nations differ in their abilities to produce. One reason is that the education, experience, health, and motivation of workers are different among nations.

An entrepreneur is a person who provides a special type of labor. An **entrepreneur** is a business leader who seeks to make profits by combining resources to produce new goods and services. An entrepreneur is a motivated person who is willing to take risks to make money. These risks include starting new businesses or creating new products. Few people are willing to make decisions that involve above-average chances for failure. An important contribution of entrepreneurs is that they help create a growing economy.

Local Natural Resources

What are the natural resources in your area? Those resources are an important factor for just about every aspect of your life. Natural resources can provide energy, crops, and livestock used for food. They can also provide ingredients for manufacturing. Natural resources even attract tourists who bring added revenue to your state.

Investigate Your Local ECONOMY

Try it Out

Make a list of five important natural resources (land) found in your state. Which industries use these natural resources? What is the impact of these natural resources on the industries in your local economy? Report your results to the class.

The birth of the Levi Strauss Company is a good illustration of a successful entrepreneur. In 1853 at the age of 24, Levi Strauss sailed from New York to join the California Gold Rush. His intent was not to dig for gold, but to sell cloth. When he arrived in San Francisco, he had sold most of his cloth to people on the ship. The only cloth he had left was a roll of canvas for tents and covered wagons. On the dock, he met a miner who wanted sturdy pants that would last while digging for gold. So Strauss made the miner a pair from the canvas. Later, a customer gave Strauss the idea of using little copper rivets to strengthen the seams. Strauss knew a good thing when he saw it. He hired workers, built factories, and became one of the largest pants makers in the world. As a reward for taking risks, the Levi Strauss Company earned profits and he became rich and famous.

NET Bookmark

Visit www.cengage.com/school/economics/personalfinance and click on the link for Chapter 1. Read the article on the Chisholm Trail. What was the importance of this trail and what motivated those who traveled it? Relate this trail to land, labor, entrepreneurship, and capital.

www.cengage.com/school/economics/personalfinance

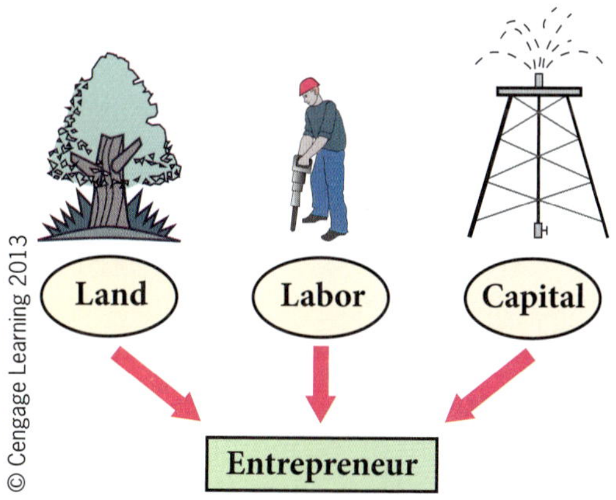

Figure 1-1

The Three Categories of Resources

Resources are the basic categories of inputs organized by an entrepreneur (a special type of labor) to produce goods and services. Economists divide resources into the three categories of land, labor, and capital.

Capital

Capital means human-made goods that are used to produce other goods and services. Before the Industrial Revolution, capital meant a tool, such as a hoe, an axe, or a bow and arrow. These items served as capital to build a house or provide food for the dinner table. Today, capital consists of factories, machinery, robots, trucks, roads, and warehouses. Other examples are high school buildings and the printing presses used to produce this textbook.

The term capital, as it is used in the study of economics, can be confusing. Economists know that capital in everyday conversations means money. In the study of economics, capital does not refer to money. Stated simply, money is not capital because in-and-of itself money produces nothing. Money is therefore not a resource. Instead, money is used to buy land, labor, and capital. These are the resources that directly produce goods and services, and not money.

CHECKPOINT

Why is money not considered capital in economics?

LO 1-3 Economics: The Study of Scarcity and Choice

Scarcity forces people to make choices. Those choices provide the basis for the definition of economics. **Economics** is the study of how society chooses to use its scarce resources for the production of goods and services to satisfy unlimited wants. In turn, the condition of scarcity causes the effect of people making choices. You may be surprised by this definition. People often think economics means studying supply and demand, the stock market, money, and banking. In fact, there are many ways you could define economics. But economists accept the definition given here because it includes the connection between scarcity and choices. The cause-and-effect chain shown in Figure 1-2 shows that unlimited wants cause the effect of scarcity.

Figure 1-2

Unlimited Wants, Scarcity, and Choices

The cause and effect chain shows that unlimited wants cause the effect of scarcity. In turn, the condition of scarcity causes the effect of people making choices.

Society makes two kinds of choices: macro choices and micro choices. The prefixes macro and micro come from the Greek words meaning "large" and "small," respectively. Based on the macro and micro concepts, economics consists of two main branches: macroeconomics and microeconomics.

Macroeconomics

"Looking at the forest rather than the trees" describes macroeconomics. **Macroeconomics** is the branch of economics that studies decision making for the economy as a *whole*, rather than individual parts. Macroeconomics applies an overview of an economy. It examines nationwide measures, such as unemployment and growth of the economy. Macroeconomic decision making considers such "big picture" policies as the effect that federal tax cuts will have on unemployment. A macro view may also examine the effect of an oil spill on the national average of consumer prices.

Microeconomics

Examining individual trees, leaves, and pieces of bark, rather than looking at the forest, illustrates microeconomics. **Microeconomics** is the branch of economics that studies decision making by *individuals, families*, or *businesses*. Microeconomics applies a microscope to study specific parts of an economy as one would examine cells in the body. An example of microeconomic analysis would be to study the market for ostrich eggs. Will sellers decide to supply more or less ostrich eggs to the market when the price of eggs changes? Will consumers of these eggs decide to buy more or less at a new price? Macroeconomics, on the other hand, would not consider only the ostrich egg market. It would look only at the total of all goods and services exchanged in an economy.

CHECKPOINT

What is the difference between macroeconomics and microeconomics?

FreeSoulProduction/Shutterstock.com

Math CONNECTION

Covering Labor Needs

sjlocke/iStockphoto.com

You own a corner convenience market. Your store is open seven days a week, from 6 A.M. to 2 A.M. Each employee works a 6-hour shift. You recently had some employees quit and now you have 4 employees that can each work 5 days a week. Do you need to hire more people and, if so, for how many hours a week?

SOLUTION

Find the number of hours the store is open each week.

6 A.M. to 6 P.M. = 12 hours **6 P.M. to 2 A.M. = 8 hours**

20 hours	number of hours open each day
× 7	number of days open each week
140 hours	total number of hours of labor needed each week

Find the number of hours the employees can work each week.

6 hours	number of hours in a shift
× 5	number of days worked each week
30 hours	total number of hours one employee works each week
30 hours	number of hours for one employee
× 4	number of employees
120 hours	total number of hours all employees work each week

Because 120 < 140, one more employee is needed to work 20 hours a week.

TRY IT

If you hire one more employee, but decide to have the store open 24 hours a day, would you have enough hours of labor from the 5 employees? Explain your answer.

1-1 Assessment

Key Concepts

LO 1-1 1. Free markets exist when consumers and businesses are able to buy and sell products with a __?__ of government restrictions.

LO 1-1 2. **TRUE OR FALSE** Rich individuals and countries do not have the problem of scarcity.

LO 1-2 3. Entrepreneurship is a special type of __?__.

LO 1-3 4. **TRUE OR FALSE** Microeconomics studies decision making by examining specific parts of an economy.

Think About It

LO 1-1 5. Explain how businesses and consumers benefit from free markets in the American economy.

LO 1-1 6. If you won one million dollars in a lottery, would you escape the scarcity problem?

LO 1-2 7. Computer software programs are an example of which resource? Explain.

LO 1-2 8. What are the three scarce economic resources or factors of production? Give an example of each.

LO 1-2 9. Explain why scarcity is a basic problem faced by all societies and how it forces societies to make choices.

LO 1-3 10. Which of the following are microeconomic issues? Which are macroeconomic issues? Explain.
   a. How will an increase in the price of Cola A affect the quantities sold?
   b. What will cause the nation's prices for goods and services to fall?
   c. How does a quota or limit on textile imports affect the textile industry?
   d. Does a large federal budget deficit reduce the rate of unemployment in the economy?

Make Academic Connections

LO 1-1 11. **INTERNATIONAL STUDIES** Research a wealthy country and a less-developed country. Find examples of scarcity in each country.

LO 1-2 12. **COMMUNICATION** Write a five-minute speech on an idea you have for starting a new business and becoming a successful entrepreneur.

LO 1-2 13. **MANAGEMENT** Choose a company that interests you. Research this company and explain how it uses resources to produce products or services and earns profits.

LO 1-2 14. **SCIENCE** Conduct a study of energy sources. Discuss which sources of energy should be used more in the future.

Teamwork

LO 1-1 15. Work in groups. Decide on a new product that students in your school would buy. Present the product idea to the class and explain how to use scarce resources to produce the product.

Unit 1 Project: Free Markets

SHOWCASE FREE MARKETS IN AMERICA Prepare a collage of pictures that describe what it is like to live in an economic system based on free markets. For each picture include a caption to explain what it means to you. For example: "The availability of goods and services allows choices." Include pictures of entrepreneurs and the factors of production.

yienkeat/Shutterstock.com; Chad Baker/Ryan McVay/Photodisc/Getty Images

1-2 Principles and Goals of Free Markets

Learning Objectives

LO 2-1 **Identify** the main principles of a free market system.

LO 2-2 **Describe** the goals of the free market system.

LO 2-3 **Explain** the three economic questions that all economies must answer.

Vocabulary

private property rights, p. 14
consumer sovereignty, p. 15
voluntary exchange, p. 16
self-interest, p. 16
standard of living, p. 17
***What* question,** p. 18
***How* question,** p. 19
***For Whom* question,** p. 19

© Aleksandar Vrzalski/ iStockphoto.com

REAL-WORLD FOCUS

James wants to buy a used car. He has visited car lots and has checked values and prices online. He reads the ads in papers and online offering cars for sale. He finally found his ideal choice at a used car lot. The asking price is much higher than James believes is a fair price based on mileage, features, and condition of the car. James has offered what he believes to be a fair price, but the car dealer has refused to accept his offer.

WORK AS A TEAM Does James have to pay the high price being asked at the car lot? What can he do? What would you do?

Phelps Lake is located at the entrance of Death Canyon in the southern region of Grand Teton National Park in Wyoming.

DO YOU THINK Phelps Lake is private or public property? Why?

Jason Patrick Ross/Shutterstock.com

yienkeat/Shutterstock.com

LO 2-1 Principles of Free Markets

In the previous lesson, the story of Levi Straus illustrates the free market system. Owners freely choose to start a business for profit. Workers voluntarily choose to exchange their labor for pay. Consumers make their own decisions on whether or not to purchase the products offered for sale. Why has America been such an economic success? A key factor has been the American tradition of the free market. This system operates according to the following five main principles. See Figure 1-3.

Principle 1 The Right to Own Private Property

Private property rights are the rights of individuals and groups to own businesses and resources. Private property may be land or factories that an individual, family, or business owns. It also includes money, ideas for inventions, and intellectual property, such as songs. Private property allows individuals to own the means to borrow money, take risks, invest money, and create personal wealth. This differs from *public property,* such as a park or library, owned by the government rather than an individual. The framers of the Constitution ensured the right to own private property. The Constitution declares that no person may be deprived of "life, liberty, or property without due process of law." It also says that "just compensation" must be paid to owners when private property is taken for public use.

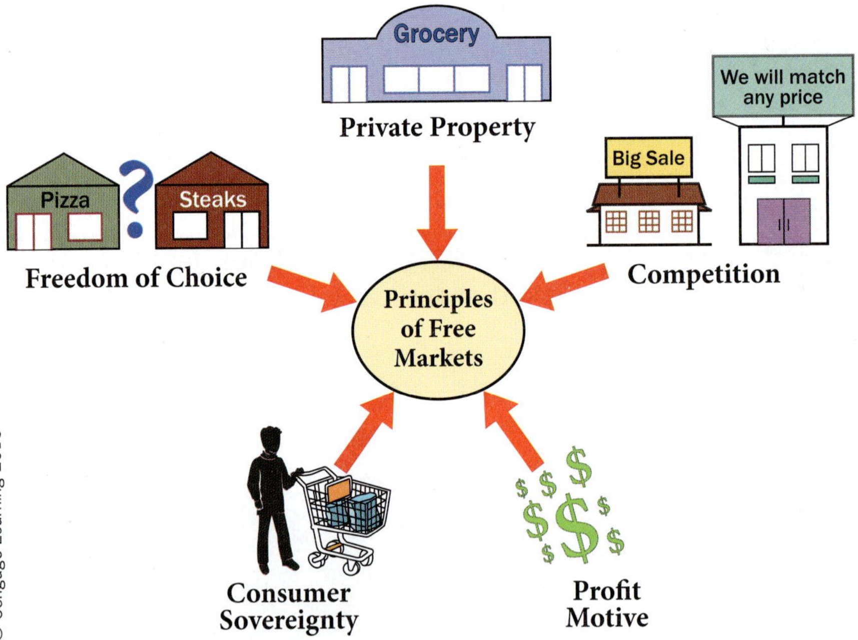

Figure 1-3
Principles of Free Markets
Basic principles of the free market system are private property rights, the profit motive, competition, consumer sovereignty, and freedom of choice.

Principle 2 The Profit Motive

The major reason enterprising people start a new business is to make a profit. By increasing the difference between income and expenses, profit rewards firms that use financial discipline. In Cuba and North Korea, for example, the government highly restricts or eliminates the profit motive. In fact, this is one reason these countries have poor economic performances.

Principle 3 Competition

Profitable businesses in free markets must face the rivalry of other businesses. Businesses compete by offering better products and lower prices. Such competition results in a great variety of goods and services at low prices. This large selection of products would not exist without competition among sellers.

Principle 4 Consumer Sovereignty

In a free market economy, the consumer has the power to decide whether any business succeeds or fails. **Consumer sovereignty** is the freedom of consumers to cast their dollar votes to buy, or not to buy, at prices set in competitive markets. In short, in a free market system, consumers are the supreme authority. Through their buying in the marketplace, consumers signal what products businesses should offer for sale. If consumers spend their money on iPhones, then sellers of these products are likely to make profits. If consumers no longer want Blackberries, then they will disappear from the shelves because there is no profit to be made from offering them for sale.

ETHICS in Action!

What is Ethics?

Ethics is the study of right and wrong. When people act ethically, they are doing the right thing regardless of whether the law requires them to act in this way. What is legal and what is ethical can be entirely different things. The law does not require you to do good. But it does require you do no harm to others. This is the *moral minimum*. As an individual you are not required to donate blood. But when you do, it makes it possible for others to live. If you saw a woman leave her purse on a park bench, the law does not require you to pick it up and run after her to return it; but your ethical values might. Much of what you believe is ethically correct behavior is determined by the values held by the society in which you live. In some nations taking bribes for doing your job is an accepted practice for government officials. In the United States such actions are both unethical and against the law.

Businesses, as well as individuals, make ethical decisions. It could be expensive for a firm to discard its waste in an environmentally safe way but its owners could make the ethical choice to do this even if they were not required to by law. Businesses are not required to make charitable contributions or provide free services that benefit the community. Many argue, however, that doing so is a matter of social responsibility. They believe that businesses earn profits from the community and should therefore be expected to give part of their earnings to benefit the community. Leading an ethical life is its own reward. It allows people to feel good about themselves and is likely to cause them to be respected by other members of their communities.

Think Critically

1. **Is it important for businesses to have ethical goals as well as profit-making goals? Why or why not?**
2. **What would the world be like for individuals and for businesses if everyone did just the moral minimum?**

Principle 5 Freedom of Choice

Free markets allow **voluntary exchange.** Buyers and sellers decide what to buy and sell with a minimum of government intervention. Free markets allow everyone to compete in the marketplace. The free market system provides the right of people to enter into agreements or contracts with others. There is freedom to enter any field of employment or business. Such exchanges allow both buyers and sellers to be guided by their own self-interests. **Self-interest** is the focus of buyers and sellers on their own personal benefit. For example, the government does not set the price of Dallas Cowboy tickets or force fans to buy them.

CHECKPOINT

How does a hair salon relate to the principles of free markets?

LO 2-2 Economic Goals and Free Markets

Different societies choose different goals for their economies. These goals are based on values or collective judgments on what is important for their economies to accomplish. Look at the following six economic goals and see how free markets achieve them.

Michael-John Wolfe/Shutterstock.com

Members of the Writers Guild of America walk the picket line while on strike.

Economic Freedom

The free market system achieves economic freedom because government intervention is minimal. A critical question one must ask is: What personal freedoms do people have? Personal economic freedoms include the right to make one's own economic choices. These choices include the right to own property and start a business. Consumers have the right to spend or save money as they decide. Workers are allowed to change jobs, join unions, and go on strike.

Economic Efficiency

Economic efficiency means producing the most goods and services from limited resources. To wisely deal with scarcity, top priority must be given to avoid wasting resources. In a free market system, workers earn the highest possible income for their given talents. Businesses also have the incentive to reduce waste, to lower costs, and to increase profits. Schools and other government institutions must consider economic efficiency to achieve the best public services possible from the economic resources they acquire.

Economic Security

A free market system with no government intervention would provide incomes only to those who directly contributed to production. Anyone who is too old, disabled, lacks savings, or who does not contribute to current production must depend on outside assistance. Economic security is the protection against economic hardships. Society must decide on how to provide such protection. In response to the Great Depression of the 1930s, when many people were out of work, the government decided to provide Social Security benefits for retired persons and unemployment compensation for those who have lost jobs. Society provides funding for programs to help the mentally and physically challenged find living arrangements and job training. Economic security is provided for victims of "acts of nature," such as floods, earthquakes, or hurricanes.

Caitlin Mira/Shutterstock.com

People living in this town along the Mississippi River could not avoid flooding when a levee failed.

Economic Equity

Each society must decide the best way to divide its economic pie. Economic equity is difficult to define and deals with what people perceive to be "fair" or "unfair." This goal asks which groups of people are better or worse off in an economic system. Who has the chance to engage in economic activity? Who gains and who loses? Who owns wealth and who does not? Equity concerns the question, "Is there an equal opportunity for each person to participate in and benefit from the system?"

Full Employment and Stable Prices

Another important goal is for everyone who wants a job to have one. Since the Great Depression, a major goal of the United States has been to achieve low unemployment. The Employment Act of 1946 declared that the federal government work to use the free market system to provide the unemployed with useful employment opportunities. Later, Congress amended this act to include the goal of stable prices. This goal is to avoid rising prices for goods and services. As prices rise, it takes more money to buy goods and services.

Economic Growth

An economy must grow for its citizens to improve their standard of living. The **standard of living** is the level of economic well-being of people. When an economy grows, jobs are easy to find, and unemployment falls. The economy produces a greater volume of goods and services, which causes the standard of living to rise. Economic growth is necessary to provide more jobs and income for people. A brief description of each economic goal is given in Figure 1-4.

Figure 1-4
Economic Goals

Goal	Brief Description
Economic freedom	Freedom to own property, start a business, change jobs, and spend money as one chooses
Economic efficiency	Production of the most goods and services with scarce resources
Economic security	Protection against economic hardships such as unemployment, old age, mental or physical disability, or natural disasters
Economic equity	The fair division of the economic pie among the population
Full employment and stable prices	Provision of jobs and avoidance of rising prices for goods and services
Economic growth	Growth of the economy to improve the standard of living

CHECKPOINT

Why is the economic goal of security important when the economy experiences a downturn?

LO 2-3 Three Fundamental Economic Questions

Because of scarcity, whether rich or poor, every nation must answer the same three fundamental economic questions:

1. What products will be produced?
2. How will the products be produced?
3. For whom will the products be produced?

A pharmacist consults with a patient regarding his prescribed medication.

What to Produce?

The ***What* question** requires an economy to decide the mix and quantity of goods and services that it will produce. Should society devote its limited resources to producing more health care and fewer military goods? Should society produce more Apple iPads and fewer PCs? Should more capital goods be produced instead of consumer goods? Or should small hybrid cars and fewer SUVs be produced? The problem of scarcity restricts the ability to produce everything you want. In the United States, free enterprise featuring consumer sovereignty answers the *What* question. In Cuba and North Korea, the government, not the consumer, answers this question.

gerenme/iStockphoto.com

A robotic arm works on a production line in an automobile assembly plant.

How to Produce?

After deciding which products to make, the second question for society to decide is the ***How* question**. An economy must decide which combination of technology and resources to use for producing goods and services. For instance, a towel can be sewn primarily by hand (labor). It can also be made partially by hand and partially by machine (labor and capital). Or towels can be made primarily by machine (capital). In short, the *How* question asks whether production will be more or less *capital-intensive*. The *How* question also concerns choices among resources used for production. Should you produce electricity from oil, solar power, or nuclear power?

Education plays an important role in answering the *How* question. Education improves the ability of workers to perform their work. For example, how does the United States improve its robotics? Robotics requires engineers and employees with the proper training in the installation and operation of robots.

For Whom to Produce?

Once the *What* and *How* questions are resolved, the third question is the ***For Whom* question.** An economy must decide which people receive the goods and services produced. This question concerns how the economic pie is divided. Who is fed well? Who drives a Mercedes? Should economics teachers earn a salary of $1 million a year? The *For Whom* question means that society must have a method to decide who will be "rich and famous" and who will be "poor and unknown."

In a free market system, price is a method used to decide who will receive the goods and services that are produced. Those who earn sufficient money will be able to buy a certain amount of products. Those who earn more money are able to buy more products, as well as more expensive products.

CHECKPOINT

Why must a society answer the three basic economic questions?

Global View

Will Cuba Become a More Free Market Economy?

Karmira/Shutterstock.com

Cuban artisans sell iconic portraits to tourists near Havana's old harbors.

Cuba often experiences daily power blackouts, and other economic hardships such as inadequate housing and fuel. Aid from the former Soviet Union ended in 1990. This loss of support combined today with the effects of U.S. trade restrictions have forced Fidel Castro, and the country's new leader, Raul Castro, to reluctantly adopt limited free market reforms. The dollar has been legalized, and the Cuban government has poured its resources into tourism. Cuba has built several new state-owned hotels and restored historic sections of Havana. Cuba also operates special medical tourist hospitals that treat foreigners and diplomats, while excluding Cubans.

Few Cubans have dollars and many are earning them by turning to illegal schemes, such as driving unregistered cabs, or selling Cuba's famous cigars and coffee. Other Cubans have abandoned state jobs and opened small businesses under the new rules. These small-scale businesses cannot employ anyone beyond family members of the owner. Spare rooms in houses can be rented, and artisans can sell their work to tourists. In addition, state farm enterprises have been broken into worker-owned units, and the government allows farmers to sell produce left over after they have met the state's quota. As a result of this limited free market, some farmers have become venture capitalists, and more food, and a greater variety of food is becoming available.

In 2008, a series of changes opened access to cell phones, Internet, computers, and DVD players. Cubans are now also allowed to patronize tourist hotels. However, such luxuries are too expensive for most Cubans. In 2009, to improve its woeful transportation system, Cuban owners of classic American cars were recruited by the government to apply for taxi licenses. These taxis were allowed to set their own fares. In spite of the private enterprise reforms, there are still highly restrictive regulations. For example, restaurants in Havana are limited to 12 seats and cannot expand regardless of demand.

Think Critically

1. **How does Cuba answer the three fundamental economic questions? Compare Cuba's economy to the goals and principles of the free market system.**
2. **Do you believe the communications revolution (cell phones and Internet) has encouraged more rapid change in the Cuban economy? Explain your answer.**

1-2 Assessment

Key Concepts

LO 2-1 1. Free markets allow __?__ because buyers and sellers decide what to buy and sell with minimum government intervention.

LO 2-2 2. **TRUE OR FALSE** Economic efficiency means providing income only to those with jobs.

LO 2-3 3. The __?__ means an economy must decide the mix and quantity of goods and services it will produce.

LO 2-2 4. **TRUE OR FALSE** The standard of living is the level of economic well-being of people.

LO 2-3 5. The __?__ decides which combination of technology and resources to use for producing goods and services.

Think About It

LO 2-1 6. Describe each of the five principles of a free market system.

LO 2-1 7. When someone uses a credit card to make a purchase, which principle best illustrates this transaction?

LO 2-2 8. Describe each of the six goals of a free market system and how they would benefit society.

LO 2-2 9. When a hurricane destroys people's homes, which economic goal would help the recovery?

LO 2-3 10. What are the three basic economic questions that must be answered by every society and how are they answered in the U.S. economy?

LO 2-3 11. Your class decides to earn money by washing cars. Relate this enterprise to the *What*, *How*, and *For Whom* questions.

Make Academic Connections

LO 2-2 12. **SOCIAL STUDIES** Conduct a survey of at least three people of varied ages. Give them a list of the five principles of free markets and ask, "How do any of these principles affect your life?" As a class, compare and discuss the results.

LO 2-2 13. **RESEARCH** Find a recent news story that illustrates one of the goals of an economy. Write a report describing how this story relates to an economic system goal.

LO 2-3 14. **INTERNATIONAL STUDIES** Research Cuba, Brazil, or Argentina and write a report on how it answers the three basic economic questions.

Teamwork

LO 2-3 15. Divide into groups. Brainstorm and list ten examples of how the United States is a free market system. Compare your list to Cuba.

LO 2-1 16. Work in five groups. Each group represents one of the following: business owner, teenage shopper, disabled worker, retired person, and business employee. Discuss the advantages and disadvantages of the free market system for these people.

Unit 1 Project: Free Markets

PRESENT PRINCIPLES OF FREE MARKETS Create a PowerPoint presentation that describes the principles of free markets. For each principle, include an example of how you benefit as a consumer when these principles are supported by the economic system of the free market system.

yienkeat/Shutterstock.com; Chad Baker/Ryan McVay/Photodisc/Getty Images

1-3 Types of Economic Systems

Learning Objectives

LO 3-1 **Understand** the basic characteristics of economic systems including traditional, free markets, socialism, and communism.

LO 3-2 **Describe** how a mixed economy involves different types of systems.

Vocabulary

economic system, p. 23
traditional economy, p. 23
market economy, p. 23
invisible hand, p. 25
capitalism, p. 25
command economy, p. 25
socialism, p. 26
communism, p. 26
mixed economy, p. 27
nationalization, p. 27

© Aleksandar Vrzalski, iStock.

REAL-WORLD FOCUS

Alisa likes to make jewelry from marbles, buttons, and other items she finds around the house. She sells the jewelry to friends and neighbors and makes money, but she would like to expand. A local craft fair is coming up where residents and tourists buy handmade crafts. A local boutique owner admires Alisa's work. She suggests that, if Alisa really wants to make money, she should try a more sophisticated look. The boutique owner offers to buy beads, string, hooks, and other supplies, as long as she approves Alisa's designs before the jewelry is made.

WORK AS A TEAM What should Alisa think about? Should she stick with what she knows or should she try something new?

leungchopan/Shutterstock.com

Under a 99-year lease originally signed in 1898, The United Kingdom transferred Hong Kong to the People's Republic of China in 1997.

DO YOU THINK Hong Kong's economic system would now be classified as capitalism, communism, or socialism?

yienkeat/Shutterstock.com

LO 3-1 The Importance of Economic Systems

North Korea and South Korea share the same language and historical background. South Korea today is a modern economy while people are starving in North Korea. This difference relates to their differing economic systems. An **economic system** is the methods used to answer the *What*, *How*, and *For Whom* questions. The decision-making process involves many aspects of a nation's culture. These include its laws, form of government, ethics, religions, and customs. Economists have established a simple way to classify economic systems into three basic types: (1) traditional, (2) market, and (3) command.

The Traditional Economy

The traditional economy has been used for making economic decisions throughout history, and is still used today in certain societies. A **traditional economy** answers the *What*, *How*, and *For Whom* questions the way they have been answered for generations. People in this type of society learn that copying the previous generation allows them to feel accepted. People in such a society believe that what has been good for centuries is still good today.

Traditional systems that are used today include the Inuit of Canada, native people of Brazil's rain forest, and the Amish of Pennsylvania. In these societies, the way past generations decided what crops to plant has not changed. Neither has how crops are harvested and to whom they are distributed. People perform their jobs in the manner established by their ancestors. The Amish are well known for rejecting tractors and using horse-drawn plows. They also reject Social Security because their society voluntarily redistributes wealth to members who are needy.

Delmas Lehman/iStockphoto.com

A horse and carriage makes its way from an Amish farm to a Pennsylvania town.

The benefit of the traditional approach is that it reduces friction among members. This is because relatively little is disputed. People in this system may cooperate more freely with one another. Today, the Amish and other traditional economies appear very satisfied with their relatively uncomplicated systems. Critics argue that the traditional system restricts individual initiative. Therefore, it does not lead to advanced goods, new technologies, and a higher standard of living.

The Market Economy

A **market economy** does not use customs or central planners to answer the three basic economic questions. It answers the *What*, *How*, and *For Whom* questions based only on voluntary buying and selling in markets. Without the restrictions of central planning by a government, free markets coordinate the buying and selling for millions of consumers and producers.

PROFILE

Adam Smith
Father of Modern Economics

Hulton Archive/iStockphoto.com

The Scottish economist Adam Smith explained the power of a market economy. In 1776, the same year that the American colonies declared their political independence, Smith published *The Wealth of Nations*. This book presented a blueprint for using markets to improve economic performance. Smith spent over 10 years observing the real world. Then he wrote about how nations could best improve their material well-being. Smith concluded that the answer was to use free markets because they provide incentives for everyone to follow his or her self-interest.

Smith is the father of modern economics. He intended to write a book that would influence popular opinion. Unlike many famous works, *The Wealth of Nations* was an immediate success. The basic philosophy of his book is "the best government is the least government." This belief is known as *laissez faire*, a French expression meaning "allow to act." Adam Smith believed the role of the government should be limited. The government should provide national defense, education, maintain roads, enforce contracts, and little else. Smith also advocated free trade among nations. He also rejected the idea that nations should impose trade barriers. During Smith's lifetime, European nations, such as England, France, and Spain, intervened to control economic activities. In *The Wealth of Nations*, he argued that economic freedoms are natural rights. He believed that free competition among people who follow their self-interests would best benefit society. The "invisible hand" of markets free from government interference produces the greatest amount of products exchanged. Smith asked the question implied in the title of his book. Why are some nations richer than others? He explained that any nation's wealth is not really the amount of gold or silver it owns. Instead, he argued that it is the ability of people to trade in free markets that creates a nation's wealth. The founding fathers of the United States were well acquainted with Smith's work and his influence on the world was profound.

THINK CRITICALLY

1. **How do Smith's ideas favor a market economy?**

2. **A famous quote from Adam Smith is "It is not from the benevolence of the butcher, the brewer, or the baker, that we expect our dinner, but from their regard to their own interest." How does this quotation relate to free markets?**

yienkeat/Shutterstock.com

Adam Smith in his famous book, *The Wealth of Nations,* said that the market economy seemed to be controlled by an **invisible hand**. This phrase means that the best interests of a society are served by markets guided by self-interest. Guided by an invisible hand, producers must compete with one another to earn consumers' money. A competitive marketplace provides profits as a reward for efficient producers. Losses punish inefficient producers. Smith saw profit as the necessary driving force in a market system. Profit leads manufacturers to sell products at the lowest prices. Consumers compete with one another to buy in their self-interests the best goods at the lowest price. Competition, not a central authority, regulates the economy.

Critics contend that competitive markets result in very wealthy and very poor people. In a market economy, output is divided in favor of people who earn higher incomes and own property. Supporters argue that this inequality gives people an incentive to strive for the reward of earning more income and owning property. The popular term for the market economy is capitalism. **Capitalism** is an economic system based on private ownership of resources and markets. Capitalism is also called the *free market or free enterprise system* and best describes the economic system of the United States.

More recent authors have promoted free markets. Friedrich von Hayek, an Austrian economist who was a 1974 recipient of the Nobel Prize for Economics, wrote *The Road to Serfdom.* He argued that political and economic freedoms are inseparable.

Milton Friedman was a champion of personal freedom and free markets. In 1976 he won the Nobel Prize for Economics. Two of his important books are *Capitalism and Freedom* and *Free to Choose,* which he wrote with his wife, Rose.

The Command Economy

In a **command economy**, the *What, How*, and *For Whom* questions are answered by a dictator or central authority. The former Soviet Union and China in the past, along with Cuba and North Korea today, are examples of command economies. Politically selected committees make virtually all economic decisions. They decide on such matters as the number, color, size, quality, and price of automobiles, tanks, brooms, and sweaters. These authorities might decide to produce modern weapons instead of schools. Or, like the ancient pharaohs of Egypt, they might decide to devote resources to build monuments to themselves, like the pyramids.

Kim Il Sung Square in Pyongyang, North Korea sits on the banks of the Taedong River.

Socialism and Communism

The idea of socialism has existed for thousands of years. Its basis is the command system. **Socialism** is an economic system based on government ownership of resources and centralized decision making. Under socialism, a government owns and controls major industries, such as steel, electricity, and agriculture. Socialism exists in China, Venezuela, and many less-developed countries. Modern examples of socialism and communism can be traced to Karl Marx. Marx was a nineteenth-century German philosopher, revolutionary, and economist. Marx rejected the concepts of private property, self-interest, and profit.

Solodov Alexey/Shutterstock.com

A portrait of Karl Marx is printed on this 1983 USSR stamp.

Marx wrote the *Communist Manifesto*, published in 1848. A massive work followed, titled *Das Kapital*, which was published in three volumes between 1867 and 1894. These two works made Karl Marx the most influential economist in the history of socialism. In fact, he devoted his entire life to a revolt against capitalism. As Marx understood the ideas proposed in *The Wealth of Nations*, profits were unjust payments made to owners of firms—the capitalists. Marx predicted that, over time, the market system would destroy itself.

Marx believed that private ownership would produce a class struggle between a few "haves" and many "have-nots." He stated in the *Communist Manifesto*, "The history of all existing society is the history of class struggle." In Marx's vision, capitalists were the oppressors, and the workers were the oppressed. Wealthy owners exploited workers by paying starvation wages to increase profits. Business owners forced laborers to work in unsafe conditions. Marx predicted the workers would rise up in a revolution against the owners of capital. Marx believed communism to be the ideal system that would evolve in stages from capitalism through socialism. **Communism** is a classless economic system in which all resources are owned by the workers. There is no government and people share production according to their needs. In Marx's view, this is the highest form of socialism toward which the revolution should strive.

Under communism, private property that encourages self-interest does not exist. There is no struggle between classes of people and everyone cooperates. There is no reason to commit crime, and police, lawyers, and courts are unnecessary. Marx believed that those who work hard, or are more skilled, will be public spirited. Any "haves" will give voluntarily to "have-nots" until everyone has exactly the same. Marx believed people would be motivated by this principle: "From each according to his ability, to each according to his need." There would be no reason for governments. World peace would evolve as people accepted cooperation and rejected profits and competition. Actually, no nation has achieved the ideal communist society described by Marx. Nor has free enterprise self-destructed as he predicted. The 1917 communist revolution in Russia did not fit Marx's theory. At that time, Russia was an underdeveloped country. It was not an industrial country filled with greedy capitalists who exploited workers.

CHECKPOINT

How are socialism and communism different?

LO 3-2 The Mixed Economy

A **mixed economy** is a system that answers the *What*, *How*, and *For Whom* questions through a mixture of traditional, command, and market systems. In the real world, no nation is a pure traditional, command, or market economy. Even primitive tribes employ a few markets in their systems. For example, members of a tribe may exchange shells for animal skins. In China, many private businesses and farms operate in free markets. The United States is best described as a market economy. It is also a blend of the other two systems. As mentioned earlier, the Amish operate a well-known traditional economy in the United States. The draft during wartime is an example of a command economy. The government uses the draft to obtain involuntary labor. Taxes are "commanded" from taxpayers to fund government programs, such as national defense and Social Security. Federal agencies regulate environmental quality, food safety and other activities. The economic systems of most nations do not perfectly fit one of the basic definitions. So what term best describes real-world economies? A description is that most countries employ a mix of the basic types of systems. Figure 1-5 places countries between the two extremes. Pure socialism is on the left and pure free enterprise on the right.

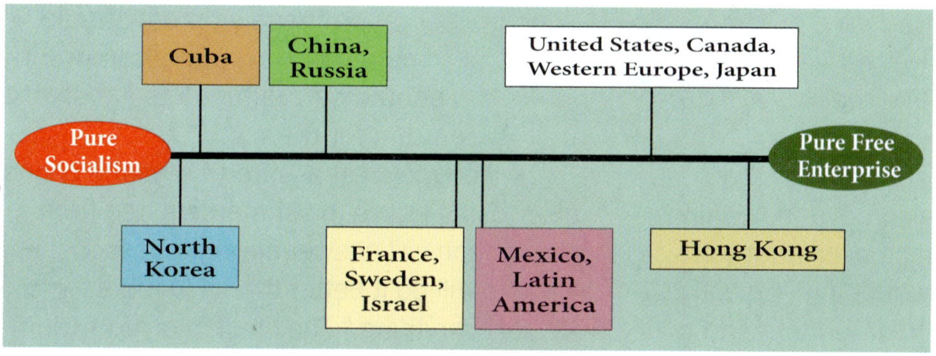

Figure 1-5

A Classification of Economic Systems

No nation has an economic system that is pure socialism or pure free enterprise. All nations mix government ownership and reliance on markets. North Korea and Cuba are closest to pure socialism. Hong Kong comes closest to pure free enterprise. Other nations are between these two extremes based on their uses of government ownership versus markets.

Changes in the Role of Government

Over time, the role of government in the U.S. free market system has changed. The United States has a history of nationalization. **Nationalization** is the act of transforming a private enterprise into a government enterprise. Most were temporary. But one has endured. Amtrak is a government-owned corporation created in 1971 after railroads petitioned to abandon unprofitable passenger service. Also, the Resolution Trust Corporation (RTC) was established in 1989 to take over more than 1,000 failed savings and loans (S&L) institutions with bad loans and foreclosed homes. After fulfilling its mission to sell the assets of these S&Ls, the RTC was closed in 1995. The recent financial crisis has generated several nationalizations. General Motors provides a prime case. With GM facing bankruptcy in 2009, the U.S. government replaced the CEO and took a 60 percent controlling share, with Canada a 12.5 percent share, and United Auto Workers (UAW) 17.5 percent. Existing stockholders were given zero shares. This nationalization was very controversial. What will happen in the future? Will more economies move toward free enterprise or socialism?

CHECKPOINT

How do a traditional, a command, and a market economy view the importance of self-interest?

Choosing an Economic System on Another Planet

Suppose life is discovered on a new planet. The chief of their society learns of the successful economy of the United States. An economist is summoned to learn the secret. Sitting at the head of a huge oval table, the chief addresses the economist, "Our economic system depends on tradition and command. It works, but not nearly as well as the U.S. economy. Our men and women lead a highly traditional way of life. Men farm and hunt like their forefathers. Women work only in the home following the role approved by their elders. There is no confusion over how things are done. There is no chaos over what work, or what output will be produced. People are simply assigned jobs by their leaders and told how much to produce. Likewise, people are told to work on community projects for our planet's benefit. If anyone refuses to follow instructions, they are shunned or banished. Tell me, how could there possibly be a better way to organize our economy?" The economist responds, "Yes, there is definitely a better way. Replace tradition and command systems with the 'invisible hand' of the market system. This idea was explained long ago by Adam Smith, the father of modern economics."

The chief is puzzled. "I have never heard of Adam Smith or the market economy. In a nutshell, explain to me how it differs from our system." "Very well," says the economist. "In a market economy, each person decides what to do based on price signals." The chief is horrified and takes offense. "But what happens when they do not choose correctly? Let's talk about something specific, like computer production. Unless you designate people to make computers, how will the right number select this job? What if women want to work in this industry? Who decides how much these workers should be paid? How many computers should be produced to satisfy the demand for them?"

"You may rest assured," says the economist, "using prices to set markets free from intervention will answer all your questions, and markets will do it better than if leaders try to control everything." The chief interrupts triumphantly, "Do you really expect me to believe that without the leaders, the right number will be bought and sold?" "Ah, exactly!" The economist quickly answers. "The market will automatically do all these wonderful things. People will be more motivated by their self-interests rather than by tradition or central authority. In short, the system runs itself." "The economy runs without my leaders' directions!" says the chief. "That's absurd, and you have wasted my time. I thought you had a meaningful proposal. Good day!"

Think Critically

Why might the leader find a market system inconceivable?

1-3 Assessment

Key Concepts

LO 3-1 1. The __?__ economic system answers the *What*, *How*, and *For Whom* questions the way they always have been answered.

LO 3-1 2. **TRUE OR FALSE** The *invisible hand* is a phrase that expresses the belief that the best interests of society are served by markets guided by self-interests.

LO 3-1 3. The economic system based on government ownership of resources and centralized decision making is __?__.

LO 3-1 4. **TRUE OR FALSE** According to Karl Marx, the highest form of socialism is communism.

Think About It

LO 3-1 5. Give an example of how a nation's culture affects its economic system.

LO 3-2 6. Make a chart showing the advantages and the disadvantages of any two of the three basic types of economic systems.

LO 3-1 7. Suppose you are a farmer. Explain why you would be motivated to work in traditional, command, and market economies.

LO 3-2 8. The United States is primarily a market economy. Give an example of elements of a traditional and a command economy in the United States.

Make Academic Connections

LO 3-1 9. **INTERNATIONAL STUDIES** Research the Inuit of Canada and the Amish of Pennsylvania. Write a report giving examples of a traditional economy for each of these societies.

LO 3-1 10. **COMMUNICATION** Create a chart listing the advantages and disadvantages of self-interest and competition to guide the market. Give examples from your own experiences.

LO 3-2 11. **SOCIAL STUDIES** Imagine the United States becomes a centrally planned economy like the former Soviet Union. Write a paper on what everyday life might be like.

Teamwork

LO 3-2 12. Work in two groups. One group plays the part of central planners for a command economy. The other group represents a market economy. Each group reports how their country will build a new factory and answers the *What*, *How*, and *For Whom* questions.

LO 3-2 13. Work in four groups. Each group represents one of the following: a traditional, a command, a market, or a mixed economy. Create a scenario that illustrates how the assigned system makes an economic decision.

Unit 1 Project: Free Markets

THE STORY OF ECONOMIC GOALS Write a poem, song lyrics, or a short story describing life in America based on the economic goals of people and businesses in free markets, and how those goals are met through the economic system. Include historical, as well as current events, to describe how the economic goals of freedom, efficiency, security, equity, full employment, and economic growth are met.

Chapter 1

Summary

1-1 WHAT IS A FREE MARKET?

1. Free markets exists when consumers and businesses are free to buy and sell products with minimum government restrictions. Free markets involve the relationship between scarcity and resources.
2. Resources are the basic categories of inputs used to produce goods and services. Economists divide resources into three categories: land, labor, and capital. An entrepreneur is a business leader who seeks profits by combining resources to produce new goods and services.
3. Economics is the study of how society chooses to use its scarce resources to the production of goods and services to satisfy unlimited wants. Macroeconomics is the branch of economics that studies decision making for the economy as a whole. Microeconomics is the branch of economics that studies decision making by individuals, families, or businesses.

1-2 PRINCIPLES AND GOALS OF FREE MARKETS

4. The main principles of free market systems are: private property rights, the profit motive, competition, consumer sovereignty, and freedom of choice (voluntary exchange).
5. The economic goals of free market systems are: economic freedom, economic efficiency, economic security, economic equity, full employment and stable prices, and economic growth.
6. An economy must respond to three basic questions: What to produce; How to produce; and For whom to produce.

1-3 TYPES OF ECONOMIC SYSTEMS

7. A traditional economy is an economic system that answers the *What*, *How*, and *For Whom* questions the way they have been answered for generations.
8. A command economy is an economic system that answers the *What*, *How*, and *For Whom* questions by a dictator or central authority. One form of a command economy is socialism. Karl Marx, a nineteenth-century German economist, believed that communism would evolve from socialism.
9. A market economy is an economic system that answers the *What*, *How*, and *For Whom* questions based on voluntary exchange in markets. Capitalism is an economic system based on private ownership of resources and markets. It is also called the free market or free enterprise system.
10. A mixed economy is an economic system that answers the *What*, *How*, and *For Whom* questions through a mixture of traditional, command, and market systems.

Chapter 1 Assessment

Vocabulary Review

Match each statement with the term that best defines it. Some terms may not be used.

1. The freedom of consumers and businesses to buy and sell goods and services with a minimum of government restrictions
2. Human-made goods that are used to produce other goods and services
3. The branch of economics that studies decision making by individuals, families, and businesses
4. The freedom of consumers to buy, or not to buy, at prices set in competitive markets
5. Buyers and sellers decide what to buy and sell with minimum government intervention
6. The methods used to answer *What*, *How*, and *For Whom* questions
7. The basic categories of inputs used to produce goods and services
8. An economic system that answers the *What*, *How*, and *For Whom* questions by a dictator or central authority
9. A phrase that expresses the belief that the best interests of society are served when consumers and producers compete in markets guided by self-interests
10. The act of transforming a private enterprise into a government enterprise
11. An economic system based on government ownership of resources and centralized decision making
12. The condition in which human wants are forever greater than the available supply of time, goods, and resources needed to fill them
13. A leader who seeks to make profits by combining resources to produce new goods and services
14. The rights of individuals and groups to own businesses and resources
15. The study of how society uses its scarce resources for the production of goods and services to satisfy unlimited wants

Vocabulary

a. capital
b. capitalism
c. command economy
d. communism
e. consumer sovereignty
f. economics
g. economic system
h. entrepreneur
i. free market
j. invisible hand
k. labor
l. land
m. macroeconomics
n. market
o. market economy
p. microeconomics
q. mixed economy
r. nationalization
s. private property rights
t. resources
u. scarcity
v. self-interest
w. socialism
x. standard of living
y. traditional economy
z. voluntary exchange

Review Your Knowledge

LO 1-1 **16.** The condition of scarcity
a. cannot be eliminated
b. prevails in poor economies
c. prevails in rich economies
d. all of the above are true

LO 1-2 **17.** A textbook is an example of
a. capital
b. a natural resource
c. labor
d. none of the above

LO 1-3 **18.** The subject of economics is primarily the study of
a. the government decision-making process
b. how to operate a business successfully
c. decision making because of the problem of scarcity
d. how to make money in the stock market

LO 1-3 **19.** Which of the following is included in the study of macroeconomics?
a. salaries of college professors
b. computer prices
c. unemployment in the nation
d. silver prices

LO 3-1 **20.** What type of economic system is commonly described as being controlled by an "invisible hand"?
a. a traditional economy
b. a command economy
c. a market economy
d. a communist economy

LO 2-1 **21.** Consumer sovereignty means
a. customers decide whether any business succeeds or fails
b. consumers are not free to spend their money as they wish
c. businesses and not consumers have the market power
d. government agencies decide which products consumers do not want

LO 2-3 **22.** Which fundamental economic question requires society to choose the technological and resource mix used to produce goods?
a. *What to Produce* question
b. *Why to Produce* question
c. *How to Produce* question
d. *For Whom to Produce* question

LO 3-1 **23.** What famous economist said that the market economy seemed to be controlled by an invisible hand?
a. Friedrich von Hayek
b. Adam Smith
c. Karl Marx
d. Milton Friedman

LO 3-1 **24.** Who predicted that the exploitation of workers would cause capitalism to self-destruct?
a. Charles G. Guth
b. T. Boone Pickens
c. Karl Marx
d. Adam Smith

Digging Deeper with Economics e-Collection

One American dream is that of owning your own business. Because of the free market system, anyone in the United States can become an entrepreneur. Some entrepreneurs are successful because they provide a product that meets consumer demand. Others start a business that does not meet consumer demand and find failure. Access the Gale Economics e-Collection at **www.cengage.com/school/economics/personalfinance.** Find entrepreneurs that successfully started a business. Choose a few entrepreneurs and find out how they got their ideas and how they financed their startup costs. Prepare a demonstration about one these businesses and show the history of the business and the entrepreneur.

Think About It

LO 1-1 **25.** To a greater or lesser degree, scarcity exists in every level of society. Even the wealthy do not have everything that they want. Because of scarcity, society needs to make choices about what, how, and for whom to produce. Can scarcity ever benefit society? Why or why not?

LO 2-1 **26.** Customer sovereignty asserts that the consumer can have a say in the success or failure of a certain product. By making thoughtful choices when buying, consumers can influence competition between manufacturers, pricing, and quality. Think about recent purchases you have made and the reasons why you made them. Discuss the power and responsibility that you have as a consumer.

LO 3-2 **27.** Nationalization refers to the transformation of a private enterprise into a government enterprise. Because of recent economic developments, the U.S. federal government stepped in and assumed control of the General Motors Corporation. Under what, if any, conditions should the government nationalize a private company?

Make Academic Connections

LO 3-1 **28. HISTORY** Adam Smith wrote in eighteenth-century Britain during a period known as the Enlightenment. Thinkers emphasized the power of the human mind or reason to explore, measure, and understand the world around them. Research this period in history. Who were the leading thinkers and scholars? What were some significant events? Discuss Enlightenment thought that contributed to the rise of economics.

LO 1-2 **29. ECONOMICS** Research your local economy and learn about the leading producers of goods and services in your area. What popular clothing, food, sports equipment, or media products are being sold? What entrepreneurs contributed to the success of these products? Choose one and write a one-page summary about what you learned.

LO 3-1 **30. SOCIAL STUDIES** Investigate the economy of your school or neighborhood. See if you can identify examples of traditional, market, and command economic systems at work. Present your findings.

LO 3-1 **31. DEBATE** Stage a debate between Karl Marx and Adam Smith. Structure the debate so it resembles those seen during political elections. You will portray Marx or Smith, members of the press, or a moderator. Members of the press will pose questions to each debater, and then the other will respond. Members of the audience can pose questions as well. Vote on whether Marx or Smith won the debate.

Extend Your Learning

LO 2-3 **32. GRAPHIC ORGANIZER** Complete the graphic organizer with the three basic questions any economic system must answer. Explain what each question means by giving three examples of the free market system that answer each question.

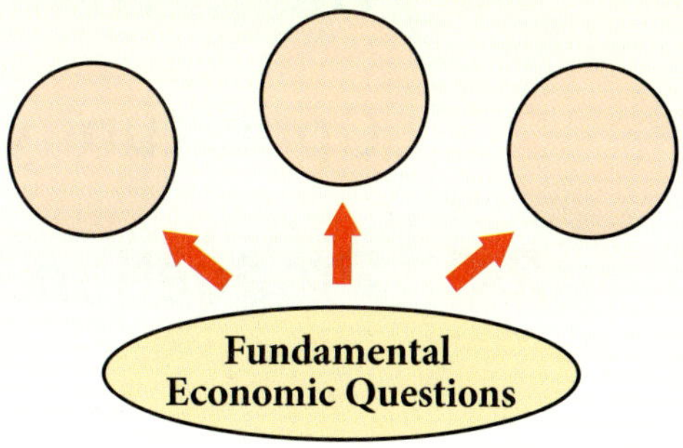

Atno Ydur/iStockphoto.com

chapter 2

Understand Decision Making

yienkeat/Shutterstock.com

MARKETS *in Action!*

Steven Spielberg DreamWorks Studios

Born in Cincinnati, Ohio, in 1946, Steven Spielberg is widely known for his films—from science fiction and adventure films to historical depictions of serious societal issues including the Holocaust, the horrors of war, slavery, and terrorism.

Spielberg is a film director, producer, screenwriter, video game designer, and studio executive. He won Best Director awards for *Schindler's List* (1993) and *Saving Private Ryan* (1998). He also directed films that became the highest-grossing films ever made. To date, Spielberg-directed films have grossed more than $8.5 billion and his personal fortune is estimated to exceed $3 billion.

Spielberg had modest beginnings. His mother owned a restaurant and was a concert pianist. His father was an electrical engineer. During his early teen years, Spielberg made amateur 8-mm adventure films with his friends. He charged 25 cents for admission to his home films while his sister sold popcorn. At age 16, Spielberg wrote and directed his first independent film, a science fiction adventure called *Firelight*, which would later inspire his film *Close Encounters*. Following high school, Spielberg moved to California where he became a student of film at California State University (Long Beach). His actual career began at Universal Studios as an unpaid, seven-day-a-week intern of the editing department. In 2002, 35 years after first starting college, Spielberg finished his degree in Film Production and Electronic Arts. In 2003, Spielberg gained his star on Hollywood's Walk of Fame.

Based on the strength of his work, Universal hired Spielberg to do TV films. It was the movie *Jaws* that brought Spielberg to the big screen. He teamed with *Star Wars* creator George Lucas and produced the Indiana Jones films. His career is filled with awards for creativity, originality, and amazing cinematography. Today he is one of the most highly respected and highest grossing film producers of all time. Most of his films deal with ordinary characters finding themselves in extraordinary circumstances. A strong and consistent theme is his family-friendly sense of wonder, optimism, and good character portrayals.

When developing his first film project, Steven Spielberg started with an idea. He identified the need (problem) as a film he could create, which others would want to see, and that could make a profit. His first film, at age 16, generated a profit of $100 from ticket and popcorn sales. This success marked the beginning of a long career in entertainment.

Devils Tower National Monument, located in Wyoming, was the location used in Steven Spielberg's 1977 film *Close Encounters of the Third Kind* for the place where the aliens landed.

Mike Norton/Shutterstock.com

Think Critically

1. Do you think most entrepreneurs begin with identifying a need or problem, developing a plan or model, and then collecting information to test that model? Why is it important?
2. Explain why (or why not) a step-by-step plan adds value to a business idea.

yienkeat/Shutterstock.com

2-1 The Economist's Toolkit

Learning Objectives	Vocabulary
LO 1-1 Understand how economists use economic models.	**model,** p. 37
LO 1-2 Evaluate economic activity using graphs.	**assumption,** p. 37
LO 1-3 Explain why economists can disagree.	**direct relationship,** p. 38
	inverse relationship, p. 40
	positive economics, p. 42
	normative economics, p. 42

© Aleksandar Vrzalski/iStockphoto.com

REAL-WORLD FOCUS

Marty needs a new laptop. He wants a wide screen so he can have multiple websites open at once. The computer must be powerful enough to download extensive graphics, programs, music, and visual displays. He wants it to be small enough to carry in his backpack. He has looked at several options, but finds the computers difficult to compare in terms of value and price.

ifong/Shutterstock.com

WORK AS A TEAM What should Marty do to narrow his choices and make the best decision? What steps would you take to narrow the focus?

Ints Vikmanis/Shutterstock.com

Normally, there are more rainy days in the spring than any other time of the year.

DO YOU THINK the relationship between the number of umbrellas sold and the number of rainy days is a direct relationship or an inverse relationship?

yienkeat/Shutterstock.com

1-1 The Methodology of Economics

This lesson introduces three tools of analysis used by economists. These tools include model building, graphs, and positive versus normative analysis. Economists use a step-by-step method for solving problems. Step 1 is to identify the problem. Step 2 is to develop a model by selecting the variables based on an assumption. Step 3 is to collect data and test the model. Figure 2-1 summarizes the model-building process.

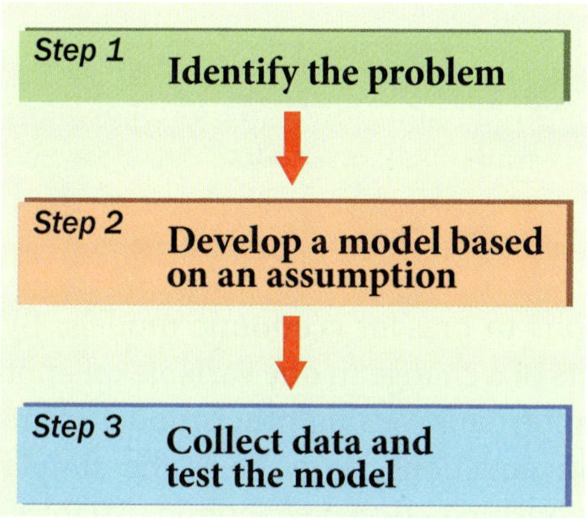

Figure 2-1

Steps in the Model-Building Process

The first step is to identify the problem. The second step is to develop a model by selecting the variables. A model is based on an assumption that eliminates variables that complicate the model. The third step is to collect data and test the model.

Step 1 Identify the Problem

The first step is to define the problem. Suppose an economist wishes to investigate why motorists cut back on gasoline consumption. Assume customers purchased 400 million gallons per day in May. In December, they purchased 300 million gallons per day. The economist needs to investigate the question of why 100 million fewer gallons were purchased in December.

Step 2 Develop a Model

The second step is to build a model. A **model** is a simplification of reality used to understand the relationship between variables. A model is also called a *theory*. A model emphasizes those variables that are most important by assuming that all other variables remain unchanged. Using a model makes the relationship between the chosen variables easier to understand.

Consider a highway map as an example of a model. To find the best route to drive between two distant cities, you do not need to see all the roads, potholes, trees, stoplights, schools, hospitals, and firehouses. Too much detail may make it difficult to choose the best route. In this case, the model consists of two variables, the price of gasoline and the quantity of gasoline consumed. The economist believes that when the price rises, the quantity consumers buy falls. All other possible causes for the decline in gasoline sales are ignored.

The Capital of Texas Highway, also known as Loop 360, is near the city of Austin.

A model must include an assumption. An **assumption** is something that is accepted as being true. Here the assumption is that consumer incomes and other variables do not change when gasoline prices rise. If they did, the reason for reduced gasoline consumption could be one of these variables and not the price.

An economic model is useful only if it yields accurate predictions. When the evidence confirms a model, it is accepted. When the evidence does not support a model, the model is rejected.

Step 3 Test the Model

In the third step, the economist gathers data to test the model. If the price of gasoline rises, do gasoline purchases fall? An investigation reveals that the price of gasoline rose sharply between May and December. The data support the model that the quantity of gasoline consumed per month falls when its price rises. Thus, the model is valid.

CHECKPOINT

Why is an assumption important to a model?

LO 1-2 Applying Graphs to Economics

Economists use graphs to present economic models. By drawing a graph, you can analyze the effects of a change in one variable on another variable. You could describe the same information using other model forms. These include verbal statements, tables, or equations. A graph is the simplest way to present and understand the relationship between economic variables.

A Direct Relationship

Basic economic analysis concerns the relationship between two variables. The horizontal axis in Figure 2-2 represents annual income. The vertical axis shows the amount spent per year for a personal computer (PC). Both variables are expressed in thousands of dollars per year. In Figure 2-2, each point matches income and expenditures for a PC. Point *A* shows that people with an annual income of $30,000 spent $1,000 for a PC. At $120,000 per year (point *D*), $4,000 is spent annually for a PC.

The line shows the direction of change in PC expenditure as annual income changes. This relationship is positive. PC expenditure and income move along the line in the same direction. PC expenditure increases as annual income increases. As income falls, so does the amount spent on a PC. The line is a direct relationship. A **direct relationship** is a positive relationship between two variables. When one variable increases, the other variable increases. When one variable decreases, the other variable decreases. Both variables change in the same direction.

Figure 2-2

A Direct Relationship Between Variables

The line shows that the expenditure for a personal computer has a direct relationship to annual income. Annual income increases along the horizontal axis. The amount spent on a PC also increases along the vertical axis.

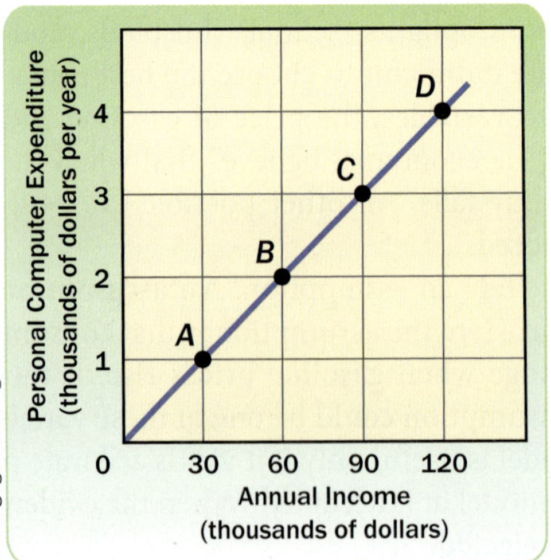

Point	Personal Computer Expenditure (thousands of dollars per year)	Annual Income (thousands of dollars)
A	$1	$30
B	2	60
C	3	90
D	4	120

Math CONNECTION

FreeSoulProduction/Shutterstock.com

Extrapolate Data from a Graph

At a local job fair, you stop at a booth advertising jobs at a warehouse. You talk to a human resource person who shows you the graph below and says, "The more hours you work, the more money you will make." You look at the graph and think to yourself, "I want this job because I will make $425 a week." From the graph you can determine how much money you can make for any number of hours worked. Each point on the line is represented by an ordered pair (x, y) where x is the number of hours worked and y is the amount of money earned. What is the ordered pair that tells you how many hours you have to work to make $425?

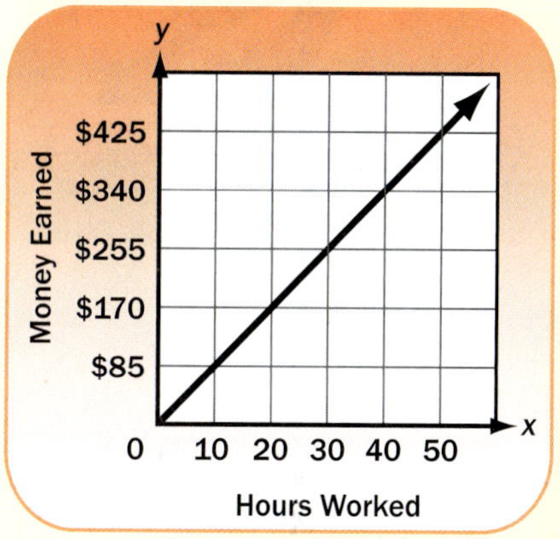

SOLUTION

The scale for the x-axis (horizontal line) is units of 10 hours. The scale for the y-axis (vertical line) is $85. Locate the line on the y-axis labeled $425. This is the location where y = $425. Look to the right (or slide your finger) along the horizontal line until you are on the graphed line. From that point, look down to the x-axis (horizontal) to find the number of hours worked. The number of hours worked is 50, which mean x = 50.

Write the ordered pair in the format (*x*, *y*). (50, $425)

You will have to work 50 hours to earn $425.

TRY IT

Write each point described in the graph above as an ordered pair.

1. working 20 hours
2. earning $340
3. earning $255
4. working 10 hours

A two-variable graph isolates the relationship between two variables. It also assumes all other variables not shown in the graph are constant or unchanged. Such factors as the price of PCs and education of buyers are held constant by this assumption.

Another tool used is data in a table arranged in rows and columns. In Figure 2-2, observe the rows in the table match each point in the graph. The columns give data for PC expenditures and annual income variables. Point *A*, for example, represents $1,000 on the vertical axis and $30,000 on the horizontal axis. The graph and the table use the same data, but have different appearances.

joshblake/iStockphoto.com

A young man plays the new Super Hero video game on a game console.

An Inverse Relationship

A company does a consumer survey for its new video game called Super Hero. Figure 2-3 shows an inverse relationship between the price and the quantity consumers will buy per year. An **inverse relationship** is a negative relationship between two variables. When the price is low, consumers purchase a greater quantity of Super Hero. When the price is high, consumers buy fewer video games. At a price of $80, the number of games purchased is 25 million (point *A*). At a price of $20, the number of games purchased is 100 million (point *D*). Stated simply, the variables move in opposite directions.

Figure 2-3

An Inverse Relationship Between Variables

The line shows an inverse relationship between the price per game and the quantity of video games consumers purchase. As the price of Super Hero rises, the quantity of Super Hero games purchased falls. At a lower price consumers purchase more Super Hero games.

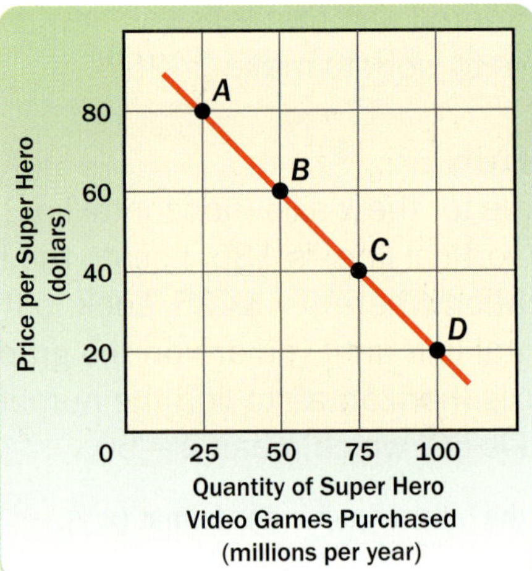

Point	Price per Game	Quantity of Super Hero Video Games Purchased (millions per year)
A	$80	25
B	60	50
C	40	75
D	20	100

ETHICS *in Action!*

Correlation and Causation

The fact that two events happen at the same time (correlation) does not necessarily mean that one of the events causes (causation) the other to happen. Consider the economic situation in the United States in the years following 2008. The U.S. economy fell into a deep recession. Thousands of people lost their homes to foreclosures. Unemployment rates grew to over 10 percent. Government borrowing skyrocketed as tax collections fell. The number of people receiving government assistance rose dramatically.

State or local government officials could do little to prevent or solve the economic problems. Nevertheless, current officeholders were blamed for economic problems by candidates who ran against them in the election campaigns of 2010. These candidates sometimes used graphs to illustrate relationships that did not exist.

Suppose a person running to replace your state's governor in 2010 used the graph below to argue that the current governor was responsible for high unemployment in your state. Clearly, there is a correlation between the current governor's election and increasing rates of unemployment. But, is there also causation? How much did the current governor do to cause the growth in unemployment and could he or she have done much to bring these rates down when unemployment was a national problem?

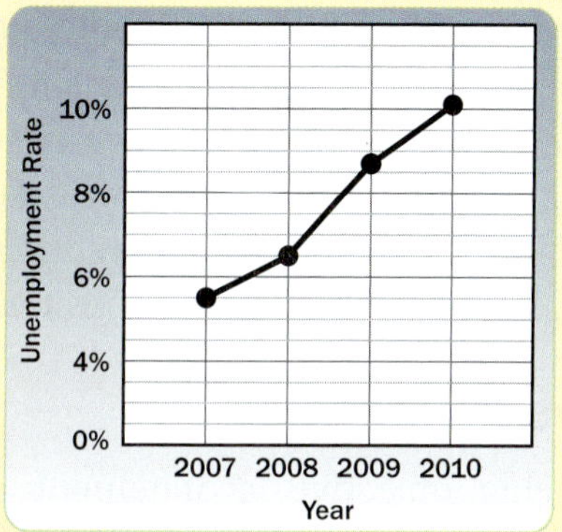

© Cengage Learning 2013

Graphs are models that show relationships between two variables. This does not mean the graphs always show the truth or are used in an ethical way.

Think Critically

1. Why should you always evaluate relationships presented in economic models to make sure they are based on reason and logic?

2. Do you believe that politicians in your community have used models in an unethical way? Explain why or why not.

In Chapter 3, the law of demand will be explained as an inverse relationship between a product's price and the quantity demanded. The law of supply in Chapter 4 is developed as a direct relationship between a product's price and the quantity demanded.

CHECKPOINT

Economists can use a graph or a table to present the same data. Do you have a preference? Why?

LO 1-3 Why Do Economists Disagree?

Why might one economist say a clean planet should be a country's priority, while another might say economic growth should be the priority? If economists use the same tools of analysis, then why do they sometimes disagree? The reason can often be explained by the difference between positive economics and normative economics.

Positive Economics

Positive economics is an analysis based on facts. Positive analysis uses statements that can be proven either true or false. Often a positive statement is expressed using the words "if" and "then." *If* the unemployment rate rises to 9 percent, *then* teenage unemployment exceeds 80 percent. This is a positive prediction that may or may not be correct. A positive statement does not have to be correct. The key is whether the statement is testable. For example, the overall unemployment rate was 9.6 percent in 2010. The rate for teenagers was 25.9 percent which is far short of 80 percent. Based on the facts, the positive statement is false.

Normative Economics

Instead of being objective, a statement can be subjective using normative economics. **Normative economics** is an analysis based on value judgments. Normative statements express an opinion on a subject. The opinion cannot be proven by facts to be true or false. Certain words or phrases are normative, such as good, bad, need, should, and ought to be.

People have individual preferences that they apply to a particular subject. They express these preferences using normative statements. One person may argue, "We ought to see that every teenager who wants a job has one." Another may say, "The minimum wage should be raised."

A young man shows his monthly earnings.

Suzanne Tucker/Shutterstock.com

Make sure to recognize statements or arguments as either positive or normative. Understanding the difference allows you to know if the statement or argument is based on facts or opinion. In your everyday life, politicians, business executives, relatives, and friends often use normative statements. When using value judgments, an economist's arguments may have no more value than others'. Biases can cloud an economist's thinking just as they can cloud yours. The *You're the Economist* on the minimum wage issue presents an illustration of the difference between positive and normative economic arguments.

CHECKPOINT

Assume an argument is based on incorrect facts. Is this a positive or normative analysis? Why?

Does the Minimum Wage Really Help the Working Poor?

You're the ECONOMIST

In 1938, Congress enacted the federal Fair Labor Standards Act, commonly known as the "minimum-wage law." Today, a minimum-wage worker who works full time still earns a deplorably low annual income. One approach to help the working poor earn a living wage might be to raise the minimum wage. Some politicians claim that raising the minimum wage is a way to help the working poor without costs to taxpayers. Others believe the costs are hidden in higher prices for products and lost jobs for teenagers, the elderly, and minorities. One study by economists examined sixty years of national data and reported evidence that minimum wage increases resulted in reduced employment and hours of work for low-wage workers.

imageegami/Shutterstock.com

A person who takes orders at a pizza shop earns minimum wage and is an example of a worker that is not likely to work full-time as the sole supporter of the family.

Does raising the minimum wage aid the working poor? Studies show that only a small percentage of minimum-wage earners are full-time workers whose family income falls below the poverty line. What these studies show is that most increases in the minimum wage go to workers who are not members of poor families. For example, many minimum-wage workers are students living at home or workers whose spouse earns a much higher income. To help only the working poor, some economists argue that the government should target only those who need assistance. Although this approach is favored by some, the task of deciding which minimum-wage workers actually need a higher wage is daunting.

Supporters of raising the minimum wage say it is outrageous that a worker can work full time and still live in poverty. Moreover, people on this side of the debate believe that opponents exaggerate the dangers to the economy from a higher minimum wage. One could argue that a higher minimum wage will force employers to upgrade the skills and productivity of their workers. Increasing the minimum wage may therefore be a winning proposition.

Think Critically

1. **Identify a positive and a normative statement given above concerning raising the minimum wage.**
2. **Give a positive and a normative argument why a business leader would oppose raising the minimum wage. Give a positive and a normative argument why a labor leader would favor raising the minimum wage.**
3. **Explain your position on this issue using positive and normative reasons for your decision. Are there alternative ways to aid the working poor?**

2-1 Assessment

Key Concepts

LO 1-2 1. A(n) __?__ relationship is a positive relationship between two variables.

LO 1-1 2. **TRUE OR FALSE** A model is based on assumptions.

LO 1-3 3. An analysis based on value judgments is __?__ economics.

LO 1-2 4. **TRUE OR FALSE** An inverse relationship between two variables means both variables move in the same direction.

LO 1-3 5. An analysis based on facts is __?__ economics.

Think About It

LO 1-1 6. Explain why it is important for an economic model to be a simplification of the real world.

LO 1-3 7. Which statements are positive economics and which are normative economics?
   a. The lottery is a better way to fund our schools.
   b. Variables *A* and *B* move in the same direction.
   c. As people's incomes rise, the number of jobs also rises.

LO 1-2 8. Draw a graph without specific data for the expected relationship between the following variables. In each case, state whether the expected relationship is direct or inverse.
   a. probability of living for ten more years and age
   b. annual income and years of education
   c. inches of snow and sales of bathing suits
   d. number of football games won and the athletic budget

LO 1-1 9. What is the purpose of economic models?

LO 1-2 10. How may graphs be used to demonstrate economic relationships?

LO 1-3 11. What is the cause of most disagreements among economists?

LO 1-1 12. Use the model-building process. Identify a problem that interests you. Next formulate a model based on assumption. Collect data to test your model. Include a description of your process and conclusion.

Make Academic Connections

LO 1-3 13. **RESEARCH** Find a statement about the economy from a businessperson, politician, and an economist. Explain why you think each statement is normative or positive.

Teamwork

LO 1-2 14. Work in four groups. Two groups represent normative economics and two groups represent positive economics. Each group brainstorms three current economic issues in terms of normative or positive analysis. A spokesperson from each group explains their examples.

Unit 1 Project: Free Markets

CREATE A MODEL Draw a map of your home, including the driveway, entrances, exits, garages, and other features. Include all usable space inside and outside. Include all major walls, rooms, furniture, and personal property. Write a one-page direction sheet that would tell a house sitter exactly what they would need to know if they would be taking care of your home for a week.

2-2 Opportunity Cost

Learning Objectives

LO 2-1 **Explain** why all decisions have trade-offs and opportunity costs.

LO 2-2 **Understand** how to perform marginal analysis.

Vocabulary

trade-off, p. 46
opportunity cost, p. 46
marginal analysis, p. 48
marginal benefit, p. 48
marginal cost, p. 48
cost-benefit analysis, p. 48
net benefit, p. 48

© Aleksandar Vrzalski/iStockphoto.com

REAL-WORLD FOCUS

Carrie has saved her money for more than a year so she can buy a new purse. She wants a designer bag that is both durable and attractive. Now that she has saved enough money, she is reluctant to make the purchase. "It feels really good having the money in my savings account," she told her friend. "I keep thinking about other ways I could spend the money. I also like the idea of growing the account and having it as a safety net. I guess that's the problem with saving money—you get used to it and hate to let it go."

Grayba Victoria/Shutterstock.com

WORK AS A TEAM Considering her original goal, why is Carrie reluctant to spend her savings on a purse? What does Carrie give up if she spends all of her savings on a purse? What would you advise Carrie to do?

The cost of dining in a restaurant should include the amount of money you leave as a tip for the server.

DO YOU THINK if you choose to get a part-time job as a cashier instead of a server in a restaurant, is the money received as tips an opportunity cost?

BrianAJackson/iStockphoto.com

yienkeat/Shutterstock.com

LO 2-1 Trade-offs and Opportunity Cost

© Cengage Learning 2013

Everyday decisions involve trade-offs. A **trade-off** is all the options given up when a decision is made. All individuals, businesses, and governments make decisions resulting in trade-offs. You make decisions involving trade-offs when deciding what to do during your summer vacation. Should you work as an aide in the library, a lifeguard at the beach, or a server at a restaurant? Working at the library would be a good educational experience. Working at the beach would be great fun. Working as a server at a restaurant would be the highest-paying option. Regardless of your choice, there are always trade-offs. Whenever you choose to use your time in a particular way, you trade this use of your time for the opportunity to do anything else during that time. Businesses and governments have trade-offs, too. Suppose a farmer decides to plant corn one year. The farmer gives up the option of planting cotton, soybeans, and other crops on the same land. If the federal government decides to purchase more military goods, it has less to spend on health, education, and clean air.

Because of scarcity, the three basic economic questions cannot be answered without sacrifice or cost. But what does the term *cost* really mean? The common response is to say that the purchase price is the cost. A movie ticket costs $8, or a shirt costs $50. However, economists define the term *cost* differently. The true cost of these decisions is the opportunity cost of a choice, not just the purchase price. **Opportunity cost** is the value of the next best option sacrificed for a chosen option. In other words, it is the cost of not choosing the best alternative. This principle states that some highly-valued opportunity must be forgone, or given up, in all decisions. The actual good or use of time given up for the chosen good or use of time is the opportunity cost. Figure 2-4 illustrates the causation chain linking scarcity, choice, and opportunity cost. Because of scarcity, people must make choices, and each choice incurs a cost (sacrifice). Once one option is chosen, the second best option is given up.

kali9/iStockphoto.com

Most of the money earned by a server comes from tips given by customers.

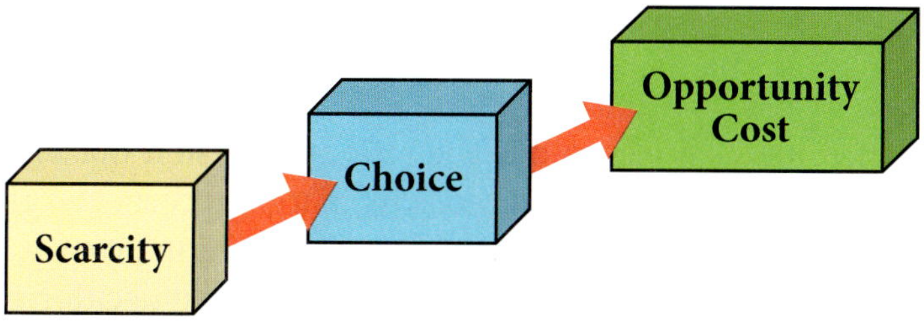

Figure 2-4

The Links Between Scarcity, Choice, and Opportunity Cost

The cause-and-effect chain shows that scarcity causes the effect of choice. Next, each choice causes the effect of opportunity cost.

All decisions have several trade-offs or options given up. Only one of these options is the opportunity cost. Think about your decision concerning how to spend your summer. Suppose you choose being a server because earning money is most important to you. Your best option not chosen is being a lifeguard at the beach. Therefore this option is the opportunity cost of choosing to be a server. Working in the library is also a trade-off, but it is not the opportunity cost.

Consider a few more examples. Suppose your economics teacher decides to become a rock star. Now all his or her working hours are devoted to creating hit music. The opportunity cost is the educational services he or she no longer provides. Opportunity cost also applies to national economic decisions. Suppose the federal government decides to spend tax revenues on a space station. The opportunity cost is the value of the next best program not funded. Assume roads and bridges are the highest-valued projects not built because of the decision to construct the space station. Then the opportunity cost of the decision to devote resources to the space station is the forgone roads and bridges and not the money actually spent to build the space station.

The opportunity cost of a space station might be roads and bridges not built.

Think of an example in your life of the relationship between time and opportunity cost. Ask yourself what you would be doing if you were not reading this book. Your answer might be watching television or sleeping. If sleeping is your second best choice, the opportunity cost of studying this text is the sleep you sacrifice. How would a professional athlete or movie star answer this question?

CHECKPOINT

Explain the difference between trade-offs and opportunity cost.

LO 2-2 Marginal Analysis

Most decisions are m*arginal* and not all-or-none. **Marginal analysis** is the decision about how much more or less to do. The rational decision maker decides on an option only if its marginal benefit exceeds its marginal cost. **Marginal benefit** is the extra gain from an additional unit of change. **Marginal cost** is the extra cost from an additional unit of change. For example, you must decide how to use your scarce time. Should you devote an extra hour to reading this book, going to a movie, watching television, texting, or sleeping? Which option do you choose? If you decide the benefit of a higher grade in economics exceeds the opportunity cost of sleep, then you use the extra hour for studying economics. When you use marginal analysis to make decisions, you are said to be "thinking at the margin."

Orchidflower/Shutterstock.com

A homeowner chooses the "do-it-yourself" option for getting the interior of her house painted.

Businesses use marginal analysis in making decisions. Hotels, for example, rent space to student groups for dances and other events. Assume you are the hotel manager and a student group offers to pay $500 to use the ballroom for an event. To decide whether to accept the offer requires marginal analysis. The marginal benefit of renting otherwise vacant space is $500, and the marginal cost is $300 for extra electricity and cleaning services. Because the marginal benefit exceeds the marginal cost, the manager accepts the offer.

Farmers also use marginal analysis. For example, a farmer must decide whether to add fertilizer when planting corn. Using marginal analysis, the farmer estimates that corn grown on an acre of land will yield about $75 per acre without fertilizer and about $100 per acre using fertilizer. If the cost of fertilizer is $20 per acre, marginal analysis tells the farmer to fertilize. The addition of fertilizer adds $25 ($100 – $75) revenue per acre to the value of each acre (marginal benefit) at a cost of $20 per acre (marginal cost). The additional fertilizer increases the profit by $5 per acre.

To evaluate choices, economists often use cost-benefit analysis. **Cost-benefit analysis** compares the additional rewards and costs of an action to determine if the benefits outweigh the costs. If there is a net benefit, the option is selected. **Net benefit** is the difference between the marginal benefit and the marginal cost of an option. Your parents often think about painting, cutting the lawn, or other possible "do-it-yourself" projects. They balance the costs and benefits of hiring someone or doing it themselves. Is investing one's time worth it? It comes down to comparing the benefits to the cost. Is the satisfaction of painting the house worth the cost of leisure time? Does the benefit of a well-kept lawn outweigh the cost of hiring someone?

The basic rule of cost-benefit analysis is that an undertaking in which a cost exceeds its benefit is an inefficient use of resources. In the free market system, undertaking projects that yield benefits greater than costs offers a much better chance of success. In the long run, any firm that does not follow the cost-benefit rule will go out of business.

CHECKPOINT

What does it mean to "think at the margin"?

PROFILE

Friedrich von Hayek
Austrian School of Economics

© Bettmann/CORBIS

Friedrich von Hayek (1899-1992) was born in Vienna, then Austria-Hungary. He served in World War I, and said this experience gave him the desire to follow an academic career devoted to avoiding mistakes that cause war. At the University of Vienna, he earned doctorates in law (1921) and political science (1923). He also studied philosophy, psychology, and economics. Hayek lived in Austria, Germany, Great Britain, and the United States. After Nazi Germany took control of Austria, he became a British subject in 1938. His academic career was spent at the London School of Economics, the University of Chicago, and the University of Freiburg.

Hayek was a Renaissance man. He made contributions to political theory and psychology as well as economics. His role in the twentieth-century collapse of socialism can be compared to the role of Adam Smith in the eighteenth century. Both were champions of the creative power of freedom and the market economy. Hayek said that the market does a remarkable job of coordinating people's actions through "spontaneous order." Hayek meant that the market was unplanned and evolved as the result of human action.

Friedrich von Hayek was a recipient of the 1974 Nobel Prize for economics. He was a key contributor to a free market school of thought called the *Austrian school*. His major book was *The Road to Serfdom*, published in 1944. This book warned of the dangers that result from government central planning, which leads to individuals losing their freedoms. The *Road to Serfdom* remains a popular and influential argument for free market economics.

One feature of the Austrian school is information economics. This includes a focus on the market adjustment process. Hayek rejected an economy directed by central authority. Instead, he advocated markets as superior transmitters of information. How are people informed of the best use of resources? The answer is that prices set in free markets give the correct information. An increase in the price of a resource signals its opportunity cost has risen. As a result, resources are allocated efficiently to their best use. In contrast, decisions on prices set by central authority are subject to human errors and are inefficient. Such central authority decisions often turn out to be against the best interest of society and its individual members.

THINK CRITICALLY

Suppose the resource is your labor and the labor market sets a higher wage rate that you could earn at another job. Relate this situation to opportunity cost and the allocation of your labor to a job.

2-2 Assessment

Key Concepts

LO 2-2 1. The decision about how much more or less to do is __?__.

LO 2-1 2. **TRUE OR FALSE** Trade-offs always exist, but opportunity cost does not.

LO 2-2 3. The difference between the marginal benefit and the marginal cost of an option is the __?__.

LO 2-2 4. **TRUE OR FALSE** Cost-benefit analysis can only be applied to money decisions.

Think About It

LO 2-1 5. Explain how scarcity forces all individuals to incur opportunity costs when they make choices.

LO 2-1 6. Explain how scarcity applies to society. Consider the choice between society choosing to produce more or less military goods and services and consumer goods and services.

LO 2-1 7. Which of the following decisions has the greater opportunity cost? Why?
   a. A decision to use an undeveloped lot in Tokyo's financial district for an apartment building.
   b. A decision to use a square mile in the desert for a gas station.

LO 2-1 8. What might be the opportunity cost of watching TV until 2 A.M. on a school night? Explain.

LO 2-2 9. What steps are involved in marginal analysis?

LO 2-2 10. Attending college is expensive, time consuming, and it requires effort. So why do people decide to attend college?

LO 2-2 11. Peaches are in season, and your local grocery store is selling them for a great low price. What would be the marginal benefit and the marginal cost of buying five pounds of peaches? Explain your answer.

Make Academic Connections

LO 2-2 12. **COMMUNICATION** Think of a decision that you had to make. Write a description of how you made that decision.

LO 2-1 13. **ENGLISH** Begin a journal with the hyphenated words used in economics such as trade-off and cost-benefit. Note one use of a hyphen joins two words to serve as a single adjective before a noun.

Teamwork

LO 2-2 14. Work in groups. Each group considers the marginal benefits and marginal costs of buying a new car. Each group reports their ideas to the class.

Unit 1 Project: Free Markets

ANALYZE A SITUATION Prepare a quantitative and qualitative analysis and present it orally. Assume you are a night clerk at a local four-star hotel. Late on Friday night, you have five out of 100 rooms available. A competitor hotel is full and their night clerk is on the phone asking if you will accept two of their customers who had confirmed reservations. They ask you to charge the confirmed price of $150 per night. You normally charge $250 per night. What do you need to consider before deciding if you will accept or reject the offer? Explain how added revenue versus added costs will help you make a decision. Explain your answer both in terms of math (marginal revenues, costs, and profits) and in terms of other factors (non-quantitative) to consider.

2-3 Production Possibilities Curve

Learning Objectives

LO 3-1 **Interpret** a production possibilities curve.

LO 3-2 **Understand** how scarcity relates to the production possibilities curve.

LO 3-3 **Demonstrate** how economic growth occurs using the production possibilities curve.

Vocabulary

production possibilities curve, p. 52
technology, p. 52
efficiency, p. 52
underutilization, p. 53
law of increasing opportunity cost, p. 54
economic growth, p. 55

© Aleksandar Vrzalski/iStockphoto.com

REAL-WORLD FOCUS

Ron just inherited $500 from his uncle. He is deciding what to do with it. His first thought is to spend it all on new camping equipment. Another option is to save it all in his bank account. The camping equipment would bring him immediate pleasure this summer. But saving the money would help provide financial security for the future. He is having a hard time deciding what to do—should he spend it all or should he save it all?

WORK AS A TEAM Is there another choice besides spending all of the money or saving all of the money? How might Ron have both an immediate pleasure and a long-term focus for this inheritance? What would you do?

Using a non-motorized lawn mower is considered to be an environmentally friendly way to cut grass.

DO YOU THINK the woman in the photo is an example of efficiency or underutilization? Explain your answer.

Groomee/iStockphoto.com

yienkeat/Shutterstock.com

LO 3-1 Production Possibilities Curve

Scarcity means that society's capacity to produce is limited. This condition can be shown in a model called the production possibilities curve. The **production possibilities curve (PPC)** shows the maximum possible output for an economy. The model has two assumptions.

1. **Fixed Resources** All resources remain unchanged. There is no way to increase land, labor, or capital. But the "rules of the game" do allow an economy to shift any resource from producing one output to producing another. For example, an economy might shift workers from producing tanks to sailboats. The number of workers remains unchanged. This transfer of labor will produce fewer tanks and more sailboats.
2. **Technology Unchanged** Technology also is assumed to be fixed or unchanged. **Technology** is the body of knowledge applied to how goods and services are produced.

Figure 2-5 uses a production possibilities curve to show an economy that produces tanks and sailboats. The economy can produce any combination of these two products shown along its production possibilities curve. Point *A* shows where all resources are used to make 80,000 tanks and zero sailboats. Another possibility is shown at point *D* where the economy uses all of its resources to produce 60,000 sailboats and zero tanks. Between points *A* and *D* are other output options for tanks and sailboats. At point *B*, the economy will produce 70,000 tanks and 20,000 sailboats. Another possibility at point *C* is to produce 50,000 tanks and 40,000 sailboats. All points along the curve illustrate maximum output levels. They are all efficient points. **Efficiency** is producing the maximum output with given resources and technology.

What happens if the economy does not use all its resources to full capacity? For example, some workers may be unemployed, or plants and equipment may

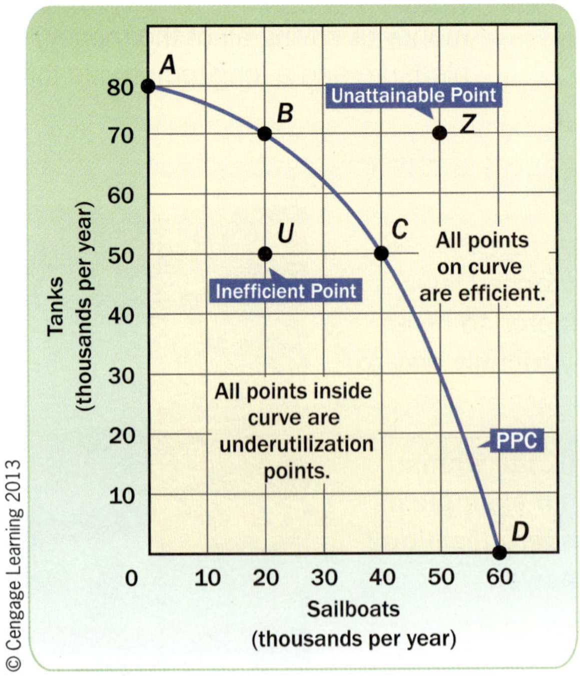

Figure 2-5

Production Possibilities Curve for Tanks and Sailboats

On the curve four different efficient combinations of tanks and sailboats an economy could produce are labeled as points *A*, *B*, *C*, and *D*. The assumption is that resources are fully used and technology is unchanged. If not, the result is inefficient points such as *U*. Points like *Z* are beyond the economy's capacity and are unattainable.

not be used to full capacity. The result is that the economy fails to reach any of the efficient points along the PPC. In Figure 2-5, point *U* illustrates an inefficient output level because the economy is operating without all its resources fully employed. At point *U*, the economy is producing 50,000 tanks and 20,000 sailboats per year. Such an economy is underproducing. It could satisfy more of society's wants if it were producing at some point along *PPC*. Any point inside the curve indicates underutilization of resources. **Underutilization** occurs when an economy fails to fully use its resources. As a result, the economy produces less than maximum output. All points inside the PPC are inefficient points because the economy is producing less than it could.

There is always a limit to the quantity of goods and services an economy is able to produce from its limited resources. Any point outside the PPC curve is impossible. These points are beyond the economy's productive capacity. Point *Z* represents an *unattainable* output. The economy cannot reach this point with its existing resources and technology.

gaspr13/iStockphoto.com

A crane lowers a new sailboat into the water for its initial launch.

CHECKPOINT

Explain why all points along the production possibilities curve are efficient points.

Technology Advances

States and large metropolitan areas may have specific robotic needs based on industries that prevail in the region. For example, a farming community has little need for robots that operate assembly lines, but would benefit from technology that provides harvesting assistance. However, states with many automobile manufacturers may have needs just the opposite of the farming community. Research new technological advances that have been produced or utilized in your state or locality in the last five years.

Investigate Your Local ECONOMY

Try it Out

Are there any new technological advances expected soon? Explain how these technological advances would affect a production possibilities curve and produce economic growth.

LO 3-2 Opportunity Costs and the Production Possibilities Curve

The concept of opportunity cost also can be explained with a PPC graph. Figure 2-6 presents an economy producing tanks and sailboats. Using marginal analysis, sailboat output increases by 20,000 increments along the horizontal dashed arrows. The 10,000 sailboats increments are read along the horizontal axis between 0–20,000, 20,000–40,000, and 40,000–60,000. Moving down from point *A* to point *B*, the opportunity cost is 10,000 tanks. This opportunity cost is shown by the vertical arrow between 80,000 and 70,000 tanks. Recall that opportunity cost is the best option given up. Here more sailboat output requires giving up tank output. Between point *B* and point *C*, the opportunity cost is 20,000 tanks. This opportunity cost is shown by the vertical dashed arrow reading down from point *B* between 70,000 and 50,000 tanks. The opportunity cost of moving from point *C* to point *D* is 50,000 tanks. This opportunity cost is shown by the vertical dashed arrow reading down from point *C*. Where the PPC touches the horizontal axis, zero tanks are produced.

Figure 2-6

Opportunity Costs and the Production Possibilities Curve

Using marginal analysis, the graph shows additional increases of 20,000 sailboats produced between points. The decreases of tank output represent the opportunity cost of the gains in sailboat output. Between points *A* and *D*, sacrifice of tank output rises from 10,000 (point *A* to point *B*) to 50,000 (point *C* to point *D*).

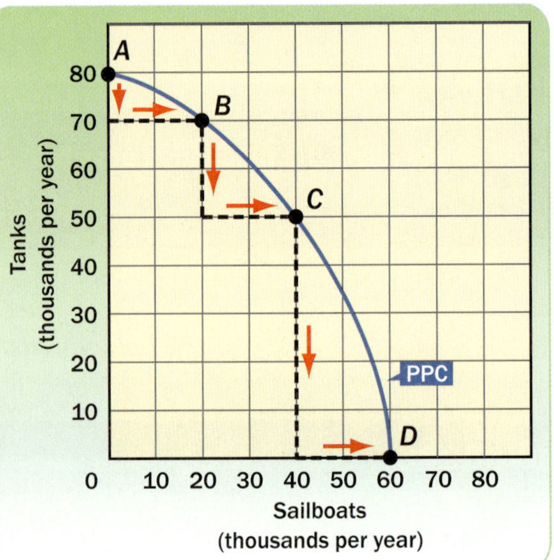

Notice the number of tanks that must be given up in order to produce each additional 20,000 boats is increasing. This situation illustrates the law of increasing opportunity cost. The **law of increasing opportunity cost** states that the opportunity cost increases as production of an output expands. As more of an economy's resources are devoted to producing one product, ever greater quantities of production of the other product must be given up. This law exists because not all resources are equally suited to all

NET Bookmark

Access www.cengage.com/school/economics/personalfinance and click on the link for Chapter 2. On the Bureau of Labor Statistics website locate o[n] Subject Areas to locate the unemployment rate. W[hat] is the trend in the unemployment rate over the last two years? How would this trend be reflected in the nation's production possibilities curve?

www.cengage.com/school/economics/personalfin[ance]

types of production. Some resources are better suited to producing tanks than boats. If these resources are used to produce boats, they will not be used effectively and increasing quantities of them must be used to produce each additional boat.

CHECKPOINT

Explain the condition of scarcity and opportunity costs in terms of the production possibilities curve.

LO 3-3 Sources of Economic Growth

An economy's production capacity is not always fixed. If resources increase or technology advances, this creates economic growth. Economic growth occurs when the production possibilities curve shifts outward. **Economic growth** is the ability of an economy to produce greater levels of output. When economic growth occurs the assumption that resources and technology are fixed is removed.

Changes in Resources

One way to achieve economic growth is to gain resources. Any increase in resources shifts the production possibilities curve outward. Building new factories and increasing the number of workers are examples. In Figure 2-7, assume curve PPC_1 represents an economy in a given year. When new sources of labor and capital are obtained, the economy has an expanded capacity. It can now produce any combination along the expanded curve, PPC_2.

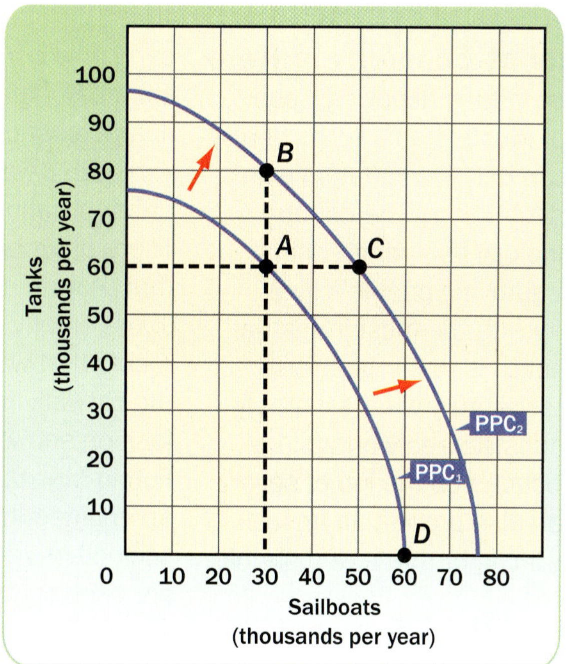

Figure 2-7

Outward Shift of the Production Possibilities Curve for Tanks and Sailboats

More resources or technological advances shift the PPC outward from PPC_1 to PPC_2. This economic growth allows the economy to produce more of both tanks and sailboats between points *B* and *C* compared to point *A*.

What is the importance of an outward shift? At point *A* on PPC_1, the economy produces 60,000 tanks and 30,000 sailboats per year. If the curve shifts outward to the new curve PPC_2, output can expand. One option is to produce at point *B* and increase tank output to 80,000 per year. Another possibility is to increase sailboat output to 50,000 per year at point *C*. Yet another choice is to produce more of both at some point between points *B* and *C*. Being able to produce more output increases the standard of living.

Technological Change

Another way to achieve economic growth is new knowledge that makes an economy more productive. The invention of the wheel vastly improved people's ability to produce. Technological change makes it possible to shift PPC_1 outward to PPC_2. The reason is that the economy can produce more from the same resources. One source of technological change is inventions. Computer chips, satellites, and the Internet are examples of new science and engineering knowledge that have increased the ability to produce. Technological change also results from entrepreneurship. Seeking profits in a free market system, entrepreneurs create new and better products. Henry Ford changed the auto industry by pioneering the use of the assembly line. Entrepreneurs are important because they transform new ideas into ways to increase production.

CHECKPOINT

Explain how changing an assumption shifts the production possibilities curve.

Global View

In Japan the Robot Economy Is Here

Japan is an efficient industrial powerhouse known for quality products produced by dedicated workers. Japan has a fascination with advances in robot technology. The country regards robot technology as strengthening the economy and improving people's lives. Japan is the country with the most industrial robot workers. Robotics is to the Japanese economy in the 21st century what assembly lines were to the industrialized world in the 20th century. A robot can do the job of several workers. Robots can also provide an answer for the nation's declining birthrate and shrinking workforce.

Japan has all types of robots. There are humanoid robots, animal robots, social robots, security robots, domestic robots, rescue robots, and so on. There are robot dogs that bark, wag their tails, and run. There are also mountable robots that carry passengers around. A Japanese robotics expert has unveiled a robot of himself. This humanoid robot is designed down to the tiniest detail in its creator's image. It can shrug or scowl and carry on a conversation. Robots' characteristics vary with different applications. There are robots that provide help to the elderly, and robots that walk the catwalk in fashion shows. Fumio Miyazaki, an engineering science professor, predicts that Japanese scientists will provide thousands of humanoids that could be working alongside humans by the end of 2020s.

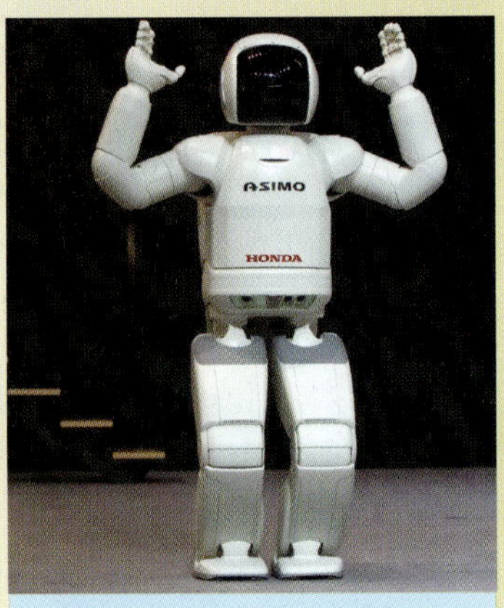

DenisKlimov/Shutterstock.com

Honda presented an ASIMO humanoid robot at an international motor show in 2008. ASIMO stands for Advanced Step in Innovative Mobility.

Think Critically

How do advances in robot technology affect Japan's production possibilities curve?

2-3 Assessment

Key Concepts

LO 3-3 1. An outward shift of a production possibilities curve illustrates __?__.

LO 3-1 2. **TRUE OR FALSE** All points inside a production possibilities curve are inefficient.

LO 3-2 3. Opportunity costs and __?__ can be illustrated on a production possibilities curve.

LO 3-3 4. **TRUE OR FALSE** An advancement in technology will not shift a production possibilities curve outward.

Think About It

LO 3-1 5. What do points outside, along, and inside the production possibilities curve represent?

LO 3-1 6. Explain the statement "There is no such thing as a free lunch" in relation to the production possibilities curve.

LO 3-1 7. What does the production possibilities curve on page 54 demonstrate?

LO 3-2 8. How does scarcity of resources determine the location of a production possibilities curve?

LO 3-3 9. How can economic growth be shown on a production possibilities curve?

LO 3-3 10. What might cause the production possibilities curve to shift outward?

Make Academic Connections

LO 3-3 11. **COMMUNICATION** Write a paper on the effect you think the Internet has on the production possibilities curve.

LO 3-2 12. **MATH** The table shows the production possibilities for pies and chairs. Fill in the opportunity cost (pies forgone) of producing the first through the fifth chair.

Combination	Pies	Chairs	Opportunity Cost
A	30	0	
B	26	1	__?__
C	21	2	__?__
D	15	3	__?__
E	8	4	__?__
F	0	5	__?__

Teamwork

LO 3-1 13. Work in groups. Each group acts as a country that can produce only two products. Assume that resources and technology are fixed. Identify the two products. Make up logical numbers for combinations of these two products. Use these values to draw a production possibilities curve that conforms to the law of increasing opportunity costs (bends away from the origin). Each group presents and explains to the class where on the PPC its country will produce.

Unit 1 Project: Free Markets

CONSIDER POSSIBILITIES You operate a plant nursery. You want to increase your production of roses and/or tomato plants by adding two more acres of land. Prepare a production possibilities curve for the additional two acres of land. One axis should represent production of roses. The other should represent production of tomato plants. Some of the land is wet and not appropriate for roses. Some of it is too alkaline for tomatoes. Make up production amounts for these two plants that are reasonable and which conform to the law of increasing opportunity costs. Label and explain your graph.

Chapter 2 Summary

2-1 THE ECONOMIST'S TOOLKIT

1. An economic problem-solving method begins with identifying a problem. The second step is building a model. A model is a simplification of reality used to understand the relationship between two variables. A model must have an assumption, something accepted as being true. The third step involves testing the model to see whether or not the model is true.
2. Positive economics is an analysis based on facts. Normative economics is an analysis based on value judgments. Knowing the difference will help you decide whether a statement is based on facts or on opinions.
3. Graphs illustrate the relationships between variables. A direct relationship is positive in that both variables move in the same direction. They both increase or both decrease. An inverse relationship is negative in that as one variable increases, the other variable decreases.

2-2 OPPORTUNITY COST

4. Whenever you make a decision, you get something (trade-off) and you give up something (opportunity cost). Decisions involve making sacrifices, or giving up of options, for consumers, for businesses, and for the government.
5. Marginal analysis involves comparing the marginal (added) benefit to the marginal (added) cost of a decision. It is what you will gain (or lose) if you make one additional unit of change.
6. Cost-benefit analysis is the process of comparing added costs to added benefits to decide whether or not the added cost is equal to or greater than the added benefits. Generally, when the added cost exceeds the added benefit, such action is not a good idea.

2-3 THE PRODUCTION POSSIBILITIES CURVE

7. The production possibilities curve shows the maximum possible output of two products for an economy. It is based on the assumption that all resources and technology remain unchanged. If either of these variables was not held constant, the model would not accurately measure the most efficient or maximum combinations of output based on the data supplied.
8. The production possibilities curve demonstrates how society's resources at a point in time can be underutilized (not fully used). Points inside the curve demonstrate an inefficient use of resources.
9. The law of increasing opportunity costs explains how opportunity cost increases as production of an output expands. Economic growth occurs when the production possibilities curve shifts outward, which allows an economy to produce greater levels of output. Sources of economic growth include new resources, such as new factories or new workers, and new technological advances, such as better or faster tools used for production.

Chapter 2

Assessment

Vocabulary Review

Match each statement with the term that best defines it.

1. A simplification of reality used to understand the relationship between variables
2. Something that is accepted as being true
3. An analysis based on facts
4. An analysis based on value judgments
5. A positive relationship between two variables
6. A negative relationship between two variables
7. When an economy fails to fully use its resources, it produces less than maximum output
8. The value of the next best option sacrificed for a chosen option
9. The decision about how much more or less to do
10. The extra gain from an additional unit of change
11. Knowledge applied to how goods and services are produced
12. The extra cost from an additional unit of change
13. An analysis that compares the additional rewards and costs of an action
14. The difference between the marginal benefit and the marginal cost of an option
15. An economy produces the maximum output with given resources and technology
16. An outward shift of the production possibilities curve, which allows an economy to produce greater levels of output
17. A curve that shows the maximum possible output for an economy
18. Opportunity cost increases as production of an output expands
19. All options given up when a decision is made

Vocabulary

a. assumption
b. cost-benefit analysis
c. direct relationship
d. economic growth
e. efficiency
f. inverse relationship
g. law of increasing opportunity cost
h. marginal analysis
i. marginal benefit
j. marginal cost
k. model
l. net benefit
m. normative economics
n. opportunity cost
o. positive economics
p. production possibilities curve
q. technology
r. trade-off
s. underutilization

Review Your Knowledge

LO 1-3 **20.** The statement, "Crime has decreased in the last five years," is
  a. obviously wrong, and therefore, cannot be a positive statement
  b. normative since it can be answered by looking at the facts
  c. positive because it is testable
  d. not interesting because all normative statements are not important

LO 1-2 **21.** A direct relationship exists when
  a. there is no association between two variables
  b. one variable increases and there is no change in the other variable
  c. one variable increases and the other variable increases
  d. one variable increases and the other variable decreases

LO 2-1 **22.** The highest valued alternative that must be given up to choose an option is the
  a. opportunity cost
  b. utility cost
  c. scarcity expense
  d. disutility option

LO 2-1 **23.** When deciding whether to buy a second car, using marginal analysis means the purchaser compares
  a. the benefits expected from two cars with the cost of both
  b. the additional benefits expected from a second car with the cost of the two cars
  c. the dollar cost of the two cars with the potential income the cars will generate
  d. the additional benefits of the second car with the additional cost of the second car

LO 1-1 **24.** "The government should provide health care for all citizens." This statement is an illustration of
  a. positive economic analysis
  b. correlation analysis
  c. fallacy of association analysis
  d. normative economic analysis

LO 3-1 **25.** Any point on the production possibilities curve illustrates
  a. minimum production combinations
  b. maximum production combinations
  c. economic growth
  d. unattainable production combinations

LO 3-3 **26.** The law of increasing opportunity costs exists because
  a. not all resources are equally suited to all types of production
  b. some products require large amounts of resources to produce
  c. it takes longer to make some products than it does to make others
  d. the price of some products is greater than for other products

LO 3-3 **27.** Which of the following would cause the production possibilities curve for computers and education to shift outward?
  a. A choice of more computers and less education
  b. A choice of more education and less computers
  c. A reduction in the labor force
  d. An increase in the quantity of resources

Digging Deeper with Economics e-Collection

Minimum wage is a controversial issue. Some unions would like to require contracts that include a living wage instead of a minimum wage. Access the Gale Economics e-Collection at www.cengage.com/school/economics/personalfinance. Research the concept of a living wage. Summarize the arguments. Determine where you stand on this issue. Present your results on a poster or give a slide presentation.

Think About It

LO 1-2 **28.** A direct relationship tells you that as one variable changes, another will move in the same direction. In other words, if sales increase, production costs will also increase. Why is it important to be able to predict how variables will change?

LO 1-2 **29.** Every decision you make costs you something. List three decisions you made today and explain (a) what you got, and (b) what you gave up.

LO 3-1 **30.** The production possibilities curve shows that some outputs are not possible (unattainable), while others are inefficient. Why are some outputs not attainable in any given economy?

Make Academic Connections

LO 1-3 **31. COMMUNICATIONS** When interest rates rise, individuals should buy less. This statement is based on the assumption that as the cost of credit increases, consumers will charge less and will save more money. Is this a positive or normative statement? Explain. What might happen to cause consumers to buy more (on credit as well as with cash) despite the rising interest rates?

LO 2-1 **32. SOCIAL STUDIES** During tough economic times people often have to make difficult choices. Being forced to choose between paying the utility bill or feeding the family may result in a short-term solution to one problem that creates a long-term outcome in another area. Explain how today's choices by societal members can affect other people (and businesses) as well as the future well-being of individuals.

LO 3-1 **33. TECHNOLOGY** New technological advances make it possible for individuals (as well as companies) to be more efficient and productive. List five products your parents enjoy that were not a part of the lives of their parents. List five products you enjoy that were not available twenty years ago. Next to each, briefly explain how that product or invention has enhanced lives.

LO 3-3 **34. HISTORY** When the United States entered World War II it faced the huge task of preparing for war. Consumer goods were in short supply and ration coupons were issued to limit purchases of these goods. Explain the period during World War II in terms of a production possibilities model.

Extend Your Learning

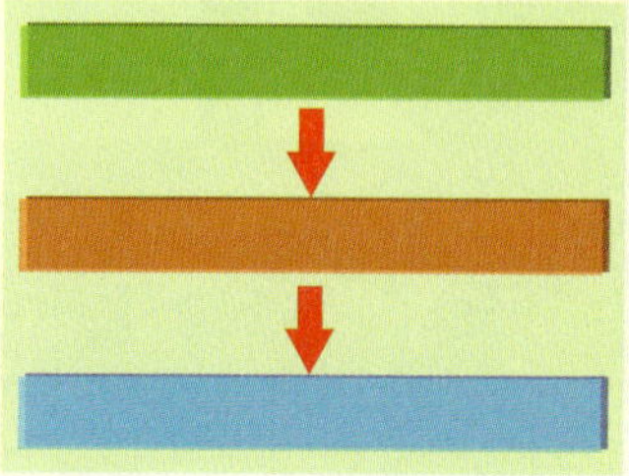

LO 1-1 **35. MODEL BUILDING** On your own paper, sketch a copy of the model-building process shown. Label the steps in the boxes and explain each step.

LO 3-1 **36. GRAPHING EXERCISE** An economy can produce either computers or pizzas. The more it makes of one product, the less it is able to make of the other. The table shows different combinations of the two products it could manufacture per year. Use these data to construct a production possibilities curve for this nation. (Label the vertical axis for computers.)

Combinations of Computers and Pizzas an Economy Could Produce (millions per year)

Combination	Computers	Pizzas
A	80	0
B	70	200
C	40	400
D	0	500

UNIT 2 Free Markets in Action

Unit 2 continues building on your foundation of knowledge about the free market system. The chapters in this unit provide essential concepts for how free markets work. Chapter 3 and 4 explain the market demand and supply curves. In Chapter 4 you will learn how the interaction of demand and supply sets prices for goods and services. Here, you will also learn the effects of government regulation on markets. Chapter 5 discusses different types of markets, each with its own set of characteristics.

yienkeat/Shutterstock.com

UNIT 2 Project

Tools of Free Markets

Project Objectives

PARTNERSHIP FOR 21ST CENTURY SKILLS

- Analyze the economic rights and responsibilities of individuals as consumers.
- Analyze the consequences of an economic decision made by an individual consumer.
- Use appropriate mathematical skills to interpret social studies information.
- Analyze information by sequencing, categorizing, identifying cause-and-effect relationships, comparing, contrasting, finding the main idea, summarizing, making generalizations and predictions, and drawing inferences and conclusions.

chapter 3

Presentation of Demand, p. 80

Prepare a demand schedule for a product that you or your family (or group) purchase on a regular basis.

Elasticity Correlation, p. 87

Create a PowerPoint presentation to compare and contrast the price elasticity of demand—elastic, inelastic, and unitary elastic.

chapter 4

Presentation of Supply, p. 106

Prepare a supply schedule for a product that you as a business owner would be willing and able to produce on a regular basis.

Market Equilibrium, Ceilings, and Floors, p. 123

Research the impacts of ceilings and floors (surplus and shortage) throughout the history of the United States.

chapter 5

Price Makers and Takers, p. 138

Prepare a chart that lists four products your group has purchased in the last year.

Market Structures in a Wheel, p. 147

Draw a wheel to describe the types of market structures as perfect competition, monopoly, monopolistic, or oligopoly.

Project Wrap-up

Create a brochure, flyer, or newsletter that defines, describes, and explores the concepts of demand, movement along a demand curve versus a shift in demand, supply, movement along a supply curve versus a shift in supply, price elasticity of demand, the four market structures, and the role of government in the free market system. Have a target audience in mind. Save a copy of all work completed to include in your economics portfolio.

Comstock/Jupiter Images

yienkeat/Shutterstock.com

chapter 3

Market Demand

3-1 The Law of Demand

3-2 Shifts in the Demand Curve

3-3 Elasticity of Demand

MARKETS *in Action!*

Vera Wang
Vera Wang Fashions

The daughter of Chinese immigrants, fashion designer Vera Wang was born in New York City in 1949. She completed a degree in art history and was a talented figure skater. Following college, she worked for *Vogue* magazine where she was able to excel due to her natural instincts for fashion. She was promoted to senior fashion editor at the age of 23, a job she held for 15 years.

In 1987, Wang left *Vogue* to become a design director for accessories at Ralph Lauren. Seeing there was very little to choose from in bridal wear, she sketched her own design for a bridal gown that would cost $10,000. It was a great success and gave Wang the courage to step out on her own. The next year with some financial backing from her father, Wang opened her own bridal boutique in a hotel on Madison Avenue in New York City. Catering mostly to the wealthy, celebrities, and elite, Wang initially offered couture (high fashion, one-of-a-kind) gowns. Over the next few years, Wang developed her skills and launched a signature line of sophisticated bridal wear.

Wang has designed specialty clothing for figure skaters, elegant evening wear, and Vera Wang Made to Order—a collection of designs available only at her Manhattan boutique. In 1994, Wang started her own label. Her client list is long and distinguished, especially for special events such as Oscar night.

Her bridal and evening apparel sells at upscale retailers nationwide. Wang balances modern designs with traditional elegance, and has acquired a large following of celebrities. When it's time for a special occasion demanding a unique design, the Vera Wang label commands respect and makes the short list for many who want to wear something memorable and elegant.

Today, Wang is one of the top designers of bridal wear in America. She has received many awards for her achievements. In the fashion world, Vera Wang has made her spot in history as a fashion designer of high-end, expensive products. People who buy expensive wedding gowns and evening dresses are less concerned about the financial cost and more concerned about image and brand recognition. They will pay a higher price for the label and the "name" product. They will pay large amounts to wear something that is unique, striking, high quality, and the latest design.

Vera Wang poses for photographers before an awards ceremony.

stocklight/Shutterstock.com

Think Critically

1. What decision process might Vera Wang use to set the right price for the products she designs?
2. How important is it to understand the prospective customers and be able to predict the demand for a product? Explain.

yienkeat/Shutterstock.com

3-1 The Law of Demand

Learning Objectives	Vocabulary
LO 1-1 Explain the law of demand and how a demand schedule is represented in a demand curve.	**demand,** p. 67
LO 1-2 Understand the difference between an individual and a market demand curve.	**quantity demanded,** p. 67
	law of demand, p. 67
	demand schedule, p. 67
	demand curve, p. 68
	individual demand curve, p. 69
	market demand curve, p. 69

REAL-WORLD FOCUS

Michael and Zoe love to buy and eat their favorite brand of individual frozen pizzas. "I can eat ten of those a week," Michael told Zoe, "but lately I've been eating fewer pizzas because I can't afford them. Today I can buy only three for the same amount I spent to buy four pizzas last year."

"That's right," said Zoe. "I've cut back too. And you know what else? I've noticed that the pizzas are smaller. There's less to eat and each pizza has a higher price too! I'm thinking about switching to a different brand. Or maybe to a different type of snack food. Are you getting tired of pizza?"

WORK AS A TEAM Why are Michael and Zoe cutting back on their purchases of pizzas? What items in the grocery store have you noticed are more expensive? What can consumers do when the price rises? What would you do?

As this mother and daughter shop for a frozen pizza, they have a wide variety of choices of brands and toppings to consider.

DO YOU THINK a store manager uses an individual demand curve or a market demand curve to decide how many of each type of pizza to stock? Why?

LO 1-1 The Demand Curve

Economics might be referred to as "graphs and laughs" because economists are fond of using graphs to explain production possibilities, demand, and other concepts. Unfortunately, some students taking economics courses say they miss the laughs.

Estelle/Shutterstock.com

Consumer demand for gasoline changes as the price per gallon rises and falls.

Recall the example of gasoline in Lesson 2-1. How many gallons of gasoline will people buy each week if the price is $6 per gallon? What if the price is $4 per gallon? What if it is $3? The answer depends on demand. **Demand** is the relationship between the price and the quantity demanded for a good or service, when other variables are held constant. In a market, demand is the buying side. Demand is based on the assumption that other variables remain constant or unchanged. **Quantity demanded** is the amount of goods and services purchased at a given price.

In a free market system, consumers serve their best interest by buying at the lowest price. Figure 3-1 reveals an important law in economics called the law of demand. What does this law say? The **law of demand** states there is an inverse relationship between the price of a good or service and the quantity buyers purchase. The law of demand makes good sense. When a product goes on sale consumers buy (demand) more because the price has been reduced.

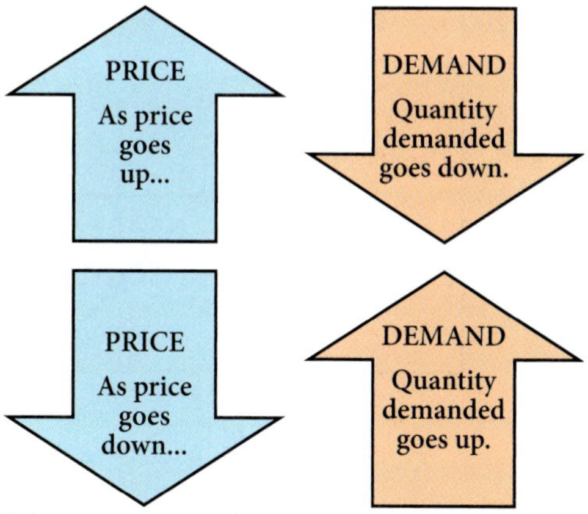

Figure 3-1

The Law of Demand

The law of demand states there is an inverse relationship between change in price and the quantity demanded.

A **demand schedule** is a table that lists the quantity of a good or service consumers purchase at various possible prices. Figure 3-2 on the next page illustrates an individual's demand for DVDs. The first column lists points observed. The second column shows the prices per DVD. And the third column gives the quantity demanded at each price. Bob, a senior at Marketplace High, loves watching movies on DVDs. At a price of $20, Bob's quantity demanded is 4 DVDs per year. Following the law of demand, as the price falls from $20 to $5, the quantity of DVDs Bob is willing to purchase increases from 4 to 16.

Figure 3-2

Bob's Demand Schedule for DVDs

Bob's demand schedule shows how many DVDs he is willing to purchase at different prices. As the price of DVDs declines, the quantity demanded increases. The inverse relationship between price and quantity demanded conforms to the law of demand.

Point	Price per DVD	Quantity Demanded per Year
A	$20	4
B	15	8
C	10	12
D	5	16

In Figure 3-3, the **demand curve** is formed by the line connecting points that represent possible combinations of price and quantity purchased by consumers. By moving along the curve, you can find the quantity demanded by a buyer at any possible selling price. The price and quantity possibilities for Bob are transferred from the data in the table in Figure 3-2. Bob's demand curve shows that at a price of $15 his quantity demanded is 8 DVDs annually (point *B*). At the lower price of $10, Bob's quantity demanded increases to 12 DVDs per year (point *C*).

Until you know the actual selling price, you do not know how many DVDs Bob will buy. The demand curve is a summary of Bob's buying intentions. Once you know the market price, a look at the demand curve tells you how many DVDs Bob will buy. Although you might never have thought about demand curves, they represent relationships between price and the quantity demanded that exist in the real world. There are demand curves for iPhones, concert tickets, orange juice, and every other product you and other consumers buy.

Figure 3-3

Bob's Demand Curve for DVDs

Bob's demand curve is plotted from the table in Figure 3-2. This curve shows an inverse relationship between the price per DVD and the quantity demanded. The model assumes other variables are held constant.

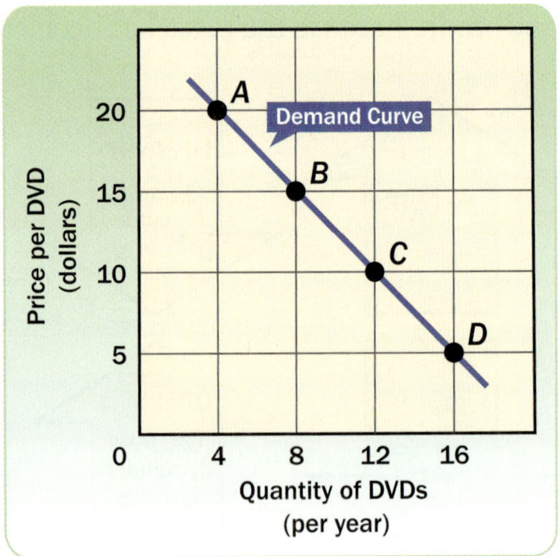

CHECKPOINT

If the price of DVDs is $5, how many would you buy per year? If the price rose to $20, how many would you buy? Does your answer confirm the law of demand?

LO1-2 Market Demand

To change from an individual demand curve to a market demand curve, total the individual demand curves. An **individual demand curve** is the demand for a single consumer. The **market demand curve** is the sum of all the individual demand curves in a market. Suppose the owner of Zap Mart, a small retail chain of stores, must decide what to charge for DVDs and hires a consumer research firm. For simplicity, assume Fred and Mary are the only two buyers in Zap Mart's market. They are sent a questionnaire that asks how many DVDs each would be willing to purchase at several possible prices. Figure 3-4 reports their responses in graphical form and in a table. The table gives Fred and Mary's responses at various prices. To simplify, the graphs show their responses at only \$20 and \$5 per DVD.

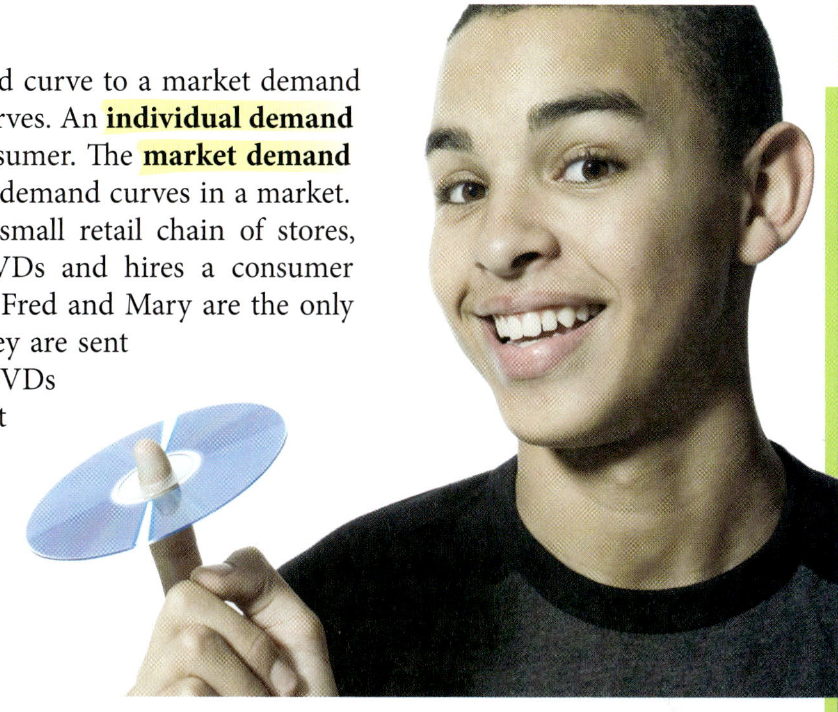

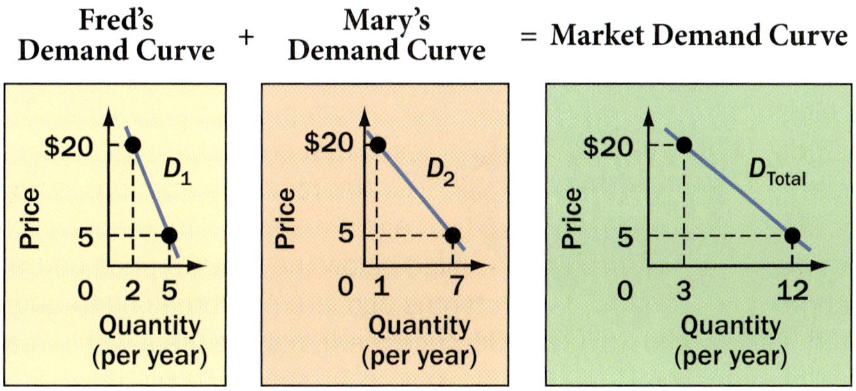

Figure 3-4

Market Demand Curve for DVDs

Individual demand curves differ for consumers Fred and Mary. Assuming they are the only buyers in the market, the market demand curve, D_{total}, is derived by summing the individual demand curves, D_1 and D_2.

Market Demand Schedule for DVDs

Price per DVD	Quantity Demanded per Year		
	Fred +	Mary =	Total Demand
\$20	2	1	3
15	3	3	6
10	4	5	9
5	5	7	12

The market demand curve, D_{total}, in Figure 3-4 is the sum of the individual demand curves, D_1 and D_2, for each possible price. At a price of \$20, for example, sum Fred's 2 DVDs demanded per year and Mary's 1 DVD demanded per year. The total quantity demanded at \$20 is 3 DVDs per year. Repeating the same process for other prices generates the market demand curve, D_{total}. At a price of \$5, the total quantity demanded is 12 DVDs.

Like the individual demand curve, the law of demand applies to market demand. When the price rises, the quantity demanded goes down. And if the price falls, the quantity demanded goes up. Also, like the individual demand curve, the assumption for market demand is that all other variables are constant. In the next lesson, you will see the effect on demand when this assumption is changed.

CHECKPOINT

Suppose you own a pizza company. How would you determine the market demand for your company's pizza?

PC Prices: How Low Can They Go?

Radio was in existence for 38 years before 50 million people tuned in. Television took 13 years to reach that benchmark. Sixteen years after the first PC kit came out, 50 million people were using one. Once opened to the public, the Internet crossed that line in four years. Before 1999 there were no blogs and now there are millions. Today, over 80 percent of U.S. households have a computer. Following is a simulated newspaper article:

We have reached a situation where the market is saturated. People who need computers have them. Computer companies are living on sales of replacements. But that doesn't give them the kind of growth they seek. Companies have been narrowing profit margins for the last couple years. Now the more aggressive companies have decided to try to gain market share by cutting prices to the bone. This is an all-out battle for market share. An analyst observed that consumers can pick up good deals on desktop and notebook PCs by following the price cut wars. Prices are falling at the right time for users to get good value for their investments. Dell, Gateway, and Asus offer basic computers for less than $300 that outperform most middle-of-the-road PCs from only a few years ago. Personal computers, which tumbled below the $1,000-price barrier just months ago, are now breaking through the $400-price mark, putting them within reach of the average U.S. family. The plunge in PC prices has been astonishing, said an analyst based in Boston. Today's computers priced below $400 have equal or greater power than PCs that cost $1,500 or more just a few years ago. These new computers work well for word processing, spreadsheet applications, and Internet access, the most popular computer uses. As the price has dropped, sales have risen from 300 million to 400 million personal computers per year.

Darrin Henry/Shutterstock.com

Think Critically

How does this article demonstrate the law of demand? Is there a possible violation of the "other factors held constant" assumption?

3-1 Assessment

Key Concepts

LO 1-1 1. The law of demand states there is an __?__ relationship between the price of a good or service and the quantity buyers purchase.

LO 1-1 2. **TRUE OR FALSE** The concept of demand is based on the responses of sellers to price changes.

LO 1-1 3. Quantity demanded is the __?__ of goods and services purchased at a given price.

LO 1-2 4. **TRUE OR FALSE** A market demand curve is the sum of all the individual demand curves in a market.

Think About It

LO 1-1 5. What is the most important factor you consider when buying something?

LO 1-1 6. Why do consumers buy less of a good at a higher price and more at a lower price?

LO 1-1 7. Compare the law of demand to a seesaw with one end labeled "Price" and other labeled "Quantity Demanded."

LO 1-2 8. How is the law of demand illustrated by a demand schedule and a demand curve?

LO 1-2 9. How are individual demand curves used to construct a market demand curve?

LO 1-2 10. Every year many retailers have Black Friday sales when they offer to sell many products at substantial discounts. Explain what these sales do to the quantity of products these businesses are able to sell. Explain why you believe retailers do this.

Make Academic Connections

LO 1-2 11. **MARKETING** Ralph is the sales manager of a small chain of retail shoe stores. The owner has conducted a consumer survey and given Ralph the data in the table at the right. Using the data in the table, draw a demand curve graph. How does your graph illustrate the law of demand?

Price	Quantity Demanded
$125	100
100	200
75	300
50	400
25	500

Teamwork

LO 1-1 12. Work in groups. Brainstorm a list of five goods or services. Then make a demand schedule listing how many of each item you would purchase at various possible prices.

LO 1-1 13. Work in groups. Create a skit that illustrates the law of demand. Perform your skit for the class.

3-2 Shifts in the Demand Curve

Learning Objectives

LO 2-1 Explain the difference between change in quantity demanded and change in demand.

LO 2-2 Identify demand shifter variables that cause changes in demand.

Vocabulary

change in quantity demanded, p. 73
change in demand, p. 73
normal good, p. 76
inferior good, p. 76
substitute, p. 77
complement, p. 77

REAL-WORLD FOCUS

© Aleksandar Vrzalski/iStockphoto.com

Jerod used Brite White toothpaste because he believed it helped him keep his teeth free of plaque and discoloration. Last week he read an article in the newspaper that said the Brite White brand had been reported as possibly being unsafe. According to the article, the toothpaste might have harmful abrasives that could lead to breakdown of tooth enamel. This week, Jerod did not buy the toothpaste, and neither did any of his friends. He noticed that the price was lower, but still, he would not buy it.

WORK AS A TEAM Why is Jerod hesitant to buy the toothpaste? Would you buy a product that had recently been cited for safety issues? Would you change your mind with a lower price? List reasons, other than price, why you would buy more or less of a good or service. Explain your reasoning.

Natalia Bratslavsky/Shutterstock.com

Lobster, whether purchased in a store or a restaurant, has a high price compared to most other options for protein.

DO YOU THINK lobster is classified as a normal good or an inferior good? Why?

yienkeat/Shutterstock.com

LO 2-1 Difference Between Change in Quantity Demanded and Change in Demand

Price is not the only variable that determines how much of a good consumers buy. Recall from Lesson 2-1 that variables in a model are subject to the other variables held constant assumption. If you relax this assumption, a variety of factors can influence the position of the demand curve. These variables or factors are *demand shifters* or *non-price determinants*. These include (1) the number of buyers, (2) tastes, (3) income, (4) expectations, and (5) prices of related goods. Before discussing these demand shifter factors, the terms change in quantity demanded and change in demand need explanation.

Bobby Deal/RealDealPhoto/Shutterstock.com

As the demand for DVDs increases, more DVDs must be produced and packaged for purchase.

A change in quantity demanded results solely from a change in the price. A **change in quantity demanded** is a movement between points along a demand curve. This change is based on the assumption that all other demand shifter factors remain constant. Figure 3-5 shows the market demand curve for DVDs per year. At the price of \$15, the quantity demanded is 20 million DVDs per year, which is point *A* on the demand curve. At a lower price of \$10, the quantity demanded increases to 30 million DVDs per year, which is point *B*. This relationship on the demand curve is a movement along the curve from point *A* to point *B*. Stated another way, the price decrease causes an increase in the quantity demanded of 10 million DVDs per year. This decrease is the difference between 30 million DVDs at point *B* and 20 million DVDs at point *A*.

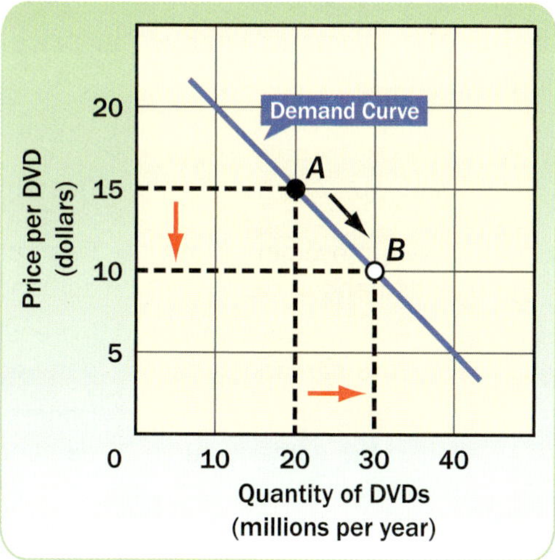

Figure 3-5

Change in Quantity Demanded

If the price is \$15 (point *A*), the quantity demanded by consumers is 20 million DVDs. If the price decreases to \$10 (point *B*), the quantity demanded increases from 20 million to 30 million DVDs. The change between point *A* and point *B* is a movement along the curve.

A **change in demand** is an increase (rightward shift) or a decrease (leftward shift) in the demand curve. If one of the five demand shifter factors changes, it causes the demand curve to shift. Comparing Figures 3-5 and 3-6 is helpful in seeing the difference between a change in quantity demanded and a change in demand. In part (a) of Figure 3-6, suppose the market demand curve for DVDs is initially at D_1 and there is a shift to the right. This shift can also be stated as an increase in demand from D_1 to D_2, which means that at all possible prices consumers are buying more than before the shift. At $15 per DVD, 30 million DVDs (point *B*) will be purchased, rather than 20 million DVDs (point *A*). At other points along the initial demand curve D_1, a greater quantity demanded exists on the new curve D_2.

In part (b) of Figure 3-6, a change in some demand shifter factor causes demand curve D_1 to shift leftward to D_3. This decrease in demand means that at all possible prices consumers will buy a smaller quantity than before the shift. For example, at point *A* 20 million DVDs are bought at the price of $15. After the leftward shift in the demand curve, 10 million DVDs are purchased at $15 (point *B*). At all points along D_1, a smaller quantity is demanded on the new curve D_3.

Figure 3-6

Change in Demand

Part (a) illustrates an increase (rightward shift) in demand. A change in some demand shifter can cause an increase in demand from D_1 to D_2. Part (b) shows a decrease (leftward shift) in demand from D_1 to D_3.

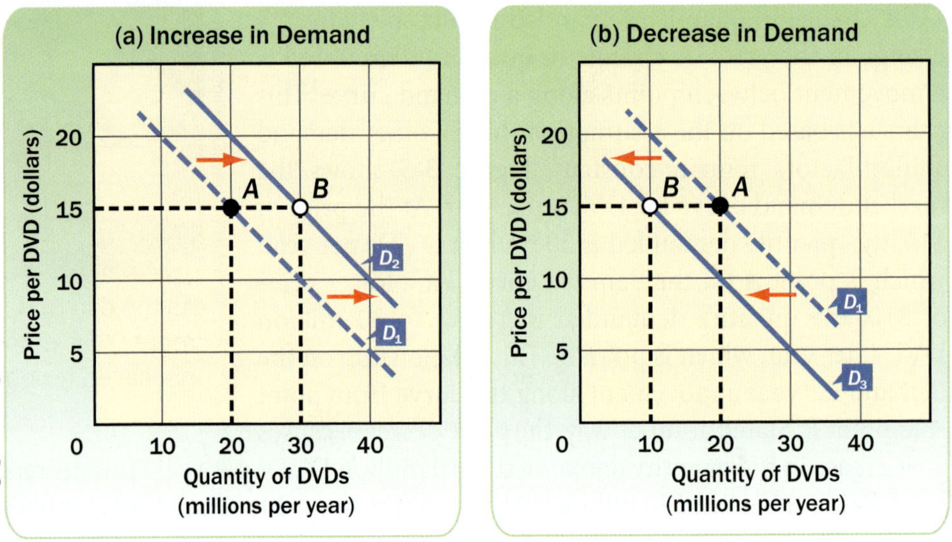

Figure 3-7 summarizes the effects of changes in price and demand shifter factors on the demand curve.

Figure 3-7

What Happens When Price and Demand Shifter Factors Change

Change	Effect	Description
Price Increases	Upward movement along the demand curve	Decrease in the quantity demanded
Price Decreases	Downward movement along the demand curve	Increase in the quantity demanded
Demand Shifter Factors	Leftward or rightward shift in the demand curve	Decrease or increase in demand

CHECKPOINT

What is the difference between a movement along a demand curve and a shift of a demand curve?

LO 2-2 Demand Shifter Factors

It is important to distinguish between a change in quantity demanded and a change in demand. An increase in demand (rightward shift) or decrease in demand (leftward shift) is not caused by a change in price. Instead, a shift is caused by a change in one of the following demand shifter factors.

Number of Buyers

Look back at the market demand curve in Figure 3-4 in Lesson 3-1. Imagine the effect of adding more individual demand curves to the individual demand curves of Fred and Mary. At all possible prices, there are extra quantities demanded by the new customers. This change causes the market demand curve for DVDs to shift rightward (an increase in demand). Population growth increases the number of buyers, which shifts the market demand curve rightward. Conversely, a population decline shifts market demand curves leftward (a decrease in demand).

Tastes

A favorable or unfavorable change in consumer tastes shifts the demand curve. Fads, fashions, advertising, and new products influence consumers to buy more or less at possible prices. Beanie Babies became the rage soon after they first came to market in 1993. Their demand curve quickly shifted to the right. When people tire of a product, the demand curve shifts leftward. The physical fitness trend has increased the demand for health clubs and exercise equipment. On the other hand, have you noticed many stores selling hula hoops? Advertising can also

Global View

China's Economy Impacts the World Demand for Oil

China is a huge nation transforming itself swiftly into a powerful player in the global economy. Swarms of bicyclists once synonymous with urban China are being pushed off the road by consumers who now can afford cars and trucks. Rolls-Royce and Bentley, the ultra-luxury cars, have expanded into China, and it is estimated that by 2030 China will have more cars on the road than the United States. More Chinese are traveling by air. Consequently, the Chinese are buying more Boeing airplanes and American-made cars. Also, China manufactures most of the world's copiers, microwave ovens, DVD players, and shoes. To keep up with these demands, China is consuming huge quantities of resources such as crude oil, copper, steel, and aluminum.

Think Critically

Consider the market demand curve for oil in terms of a global market. In this case, each consumer of oil is a country and the total market curve is total world demand. What is the impact of China's rising demand for oil?

influence consumers' tastes for a product. As a result, consumers are more likely to buy more at every price, and the demand curve shifts to the right. Concern for global climate change has increased the demand for hybrid cars and recycling.

Income

There are two possible categories for the relationship between changes in income and changes in demand: (1) normal goods and (2) inferior goods.

A **normal good** is any good for which there is a direct relationship between changes in income and its demand curve. For many goods and services, an increase in income causes buyers to purchase more. As buyers receive higher incomes, the demand curve shifts rightward. Examples of items that are in greater demand with higher incomes are new cars, steaks, brand-name products, designer clothes, and DVDs. A decline in income has the opposite effect, and the demand curve shifts leftward. What would you buy more of if your income increased?

An **inferior good** is any good for which there is an inverse relationship between changes in income and its demand curve. A rise in income results in reduced purchases of an inferior good at any possible price. Reduced prices might happen with such inferior goods as generic brands, discount clothing, and used cars. Conversely, a fall in income causes the demand curve for inferior goods to increase (shift rightward). Instead of buying steaks, for example, people buy more hamburger meat. What would you buy less of if your income rose sharply?

Expectations of Buyers

What is the effect on demand in the present when consumers anticipate future changes in prices? What happens when a war breaks out in the Middle East? Expectations that there will be a shortage of gasoline induce consumers to say "fill-er-up" at every opportunity. As a result, demand increases. Suppose college students learn that the prices of the textbooks will double soon. Their likely response is to buy now, which causes an increase in demand for textbooks.

The threat of bad weather or a natural disaster can affect the demand for some goods and services. Suppose a hailstorm destroys a substantial portion of the

Population Growth

A population can be described by its size and how it is growing or declining. More importantly, you can define a population by describing the ages, sex, and ethnic diversity of the individuals that make up the population. Each local area will have a different composition of its population. Study trends in the composition of the population in your local area.

Investigate Your Local ECONOMY

Try it Out

What are the changes in composition of population in your local area? Draw the demand curves for five products that you believe might be shifted by these population changes. Share your list with the class.

peach crop. Consumers reason that the reduction in available supply will soon drive up prices. They stock up before the higher price peaches hit the store shelves. This change in expectations causes the demand curve for peaches to increase. Prior to Hurricane Katrina hitting New Orleans, sales of batteries and flashlights soared.

NET Bookmark

Access www.cengage.com/school/economics/personalfinance and click on the link for Chapter 3. Go to The Conference Board and read the latest Consumer Confidence Index report. What demand shifter variable is affected by consumer confidence? Based on this report, what might be the effect on the demand curves for automobiles and generic brands?

www.cengage.com/school/economics/personalfinance

Prices of Related Goods

Possibly the most confusing demand shifter factor is the influence of other prices on the demand curve. This confusion exists when one fails to distinguish between changes in quantity demanded and changes in demand. Remember that the other variables held constant assumption holds all prices of other goods constant. Therefore, movement along a demand curve occurs solely in response to changes in its "own" price. When you draw the demand curve for Coca-Cola, the prices of Pepsi-Cola and other colas remain unchanged. Therefore, an increase or decrease in the price of Coca-Cola causes a movement along its demand curve. What happens if you relax the assumption and the price of Pepsi rises? Many Pepsi buyers switch to Coca-Cola and the demand curve for Coca-Cola shifts rightward (an increase in demand). Coca-Cola and Pepsi-Cola are one type of related goods called **substitutes**. Substitutes are goods that compete for consumer purchases. There is a direct relationship between a price change for one good and the demand for its "competitor" good. Examples include margarine and butter, domestic cars and foreign cars, email and the U.S. Postal Service, and Internet movie downloads and DVDs.

DVDs and DVD players illustrate a second type of related goods called complements. **Complements** are goods that consumers purchase together with another good. There is an inverse relationship between a price change for one good and the demand for its "go together" good. Although buying a DVD and buying a DVD player can be separate decisions, these two purchases are related. The more DVD players consumers buy, the greater the demand for DVDs. What happens when the price of DVD players falls sharply? The market demand curve for DVDs shifts rightward (an increase in demand) because new owners of players add their individual demand curves to those of persons already owning players and buying DVDs. Conversely, a sharp rise in the price of Hewlett-Packard (HP) DeskJet color printers decreases the demand for color ink cartridges for these machines. Figure 3-7 provides further real-world examples of the demand shifter factors.

Figure 3-8 on the next page provides a summary of real-world examples of the demand shifter factors.

CHECKPOINT

Consider a normal good that you consume. Also think of a good that you consume that is an inferior good. What would happen to your demand for each of these products if your income rose sharply?

Figure 3-8

Demand Shifter Factors with Real-World Examples

Demand Shifter Factors	Relationship to Changes in Demand Curve	Shifts in the Demand Curve with Examples	
1. Number of Buyers	Direct	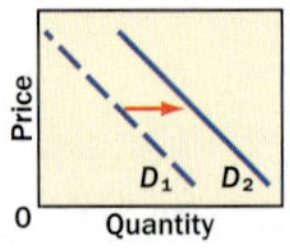 Immigration from Mexico increases the demand for Mexican food products in grocery stores.	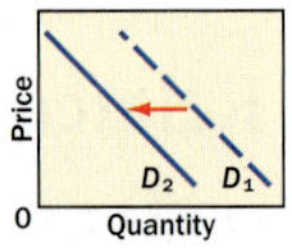 A decline in the birthrate reduces the demand for baby clothes.
2. Tastes	Direct	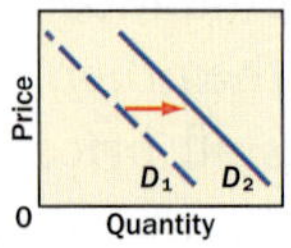 For no apparent reason, consumers want Beanie Babies and demand increases.	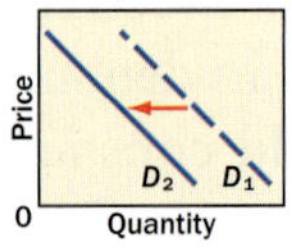 After a while, the fad dies and demand declines.
3. Income **a.** Normal Goods	Direct	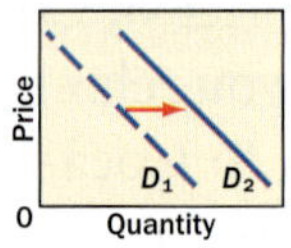 Consumers' incomes increase, and the demand for steaks increases.	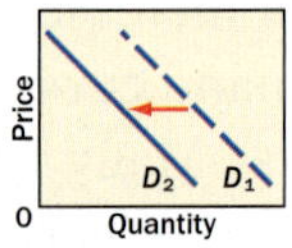 A decline in income decreases the demand for air travel.
b. Inferior Goods	Inverse	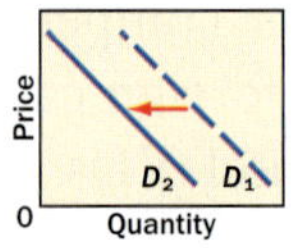 Consumers' incomes increase, and the demand for hamburger decreases.	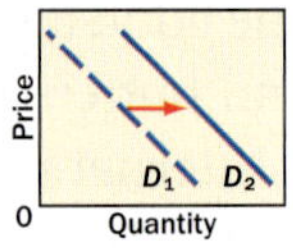 A decline in income increases the demand for bus service.
4. Expectations of Buyers	Direct	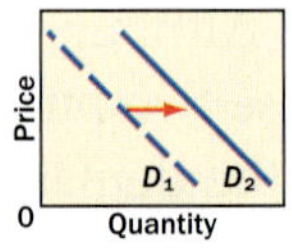 Consumers expect gasoline prices will rise, so they fill their tanks and the demand for gas increases.	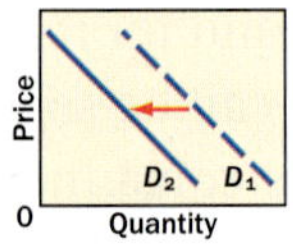 Later consumers expect the price of gasoline to fall, and the demand for gas decreases.
5. Prices of Related Goods **a.** Substitute Goods	Direct	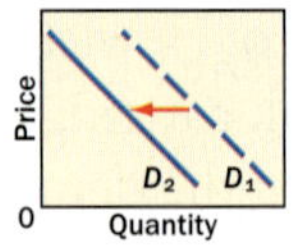 A reduction in the price of tea decreases the demand for coffee.	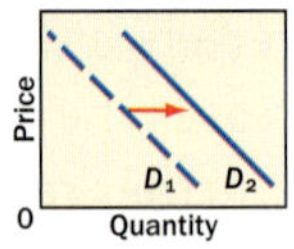 An increase in the price of airfares causes higher demand for bus transportation.
b. Complementary Goods	Inverse	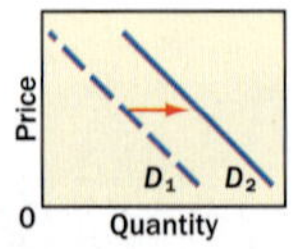 A decline in the price of cellular service increases the demand for cell phones.	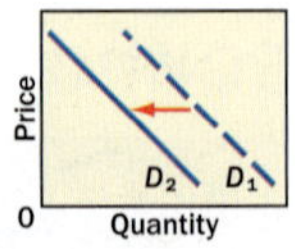 A higher price for peanut butter decreases the demand for jelly.

PROFILE

Caleb D. Bradham
Founder of Pepsi-Cola

AP Photo/HO

In 1891 Caleb D. Bradham arrived in New Bern, North Carolina and began his career as a teacher. He was a graduate of the University of North Carolina and studied to be a doctor at the University of Maryland. The failure of his father's business forced Bradham to leave school to earn his own living. At the age of 26, Caleb believed that fortune came to those who are willing to apply themselves to new ideas. Drugstores at the turn of the century were social centers where friends and business acquaintances met at the soda fountain to discuss issues of the day. New Bern had no drugstore, therefore young Bradham decided to open one and become a pharmacist. He began tinkering with a drink for his customers using new flavor combinations. One particular soda he mixed proved to be so popular that it was called "Brad's Drink" in his honor. Bradham changed its name to Pepsi-Cola because the drink aided digestion like a pepsin enzyme. He purchased his own building and a bottling machine to manufacture his product. Pepsi was a great success. But World War I brought about an end to Bradham's good fortunes because sugar became very scarce. This led to a series of financial problems ending in bankruptcy in 1923. A Wall Street stockbroker, Roy C. Mergargel, purchased Pepsi and struggled to make Pepsi a success. However, the stock market crash in 1929 ended his dream. On June 8, 1931, Pepsi-Cola again declared bankruptcy.

Charles G. Guth was president of a company which owned over 200 candy stores with soda fountains. These fountains used over 30,000 gallons of Coca-Cola syrup per year. Guth argued that this volume deserved a discount price from Coca-Cola. They refused and Guth bought Pepsi-Cola. Even though Guth had purchased Pepsi to spite Coca-Cola, he offered to sell Pepsi to Coca-Cola. They declined the offer. However, a new idea caused sales to skyrocket. Guth introduced a 12-ounce bottle and cut the price from 10 cents to 5 cents while Coca-Cola was selling its 6-ounce bottle for 5 cents. Pepsi also introduced advertising with the jungle "Pepsi Cola hits the spot, twelve full ounces, that's a lot, twice as much for a nickel, too."

The final hurdle for the Pepsi-Cola Company came when they won their trademark court battle with Coca-Cola. Coke's claim was that Pepsi did not have the legal right to use the word "cola." Over the years, Pepsi-Cola grew to become PepsiCo, Inc. with ownership of Frito-Lay, Tropicana, Quaker Oats, Gatorade, and many other brands. Indeed, it was a long and difficult journey from Caleb Bradham's drugstore to today's global business.

THINK CRITICALLY

Relate the story of the birth of Pepsi to changes in demand shifter factors.

yienkeat/Shutterstock.com

3-2 Assessment

Key Concepts

LO 2-2 1. Goods that compete for consumer purchases are called __?__.

LO 2-2 2. **TRUE OR FALSE** A normal good's demand curve shifts rightward (increases) when consumers' incomes increase.

LO 2-1 3. A movement between points along a stationary demand curve is caused by a change in __?__.

LO 2-1 4. **TRUE OR FALSE** A change in demand is a movement along a stationary demand curve.

Think About It

LO 2-2 5. What would happen to the demand curve for bus tickets if the price of gasoline per gallon doubles? Which demand shifter factor is affected?

LO 2-2 6. What happens to the demand curve for good X when a famous movie star appears in the media announcing that good X is the best product he or she has ever used?

LO 2-2 7. Consider the demand curve for surf boards at the beach. Explain what happens to this demand curve during the summer. What demand shifter factor is affected?

LO 2-1 8. What is the difference between a change in the quantity of a product that is demanded and a change in demand for that product?

LO 2-2 9. What are the five demand shifter variables? Describe a situation for each that illustrates how it works.

Make Academic Connections

LO 2-1 10. **MATH** Draw two graphs to illustrate the difference between a decrease in the quantity demanded and a decrease in demand for Mickey Mantle baseball cards. Give a possible reason for change in each graph.

LO 2-2 11. **HISTORY** During the Great Depression of the 1930s and other economic downturns throughout history, there were increases in the demand for inferior goods. Explain why these increases happened.

Teamwork

LO 2-2 12. Work in pairs or small groups. Discuss the benefits of buying a new car versus a used car. Take a poll to see how many students would choose a new car and how many would choose a used car. Share your ideas on the pros and cons of buying a new car compared to a used car. What would happen to the demand for used cars in the United States if the price of many imported cars increased rapidly after a natural disaster in Japan? What is the connection to a demand shifter factor?

Unit 2 Project: Tools of Free Markets

PRESENTATION OF DEMAND Prepare a demand schedule for a product that you or your family (or group) purchase on a regular basis. Transfer the demand schedule to a demand curve. Propose a scenario in which your total demand for the product would increase dramatically and prepare a new demand curve. Propose a scenario in which your total demand for the product would decrease dramatically and prepare a new demand curve. Explain the law of demand, your demand schedule, demand curve, and shifts in demand within an Excel worksheet.

yienkeat/Shutterstock.com; Chad Baker/Ryan McVay/Photodisc/Getty Images

3-3 Elasticity of Demand

Learning Objectives

LO 3-1 Understand the difference between elastic, inelastic, and unitary elastic demand.

LO 3-2 Explain how total revenue is related to price elasticity of demand.

Vocabulary

total revenue, p. 82
elasticity of demand, p. 82
elastic demand, p. 82
inelastic demand, p. 83
unitary elastic demand, p. 84

REAL-WORLD FOCUS

© Aleksandar Vrzalski/iStockphoto.com

Lisa wants to buy tickets to a professional sporting event. Most tickets are sold to season ticket holders. Standing outside the stadium, some season ticket holders are re-selling their $50 tickets for $75 or more. Lisa does not want to pay more than the original price, but if she wants to attend the event, she doesn't have a choice. The tickets are in short supply and will sell out rapidly at the gate.

WORK AS A TEAM Why do sports tickets, in short supply, sell for more than the original price? What can Lisa do to avoid the higher prices? Would you pay the 50 percent higher price? Why or why not?

Many theaters offer lower-priced tickets for movies shown during the morning and afternoon hours. These shows are often called matinees.

DO YOU THINK matinee movies are an example of elastic demand or inelastic demand?

Rafael Ramirez Lee/Shutterstock.com

yienkeat/Shutterstock.com

LO 3-1 Why Elasticity of Demand Matters

Suppose you are the manager of the Steel Porcupines rock band. You are considering raising the ticket price, and you wonder how fans will react. You know the law of demand. When the price of a ticket rises, the quantity demanded goes down. You need to know how many tickets fans will purchase if the band boosts the ticket price. If the lawn seating ticket price for a Steel Porcupines concert is \$25, you will sell 20,000 tickets. At \$30 per ticket, only 10,000 tickets will be sold. A \$5 increase per ticket cuts the number of tickets sold in half.

Should the band charge a higher price and sell fewer tickets or charge a lower ticket price and sell more tickets? The answer depends on changes in total revenue, or sales, as you move along the demand curve. **Total revenue** is the total dollars a firm receives from the sale of a good or service. It is equal to the price multiplied by the quantity demanded. At \$30 per ticket, sales will be \$300,000 (\$30 × 10,000 tickets). If you charge \$25, the group will take in \$500,000 (\$25 × 20,000 tickets) for a concert. What happens at \$20 per ticket or other possible prices? You need to measure the relative size of changes in the price and the quantity demanded. You must calculate and compare the percentage change in quantity demanded that is caused by a percentage change in price.

Calculating Elasticity of Demand

Economists use an elasticity of demand formula to measure consumer responsiveness to a change in price. **Elasticity of demand** is the ratio of the percentage change in the quantity demanded of a product to a percentage change in its price. Elasticity of demand explains how strongly consumers react to a change in price. Think of quantity demanded as a rubber band. Elasticity of demand measures how "stretchy" the rubber band is when the price changes. The following formula is used to measure the degree of elasticity of demand. This number tells the responsiveness of changes in quantity demanded to changes in price.

$$\textbf{Elasticity of demand} = \frac{\textbf{percentage change in quantity demanded}}{\textbf{percentage change in price}}$$

Computing the percentage change in quantity demanded or price can be simplified using the following formula. Ignore any negative sign.

$$\textbf{Percentage change} = \frac{\textbf{Original number} - \textbf{New number}}{\textbf{Original number}} \times \textbf{100}$$

Elastic Demand

Elastic demand exists when the percentage change in quantity demanded (numerator) is greater than the percentage change in price (denominator). If so, demand is elastic and its value is greater than 1. Suppose the Steel Porcupines' demand curve is shown in Figure 3-9. Assume the band lowers its ticket price from \$25 to \$20 (point *A* to *B*). The quantity demanded increases from 20,000 to 30,000. This change means that a 20 percent reduction in ticket price brings a 50 percent increase in quantity demanded. Thus, demand is elastic because it is 2.5, which is greater than 1. In this case, the numerator (50%) of the elasticity formula exceeds the denominator (20%).

$$\text{Percentage change in quantity demanded} = \frac{20{,}000 - 30{,}000}{20{,}000} \times 100 = 50\%$$

$$\text{Percentage change in price} = \frac{\$25 - \$20}{\$25} \times 100 = 20\%$$

$$\text{Elasticity of demand} = \frac{50\%}{20\%} = 2.5$$

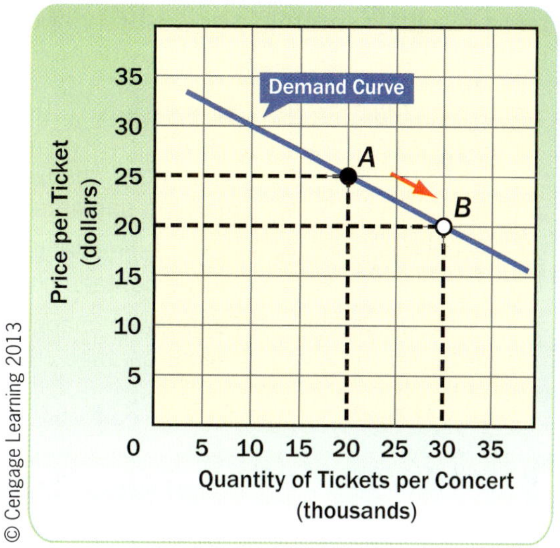

Figure 3-9

Elastic Demand Curve

A change from point *A* to point *B* results in an elasticity of demand of 2.5. Since this number is greater than 1, demand is elastic.

Inelastic Demand

Inelastic demand occurs when the percentage change in quantity demanded (numerator) is less than the percentage change in price (denominator). Demand is inelastic when the elasticity value is less than 1. The change in elasticity along the demand curve in Figure 3-10 is inelastic. Note that it is steeper than the elastic demand curve in the previous figure. The quantity demanded is less responsive to a change in price. Here a fall in ticket price from \$30 to \$20 causes the quantity demanded to increase by 5,000 tickets (20,000 to 25,000 tickets). In this case, a 33 percent fall in the ticket price causes a 25 percent rise in the quantity demanded. This change means the elasticity of demand value is 0.76, and demand is inelastic because it is less than 1. Here the numerator (25%) is less than the denominator (33%).

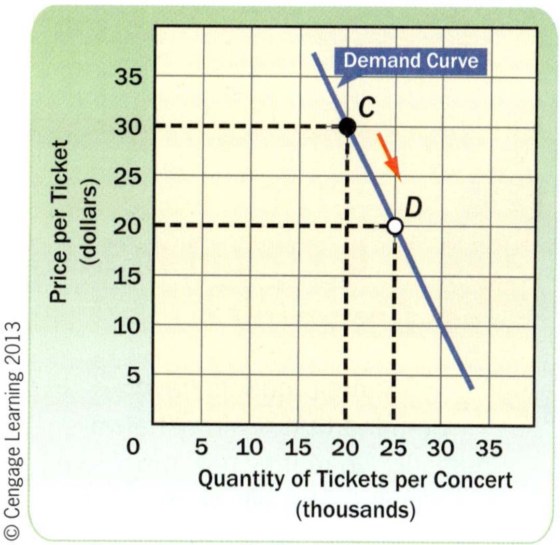

Figure 3-10

Inelastic Demand Curve

A change from point *C* to point *D* gives an elasticity of demand value of 0.76. Since this number is less than 1, demand is inelastic.

$$\text{Percentage change in quantity demanded} = \frac{20{,}000 - 25{,}000}{20{,}000} \times 100 = 25\%$$

$$\text{Percentage change in price} = \frac{\$30 - \$20}{\$30} \times 100 = 33\%$$

$$\text{Elasticity of demand} = \frac{25\%}{33\%} = 0.76$$

Unitary Elastic Demand

Most demand curves have a range where demand is elastic at relatively high prices. As the price falls, demand typically becomes less elastic until it is inelastic. There is a point between these two ranges where demand is unitary elastic. This point occurs when a percentage change in price results in the same percentage change in the quantity demanded. **Unitary elastic demand** is when the percentage change in quantity demanded is equal to the percentage change in price. This change means the numerator of the elasticity formula equals the denominator. Unitary demand is the dividing point between elastic and inelastic demand. This is the point on the demand curve where total revenue is at its maximum. Figure 3-11 presents a summary of elasticity of demand definitions.

Figure 3-11

Elasticity of Demand Definitions

Demand	Definition
Elastic	Percentage change in quantity demanded is greater than the percentage change in price
Inelastic	Percentage change in quantity demanded is less than the percentage change in price
Unitary Elastic	Percentage change in quantity demanded is equal to the percentage change in price

CHECKPOINT

Assume the elasticity of demand for used cars is 3. What does this mean?

ETHICS *in Action!*

Is It Ethical to Take Advantage of Inelastic Demand?

Some products have demand that is almost always inelastic. No matter how much the price is raised consumers will continue to buy it and its total revenue will increase. This demand exists for unique products that consumers are desperate to buy. New life-saving medicines often have this type of demand. People who are afflicted with terminal cancer would probably pay any price for a medicine that would save their lives. When pharmaceutical businesses have this type of pricing power is it ethical for them to maximize their total revenue?

Some government leaders have suggested that a solution would be to limit the amount pharmaceutical producers could charge for their products. This would create maximum prices for life-saving medications. Although such a policy might make drugs less expensive in the short-run, some argue that it would discourage costly research and development of new drugs.

Think Critically

1. **Why are firms that produce products with very inelastic demand said to have a great deal of "market power"?**
2. **What are three other products that have very inelastic demand? Explain. Why would most businesses prefer to have products with inelastic demand?**

LO 3-2 Total Revenue Test

Businesses need to know about elasticity of demand because it determines the size of total revenue or sales. The elasticity of demand for a typical demand curve varies as you move from left to right along the curve. Look at Figure 3-12. The changes in elasticity along the demand curve in part (a) correspond to the total revenue curve in part (b). Begin at $40 on the demand curve, and move down from price to price. The table in Figure 3-12 lists variations in the total revenue and elasticity of demand at different ticket prices.

As you move down the upper segment of the demand curve, elasticity of demand is elastic, and total revenue rises. For example, between $30 and $25, total revenue increases from $300,000 ($30 × 10,000 tickets) to $375,000 ($25 × 15,000 tickets). At $20, price elasticity is unitary elastic, and total revenue is maximized at $400,000. As you move down the lower segment of the demand curve, elasticity of demand is inelastic.

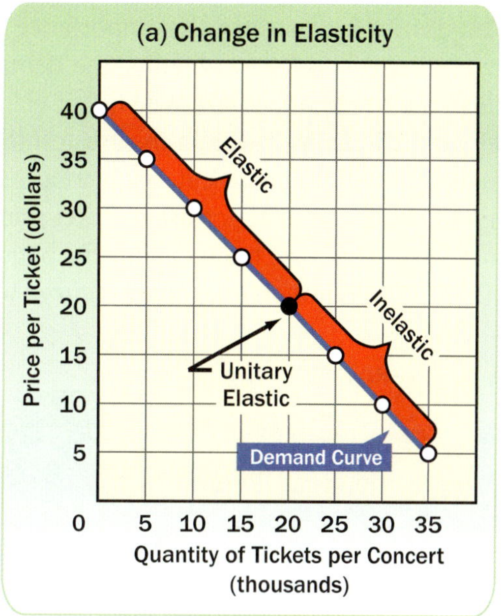

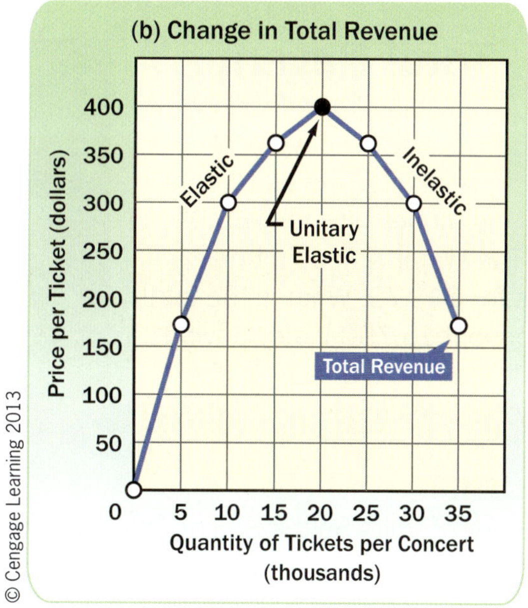

Figure 3-12

How Total Revenue Changes along a Demand Curve

Part (a) shows a typical demand curve and its three elasticity ranges. Above $20, demand is elastic. As price decreases in this range, total revenue increases. At $20, demand is unitary elastic, and total revenue is at its maximum. Below $20, price range, demand is inelastic. As price decreases in this range, total revenue decreases. The total revenue curve plotted in part (b) traces its relationship to elasticity of demand in part (a).

Price	Quantity (thousands of tickets)	Total Revenue (thousands of dollars)	Elasticity of Demand
$40	0	$ 0	
35	5	175	Elastic
30	10	300	Elastic
25	15	375	Elastic
20	20	400	Unitary elastic
15	25	375	Inelastic
10	30	300	Inelastic
5	35	175	Inelastic

Over this range total revenue falls. Between $15 and $10, for example, total revenue decreases from $375,000 to $300,000.

Figure 3-12 illustrates the importance of elasticity of demand to a business. The band needs to know whether the demand for its concert is elastic or inelastic at different ticket prices. Knowledge of elasticity of demand helps the band make pricing decisions that result in the greatest total revenue. If the ticket price is $30 and demand is elastic, a price cut raises total revenue. If the current price is $15, then demand is inelastic. An increase in ticket price here would also increase total revenue. Note that to maximize total revenue the band would charge $20 per ticket. This is the unitary elastic point on the demand curve where total revenue equals $400,000.

CHECKPOINT

Summarize in your own words the relationship between elasticity of demand and total revenue.

FreeSoulProduction/Shutterstock.com

Math CONNECTION

Total Revenue

Sunshine Lawn Products produces two types of sprinklers. The Water Saving model sells for $35.99. The Water & Feed model sells for $42.79. What is the total revenue if 15,750 Water Saving models are sold and 11,500 Water & Feed models are sold?

carballo/Shutterstock.com

SOLUTION

Number of Units Sold × Selling Price of Unit = Revenue

Revenue from Water Saving models	**15,750 × $35.99 = $566,842.50**
Revenue from Water & Feed model	**11,500 × $42.79 = $492,085**
Add revenues.	**$566,842.50 + $492,085 = $1,058,927.50**

Sunshine Lawn Products will generate $1,058,927.50 in revenue.

TRY IT

1. Milano's Deluxe Frozen pizzas sell for $7.69 each. The company sold 789,115 last year. Find the total revenue generated.
2. Backyard Firepits sold 4,088 of Wildfire pits at a price of $89 each. The company sold 10,265 of the Patio pits for $68 each. Find the total revenue.

3-3 Assessment

Key Concepts

LO 3-1 1. If the percentage change in quantity demanded is less than the percentage change in price, demand is __?__.

LO 3-2 2. **TRUE OR FALSE** The total dollars received by a business from the sale of a good or service is its total revenue.

LO 3-2 3. Total revenue equals the __?__ multiplied by the quantity demanded.

LO 3-1 4. **TRUE OR FALSE** If the percentage change in quantity demanded is equal to the percentage change in price, demand is unitary elastic.

Think About It

LO 3-1 5. If the price of a good or service increases and the total revenue received by the seller declines, is the demand for this good over this segment of the demand curve elastic or inelastic? Explain.

LO 3-1 6. What is the elasticity of demand for used cars if the price rises by 10 percent and the quantity demanded falls by 30 percent? Is demand for used cars elastic, inelastic, or unitary elastic?

LO 3-2 7. Suppose a movie theater raises the price of popcorn 10 percent, but customers do not buy any less popcorn. What does this tell you about the price elasticity of demand? What will happen to total revenue as a result of the price increase?

LO 3-2 8. What would happen to the quantity of a product that is demanded if there was a 5 percent increase in price when demand is elastic, inelastic, or unitary elastic?

LO 3-2 9. How would total revenue be affected by a 5 percent increase in price if the demand was elastic, inelastic, or unitary elastic?

Make Academic Connections

LO 3-1 10. Consider the demand schedule shown. What is the elasticity of demand value between the following prices? Is demand elastic or inelastic?

a. $P = \$25$ and $P = \$20$
b. $P = \$20$ and $P = \$15$
c. $P = \$15$ and $P = \$10$
d. $P = \$10$ and $P = \$5$

Price	Quantity Demanded	Elasticity Value
$25	20	
20	40	__?__
15	60	__?__
10	80	__?__
5	100	__?__

Teamwork

LO 3-1 11. Work in groups. Make a list of five products students purchase. Consider how the quantity demanded for each item will change if the price increases 10 percent. What if the price doubles? Classify the demand for each product as elastic or inelastic.

Unit 2 Project: Tools of Free Markets

LO 1-1 **ELASTICITY CORRELATION** Create a PowerPoint presentation that compares and contrasts the price elasticity of demand—elastic, inelastic and unitary elastic—as described in Chapter 3. Cite products or services that meet the criteria for elastic and inelastic demands, present the elasticity formulas, and explain how sellers set prices based on elasticity of demand.

Chapter 3

Summary

3-1 THE LAW OF DEMAND

1. The law of demand states that as prices rise, the quantity demanded falls. Demand is the willingness and ability of consumers to buy. A demand schedule lists the quantity demanded at various price levels. It is used to plot a demand curve which slopes downward to the right.
2. An individual demand curve shows the demand for a product by a single consumer. The market demand curve shows overall demand or the sum of all individual demand curves within a market.
3. The law of demand applies to both the individual demand curve and market demand curve. As prices rise, the quantity demanded declines.

3-2 SHIFTS IN THE DEMAND CURVE

4. A change in quantity demanded results from a change in price. When prices rise, the quantity demanded declines. When prices fall, the quantity demanded grows. A change in quantity demanded is a movement between points along a single demand curve.
5. A change in demand is an increase or decrease in total demand. The demand curve shifts or moves toward the right when there is an increase in demand. The demand curve shifts or moves to the left when there is a decrease in demand. A change in demand means there is a market shift. As a group, consumers are buying fewer products at all price levels with a shift to the left (decrease in demand). As a group, consumers are buying more products at all price levels with a shift to the right (increase in demand).
6. A change in demand is created when the number of buyers in the market changes, when consumer tastes and preferences change, when income levels change, when expectations of buyers change, or when prices of related goods change.

3-3 ELASTICITY OF DEMAND

7. Elasticity measures the responsiveness of the quantity demanded to changes in price. Knowledge of a product's elasticity allows a firm to project how a change in a product's price will impact the total revenue its sales generate.
8. To calculate elasticity, divide the percentage change in quantity demanded by the percentage change in price. If elasticity is less than one, the product is said to be inelastic (demand is not responsive to price changes). If elasticity is greater than one, the product is said to be elastic (demand is responsive to price changes).
9. Unitary elasticity results when the percentage change in quantity demanded is equal to the percentage change in price. The percent decrease in price brings the same percent increase in quantity demanded resulting in the maximum revenue. Elasticity of demand helps a business decide what price to charge and how it will affect sales and total revenues that can be collected.

Chapter 3

Assessment

Vocabulary Review

Match each statement with the term that best defines it.

1. The percentage change in quantity demanded is greater than the percentage change in price
2. A table that indicates the quantity of a good or service consumers purchase at various possible prices
3. Any good with a demand curve that shifts rightward (increases) when consumers' incomes increase
4. The total dollars a firm earns from the sale of a good or service. It is equal to the price multiplied by the quantity demanded
5. The sum of all the individual demand curves in a market
6. A movement between points along a demand curve because of a change in price
7. The percentage change in quantity demanded is equal to the percentage change in price. Therefore, the elasticity of demand is equal to 1
8. A good that competes with another good for consumer purchases
9. The relationship between the price and the quantity demanded for a good or service, other variables held constant
10. The line connecting possible combinations of price and quantity purchased by consumers
11. A good that is used together with another good
12. The percentage change in quantity demanded is less than the percentage change in price. Therefore, the elasticity of demand is less than 1
13. Any good with a demand curve that shifts leftward (decreases) when consumers' incomes increase
14. The ratio of the percentage change in the quantity demanded of a product to a percentage change in its price
15. The law that states there is an inverse relationship between the price of a good or service and the quantity buyers purchase
16. An increase (rightward shift) or a decrease (leftward shift) in the demand curve. The shift is caused by a change in a demand shifter factor
17. The demand curve for a single consumer
18. The amount of goods and services purchased at a given price

Vocabulary

a. change in demand
b. change in quantity demanded
c. complement
d. demand
e. demand curve
f. demand schedule
g. elastic demand
h. elasticity of demand
i. inelastic demand
j. inferior good
k. individual demand curve
l. law of demand
m. market demand curve
n. normal good
o. quantity demanded
p. substitute
q. total revenue
r. unitary elastic demand

Review Your Knowledge

LO 1-1 **19.** The law of demand refers to the
- a. inverse relationship between the price of a good and the quantity demanded
- b. price increase that results from an increase in demand for a good of limited supply
- c. inverse relationship between the price of a good and the quantity offered for sale
- d. increase in the quantity of a good available when its price increases

LO 1-1 **20.** A demand curve is a graph that shows combinations of
- a. price and quantity demanded
- b. demand and supply schedules
- c. leakages and injections
- d. price and technology

LO 1-2 **21.** The market demand is the
- a. sum of all individual demand curves in a market
- b. sum of all individual prices in a market
- c. sum of all individual demand curves and supplies in a market
- d. vertical sum of all individual demand curves

LO 2-1 **22.** A movement along a demand curve is caused by a change in
- a. income
- b. price
- c. demand
- d. tastes

LO 2-1 **23.** When the demand for a product has increased, the
- a. demand curve has shifted to the right
- b. price of the product has fallen and, consequently, consumers are buying more of it
- c. cost of producing the product has risen
- d. amount of the product that consumers are willing to purchase at various prices has decreased

LO 2-2 **24.** If the demand for a good increases because consumer income increases, the good is a (an)
- a. inferior good
- b. normal good
- c. necessity good
- d. luxury good

LO 2-2 **25.** Assuming that bus travel is an inferior good, a decrease in consumer income will cause
- a. a downward movement along the demand curve for bus travel
- b. no change in the demand curve for bus travel
- c. an upward movement along the demand curve for air travel
- d. a rightward shift in the demand curve for bus travel

LO 3-1 **26.** Elasticity of demand refers to the ratio of the
- a. percentage change in price of a good in response to a percentage change in quantity demanded
- b. percentage change in price of a good to a percentage increase in income
- c. percentage change in the quantity demanded of a good to a percentage change in its price
- d. none of the above

LO 3-2 **27.** If a decrease in the price of movie tickets increases the total revenue of movie theaters, this is evidence that demand is
- a. elastic
- b. inelastic
- c. unitary elastic
- d. neutral elastic

LO 3-1 **28.** If a 5 percent decrease in the price of a good produces a 5 percent increase in the quantity demanded, the price elasticity of demand is
- a. constant elastic
- b. elastic
- c. inelastic
- d. unitary elastic

Digging Deeper with Economics e-Collection

Price elasticity of demand is an important consideration for business owners. Raising or lowering prices can cause increased profits or loss of profits. For example, when a price elasticity of demand for a product is inelastic, lowering the price can cause lowered total revenues. Thus, a seller of an inelastic product would not choose to lower prices. Access the Gale Economics e-Collection at **www.cengage.com/school/economics/personalfinance**. Research and make a list of three to five products. Prepare diagrams and charts that show the different types of elasticity and how they affect the prices charged for these products.

Think About It

LO 1-1 **29.** The law of demand says that lower prices will result in an increase in the quantity demanded. Can you think of products where this is not true (higher prices result in an increase in the quantity demanded)?

LO 2-1 **30.** When an existing product is found in research studies to bring new and unexpected health benefits, the demand can increase dramatically (causing a rightward shift in demand). What might happen to cause a leftward shift in demand for that same product?

LO 3-1 **31.** A popular soft drink lowers its price during a period of time when the temperature is hot. What is likely to happen to demand for the soft drink? What type of elasticity is this?

Make Academic Connections

LO 1-2 **32.** **COMMUNICATIONS** Cell phone technology allows consumers to use their phone as a GPS. Explain how this technological advancement has affected the demand for cell phones.

LO 2-2 **33.** **SOCIAL STUDIES** During tough economic times, people buy more inferior goods. When the economy gets better (and people are more optimistic) they resume the purchase of normal goods. Explain why people shift their purchasing strategies (demand) depending on their income.

LO 3-1 **34.** **MATH** When the price of acrylic nails is reduced from $25 to $20, the resulting change in the quantity of these products demanded increases from 30 customers to 40. Compute the percentage change in quantity demanded, the percentage change in price, and the elasticity of demand.

Extend Your Learning

35. You are the store manager. From a consumer survey, the demand curve information for athletic shoes per month is given as follows. If you decrease the price from $100 to $75 (25%), the quantity demanded increases from 100 to 150 pairs per month (50%). What is the elasticity of demand? Is demand elastic, unitary elastic, or inelastic? Will the store's total revenue increase, decrease, or remain unchanged as a result of the price decrease?

yienkeat/Shutterstock.com

shotbydave/iStockphoto.com

chapter 4

Market Supply and Price Determination

yienkeat/Shutterstock.com

MARKETS *in Action!*

Fred Smith FedEx Founder

Frederick W. Smith is a classic success story. Fred went to Yale University. He had a new idea to start an overnight delivery service to compete with the U.S. Postal Service. He secured venture capital, worked like crazy, and made a fortune building FedEx. The Smithsonian Institution rendered its ultimate award when it obtained an early FedEx jet for its collection. For a time, this jet was displayed in the Air and Space Museum in Washington, D.C., not far from the Wright brothers' first airplane.

Smith's business plan began with a college economics term paper. His paper spelled out an overnight parcel delivery system that would beat the U.S. Postal Service. People, he said, would pay much more if their packages would arrive at their destinations the next morning. To accomplish his plan, planes would converge nightly on Memphis, Tennessee. The planes would carry packages accepted at any location throughout the nation. Smith chose this city for its central U.S. location. Also, due to its location, there is little bad weather to cause landing delays. In the morning hours, all items would be unloaded, sorted, and rerouted to other airports. From those airports, vans would battle rush-hour traffic to make deliveries before the noon deadline.

Smith's college term paper didn't get a particularly good grade. Perhaps the professor thought the idea was too risky. Lots of other people certainly agreed. After college and a tour as a Marine pilot in Vietnam, the 24-year-old Smith began selling his plan to skeptical financiers. With $4 million of his family's money, he persuaded a few bankers to lend him $80 million. Up to that time, this was the largest venture capital package ever assembled. In 1973, delivery service began with 33 jets connecting 25 cities. But on the first night only 86 packages showed up for delivery.

It was years before Smith looked like a genius. The company posted a $27 million loss the first year. Then a 1981 decision to add letters to its package delivery service brought success. Today, Smith's basic strategy hasn't changed. However, the scale of the operation has exploded. FedEx is the world's largest express transportation company serving over 200 countries.

Fred Smith believed that people wanted faster and better service for packages than could be delivered by the post office. He believed he could deliver that service for a better price.

Originally, all FedEx planes would be in Memphis, TN nightly where packages were unloaded, sorted, and rerouted to other airports for delivery by noon the next day.

Denise Kappa/Shutterstock.com

Think Critically

1. Smith's price for package mail was not set by the government. How do you think Smith estimated the price for his new service?
2. What steps do you think he took in setting the right price?
3. Why do you suppose many new businesses don't make a profit in their first few years of business?

yienkeat/Shutterstock.com

4-1 The Law of Supply

Learning Objectives

LO 1-1 **Explain** the law of supply.

LO 1-2 **Understand** the difference between an individual and a market supply curve.

Vocabulary

supply, p. 95
quantity supplied, p. 95
law of supply, p. 95
supply schedule, p. 95
supply curve, p. 95
individual supply curve, p. 96
market supply curve, p. 96

© Aleksandar Vrzalski/iStockphoto.com

REAL-WORLD FOCUS

Betty works at her parents' bakery. Every Saturday morning, she goes to work with her parents at 3 A.M. and helps them prepare strudel, bread, rolls, desserts, and cookies. Betty's parents told her that weekends require a larger inventory of their baked goods. They explained that the Saturday Market which is just a block away brings more people to the store. Opening the store an hour before the market opens allows them to sell large quantities of baked goods. Throughout the day they are also able to serve many more customers. Their product line is larger than during the week, and it is priced higher. Because they can charge a higher price, they are able to make higher profits on weekends than the rest of the week.

WORK AS A TEAM Why would the bakery charge higher prices on Saturday than the rest of the week? What would you to do to encourage some of the Saturday customers to come back during the week?

val lawless/Shutterstock.com

In the bakery business, baked goods have to be prepared in advance. On any given day, sales are limited to the number of items ready to be sold at the time the store opens.

DO YOU THINK the owner of a bakery uses the law of supply to set the prices for his products?

yienkeat/Shutterstock.com

LO 1-1 The Supply Curve

In everyday conversation, the term supply refers to a specific quantity. A "limited supply" means there are only so many items for sale. This meaning of supply is not the economist's definition. To economists, **supply** is the relationship between the price and quantity supplied for a good or service. Like demand, supply is based on the assumption that other variables remain unchanged. **Quantity supplied** is the amount of goods or services sellers offer for sale at a given price.

In a free market system, sellers have a profit incentive to charge higher prices. Figure 4-1 illustrates an important law in economics called the law of supply. The **law of supply** states there is a direct relationship between the price of a good and the quantity sellers offer for sale. At a higher price, suppliers devote more resources to a product. The result is a greater quantity supplied.

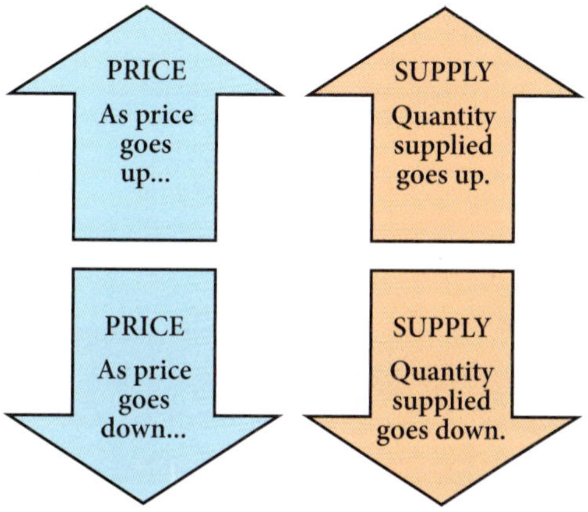

Figure 4-1

The Law of Supply

The law of supply states there is a direct relationship between changes in price and the quantity supplied.

Interpreting the individual supply schedule in Figure 4-2 and a demand schedule are similar. A **supply schedule** is a table that lists the quantity of a good or service sellers offer for sale at possible prices. Each point in the first column represents a price and quantities supplied are in the other two columns. At a price of $10 per disc, the quantity supplied by the seller, Entertain City, is 30,000 DVDs per year. At the higher price of $15, the quantity supplied increases to 40,000 DVDs. Following the law of supply, as the price rises, the quantity supplied also rises.

Point	Price per DVD	Quantity Supplied (thousands per year)
A	$5	20
B	10	30
C	15	40
D	20	50

Figure 4-2

Entertain City's Supply Schedule for DVDs

The supply schedule for an individual seller shows the quantity of DVDs offered for sale at different prices. As the price of DVDs rises, a seller has an incentive to increase the quantity of DVDs supplied. The direct relationship between price and quantity supplied conforms to the law of supply.

Why are sellers willing to sell more at a higher price? The incentive of profits motivates sellers. As the price of a good rises, there is greater *profit*. If the price falls, there is less profit and businesses offer less quantity for sale. In Figure 4-3, the **supply curve** is formed by the line connecting possible price and quantity supplied responses of sellers. It allows you to find the quantity supplied for a seller at possible selling prices by moving along the curve. The price and quantity combinations for Entertain City are taken from the data in the table in Figure 4-2. Entertain City's supply curve shows that at a price of \$20 per DVD (point *D*) the quantity supplied is 50,000 DVDs. At the lower price of \$5, Entertain City's quantity supplied decreases to 20,000 DVDs (point *A*).

Figure 4-3

Entertain City's Supply Curve for DVDs

Entertain City's supply curve is from Figure 4-2. The supply curve shows a direct relationship between price per DVD and the quantity supplied. The model assumes other variables are held constant.

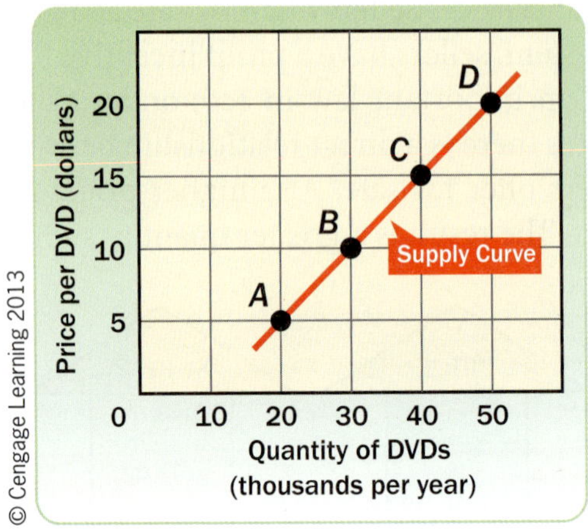

CHECKPOINT

Assume you are in the pizza business and you believe that you could sell pizzas at a higher price. How does the law of supply relate to the number of pizzas you would be willing to offer for sale at a higher price?

LO 1-2 Market Supply

To construct a market supply curve, follow the same procedure used to derive a market demand curve. An **individual supply curve** is the supply for a single seller. To change from an individual supply curve to a market supply curve, total the individual supply curves. A **market supply curve** is the sum of all the individual supply curves in a market.

Assume Entertain City and High Vibes Company are the only two firms selling DVDs in a given market. In Figure 4-4, the market supply curve, S_{Total}, slopes upward to the right. The table reports price-quantity responses at various prices. For simplicity, the graphs show only sellers' responses at \$25 and \$15 per DVD. For example, at a price of \$25, Entertain City will supply 25,000 DVDs, and High Vibes will supply 35,000 DVDs. Summing the two individual supply curves, S_1 and S_2, the total of 60,000 DVDs is plotted on the market supply curve, S_{Total}. Similar calculations at other prices generate a market supply curve. This curve shows the total amount of DVDs these businesses offer for sale at different possible selling prices. The law of supply applies to the market supply curve. When the price rises, the quantity supplied goes up. And if price falls, the quantity supplied goes down. Also, like the individual demand curve, the assumption is that all other variables are constant.

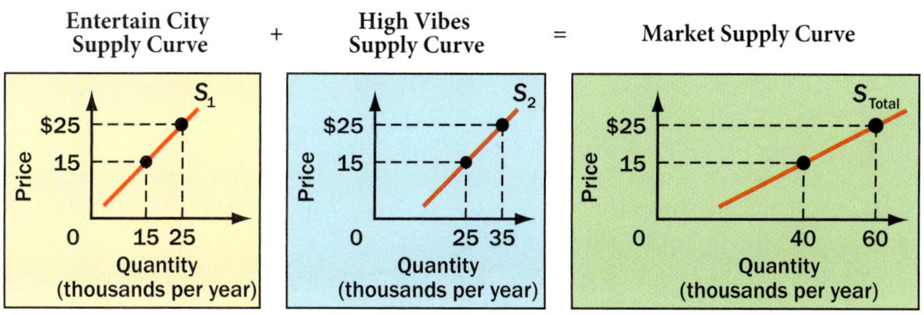

Price per DVD	Quantity Supplied per Year: Entertain City	High Vibes	Total Supply
$25	25	35	60
20	20	30	50
15	15	25	40
10	10	20	30
5	5	15	20

Figure 4-4

Market Supply Curve and Schedule for DVDs

Individual supply curves differ for sellers Entertain City and High Vibes. Assuming they are the only sellers, the market supply curve, S_{Total}, is obtained by summing the individual supply curves, S_1 and S_2.

CHECKPOINT

Explain the difference between an individual supply curve and a market supply curve.

Ostrich Farmers Stuck Their Necks Out

Ostrich farmers in Iowa, Texas, Oklahoma, and other states in the Midwest "stuck their necks out." Many invested millions of dollars converting a portion of their farms into breeding grounds for ostriches. The reason was that mating pairs of ostriches were selling for $75,000 during the late 1990s. Ostrich breeders claimed that ostrich meat would become the low cholesterol, low-fat health treat, and ostrich prices rose. The high prices for ostriches fueled profit expectations.

Adam Smith concluded that competitive forces are like an "invisible hand" that leads producers who are pursuing their own interests. When the profit potential looked good, firms entered this market and started raising ostriches. Over time the population of these birds exploded and the price of a breeding pair plummeted to a few thousand dollars. Profits tumbled, and the number of ostrich farms declined.

A decade later demand increased because mad cow disease plagued Europe. People bought alternatives to beef. Suppliers could not meet the demand for ostrich burgers. Profits rose again, causing farmers to once more increase supply by investing in ostriches.

Think Critically

Relate the ostrich scenario described to the law of supply.

4-1 Assessment

Key Concepts

LO 1-1 1. The law of supply states there is a __?__ relationship between the price of a good or service and the quantity sellers offer for sale.

LO 1-1 2. **TRUE OR FALSE** The concept of supply is based on the responses of buyers to price changes.

LO 1-1 3. Quantity supplied is the __?__ of goods and services sellers offer for sale at a given price.

LO 1-2 4. **TRUE OR FALSE** A market supply curve is the sum of all the individual supply curves in a market.

Think About It

LO 1-1 5. What is the most important factor sellers consider when offering a good for sale?

LO 1-1 6. Why might sellers offer more of a good at a higher price and less at a lower price?

LO 1-2 7. Two businesses offer fresh-baked apple pies for sale. At a price of $10 the Knife and Fork is willing to offer 50 apple pies for sale while the Green Garden offers 30 similar pies. What is the quantity of fresh-baked apple pies supplied in this market at a price of $10? How did you find your answer?

LO 1-1 8. Describe a situation that demonstrates the law of supply.

LO 1-2 9. Explain how a market supply curve would be constructed from the individual supply curves of all businesses in a market.

LO 1-2 10. Imagine you own a store that stocks winter gloves. Weather experts have predicted an exceptionally cold winter so consumers are willing to pay much more for the products you offer for sale. Explain what this would do to the quantity of gloves you would be willing to supply to your market. Describe how this event could be shown on a supply curve for the products you offer for sale.

Make Academic Connections

LO 1-1 11. **MARKETING** Ralph is the sales manager of a small chain of retail shoe stores. The owner has reviewed costs and profits to determine how many pairs of athletic shoes to offer for sale at various prices each week. The results of this research appear in the supply schedule below. Use this data to construct the supply curve for athletic shoes.

Price	Quantity Supplied
$125	500
100	400
75	300
50	200
25	100

Teamwork

LO 1-2 12. Work in groups. Each group determines a product to sell and sets five different possible prices above and below the current market price for the selected product. Create individual supply schedules that show how many units of the product each member of the group would be willing to supply at each of the five different prices. Combine the individual schedules into a market supply schedule. Finally, transform the data into a market supply curve for the product.

4-2 Shifts in the Supply Curve

Learning Objectives

LO 2-1 Explain the difference between changes in quantity supplied and changes in supply.

LO 2-2 Identify supply shifter factors that cause changes in supply.

Vocabulary

change in quantity supplied, p. 100
change in supply, p. 100
excise tax, p. 102
subsidy, p. 102

© Aleksandar Vrzalski/iStockphoto.com

REAL-WORLD FOCUS

Raoul mows lawns during his summer vacations. He has a number of regular customers who pay him to mow their lawns once a week. He also has a limited amount of time to do special jobs. Mrs. Adams, one of his neighbors, also hires Raoul to weed her yard. This coming summer, Raoul plans to do an internship for a local business owner. He knows that he will have less time to mow lawns and do special jobs. He believes he will be able to maintain his regular customers, but he has told Mrs. Adams he can't weed her yard. Mrs. Adams really likes Raoul's work and has offered to pay him twice the previous rate. Now Raoul is reconsidering his decision.

WORK AS A TEAM Why is Raoul reconsidering his summer schedule? Is there a way he could also do the special job for Mrs. Adams without losing his regular customers or giving up the internship? What is Raoul's basic problem regarding his decision?

The tax assessed for each vehicle manufactured is based on the manufacturer's list price in the year it is manufactured.

DO YOU THINK the amount of the tax assessed on a vehicle is included in the price displayed by the dealer?

Mr Doomits/Shutterstock.com

LO 2-1 Difference Between Changes in Quantity Supplied and Changes in Supply

A **change in quantity supplied** results solely from a change in price. It is a movement between points along a stationary supply curve. This change is based on the assumption that all other supply shifter factors remain constant. In Figure 4-5, at the price of \$10, the quantity supplied is 30,000 DVDs per year (point *A*). At the higher price of \$15, sellers offer a larger quantity supplied of 40,000 DVDs per year (point *B*). The change between point *A* and point *B* is a movement along the curve. Economists describe the effect of the rise in price as an increase in the quantity supplied of 10,000 DVDs per year.

Figure 4-5

Change in Quantity Supplied

The figure shows the market supply curve for DVDs per year. If the price is \$10 at point *A*, the quantity supplied is 30,000 DVDs. If the price increases to \$15 at point *B*, the quantity supplied increases from 30,000 to 40,000 DVDs. The change between point *A* and point *B* is a movement along the curve.

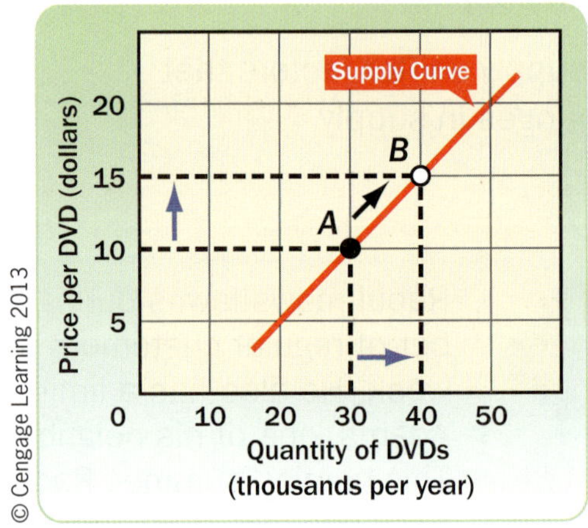

A **change in supply** is an increase (rightward shift) or a decrease (leftward shift) in the quantity supplied at each possible price. If one of the six supply shifter factors changes, the impact is to alter the supply curve's location. In Figure 4-6(a), the rightward shift (an increase in supply) from S_1 to S_2 means that at all possible prices sellers offer a greater quantity for sale. At \$15 per DVD, for instance, sellers provide 50,000 for sale annually (point *B*), rather than 40,000 (point *A*).

Another case in Figure 4-6(b) is that a supply shifter factor changes and causes a leftward shift (a decrease in supply) from supply curve S_1 to S_3. As a result, a smaller quantity will be offered for sale at each possible price.

Figure 4-6

Change in Supply

Part (a) illustrates an increase (rightward shift) in supply. A change in a supply shifter can cause an increase or decrease in supply from S_1 to S_2. Part (b) shows a decrease (leftward shift) in supply from S_1 to S_3.

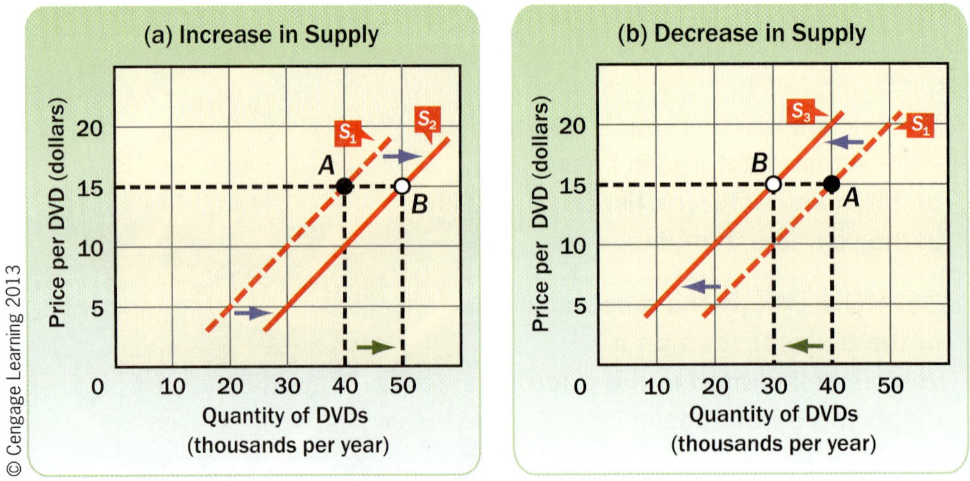

Change	Effect	Description
Price Increase	Upward movement along the supply curve	Increase in the quantity supplied
Price Decrease	Downward movement along the supply curve	Decrease in the quantity supplied
Supply Shifter Factors	Leftward or rightward shift of the supply curve	Decrease or increase in supply

Figure 4-7
What Happens When Price and Supply Shifter Factors Change

CHECKPOINT

What is the difference between a movement along a supply curve and a shift of a supply curve?

LO 2-2 Supply Shifter Factors

As in demand theory, the price of a product is not the only factor that influences how much sellers offer for sale. Once you relax the other variables held constant assumption, there are six principal *supply shifter factors* that can shift or move the supply curve's position. These variables or factors are also called *non-price determinants.* The factors include (1) the number of sellers, (2) technology, (3) resource prices, (4) taxes and subsidies, (5) expectations of producers, and (6) prices of other goods the firm could produce.

Number of Sellers

What happens when frost ruins the orange crop? The damaging effect of the weather may force orange growers to lose that year's crop, and supply decreases. When the government eases restrictions on hunting alligators, the number of alligator hunters increases. As a result, the supply curve for alligator meat and skins increases. Internationally, the United States may decide to lower trade barriers on textile imports. This action increases supply by allowing new foreign firms to add their individual supply curves to the U.S. market supply curve for textiles. Conversely, higher U.S. trade barriers on textile imports shift the U.S. market supply curve for textiles leftward.

Robotic arms are used in the process of DVD replication.

Technology

Never has society experienced such an explosion of new production techniques. Throughout the world, new and more efficient

With advances in technology, dairy farmers use computers that automate the process of milking cows.

technology is making it possible to manufacture more products at any possible selling price. New more powerful computers reduce production costs and increase the supply of all sorts of goods and services. For example, computers now control the milking of cows. Computers admit the cows into the milking area and activate lasers to guide milking cups into place. Dairy farmers no longer must wake up at 5:30 A.M. Cows can be milked day or night. As this technology spreads across the United States, it will be possible to offer more milk for sale at each possible price. Therefore, the entire supply curve for milk will shift to the right.

Resource Prices

Natural resources, labor, capital, and entrepreneurs are all required to produce products, and the prices of these resources affect supply. Suppose many firms are competing for computer programmers to design their software programs, and the salaries of these highly-skilled workers increase. This increase in the price of labor adds to the cost of production. Along the original supply curve, extra costs must be added to each possible price. As a result, the supply of computer software shifts leftward (decreases) because sellers must charge more than before for any quantity supplied. Any reduction in production costs caused by a decline in the price of resources will have an opposite effect on the supply curve and it shifts rightward (increases). Along the original supply curve, cost declines so the price can be reduced at each possible supply level.

Taxes and Subsidies

Certain taxes, such as excise taxes, have the same effect on supply as an increase in the price of a resource. An **excise tax** is a tax paid by the seller on the production or sale of a good or service. The impact of an increase in the tax is similar to a rise in the cost of labor or any other productive resource. The higher tax imposes an additional cost on producers, and the supply curve shifts leftward. Conversely, a subsidy for a productive resource has the same effect as lower costs for resources or a technological advance. A **subsidy** is a payment from the government to support a business that reduces its costs. As a result the firm's supply curve shifts rightward. Note that subsidies and excise taxes are forms of government regulation that influence supply in opposite directions.

NET Bookmark

Access www.cengage.com/school/economics/personalfinance and click on the link for Chapter 4. Go to Economagic, which is a rich source of economic data. Observe the trend in the price per barrel of crude oil for a twelve-month period. Which supply shifter variable is affected by the cost of crude oil? Based on the recent trend in the price of crude oil, analyze the effect on the supply curve for plastics.

www.cengage.com/school/economics/personalfinance

The Europoort area in the Port of Rotterdam is an industrialized port where oil is stored in large spherical containers.

Expectations of Producers

Expectations affect both current demand and current supply. Suppose a war in the Middle East causes oil producers to believe that oil prices will rise dramatically. Their initial responses could be to hold back a portion of the oil in their storage tanks. The reason is so they can sell the stored oil later and make greater profits when oil prices rise. One approach used by the major oil companies might be to limit the amount of gasoline delivered to independent distributors. This response by the oil industry shifts the current supply curve to the left. Now suppose farmers anticipate the price of wheat will soon fall sharply. Their reactions are to sell their inventories stored in silos immediately before the price declines. Such a response shifts the supply curve for wheat to the right.

Prices of Other Goods the Firm Could Produce

Businesses are always considering shifting resources from producing one good to producing another good. A rise in the price of one product relative to the prices of other products sends signals to suppliers. The signal is that switching production to the product with the higher relative price yields higher profit. Suppose the price of corn rises due to government incentives to use corn to produce ethanol. If the price of wheat remains the same, then many farmers will divert more of their land to corn and less to wheat. The result is an increase in the supply of corn and a decrease in the supply of wheat. This shift happens because the opportunity cost of growing wheat, measured in forgone corn profits, increases. Figure 4-8 gives other real-world examples of supply shifter factors.

CHECKPOINT

Which supply shifter factor is affected by an increase in the price of oil? Does this change cause an increase or decrease in the supply curve for airline tickets?

Figure 4-8

Supply Shifter Factors with Real-World Examples

Supply Shifter Factors	Relationship to Changes in Supply Curve	Shifts in the Supply Curve with Examples	
1. Number of Sellers	Direct	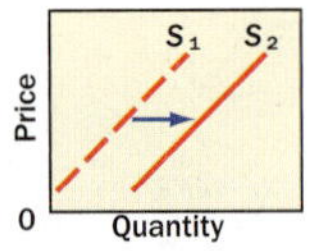 The U.S. lowers trade restrictions on foreign textiles, and the supply of textiles in the U.S. increases.	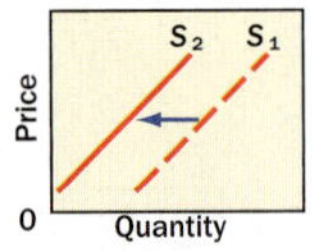 A severe drought destroys the orange crop, and the supply of oranges decreases.
2. Technology	Direct	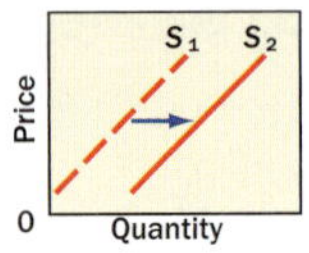 New methods of producing automobiles reduce production costs, and the supply of automobiles increases.	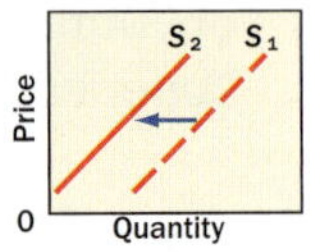 Technology is destroyed in war, and production costs increase; the result is a decrease in the supply of good *X*.
3. Resource Prices	Inverse	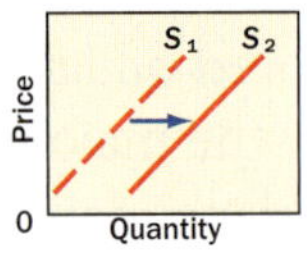 A decline in the price of computer chips increases the supply of computers.	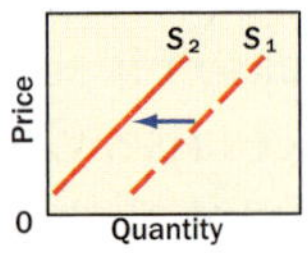 An increase in the cost of farm equipment decreases the supply of soybeans.
4. Taxes and Subsidies	Inverse and Direct	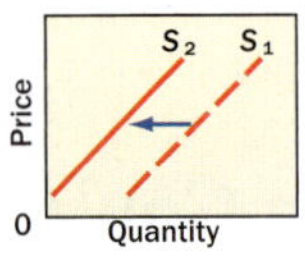 An increase in the per-gallon tax on gasoline reduces the supply of gasoline.	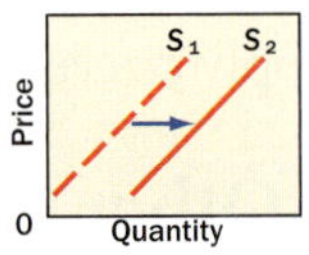 A government payment to dairy farmers per gallon produced increases the supply of milk.
5. Expectations	Inverse	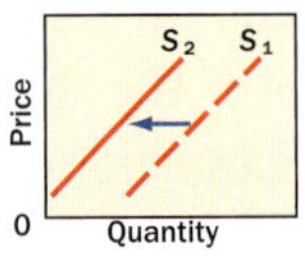 Oil companies anticipate a rise in future oil prices, which causes these companies to decrease their current supply of oil.	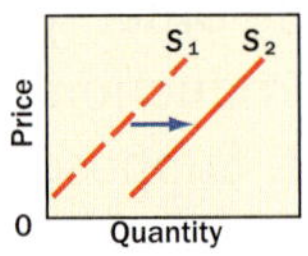 Farmers expect the future price of wheat to decline, so they increase the present supply of wheat.
6. Prices of Other Goods and Services	Inverse	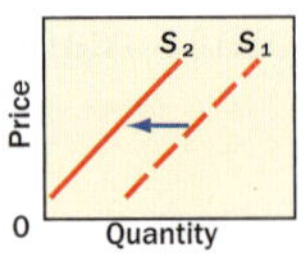 A rise in the price of brand-name drugs causes drug companies to decrease the supply of generic drugs.	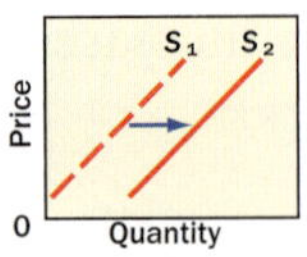 A decline in the price of tomatoes causes farmers to increase the supply of cucumbers.

PROFILE

Alfred Marshall
Classical Economist

By kind permission of the Marshall Library of Economics, University of Cambridge

Alfred Marshall (1842-1924) was born in London, England. His father was a cashier at the Bank of England and Marshall grew up in a middle class family. His father urged Marshall to become a clergyman. However, he abandoned plans to enter the clergy and graduated with a M.A. in mathematics at Cambridge in 1865. Marshall planned to pursue a career in physics, but he became interested in ethics, and studied this subject for a year in Germany. Later he turned to economics as a means for implementing ethics. Marshall's view was that the role of economics was to improve material conditions, which is tightly connected to ethical, social, and political influences. Marshall believed economics plays an essential role in advances for the working class. His vision, for example, was for economics to contribute to the reduction of poverty and inequality. This philosophy influenced his work.

In 1875, Marshall became a professor at Cambridge and attempted to develop the subject of political economy. He married a former student who had also become a professor in economics at Cambridge. His marriage made him ineligible to continue at Cambridge so he accepted a teaching position at another college. Years later he returned to Cambridge and remained until he retired in 1908.

While at Cambridge, Marshall became interested in the work of Adam Smith and other classical economists. In time he became one of the most influential economists of his era. Marshall's contribution was to apply his mathematical training to economics. However, he did not want mathematics to overshadow economics for the public. In 1890, he published *Principles of Economics*. This text was the leading economics text for decades. Among Marshall's most important contributions are explaining price elasticity of demand and how markets set prices. Marshall described the market as a pair of scissor blades. Today economists also owe Marshall for showing how factors change and shift demand and supply curves.

THINK CRITICALLY

1. **How do demand and supply act as blades of the scissors in Marshall's quote?**
2. **Explain Marshall's view that the role of economics is tightly connected to ethical, social, and political influence.**

yienkeat/Shutterstock.com

4-2 Assessment

Key Concepts

LO 2-2 1. A payment from government to support a business is called a __?__.

LO 2-1 2. **TRUE OR FALSE** A movement between points along a stationary supply curve because of a change in price is an increase in supply.

LO 2-2 3. A tax on the production or sale of a good or service is an __?__ tax.

LO 2-2 4. **TRUE OR FALSE** A shift in the supply curve is caused by a change in a supply shifter factor.

Think About It

LO 2-1 5. Draw graphs to illustrate the difference between a decrease in quantity supplied and a decrease in supply for condominiums. Give a possible reason for change in each graph.

LO 2-2 6. Predict whether there is an increase or decrease in supply for each of the following situations.
   a. Several new companies enter the cell phone industry.
   b. Farmers decide what crop to plant and learn that the price of corn has fallen relative to the price of cotton. What is the impact on the supply of cotton?
   c. Gasoline lobbyists convince Congress to remove the tax paid by sellers on each gallon of gasoline.
   d. A new type of robot is invented that will pick peaches.
   e. A computer game company anticipates the future price of its games will rise much higher than the current prices.

LO 2-1 7. Describe each of the six supply shifter factors.

Make Academic Connections

LO 2-2 8. **RESEARCH** Investigate a world event that could have an impact on the supply of a product you consume. Describe this event and explain how it would shift the supply curve.

LO 2-2 9. **TECHNOLOGY** Choose a single product that you buy, and write a paragraph that discusses whether the creation of the Internet has shifted the supply curve for this product.

Teamwork

LO 2-2 10. Work in six groups. Each group chooses one of the supply shifter factors. Each group assumes they are sellers of surf boards and brainstorms scenarios that show how the assigned factor affects the supply curve for surf boards. Each group prepares a graph to illustrate the scenario and shares the analysis with the class.

Unit 2 Project: Tools of Free Markets

PRESENTATION OF SUPPLY Prepare a supply schedule for a product that you as a business owner would be willing and able to produce. Transfer the supply schedule to a supply curve. Propose a scenario in which your total supply would increase dramatically and prepare a new supply curve. Propose a scenario in which your total supply would decrease dramatically and prepare a new supply curve. Explain the law of supply, your supply schedule, supply curve, and shifts in supply.

yienkeat/Shutterstock.com; Chad Baker/Ryan McVay/Photodisc/Getty Images

4-3 The Free Market Price

Learning Objectives

LO 3-1 Understand how a free market determines equilibrium prices.

LO 3-2 Analyze how changes to demand and supply affect the equilibrium price.

Vocabulary

surplus, p. 108
shortage, p. 109
disequilibrium, p. 109
equilibrium, p. 110

© Aleksandar Vrzalski/iStockphoto.com

REAL-WORLD FOCUS

Emily likes to have her nails manicured once a week. She often has special colors or designs applied for special occasions. For regular manicures, Emily goes to one shop, but for special designs she goes to a different shop across town. Most of her friends also use that shop across town. Recently, her regular manicurist explained that her shop will start offering some special designs that may interest Emily. When she compared prices, she found that she would be able to get the work done for about the same price, but that the total cost would be less because she wouldn't have to drive or get a ride across town.

WORK AS A TEAM What would cause Emily to reject the special designs at her regular manicurist's shop? Why is Emily concerned about the cost of driving across town? How might her regular manicurist maintain and increase business profits?

Taking inventory is one way retailers record the number of items available for sale. When inventory shows stock on an item is low, more items need to be ordered.

DO YOU THINK retailers order more of an item to sell when they have a surplus or a shortage of that product? Explain your answer.

yienkeat/Shutterstock.com

spflaum/Shutterstock.com

LO 3-1 Free Market Equilibrium

Recall from Lesson 1-1 that a market is any place or method used by buyers and sellers to exchange goods and services. Also recall that microeconomics studies decision making by individuals, families, and businesses. Here micro analysis is applied to an individual market. Consider the retail market for athletic shoes. Figure 4-9 displays market demand and supply data for this product. Notice in column 1 of the table that price serves as a common variable for both supply and demand. Columns 2 and 3 list the quantity demanded and the quantity supplied for pairs of athletic shoes per month at various possible prices. This data is used for the graphs in part (a) and part (b).

Figure 4-9

Demand, Supply, and Equilibrium for Athletic Shoes (pairs per month)

In part (a) a surplus occurs because the quantity supplied (200,000) is greater than the quantity demanded (100,000). As a result, the price falls to $75. In part (b) a shortage exists because the quantity demanded (200,000) exceeds the quantity supplied (100,000). Here, the price rises to $75.

(1) Price per Pair	(2) Quantity Demanded	(3) Quantity Supplied	(4) Difference (3) – (2)	(5) Market Condition	(6) Pressure on Price
$125	50,000	250,000	+200,000	Surplus	Downward
100	100,000	200,000	+100,000	Surplus	Downward
75	150,000	150,000	0	Equilibrium	Stationary
50	200,000	100,000	−100,000	Shortage	Upward
25	250,000	50,000	−200,000	Shortage	Upward

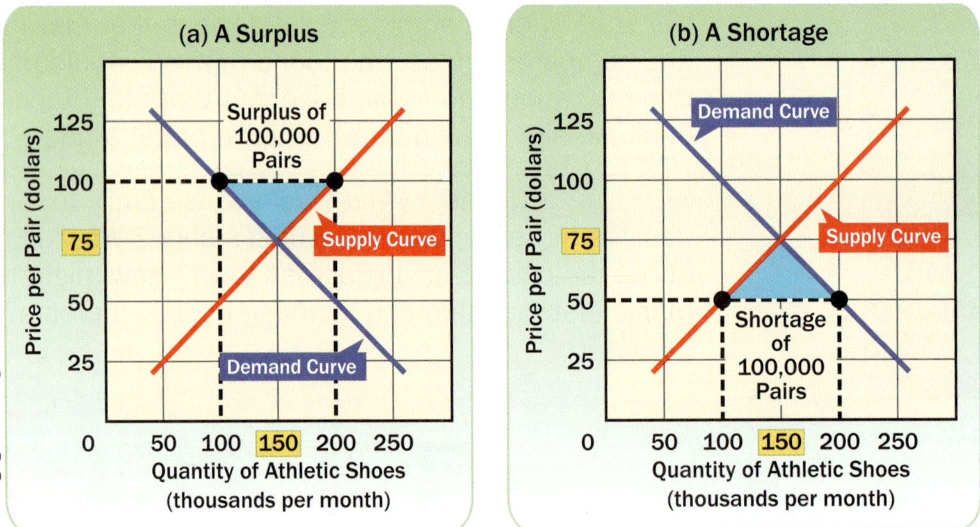

There is an important question for market supply and demand analysis. Which selling price and quantity will prevail in the market? What will happen if retail stores supply 250,000 pairs of athletic shoes and charge $125 a pair? As shown in the table, at this relatively high price for athletic shoes, consumers purchase only 50,000 pairs. As a result, 200,000 pairs of athletic shoes remain on the shelves of sellers (column 4) as unsold inventory. The market condition is a surplus (column 5). A **surplus** occurs at any price at which the quantity supplied is greater than the quantity demanded.

How will retailers react to excess supply? Free market competition forces sellers to bid down their selling prices to attract more sales (column 6). If sellers cut the selling price to $100 shown in part (a), there will still be an unwanted surplus of 100,000 pairs of athletic shoes. Pressure on sellers to cut their selling prices will continue.

Now assume sellers slash the price of athletic shoes to $25 per pair. This price is very attractive to consumers, and the quantity demanded shown in the table is 200,000 pairs of athletic shoes. Sellers will provide only 50,000 pairs at this price. The good news is consumers buy these 50,000 pairs of athletic shoes at $25. The bad news is that potential buyers are willing to purchase 200,000 more pairs at that price. But they cannot because the shoes are not on the shelves for sale. This out of stock condition signals the existence of a shortage. A **shortage** occurs at any price at which the quantity supplied is less than the quantity demanded.

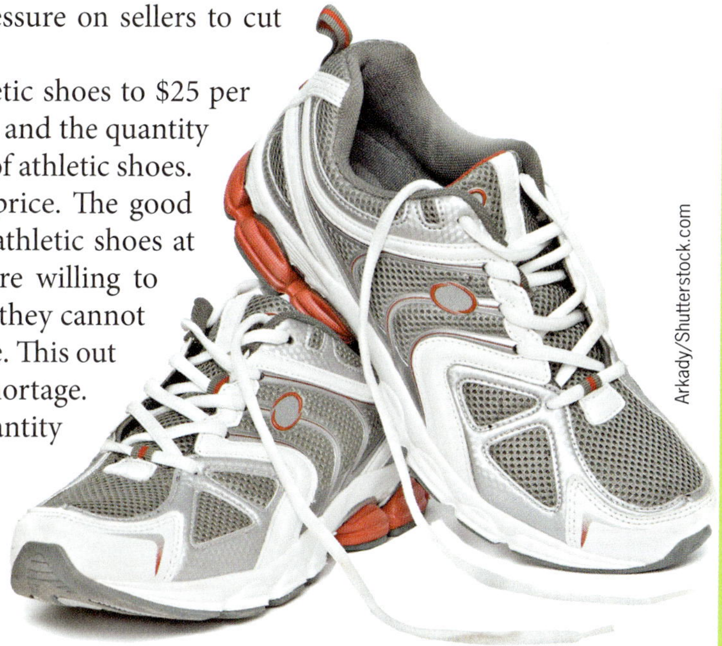

Arkady/Shutterstock.com

In the case of excess demand, unsatisfied consumers compete to obtain the product by bidding to pay a higher price. Sellers are seeking the higher profits that higher prices make possible. They gladly respond by setting a higher price such as $50 shown in part (b) and increasing the quantity supplied to 100,000 pairs. At $50, the shortage of 100,000 pairs persists because the quantity demanded of 200,000 pairs still exceeds the quantity supplied. The price of $50 will also be temporary. The unfulfilled quantity demanded provides an incentive for sellers to raise their selling prices and offer more athletic shoes for sale.

Equilibrium Price and Quantity

Surplus and shortage conditions create disequilibrium. **Disequilibrium** occurs at a market price at which the quantity demanded does not equal the quantity supplied. Disequilibrium is a temporary condition in a free market. Sellers are free to sell their products at any price. Trial and error makes all possible

Surplus and Shortage

The goal for suppliers and sellers is to identify the equilibrium for their products to avoid surpluses and shortages. In all markets and for all products, this goal is not easily obtained. Evidence of surpluses and shortages are on the shelves of retailers. While at a local shopping center, make a list of three goods that are in surplus and three goods that are in shortage.

Investigate Your Local ECONOMY

Try it Out

Do you think the reason was excess supply, excess demand, or simply a stocking error? Share your observations in class.

price-quantity combinations unstable except at equilibrium. **Equilibrium** occurs at a price at which the quantity demanded and the quantity supplied are equal. At the equilibrium price there is no surplus or shortage.

In Figure 4-10, $75 is the equilibrium price, and 150,000 pairs of athletic shoes is the equilibrium quantity per month. When the price per pair is $75, the market supply curve and the market demand curve intersect at point *E*. At this point the quantity demanded equals the quantity supplied at 150,000 pairs per month. At the equilibrium price there is no surplus or shortage.

Equilibrium means that the forces of supply and demand are "in balance." There is no reason for price or quantity to change, other variables held constant. In short, all prices and quantities except a unique equilibrium price and quantity are temporary. Once the price is $75, it will not change unless a demand or supply factor changes. In the next lesson, you will learn how equilibrium changes over time.

Figure 4-10

The Market Equilibrium for Athletic Shoes

Only at the equilibrium price of $75 is the quantity demanded equal to the quantity supplied of 150,000 pairs of athletic shoes per month.

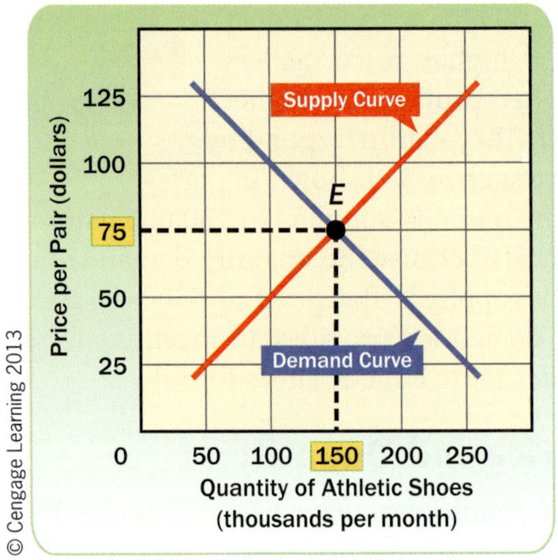

Rationing Function of the Price System

The analysis leads to an important conclusion. The predictable or stable outcome in the athletic shoes example is that the price will eventually come to rest at $75 per pair. All other factors held constant, the price may be above or below $75, but the forces of surplus or shortage guarantee that any price other than the equilibrium price is temporary. This is how the free enterprise system operates. The price system uses the forces of supply and demand to create equilibrium through rising and falling prices. Price plays a *rationing* role. The price system is important because it is a mechanism for distributing scarce goods and services. At the equilibrium price of $75, only those consumers willing to pay $75 per pair get athletic shoes. There will be no shoes produced for buyers who are unwilling or unable to pay that price.

CHECKPOINT

Why would you prefer a world with all markets in equilibrium?

LO 3-2 Changes in Market Equilibrium

Using market supply-and-demand analysis is like putting on glasses if you are nearsighted. Suddenly, the fuzzy world around you comes into clear focus. Many people believe that prices are set by sellers adding a certain percentage to their costs. If sellers' costs rise, they simply raise these prices by that percentage. In free markets, there is more to the story.

jgroup/iStockphoto.com

One reason cruises are a popular form of vacationing is that meals and entertainment are included in the price of the ticket.

Changes in Demand

The Caribbean cruise market is shown in Figure 4-11 part (a). Assume market supply, *S*, is constant and market demand increases from D_1 to D_2. Why has the demand curve shifted rightward? Assume the popularity of cruises has suddenly risen sharply due to advertising. Given supply curve *S* and demand curve *D*, the initial equilibrium price is $600 per cruise. The initial equilibrium quantity is 8,000 cruises per year, shown as point E_1. After advertising, the new equilibrium point, E_2, becomes 12,000 cruises at a price of $900 each. Thus, the increase in demand causes both the equilibrium price and the equilibrium quantity to increase.

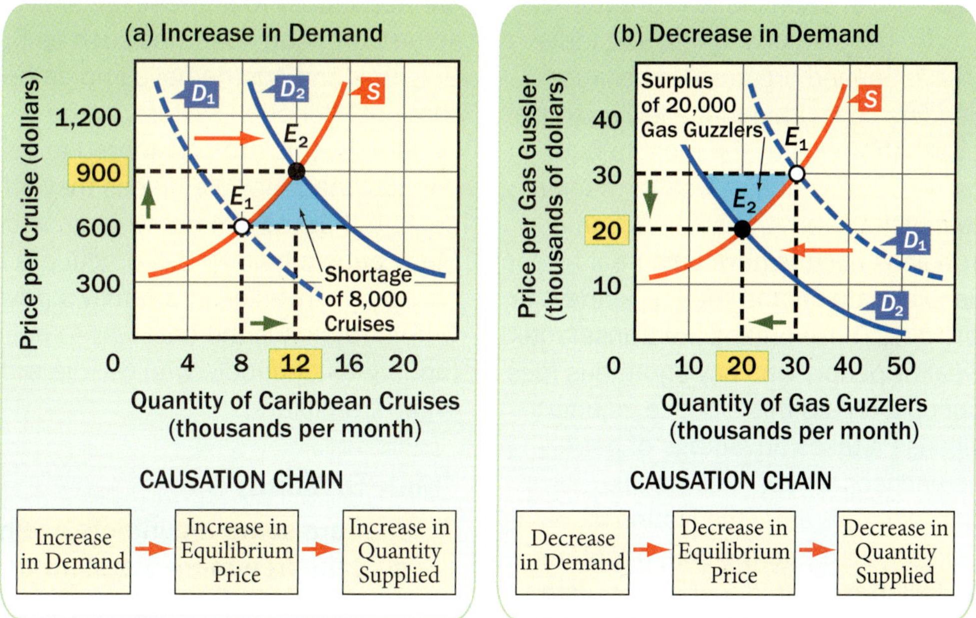

Figure 4-11

How Shifts in Demand Change Market Equilibrium

In part (a), demand for Caribbean cruises increases, and the demand curve shifts rightward from D_1 to D_2. A shortage encourages firms to move upward along the supply curve to a new equilibrium at E_2.

Part (b) illustrates a decrease in the demand for SUVs. A surplus forces sellers to move downward along the supply curve to a new equilibrium at E_2.

It is important to understand the force that caused the equilibrium to shift from E_1 to E_2. When demand initially increased from D_1 to D_2, there was a temporary shortage of 8,000 cruises at $600 per cruise. Firms in the cruise business responded to the excess demand by hiring more workers. They also offered more cruises to the Caribbean, and raised the price. The cruise lines therefore moved upward along the supply curve (increasing quantity supplied). After trial and error, Caribbean cruise sellers increased their prices and quantities supplied until a shortage no longer existed at point E_2. The increase in demand caused both the equilibrium price and the equilibrium quantity to increase.

What will happen to the demand for gas-guzzling automobiles (for example, SUVs) if the price of gasoline triples? Gasoline and automobiles are complements. This relationship means a rise in the price of gasoline decreases the demand for gas guzzlers from D_1 to D_2 in Figure 4-11 part (b). At the initial equilibrium price of $30,000 per gas guzzler ($E_1$), the quantity supplied now exceeds the quantity demanded by 20,000 automobiles per month. This unwanted inventory forces automakers to reduce the price and quantity supplied. As a result of this movement downward on the supply curve, market equilibrium changes from E_1 to E_2. The equilibrium price falls from $30,000 to $20,000. The equilibrium quantity falls from 30,000 to 20,000 gas guzzlers per month.

ETHICS *in Action!*

Using the Market Approach to Organ Shortages

There is a global market in human organs in spite of attempts to prevent these transactions. China and India have banned organ sales because their leaders concluded that allowing those who could afford to pay the most to buy organs would prevent less wealthy people from benefitting from transplants. Some unscrupulous doctors have paid healthy poor people to donate organs such as kidneys or partial livers. These organs are transplanted into wealthy people who pay enormous fees. Most people regard this practice as unethical because it takes advantage of poor people and jeopardizes their health.

In the United States, the National Transplant Organ Act made the sale of organs illegal. Still, the organ donor distribution system continues to suffer from shortages. The United Network for Organ Sharing (UNOS) reports that there are over 100,000 patients waiting for organs. Many of these people die before an organ becomes available. There are simply more people who need transplants than there are donations. To address the shortage, some European countries such as Spain, Belgium, and Austria have implemented an "opt-out" donation system. In the "opt-out" system, people are considered to be organ donors when they die unless they officially declare that they do not wish to be donors. Many people believe this practice is unethical and an invasion of a family's privacy. Others think it is the best way to help the thousands of people who will die without an organ transplant.

Think Critically

1. **What are some arguments against using the free market system to distribute organs?**
2. **Do you believe it is ethical to allow those who can afford to pay the most to be first in line to receive organ transplants? Explain.**

Changes in Supply

Assume demand remains constant and allow the supply curve to shift. In Figure 4-12 part (a), begin at point E_1 in a market for babysitting services. The equilibrium price is \$9 per hour and 4,000 babysitters are hired per month. Next, assume there is a population shift and the number of people available to babysit rises. This increase in the number of sellers shifts the market supply curve rightward from S_1 to S_2. This shift creates a temporary surplus of 4,000 babysitters at point E_1 who offer their services but are not hired. The unemployed babysitters respond by reducing the price and the number of babysitters available for hire. This change is a movement downward along S_2. As the price falls, buyers move down along the demand curve and hire more babysitters per month. When the price falls to \$6 per hour, the market is in equilibrium again at point E_2, instead of E_1. Now consumers hire 6,000 babysitters per month.

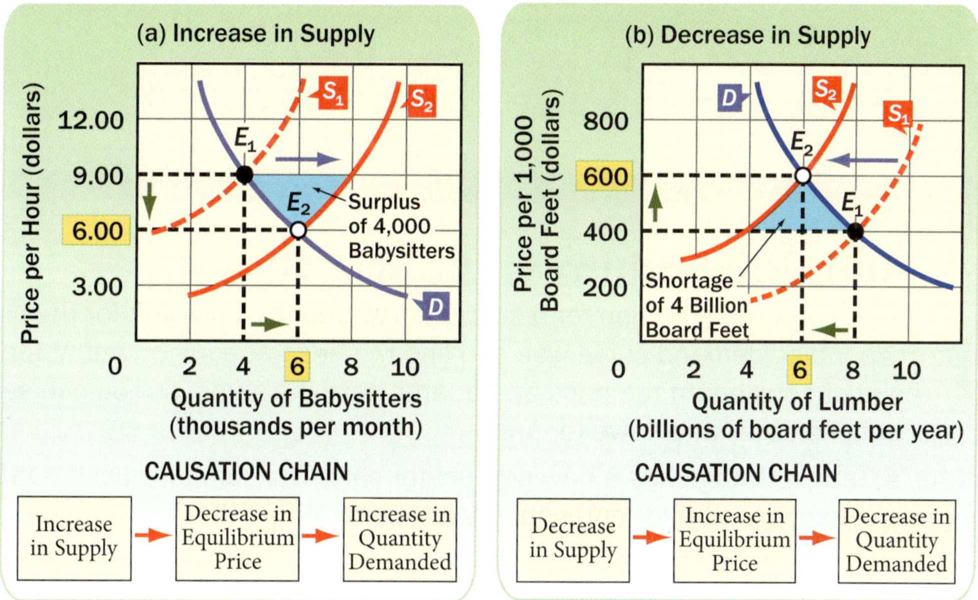

Figure 4-12

How Shifts in Supply Change Market Equilibrium

In part (a), begin at equilibrium E_1 in the market for babysitters. Assume an increase in the number of babysitters shifts the supply curve rightward from S_1 to S_2. A surplus condition causes a movement downward to a new equilibrium at E_2. At E_2, the equilibrium price declines, and the equilibrium quantity rises.

In part (b), forest fires cause the supply curve for lumber to shift leftward from S_1 to S_2. This shift in supply results in a temporary shortage of 4 billion board feet per year. Customer bidding for the available lumber raises the price. As a result, the market moves upward along the demand curve to a new equilibrium at E_2, and the quantity demanded falls.

Figure 4-12 part (b) illustrates the market for lumber. Suppose this market is at equilibrium at point E_1. Here the going price is \$400 per thousand board feet, and 8 billion board feet are bought and sold per year. Now suppose extensive fires in western states destroy huge forests. This disaster causes the market supply curve to shift leftward from S_1 to S_2. A temporary shortage of 4 billion board feet of lumber exists at point E_1. Suppliers respond by hiking their prices from \$400 to \$600 per thousand board feet. A new equilibrium is established at E_2, where the quantity is 6 billion board feet per year. This higher cost of lumber, in turn, raises the price of a new home.

Evgeny Dubinchuk/Shutterstock.com

When fire destroys a forest, a shortage of lumber causes a shift in the market supply of board feet of lumber.

Figure 4-13 gives a concise summary of the impact of changes in demand or supply on market equilibrium.

Figure 4-13

Shifts in Demand or Supply Change Market Equilibrium

Change	Effect on Equilibrium Price	Effect on Equilibrium Quantity
Demand Increase	Increases	Increases
Demand Decrease	Decreases	Decreases
Supply Increase	Decreases	Increases
Supply Decrease	Increases	Decreases

CHECKPOINT

A hotel room in Myrtle Beach, South Carolina charges $75 a night in February, but $200 a night in July. Why is there a difference in price?

Math CONNECTION

Find Equilibrium without a Graph

If you know the equation for a supply curve and the equation for the corresponding demand curve, you can find the price at equilibrium. At the point of equilibrium the price and quantity are the same, so you can set the equations equal and solve for price.

Gary's Gadget Garage has a new product for sale. The company used q to represent quantity and p to represent price to determine the supply equation as $q = 8 + 2p$ and the demand equation as $q = 20 - 4p$. What is the price at which the product should sell so the quantity supplied by the seller is the same as the quantity wanted by the buyers?

SOLUTION

$8 + 2p = 20 - 4p$ Set the right sides of the two equations equal.

$8 + 2p + 4p = 20$ Solve for p. Add $4p$ to each side of equation.

$6p = 20 - 8$ Subtract 8 from each side of equation.

$p = 2$ Divide each side of equation by 2.

Gary's Gadget Garage should sell the product for $2.

TRY IT

1. What is the price at the equilibrium given the supply equation for an app for a smartphone is $q = 13p + 300$ and the demand equation is $q = 450 - 12p$?
2. What is the price at the equilibrium given the supply equation for a bag of snack chips is $q = 3.25p + 16$ and the demand equation is $q = 52 - 5.75p$?

4-3 Assessment

Key Concepts

LO 3-2 1. A market price at which the quantity demanded equals the quantity supplied is called __?__.

LO 3-1 2. **TRUE OR FALSE** A surplus occurs at any price above the equilibrium price.

LO 3-2 3. A market price at which the quantity demanded does not equal the quantity supplied is called __?__.

LO 3-1 4. **TRUE OR FALSE** A shortage occurs at any price where the quantity supplied is greater than the quantity demanded.

LO 3-2 5. Assume a stationary demand curve and a supply shifter factor changes and shifts the supply curve rightward. The result will be a (an) __?__ in equilibrium price and a (an) __?__ in equilibrium quantity.

Think About It

LO 3-2 6. Explain why the market price may not be the same as the equilibrium price.

LO 3-1 7. How would the owner of a wedding dress shop react if she had 50 wedding dresses that she could not sell at the current price?

LO 3-1 8. What change in price per cake would a cake shop owner make if the quantity of cakes per month offered for sale equals the quantity demanded?

LO 3-2 9. There is a shortage of college basketball and football tickets for some games, and a surplus of tickets to other college sporting events. Why do shortages and surpluses exist for different games?

LO 3-1 10. Explain how a free market determines equilibrium.

LO 3-2 11. Describe a situation that demonstrates how a change in demand causes equilibrium for a product to change and another situation for how a change in supply causes a change in equilibrium.

Make Academic Connections

LO 3-2 12. **MARKETING** Find an advertisement for a well-known product. Explain what the company is trying to do. Your answer must include the effect on the demand curve, equilibrium price, and equilibrium quantity.

LO 3-2 13. **GOVERNMENT** Suppose the federal government is considering actions it could take to reduce the price of gasoline. One option being considered is to reduce the excise tax. How would this policy affect the equilibrium price per gallon and quantity of gasoline?

Teamwork

LO 3-2 14. Work in groups. Each group selects one of the following situations. Predict the direction of change for either supply or demand. Each group draws a graph and explains the change in equilibrium.

   a. Several new companies enter the cell phone industry.
   b. Consumers suddenly decide SUVs are unfashionable.
   c. The U.S. Surgeon General issues a report stating that tomatoes prevent the common cold.
   d. Frost threatens to damage the coffee crop, and consumers expect the price to rise sharply in the future.
   e. The price of tea falls and the effect on the coffee market.

yienkeat/Shutterstock.com; Chad Baker/Ryan McVay/Photodisc/Getty Images

4-4 Role of Government in a Free Market System

Learning Objectives

LO 4-1 **Evaluate** the effect of price ceilings and price floors on a market.

LO 4-2 **Discuss** government regulation and deregulation in the U.S. free market system.

Vocabulary

- **price ceiling,** p. 117
- **rent control,** p. 117
- **price floor,** p. 118
- **minimum wage,** p. 118
- **regulation,** p. 119
- **deregulation,** p. 120

REAL-WORLD FOCUS

Jim has worked for his current employer for almost three years. He started as a part-time employee at an entry-level job. He was paid minimum wage. Now, Jim works full-time and makes $3 an hour above his starting pay. His friend Bob was just hired by the same company as a part-time worker and his starting pay is the same as Jim's current pay. Jim is happy for his friend, but he is not happy with his employer.

WORK AS A GROUP What reasons might Jim's employer have for paying Bob more money as a new hire? Why is Jim unhappy? What can Jim do?

© Aleksandar Vrzalski/iStockphoto.com

Andy Z./Shutterstock.com

New York City has a large population with a lot of people living in the downtown areas.

DO YOU THINK New York City has some form of rent control?

yienkeat/Shutterstock.com

LO 4-1 Can the Laws of Supply and Demand Be Repealed?

The government intervenes or regulates some markets with the objective of preventing prices from rising to the equilibrium price. In other markets, the government's goal is to intervene and maintain a price higher than the equilibrium price. Market supply-and-demand analysis is a valuable tool for understanding what happens when the government regulates prices.

Price Ceilings

A **price ceiling** is a legally established highest price a seller can charge for a good or service. What happens if the government prevents the price system from setting a market price "too high" by mandating a price ceiling?

Rick S/Shutterstock.com

San Francisco is one of the cities in the United States where the government has mandated a price ceiling on the rent charged for an apartment.

CASE 1: RENT CONTROLS Rent controls are an example of the imposition of a price ceiling in the market for rental units. A **rent control** is a price ceiling placed by government on rent. New York City, Washington, D.C., Los Angeles, San Francisco, and other communities in the United States have some form of rent control. The rationale for rent controls is to provide an essential service. Otherwise rent would be unaffordable to many people at the equilibrium rental price.

Figure 4-14 is a supply and demand graph for the quantity of rental units demanded and supplied per month in a city. Begin the analysis by assuming no rent controls exist and equilibrium is at point *E*. The monthly rent is $1,200 per month and 6 million units are occupied. Next, assume the city council imposes a rent control (ceiling price). This law forbids any landlord from renting a unit for more than $800 per month. What does market supply-and-demand theory predict will happen? At the low rent ceiling of $800, the quantity demanded of rental units will be 8 million. But the quantity supplied will be only 4 million. The price ceiling creates a lasting market shortage of 4 million rental units. The reason is that suppliers cannot raise the rental price without being subjected to legal penalties.

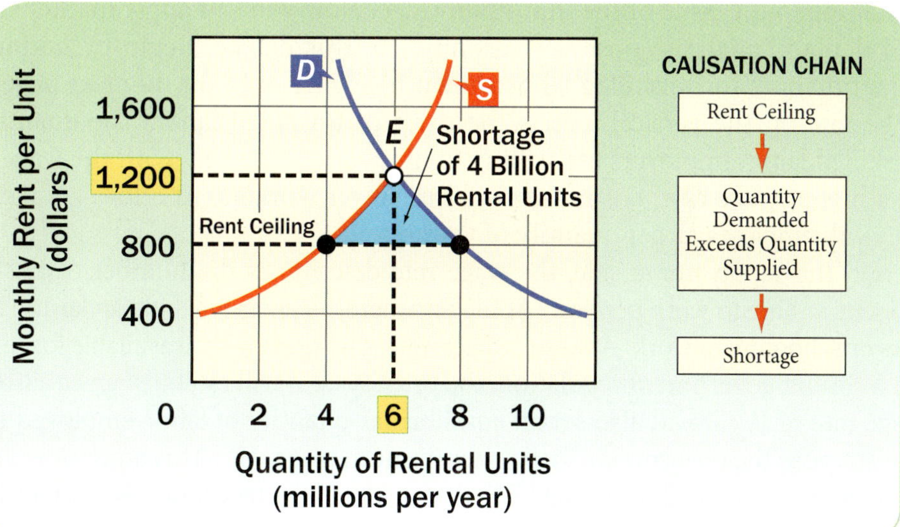

Figure 4-14

Rent Control Results in a Shortage of Rental Units

If no rent controls exist, the equilibrium rent for an apartment is $1,200 per month at point *E*. If the government imposes a rent ceiling of $800 per month, a shortage of 4 million rental units occurs.

What is the impact of rent controls on consumers? First, consumers must spend more time on waiting lists and searching for rental housing. Second, an illegal market, or *black market*, can arise because of the shortage of rental units. Because the price of rental units is artificially low, the profit motive encourages tenants to risk breaking the law. One violation is that a tenant might sublet a rental unit to the highest bidder over $800 per month.

From the seller's perspective, rent control encourages two undesirable effects. First, faced with a mandated low rent, landlords may cut maintenance expenses. Over time, housing deterioration will reduce the stock of rental units. Second, landlords may use discriminatory practices to replace the price system. Excess demand at the controlled price encourages landlords to use preferences based on pet ownership or family size to determine how to allocate scarce rental space.

CASE 2: GASOLINE PRICE CEILING The government placed ceilings on most nonfarm prices during World War II and imposed rationing for most essential goods. In 1971, President Nixon "froze" virtually all wages, prices, and rents until 1973 in an attempt to control rising prices. As a result of an oil embargo in late 1973, the government imposed a price ceiling of 55 cents per gallon of gasoline. To deal with the resulting shortage, nonprice rationing schemes were introduced in 1974. Some states used a first come, first served system. Other states allowed consumers with even numbered license plates to buy gas on even numbered days. Those with odd numbered license plates could buy on odd numbered days. Gas stations were required to close on Friday night and not open until Monday morning. Regardless of the scheme, long waiting lines for gasoline formed, just as the supply-and-demand model predicts.

Price Floors

The other side of the price-control coin is a price floor set by government if it fears the free enterprise price would be "too low." A **price floor** is a legally established lowest price a seller can charge for a good or service. The minimum wage is an example of a price floor. A **minimum wage** is a legally established lowest hourly wage rate that can be paid to workers.

In Lesson 2-1, the *You're the Economist* applied *normative* and *positive* reasoning to the issue of the minimum wage. Now you can apply market supply and demand analysis (positive reasoning) to this debate. Begin by noting the demand curve for unskilled labor shown in Figure 4-15 on the next page. The wage rate on the vertical axis is the price of unskilled labor. The quantity of unskilled labor employers are willing to hire varies inversely with the wage rate. At a higher wage rate, businesses will hire fewer workers. At a lower wage rate, they will employ a larger quantity of workers.

On the supply curve side, the wage rate determines the number of unskilled workers willing to work per year. At higher wages, workers will give up leisure activities or schooling to work. At lower wages, fewer workers will be available for hire.

Without government regulation, the price system will establish an equilibrium wage rate of W_e. It will also set an equilibrium quantity of labor employed of Q_e. But suppose the government enacts a minimum wage, W_m. This amount is a price floor above the equilibrium wage, W_e. The intent of the legislation is to make lower paid workers better off with a higher wage rate. But consider the undesirable

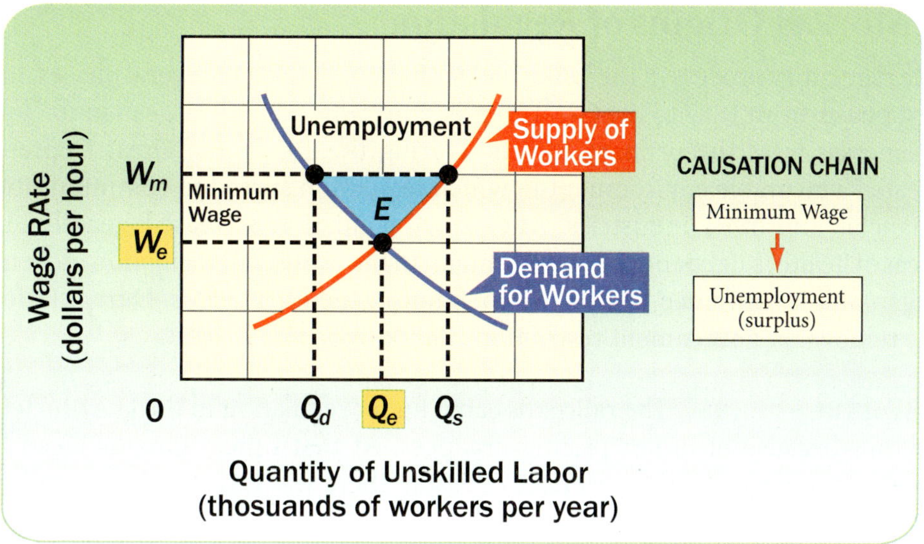

Figure 4-15

A Minimum Wage Results in a Surplus of Labor

When the government sets a wage-rate floor above the equilibrium wage, a surplus of unskilled labor develops. The supply curve is the number of workers offering their labor services per year at possible wage rates. The demand curve is the number of workers employers are willing and able to hire at various wage rates. At the minimum wage of W_m, there is a surplus of unemployed workers, $Q_s - Q_d$.

consequences. One result is that the number of workers willing to offer their labor increases upward along the supply curve to Q_s. But there are fewer jobs because the number of workers companies are willing to hire decreases to Q_d on the demand curve. The predicted outcome is a labor surplus of unskilled workers who are unemployed. Also, employers are encouraged to substitute machines and skilled labor for unskilled labor. The minimum wage can therefore be counterproductive. Employers lay off the lowest skilled workers, who ironically are the type of workers minimum wage legislation intends to help. Also, loss of minimum wage jobs represents a loss of entry-level jobs to those who seek to enter the workforce.

Supporters of the minimum wage are quick to point out that those employed (Q_d) are better off. Although the minimum wage causes a reduction in employment, some argue that better pay is worth the loss of some jobs.

CHECKPOINT

Why wouldn't the government set the minimum wage at $10,000 per hour? What are they afraid of? What would happen to employment if the minimum wage price floor were eliminated?

LO 4-2 Regulation of the Free Market System

"People of the same trade seldom meet together, even for merriment and diversion, but the conversation ends in a conspiracy against the public, or in some contrivance to raise prices." — Adam Smith

Adam Smith in the *Wealth of Nations* knew that there was a role for government in the free market system. For example, businesses without government interference could agree to fix prices. Today this action would be a violation of the 1890 Sherman Antitrust Act. Price fixing harms consumers who pay more than they otherwise would pay. In fact, regulation affects virtually every business and consumer. **Regulations** are government rules or laws designed to control business. Food quality is regulated, activities that impact the environment are regulated, airline safety is regulated, and most industries must deal with some form of regulation.

Historical Origins of Regulation

The regulatory process in the United States has gone through several phases. In the first phase, from 1887 to the Great Depression, railroads and large manufacturing businesses were the primary targets. During the 1930s, the Great Depression created a favorable environment in which regulation spread to communications, financial, and other industries. After 1970, regulation increased steadily in the areas of health, safety, and the environment. In the 1980s, a deregulation movement began and it continued to have momentum in the early 2000s. **Deregulation** is the removal of government restrictions or controls on a market.

THE EARLY YEARS The railroads came under regulation in the late nineteenth century because of unfair pricing practices. At that time, railroads faced little competition from other carriers. As a result, there was little to prevent railroads from overcharging. Railroads also practiced price discrimination against isolated rural customers. Rural customers were charged higher rates for short hauls than city customers were for long hauls.

In 1887, the Interstate Commerce Commission (ICC) was established to regulate rail prices and to cut the costs of rail transportation by reducing duplicate trains, depots, and tracks. Another example of early government regulation was the Food and Drug Administration (FDA) that was established in 1906 to oversee the safety of food and drugs.

THE GREAT DEPRESSION ERA During the 1930s, regulation was extended to other industries. All surface transportation, including trucks, barges, and oil pipelines, came to be regulated by the ICC. The Civil Aeronautics Board (CAB) was created in 1938 to regulate air travel, and the Federal Communications Commission (FCC) was established in 1934 to regulate telephones, telegraphs, and broadcasting industries. In 1934, as a result of the stock market crash of 1929, the Securities and Exchange Commission (SEC) was created. Its role is to combat fraud and malpractice in the securities industry.

THE HEALTH, SAFETY, AND ENVIRONMENT ERA The Occupational Safety and Health Administration (OSHA) was created in 1970 to reduce the incidence of injury and death in the workplace. This agency cites and fines employers who violate safety and health rules. In the same year, the Environmental Protection Agency (EPA) was established to set and enforce pollution standards. In 1972, the Consumer Product Safety Commission (CPSC) was established to protect the public against injury from unsafe products. The CPSC has the power to ban the sale of hazardous products.

The Deregulation Trend

In the 1970s, higher production costs resulting from regulation generated widespread dissatisfaction with government regulation. The result was a movement toward deregulation in the late 1970s and 1980s. Initially, the major thrust of deregulation was in the transportation and telecommunications industries. The Interstate Commerce Commission (ICC) was abolished in 1995.

Global View

Should the Government Regulate Job Offshoring?

Certain jobs can be globally resourced, which means they can be performed anywhere in the world. A company has the choice of having a job performed by its own employees in the U.S. where the product is sold, or in another country. *Offshoring* occurs when a U.S. company hires employees in another country to perform jobs once done by the company's American employees. Suppose, for example, a U.S. company hires engineers in India to do jobs once done for this company in the United States. The result may be that the average salary paid by the company to these engineers drops $100,000 per year. A benefit is that the company reduces it costs although some Americans lose their jobs and must find new employment.

Some people believe the government should pass laws to restrict businesses' ability to send jobs out of the United States causing laid off U.S. workers. Some suggest that this practice simply be made illegal. Others believe that businesses should be required to pay a large tax when they offshore jobs. Either of these suggested laws would cause production costs for U.S. firms to be higher than they otherwise might be. This would probably result in higher prices for U.S. consumers.

Think Critically

Do you believe the costs or benefits of restricting U.S. businesses' ability to offshore jobs would be greater? If you had the power to make the law, what would you do? Explain your answer.

The Civil Aeronautics Board (CAB) was established in 1938 to regulate airline fares and air routes. The CAB set both fares and routes so that airlines could not compete. Instead of free enterprise, airlines would attempt to boost profits by lobbying the CAB for higher fares. In addition to eliminating price competition between established airlines, the CAB restricted entrants into the industry. From 1938 until 1977, the CAB did not award a major route to any new airline. The CAB was abolished in 1984. The Federal Aviation Administration (FAA) still regulates the safety of air service.

Successful deregulation of an industry would be expected to provide the following two results.

- The average price of the service falls.
- The volume and variety of services rises.

The Airline Deregulation Act of 1978 provided these results by changing the structure of the airline industry. This act removed regulated airfares and restrictions against competition in air travel markets. Price competition followed and produced the expected results of lower fares and greater quantity of service. The average passenger price per mile for a flight declined from 1978 to less than half that rate today. This decline saved consumers billions of dollars in lower fares. Over this same period, passenger-miles flown per year more than tripled. Today, deregulation continues to exert downward pressure on fares. And old-guard airlines scramble to compete with low-cost carriers such as Southwest and Jet Blue. Low-fare tickets, e-tickets, and frequent flyer miles are popular. Airlines have been able to increase profits by charging fees for food, baggage, and other services that were once included in the fare. By reducing routes, reorganization, and lowering costs, they have also improved profitability.

In telecommunications, the most important case was the deregulation and dismantling of AT&T. As a result of an antitrust lawsuit, AT&T was broken up and forced to compete with other companies for long-distance service. In 1996, Congress passed a telecommunications bill that made additional changes in U.S. telecommunications. This bill deregulated cable television rates. It allowed local and long-distance telephone companies and cable companies to compete. This bill also required television manufacturers to equip new sets with a computer chip to block shows parents do not wish their children to watch.

The principal functions of the federal regulatory agencies discussed are summarized in Figure 4-16.

Figure 4-16
Federal Regulatory Agencies

Agency	Year Created	Function
Food and Drug Administration (FDA)	1906	Protects the health of the nation against impure and unsafe foods, drugs, and cosmetics. Develops policy regarding labeling of all drugs.
Federal Trade Commission	1914	Enforces antitrust laws and monitors unfair business practices, including deceptive advertising.
Securities and Exchange Commission (SEC)	1934	Provides for complete financial disclosure and protects investors in stock and other securities against fraud.
Federal Communications Commission (FCC)	1934	Regulates television, radio, telephone, telegraph service, satellite transmissions, and cable TV.
Occupational Safety and Health Administration (OSHA)	1970	Enforces rules in cases involving safety and health violations in the workplace.
Environmental Protection Agency (EPA)	1970	Regulates pollution in the areas of air, water, waste, noise, radiation, and toxic substances.
Consumer Product Safety Commission (CPSC)	1972	Protects the public against unreasonable risks of injury from consumer products.

CHECKPOINT

How can laws and regulation improve the operation of the free market system?

4-4 Assessment

Key Concepts

LO 4-1 1. A price __?__ is a legally established lowest price a seller can charge for a product.

LO 4-1 2. **TRUE OR FALSE** A rent control is a price ceiling placed by the government on rent.

LO 4-1 3. A price __?__ is a legally established highest price a seller can charge for a product.

LO 4-2 4. **TRUE OR FALSE** A minimum wage is a market determined average wage paid to unskilled workers.

Think About It

LO 4-1 5. Market researchers estimate the supply of and the demand for milk are as follows:

Demand and Supply Schedule (millions of gallons per month)

Price	Quantity Demanded	Quantity Supplied
$10	100	500
8	200	400
6	300	300
4	400	200
2	500	100

a. Graph the demand for and the supply of milk. Identify the equilibrium point as *E*. Use dotted lines to connect *E* to the equilibrium price on the price axis and the equilibrium quantity on the quantity axis.

b. Assume the government sets a price ceiling of $4 per gallon. Show and explain how this affects your graph. What objective is the government trying to achieve by establishing such a price ceiling? What are the actual results likely to be?

LO 4-1 6. What results do price ceilings that are below a product's equilibrium price cause?

LO 4-1 7. What results do price floors that are above a product's equilibrium price cause?

LO 4-2 8. Describe examples of regulation and deregulation of an industry in the U.S. economy.

Make Academic Connections

LO 4-1 9. **HISTORY** President Franklin Roosevelt established the Office of Price Administration and Civilian Supply (OPA) in 1941 before the United States entered World War II. The OPA set up a large bureaucracy to administer price and rent controls. Research this and report the effect.

Teamwork

LO 4-2 10. Work in groups. Each group investigates one of the federal regulatory agencies in Figure 4-16. Research to find examples of how that regulatory agency affects their lives. Give a group presentation to share the examples with the class.

Unit 2 Project: Tools of Free Markets

MARKET EQUILIBRIUM, CEILINGS, AND FLOORS Present a visual display chart and story board of the supply-and-demand curves for wages and rent, their market equilibrium prices, and the result of imposed ceilings and floors. Explain the economic results of these government interferences in the setting of price and the requirement of making goods and services available.

Chapter 4

Summary

4-1 THE LAW OF SUPPLY

1. The law of supply states that there is a direct relationship between selling price and the quantity made available for sale. Producers are willing to supply more products with a high price and fewer with a low price.
2. A supply schedule lists the quantity of goods offered at possible prices. The supply curve is the line on a graph that connects points that represent different combinations of price and quantity supplied. It is prepared from the supply schedule.
3. Individual market supply refers to the quantity a single seller is willing to supply. Market supply refers to the total supply of a product available in the economy.

4-2 SHIFT IN THE SUPPLY CURVE

4. The change in quantity supplied results from a change in price. It is a movement along the same supply curve.
5. A change in supply is represented by a movement of the supply curve to the right or the left. This movement is caused by a change in one or more of the supply shifters. These include changes in the number of sellers, technology, resource prices, taxes and subsidies, expectations, and prices of other goods. The supply curve shifts outward to the right when overall supply increases and inward to the left when overall supply decreases.

4-3 THE FREE MARKET PRICE

6. Where market supply and market demand curves intersect is the point of equilibrium. When a price is set higher than the market equilibrium price, a surplus is created because there is a greater quantity supplied than is demanded. When a price is set lower than the market equilibrium price, a shortage is created because a smaller quantity is supplied at the lower price than is demanded.
7. Within a free market system, price is the mechanism to determine who will get what products. Only those who can pay the price will receive the goods or services. This is a rationing process.

4-4 ROLE OF GOVERNMENT IN A FREE MARKET SYSTEM

8. A price ceiling (set by government) is a price that is higher than the market price. With a price ceiling, sellers cannot charge more than the set price. A price floor (set by government) is a price that is lower than market price. With a price floor, sellers cannot sell below the set price.
9. Free enterprise is regulated in ways to protect consumers. For example, price fixing would create higher prices than those set by the market. Over the history of this country, many regulations have been passed by government.
10. Deregulation occurs when laws are passed to take away government controls over business activities and prices. Successful deregulation should bring lower prices to consumers through greater competition.

Chapter 4

Assessment

Vocabulary Review

Match each statement with the term that best defines it. Some terms may not be used.

1. A legally established lowest price that a seller can charge for a good or service
2. The line connecting the possible prices and corresponding quantities supplied by sellers
3. An excess of unsold products that occurs when the quantity supplied is greater than the quantity demanded
4. A movement between points along a stationary supply curve because of a change in price
5. A price ceiling placed by the government on rent
6. A market price at which the quantity demanded equals the quantity supplied. At this price, there is no surplus or shortage
7. The law that states there is a direct relationship between the price of a good and the quantity sellers offer for sale
8. A legally established highest price that a seller can charge for a good or service
9. Unsatisfied demand for products that occurs when the quantity demanded exceeds the quantity supplied
10. An increase (rightward shift) or a decrease (leftward shift) in the supply curve
11. A tax paid by a seller on the production or sale of a good or service
12. A table that lists the quantity of a good or service offered for sale at possible prices
13. The act of removing government restrictions on a market
14. A payment from the government to a business that reduces its costs
15. A curve that shows the sum of all the individual supply curves in a market
16. A price floor for hourly wages
17. Created by surplus and shortage conditions
18. The relationship between the price and quantity supplied for a good or service
19. The amount of goods or services sellers offer for sale at a given price

Vocabulary

a. change in quantity supplied
b. change in supply
c. deregulation
d. disequilibrium
e. equilibrium
f. excise tax
g. individual supply curve
h. law of supply
i. market supply curve
j. minimum wage
k. price ceiling
l. price floor
m. quantity supplied
n. regulation
o. rent control
p. shortage
q. subsidy
r. supply
s. supply curve
t. supply schedule
u. surplus

Review Your Knowledge

LO 1-1 **20.** According to the law of supply
a. producers are willing to supply larger quantities of a good as its price increases
b. a direct relationship exists between the price of a good and the quantity buyers choose to buy
c. an inverse relationship exists between the price of a good and the quantity buyers wish to buy
d. an inverse relationship exists between the price of a good and the quantity producers supply

LO 2-1 **21.** When economists say there is a decrease in the supply of a product, they mean
a. the supply curve has shifted to the left
b. the product price has decreased causing suppliers to produce less of the product
c. producers are willing to sell more of this product at each possible price
d. the supply curve has shifted to the right

LO 3-1 **22.** If a surplus of a product currently exists in the market
a. the market price is too low
b. the quantity demanded exceeds the quantity supplied at the current price
c. the quantity supplied exceeds the quantity demanded at the current price
d. there is a shortage of the product

LO 2-1 **23.** A technological improvement in producing good X would be a shift in the
a. supply curve for good X to the right
b. supply curve for good X to the left
c. demand curve for good X to the right
d. demand curve for good X to the left

LO 3-2 **24.** If equilibrium is present in a market,
a. there is either a shortage or a surplus
b. the quantity demanded equals quantity supplied
c. the quantity demanded exceeds quantity supplied
d. the quantity supplied exceeds quantity demanded

LO 2-1 **25.** Which of the following will decrease the supply of motorcycles?
a. An increase in the population aged 16 to 35, the primary consumers of motorcycles
b. An increase in taxes imposed on motorcycle production
c. A technological improvement reducing the production costs of motorcycles
d. A government study that reveals motorcycle riders, on average, live 10 years longer than those who don't ride motorcycles

LO 4-1 **26.** A price ceiling that sets the price of a good below the equilibrium price will cause
a. an increase in demand
b. a decrease in supply
c. a shortage of the good
d. all of the above

Digging Deeper with Economics e-Collection

When technology improves, products can be produced at a lower price. Access the Gale Economics e-Collection at **www.cengage.com/school/economics/personalfinance**. Read about advances in technology used in American production. Prepare a report about a product that has decreased in price over time, even though the quantity supplied was increasing. Find a decrease that can be attributed to changes in technology that allowed for greater efficiencies. Include photos or drawings of the product and review the history of development of the product through its product life cycle.

Think About It

LO 1-1 **27.** People go into business to make a profit. The price they set for their product or service is the one that will maximize profit. If they charge too much, their profits will drop. Why?

LO 2-1 **28.** Technology allows more and better products to be produced at a lower cost. When you buy a product that is first introduced to the market, your price is often higher than if you wait for a year or longer. Why?

LO 3-1 **29.** Assume a new and exciting car is introduced that gets 90 miles per gallon of gasoline. But the price of the car is $80,000. Most consumers would like to save money on gas but cannot afford to buy the car. Explain how this is the rationing function of price.

LO 4-1 **30.** A price ceiling can have negative effects. It prohibits sellers from charging the market price. Suppose a producer of milk can only charge $2 per gallon. What might be some negative consequences?

LO 4-2 **31.** Prior to airline deregulation, critics argued that airline safety would suffer. Instead, the accident rate involving fatalities has fallen. Give a rationale for why the critics' prediction did not come to pass.

Make Academic Connections

LO 2-2 **32.** **SOCIAL STUDIES** When the cost of resources increases (because they become more difficult to extract from the earth), prices charged increase due to a short supply. Explain who gets hurt when gas prices reach $5 or more per gallon. What is the effect on the economy?

LO 3-3 **33.** **COMMUNICATION** Extreme weather conditions have caused crop damage across the country. In addition, gas prices are at an all-time high. Explain why prices in grocery stores are increasing rapidly. Are there strategies consumers can use to limit the financial damage?

LO 4-4 **34.** **ETHICS** Government regulations are often imposed to prevent unethical practices such as price fixing and violation of safety standards. Explain how lack of regulation can cause financial damage to consumers as well as businesses. An example is the financial meltdown in 2007–2008 that caused the Great Recession.

Extend Your Learning

LO 4-2 **35.** Suppose the government became concerned about the income of apricot farmers. To boost their incomes by setting the price above the equilibrium price, it imposed a price floor of $20 per bushel. Given the data in the table below for an apricot farmer, what is the equilibrium price? What is the effect of such a regulation? Draw a graph that demonstrates the impact of this regulation.

Demand and Supply Schedule for Apricots (millions of bushels per month)

Price	Quantity Demanded	Quantity Supplied
$25	50	250
20	100	200
15	150	150
10	200	100
5	250	50

© Richard Levine/Alamy

chapter 5

Market Structures

yienkeat/Shutterstock.com

MARKETS *in Action!*

Walt Disney
American Entrepreneur

Born Walter Elias Disney on December 5, 1901, Walt Disney became the co-founder (with his brother Roy Disney) of one of America's most prominent film and entertainment corporations. Walt himself was a film producer, director, screenwriter, voice actor, animator, entrepreneur, international icon, and philanthropist. Today, Mr. Disney's multi-national company brings in annual revenues of more than $35 billion.

During his teen years at McKinley High School in Chicago, Walt Disney was the cartoonist for the school newspaper. In 1919, Disney moved to Kansas City to begin his artistic career. He started by drawing political caricatures and comic strips for a newspaper. While working at the Kansas City Film Ad Company, Disney made commercials based on cutout animation. His career in film production had begun. Disney and his brother pooled their money to set up a cartoon studio in Hollywood called Disney Brothers Studio.

By 1932, Mickey Mouse was well known and Disney received an Academy Award for the cartoon series which was made into color in 1935. Supporting characters were created, including Donald Duck, Goofy, Minnie Mouse, and Pluto. The years 1937–1941 were known as the "golden age of animation." Disney introduced *Snow White,* the first full feature cartoon movie. Disney Studios flourished for the next twenty years, but Disney was visioning a new direction. Planning for Disneyland began in the late 1940s; the park opened in 1955. An enormous success, Disney continued innovations and updating. He was planning Walt Disney World (which opened in 1971) at his death in 1966.

Disney's innovative ideas span many different types of entertainment and media. Most people recognize the name Disney from the theme parks located in the U.S., Japan, China, and Europe. His namesake Disneyland and Disney World theme park properties provide hotel and food services, entertainment, and shopping, both inside and outside the parks. Disney retail stores are located throughout the country. The stores contain Disney label merchandise from clothing to movies. Disney movie studio productions include action, adventure, comedy, and animated cartoons. Disney movies have won entertainment industry awards for directing, music, graphic arts, acting, and creative design.

Walt Disney was successful because he was able to diversify by making his products different from the competition. Disney companies are still producing award-winning pictures, music, and product designs.

Behind Minnie Mouse sits Cinderella's castle in Disney World in Orlando, FL.

umoments/Shutterstock.com

Think Critically

1. Visit the official Disney website and be prepared to discuss the products and services being advertised.
2. How did Walt Disney continue innovating during his lifetime? Why is it important to innovate?

yienkeat/Shutterstock.com

5-1 Perfect Competition and Monopoly

Learning Objectives

LO 1-1 **Explain** the characteristics of perfectly competitive markets.

LO 1-2 **Describe** the characteristics of a monopoly.

Vocabulary

market structure, p. 131
perfect competition, p. 131
barrier to entry, p. 131
price taker, p. 132
monopoly, p. 133
natural monopoly, p. 136
price maker, p. 137

© Aleksandar Vrzalski/iStockphoto.com

REAL-WORLD FOCUS

Rachel works at her uncle's farm in the summer. Uncle Ned operates a roadside stand where he sells farm products. The prices are lower than prices charged in grocery stores. "In the store, I would pay $3 for a small box of raspberries," Rachel told her uncle. "Why are you charging $2 when the market price appears to be $3? In fact, yours are fresher and better than the ones in the store, so they should cost more."

WORK AS A TEAM Farmers at roadside stands are selling products directly to consumers. Who are their competitors? How do they set their prices? Why would Uncle Ned charge a price that is lower than local stores?

Moises Fernandez Acosta/Shutterstock.com

In many major metropolitan areas, the power plant that supplies electricity to the city and surrounding suburbs is located on the banks of a river.

DO YOU THINK a power plant is a price maker or price taker?

yienkeat/Shutterstock.com

LO 1-1 Characteristics of Perfect Competition

Firms sell goods and services under different market conditions, which economists call market structure. A **market structure** describes the key characteristics of a market, which include the number of firms and the similarity of the products they sell. This description includes how easy or difficult it is for new firms to enter the market. Examination of the business sector of the economy reveals firms operating in different market structures. You will study four market structures. The first is perfect competition. **Perfect competition** is a market structure in which a large number of small firms sell identical products, and entry into the market is easy. Figure 5-1 gives a summary of the characteristics of perfect competition. Following is a discussion of each of these characteristics.

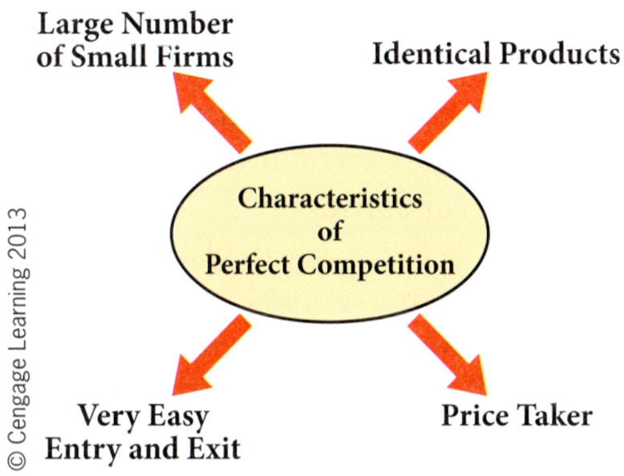

Figure 5-1
Characteristics of Perfect Competition

Large Number of Small Firms

How many sellers comprise a large number? And how small is a small firm? Certainly, one, two, or three firms in a market would not be a large number. In fact, the exact number cannot be stated. This condition is fulfilled when each firm in a market has no significant share of total output. Therefore, no firm has the ability to affect the market price of its product. For example, there are thousands of small egg farmers in the United States. If any single egg farmer raises the price, the going market price for eggs is unaffected. Each farmer is too small relative to the total market to affect the market price.

Identical Product

In a perfectly competitive market, all firms produce a standardized or identical product. Farmer Brown's wheat is identical to Farmer Jones's wheat. Buyers may believe the transportation services of one independent trucker are about the same as another's services. This assumption rules out individual firms advertising because all firms have identical products.

Very Easy Entry and Exit

Very easy entry into a market means that a new firm faces no barriers to entry. A **barrier to entry** is an obstacle that makes it difficult for a new firm to enter a market. Barriers can be financial, technical, or government-imposed barriers, such as licenses, permits, and patents. Anyone who wants to try his or her hand at raising chickens needs only a plot of land and chicken feed. By the same token, individual firms in perfect competition are just as free to leave or exit a market if they are not successful.

No real-world market exactly fits the three assumptions of perfect competition. The perfectly competitive market structure is an ideal model. However, some actual markets are fairly close to the model. Examples include farm products and the stock market.

The Perfectly Competitive Firm as a Price Taker

Suppose a firm operates in a market that conforms to all three of the requirements for perfect competition. This assumption means that the perfectly competitive firm is a price taker. A **price taker** is a seller that has no control over the price of the product it sells. The firm's price of its product is determined by market supply and demand conditions. Therefore, individual firms have no influence. A small firm that is one among many firms, sells a homogeneous product, and is exposed to competition from new firms entering the market. These conditions make it impossible for the perfectly competitive firm to have the market power to affect the market price. Instead, the firm must adjust to, or take, the market price.

eliandric/iStockphoto.com

A wheat farmer takes his laptop to the fields with him to check the daily market price of wheat.

Figure 5-2 is a graph of the market supply and demand for wheat. The equilibrium price and quantity are $6 per bushel, and 300,000 bushels per day. In fact, wheat farmers check daily reports and know the market price of wheat.

When a firm in perfect competition tries to raise its price one penny higher than $6, no buyer will purchase its product. The reason is that so many other firms are selling the same product at $6 per bushel. The perfectly competitive firm will not set the price above the prevailing market price and risk selling zero output. Nor will the firm set the price below the market price. The reason is a lower price would reduce the firm's total revenue (sales). The firm can sell all it chooses to produce at the market price of $6.

Figure 5-2

Market Supply and Demand Set the Firm's Price in Perfect Competition

In perfect competition, the firm is a price taker. It must sell at the market determined equilibrium price of $6 per bushel of wheat.

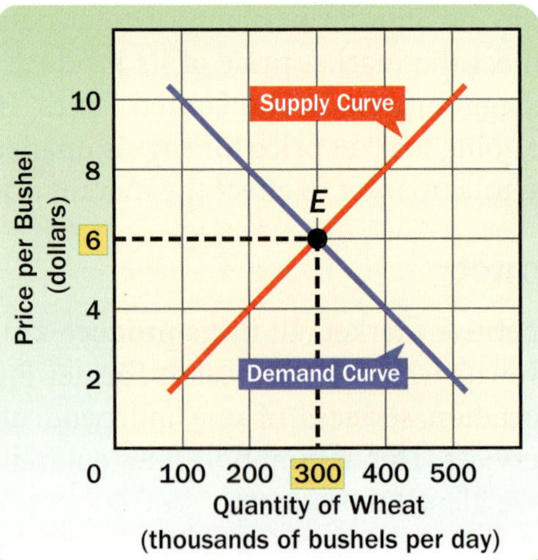

CHECKPOINT

Do all sellers in perfect competition have to sell their products at the equilibrium price? Compare a farmer selling wheat and a shop selling skateboards.

FreeSoulProduction/Shutterstock.com

Math CONNECTION

Pricing to Cover Expenses and Make a Profit

Congrat Frames produces special picture frames for seniors to display graduation photos. The owner spends $250,000 to produce 18,000 frames. What is the minimum price that can be charged when $0 profit is made? Use the minimum price to set a price per frame. What is the profit made on each frame?

SOLUTION

Total Costs ÷ Number of Frames Produced = Minimum Price per Frame

$250,000 ÷ 18,000 = $13.89 Round quotient to the nearest cent.

The minimum price is $13.89. A price of $19.99 will bring profit on each frame.

$19.99 – $13.89 = $6.10 Subtract minimum price from chosen price.

Congrat Frames will make a profit of $6.10 on each frame sold.

TRY IT

Find the minimum price for each item. Name a price and profit made per item.

1. Specialty Stickers spends $132,500 to produce 450,000 stickers.
2. Cupcake Corner spends $8.60 to make two dozen cupcakes.

LO 1-2 Monopoly

NoDerog/iStockphoto.com

In this game of Monopoly, the hat and shoe players have to pay another player because they landed on developed property.

Playing the popular board game of Monopoly teaches some of the characteristics of monopoly. In the game version, players win by gaining as much economic power as possible. They strive to own railroads, utilities, Boardwalk, Park Place, and other valuable real estate. Each player tries to bankrupt opponents by having hotels that charge high prices. A player who lands on another player's property has no choice. The player must either pay the price or lose the game.

Perfect competition and monopoly are polar extremes. The word *monopoly* is derived from two Greek words meaning "single seller." **Monopoly** is a market structure in which a single seller sells a unique product. A monopoly has the market power to set its price and not worry about competitors. Under monopoly, the consumer has a simple choice. The consumer must either buy the monopolist's product by paying the asked price or do without it. Entry into the market is impossible. Unlike perfect competition, there are no competitors for the monopolist's product. Monopoly, like perfect competition, corresponds only approximately to real-world markets. But it serves as a useful benchmark model.

Figure 5-3 gives an illustration of the characteristics of monopoly. Following are brief descriptions of each monopoly characteristic.

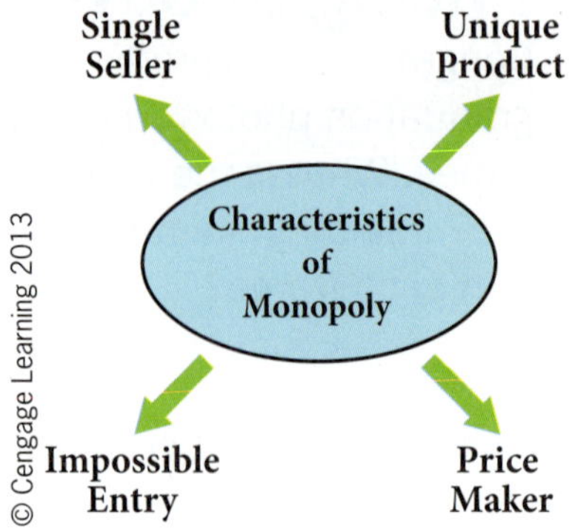

Figure 5-3
Characteristics of Monopoly

Single Seller

In perfect competition, many firms compete in a market. In contrast, a monopoly means that a single firm provides the total supply of a product in a given market. Local monopolies are common examples. A campus bookstore, cable television company, and electric power company may be local monopolies. The only gas station, drug store, or grocery store in Nowhere County, Utah, and a hotdog stand at a football game are also examples of monopolies. Nationally, the U.S. Postal Service monopolizes first class mail.

Unique Product

A unique product means the monopolist faces little or no competition. In reality, however, there are few perfect monopolies. For example, college students can buy used textbooks from sources other than the campus bookstore. Textbooks can be purchased over the Internet, and satellite television competes with cable television. Natural gas, oil furnaces, and solar energy are competition for electric heat. Similarly, the fax machine and email are competition for mail service, and people can bring food from home to the football game.

Impossible Entry

In perfect competition, there are no barriers to prevent new firms from entering a market. In the case of monopoly, extremely high barriers make it very difficult or impossible for new firms to enter a market. Following are the three major barriers to entry that prevent new firms from competing with a monopoly.

1. OWNERSHIP OF A VITAL RESOURCE Sole control of a strategic input is one way a monopolist can prevent a newcomer from entering a market. A famous historical example is Alcoa's monopoly of the U.S. aluminum market. Its monopoly lasted from the late 19th century until the end of World War II. The source of Alcoa's monopoly was its control of bauxite ore, necessary to produce aluminum. Today, it is difficult for a new professional sports league to compete with the National Football League (NFL) because the NFL teams have contracts with the best players and leases for the best stadiums.

2. LEGAL BARRIERS The most effective barriers protecting a firm from potential competitors are government franchises and licenses. The government permits a single firm to provide a certain product and by law excludes competing firms. For example, water and sewer services, natural gas, and cable television operate under monopolies granted by state and local governments. In many states, the state government runs monopoly liquor stores and lotteries. The U.S. Postal Service has a government franchise to deliver first class mail.

Government granted licenses restrict entry into some industries and occupations. For example, the Federal Communications Commission (FCC) must license radio and television stations. In most states, physicians, lawyers, dentists, nurses, taxicabs, and businesses are required to have licenses.

Patents and copyrights are another form of government barriers to entry. The government grants patents to inventors. This legally prohibits other firms from selling the patented product for 20 years. Copyrights give creators of literature, art, music, and movies exclusive rights to sell their works. The purpose behind granting patents and copyrights is to encourage innovation and new products. This barrier guarantees exclusive rights to profit from new ideas for a limited period.

ewenjc/iStockphoto.com

A water processing plant is an example of a monopoly that exists due to laws that exclude competition.

Global View

Is DeBeers's Diamond Monopoly Forever?

"Diamonds are forever," has been a DeBeers slogan, but is the diamond monopoly forever? DeBeers, a South African corporation, is close to a world monopoly. It owns the world's largest diamond mine, which was discovered in 1866 on a farm in South Africa owned by Johannes DeBeers. Through its Central Selling Organization (CSO) headquartered in London, DeBeers controlled 80 percent of all the diamonds sold in the world. DeBeers controlled the price of jewelry-quality diamonds by requiring suppliers in Russia, Australia, Congo, Botswana, Namibia, and other countries to sell their rough diamonds through DeBeers's CSO. Why did suppliers of rough diamonds allow DeBeers to set the price and quantity of diamonds sold throughout the world? The answer was that the CSO could put any uncooperative seller out of business. All the CSO had to do was to reach into its huge stockpile of diamonds and flood the market with the type of diamonds being sold by an independent seller. As a result, the price of diamonds plummeted in the competitor's market, and it ceased to sell diamonds.

In recent years, DeBeers has lost some of its control of the market. Reasons for this change are mines in Australia became more independent, diamonds were found in Canada, and Russian mines began selling to independents. In 2001, DeBeers reversed its policy by closing CSO and promoting DeBeers's own brand of diamonds rather than controlling the world diamond supply. DeBeers proclaimed its strategy to be "the diamond supplier of choice." Will this monopoly continue? It is an interesting question.

Think Critically

Compare DeBeers to the characteristics of a monopoly. What is your conclusion?

3. NATURAL MONOPOLY A monopoly can emerge naturally because of the fall in average cost as the quantity sold rises. As a firm becomes larger, its cost per unit of output may decline compared to costs of a smaller competitor. This "survival of the fittest" cost advantage forces smaller firms to leave the market. New firms cannot hope to produce and sell output at a price that is equal or close to that of the monopolist. They will therefore not enter that market. Thus, a monopoly can arise over time and remain dominant in a market. This can happen even though the monopolist does not own an essential resource or obtain legal barriers.

Economists call the situation in which one seller emerges in a market because of lower average cost a natural monopoly. A **natural monopoly** is a market in which the average cost of production is lowest when only one firm supplies a good or service. A single firm can supply the entire market demand at a lower cost than two or more smaller firms. Public utilities, such as the natural gas, water, and cable televisions, are examples of natural monopolies. The government grants these industries an exclusive franchise in a geographic area.

Consumers can benefit from the cost savings that occur with only one firm in a market. The single firm operates with lower cost and sells a larger output. The government then regulates these monopolies through a board of commissioners to prevent setting the price too high.

Figure 5-4 illustrates the average cost curve for a natural monopoly. A single firm can produce 100 units at an average cost of \$15. Total cost is \$1,500 (\$15 × 100 units). If two firms each produce 50 units, the same 100 units are produced. The total cost rises to \$2,500 and average cost per unit is higher at \$25. With five firms producing 20 units each, the total cost of 100 units rises to \$3,500. The average cost is still higher at \$35. Therefore, a single seller produces at the lowest average cost and total cost.

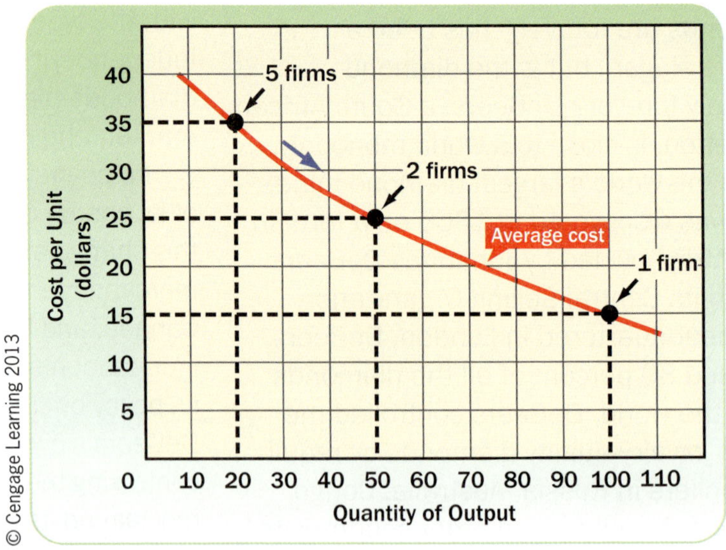

Figure 5-4

Single Seller Minimizes Costs in a Natural Monopoly

In a natural monopoly, a single firm can produce at a lower cost than two or more firms because the average cost curve for any firm decreases. One firm can produce 100 units at an average cost of \$15 and a total cost of \$1,500. Two firms can produce 100 units of output (50 units each) for a total cost of \$2,500. Five firms can produce the same output for a total cost of \$3,500.

The Monopolist as a Price Maker

As explained earlier, a perfectly competitive firm is a price taker. Given the characteristics of the perfectly competitive market structure, the firm has absolutely no control over price. This condition is not true for monopoly. Since a monopolist is the only seller in a market, and it faces the entire market demand curve, it does not worry about checking daily reports to find out the market price of its product. The monopolist is not concerned about the intersection of the market demand and supply curve for its product. The monopolist is a price maker. A **price maker** is a seller that does not consider competition when setting its price.

Since the monopoly firm is a price maker, it can choose any price along its market demand curve. Which price would you choose? The monopolist considers its costs and total revenue and chooses the price that generates the greatest profit. It should be noted that in government-regulated monopolies such as water, natural gas, and cable television, maximum profit may be sacrificed. In the public interest, lower regulated prices are often imposed.

CHECKPOINT

How does the government create monopolies? Are all monopolies created by the government?

ETHICS *in Action!*

Natural Disasters and Monopoly Power

Natural disasters such as earthquakes, hurricanes, or tornados can create situations that temporarily offer great monopoly power to some businesses. Consider hurricane Katrina that devastated the gulf coast of the United States in 2005 as an example. This storm came ashore near New Orleans on August 25. Its tidal surge breached the city's levies, flooding nearly two-thirds of New Orleans. Virtually all roads in and out of the city were impassable. Thousands of people sought refuge in the Superdome, which had lost large parts of its roof.

Help from outside took days to arrive and was inadequate. Shortages of most products including food and water were extreme. In this situation some individuals sought to earn a quick profit by charging inflated prices for basic human needs. Even when these immediate needs were met, other shortages occurred. Building materials that could be used to protect people's belongings or create a shelter were almost impossible to find. The few businesses that had tarps or plywood to sell could have charged almost any price and still have had more customers than they could serve. Most businesses set prices that were no higher than normal, but a few took advantage of the situation because they had the power to do so. The practice of charging exorbitant prices for products people desperately need is *price gouging*. In most places it is against the law. Even if it was not illegal, price gouging is considered unethical by most people.

Think Critically

1. **Is it ethical to charge high prices for products that are in short supply because of a natural disaster? Explain why higher prices might increase the quantity of these goods consumers could purchase over time.**
2. **What do you believe the government should do to businesses that price gouge? Why may it be difficult to determine when price gouging is taking place?**

5-1 Assessment

Key Concepts

LO 1-2 1. A market in which the average cost of production is lowest when only one firm supplies a product is a __?__ monopoly.

LO 1-1 2. **TRUE OR FALSE** A price taker is a seller that has no control over the price of the product it sells.

LO 1-2 3. A seller that does not consider competition when setting its price is a price __?__.

LO 1-1 4. **TRUE OR FALSE** A barrier to entry is any obstacle that makes it difficult for a new firm to enter a market.

LO 1-1 5. A market structure in which a large number of small firms sell identical products, and entry into the market is very easy is __?__ competition.

LO 1-2 6. **TRUE OR FALSE** A market structure in which a single seller sells a unique product, and entry into the market is very easy is called a monopoly.

LO 1-1 7. The key characteristics of a market, including the number of firms, the similarity of products they sell, and how easy or difficult it is to enter the market is the __?__.

Think About It

LO 1-1 8. Does a Kansas wheat farmer fit the perfectly competitive market? Explain.

LO 1-1 9. Explain why a perfectly competitive firm would or would not advertise.

LO 1-2 10. Using the three characteristics of monopoly, explain why each is a monopolist.
a. cable television company b. water company c. U.S. Postal Service
d. The NFL team or the NBA team in a particular city

LO 1-2 11. Explain why you agree or disagree with the following statement: "All monopolies are created by the government."

LO 1-2 12. Suppose an investigator finds that the prices charged for drugs at a hospital are higher than the prices charged for the same products at drugstores in the area served by the hospital. What might explain this situation?

LO 1-1 13. What are the characteristics of a market that has perfect competition?

LO 1-2 14. What are the characteristics of a market that is dominated by a monopoly?

Make Academic Connections

LO 1-1 15. **MATH** Suppose the market equilibrium price of wheat is $9 per bushel in a perfectly competitive market. Draw the market supply and demand curves facing a single wheat farmer. Explain why the wheat farmer is a price taker.

Teamwork

LO 1-2 16. In small groups, brainstorm a list of goods that you (or your family) purchase from a monopoly. Compare your answers with other groups.

Unit 2 Project: Tools of Free Markets

PRICE MAKERS AND TAKERS Prepare a chart that lists four products your group has purchased in the last year. Identify the manufacturers and sellers of those products as price makers or price takers. Include pictures of the products in a display that lists the prices paid along with any competition that has developed in response to consumer demand.

5-2 Monopolistic Competition and Oligopoly

Learning Objectives

LO 2-1 **Explain** the characteristics of monopolistic competition markets.

LO 2-2 **Describe** the characteristics of oligopoly markets.

Vocabulary

monopolistic competition, p. 140
product differentiation, p. 141
oligopoly, p. 143
cartel, p. 145

REAL-WORLD FOCUS

© Aleksandar Vrzalski/iStockphoto.com

Jung works at his parents' bird shop every weekend and during school breaks. The store sells a unique blend of bird seed compared to other stores in the area. The average selling price is $10 per bag. His parents mix the feed using a special blend that has been used by the family for dozens of years and is guaranteed to attract numerous types of birds. Customers come from long distances to buy this unique bird seed. "We charge a price that represents our costs plus a reasonable profit," his mother told him.

WORK AS A TEAM When a product is different this gives the seller a degree of control over the price of its product. Why wouldn't they set the price very high such as $50 per order? Why do customers continue to buy their products?

Each day thousands of travelers check in and drop off baggage at airline ticket counters in the main terminal of this international airport.

DO YOU THINK airlines use product differentiation to attract customers? Describe a differentiation that would appeal to travelers.

yienkeat/Shutterstock.com

Elena Elisseeva/Shutterstock.com

LO 2-1 Monopolistic Competition

Suppose your favorite restaurant is Ivan's Oyster Bar. Ivan's does not fit either of the two extreme models in the previous lesson. Instead, Ivan's characteristics are a blend of monopoly and perfect competition. For starters, like a monopolist, Ivan's is a price maker. Ivan's has some control over its prices. It can charge a higher price for seafood. Ivan's may lose some customers, but many loyal customers will keep coming back. The reason is that Ivan's distinguishes its product from the competition. Ivan advertises first-rate service, a great salad bar, and other attributes. Like a monopolist, Ivan's has a degree of market power to maximize profit. But like a perfectly competitive firm, Ivan's is not the only place to buy a seafood dinner in town. It must share the market with many other restaurants within an hour's drive.

Economists define **monopolistic competition** as a market structure characterized by many small sellers, a differentiated product, and easy market entry. Monopolistic competition fits many real-world markets. Figure 5-5 provides a summary of the characteristics of monopolistic competition. Following are brief descriptions of each monopolistic competition characteristic.

Figure 5-5

Characteristics of Monopolistic Competition

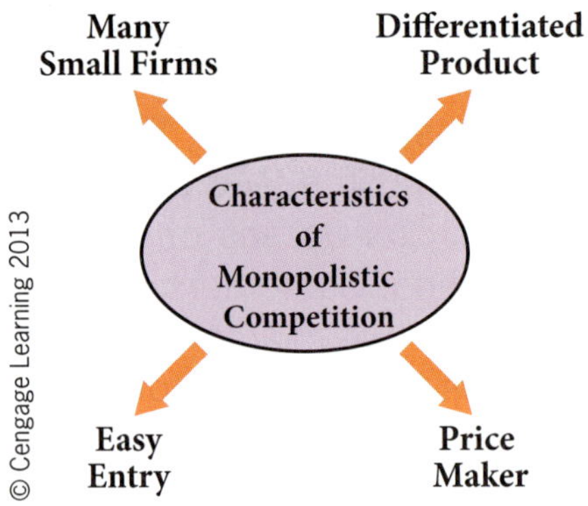

To serve the best salmon in town, a restaurant owner will likely personally select the filets at the fish market, or he may catch the fish himself.

Many Small Firms

Under monopolistic competition and perfect competition, the exact number of firms cannot be stated. But in monopolistic competition the number of sellers is smaller than in perfect competition. In this market structure consumers have many different but similar varieties of products from which to choose. The prices are not identical but are competitive. No single seller has a large enough share of the market to completely control prices. Ivan's Oyster Bar is an example of a monopolistic competitor. Ivan assumes that his restaurant can set prices slightly higher without fear that competitors will react by changing their prices. If any single seafood restaurant raises its price, the going market price for seafood dinners increases by a very small amount.

Differentiated Product

The key feature of monopolistic competition is **product differentiation**, which is the process of creating differences between similar goods and services. Although the products of each firm are highly similar, the consumer views them as somewhat different. There may be 25 seafood restaurants in a given city, but they are not all the same. They differ in location, atmosphere, quality of food, quality of service, and so on.

Product differentiation can be real or imagined. It does not matter which is correct as long as consumers believe differences exist. Many customers think Ivan's has the best seafood in town even though other restaurants offer a similar product. The importance of this viewpoint is that consumers are willing to pay a slightly higher price for Ivan's seafood. This gives Ivan the incentive to appear on local TV cooking shows. He also buys ads showing him personally catching the seafood he serves.

Product differentiation is an important characteristic of monopolistic competition that distinguishes it from perfect competition and monopoly. Under perfect competition, there is no product differentiation. This is because the product is identical for all firms. Likewise, the monopolist has little incentive to engage in product differentiation because it has no competition. Advertising expenses would simply reduce profits.

NET Bookmark

Access www.cengage.com/school/economics/personalfinance and click on the link for Chapter 5. Visit Kimberly-Clark, maker of Kleenex, and click on Our Brands. Facial tissues, according to some analysts, are a product with low customer loyalty. What is Kimberly-Clark doing to increase product differentiation and brand loyalty?

www.cengage.com/school/economics/personalfinance

Easy Entry

Unlike a monopoly, firms in a monopolistically competitive market face low barriers to entry. But entry into a monopolistically competitive market is not as easy as entry into a perfectly competitive market. Persons who want to enter the seafood restaurant business can get loans, lease space, and start serving seafood without too much trouble. These new seafood restaurants may initially have difficulty attracting consumers. The reason is Ivan's established reputation as the best seafood restaurant in town. Ivan's product is differentiated.

Monopolistic competition is by far the most common market structure in the United States. Examples include retail firms, such as grocery stores, hair salons, gas stations, mini-marts, diet centers, and restaurants.

timegoodwin/iStockphoto.com

This restaurant owner uses a neon sign to attract customers who are looking for a seafood restaurant.

Monopolistic Competition

Monopolistic competition can be found in every small town, mid-size community, and large city in the United States. These businesses establish themselves based on the needs and interests of the people that live nearby. You can watch television commercials, notice billboards along the roadsides, or read local newspaper advertisements to find numerous monopolistic competition firms. Find five examples of businesses in your local community that are in a monopolistic competition market.

Investigate Your Local ECONOMY

Try it Out

Examine how each business differentiates its good or service from its competitors. Prepare a report of your findings.

whitemay/iStockphoto.com

Outdoor menu boards are one way to advertise both menu items and prices to customers passing by.

The Monopolistically Competitive Firm as a Price Maker

Given the characteristics of monopolistic competition, you might think the monopolistic competitor is a price taker. But it is not. Firms in the market are price makers. The primary reason is that their products are differentiated. This gives the monopolistically competitive firm, like the monopolist, limited control over its price. When the price is raised, brand loyalty ensures some customers will remain steadfast. A key reason is advertising.

Firms in this market use ads to differentiate their products. The firm's goal is to convince customers that its product is really different, and better than its rivals' products. These ads often feature great taste, a higher quality of service, or new products to win customers. Ads proclaim that products make you smarter, better looking, or nicer to be around. Graphically, the firm hopes advertising will make the demand curve shift rightward by changing consumers' tastes in favor of its product. As a result, total revenue rises, and the firm makes more profit.

CHECKPOINT

As a consumer, from which market would you prefer to buy a product: perfect competition, monopoly, or monopolistic competition? Why?

LO 2-2 Oligopoly—Competition among the Few

Many manufacturing industries, such as steel, aluminum, automobiles, and aircraft, are best described as oligopolistic. This is the "big business" market structure, in which firms aggressively compete. They bombard consumers with advertising on television and fill mailboxes with advertisements. Economists define an **oligopoly** as a market structure characterized by a few large sellers, either of an identical or differentiated product, and difficult market entry. Like monopolistic competition, oligopoly is found in real-world markets. Figure 5-6 shows the characteristics of oligopoly. Following is a discussion of each of these characteristics.

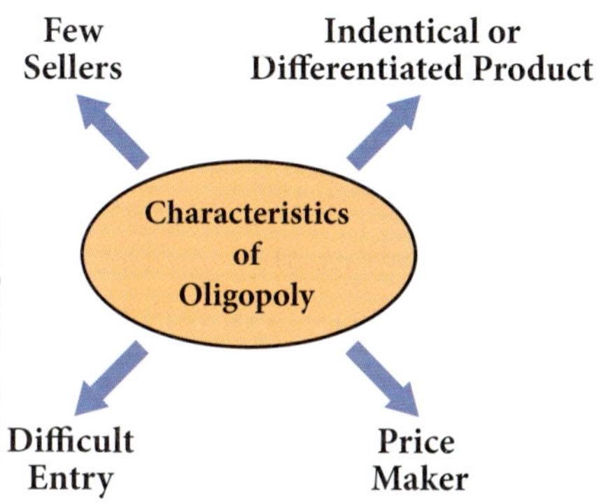

Figure 5-6 Characteristics of Oligopoly

Few Sellers

The Ford Motor Company showcases its Focus ST at an auto show.

Oligopoly is competition "among the few." The "Big Three" or "Big Four" is used to mean that three or four firms dominate a market. But what does "a few" firms really mean? Does this mean at least two, but less than ten? As with other market structures, the answer is there is no specific number of firms that must dominate a market before it is an oligopoly. Basically, an oligopoly is a market in which an action by one firm generally causes a reaction from other firms. When Ford considers a price hike or a style change, it must predict how General Motors (GM), Toyota, and other major automobile producers will change their prices and styling in response. Therefore, decisions under oligopoly are more complex than under perfect competition, monopoly, and monopolistic competition.

Identical or Differentiated Product

Under oligopoly, firms can produce either an identical or a differentiated product. The steel produced by USX is identical to the steel from Republic Steel. The oil sold by Saudi Arabia is identical to the oil from Alaska. Similarly, zinc, copper, and aluminum are standardized or identical products. But cars produced by the major automakers are differentiated products. Tires, soup, detergents, and breakfast cereals are also differentiated products sold in oligopolies.

Major oligopolists often compete using advertising to display product differentiation. Instead of slugging it out with price cuts, oligopolists may try to lure business away from their rivals through better advertising campaigns and improved products. This model of behavior explains why advertising expenditures often are large in the cigarette, soft drink, athletic shoe, and automobile industries. It also explains why the research and development (R & D) function is so important to oligopolists. For example, much of their engineering efforts are aimed at developing new products and improving existing products.

Social Networking Sites: The New Advertising Game

You're the ECONOMIST

A key characteristic of market structures is that firms use advertising to promote product differentiation. Television commercials are considered a very effective method of mass-market advertising. This explains why TV networks charge such high prices for commercial airtime during prominent events, such as the Super Bowl football game. However, the days when television commercials dominate the advertising world could be fading away. Don't want to be bothered by those advertisements? It's easy: Just press the fast forward button on the remote control of a digital video recorder (DVR). Advertisers are therefore struggling to figure out other ways to get the attention of consumers. One idea is to tap into the popularity of social networking sites such as Facebook, Twitter, MySpace, YouTube, and sites that target specific audiences. These sites connect individuals with others who interact through personal profiles, games, video clips, and more.

The challenge for Web economy entrepreneurs is to earn profits by differentiating their products using innovative ways to include advertising. The search engine is a highly successful business model. If someone Googles for golf clubs, sponsored links for golf clubs appear on the screen. Social networks provide the prospect of tailoring ads to people's specific interests. Suppose a golf club company pays Facebook for a page where you and your friends can register and play a video game of golf. What does the company get out of it? They get a database of tens of thousands of names, all potential customers. However, some ideas are not winners. Facebook used a new approach that informed friends whenever a member purchased something from online retailers. Consumers protested claiming that this was an invasion of their privacy, and the program was abandoned. Now consider this idea. Imagine being at a concert and text messaging a shout-out to your friends. Your message appears during the concert next to the stage on a big screen with a large ad from a company. Is this a good idea?

Think Critically

Advertising is tasteless, offensive, and a nuisance that wastes resources. Give three arguments against this idea.

Why might oligopolists compete through product differentiation rather than price competition? The answer is that each oligopolist perceives that its rival will easily and quickly match any price reduction. In contrast, it is much more difficult to combat a clever and important product improvement.

Difficult Entry

Similar to monopoly, formidable barriers to entry in an oligopoly protect firms from new producers entering the market. These barriers include significant financial requirements, control over an essential resource, patent rights, and other legal barriers.

Review of the Four Market Structures

Now you are prepared to compare the four market structures. Figure 5-7 summarizes the characteristics and gives examples of each market structure.

Market Structure	Number of Sellers	Type of Product	Entry Condition	Control of Price	Examples
Perfect Competition	Large	Identical	Very easy	Price taker	Agriculture, stocks
Monopoly	One	Unique	Impossible	Price maker	Public utilities, first class mail
Monopolistic Competition	Many	Differentiated	Easy	Price maker	Retail trade, restaurants
Oligopoly	Few	Identical or differentiated	Difficult	Price maker	Auto, steel, oil

Figure 5-7
Comparison of Market Structures

The Cartel

A way to avoid price wars is for oligopolists to agree to a peace treaty. Instead of competing, firms openly or secretly conspire to form a monopoly called a cartel. A **cartel** is a group of firms that formally agree to reduce competition by coordinating the price and the output of a product. The goal of a cartel is to reap monopoly profits by replacing competition with cooperation. Cartels are illegal in the United States, but not in other nations. The best known cartel is the Organization of the Petroleum Exporting Countries (OPEC). The members of OPEC divide "black gold" output among themselves according to quotas openly agreed upon at meetings of the OPEC oil ministries. Saudi Arabia is the largest producer and has the largest quota.

CHECKPOINT

In the cereal aisle, notice there are many different brands of the same product (cereal) on the shelves. Each brand is slightly different from the others. Is the breakfast cereal market structure monopolistic competition or oligopoly?

PROFILE

Joan Robinson
British Economist

Photo courtesy of Ramsey and Muspratt

Joan Robinson was born in England in 1903 and studied economics at Cambridge. After her graduation in 1925, she became a lecturer and then a professor of economics at the University of Cambridge. At this time only the extreme theories of perfect competition and monopoly existed in economic theory. Most economists and political leaders failed to recognize that the majority of businesses in the real world were not perfect examples of either of these types of market structure. Economic theories and government policies were generally supportive of the idea that the market should be allowed to operate with as little government involvement as possible. During the Great Depression of the 1930s, many people came to believe that this idea was mistaken because market forces didn't seem to be solving the nation's economic problems.

Robinson was one of a few economists who suggested that older classical economic theories should be replaced because they failed to explain what was happening in the economy or what should be done to improve the situation. She explained that most businesses would not invest in new factories, hire additional workers, or spend the money necessary to develop new and better products when they were not sure they could sell the products they produced at a price that would earn them a profit. In this situation, Robinson and others encouraged the government to stimulate demand through increased government spending or tax reductions. This policy was intended to encourage greater production and employment even if it required the government to temporarily go into debt.

One of Robinson's greatest contributions was to introduce the idea of monopolistic competition. She did this in her first major book, *The Economics of Imperfect Competition*, published in 1933. This book led to a new economic understanding that was often called the *monopolistic competition revolution.* In her model firms that compete with each other have some degree of monopoly power. In fact, most industries in the real world are neither perfectly competitive nor complete monopolies. Instead, firms compete using product differentiation and advertising.

THINK CRITICALLY

Joan Robinson was one of the first to write about monopolistic competition and oligopoly. Why do you think that she used the term "imperfect competition" in the title of her book?

5-2 Assessment

Key Concepts

LO 2-2 1. A group of firms that formally agree to reduce competition by coordinating the price and output of a product is called a(n) __?__.

LO 2-1 2. **TRUE OR FALSE** Product differentiation is the process of creating differences between similar goods and services.

LO 2-2 3. A(n) __?__ is a market structure characterized by a few large sellers, either identical or a differentiated product, and difficult market entry.

LO 2-1 4. **TRUE OR FALSE** Product differentiation does not occur in an oligopoly.

LO 2-1 5. A firm in monopolistic competition is a price __?__.

Think About It

LO 2-1 6. Which market structure do most real-world markets approximate?

LO 2-2 7. List four goods or services produced by an oligopolist that you have purchased. Why are these markets oligopolistic rather than monopolistically competitive?

LO 2-2 8. What might be the difference in products between oligopolists that advertise and those that do not?

LO 2-2 9. Evaluate the following statement: "A cartel will put an end to price war, which is a barbaric form of competition that benefits no one."

LO 2-1 10. What are the characteristics of a market that has firms operating in monopolistic competition?

LO 2-2 11. What are the characteristics of a market that is an oligopoly?

Make Academic Connections

LO 2-2 12. **HISTORY** The 1988 movie *Tucker: The Man and His Dream* is based on the saga surrounding the Tucker car's production. Research the Tucker car produced in 1948. What speculation exists concerning the failure of competition in this oligopoly?

LO 2-2 13. **HISTORY** Throughout history cartels have been unsustainable. The average life of a cartel is from 5 to 8 years. Why do cartels tend not to last long? Research and make a list of international cartels that you find which exist today.

Teamwork

LO 2-1 14. Work in six groups. Three groups choose a monopolistic competition market structure and three groups choose an oligopoly market structure. Look at advertisements on billboards, magazines, and other sources. Share your findings in terms of product differentiation and nonprice competition with the class.

LO 2-1 15. Work in groups, considering the local market. As a group, decide what business to start to seek profit opportunities. Decide how to differentiate your business from the competition. Create a brochure that will sell your business to customers.

Unit 2 Project: Tools of Free Markets

MARKET STRUCTURES IN A WHEEL Draw a wheel with five spokes. Within the spokes describe the types of market structures: perfect competition, monopoly, monopolistic competition, and oligopoly. Insert characteristics of each market structure and give an example of a product or service provided by sellers. In the fifth spoke describe what you believe would be the perfect market structure for you as a new business owner.

Chapter 5 Summary

5-1 PERFECT COMPETITION AND MONOPOLY

1. Perfect competition is a market structure where a large number of small companies are selling identical products. Entry into and exit from the market are easy and inexpensive. Because there are many sellers of an identical product, the price for consumers is the lowest possible.
2. Companies operating in perfect competition are price takers. This means that sellers have no control over price. They must be able to produce and sell products for the prevailing market price.
3. In a monopoly, there is only one seller of a product. The product being produced is unique. Thus a local monopoly is able to provide the total supply of a product in a given market. There are extremely high barriers to entry for new firms to enter the market.
4. Those who own a unique and vital resource are able to create a monopoly. When there are laws, rules, and regulations restricting entry into a market, the monopoly is preserved.
5. A natural monopoly may be formed when a single company in a market results in the lowest possible cost of production. Competition falls away when they cannot offer a competitive price with the market leader. Thus a natural monopolist is a price maker, which means it can set its own price without regard to competition.

5-2 MONOPOLISTIC COMPETITION AND OLIGOPOLY

6. A market that has many small sellers, a differentiated product, and easy market entry is said to be monopolistic. There are fewer sellers than in perfect competition, but the products are not identical. Because of differentiation (creating differences between products), higher prices can be maintained by some sellers.
7. Monopolistic competition involves low barriers to entry. Still any new companies must convince customers of other businesses to try their products and compare values. As price makers, these companies must present a compelling story to justify their prices.
8. An oligopoly has few sellers who are large and powerful. Entry into this marketplace is very hard to do. It would require extremely large sums of capital. Thus a few large sellers create a market of identical or very similar products that they often differentiate from competitors. Price competition is rare in this market.
9. In some cases, large sellers band together to form cartels or mutual agreements to control supply, competition, and output of products. This allows them to set prices and to dominate the production of goods in world marketplaces. These price makers are able to control output and supply to their advantage so long as there is no competing or alternate source of product that consumers can access.

Chapter 5

Assessment

Vocabulary Review

Match each statement with the term that best defines it.

1. A market structure characterized by a few larger sellers, either identical or a differentiated product, and difficult market entry
2. A market structure in which a single seller sells a unique product, and entry into the market is impossible
3. The key characteristics of a market, including the number of firms, the similarity of products they sell, and how easy or difficult it is for new firms to enter the market
4. A market structure characterized by many small sellers, differentiated product, and easy market entry
5. Any obstacle that makes it difficult for a new firm to enter a market
6. A seller that does not consider competitors when setting its price
7. A group of firms that formally agree to reduce competition by coordinating the price and the output of a product
8. A market in which the average cost of production is lowest when only one firm supplies a good or service
9. A seller that has no control over the price of the product it sells. The seller can sell all its output at the equilibrium prices, but none at other prices
10. A market structure in which a large number of small firms sell identical products, and entry into the market is very easy
11. The process of creating differences between similar goods and services

Vocabulary

a. barrier to entry
b. cartel
c. market structure
d. monopolistic competition
e. monopoly
f. natural monopoly
g. oligopoly
h. perfect competition
i. price maker
j. price taker
k. product differentiation

Review Your Knowledge

LO 1-1 12. A firm operating in a perfectly competitive market is a price taker because
  a. no firm has a significant market share
  b. no firm's product is different
  c. setting a price higher than the going price results in zero sales
  d. all of the above

LO 2-1 13. A monopolistically competitive market is characterized by
  a. many small sellers selling a differentiated product
  b. a single seller of a product that has no competition
  c. very strong barriers to entry
  d. firms with no control over their prices

LO 1-1 14. In the perfectly competitive market, all firms in the market are assumed to be producing
a. identical products
b. differentiated products
c. products that are heavily advertised
d. complementary products

LO 1-1 15. Market structure is defined by the
a. number of firms in each market
b. similarity of the product sold
c. ease of entry into the market
d. all of the above

LO 1-2 16. A market in which total costs are kept to a minimum because only one firm serves the whole market is a
a. natural monopoly
b. competitive monopoly
c. patent monopoly
d. limit monopoly

LO 1-2 17. Which of the following best fits the definition of a monopoly?
a. General Motors
b. Exxon Mobile
c. Local electric utility
d. AT&T

LO 2-1 18. Which of the following most closely approximates the conditions of a monopolistically competitive market?
a. The market for Grade A eggs, which is characterized by a large number of firms producing an identical product.
b. The restaurant industry, which is characterized by firms producing a differentiated product in a market with low entry barriers.
c. Local cable television service, where a licensed supplier competes with firms offering satellite service.
d. The market for jumbo aircraft, where one major domestic firm competes with one major foreign firm.

LO 1-1 19. Which best illustrates a perfectly competitive market?
a. Soft drinks
b. Automobiles
c. Electric power
d. Soybean farmers

LO 1-2 20. A monopoly is
a. a seller of a highly advertised and differentiated product in a market with low barriers to entry in the long run.
b. the only seller of a good for which there is no competition in a market with high barriers to entry.
c. the only buyer of a unique raw material.
d. the producer of a product subsidized by the government.

LO 2-1 21. Product differentiation
a. refers to the attempt of firms to make their products look like those of the other firms in the industry
b. refers to the attempt of firms to make differences in similar products look different in the minds of the consumers
c. is a common characteristic of a perfectly competitive market structure
d. is only employed in a monopoly market structure

LO 2-2 22. The automobile, steel, and oil markets are all examples of
a. perfectly competitive markets
b. monopolies
c. monopolistically competitive markets
d. oligopolies

LO 2-2 23. A cartel
a. is a group of firms formally agreeing to control the price and the output of a product
b. has as its primary goal to earn monopoly profits by replacing competition with cooperation
c. is illegal in the United States, but not in other nations
d. all of the above

Digging Deeper with Economics e-Collection

Price is only one way sellers compete with other sellers. Another way is differentiation—making your product different from your competitors—so that consumers will see the value and choose your product. Access the Gale Economics e-Collection at **www.cengage.com/school/economics/personalfinance**. Research to find two products, one that has been around for a long time and one that is new within the last year or two. Prepare a visual display comparing the products of two or more producers, explaining how the sellers have focused on differentiation.

Think About It

LO 1-1 **24.** In perfect competition, a seller must be a price taker. Why would you want to enter into this market as a seller?

LO 1-2 **25.** In a monopoly, entry into the market by a competitor is impossible. Why?

LO 2-1 **26.** Product differentiation is important in both monopolistic and some oligopolistic forms of competition. How do consumers benefit from this type of competition?

LO 2-2 **27.** When formidable barriers to entry into a market exist, it is difficult for entrepreneurs to develop and sell a competing product. Are there ways for new businesses in these markets to succeed and earn profits? How?

Make Academic Connections

LO 2-2 **28.** **ETHICS** In some industries, especially high-tech, dominant firms buy up small businesses and their patents for the purpose of eliminating competition. They do not develop that product line. Instead they kill it so it will not compete with their own products. Is this practice in the best interest of consumers? Explain why or why not.

LO 1-1 **29.** **RESEARCH** Over time, new products are developed that replace old ideas. Do research on an industry or business that has changed rapidly over time. For example, AT&T first began with telegraph lines. Then hard-line phone lines were stretching across the country. Today wireless has replaced that technology. Explain how these changes affect companies as well as consumers.

LO 2-1 **30.** **COMMUNICATION** For some products and services, consumers can have a great deal of influence over prices in the market. In other industries, they have little or no influence. Describe each type of market structure and how consumers influence prices in that market.

Extend Your Learning

31. On your own paper complete the following comparison of market structures table.

Market Structure	Number of Sellers	Type of Product	Entry Condition	Control of Price	Examples
Perfect Competition	__?__	__?__	__?__	__?__	__?__
Monopoly	__?__	__?__	__?__	__?__	__?__
Monopolistic Competition	__?__	__?__	__?__	__?__	__?__
Oligopoly	__?__	__?__	__?__	__?__	__?__

UNIT

3 Business in Action

Chapter 6 Business Organizations
Chapter 7 Business Ownership

Unit 3 explores how American business works. In Chapter 6, you will learn how businesses started and evolved in America, from original colonies through today's information age. You will also discover the three major types of business ownership: proprietorships, partnerships, and corporations. Within the structures of proprietorships and partnerships, you will also look at options available in states to become LLCs (limited liability companies) and LLPs (limited liability partnerships). Discovering self-employment and how to start and successfully run a business are covered in Chapter 7. You will learn about starting a new business, buying an existing business, or buying a franchise. For new business ventures, you will need to prepare a business plan. The overall plan includes many parts so you can convince lenders and investors to be a part of your business's success. Finally, you will learn about reasons why businesses fail and ways to avoid falling victim to these occurrences. Good planning and research up front will help ensure that your business will be profitable and successful for years to come.

UNIT 3 Project

Going into Business

Project Objectives

PARTNERSHIP FOR 21ST CENTURY SKILLS

- Apply critical-thinking skills to create models and evaluate economic activity
- Use standard grammar, spelling, sentence structure, and punctuation
- Transfer information from one media to another, including written to visual and oral
- Create a written, oral, and visual presentation of business and economic information

chapter 6

Timeline of Business Development from 1776, p. 161

Prepare a timeline of business development events since this country was formed to present day.

Create a Business, p.169

Create a new product or service, or a new way to use an existing product or service. Consider possible customers of the business and what needs or wants you would be meeting.

Display of Types of Business Organizations, p. 183

Create a chart or visual display that lists and explains the pro's and con's of the various types of business organization: proprietorships, LLCs, partnerships, LLPs, and corporations.

chapter 7

Prepare a Resume, p. 200

Compile information about yourself, your training, and your expertise. Prepare a resume that you can share with potential business partners.

Business Plan Introduction, p. 208

Download a sample business plan from www.cengage.com/school/economics/personalfinance and analyze the Introduction section. Create an introduction for your business plan.

Business Plan Requirements, p. 215

Explore the contents of an entire business plan, considering information you need, sources of the information, and types of data that would need to appear in the report.

Project Wrap-up

Create a poster, newsletter, website, oral report, slide presentation, or video that explains your business idea, describes how your new business will create value and meet your customers' needs, and states how your business will be organized and how it will operate. Save a copy of all work completed in your economics portfolio.

yienkeat/Shutterstock.com; Alex Raths/iStockphoto.com

Blend Images/Jupiter Images

chapter 6

Business Organizations

yienkeat/Shutterstock.com

MARKETS *in Action!*

The Story of UPS

United Parcel Service started as a messenger company in 1907. Today, they deliver packages in more than 200 countries around the world.

The company began in Seattle, Washington when 19-year-old James E. Casey borrowed $100 from a friend and started the American Messenger Company. Jim had worked for other messenger service companies in the area, and he believed he could do a better job with his own company. He delivered packages, notes, baggage, and even trays of food from restaurants. Only a few cars existed at that time. He delivered goods on foot and using horses and wagons. Jim and his partner, Claude Ryan, ran the service from a humble office located under the sidewalk. Jim's brother and a handful of teenagers were the company's employees. The company did well, providing round-the-clock service at low rates.

In 1913, the company acquired its first car: a Model T Ford. In 1916, Charlie Soderstrom joined the partnership, bringing automobiles, expertise, and the color brown. In 1919, three of Seattle's largest department stores were regular customers of this company, which was then called Merchants Parcel Company. That same year, the company expanded to Oakland, California, and adopted its present name, United Parcel Service (UPS). In 1922, UPS acquired a company in Los Angeles with an innovative practice known as the "common carrier" service.

In 1930, UPS expanded to the East Coast. As the population migrated to suburbs in the 1940s and 50s, UPS expanded into delivery to consumers. This expansion put them in direct competition with the U.S. Postal Service. In the 1970s, UPS expanded its services to include air operations, offering two-day services to major U.S. cities. By 1980, UPS was delivering coast-to-coast. By 1985, UPS Next Day Air service was available. UPS also offered international service, delivering to more than 185 countries and territories. By 1993, UPS was delivering 11.5 million packages and documents a day with more than 1 million regular customers.

On November 10, 1999 UPS offered shares of stock to the public for the first time. The IPO (initial public offering) was one of the most successful in history. UPS's continual upgrading and reinventing itself and its mission has led to its being a leading provider of air, ocean, ground, and electronically-monitored delivery services.

Roberto Schmidt/AFP/Getty Images

Think Critically

1. UPS's founder started a business as a teenager. Using what you learned from this case, what do you see as the key to starting up a successful business?
2. What personal traits do you think business owners have in common?

yienkeat/Shutterstock.com

6-1 Business in America

Learning Objectives	Vocabulary
LO 1-1 **Identify** the beginnings of business in America, from farming to the Gilded Age. **LO 1-2** **Discuss** the evolution of business activity in the Twentieth Century.	**barter,** p. 157 **industrialization,** p. 157 **specialization,** p. 157 **mechanization,** p. 158 **productivity,** p. 159 **branding,** p. 159

© Aleksandar Vrzalski/iStockphoto.com

REAL-WORLD FOCUS

Bill has had several jobs as a mechanic. He loves the work, but he really doesn't want to work for someone else. He believes he could provide better customer service if he worked for himself. He already owns his own tools and could work from his garage. He's wondering if he should start his business as a sole proprietorship or if he should start as an LLC or a Subchapter S corporation. His friend Allen suggests he just get started repairing cars and worry about "the rest" later. While Bill is great at fixing cars, he really isn't sure about "the rest."

WORK AS A TEAM Bill has the skills and the desire to own his own business. Is he right to decide up front how to organize the business? What would you suggest he do about "the rest" (such as billing, parts inventory, getting a business license, and so on)?

Celso Pupo/Shutterstock.com

The National Soft Drink Association reports the average person consumes more than six hundred 12-oz. soft drinks each year.

DO YOU THINK the soft drink industry has done a good job of branding their products? Explain your answer.

yienkeat/Shutterstock.com

LO 1-1 From Agriculture to Enterprise

When the United States first began, farming and hunting provided the means of survival. People lived in small villages and worked together to provide for the common good. As the nation grew, it passed through several eras to become what it is today.

The First Era: Colonies

In order to meet needs of food, clothing, and shelter, trading and bartering was a common means of business activity from the early 1600s to the mid 1700s in America. **Barter** is the process of exchanging one product for another. If a family who grew corn and potatoes needed clothing, they would exchange bushels of produce for yards of fabric. Much of what people consumed, they made themselves. What they couldn't make, they bartered or traded, or used what they brought with them from their previous home land. This first wave or era worked well when the country was young. As the nation grew, it soon became apparent that things were going to change. In the mid 1700s, the country entered a new era.

The Second Era: Factories

The industrial revolution in America began in the mid 1700s and flourished through the mid 1800s. A growing population demanded more goods and services. Businesses popped up to meet those needs. People with skills started companies to make and sell products. Many people started working in factories and earning a paycheck.

With a paycheck, citizens could buy what they needed. **Industrialization** is the process of making large quantities of goods and services in factories. People are able to specialize in a small number of tasks, rather than making almost everything they consume. **Specialization** occurs where workers are doing just a few tasks and learning to do them well. This process leads to efficiency and the ability to make more and better products at a lower cost.

Lucian Coman/Shutterstock.com

In some factories, garments are sewn by individuals and in other factories garments are made on a production line.

As people left their homes to work for businesses, cities began to grow and society evolved. This evolution allowed people to do what they did well and earn money doing it. With the money, people could buy the things they still needed.

The Third Era: The Gilded Age

The new industrial age brought with it strong profit and growth incentives. Often dubbed "The Gilded Age," many strong leaders emerged to build new businesses and create great wealth. After the Civil War and until about 1917, the U.S. economy grew at the fastest rate in history. New towns were formed and super-rich industrialists were created. Examples of well known entrepreneurs of the era include Cornelius Vanderbilt, Andrew Carnegie, John Jacob Astor, John D. Rockefeller, Andrew Mellon, and J.P. Morgan.

Nancy Kennedy/Shutterstock.com

The Vanderbilt Mansion, which is a historic site, is located in Hyde Park, NY. It stands as an example of the changes that took place in America in the years after the Civil War.

Called "robber barons" by critics, the wealthy of this period also were creative. They provided new products and services, from transportation to communication. Many immigrants were hired, urban life was created and sustained, and business was transformed. These industrial titans raised the overall standard of living in the entire country. It should not be surprising that they enjoyed the benefits of their own efforts.

These wealthy barons built mansions and enormous buildings to reflect success and affluence. These business owners also dominated markets and put competitors out of business. They controlled prices and workers, and in many cases, did great damage to the environment along the way.

CHECKPOINT

Why did America move from bartering and trading into an economy based on specialization?

LO 1-2 The Twentieth Century

The new century began with a bang in America. Increased **mechanization,** the use of tools and machines, made it possible to make more, better, and cheaper products. Workers progressed from hand laborers to semi-skilled workers. Careers in farming gave way to skilled workers using machines, middle managers, and white collar jobs. While farming and agriculture were still important businesses, many workers were looking for ways to support their families working in the factories, mills, and growing industries. By mid-century, large numbers of people were seeking a college education or other vocational training. Most notably, women began entering the job market in large numbers, changing the business world in major ways.

The Fourth Era: Mass Production

Business in the early 1900s focused on the ways to increase productivity. **Productivity** is the value of outputs compared to the cost of inputs. As outputs (what you can produce) go up, while the cost of labor and materials doesn't increase as fast, productivity grows.

In 1913, Henry Ford introduced the assembly line which quickly changed the way America made its products. For the first time, the average consumer would be able to buy a car. During this era, business focused on efficiency, without much thought toward what consumers might want or prefer. For example, if someone wanted a car, the choice of colors was black, black, or black. Still, it was an era of wonder. New products were making their ways into the lives of common Americans. The middle class grew in numbers and importance.

© Bettmann/CORBIS

A Model-T Ford is coming off the assembly line in 1927.

The Fifth Era: Consumerism

Following World War II (1945), it became clear that businesses had to think more about what consumers wanted and how to meet those demands. The country was growing, and people were buying things to enhance the quality of their lives. But it wasn't business as usual. The new era required that businesses rethink how they would use their resources to make profits. Product branding and differentiation had begun. **Branding** gives recognition that leads to customer loyalty. Brand names gained recognition, from Coca-Cola to Chevrolet. People saw their quality of life increase greatly. They worked and enjoyed new, faster, better ways of getting things done. This era continued until the late 1970s when a new age began—the information age.

The Sixth Era: Information

The late 1970s brought a marvelous (and world-changing) invention into American households. It was a new day that began with an Atari and the TRS 80 personal computer. These original technologies were simple and limited in power and scope, but the computer gaming era had also begun. Within a short time, most Americans had welcomed computer technology into their homes.

The information age is characterized more with building *relationships*. Businesses that will thrive in the future will predict what consumers want now and what they will want in the future. Businesses will "re-invent" themselves to meet those changing and emerging needs.

As the U.S. moves from the information age into the new era that will soon follow, citizens must wonder what the new business environment will be like in the future. One thing seems sure: jobs, lives, products, and businesses will continue to evolve and change. Those individuals and businesses that can adapt and be proactive will be in a position to thrive. Those who ignore or resist change will not prosper.

CHECKPOINT

What is the relationship between entrepreneurship and the free market system?

ETHICS in Action!

Business and Social Responsibility

Businesses make profits because they sell goods and services to consumers. It is arguably the number one job of companies to increase investor wealth. At the same time, do businesses have social responsibilities to the citizens, neighborhoods, and towns which support them?

Social responsibility refers to doing the right thing, ethically, to support and care for the community that you serve. When a business does more harm than good, should they be held accountable for the damage they cause? For example, assume a company comes into a local area and manufactures a product to sell. They hire local workers and help the local economy. In the process of making the product, they dump pollutants into the air and water surrounding the company. As a result, people who live close to the plant are harmed. This is known as a *negative externality*, which is an unintended but direct consequence of the business.

Think Critically

1. **Should the business be held accountable for injuries suffered by local residents?**
2. **What would you do if you were a consumer? The business owner?**
3. **What responsibilities do businesses have to the communities that support them?**

6-1 Assessment

Key Concepts

LO 1-1 1. What is meant by bartering?

LO 1-1 2. How did industrialization lead to a better lifestyle for workers and their families (working away from home)?

LO 1-2 3. How does productivity measure efficiency in a nation?

LO 1-1, 1-2 4. List and briefly describe each of the six eras that the American economy has passed through.

Think About It

LO 1-1 5. Urbanization is the creation of cities. Many people moved from farms and farming to work for an employer in a city. Discuss how this can be both good and bad for a country and its society.

LO 1-1 6. How does specialization lead to greater efficiency (higher output at a lower cost)? Why is efficiency important?

LO 1-1 7. In the Gilded Age, there were no personal income taxes. Property taxes were also absent or very low. Most of the mansions built during the Gilded Age now belong to government agencies and are open to the public. Explain why these residences are no longer held privately.

Make Academic Connections

LO 1-1 8. **HISTORY** The Gilded Age also brought government laws, such as antitrust (1898) to control the size and domination of companies in the market. Research the Gilded Age, and write a paper describing the era. Include a discussion of how new laws to regulate business and protect consumers created more balance in the economy.

LO 1-2 9. **SOCIAL STUDIES** The generation born between 1946 and 1964, the age of consumerism, is called the Baby Boomers. Interview two or three "Boomers". Ask them how the economy has changed since they were young. Present an oral report of your findings about what they said. Explain why the average standard of living increased dramatically during this time period.

LO 1-2 10. **TECHNOLOGY** Today's marketplace is consumed with technology. Prepare a poster board, timeline, or other graphic display to show how technology has enhanced your life. Include the technological improvements you have experienced in the last several years.

Teamwork

LO 1-1 11. Prepare a biographical sketch of one of the super-rich industrialists and financiers who prospered in the Gilded Age, such as John D. Rockefeller, Henry Rogers, or Andrew Carnegie, and present it to the class, sharing both the positive and negative aspects of life and career.

Unit 3 Project: Going into Business

TIMELINE OF BUSINESS DEVELOPMENT FROM 1776 Prepare a timeline of business development events since this country was formed to present day. Include major events, such as wars, new laws that were passed, constitutional amendments, presidential elections, transportation systems, inventions, and discoveries. Do research online and through personal interviews, history books, and other sources. Your timeline can be an electronic display or a poster board. Use pictures, diagrams, and graphic displays.

6-2 Proprietorships in America

Learning Objectives

LO 2-1 **List and explain** the advantages of the proprietorship form of business ownership.

LO 2-2 **List and explain** the disadvantages of proprietorships.

LO 2-3 **Describe** the advantages of a limited liability company.

LO 2-4 **Describe** the disadvantages of a limited liability company.

Vocabulary

sole proprietorship, p. 163
business tax deduction, p. 163
business license, p. 164
unlimited liability, p. 165
collateral, p. 165
limited liability company (LLC), p. 166

REAL-WORLD FOCUS

Mackenzie works at her parents' ice cream store. The business is organized as a proprietorship. When a customer slipped and fell in the store last year, the store was liable for her medical costs. The store's liability insurance paid most of the claim, but now Mackenzie's parents are worried about future claims. Recently, she overheard her mother say, "If someone sues us, we could lose more than the business. We could lose our house and our personal bank accounts." Her parents are thinking about selling the business.

WORK AS A TEAM Mackenzie wants to know: Are her parents right? If so, what can they do (other than sell the business)?

© Aleksandar Vrzalski/ iStockphoto.com

Benjamin Haas/Shutterstock.com

A fleet of company vehicles are cars or trucks owned by a company and used for business purposes.

DO YOU THINK a fleet of trucks could be used as collateral?

yienkeat/Shutterstock.com

LO 2-1 Proprietorships: The Good News

When a person decides to go into business, one of the first choices to make is the form of business ownership. This choice affects more than just the initial costs of starting a business. It also affects how the business operates on a daily basis, how taxes are paid, and how profits are divided among owners. Numerically, there are more sole proprietorships than any other form of business ownership. Today, there are more than 20 million proprietorship businesses in America. There are many reasons for the decision to start a business as a sole proprietor.

YinYang/iStockphoto.com

The owner of this flower and garden store carries newly arrived blooming plants into her showroom.

The Owner Is in Control

Most business owners agree: they want to be captain of their own ship. They want to give orders, not take orders. They want to control what goes on in their own business. In a **sole proprietorship**, the business is owned and managed by a single person. That person is accountable to no one except him- or herself. That means the owner makes all the decisions and controls what the company does and does not do.

For many people, pride of ownership is also important. They want to work for themselves. They want to see what they are able to do. They have drive and ambition and it's important to be able to do things their way. To quote one successful entrepreneur:

> "You can make a living working for others. You can make a life working for yourself."

The Owner Keeps the Profits

One of the most important reasons why people go into business for themselves is so they can keep all of the business's income, called *profits*. Thus, all the earnings of the company are the income of the owner.

The Owner Enjoys Tax Advantages

The tax return of the business and the owner appear on the same tax form. In other words, the company does not pay taxes separately from the owner. Instead, all earnings of the business are taxed as income of the owner.

Business owners are allowed to write off expenses for costs that are related to the business. A write-off, or **business tax deduction**, allows business owners a favored tax status. Business deductions lower taxable income. For example, a business owner may use his or her car for business purposes. The business use of that vehicle becomes an expense of the business, which lowers the amount of income that will be taxed.

mangostock/iStockphoto.com

The sole proprietor of a café stands at the pastry counter and showcases her signature desserts.

The Business Is Easy to Set Up

The paperwork and costs of forming a sole proprietorship are very small. No special forms are needed. There are no fees, except for small expenses, such as a business license that may be required in some local areas. A **business license** is a document issued by a local government unit that allows business activities within a certain geographic area. In some cases, the owner must also file paperwork applying for an *assumed business name.* This process allows the owner the right to use a particular name, such as "Bill's Bumper Stickers." Anyone can file and obtain these privileges for a small fee.

CHECKPOINT

What tax advantages are available to the owner of a proprietorship?

Black-Owned Businesses in America

You're the ENTREPRENEUR

According to the Census Bureau, black-owned firms are growing faster, both in number and in sales, than companies in America overall. The number of black-owned businesses increased 60% between 2002 and 2007, while sales increased 55% versus 35% for all businesses. The Census Bureau concluded that "black-owned businesses continue to be one of the fastest-growing segments of the economy."

Despite the growth, however, black-owned businesses are less than 10% of all businesses in America. They tend to be smaller, often with fewer than five employees. New York has the greatest number of black-owned businesses, followed by Georgia and Florida. The tough recession of 2008 and 2009 has caused many businesses to fail. At the same time, layoffs have led to an increase in the exit from the corporate world to starting up one's own business, especially among African-Americans. The Census Bureau conducts its business owners survey every five years. It defines a black-owned business as a privately held company in which blacks own at least 51% of the business stock.

Think Critically

1. **Why are black-owned businesses growing in America?**
2. **How can corporate employees move from being an employee to becoming a business owner?**

maukun, Shutterstock

LO 2-2 Proprietorships: The Bad News

There are also some negative things about proprietorships to consider. Business owners must think about these things before deciding that a sole proprietorship is the best way to form their business.

The Owner Is Liable

The business owner has total liability for what the business does. The debts of the business are the debts of its owners. If the business fails, the owner is responsible. If the business gets sued, the owner will also have to pay. This type of situation is known as **unlimited liability**, which means as a proprietor your assets (even your car and your home) are at risk.

The Owner Has Limited Resources

The financial resources of the owner and the business are the same. Thus, it can be hard to pay for growth. Banks will not lend money to business owners when the risk is high. Suppliers, called *vendors*, may be hesitant to provide products and supplies on credit. If the owner hires workers, she or he is responsible to pay those wages. The sole proprietor often must rely on resources such as personal bank loans, personal lines of credit, and personal credit cards. Unless the business owner has collateral to lower the risk, these types of loans are hard to get. **Collateral** is assets that have value and can be sold for cash.

visi.stock/Shutterstock.com

A banker points out specific details of a business loan to a woman who is borrowing money to start a sole proprietorship.

The Owner Must Work Hard

The owner of a business often works much longer hours than people who work for wages. The survival of the business depends on it. This heavy *workload* can be discouraging and tiring. But the owner knows extra effort is required for the business to succeed. Due to limited resources, the owner may even be doing work where he or she lacks expertise. For example, the business owner may know a lot about repairing furniture. But she or he may not know how to do a good price quote or how to collect an account. Neglecting these parts of the business could cause the business to suffer.

Lack of Permanence

The sole proprietorship exists only as long as its owner. If the owner dies, retires, or must leave the business, that is the end of the company. Even if the company continues in business (under a new owner), it is then a new proprietorship. Because the success of a proprietorship depends so much on its owner, there often is nothing to sell when the original owner wants to leave. Even a "mom and pop," which is a business where a couple is the proprietor, has nothing to sell when the owners want out of the business. If one owner of a "mom and pop" business dies or leaves the business, it can be difficult for the other one to carry on.

CHECKPOINT

What is meant by "unlimited liability" of the owners or proprietors?

LO 2-3 The LLC: Good News

The **limited liability company** (LLC) is a relatively new form of business ownership. It creates a sole proprietorship without unlimited liability. The LLC is not a corporation, nor is it a partnership. It is formed by filing a document with the state called "articles of organization." This procedure requires the owner(s) to write up an operating agreement and pay a filing fee. The process may sound simple, but it usually means a lot of time reading and studying whether or not it is something worth the time, trouble, and cost.

biffspandex/iStockphoto.com

Five owners of a new start-up LLC pose for a snapshot that will accompany an article about their business in the local newspaper.

Limited Liability

Unlike a sole proprietorship, all owners of the LLC have *limited liability*. That means the owners' personal assets are not at risk. If the company is sued, owners do not incur personal liability to pay those debts. This possibility of a lawsuit is the primary reason most individuals consider the LLC over a simple sole proprietorship. It may well be worth the paperwork, time, and cost of setting up the business.

Tax Advantages

Like the sole proprietorship, the owners pay taxes on income they receive from the business. There is no separate tax on the business itself. This type of organization eliminates any "double taxation" where the business pays income tax and then the owners pay income tax on the same amount of income.

Simplicity of Operation

LLCs operate just like a sole proprietorship. They do not have to hold special meetings or meet paperwork requirements like corporations.

Flexible Ownership

LLCs can have any number of owners—not just a single person or a couple. Owners can even be foreign investors or other companies, making it different from corporations and sole proprietors.

CHECKPOINT

What is the main reason why entrepreneurs consider LLCs over sole proprietorships?

LO 2-4 The LLC: Bad News

Of course, there are always two sides to every coin. LLCs are no exception. There are several significant limitations to the LLC form of ownership.

Complexities Take Time to Understand

The LLC is more complex than sole proprietorship. Owners must read and understand what they are getting into. The time required is well worth it. When owners set up a company correctly in the first place, it is much easier to deal with events that occur later. Understanding the LLC and the decisions to be made up front (like who will be involved) will take time.

Costs Are Higher

Unlike the sole proprietorship, annual franchise taxes (fees) must be paid to the state where the LLC is organized. In addition, setting up an LLC will likely require the services of an attorney or a tax accountant and require an investment of several thousand dollars.

Stephen Coburn/Shutterstock.com

Two men who are starting an LLC meet with their tax accountant to review the plan for their investment.

Restrictions Can Be Confusing

Because LLCs are created in individual states, they also differ by state. In some states, certain businesses cannot form LLCs, such as banks, insurance companies, and nonprofit organizations. There are also significant differences among states in areas such as how ownership interests can be transferred (how one owner can leave the business). While someday there may be a uniform law for LLCs in all states, currently there is no such law.

CHECKPOINT

What is the main reason why entrepreneurs get discouraged with LLCs?

PROFILE

Phil Knight
Co-Founder of Nike

© Mark Peterson/CORBIS

Born in 1938 in Portland, Oregon, Phil Knight's current stake in Nike Corporation gives him an estimated net worth of more than $10 billion, making him one of the richest persons in the world. In 2006, Knight made the largest donation in history (at that time) to Stanford University's School of Business.

It was at Stanford that Knight realized he would be an entrepreneur. In his Small Business class, Knight developed a love for something other than sports—he discovered he was an entrepreneur. Knight recalls in a *Stanford Magazine* article "That class was an 'aha' moment... [my professor] defined the type of person who was an entrepreneur—and I realized he was talking to me." In this same class, Knight learned how to create a business plan.

After graduation with a Masters of Business Administration from Stanford in 1962, Knight visited Japan where he discovered running shoes that were both high in quality and low in cost. Within a year, he partnered with Bill Bowerman (of Eugene, Oregon) to design and sell better running shoes and market them in the United States. Knight's first sales were made out of a now legendary green Plymouth Valiant at track meets across the Northwest.

By 1969, early sales allowed Knight to quit his job as an accountant to work full time at his new company (Blue Ribbon Sports). That name was later changed to *Nike*, named after the Greek winged goddess of victory. Though designed in the U.S., the shoes were manufactured in south-east Asian countries, where factories create jobs. Nike did not own factories but bought products from them.

While Nike started as an idea (a partnership) in 1964, it made a successful IPO (initial public offering) in 1980. During the span of his long entrepreneurial life, Phil Knight has made a large contribution to the athletic shoe industry, made large sums of money, and given money to a diversity of worthy causes, including medical research.

Knight is also known as a philanthropist. *Philanthropy* is the act of giving to charitable organizations for the betterment of mankind. In 2006, Knight donated $105 million to the Stanford Graduate School of Business. In 2008, Knight pledged $100 million to the OHSU (Oregon Health Sciences University) Cancer Institute, the largest gift in the history of the institution. In recognition for the contribution, the university renamed it the OHSU Knight Cancer Institute.

THINK CRITICALLY

1. **Explain how a concept or idea can become the basis of a billion-dollar company.**
2. **Many corporate founders and executives give large sums of money to worthwhile causes. Explain how philanthropy helps the American economy.**

yienkeat/Shutterstock.com

6-2 Assessment

Key Concepts

LO 2-1 1. What are three reasons why people go into business for themselves?

LO 2-2 2. What are three disadvantages of being a sole proprietor?

LO 2-3 3. Why would a sole proprietor consider an LLC form of ownership?

Think About It

LO 2-1 4. Most small business owners like to be in control of their lives including when they go to work and how they work. Business owners do not work less than employees (hired workers). Most owners work considerably more hours than they did as employees. Do you think they feel more or less satisfaction with a harder and longer work day? Why?

LO 2-1, 2-2 5. The U.S. Tax Code has many features that favor businesses, such as the ability to write off expenses. These deductions are available to anyone who owns a business, even a part-time business in addition to one's full-time employment. Does this sound appealing to you? Explain.

Make Academic Connections

LO 2-2 6. **RESEARCH** Proprietors can find it hard to borrow money for the business. Whether they are starting or growing a business, getting resources often means personal credit and using personal assets as collateral. Talk to local small business owners and ask how they got started financially. Prepare an oral report to share your findings.

LO 2-3, 2-4 7. **ETHICS** An LLC offers a major advantage to a proprietor. With limited liability, the proprietor has much less risk in the event the business fails. When businesses fail, employees get laid off. Do businesses have a social responsibility in the community? To their employees?

Teamwork

LO 2-1, 2-2, 2-3, 2-4 8. Consider a small side business that you or a friend could undertake while in school. It could be on weekends or during summer vacation. Describe the activity, its costs, and how much money you might be able to make. How long would it take you to set up your business? From whom would you need help getting started? Prepare a presentation explaining your business to a person who would lend you money to get started.

LO 2-1, 2-2, 2-3, 2-4 9. Do Internet research about proprietorships and LLCs. Write a paper about how many there are today compared to ten years ago. Explain what's good and bad in the economy and advantages or disadvantages of going into business today. Are there more or less small business start-ups? The Small Business Administration (SBA) is a good place to look for information.

Unit 3 Project: Going into Business

CREATE A BUSINESS Create a new product or service, or a new way to use an existing product or service. Consider possible customers and what needs or wants you would be meeting. Think of creative ways to describe and sell your product or service. Consider emotional as well as rational appeals. Present your idea: (a) prepare a slide show using animation, (b) create a three-minute podcast that includes ideas expressed through music, or (c) demonstrate your idea in a three-minute infomercial.

yienkeat/Shutterstock.com; Chad Baker/Ryan McVay/Photodisc/Getty Images

6-3 Partnerships in America

Learning Objectives

LO 3-1 **Discuss** the characteristics of a general partnership, including advantages and disadvantages.

LO 3-2 **Discuss** the characteristics of a limited partnership.

LO 3-3 **Describe** the concept of a limited liability partnership.

Vocabulary

partnership, p. 171
general partnership, p. 171
partnership agreement, p. 171
limited partnership, p. 174
limited liability, p. 174
limited liability partnership (LLP), p. 175

REAL-WORLD FOCUS

Alice and Bob have a general partnership where both of them work in the business. Alice makes pizzas while Bob works at the counter filling customer orders. They put equal amounts of money into the business and they share the profits equally. Lately, Bob has been thinking it's time to expand the business. He wants to open another pizza place across town. He thinks Alice can run the current store, and he will run the new one. Alice isn't so sure it is a good idea. Sales are good, but she feels that another store is too risky.

WORK AS A TEAM What kinds of issues do Alice and Bob need to talk about? Will they have to revise their partnership agreement? What might their new agreement need to contain? What would happen if Alice decided she no longer wanted to be a general partner?

© Aleksandar Vrzalski/iStockphoto.com

Maxim Petrichuk/Shutterstock.com

Many actors and athletes are part owners in upscale restaurants in cities around the country.

DO YOU THINK a famous person who is a limited partner of a restaurant has daily responsibilities in running the business?

yienkeat/Shutterstock.com

LO 3-1 General Partnerships

When two or more people go into business together as co-owners, it is called a **partnership**. This form of ownership is less common than proprietorships or corporations, but still there are nearly 2.5 million of them in America today. There are three types of partnerships: general, limited, and LLPs.

Manager Rights Are Clear

In a **general partnership**, all partners will help manage the company. They will all share in the profits (or losses) from the business. In America, there is no maximum number of partners in a general partnership. But the most common number of people who are in general partnerships is two people. With just two people, it is really clear who is taking care of what. It is also clear how profits will be split. This split is often a 50/50 split: each partner manages half of the business, and each partner will receive half of the profits.

Manager Duties Are Clear

Partnerships begin with a written agreement. The **partnership agreement** clearly states what each partner has agreed to do. This agreement is drawn up by an attorney or a standard form is used. The agreement covers the basics:

- Name of the company
- Nature of the business
- Length of the agreement (usually perpetual)
- Financial investment of each partner
- Specific duties and responsibilities of each partner
- How profits and losses are shared by partners
- What will happen in the event a partner wishes to leave the partnership
- What will happen if there is a dispute or disagreement between the partners

Advantages of General Partnerships

There are several reasons why people form a business together rather than alone. One significant advantage is that two or more partners can pool their resources, which likely increases the amount of investment available. It also increases the credit ability—each partner brings a credit line to access for the company.

When two people work together, the *workload* is much less on each person. Shared responsibilities and shared tasks also mean that each partner can do the things she or he does best. Many of these skills complete or complement the skills of the other partner.

General partnerships are easy to set up. The basic contract is simple to read and understand. Although it is a legal document, it isn't expensive because it is a standard agreement that is quick to prepare.

Like a proprietorship, the partnership itself does not pay taxes. The partnership does file a tax return, but it is an informational return. In other words, it lists the income and expenses of the business. It divides them between the partners and each partner then reports the income on their tax returns. Thus, like proprietorships, there is no double taxation of earnings.

Figure 6-1 lists how a general partnership agreement would specify rights and duties of general partners. In some cases, partners may contribute more cash but have less responsibility, and yet still share profits 50/50.

Figure 6-1

General Partnership Agreement

Item	Partner	Contribution	Percent
Financial Investment			
	Bill	$30,000	60%
	Rich	$20,000	40%
General Duties			
HR/hiring	Bill	All	100%
Production	Rich	All	100%
Customers	Bill	Half	50%
	Rich	Half	50%
Vendors	Rich	Contracts	80%
	Bill	Verification	20%
Division of Profits (Losses)			
	Bill		50%
	Rich		50%

Two partners discuss with an attorney how to bring a new partner into their business.

Disadvantages of General Partnerships

Like all forms of ownership, general partnerships also have some limitations. Most of these limitations can be cleared up if the partnership agreement is well written. Clearly expressing your intent on the way into an agreement is far more important than trying to figure out what to do on the way out.

The most serious disadvantage is the *unlimited liability* of both general partners. Just like a proprietorship, each partner is fully liable personally for the debts of the partnership. Under *mutual agency*, each partner is 100% liable, even for debts and obligations created by the other partner. In other words, one partner can act on behalf of the other. Both are responsible for each other's debts and obligations. If one partner should have more wealth than the other, that person can lose it all.

In the event there is a dispute, it may be hard for one partner to leave the business. The partnership agreement should address this issue. The partner who wishes to leave must abide with what he or she has agreed to do. If he or she does not, the remaining partner(s) can sue him or her for breach of contract.

Partnerships usually terminate if one partner leaves or a new partner joins. A new partnership is formed, and a new agreement is written. Well-written agreements are crucial to the success of partnerships.

CHECKPOINT

What do all partnerships have in common?

Math CONNECTION

General Partnerships Other Than 50/50 Splits

When a general partnership has two or more owners, the fraction of the business owned by each partner often depends on the amount of money each partner initially invests. To determine the fractional split of a partnership, the fraction for each partner is written

$$\frac{\text{amount invested by one partner}}{\text{total amount invested by all partners}}$$

Jennifer, Tom, and Howard decide to open a business that cleans office spaces. The business was Jennifer's idea and she invested $7,500 to the start-up funds. The two men joined with Jennifer by investing money at the start up. Tom put in $10,000 and Howard added $6,500. What part of the business does each partner own?

SOLUTION

Find the total amount invested.

$7,500	Jennifer's investment
$10,000	Tom's investment
+ $6,500	Howard's investment
$24,000	Total investment

Write a fraction for each owner.

Jennifer $\quad \frac{7{,}500}{24{,}000} = \frac{7{,}500 \div 1{,}500}{24{,}000 \div 1{,}500} = \frac{5}{16}$

Tom $\quad \frac{10{,}000}{24{,}000} = \frac{10{,}000 \div 2{,}000}{24{,}000 \div 2{,}000} = \frac{5}{12}$

Howard $\quad \frac{6{,}500}{24{,}000} = \frac{6{,}500 \div 500}{24{,}000 \div 500} = \frac{13}{48}$

You can check the fractions. Their sum should be 1 to represent 100% ownership.

$$\frac{5}{16} + \frac{5}{12} + \frac{13}{48} = \frac{5 \times 3}{48} + \frac{5 \times 4}{48} + \frac{13}{48} = \frac{15 + 20 + 13}{48} = \frac{48}{48} = 1$$

TRY IT

What part of the business does each partner own? Use addition to check your fractions.

1. Mr. Ferandez invested $125,000. Mrs. Fields invested $325,000. Mrs. Samuels invested $350,000.
2. Craig, Robert, and Evelyn each invested $9,200.
3. Helen invested $2,200. Tina invested $3,500. Michia invested $2,300.

LO 3-2 Limited Partnerships

A **limited partnership** is a business where there is at least one general partner and at least one limited partner. A limited partner is one who contributes money but does not participate fully in the business. The limited partner is entitled to a part of the profits (as stated in the agreement). But the limited partner does not have management or daily responsibilities.

Monkey Business Images/Shutterstock.com

A general partner speaks with a limited partner who is not involved with daily responsibilities of running the business.

Liability Is Different

Limited partners may only contribute money or property. Limited partners may *not* actively manage the company. Because they are not the managers, they will have limited liability. **Limited liability** means they will be held liable for debts or obligations of the company only to the extent of their financial investment in the company. In other words, as long as they do not participate in general management, their personal assets will not be at risk.

Roles Are Different

In a limited partnership, the general partner(s) have the same rights and responsibilities as in the general partnership. They may contribute money, property, and personal services to the partnership. They also have the *full responsibility* for managing the company. They also have the unlimited liability for all of the debts and obligations of the company.

Figure 6-2 illustrates how a limited liability partnership might divide up rights and duties between general and limited partners.

Figure 6-2
Limited Partnership Agreement

Item	Partner	Contribution	Percent
Financial Investment			
	Anna, GP	$10,000	25%
	Lisa, LP	$30,000	75%
General Duties			
	Anna		100%
	Lisa		0%
Division of Profits (Losses)			
	Anna		40%
	Lisa		60%

CHECKPOINT

How much personal liability does a limited partner have?

LO 3-3 Limited Liability Partnerships (LLPs)

Like the limited liability company, the limited liability partnership is a relatively new form of business organization. The **limited liability partnership (LLP)** is an ownership plan that allows general partnerships to provided limited financial liability for general partners.

Advantage to General Partners

The main advantage of an LLP is that it protects *all* partners. Thus all partners can take an active role in managing the business, and all partners will have some form of limited liability.

Liability Protection and Requirements Vary by State

Like the LLC, the LLP is different on a state-by-state basis. The amount of liability protection varies by state. In some states, LLPs offer a "full shield" of protection. This "shield" means that partners have full protection from all claims against the company, unless there is personal negligence or malpractice. Other states provide a "partial shield" from claims. Like the LLC, some states allow certain types of companies to become LLPs but not others. For example, in California only accountants, lawyers, and architects can become LLPs.

CHECKPOINT

What is the main advantage to a limited liability partnership?

Business Partnerships

Investigate Your Local ECONOMY

In your local area there are many partnerships. Some are professional services, such as law and accounting firms. Others may be less obvious, from bakeries to restaurants or hair salons.

Make a list of local businesses that are partnerships. Include the type of product or service they provide. In groups, make appointments to visit and ask questions about the business. Ask how they got started and why they chose a partnership form of business. If they are willing, ask a partner to come speak to your class about the advantages and disadvantages of their business organization.

Try it Out

Be a partner with another student to accomplish a group project. Divide up responsibilities and when the project is finished, evaluate the process. What went well and what were the rough spots? What would you do differently?

6-3 Assessment

Key Concepts

LO 3-1, 3-2 1. How is a general partner different from a limited partner?

LO 3-1 2. What items are contained in a partnership agreement?

LO 3-1 3. List two advantages of a partnership over a proprietorship.

LO 3-1 4. List two disadvantages of a general partnership.

LO 3-2 5. What is a limited partnership? How is it different from a general partnership?

LO 3-3 6. What is the main purpose of the limited liability partnership (LLP)?

Think About It

LO 3-1 7. Going into business with another person has many advantages, such as sharing the workload and sharing the costs. Would you be interested in a partnership to do a temporary business arrangement, such as opening a vending stand for the summer? Why or why not?

LO 3-1 8. In a general partnership, both partners are fully liable for the debts of the business, including debts incurred by the other partner. What are the risks of this type of mutual agency?

Make Academic Connections

LO 3-1 9. **BUSINESS LAW** The partnership agreement controls what will happen if there is a dispute between partners. Agreements must clearly and accurately explain each partner's duties and rights. Do research to answer these questions: How much do you think an agreement should cost? What would you want the agreement to say about a disagreement where one partner wanted to leave the business?

LO 3-2 10. **COMMUNICATION** Write an essay discussing partnerships. Answer these questions: What is the main advantage of a limited partnership? Why would a person invest money only (not do any of the work) into a limited partnership? Why would a person be willing to be a general partner and do all of the work themselves?

LO 3-3 11. **RESEARCH** Look up the LLP laws in your state. Write an outline of the steps, costs, and requirements. Be prepared to explain the results of your study, citing your sources of information.

LO 3-1 12. **MATH** Assume you entered into partnership with your friend. Each of you contributed $5,000 and you had a limited partner who contributed $20,000. Your agreement states you will share profits in proportion to your original investment. If profits are $15,000, how much will go to each of the three partners?

Teamwork

LO 3-1 13. Consider entering into a partnership agreement with another person. Write the outline of your partnership agreement, listing all of the basic items that would be covered in the agreement (name of company, nature of business, and so on).

LO 3-1, 3-2, 3-3 14. Do Internet research about all types of partnerships in America. Are they increasing or decreasing? About how much in revenue do partnerships generate each year? What types of businesses are most likely to enter into partnerships?

LO 3-1, 3-2, 3-3 15. Interview a person who is a partner in a business. Ask what type of partnership it is, what problems have they experienced, what are their future plans, and so on. Ask how they would set up their partnership differently if they had to do it over.

6-4 Corporations in America

Learning Objectives

LO 4-1 **Describe** the four types of corporations, three of which are profit-seeking.

LO 4-2 **Discuss** how corporations are formed and how they operate.

LO 4-3 **List** and define the advantages and disadvantages of the corporate form of organization.

Vocabulary

C corporation, p. 178
dividends, p. 178
S corporation, p. 179
stockholders, p. 180
common stock, p. 180
preferred stock, p. 181

© Aleksandar Vrzalski/iStockphoto.com

REAL-WORLD FOCUS

Fred, Max, and Jim are three brothers who have been farming together as a partnership. Now that their families are growing up, the brothers are considering whether it would be a good idea to become an S corporation. They want the farm to remain a family business. Fred isn't sure he can take the time to learn about corporations. Max feels that it is time to look into the change. Jim is a good farmer, but he doesn't have anything to do with the "business end."

WORK AS A TEAM What things should these partners consider when thinking about becoming an S corporation? Is it a good idea to switch?

Christian Lagerek/Shutterstock.com

Giant pipelines channel oil at the site of this oil refinery.

DO YOU THINK a major oil refinery is registered as a C corporation or an S corporation?

yienkeat/Shutterstock.com

LO 4-1 Types of Corporations

A *corporation* is a legal entity that is most often created under state laws. Unlike a proprietorship or a partnership, a corporation is separate and distinct from its owners. It can legally enter into agreements, own property, and borrow money. It can even sue and be sued. A corporation is a form of ownership that allows for the company to go on long after the original owner has departed. There are three types of profit-seeking corporations: the C corporation, the private corporation, and the S corporation.

nazdravie/iStockphoto.com

The headquarters for the world's largest consumer goods producer, P&G, has been located in Cincinnati, Ohio since 1897.

C Corporations

A **C corporation** is organized to sell stock to the general public. It is the most common type of corporation and what most people think of when they say "corporation." The stock of these companies is sold on the stock markets and stock exchanges. Anyone can buy it, including individuals. Because shares of stock are sold to the public, C corporations are subject to the rules and regulations of the Securities and Exchange Commission (SEC).

The purpose of the SEC, a federal agency, is to protect consumers who purchase stock from publicly traded companies. The SEC requires publicly held companies to publish an annual report and to have audited financial statements. Much information can be found about these companies at their websites and at the SEC website. While numerically C corporations are fewer than proprietorships and partnerships, they do a lion's share of the business in terms of income. Most of the major companies in America are C corporations.

Companies such as Coca-Cola, McDonald's, Microsoft, and Walmart measure their profits in billions of dollars every year. C corporations file income tax returns and pay corporate tax rates on earnings. **Dividends** are returns to owners of the profits earned by the company. Dividends are taxable income to those who receive them. Business and individuals paying taxes on the same money is the concept of "double taxation."

Private Corporations

A *private corporation* is a large business that is closed to public investment. These companies operate like C corporations, but because they do not sell stock to the public, they are not regulated by the SEC, and they do not have to meet specific reporting requirements. They are generally limited in number of shares they can sell. Not all states allow this type of corporation. An example of a large but private corporation is Mars, Incorporated. They make Snickers candy bars and other snack foods.

S Corporations

An **S corporation** is a small business entity that is created under state laws. Most proprietorships or partnerships become an S corporation in order to avoid unlimited liability. An S corporation does not sell stock to the general public, and it is often referred to as a "family business corporation." State laws control what it can and cannot do, what paperwork must be filed, and how often the corporate officers must meet.

One major advantage of the S corporation is that income passes through to owners (the corporation does not pay taxes on earnings). Thus, there is no double taxation. One popular form of S corporation is the PC (professional corporation). A group of lawyers, doctors, engineers, psychiatrists, or other professionals may decide to incorporate. These corporations carry professional malpractice or "errors and omissions" insurance coverage. You would see their designation as, "Miller and Adams, Architects, PC."

Global View

Forms of Business in Spain

Laws about business ownership are different around the world. In Spain there are six forms of business ownership. These forms include sole proprietorships, stock corporations, limited liability companies, workers' partnerships, joint ventures, and branches.

Foreign persons are allowed to start a business in Spain. They are required to have legal capacity to carry on business in their home country. All businesses (including sole proprietorships) must be registered at the Spanish Corporate Registry (Registro Mercantil). There are steps to be followed to set up a business entity which include:

- Registering the company name (getting a certificate issued by the Central Commercial Registry)
- Applying for a CIF (company tax identification code) at the tax office (Delegacion de Hacienda)
- Depositing a minimum amount into a bank account in the company's name
- Filing appropriate paperwork (for a corporation this includes a deed of incorporation, paying a transfer tax, registering with the Corporate Registry, and registering to pay the Spanish Tax on Economic Activity).

Many new businesses require the assistance of a lawyer in order to set up their business in Spain.

Think Critically

1. **Why do countries have different laws that regulate business activities?**
2. **Going into business can be a complicated process. What steps would you take if you decided to open a business in your local area?**

Nonprofit Corporations

Some businesses do not operate for profit. They exist to provide a public service of some type. For example, Boy Scouts of America, United Way, Red Cross, Salvation Army, hospitals, and other types of service groups organize themselves as nonprofits. These corporations do not pay federal or state income taxes. People who donate money or other items to them receive a tax deduction, making it easier for these groups to raise funds. As nonprofits, these organizations file annual reports of receipts and payments. They do not pay dividends. They must keep accurate records and file paperwork to prove and keep their nonprofit status.

CHECKPOINT

Which form of corporation is the most common type for large businesses?

LO 4-2 Forming a Corporation

A corporation is born when the paperwork is filed with the state. The paperwork called *articles of incorporation* contains information about the company, its owners, its purpose, and the stock that will be issued. The person filing the paperwork is called the incorporator. Filing fees are determined by the size of the company. Larger companies pay higher filing fees. The size of the company is measured by the revenue that it will generate. Small S corporation fees are a few hundred dollars. Large C corporations incur fees in the thousands. These fees vary by state.

Each corporation must also have bylaws. *Corporate bylaws* are the basic rules and procedures that govern how the company will operate. Every state has its own bylaws requirements too. Some states are known for their simple forms, inexpensive fees, and low corporate tax rates. These "corporate friendly" states (such as Delaware) end up with a lot of corporate filings.

Golden Pixels LLC/Shutterstock.com

The chairman of the board passes out annual reports to members of the board.

Stockholders Are Owners

Stockholders, or those who buy shares of stock, own corporations. There are two classes of stock—common stock and preferred stock.

COMMON STOCK Those who own **common stock** take the biggest risk. If the company does well, they will likely receive good dividends. If the company does poorly, they will not. If the company goes bankrupt, the common stockholders could lose their stock value. Common stockholders are not personally liable for a corporation's debts. The most they can lose is the value of their stock.

PREFERRED STOCK **Preferred stock** typically has a guaranteed annual dividend. The preferred stockholders get dividends before common stockholders. If there is no dividend in a given year (because there are no profits), in future years the preferred stockholders get their dividends in arrears before common stockholders get dividends. This type of preferred stock is called *cumulative*. In the event a company goes bankrupt, the preferred stockholders are paid before any common stockholders.

NET Bookmark

Access www.cengage.com/school/economics/personalfinance and click on the link for Chapter 6. The Securities and Exchange Commission (SEC) is a federal agency. Visit their website to find information, such as annual filings with the SEC, about publicly held companies. Click on More in the menu along the left side of the screen. Under Filings and Form you can search Company Filings. Choose a corporation you would consider a good investment and gather information about that company. In addition to learning a company's address, operation sites, and entities, much information is available for public viewing. As a potential investor, why would you want or need to know the type of information disclosed by the SEC? How would this information affect your decision to buy stock in this company?

www.cengage.com/school/economics/personalfinance

The Board Makes Decisions

The common stockholders also vote for the board of directors. The *board of directors*, who are holders of common stock, oversee the operation of the company and protect stockholder interests. It is the board of directors who declares dividends that will be paid to stockholders. The board also sets the company's mission, sets objectives, and works with the president and CEO (chief executive officer) who manages the day-to-day operations.

CHECKPOINT

Who elects the board of directors of a corporation?

LO 4-3 The Good and the Bad

Corporations have both advantages and limitations. For the company that will grow to be very large, the corporate form of organization is still the one that has the most advantages relative to its limitations.

Advantages of Corporations

The biggest advantage of corporate ownership is *limited liability*. Owners of stock are not personally liable for debts of the company or its obligations. Their personal assets are protected.

Corporations have *perpetual life*. Corporations will continue to operate as long as they are financially sound and as long as the majority of stockholders want them to continue.

Ownership can be easily transferred. If owners of stock in public corporations wish to sell their stock, they can do so quickly and easily. Stock markets and stock exchanges permit daily transfer of ownership.

Corporations can raise large sums of cash, either through the sale of stock or through borrowing money. This ability to raise large sums of money gives corporations the ability to grow and be very competitive.

Donald R. Swartz/Shutterstock.com

New York City is the home to many corporate headquarters.

Corporations can hire specialized management and the most highly qualified employees. They often offer very attractive salary and benefit packages and are able to keep talented staff.

Disadvantages of Corporations

Corporations are very complex and establishing one can be very expensive. Requirements can be very strict and ongoing costs can be high. In most states, corporations must hold annual meetings of the board of directors and keep accurate minutes to document their decisions.

Corporations are subject to *double taxation.* In other words, the corporation pays taxes on its earnings. Then when it distributes dividends (sharing profits with owners), those dividends are also taxed as income. In other words, the same income is taxed twice.

Corporations are subject to government regulation. C corporations are the most highly regulated. The SEC requires "transparency" in reporting results of operations and current financial position. Failure to comply often results in quick and severe penalties and fines.

Corporations often get very large and complex. Goals of managers may be different from increasing shareholder wealth. When this happens, the owners are not benefiting from their investment as much as they could. Corporations can also be less sensitive to needs of communities and other stakeholders. A *stakeholder* is a person who is affected by acts of the corporation, from employees to customers, vendors, and creditors.

CHECKPOINT

What is meant by double taxation?

6-4 Assessment

Key Concepts

LO 4-1 1. What are three types of profit-seeking corporations?

LO 4-1 2. What is a nonprofit corporation? What does it do?

LO 4-2 3. Why would a small business incorporate as an S corporation?

LO 4-2 4. What are the two classes of stock in a public corporation?

LO 4-3 5. What is meant by "the corporation has perpetual life"?

Think About It

LO 4-2 6. Profit-seeking C corporations are tightly regulated by the SEC (Securities and Exchange Commission). Why does the SEC require that annual reports and audited financial statements be available for the public to see?

LO 4-3 7. Why do profit-seeking C corporations pay dividends to their stockholders? They are not required by law to pay dividends from their earnings, yet most C corporations pay consistent dividends. What is their purpose?

LO 4-1 8. What is the mission of nonprofit corporations? Do you believe they fulfill their mission and deserve their tax-free status? Explain your reasoning and give an example of a nonprofit company that you have studied.

Make Academic Connections

LO 4-1 9. **SOCIAL STUDIES** Corporations affect the lives of people around them. Some people are customers, others work for them. Write an analysis explaining how a stakeholder is different from a stockholder.

LO 4-1 10. **HISTORY** Stocks of public corporations have been traded on stock exchanges for centuries. In the late 1500s, British merchants were experimenting with joint stock companies. The Dutch East India Company was formed in 1602. Explore the historical development of stock exchanges. Prepare a timeline or report describing the evolution.

LO 4-2 11. **ETHICS** The board of directors has a responsibility to common stockholders to protect their interests. What happens when a board of directors turns the other way and allows questionable practices to occur? What can stockholders do about it?

Teamwork

LO 4-2 12. Pick a profit-seeking corporation and study its history for the past 10 years. What kinds of things has the company done to improve and grow? How is it continuing to change and evolve to meet new and changing customer needs?

Unit 3 Project: Going into Business

DISPLAY OF TYPES OF BUSINESS ORGANIZATIONS Create a chart or visual display that lists and explains the pro's and con's of the various types of business organization: proprietorships, LLCs, partnerships, LLPs, and corporations. Use pictures, diagrams, icons, and color to enhance your display. Review the major advantages and disadvantages of each form of business ownership. Include a legend and other map features.

Chapter 6

Summary

6-1 THE EVOLUTION OF BUSINESS IN AMERICA

1. Bartering and trading was the first method of exchange, but as the economy grew, new forms were needed. Factories led to a new industrial age that brought vast changes and improved quality of life. Those who were able to profit from the growth and expansion were able to amass enormous wealth.
2. Mechanization and mass production led to greatly improved lifestyles for all Americans. Consumers took their rightful place in the economy in demanding goods and services. The information age currently drives business.

6-2 THE PROPRIETORSHIP FORM OF OWNERSHIP

3. The sole proprietorship is the most common type of business. The owner keeps the profits and controls the business activity. The owner is also personally responsible for all the debts and has limited resources.
4. The limited liability company (LLC) gives the owner protection from personal liability for business debts. Each state has different laws and the rules can be complex.

6-3 THE PARTNERSHIP FORM OF OWNERSHIP

5. A partnership is two or more people co-owning a business. General partnerships are common, with all partners assuming full debt responsibility. Limited partnerships have general partners and limited partners. The limited partners are not liable for business debts.
6. The limited liability partnership (LLP) gives liability protection to general partners as well as limited partners. State requirements differ and the LLP can be hard to understand.

6-4 THE CORPORATE FORM OF OWNERSHIP

7. Corporations do most of the dollar value of business in this country. The C corporation is the profit-seeking company that sells stock to the general public. It is highly controlled by the SEC. C corporations pay dividends to their stockholders. C corporations pay taxes on earnings and stockholders pay taxes on earnings as well. These tax payments are called double taxation.
8. S corporations are family businesses that are incorporated under state laws. Corporate earnings pass through to individual owners. There is no double taxation. The corporate form of ownership also provides for limited liability for owners. Personal assets are not subject to collection for business debts.
9. Corporations are formed according to state law. Articles of incorporation, along with bylaws, are filed and fees are paid. Common stockholders take the risk of ownership. They elect the board of directors and control the overall direction of the company. Preferred stockholders have a guaranteed rate of return as long as the firm earns a profit.

Chapter 6

Assessment

Vocabulary Review

Match each statement with the term that best defines it.

1. Money paid to shareholders as a share of the profits of a corporation
2. Comparing the value of outputs to the cost of inputs
3. Something of value that can be sold if a debt is not repaid
4. Stock that takes the greatest risk in a corporation
5. Doing one or a few tasks and doing them very well
6. Being responsible fully for your own debts as well as those incurred by your partner
7. People who invest in a company by purchasing stock
8. Trading something you have made or grown for something you need
9. Being personally liable for debts of the business
10. A local requirement for owners to open and run a business
11. Stock that has a guaranteed dividend rate
12. A company that by state law has limited liability for proprietors
13. Use of a recognizable name to sell products
14. A partnership with both general and limited partners
15. A business set up by the owner alone
16. Expenses that can reduce tax liability for business owners
17. A partnership with all general partners
18. Using tools and machinery in the producing of goods
19. A small, family business corporation
20. A publicly traded profit-seeking company
21. Using factories to produce large quantities of products
22. A contract specifying the rights and duties of partners
23. The protection of personal assets from business debts and obligations
24. Two or more people going into business together

Vocabulary

a. barter
b. branding
c. business license
d. business tax deduction
e. C corporation
f. collateral
g. common stock
h. dividends
i. general partnership
j. industrialization
k. limited liability
l. limited liability company
m. limited liability partnership
n. limited partnership
o. mechanization
p. partnership
q. partnership agreement
r. preferred stock
s. productivity
t. S corporation
u. sole proprietorship
v. specialization
w. stockholders
x. unlimited liability

Review Your Knowledge

LO 1-1 **25.** The process of making large quantities of goods and services in factories is
a. mechanization
b. specialization
c. industrialization
d. entrepreneurship

LO 1-1 **26.** Super-rich entrepreneurs were created in which era?
a. The Second Era: Factories
b. The Third Era: The Gilded Age
c. The Fourth Era: Mass Production
d. The Fifth Era: Consumerism

LO 1-2 **27.** The information age is characterized by
a. building relationships
b. mass marketing
c. building factories
d. consumerism

LO 2-1 **28.** The largest (numerically) type of business ownership is
a. C corporations
b. S corporations
c. partnerships
d. proprietorships

LO 2-2 **29.** When a business owner uses his car or house for business, it becomes a(n)
a. business tax deduction
b. business license
c. assumed business name
d. limited liability

LO 3-1 **30.** All partners are equally liable for debts and responsibilities in a
a. limited partnership
b. general partnership
c. LLC
d. LLP

LO 2-2 **31.** One of the biggest disadvantages of proprietorships is the
a. ease of formation of the company
b. division of profits with others
c. workload that is required
d. quick and easy profits

LO 4-1 **32.** Which of these forms of ownership has perpetual life?
a. limited partnership
b. general partnership
c. proprietorship
d. corporation

LO 3-2 **33.** Which of these may *not* participate in managing a business?
a. limited partner
b. general partner
c. sole proprietor
d. all of the above

LO 3-3 **34.** Which of these varies on a state-by-state basis?
a. articles of incorporation
b. LLC
c. LLP
d. all of the above

LO 4-3 **35.** Which of these corporations is highly regulated by the SEC?
a. nonprofit corporations
b. C corporations
c. S corporations
d. private corporations

Digging Deeper with Economics e-Collection

You can set up a corporation in any state, including a state in which you do not do business. Your business may be in Virginia, but you incorporate in Delaware. More than 900,000 businesses have incorporated in Delaware, including more than half of all publicly traded corporations in the U.S. and 63% of the Fortune 500. Access the Gale Economics e-Collection at www.cengage.com/school/economics/personalfinance. Prepare a list of well-known U.S. companies that are incorporated in Delaware. Give three reasons why they have chosen Delaware. Prepare a brochure about the advantages of incorporating in Delaware.

Think About It

LO 1-1 **36.** Business plays an important role in society. Providing quality goods and services at a reasonable price that consumers will buy is not an easy task. What ethical goals should businesses have?

LO 4-2 **37.** Make a list of top technology companies today: Apple, HP, Microsoft, and so on. Describe products they are currently selling to consumers and identify the appeal to consumers. What needs are being met?

LO 2-1, 2-3, 2-4 **38.** Owning your own business is often cited as "the American dream." Would you like to have your own business? Why or why not? Assuming you would like to start your own business, which type of business ownership appeals to you? List the positive features and limitations.

Make Academic Connections

LO 3-1, 3-2 **39. MATH** Assume you and a friend go into business together. You contribute $4,000 and your friend contributes $8,000. You decide that you will share profits in the proportion as your original investment. If profits are $20,000, how much will you receive?

LO 1-1, 1-2 **40. HISTORY** Pick a twenty-year period of time in U.S. history. Research that time, citing your sources. Prepare a presentation describing life in those 20 years. Give facts from both the consumer perspective and the business perspective.

LO 1-1 **41. SOCIAL STUDIES** Research the Gilded Age. Find out what it would have been like to live in that era. Track the life of a wealthy person who made a fortune and describe how he made money. Prepare a visual display of what life would have been like during that time, and how your chosen person lived.

LO 4-2, 4-3 **42. RESEARCH** Pick a well-known profit-seeking C corporation and write a report about its history—the founders, when it started, how it changed over time, and how it is doing today.

LO 4-3 **43. ETHICS** Corporations are criticized when they get so large that they seem to be indifferent to their employees, to the community, or to the environment. Write a paper about a corporation that has been accused of unethical behavior in the marketplace. Explain what they did (or didn't do) and discuss the impact of their actions on their stakeholders.

Extend Your Learning

LO 1-1, 1-2 **44.** Visit a factory or take a virtual tour online. Based on your observations, write a report on how the business uses technology, mechanization, and specialization to make products. How has the process changed over the years?

LO 2-1, 2-2, 2-3, 2-4 **45.** Interview a small business owner. Ask how she or he got started. Ask about the type of ownership he or she chose and how that has worked out. Ask how the company looks for new opportunities and where he or she expects to be in five or ten years. Take notes and prepare a slide presentation of your findings.

LO 4-3 **46.** Study the history of a large international company and find out how it serves the countries it profits from. Does the corporation engage in social responsibility? What are some things it does that shows it cares about its customers and other stakeholders?

mangostock/Shutterstock.com

chapter 7

Business Ownership

yienkeat/Shutterstock.com

MARKETS *in Action!*

Should You Own a Business?

Not everyone has the right personality, skill set, and risk aptitude for self-employment. When you own a business, you are the employer and you are in control.

To decide whether being a business owner is the right career goal for you, ask yourself the following questions:

1. **Am I self-motivated?** Successful business owners are able to get going and do what needs to be done without being told. They are motivated because they like to be in control and they want to succeed.
2. **Do I like people?** Business is all about serving people (customers). If people like you and trust you, they will do business with you.
3. **Am I a leader?** Business owners are able to get others to follow them. They are confident, persuasive, friendly, and passionate.
4. **Do I take responsibility**? Entrepreneurs take charge and follow through. When something goes wrong, they take responsibility and make it right. These actions are important in keeping good customer relations and repeat business.
5. **Am I willing to work hard**? Owners must be willing to work long and often hard hours to meet business goals. They don't expect others to do what they themselves would not do. Owners set the example for their employees.
6. **Can I make decisions**? Owners must make decisions easily and quickly. Sometimes you must make decisions without full information. Sometimes you will make the wrong decision. That's part of being successful—learning from your mistakes—and moving on.
7. **Am I believable**? Others must trust you and believe that you know what you are talking about. You must be able to build trust and nurture long-term relationships with customers, vendors, and creditors.
8. **Am I organized**? Business owners must account for income and expenses. They must pay taxes and understand profitability. These things require complete and accurate records.

How many times did you answer "yes"? For those you said "sometimes," are you willing to put in the time and effort to make them into "yeses"? Of course, you should also be good at what you do, it should come easy for you, and you should enjoy it. If these things are true, you will be paid to have fun!

David Davis/Shutterstock.com

Think Critically

1. What can you do now, while you are still in school, to see if owning your own business would be a good idea for you?
2. Do your parents have their own business, or do you know someone who does? What have you observed about them? Would you be happy with their lifestyle and working hours? Why or why not?

yienkeat/Shutterstock.com

7-1 Own Your Own Business

Learning Objectives	Vocabulary
LO 1-1 Identify the three types of small business and their rights and responsibilities.	**side business,** p. 191
LO 1-2 Describe the three forms of business ownership and explain how they are able to raise money.	**lifestyle business,** p. 192
	startup business, p. 192
	equity financing, p. 192
	debt financing, p. 194
	market research, p. 195
	franchise, p. 197
	royalties, p. 197

© Aleksandar Vrzalski/iStockphoto.com

REAL-WORLD FOCUS

Mary is very artistic and is able to make beautiful seasonal decorations at a low cost. She has been using her garage to make them. She stores them in her attic, and sells them at trade shows during the year. Demand has increased and Mary can sell all she can make. Last year, she took pre-orders and sold her entire stock. This year, she has decided she doesn't need to do shows any longer. Mary feels that she has a good customer base and enough orders to keep her busy. In fact, she's thinking about quitting her full-time job so she can produce more decorations.

WORK AS A TEAM What is the upside for Mary to expand her business and move it from a side business to a lifestyle business? What is the potential downside? What would you do?

Anton Balazh/Shutterstock.com

An artisan uses his woodcarving talent to create handcrafted, unique ladles that people may buy just to have a one-of-a-kind item.

DO YOU THINK creating one-of-a-kind wood carvings is the basis for a side business or a lifestyle business? Explain your answer.

yienkeat/Shutterstock.com

LO 1-1 Types of Small Business

The planning you do before you start a small business will be well worth it in the long run. There are three main types of small business to consider opening: a side business, a lifestyle business, and a business startup. Your choice will help you choose appropriate steps to take to establish and sustain a successful business.

The Side Business

Many people work for others as an employee. At this, their main job, they work full-time. In their spare time, they have a side business. A **side business** is one that is part-time. In a side business, people do something they enjoy and are good at, and the business brings in added income. Many people have some type of hobby or interest. For some people, this activity can lead to a business profit. It may be making specialized jewelry, growing vegetables, building cabinets, fixing cars, making ornaments, taking wedding pictures, giving voice lessons, or any one of thousands of ideas.

Most side businesses start small and stay small. People often think of them as hobbies. They work full-time as employees to have a steady income and benefits. They also work "on the side" doing things they love to do. They may make high quality, specialty goods that are not available in the regular marketplace. Customers buy them because they are unique and a good value. The price charged is reasonable.

Kzenon/Shutterstock.com

A carpenter uses a buzz saw as he builds bookcases for his side business.

Word of mouth is the most common method of getting customers. Satisfied customers tell others about the business, and it grows to a set level of business activity. Owners of a side business do not accept more work than they can do in their available time. The owners may (or may not) have business cards or a company logo. A *company logo* is a design or slogan that identifies a business or its product. Most side businesses have limited growth because the owners have limited time. Sometimes side businesses can develop into a lifestyle business, where you would quit your other job and work full-time using your talent.

Owners of side businesses often use their own homes, garages, and property to conduct business activities, such as making, selling, and servicing products. As property owners, they have the legal right to conduct a side business. They also have responsibilities to neighbors and others in the community. Responsibilities include maintaining safe and environmentally sound practices, obeying local laws, obtaining needed licenses, paying taxes on income earned, and being socially responsible.

A hair stylist washes a client's hair in her own salon.

The Lifestyle Business

For some owners, the business is their full-time job. They have a business that uses their skills and talents, often secured with specialized training and expertise. For example, a dentist may open his or her own practice. A hair stylist may open his or her own shop. An attorney or architect may open a practice that provides services for clients.

This type of business generally does not grow into something bigger that will be sold. It does, however, provide enough income to maintain the owner's lifestyle. A lifestyle business is one where the owner intends to keep the business small. There is income for owners and their families. The business exists for the lifetime of the owner. When the owner retires, the business closes.

A lifestyle business usually requires a specialized office or business space. Some businesses are in people's homes, but mostly, these businesses use rented space in an office building or some other location. A **lifestyle business** often has employees to do specific tasks. Lifestyle business owners have the same rights as those who occupy any commercial or retail space. Their business serves the needs of their customers. As small business owners, responsibilities include meeting contractual agreements, being a responsible business owner, providing safe working conditions for employees and customers, obeying legal regulations, paying taxes, maintaining business licenses and certifications, and providing quality goods or services to customers. People who provide professional services also have ethical responsibilities to their customers and their communities.

The owner does what he or she is trained to do. The expenses are managed to provide income. Lifestyle businesses also have limited growth. The owner rarely takes the business to the next level—a publicly held company.

The Startup Business

A company that starts small but has every intention of growing into a large corporation is a **startup business**. It is a company that will grow until it reaches full maturity. The owner starts with his or her original investment. An idea becomes a reality. A product or idea is sold and the company prospers.

As the company continues to grow, it reaches a point where large sums of cash must be raised. In order to do so, the company must be able to sell stock to the public. This type of funding is called **equity financing**. Those who buy stock in a corporation are its owners. As stockholders, they are entitled to a portion of the profits of the business and a say in how the business is run. Common stockholders are elected to the board of directors who determine the future direction of the company.

A PROFILE

Mark Zuckerberg
Founder of Facebook

AP Photo/Alexander Zemlianichenko

Time magazine's Person of the Year for 2010, Mark Zuckerberg, was chosen because he "connected more than half a billion people and mapped the social relations among them." He created a system of information exchange on the Internet, and many people's lives were changed forever.

Born in 1984 in White Plains, New York, Zuckerberg loved the classics in high school. He went to a private school where he also pursued his love of languages. He attended college at Harvard but dropped out in 2004. He became CEO and President of Facebook and the world's youngest billionaire.

Zuckerberg began using computers and writing software in middle school. He was tutored in programming languages and found a natural love of the subject. He especially loved communication tools and games. In one program he developed, he connected his father's dental office to his home, allowing computers in the office and house to communicate with each other.

Zuckerberg launched Facebook from his dorm room at Harvard in 2004. It soon spread to other schools. Zuckerberg moved to Palo Alto, California (Silicon Valley) and leased a small house that served as his office. In the summer of 2004 Peter Thiel invested in the company. Shortly afterwards, major corporations made offers to buy out Facebook. Turning down the offers, Zuckerberg said, "It's not about the money...the most important thing is to create an open information flow for people."

In 2010, more than 500 million people were using Facebook, and the rest is history. In 2010, *Vanity Fair* magazine named Zuckerberg No. 1 on its 2010 list of the Top 100 "most influential people of the information age." Also in 2010, a movie, *The Social Network*, launched depicting the founding of Facebook and the life of Zuckerberg. In 2012, Facebook prepared for its IPO (initial public offering) to raise more capital.

Think Critically

1. **What type of business enterprise was launched by Zuckerberg—a side business, a lifestyle business, or a startup business? Why did he choose this form of business?**
2. **How have social networking sites such as Facebook affected your life?**
3. **What type of new business idea can you think of that would be a new and innovative product for the future? Would you be willing to pursue taking your idea from concept to reality?**

yienkeat/Shutterstock.com

As a profit-seeking, public corporation it can also borrow money over a term from 10 to 30 years. Selling corporate bonds is a type of funding called **debt financing**. Those who lend money to the corporation in exchange for corporate bonds are entitled to regular interest payments and eventual repayment of the principal amount. Only corporations are able to generate large sums of cash from the sale of bonds and other forms of debt financing.

The stockholders are separate from the corporation itself. The original owners often have a majority interest and control the company for a time. They also have an *exit strategy*. At some point in the future, the owners will leave the management of the company. The company will carry on with its new owners and managers.

The business startup company is the most risky type of business. Each year, many of these companies fail. But those that do succeed can reap enormous benefits. Figure 7-1 compares the costs, features, and benefits of these three types of small businesses.

Figure 7-1

Comparison of Business Risk and Return

Type of Business	Dollar Investment Needed	Risk to Owner	Time Required by Owner	Likelihood of Business Failure	Potential of Great Wealth
Side	Low	Low	Low	Low	Low
Lifestyle	Medium	Medium	High	Medium	Low
Startup	High	High	High	High	High

CHECKPOINT

How is a side business different from a lifestyle business?

LO 1-2 Which Business Venture Is Best?

The next thing prospective owners need to do is decide whether to start a business, buy a business, or buy a franchise. Each choice has advantages and disadvantages.

Start a New Business

For many people, starting a new business is a very attractive option. You can do what you want and make your own decisions. You can decide how many employees to hire, what hours to stay open, and what prices to charge. You get a chance to do something new and unique. You won't be building on someone else's success, but growing a business on your own. To get started, you need a good idea of what you want to do. There are a lot of details to work out.

TYPE OF BUSINESS You may wish to start a *service business* where you provide some type of service directly to consumers. Service businesses include mowing lawns, repairing equipment, giving legal advice, cutting hair, grooming pets, doing tax returns, and so on. Numerically, there are more service businesses than any other type. To be successful, your business must provide a better or similar service to your competitors, at a similar or lower price.

A *retail business* buys products, adds a markup, and sells them to consumers. Retail businesses include grocery stores, clothing stores, department stores, toy stores, hardware stores, and so on. Retailers must be able to buy inventory that will be sold to others. They also need retail space, or a store location where customers can shop. Retail businesses are very competitive. To be successful, you need to know who you will be competing with to sell your products.

A *manufacturing company* makes the products that it sells. Many products are sold to retailers. Manufacturers include companies that make chocolate, tires, machine parts, cars, toys, dolls, and so on.

A *wholesaler* is a business that buys products from manufacturers and resells them to retailers and other customers (such as governments or consumers). New products are made and sold each year. Some become an instant success. Others do not.

Vladimir Melnik/Shutterstock.com

Equipment is shown that is used to manufacture auto tires.

PRODUCTS TO OFFER You need to decide what will make up your product line. Many businesses do **market research**, which is a study to find out what consumers will buy and what price they are willing to pay. Your choice of products offered, called the *marketing mix*, is crucial to business success.

PRICES TO CHARGE If your prices are too high, you won't be able to sell your products. If your prices are too low, you won't make a profit. Choosing the right price can be difficult. When there are already businesses selling what you will be selling, a *target price* involves setting your price at or below that of your competitors. If you can't produce and offer it at the target price, then you won't be able to sell that product.

DISADVANTAGES OF STARTING A COMPANY Starting your own company can be risky. It is hard to predict demand. There is no certainty that your products will sell. New businesses are the most risky because there is no customer base or level of ongoing activity. All customers are new customers.

Even in the best of times, success is not guaranteed. Economic conditions may change. Consumer tastes may change. The business location may not be good. Prices may be too high. A competitor may offer a better or cheaper product. Government regulations can make it difficult for a business to get started. For example, a new business may need to install walkways. Local governments may require special assessments, fees, permits, and inspections. These requirements often take long periods of time, require legal fees, and can be costly. There are many possible reasons for failure.

Buy an Existing Business

There are several reasons why buying an existing business can be a good option. One reason is that the business already has an existing customer base. Certainly you have to build on that *goodwill*, or customer loyalty base. Looking at records, a new owner can also see the history of revenues and expenses. This research removes much of the risk of buying a business.

You also will be buying the equipment and supplies. You won't have to start from scratch. You can fine tune the existing business rather than building a new one. You can learn from mistakes of the previous owner and move forward with confidence.

Many previous owners are willing to help finance the sale of an existing business. You can make a down payment and pay the rest directly to the owner on a contract of sale. If you need bank or lender financing, it is easier to get loans based on the proven record of an existing business.

HOW TO BUY AN EXISTING BUSINESS Buying an existing business can be a long and difficult process. First you must do your research. Consider the following:

- Is the business in the right location?
- Is it the right kind of business for you (does it match your skills and interests)?
- Is it properly priced?
- Does it have the right hours of operation?
- What kind of financing is available?
- Will the business meet your income expectations?

Once the business passes the initial research phase, you must then begin a negotiation process. Dealing directly with the owner may be possible. Or you may need to work through a commercial real estate broker. You also need to verify information, including suppliers, underlying mortgage, any pending legal actions, and so on. You may need the services of an attorney and/or an accountant to verify accuracy. The buying process can take several months to complete.

WendellandCarolyn/iStockphoto.com

Along the main street in this town, one business has closed its doors, but the retail space is available to purchase or lease by another business owner.

DISADVANTAGES OF AN EXISTING BUSINESS You will be paying for another person's business, including inventory, location, and goodwill. Many businesses are for sale because they are not profitable. Thus, you will have to figure out what is wrong and how to fix it. The business may have a poor reputation, difficulty with suppliers, or a poor location. Some of these obstacles may be challenging to overcome. You will need money to get started. Buying an existing business will require cash and credit. You may have to start with a very small business.

Buy a Franchise

Noodles & Company is just one franchise business in the college town of Royal Oak, MI.

RiverNorthPhotography/iStockphoto.com

A **franchise** is a legal contract that gives you the right to sell another company's product or service in a geographic area. There are more than 750,000 franchise owners in the U.S., and that number is growing. Franchising is available in almost every field. The U.S. Department of Commerce publishes the *Franchise Opportunities Handbook*. It lists more than 1,400 franchises. The FTC (Federal Trade Commission) also publishes *Buying a Franchise: A Consumer Guide*. These are good sources of information for those who are considering buying a franchise.

Often, the initial cost of running a franchise is significant. The *initial franchise fee* is what you pay for the right to operate a franchise. This fee can run several thousand dollars to a hundred thousand dollars, or more. It is nonrefundable, so if your business fails, you get nothing back. Like starting a new business, you have startup costs. Also you have to pay **royalties**, or regular payments to the franchise owner, usually based on a percentage of your profits. In addition, you are required to pay advertising costs to the franchise company to

Franchises for Sale

Investigate Your Local ECONOMY

In your local area there are many franchises, from restaurants to retail stores. You recognize their products and are willing to buy them because they are consistent from one part of the country to another. To find out if a franchise is available for purchase (to start a new business in your area), you would need to contact the franchisor for information. A good place to start is visiting with a local franchise owner. He or she can put you in contact with the franchisor, or can give you the information you need to get started. You can also check online at the franchise website. Franchise opportunities may be the right move for you.

Try it Out

Make a list of local businesses that are franchises, in the order that they would appeal to you as a potential owner. Include the type of product or service they provide. In groups, make appointments to visit and ask questions about the business. Ask how they got started and why they chose a franchise business.

support television, magazine, and other advertising of the franchise as a whole. Figure 7-2 summarizes the costs of opening a franchise for a sandwich shop.

Figure 7-2
Costs of Franchising

Costs for Initial Year of Business	
Initial franchise fee	$17,500
Annual lease of restaurant space at $2000/month	24,000
Annual lease of restaurant equipment at $1500/month	18,000
Royalty fee (8% of $70,000 profits)	5,600
Advertising contract fee, $200/month	2,400
Total franchising costs	$67,500

When buying a franchise, you have some protections. The FTC's Franchise and Business Opportunity Rule requires that sellers give specific information about the franchise. You learn about the experiences of other franchise owners, including their costs and responsibilities. You also have the financial statements of the franchise company itself. This information helps you decide whether buying the franchise is a good deal.

In South Los Angeles, residents can choose to eat at many franchise restaurants.

ADVANTAGES OF A FRANCHISE You are buying an existing business model. If you have done your research, it will be a solid and profitable business from the start. This success is because your product is well-known nationally with loyal customers. They know what to expect even though they have not been in your specific store. You will receive assistance from the franchise owner, including training, advice on operations, and help with processes and procedures.

DISADVANTAGES OF A FRANCHISE Franchise fees are costly. They reduce your profits, especially in the first year. As a *franchisee*, you have less freedom to make decisions. You must follow the business model, charge prices set by the *franchisor*, and sell only products prepared in a set way. Your business success depends on the success of the franchise as a whole. If another franchisee does something bad, it can affect your business too. Finally, the royalty agreement may allow the franchisor to end your agreement if your store does not provide a set level of profits. Your initial franchise fee is nonrefundable, even if your business fails.

CHECKPOINT

How is a side business different from a lifestyle business?

FreeSoulProduction/Shutterstock.com

Math CONNECTION

Quarterly Franchise Royalty Payments

A franchise royalty fee is calculated as a percent of gross sales. When you own a franchise, part of the agreement signed with the franchisor is that you pay royalties, usually quarterly, so that you can continually use the franchise's branding and benefit from support the main company provides to franchise owners.

As the owner of a Dairy Queen, you pay a 4.5% royalty fee quarterly. Gross sales for the third quarter of a given year are given in the table below. Find the amount of royalties you must pay to the Dairy Queen franchisor for this three month period.

July: \$86,625	**August:** \$111,375	**September:** \$61,875

SOLUTION

Add to find the total gross sales for the third quarter.

\$86,625	July sales
111,375	August sales
+ 61,875	September sales
\$259,875	Total gross sales

Multiply the total gross sales by 4.5% to find the royalty payment for the third quarter.

\$259,875	
× 0.045	Write 4.5% as a decimal.
\$11,694	Round product to the nearest dollar.

Royalty fees due to the franchisor for the third quarter of the year equal \$11,694.

TRY IT

Find royalty payment due, to the nearest dollar, for each quarter's gross sales.

1. Huntington Learning Center – royalty fee of 8%.

April: \$52,679	**May:** \$38,564	**June:** \$18,004

2. Sports Clips – royalty fee of 6%

April: \$22,645	**May:** \$30,662	**June:** \$56,774

7-1 Assessment

Key Concepts

LO 1-1 1. What is meant by a side business? Give examples.

LO 1-1 2. What is a lifestyle business? Give examples.

LO 1-1 3. What is a startup business? How is it different from a lifestyle business?

LO 1-2 4. Why is starting a new business more risky than buying an existing business?

LO 1-2 5. How is buying a franchise similar to buying an existing business?

Think About It

LO 1-1 6. If you were to have your own side business, what might you do? How would you go about setting it up? How much time would you spend on it each week? What kind of responsibilities would you have to your neighbors?

LO 1-1 7. Many people with professional designations and degrees decide to have their own business rather than work for someone else. They set up a lifestyle business. Why do you think they do this? For example, would you expect a doctor who is associated with a large medical group to make more money than a doctor with a sole practice? Why or why not?

Make Academic Connections

LO 1-2 8. **MATH** Go online and visit a franchise website (such as McDonald's or a UPS store). List and total the costs of buying the franchise. Explain how the franchisor earns money from the sale of franchise licenses.

LO 1-2 9. **COMMUNICATION** Small retail stores often have a hard time competing with large chain and department stores. Write a one-page report explaining why small businesses charge higher prices, including their costs of operation, startup, and financing.

LO 1-2 10. **RESEARCH** Search your local papers and commercial real estate listings. Make a list of businesses for sale. Write a paper about your findings: types of businesses, locations, possible reasons for the offering, asking price, financing options, and so on.

Teamwork

LO 1-1 11. As a group, list the large businesses (service, retail, or manufacturing) in your area. Pick one of them and do research about how it was founded and how it grew to its present size. Present a group report to the class.

LO 1-2 12. Do online research about a restaurant franchise in your local area. Prepare a graph or chart that explains the company's service, their profitability nationally, the cost of the franchise, and other information you are able to gather. Conclude whether you believe buying a franchise would be a profitable venture. Explain why or why not.

Unit 3 Project: Going into Business

PREPARE A RESUME As you consider starting a business, you will also have to decide whether you want to have business partners. Compile information about yourself, your training, and your expertise that will support your plan for becoming a business owner. Prepare a resume that you can share with potential business partners that will make both you and the business appealing to investors.

yienkeat/Shutterstock.com, Chad Baker/Ryan McVay/Photodisc/Getty Images

7-2 Prepare a Business Plan

Learning Objectives

LO 2-1 Identify the need for and purposes of a business plan, including rights and responsibilities of a new business.

LO 2-2 List and describe the contents of a business plan, including the expected consequences of business operations.

Vocabulary

business plan, p. 202
financing, p. 202
pro forma statements, p. 205
operations, p. 205
cover letter, p. 206
purpose statement, p. 207
executive summary, p. 207

© Aleksandar Vrzalski/iStockphoto.com

REAL-WORLD FOCUS

Andrea worked as a hair dresser for 15 years. She was a business owner of sorts. She paid rent for use of her station. She bought all of her own supplies. She also shared a percentage of her profits with the owner of the shop. Over the years, she saved her money and decided it was time to go into business for herself. She found a location in a high-traffic area near a mall. She visited her bank's loan officer and was told she needed a business plan. The bank wanted to be sure Andrea knew what she was doing in running the business itself.

WORK AS A TEAM What does Andrea have to gain by owning her own business? Are there risks involved? List things Andrea can do to make a successful transition.

Many companies choose to build office space that is larger than what is needed for their operations so they can lease to other companies to make additional revenue.

DO YOU THINK companies that build large office spaces get financing to pay for the construction?

yienkeat/Shutterstock.com

zebrik/Shutterstock.com

LO 2-1 Why Do You Need a Business Plan?

When you have knowledge and experience in something you can make or sell, you may be ready to think about going into business. You will need a business plan. A **business plan** is a written document that lists all the things you will do to ensure business success. Most lenders require that you have a business plan. It gives them assurance that you will be able to pay back the loan. The plan also helps you. When you outline how your business will work and what you will do to make it successful, it gives you a game plan for success.

The Business Plan Describes Your Goals

In the business plan, you describe what you will produce, how you will produce it, and who will buy it. The plan gives details about who will run the business, including both owner(s) and employee(s). It describes the qualifications, background, and strengths you bring to the business. It explains about how any gaps in knowledge or skills will be met—by hiring or contracting.

The business plan details your strategy to win over and keep customers. It also provides the details of financing the business. It describes how your income will exceed your costs, resulting in profits for the business.

The business plan "talks" to the reader. The reader is someone who will have a vested interest in the success of the company. The business plan details the rights and the responsibilities of the business owner. The information in the business plan is confidential. Only those who need to know should have access to your business plan.

The Business Plan Defines Your Company

A new business needs a business plan for several reasons. One reason is to meet the needs of external users. The most important reason is for the benefit of the owner.

DNY59/iStockphoto.com

YOUR STRATEGY MAP As you write about what you will do and how you will do it, you are able to think about and refine your own ideas. This *strategy map* helps you visualize what to do, the steps to take, and the importance of defining and sticking with the plan.

When you put your ideas into words, the words start to form a plan of action. Sometimes you find that you really don't have enough information. You may need to do more research. You may need to rethink certain aspects of your business. As you prepare the plan, you are thinking through your strategies. You are also discovering your weaknesses and limitations. It's better to recognize your needs and find a way to meet them now, before you actually start business. Planning gives you power to assess and solve problems before they happen.

HELPS YOU GET MONEY Most new businesses need cash. **Financing** refers to the money you need to get your business going and help it stay running. In many cases, you won't have enough money or personal resources to start a business. You need to borrow money, or finance, your business venture. The business plan specifies how borrowed money will be repaid and how investors will receive a share of the profits. A well-written business plan helps convince investors and lenders that your business will be profitable and a good investment choice.

COMMUNICATES YOUR IDEAS The business plan is a communication tool. It is designed to present your plan of action clearly and concisely. Your readers must be convinced that your plan is solid and believable. They also must believe that you are the right person to achieve the plan's objectives. What you say in the plan will convince others to help you or to work with you for joint benefit.

Jason Swarr/Shutterstock.com

Commerical property is sold and land is cleared so that construction can begin.

MANAGEMENT TOOL As you run your business, the business plan serves as your guide. It lays out your goals and objectives. It lists your hurdles and weaknesses. It also provides strategies for making good decisions. It is well thought-out ahead of time so you won't have to do that later. The plan is a vision for the future, one that will require some changes as you go along. It is a solid foundation that gives you good rationale for decisions you will make.

CHECKPOINT

How does the owner benefit from preparing a business plan?

LO 2-2 What Are the Contents of a Business Plan?

The business plan has a number of important sections that contain needed information. External users (those outside your company, such as lenders or investors) will expect to read and understand your plan in five key areas.

1. Introduction

The initial section is called the Introduction. The Introduction provides an overview (summary) of your entire plan of action. It grabs the attention of the readers and tells them the overall focus of your business in a few short but descriptive paragraphs. Filling just one or two pages, the Introduction contains basic information about the following:

BUSINESS DESCRIPTION You describe your business and what you expect to achieve. If it is making a product, you describe (in general terms) the product itself and the need it will fulfill. For a service or retail business, you describe what your business will do. You say how it is unique and different from its competitors. If there are no competitors (a new product), you tell who your customers will be and why they will buy your product. In this first part of the description, you talk about what you will do in the first year, within the short-term. You also briefly describe your medium-term goals (three to five years away), and your long-term goals (how you will succeed five to ten years from now).

NET Bookmark

Access www.cengage.com/school/economics/personalfinance and click on the link for Chapter 7. Visit the Small Business Administration (SBA) website. The website contains information to help people get started buying or building a business. The site includes templates for writing a business plan. It also includes advice about preparing finances, getting a loan, and all types of services available. What are the three types of SBA loans? Write a sentence to describe each type of loan.

www.cengage.com/school/economics/personalfinance

OWNERSHIP AND STRUCTURE This paragraph explains who will own the company and what the ownership structure will be. You may choose to form a proprietorship, a partnership, or a corporation. If you organize a partnership, you also provide information about your partner(s) and what they will contribute to the business. If you start a corporation, you explain who will own shares of stock or will be able to buy shares of stock.

SKILLS, EXPERIENCE, AND STRENGTHS This section describes your ability to successfully run the business. It includes the same information about any partner(s). You also include the background, education, and other qualities of key employees you will hire to work for your business. This section tells readers how your company will use its resources to generate profits.

ADVANTAGES OF YOUR BUSINESS The final paragraph in the Introduction describes what your proposed firm will offer that is unique and will meet needs in the marketplace. Your advantages may include a new design, a quality improvement, or a competitive price with improved features. It tells users why you will be successful and how you will match (and beat) your competition.

2. Marketing Strategy

This section describes the product or service you will offer. It talks about the market where you will operate. It describes the overall industry. And it talks about your location and why it is the best choice.

PRODUCT OR SERVICE You describe in detail the product or service you will offer. This description includes an explanation of how your product or service is unique or different from your competitors. You explain why people will want to buy your product or service. This explanation may include features of the product or what it will do for them (such as save them time or money, improve their health, make them more attractive, and so on).

terrymorris/iStockphoto.com

MARKET The market refers to how your product or service will be bought and sold. It explains your competitive environment. It describes what other products currently exist to meet demand. It talks about how many other businesses currently exist and how they are failing to meet demand.

INDUSTRY The *industry* refers to the overall field of business, such as the grocery industry, the toy industry, or the personal care services field. Each industry has potential for growth based on economic trends. There may also be new technologies that affect all businesses in the industry. This section talks about the industry as a whole and what your research shows is likely to happen.

LOCATION In this section you talk about why you chose a certain location. *Location* refers to the physical spot your business will operate—the area of town, the type of neighborhood, and the vehicle and foot traffic—and how that will be attractive to customers.

3. Financial Plan

The financial section is an outline of your financial needs and how you will meet them. It is a listing of all your projected costs. You will also predict your revenues, and your plans to maintain and grow the business. The three sections you need include risk assessment, financial statements, and funding needs.

RISK ASSESSMENT Lenders will want to know what risks you will face. They want to know the problems you expect, and how you plan to deal with them. This information includes your competition, the economy, prices and costs, and demand for your product.

FINANCIAL STATEMENTS **Pro forma statements** are estimated or budgeted results. These estimates tell a story of what will happen if funding and market conditions work to your favor. You will need to estimate how much money you will make (income statement). You will also need to estimate your financial position (balance sheet) as your operations get started and grow.

PaulaConnelley/iStockphoto.com

As part of starting a business, these owners prepare pro forma statements to prepare to be successful in their business.

FUNDING NEEDS Here, you will state how much money you need to borrow. You will also explain how you will use the money that is borrowed. As a result of the loans, you will then be able to provide a return to those who invested or loaned you money. Loans will often carry a fixed rate, while investments (such as ownership interest) will receive an estimated percentage return on their investment.

4. Operations Management

The term **operations** describes the day-to-day management of the business. It is important to know how you will manage company resources. This knowledge includes items such as your proposed hours of operation, lease or rental agreements, equipment or furnishings you will use, technology you will access, and how you will provide customer service. You describe how the company will operate and what customers can expect to receive.

An excellent place to get help in running your business is the Small Business Development Center (SBDC). Located at community colleges in some states, the SBDC receives funding from the SBA as well as state sources. They help business owners get started and operate successfully. They sponsor free and low-cost classes and workshops in topics such as using Quickbooks (an accounting software program). They also give one-on-one advice.

Another great source of operations help is from SCORE—the Service Corps of Retired Executives. This source is a group of more than 12,000 retired executives. They volunteer their time to give real-world advice to business startups. Advice and counseling are available in all areas, and especially in operations management.

5. Conclusions

Your concluding statement includes a summary of your goals and objectives. It briefly reviews your determination and commitment to the success of the business. It is a forward-looking and optimistic view of the business based on your research, expertise, and assessment of risks and opportunities.

Other Business Plan Essentials

When submitting a business plan for consideration, there are several other items you should include.

COVER LETTER A **cover letter** is a short letter that is included with your business plan. It includes a brief paragraph to the recipient stating that the business plan is enclosed. A second paragraph gives a short summary of the purpose for submitting the business plan. You can also include some brief but important information that would create interest in your plan. The closing paragraph is a courteous phrase such as "Please let me know if you need any further information," and "I look forward to hearing from you." Set up your letter as a standard business letter, with formatting as shown in Figure 7-3.

Figure 7-3
Cover Letter

ERO designs

May 15, 20--

Mr. James Stewart, Finance
First Independent Bank
2340 Wilshire Boulevard
Los Angeles, CA 90200

Dear Mr. Stewart

Enclosed is my business plan, as promised following our meeting today where we discussed funding for my startup venture.

As you will recall, I hope to fully develop the business concept into an online web business. My product line will be manufactured locally and my initial startup costs will run $50,000 for the first 90 days. I have invested $35,000 and have business assets of more then $25,000 as evidenced in the report.

Please let me know if there is any further information you may need. I look forward to hearing from you.

Sincerely

Emily Rogers

Emily Rogers, Owner

ADDITIONAL CONTENT Depending on the formality of your submission, you may consider adding other parts to your business plan. These make the document more formal. They also make it easier to read and to find information quickly.

These additions might include the following:

- Title page
- Table of contents
- Purpose statement
- Executive summary

The **purpose statement** tells the reader in a paragraph or two the exact purpose of the business plan. It may be directed toward the lender, and specifically state the requested loan amount and terms. The **executive summary** is a page-long summary of your entire business plan. It describes the business concept, the projections of profits, the needs, the amount you want to borrow, and other pertinent information. It gives the reader a quick one-page glance at the business plan. The purpose statement and executive summary are important to use when a business plan is long and will require a lot of time to read.

APPENDICES If you make reference to specific documents or data in your report, you can back it up with charts, graphs, documents, and other data. These important pieces of evidence are not a part of the report itself, but support the plan with details. You can include letters of recommendation, licenses, resumes, personal financial statements, and tax returns. You can also include charts and graphs and other visual data to support your position.

CHECKPOINT

List five topics covered in a business plan.

ETHICS *in Action!*

Truthful Applications

Loan applications, and all the supporting documents, should be truthful and forthcoming. Exaggerations, missing information, and untrue statements can lead to wrong decisions. Most lenders will verify information as much as possible, through credit reports and other electronic means.

Knowingly providing false or inaccurate information is unethical. In some cases, it can also be illegal. Knowingly providing false information that causes harm to another is a form of *fraud* and can result in legal penalties. It also can cause a loss of reputation and future difficulty building business relationships.

Think Critically

1. Should the business owner be held accountable for financial injuries caused when an investor loses money based on false representations?
2. Is it acceptable to do something that is technically legal, yet could be viewed as unethical?
3. What responsibilities do business owners have to lenders, investors, and others who are stakeholders in their startup company?

7-2 Assessment

Key Concepts

LO 2-1 1. What is the purpose of a business plan?

LO 2-1 2. List four ways a business plan defines your company.

LO 2-2 3. What are the five main sections of a business plan?

LO 2-2 4. What would be included in an appendix to a business plan?

Think About It

LO 2-1 5. The business plan is a strategy map. It helps owners visualize what the company is about and what it looks like. How does visualizing the company help a new business owner plan for the success of the company?

LO 2-2 6. The Introduction section of the business plan is hard to write. Often it is prepared last, even though it appears first. If you were writing a business plan, where would you begin? What part of the plan would be the most difficult for you to compose?

LO 2-2 7. Businesses fail or succeed within their markets. Explain what is meant by a market. How does a market change over time? What causes people to change their preferences and tastes?

Make Academic Connections

LO 2-2 8. **SOCIAL STUDIES** Business owners work long hard hours to make their business a success. Most business owners believe they work much harder as an owner than they ever did as an employee. Write a paper describing the differences in rights and responsibilities of employees of a company versus the owners of a company.

LO 2-2 9. **COMMUNICATIONS** Do research about how to write a good letter, including the introduction, body, and conclusion. Prepare a sample letter and label its parts. Present a visual display to the class.

Teamwork

LO 2-2 10. As a group, decide on a business idea. Prepare an outline of a business plan. Include the introduction and description of the business in an executive summary. Present the idea to your class, and ask how many would be willing to invest in or lend money to the business.

LO 2-1 11. Contact a local Small Business Development Center and pick up information about the help that is available to small business startups in your area. Prepare a chart or visual display board that includes brochures, sources of information, and names of local organizations (such as the Better Business Bureau or the Chamber of Commerce) that provide assistance or advice.

Unit 3 Project: Going into Business

BUSINESS PLAN INTRODUCTION Download a sample business plan from www.cengage.com/school/economics/personalfinance and analyze the Introduction section. Create an introduction for your business plan, beginning with an outline that identifies the major points to be covered in a three-page document. Describe your company in terms of a proprietorship, partnership, or corporation and how it will be competitive and thrive as a new business enterprise. Submit both the outline and the final draft of the report.

7-3 Succeed in Business

Learning Objectives

LO 3-1 **Explain** why so many new businesses fail each year.

LO 3-2 **Discuss** ways to ensure that your business will survive, including the relevance of an ethics policy.

Vocabulary

capital, p. 210
unexpected growth, p. 210
inventory, p. 210
stock-out, p. 211
unplanned investment, p. 211
price war, p. 211

© Aleksandar Vrzalski/iStockphoto.com

REAL-WORLD FOCUS

Rick and Sheila started a business three years ago. When it failed, they lost their investment. They also were stuck with personal credit card debt. They had used their lines of credit to get the business going. The business failed because of a poor economy. Their product, which sells during good economic times, was in low demand. Without sales, the company was unable to pay its *fixed costs,* such as rent, insurance, and salaries. Rick and Sheila want to try again, but they are not sure what they did wrong so they can do better this time.

WORK AS A TEAM What do you think Rick and Sheila can do to make sure their new business will survive? What would you do if you were in their shoes?

Inventory at this warehouse exceeds the space allotted on shelves to store the boxes.

DO YOU THINK the situation at this warehouse is an example of stock-out or unplanned investment?

Harald Høiland Tjøstheim/Shutterstock.com

yienkeat/Shutterstock.com

LO 3-1 Why Businesses Fail

According to the SBA (Small Business Administration), small business owners have a 50/50 chance of surviving for five years or more. Expert opinions are easy to find describing reasons for this dismal success rate.

Poor Planning

Those who don't take the time up front to make good choices often find themselves unable to deal with unexpected events. Business ownership is a serious commitment, especially in time. The planning phase is crucial. Here is where you learn about pitfalls and how to avoid them.

Insufficient Capital

In the business sense, **capital** means money, credit, and other financial resources. A company that has insufficient capital is unable to meet its obligations. It cannot grow because there isn't enough money for current operations.

© Golden Pixels LLC/Shutterstock.com

An employee takes inventory of ink supplies while working at the print shop.

Poor Location

Where your business is located is very important. A bad location can deprive the business of sufficient customers. If customers cannot get to your business, or if they cannot find it, your business will suffer from lost sales.

Unexpected Growth

Unexpected growth occurs when a business grows too fast. It may seem unlikely, but a business can grow too fast. If the business isn't prepared for the added volume, the owner can actually see expenses rise faster than revenue. For example, paying overtime to employees raises your cost of producing additional products. Your profit shrinks as you make and sell more units.

Some businesses expand too rapidly. Because they have one very successful store, they use the profits to buy another store. But the new store drains the profits and loses enough money that the entire business is no longer profitable. This failure often arises from over-confidence.

Poor Management

Managing the inventory of a business is a key success factor. When inventory is not properly managed, it can cause the business to fail. **Inventory** is an accumulated amount of the product that the company provides for sale. If the business runs out and cannot serve its customers' needs, the business experiences a shortage. A **stock-out** results in dissatisfied customers and lost profits. If a business orders or makes too many goods, then it has an excess. Excess inventory results in inventory build-up which is known as **unplanned investment**. The investment in inventory is not a planned investment. It's a forced investment. Money that could be used for other purposes is tied up in inventory costs. In many cases, inventory loses value over time. It can become obsolete and possibly unsalable.

kropic/iStockphoto.com

Busy streets in New York City may be a sign that the economy is booming.

Changes in the Economy

Successfully starting a business depends largely on the general economy. If economic conditions are favorable, the business can attract customers. However, if the economy declines, people stop buying, and if the business does not have adequate funding to last through the down period, it can fail. The economy may be favorable when the business idea begins, but economic conditions can change in a very short period of time.

Competition

When you make and sell a new product with a high profit potential, you will attract *competition*. Existing and new businesses may start offering the same product or service at a lower price. A **price war** occurs when businesses keep lowering prices in order to sell goods. Soon the price is so low there are no profits. A new business cannot survive or grow without profits.

Lack of Ethics

When customers, vendors, regulators, and others believe that a business is acting unethically, a bad public image can emerge. Once people believe a business cannot be trusted, the word spreads rapidly. A business with a bad reputation often finds itself unable to keep customers or attract new ones. Ultimately, lack of ethics can lead to business failure. At a minimum, a lack of ethics causes low morale and conflict, both internally and externally.

CHECKPOINT

What are three reasons why businesses fail?

3-2 How Businesses Succeed

Businesses that succeed seem to have several qualities in common. Those who decide to own their own business should study the reasons why business survive and thrive, even in tough economic times.

Realistic Planning

It all begins with a clear understanding of what you can expect. Plans should not be overly optimistic. Nor should they be overly pessimistic. *Realism* is the ability to see things as they are—both the good and the bad. When you are able to understand what can go wrong, you can then take action to prevent it or to lessen its impact. Do your research up front so you will know what to expect, what questions to ask, and what you can realistically expect.

Advice and Support

Consult experts and get advice from people who can help. For example, Small Business Development Centers (sponsored by the SBA) have programs to help new owners. SCORE executives give advice, counseling, and support. Getting advice early and often can make the difference. Good advice will help you find out what to do before it's too late.

Timing Is Everything

The best business idea can fail. Sometimes what seems like the worst idea can succeed. In many cases, it's being in the right place at the right time. This means understanding the economy and being able to predict what is going to happen next. There are times you should not go into business, even with a great idea.

Digital Vision/Getty Images

A company's board of directors meets to review and modify the business plan.

How Can You Protect Your Business Idea?

When you have an idea that could lead to a successful product, you must take action quickly. Sometimes that means talking to people who can help you turn your ideas into reality. You may need to build a prototype, find the right company who will buy your product, or get a patent, trademark, or copyright.

A *patent* for an invention is the grant of a property right to the inventor, used by the Patent and Trademark Office. It is good for 20 years from the date of the application. The right is to "exclude others from making, using, offering for sale, or selling an invention in the United States or from importing the invention into the United States."

A *trademark* is a word, name, symbol, or device used for a product that indicates its source and distinguishes it from others. A *servicemark* is the same except it identifies the source of a service rather than a product. Trademark rights prevent others from using a similar mark. Such protection occurs when a trademark is registered with the Patent and Trademark Office. A *copyright* is a form of protection provide for authors of "original works of authorship" including literary, dramatic, musical, artistic, and certain other intellectual work, both published and unpublished. The copyright protects the form of expression rather than the subject matter. Copyrights are registered by the Copyright Office of the Library of Congress.

The United States Patent and Trademark Office is an agency of the Department of Commerce. You can get assistance and learn about the steps to take when you have an idea or invention to protect. You can also learn about intellectual property (IP) laws, how they benefit you, and your rights as an inventor.

Think Critically

1. **How many patents, trademarks, servicemarks, and copyrights can you name? How can you identify a name or other distinguishing mark as belonging to a company or person?**
2. **Why is it important to obtain legal protections afforded by patents, trademarks, and copyrights?**

Updated and Modified Business Plan

As time goes by, you may need to revise and update your business plan. Companies need to be able to reinvent themselves—right from the start. This flexibility allows you to remain competitive, even when things change. Companies that thrive are those that stay at the forefront of change. They anticipate it and they redefine their mission as they go along. Thus the business plan is really a *work in progress*. It changes as the market changes.

Statement of Ethical Standards

An *ethics policy* is a standard of ethical conduct that is endorsed by a company. It sets out expectations and defines ethical behavior that is acceptable for internal processes, as well as external dealings. Successful companies set ethical goals as a part of their social responsibility. A company's *code of conduct* can often be found at its website. For example, General Mills Corporation's Code of Conduct begins, "General Mills' global reputation as an ethical company depends on each employee always acting consistent with the law, our policies, and our values." Their Champion's Code of Conduct is a 17-page document, available online at their website.

CHECKPOINT

What are three reasons why businesses succeed?

Global View

Funding New Businesses in China

The ChiNext stock exchange, which began operating in October, 2009, was designed for startup companies. Chase Sun Pharmaceutical was the first to sell shares to the public, bringing in more than $113 million when the exchange first opened.

According to *BusinessWeek* magazine, government regulators created ChiNext, which operates as a part of the Shenzhen exchange, to make it easier for small companies in "strategically important and emerging industries" to gain access to China's vast pool of savings. Today, more than 141 stocks trade on ChiNext. Since the exchange opened, 135 companies have raised $15 billion through initial public offerings (IPOs).

Fostering growth of small companies is part of Beijing's effort to reduce China's reliance on export of basic manufacturing goods. The goal is to create higher-value goods and services, from pharmaceuticals to automobiles. Twenty years after stock trading began in Shanghai, China's markets are booming. Chinese companies have a combined market value of over $4 trillion.

Regulators hope that ChiNext will encourage investment from private sources and venture capital firms. It should encourage new and emerging companies to go public. According to financial experts, ChiNext is helping China release the Chinese passion for innovation and entrepreneurship. It gives new products and ideas a chance, even when they are invented by ordinary people.

fotorav/iStockphoto.com

Beijing's business district is home to offices and apartment buildings.

Think Critically

1. **Why does China want to help new ideas get funding through IPOs?**
2. **Does the Chinese model sound like an idea that would work in the U.S.? Why or why not?**

7-3 Assessment

Key Concepts

LO 3-1 1. Give three reasons why businesses fail.

LO 3-1 2. Explain how poor inventory management can lead to business failure.

LO 3-2 3. Give three ways to help a business succeed.

Think About It

LO 3-1 4. Why is initial planning so important? Identify two pitfalls that small business owners can avoid by careful planning. Explain.

LO 3-1 5. Small business owners often must use personal assets, cash, and lines of credit (such as credit cards) to get started and keep their business going. When the business is in a tight spot, it is even harder to get loans. This situation can lead to business failure because the business owner cannot get cash or credit. How can small businesses avoid this dilemma?

Make Academic Connections

LO 3-1 6. **ECONOMICS** When the economy is in a downturn, people are spending less. Entrepreneurs who try to start a new business often fail in these times, even when the idea is a good one. It isn't the right place at the right time. Explain what prospective business owners can do to lessen this risk of business failure.

LO 3-2 7. **ETHICS** When you do the right thing, you are acting ethically. There may not be a legal requirement to do the right thing, but consider what it would be like if everyone acted unethically. Who could you trust? Write a statement that describes your own ethical standards. Write a second statement that you believe would be an ideal standard for a company that you do business with.

Teamwork

LO 3-2 9. Do online research and find expert opinions (from economists and business leaders) explaining why many businesses have failed in the last year. Prepare an oral report explaining what kinds of businesses have failed and reported reasons for their failures.

LO 3-2 10. Businesses that succeed most often have a good location. Pick three businesses: a service business, a retail business, and a manufacturing business. Prepare a detailed description of each business's location and explain how each location adds to the business's success.

Unit 3 Project: Going into Business

BUSINESS PLAN REQUIREMENTS Explore the contents of an entire business plan. Consider information, sources of the information, and types of data that would need to appear in the report. The purpose of the business plan is to secure financing. Prepare a PowerPoint presentation that describes the requirements you expect from a person submitting a business plan. Assume you are an individual investor or you represent a financial institution that loans money for business startups. Explain how you would evaluate the business plan and decide whether to lend the new entrepreneurs money.

yienkeat/Shutterstock.com, Chad Baker/Ryan McVay/Photodisc/Getty Images

Chapter 7

Summary

7-1 OWN YOUR OWN BUSINESS

1. Three types of small businesses include a side business, a lifestyle business, and a startup business. The side business is in addition to regular, full-time employment. It is a source of earnings that supplement the owner's primary income. The lifestyle business is a full-time job, but will not grow beyond a family business size. The startup business is designed to grow into a full corporation with an exit plan for the original owner(s).
2. New business owners can start a new business, buy an existing business, or buy a franchise. Starting your own business is the most risky because you don't have an established customer base. Buying an existing business requires good research about location, price, financing, and hours of operation. Buying a franchise can be expensive, but comes with known products and established markets.

7-2 PREPARE A BUSINESS PLAN

3. The business plan is your business concept in writing. It describes goals and defines how your company will succeed. It helps you obtain needed financing, communicate your ideas, and provides a management tool.
4. The business plan has five major sections: the business description, the marketing strategy, the financial plan, the operations management, and the conclusions. It helps prospective lenders and owners understand your plan of action and decide whether they will work with you.
5. The plan includes a cover letter and additional content as needed. This content may include a title page, table of contents, purpose statement, and executive summary. The purpose statement is a brief and directed statement toward a specific user of the business plan. The executive summary is a page-long synopsis of the entire business plan. Appendices may be used to support the document with evidence of success factors.

7-3 SUCCEED IN BUSINESS

6. Businesses fail due to poor planning, insufficient financial resources, poor location, unexpected growth, poor management, changes in the economy, and competition. One or more of these conditions can cause the business owner to be unable to continue in business.
7. Business owners can reduce their chances of failure by doing realistic up-front planning, and getting good advice from those who have had experience starting and running a business. New owners must understand the importance of timing—introducing their company, product, or service at the right time. They also need to keep their business plan updated as they go along and use it as a tool for achieving their goals.

Chapter 7

Assessment

Vocabulary Review

Match each statement with the term that best defines it.

1. Payments to franchisors from profits of their franchisees
2. A brief letter that is submitted with a business plan
3. A dangerous practice of lowering prices to increase sales
4. An overview or summary of the entire business plan
5. A business that will grow into a corporation with unlimited growth
6. A written document that details how a business will succeed
7. What happens when you make or buy too few goods to sell
8. Money you need to pay for a business to start and to grow
9. A condition that causes failure when costs rise faster than revenues
10. Goods that are kept on hand to sell to customers
11. A budgeted or expected statement of financial results
12. Money, credit, or other resources used to finance a business
13. A family-type business that will remain small
14. A condition that results when you have excess inventory that is not sold
15. How goods and services are bought and sold
16. A legal contract giving you the right to sell another company's product or service
17. A study to find out what consumers will buy
18. Money that is raised from selling ownership interest in a business
19. The day-to-day managing of a company's business
20. A paragraph that explains the exact purpose of a business plan
21. A part-time business that a person has in addition to their regular job

Vocabulary

a. business plan
b. capital
c. cover letter
d. debt financing
e. equity financing
f. executive summary
g. financing
h. franchise
i. inventory
j. lifestyle business
k. market research
l. operations
m. price war
n. pro forma statements
o. purpose statement
p. royalties
q. stock-out
r. side business
s. startup business
t. unplanned investment
u. unexpected growth

Review Your Knowledge

LO 1-1 22. Which of these is a part-time enterprise in addition to your full-time job?
a. lifestyle business
b. side business
c. startup business
d. franchise

LO 1-1 23. Which type of business will become a publicly held corporation?
a. lifestyle business
b. side business
c. startup business
d. franchise

LO 1-1 24. Which type of business has the highest risk of failure?
a. lifestyle business
b. side business
c. startup business
d. franchise

LO 1-2 25. A plan for an original owner to leave managing a company is
a. equity financing
b. exit strategy
c. debt financing
d. spreading the risk

LO 1-2 26. Which of these businesses makes the products they sell?
a. service business
b. retail business
c. wholesale business
d. manufacturing business

LO 1-2 27. Person who buys a franchise is a(n)
a. franchisee
b. franchisor
c. proprietor
d. lessor

LO 1-2 28. Which of these is an advantage of buying an existing business?
a. lower cost than starting your own
b. established customer base
c. the business may have a poor location
d. you have to pay for goodwill

LO 1-2 29. Which of these gives you the right to sell another company's product?
a. starting a new business
b. buying a franchise
c. buying an existing business
d. wholesaling

LO 2-1 30. Which part of the business plan fully describes the product or service you will offer?
a. introduction
b. financial plan
c. marketing strategy
d. exit strategy

LO 2-2 31. Which part of the business plan states how much money you will need to borrow?
a. introduction
b. marketing strategy
c. operations management
d. financial plan

LO 2-2 32. Which of these provides free business counseling by retired executives?
a. SCORE
b. SBDCs
c. Better Business Bureaus
d. SBA

Digging Deeper with Economics e-Collection

According to the Small Business Administration, more than 600,000 new businesses are started each year in the United States. Nobody goes into business planning to fail. Several characteristics of entrepreneurs are known to lead to failure more than to success. Access the Gale Economics e-Collection at **www.cengage.com/school/economics/personalfinance**. Find articles describing reasons why entrepreneurs fail. Prepare a PowerPoint presentation listing and explaining ten reasons why small businesses fail.

Think About It

LO 1-1 **33.** Most small business owners start young. They have the skills and talent. They also have the drive and ambition to work for themselves. Are you interested in owning your own business? Why or why not?

LO 1-2 **34.** Retail businesses require a large investment in inventory. Inventory is the merchandise that will be sold to customers. Inventory must meet customer needs, both in quality and quantity. If you buy lower cost merchandise, it may also be lower quality. What kinds of retail stores are in your area? Which ones have higher quality goods and higher prices?

LO 3-1 **35.** Many businesses fail each year. Visit the SBA website and look at suggestions for how to succeed. Which suggestions do you think are the most important?

LO 3-2 **36.** People like to be treated fairly in business transactions. Have you ever been treated unethically? What happened? How did you respond?

Make Academic Connections

LO 1-2 **37.** **MATH** Greg and Ted opened a new franchise store. Their profits were $50,000 last year. They paid an initial franchise fee of $12,500, paid $1,000 a month to lease equipment and space, and royalty fees of 10% of profits. Their advertising contract fee was $100 per month. What were their total franchising costs last year?

LO 3-2 **38.** **COMMUNICATIONS** A friend of yours has an idea for a new product that she would like to develop and sell. She has asked you for advice on how to get started. Write a one-page paper about what you would tell her.

LO 3-2 **39.** **SOCIAL STUDIES** Do market research within your class. Based on a new product that has been recently introduced, ask other students if they would buy it. Ask them what types of products they buy regularly and what need is being met. Ask what products they do not buy and reasons why not.

LO 2-1 **40.** **RESEARCH** Do online research to find a business plan that was successful in getting funding. Critique the plan—its strengths and weaknesses—and how the company is doing today. Present an oral report to the class which includes data from the original business plan.

Extend Your Learning

LO 1-2 **41.** Visit a local SBDC, Better Business Bureau, Chamber of Commerce, or other group that helps small businesses get started. Find out what they do and how new business owners can access their resources.

LO 2-2 **42.** Prepare an outline of a business plan. Include a brief description in each section so that your outline could be used as a template for a future business plan.

LO 3-2 **43.** Write an ethics policy statement, followed by several examples of how you would measure or evaluate ethical behavior in your company. Research ethics policies available on the Internet and cite them as sources of information to support your policy. Prepare a brochure that explains your ethics policy and why it is important to your company.

UNIT 4

Money and Banking

Chapter 8 begins the unit with a discussion of money with basic definitions for money and the money supply of the U.S. economy. Of special interest is a feature on the history of money in the colonies. The chapter concludes with an explanation for how the loans of banks influence the nation's money supply. Chapter 9 covers financial institutions and markets. It begins with individual checking and savings accounts and their maintenance, risks, costs, and rewards. Business banking is also explained, including the concept of capital formation through deposit accounts, savings, interest, and risk. Finally, the history of the labor movement is explained along with the role of labor laws and government in the labor market. Chapter 10 explores consumer credit and debt and explains how consumer buying contributes to the economy, along with the corresponding responsibilities and potential pitfalls. Also covered are credit history, ratings and reports, consumer loans, and strategies to maintain high credit scores and lower borrowing costs. A plan to avoid and eliminate credit card debt and an analysis of the costs and benefits of bankruptcy as a last resort conclude the chapter.

UNIT 4 Project

Making Sense of Money

Project Objectives

PARTNERSHIP FOR 21ST CENTURY SKILLS

- Analyze the consequences of an economic decision made by an individual consumer.
- Use standard grammar, spelling, sentence structure, and punctuation.
- Transfer information from one medium to another, including written to visual and statistical to written or visual, using computer software as appropriate.
- Create written, oral, and visual presentations of economic information.
- Attribute ideas and information to source materials and authors.

chapter 8

Printing of Money, p. 233

The Bureau of Engraving and Printing (BEP.gov) is responsible for printing paper money. Tours are available at the plants in Washington, D.C. and Fort Worth, TX.

Minting of Coins, p. 243

The United States Mint (usmint.gov) is responsible for making coins. Visit the website and explore resources available.

chapter 9

Banking Services and Fees, p. 259

Prepare a poster board display that includes brochures and data comparing banking services and fees in your local area.

Unions, Wages, and Dues, p. 273

Prepare an analysis of the economic impact unions. Include public employee unions, trade unions, and retail employee unions.

chapter 10

Making Purchase Decisions, p. 286

Prepare a step-by-step decision model that you will use when faced with a need to purchase a large-ticket item.

Avoiding Credit Problems, p. 294

Prepare a three-page report discussing recent trends in the use of credit in America.

yienkeat/Shutterstock.com

Project Wrap-up

Using Microsoft Office Publisher, create an advertisement, brochure, or flyer that describes a bank or financial institution and all the services and fees that are available for consumer and business accounts. Save a copy of all work completed to include in your economics portfolio.

Yuri Arcurs/Shutterstock.com

RusianDashinsky/iStockphoto.com

chapter 8

Money and the Banking System

yienkeat/Shutterstock.com

MARKETS *in Action!*

Henry Wells and William Fargo Wells Fargo & Company

In 1852, Henry Wells and William Fargo founded Wells Fargo & Company. The purpose was to provide banking and express service to western pioneers. The story of Wells Fargo is filled with banking innovations and contributions to the history of America. Wells Fargo's name evokes an image of a six-horse drawn stagecoach loaded with gold, silver, and money rolling across the American western frontier. In fact, Wells Fargo opened its first banking and express office in the gold rush port of San Francisco. They purchased gold dust from miners, took deposits, and offered safe transit of money, gold, silver, and mail over long distances. Soon Wells Fargo was providing reliable transportation, banking services, and mail delivery from the Pacific Ocean to the Rocky Mountains.

Wells Fargo transacted business using Pony Express, steamships, railroads, and the stagecoach where the railroad ended. In 1866, Wells Fargo created the largest stagecoach line in the world. These stagecoaches used the finest craftsmanship, including a unique suspension system to smooth the ride. Mark Twain described these coaches as "a cradle on wheels." The average speed was five miles per hour, and stagecoaches stopped to change horses every twelve miles. Home stations with meals and a change of horses were built at twelve mile intervals. To protect valuable shipments, shotgun guards were employed, including Wyatt Earp in Tombstone, Arizona. Between 1870 and 1884, bandits attempted over 300 stagecoach robberies. With the help of local law officers, Wells Fargo special agents captured, and secured convictions of most of the robbers. The transcontinental railroad was completed in 1869, and Wells Fargo switched from the stagecoach to the iron horse.

In 1888, Wells Fargo became the first nationwide express company with "ocean to ocean" service. By 1910, Well Fargo offered financial services such as money orders, traveler's checks, and transfer of funds by telegraph. Today Wells Fargo & Company is an American multinational diversified financial services company with operations around the world.

In 2010, Wells Fargo was the fourth largest bank in the U.S. It had 6,335 retail branches, 12,000 ATMs, 280,000 employees, and 70 million customers. The bank continues to grow and to redefine its mission and refine its services to its customers.

In the financial district of San Francisco, CA, Wells Fargo has multiple ATM cash machines available along the sidewalk outside the bank building.

carterdayne/iStockphoto.com

Think Critically

1. The Wells Fargo story illustrates how banking services change over time to serve customers. As in stagecoach days, what are examples of banking innovations for today's customers?
2. How do banks use technology today to meet customers' needs? How will banking change to meet your future needs?

yienkeat/Shutterstock.com

8-1 What Makes Money *Money*?

Learning Objectives

LO 1-1 **Identify** the three functions of money.

LO 1-2 **Explain** two definitions of the money supply.

Vocabulary

money, p. 225
medium of exchange, p. 225
unit of account, p. 226
store of value, p. 226
commodity money, p. 228
fiat money, p. 228
checkable deposits, p. 230
time deposit, p. 231

© Aleksandar Vrzalski/iStockphoto.com

REAL-WORLD FOCUS

Madison has two accounts at her bank, a checking account and a regular savings account. The accounts are linked together. Because Madison maintains a minimum balance in the savings account, she is able to have a free checking account. "I feel like I can't touch that savings account," she said to her banker. "It's just frozen there paying a pretty low interest rate. I realize the effective rate is higher because I can avoid monthly service fees. But I'm wondering if I could accomplish the same thing having a CD. My savings account is less than $10,000."

WORK AS A TEAM Cash along with checking accounts and time deposits are money. How are checking accounts different from time deposits? Assuming Madison increased her savings account to $10,000, would that change a measure of the money supply?

design56/Shutterstock.com

U.S. paper money is classified as a Federal Reserve Note and includes a statement that identifies it as legal tender for payment of debt.

DO YOU THINK U.S. paper money is commodity money or fiat money?

yienkeat/Shutterstock.com

LO 1-1 Exactly What Is Money?

Exactly what is money? The answer may surprise you. Imagine yourself on the small South Pacific island of Yap. You are surrounded by exotic fowl, crystal-clear lagoons, delicious fruits, and sunny skies. Now while leisurely strolling along the beach one evening, you discover a beautiful bamboo hut for sale. To pay for your dream hut, you must own a 5-foot-diameter stone that you trade with the current owner of the hut for her property.

Can exchange occur in an economy without money? It certainly can, using a trading system called *barter*. Recall from Lesson 6-1 that barter is the direct exchange of one good or service for another good or service, rather than for money. The problem with barter is that it wastes time making a transaction. Imagine for a moment that dollars and coins are worthless. Farmer Brown needs shoes, so he takes his bushels of wheat to the shoe store. Here he offers to barter wheat for shoes. Unfortunately, the store owner refuses because she wants to trade shoes for pencils, toothpaste, and coffee. Undaunted, Farmer Brown spends more time and effort to find Mr. Jones. Mr. Jones has pencils, toothpaste, and coffee he will trade for bushels of wheat. Farmer Brown's luck has improved. Now he and Mr. Jones must agree on the terms of exchange. Exactly how many pounds of coffee is a bushel of wheat worth? Assuming this exchange is worked out, Farmer Brown must spend more time returning to the shoe store. And more time yet is spent negotiating the terms of an exchange of pencils, toothpaste, and coffee for shoes.

The Three Functions of Money

Suppose citizens of the planet of Starcom want to replace their barter system. This means they must decide what to use for money. If this planet is fortunate enough to have economists, they would explain that money must conform to the following definition. **Money** is anything that people accept as payment for goods and services. Money is not limited to dimes, quarters, and dollar bills. Notice that anything meeting the three tests explained below can serve as money. This is why precious metals, beaver skins, and wampum (shells strung in belts) have all served as money.

MONEY AS A MEDIUM OF EXCHANGE In a simple society, barter is a way for participants to exchange goods and services to satisfy wants. Barter, however, requires wasting time in the process of exchange. This is time people could use for productive work. If the goal is to live in a modern economy, the most important function of money is to be widely accepted in trade for goods or services and thus serve as a **medium of exchange**. Money removes the problems of barter because everyone is willing to accept it as payment. You give up two $20 bills in exchange for a ticket to see a rock concert. All in society know that no business will refuse to trade its products for money. Money increases trade by providing a much more convenient method of exchange than a cumbersome barter system.

aldomurillo/iStockphoto.com

International currencies cover this table-top, including bills from the U.S., Europe, Argentina, Uruguay, Israel, Peru, Mexico, Cuba, Egypt, and the Philippines.

Ekspanio/iStockphoto.com

The U.S. dollars people carry in their pockets satisfy the three functions of money.

MONEY AS A UNIT OF ACCOUNT How does a wheat farmer know whether a bushel of wheat is worth one, two, or more pairs of shoes? How does a family compare its income to expenses or a business know whether it is making a profit? Government must be able to measure tax revenues collected and its spending. In each of these examples, money serves as a unit of account. The **unit of account** function of money provides a common measurement of the value for goods and services. Without dollars, there is no common measure. Without money you must decide if one pizza equals a box of pencils, 20 oranges equals one quart of milk, and so forth. You can compare the value of two items using money. If the price of one pizza is $20 and the price of a movie ticket is $10, then the value of one pizza equals two movie tickets. In the United States, the monetary unit is the dollar. In Japan, the monetary unit is the yen. Mexico has a unit of a peso. All these monetary units serve as a unit of account.

MONEY AS A STORE OF VALUE Can you save shrimp for months under your mattress and then exchange them for some product? No, after a day or so the shrimp would rot and lose all its value! Money, on the other hand, serves as a store of value because it can be exchanged for some item in the future. **Store of value** is the ability of money to hold value over time. This means you can save money and spend it in the future. However, this does not mean its value will remain constant. Over time prices often rise, and the value of money declines.

Figure 8-1 gives a summary of the functions of money with examples.

Figure 8-1
The Three Functions of Money

Function	Definition	Example
Medium of exchange	Anything that is widely accepted in exchange for goods and services	Bob uses money to buy hamburgers, video games, clothes, and sports equipment.
Unit of account	The function of money is to provide a common measurement of value for goods and services.	The price of a candy bar is $1, and the price of a video game is $60. The relative value of these two items can be compared easily using money. The video game has 60 times the value of the candy bar.
Store of value	The function of money to hold value over time.	Sue decides to save $100 instead of buying something new. Sue is confident that her money will hold its value over time and that she will be able to spend it in the future.

Are Credit Cards Money?

Credit cards, such as Visa, MasterCard, and American Express, are often called plastic money. But are these cards really money? Do credit cards conform to the three functions of money? First, credit cards are widely accepted. They serve as a means of payment in an exchange for goods or services.

Second, the credit card statement reporting spending and payments in terms of dollars, and not the card itself, serves as a unit of account. One of the advantages of credit cards is that you receive a statement listing the exact price in dollars paid for each total purchase you charged. Your credit card statement records the dollar amount you spent for gasoline, a dinner, or a trip.

But credit cards fail to meet the store of value criterion and are therefore not money. The word *credit* means receiving money today to buy products in return for a promise to pay in the future. A credit card represents a prearranged short term loan up to a certain limit. If the credit card company goes out of business or for any reason decides not to honor your card, it is worthless. Therefore, credit cards do not store value and are not money.

NET Bookmark

Access www.cengage.com/school/economics/personalfinance and click on the link for Chapter 8. Browse Historical American Currency Exhibit. Choose Portraits. Whose picture was on the $10,000 bill?

www.cengage.com/school/economics/personalfinance

Other Desirable Properties of Money

Once something has passed the three basic requirements to serve as money, there are additional hurdles to clear. First, an important consideration is scarcity. Money must be scarce, but not too scarce. Sand, for example, could theoretically serve as money. Sand is a poor choice because people can easily gather a bucketful to pay their bills. A Picasso painting is also undesirable as money. Because there are so few for circulation, people would have to use some other unit of money to complete most transactions or resort to barter.

History of Currency

Investigate Your Local ECONOMY

The first paper money used in North America was issued in 1690 by the Massachusetts Bay Colony. Soon after, other colonies issued their own paper currencies. These currencies forged the path that led to a national currency. In 1860 there were an estimated 8,000 different banks circulating currency. The federal government played no role in providing paper currency for the entire nation until 1914 with the establishment of the Federal Reserve System. Federal Reserve issued currencies in denominations from $1 to $10,000. The $100 bill is the largest denomination printed since 1946.

Try it Out

Make a list of problems that might occur if each bank in your community issued its own currency instead of using Federal Reserve notes.

Second, money should be portable and divisible. That is, people should be able to reach into their pockets and make change to buy items at various prices. Statues of George Washington might be attractive money, but they would be difficult to carry and make change. Finally, money must be uniform. An ounce of gold is an ounce of gold. But there are quality differences for beaver skins and seashells. Each exchange would involve the extra trouble of buyers and sellers arguing over which skins or shells are better or worse.

What Stands Behind U.S. Money?

Precious metals, tobacco, and other tangible goods are examples of commodity money. **Commodity money** is anything that serves as money that has market value based on the material from which it is made. This means that money itself has intrinsic worth (the market value of the material). For example, money can be pure gold or silver. Both of these metals are valuable for nonmoney uses, such as making jewelry and serving other industrial purposes.

matthiahaas/iStockphoto.com

Sheets of 100 dollar bills roll off the printing presses of the U.S. Bureau of Engraving and Printing.

Today, United States paper money and coins are no longer backed by gold or silver. Paper money was exchangeable for gold or silver until 1934. As a result of the Great Depression, people rapidly tried to get rid of their paper money. The U.S. Treasury's stock of gold dropped so low that Congress passed a law in 1934 that prevented anyone from exchanging gold for $5 and larger bills. Later, in 1963, Congress removed the right to exchange $1 bills for silver. And in the mid 1960s, zinc, copper, and nickel replaced silver in coins.

The important consideration for money is acceptability. The acceptability of a dollar is due to the fact that Uncle Sam decrees it to be fiat money. **Fiat money** is money accepted by law, and not because of its tangible value. A dollar bill contains only about three cents worth of paper, printing inks, and other materials. A quarter contains maybe 10 cents worth of nickel and copper. Pull out a dollar bill and look at it closely. In the upper left corner on the front side is small print that proclaims, "THIS NOTE IS LEGAL TENDER FOR ALL DEBTS, PUBLIC AND PRIVATE." This means that your paper money is fiat money. Notice that nowhere on the note is there any promise to redeem it for gold, silver, or anything else.

CHECKPOINT

Debit cards are used to pay for purchases, and the money is automatically deducted from the user's bank account. Are debit cards money?

Global View

Why a Loan in Yap Is Hard to Roll Over

On the tiny South Pacific island of Yap, life is easy, but the currency is hard as a rock. For nearly 2,000 years, the Yapese have used large stone wheels to pay for major purchases, such as land, canoes, and permission to marry. The people of Yap have been using stone money ever since a Yapese warrior named Anagumang used canoes to bring the huge stones over the sea in ancient times from limestone caverns on neighboring Palau. Inspired by the moon, he fashioned the stones into large circles, and the rest is history. The stone's value remained high because of the difficulty and hazards involved in obtaining them over the rough seas.

Yap is a U.S. trust territory, and the dollar is used in grocery stores and gas stations. But reliance on stone money continues. Buying property with stones is much easier than buying it with U.S. dollars. A building lot can be purchased with a 30-inch stone wheel. However, stone wheels don't make good pocket money, so Yapese use other forms of currency. Besides stone wheels, the Yapese sometimes spend gaw. Gaw consists of necklaces of stone beads strung together around a whale's tooth. They also buy things with yar, a currency made from large seashells, but these are small change.

Stone disks may change ownership during marriage, transfer of land title, or other exchanges. Yapese lean the stone wheels against their houses or prop up rows of them in village "banks." Most of the stones are smaller in diameter. Some are as much as 12 feet in diameter. Each has a hole in the center so it can be slipped onto the trunk of a fallen betel nut tree and carried. It takes 20 men to lift some wheels. Rather than risk a broken stone or their backs Yapese leave the larger stones where they are. Then they make a mental accounting that the ownership has been transferred. There are some decided advantages to using massive stones for money. They are in short supply, difficult to steal, pose formidable obstacles to counterfeiting, and serve as a tourist attraction.

© Robert Harding Picture Library Ltd/Alamy

On the island of Yap, Micronesia, there are stone money banks. Yap stones are used to pay for major purchases.

Think Critically

1. **Explain how Yap's large stones pass the three tests in the definition of money.**
2. **Briefly discuss Yap's large stones in terms of other desirable properties of money.**

LO 1-2 Money Supply Definitions

What constitutes the money supply of the U.S. economy? There are two basic methods used to measure the money supply. These definitions are officially called M1 (M-one) and M2 (M-two).

M1: The Most Narrowly Defined Money Supply

M1 is the narrowest definition of the money supply. This money definition measures purchasing power immediately available to the public without borrowing. Specifically, M1 measures the currency and checkable deposits held by the public at a given time. Currency consists of coins and paper money officially called Federal Reserve notes. Expressed as a formula:

M1 = currency + checkable deposits

Figure 8-2 shows the components of M1 and M2 money supply definitions during June 2011.

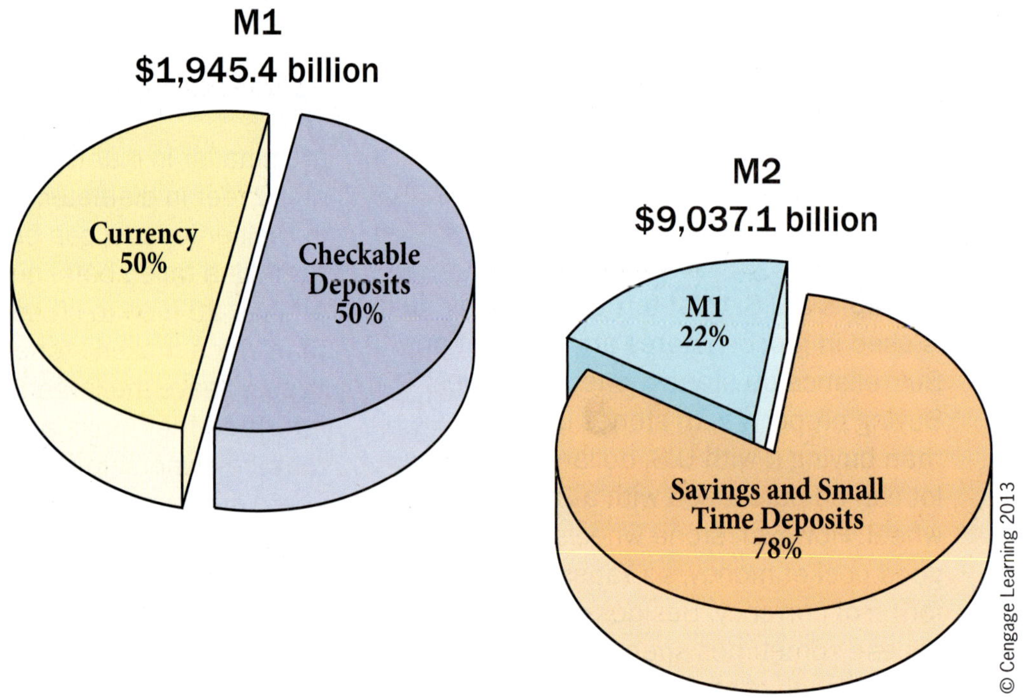

Figure 8-2

Definitions of the Money Supply, 2011

Each of the two circle graphs represents the money supply in 2011. M1 is the most narrowly defined money supply. It is equal to currency (coins and paper money) in circulation plus checkable deposits in financial institutions. M2 is a more broadly defined money supply. It is equal to M1 plus savings deposits and small time deposits of less than $100,000.

CURRENCY Currency includes coins and paper money. The public holds currency for immediate spending. The purpose of currency is to enable you to make small purchases. Currency represents 50 percent of M1.

CHECKABLE DEPOSITS Many purchases are paid for with checks rather than currency. Checks eliminate trips to the bank, and they are safer than cash. If lost or stolen, checks and credit cards can be replaced at little cost—currency cannot. Figure 8-2 shows that a major share of M1 consists of checkable deposits. **Checkable deposits** are the total money in financial institutions that can be withdrawn by writing a check. A checking account balance is a book-keeping entry. It is often called a demand deposit because it can be converted into cash "on demand." In 2011, 50 percent of M1 was made up of checkable deposits.

FreeSoulProduction/Shutterstock.com

Math CONNECTION

Interpret a Circle Graph

The sectors of some circle graphs (pie charts) are labeled with percentages, but not with amounts for each part of the whole. If you know the total amount the circle represents, you can find the amounts for each category that makes up the circle. Use the graph in Figure 8-2. Find the amount of currency for the M1 definition of the money supply.

SOLUTION

The circle represents $1,945.4 billion and has two sectors. Multiply each percent by the total to find the amount for each category.

Currency = \$1,945.4 billion × 0.50	50% = 0.50
= \$972.7 billion	
= 972.7 × 1,000,000,000	Change amount to standard form.
= \$972,700,000,000	

TRY IT

Use the graphs for the MI and M2 definitions of the money supply to find each amount. Write answers in standard form.

1. M2, Savings and Small Time Deposits
2. M1 of M2
3. How can you check that your answers are correct?

M2: A Broader Measure of the Money Supply

M2 is a broader measure of the money supply. It equals M1 plus other accounts that can easily be converted to cash and used to purchase goods and services. These include passbook savings accounts, money market accounts, mutual fund accounts, and time deposits of less than $100,000. Written as a formula:

M2 = M1 + savings deposits + small time deposits of less than $100,000

SAVINGS DEPOSITS As shown in Figure 8-2, M1 was about a little more than one fifth of M2 in 2011, with savings deposits and small time deposits constituting the remainder of M2. Savings deposits are interest bearing accounts that can be easily withdrawn. These deposits include passbook savings accounts and money market mutual funds.

SMALL TIME DEPOSITS There is a difference between a checkable deposit and a time deposit. A **time deposit** is an account with guaranteed interest for a period of time. Certificates of deposit (CDs), for example, are deposits for a specified time, with a penalty charged for early withdrawal. Where is the line drawn between a small and a large time deposit? The answer is that time deposits of less than $100,000 are considered small and therefore are included in M2.

CHECKPOINT

M1 consists of coins, paper money, and checkable deposits. Does M2 also include these components? Debit and credit cards are called "plastic money." So are debit cards or credit card balances included in the definitions of the money supply?

You're the ECONOMIST

Money Past, Present, and Future

The early colonists left behind their well-developed money system in Europe. North American Indians accepted wampum as money, which are beads of polished shells strung in belts. Soon, a group of settlers learned to counterfeit wampum, and it lost its value. As a result, the main method of trading with the Indians was to barter. Later, trade developed with the West Indies, and Spanish coins called "pieces of eight" were circulated widely. Colonists often cut these coins into pieces to make change. Half of a coin was known as "four bits." A quarter of the coin was referred to as "two bits." The first English colony to mint its own coins was Massachusetts in 1652. A striking pine tree was engraved on these coins called shillings. Other coins such as a six-pence and three-pence were produced at a mint in Boston. Several other colonies followed with their own coin issues.

The first paper money in the Americas was printed in 1690. Massachusetts soldiers returned to the colony from fighting the French in Quebec, where they had unsuccessfully laid siege to the city. The colony had no precious metal to pay the soldiers. Hundreds of soldiers threatened mutiny, and the colony decided it must issue bills of credit, which were pieces of paper promising to pay the soldiers. Other colonies followed this example and printed their own paper money. Soon paper money was being widely circulated.

In 1775, the need to finance the American Revolution forced the Continental Congress to issue paper money called "continentals," but so much was issued that it rapidly lost its value. George Washington complained, "A wagon load of money will scarcely purchase a wagon load of provisions." This statement is today shortened to the phrase "not worth a continental."

Today transactions are increasingly electronic. This raises the question of what will happen to paper money and coins. An alternative is a *smart card*. This is a piece of plastic with an embedded memory or microprocessor. Monetary value can be placed on the smart card and then it can be used to make purchases, just like using currency. It could also make credit transactions and contain medical and other information. A smart card could replace all the other cards you carry.

Think Critically

Over time the types of money people use change. Do you think smart cards will replace cash?

8-1 Assessment

Key Concepts

LO 1-2 1. An account with guaranteed interest for a period of time is a __?__ deposit.

LO 1-1 2. **TRUE OR FALSE** Medium of exchange is anything that is widely accepted in exchange for goods and services.

LO 1-1 3. Money that has market value based on the material from which it is made is __?__ money.

LO 1-1 4. **TRUE OR FALSE** Money is anything that people accept as payment for goods and services.

LO 1-1 5. Money that is accepted by law, and not because of its tangible value is __?__ money.

LO 1-1 6. **TRUE OR FALSE** Unit of account is the function of money to provide a common measurement of value for goods and services.

LO 1-2 7. The total money in financial institutions that can be withdrawn by writing a check is __?__ deposits.

Think About It

LO 1-1 8. Could each of the following items serve as money in a modern economy? Consider each as (1) a medium of exchange, (2) a unit of account, and (3) a store of value.
   a. Visa credit card
   b. Federal Reserve note (paper money)
   c. fish
   d. large stone with a hole in the center

LO 1-1 9. Consider each of the items in question 8 in terms of scarcity, portability, divisibility, and uniformity.

LO 1-2 10. What are the components of the most narrowly defined money supply in the United States?

LO 1-2 11. Distinguish between M1 and M2.

LO 1-1 12. What are the three functions of money?

LO 1-1 13. What components make up each of the two basic measures of the money supply?

Make Academic Connections

LO 1-1 14. **HISTORY** Research ancient and medieval coins. When gold and silver coins were the primary type of money in circulation merchants would often weigh their coins before accepting them. Why did they do this?

Teamwork

LO 1-1 15. Divide into six groups. Each group selects and researches four forms of money that have been used in the past, such as confederate money, wampum, and tobacco. Each group shares its findings with the class.

Unit 4 Project: Making Sense of Money

PRINTING OF MONEY The Bureau of Engraving and Printing is responsible for printing paper money. Tours are available at the plants in Washington, D.C. and Fort Worth, TX. Visit the site (in person or online) and prepare a flow chart of how money is made. Prepare a summary sheet that includes data about how old bills are replaced, plus how and why new designs are created. Explain the concept of redemption of mutilated currency and why it is important to U.S. citizens.

8-2 How Banks Create Money

Learning Objectives

LO 2-1 **Explain** how banks create money.

LO 2-2 **Understand** the calculation of the money multiplier.

Vocabulary

- **fractional reserve banking,** p. 235
- **required reserves,** p. 236
- **Federal Reserve System,** p. 236
- **required reserve ratio,** p. 236
- **excess reserves,** p. 236
- **money multiplier,** p. 241

© Aleksandar Vrzalski/iStockphoto.com

REAL-WORLD FOCUS

Rosa recently received a brochure from her bank. It contained an offer to existing customers of a $50 cash bonus to be added to their current account if they opened a new savings account and maintained an average monthly balance of $1,000 for a year. "That seems strange to me," she told her mother. "How can the bank make money if it pays me $50 cash and then it also pays me interest on my savings account?"

WORK AS A TEAM Banks make money when customers open accounts and maintain balances in those accounts. Collect brochures from local banks and credit unions. Compare fees charged on accounts to the minimum balance requirements of those accounts. Discuss and report your findings.

isak55/Shutterstock.com

A hundred dollar bill is printed with the name Federal Reserve Note and the statement declaring it legal tender. Also printed on the bill is the seal of the United States Federal Reserve System.

DO YOU THINK all denominations of paper money carry both the classification as a Federal Reserve Note and the seal of the United States Federal Reserve System?

yienkeat/Shutterstock.com

LO 2-1 The Money Creation Process

A common misconception is that banks just accept deposits and make loans. And that's about the end of the story. There is another very important chapter to tell. Banking transactions expand or contract the money supply. Without minting coins or using the printing presses to make paper money, banks can create money. That is, banks can increase the money supply (M1). Note that M1 is used throughout this text rather than M2 for simplicity. This lesson explains how getting a loan increases the size of the checkable deposits. And because M1 includes a large share of checkable deposits, the money supply increases.

Money Creation Begins

idal/iStockphoto.com

In the Middle Ages, gold was the money of choice in most European nations. One of the problems with gold is that it is a heavy commodity. This makes it difficult to use in transactions or to hide from thieves. The medieval solution was to keep it safely deposited with the people who worked with gold, called goldsmiths. This demand for their services inspired goldsmith entrepreneurs to become the founders of modern day banking.

The goldsmiths sat on their benches with ledgers close by and recorded the amounts of gold placed in their vaults. In fact, the word *bank* is derived from the Italian word for bench, which is *banco.* After assessing the purity of the gold, a goldsmith issued a receipt to the customer for the amount of gold deposited. In return, the goldsmith collected a service charge, just as you pay today for services at your bank. Anyone who possessed the receipt and presented it to the goldsmith could make a withdrawal for the amount of gold written on the receipt.

With these gold receipts in circulation, people began paying their debts with these pieces of paper, rather than actually exchanging gold. Thus, goldsmith receipts became paper money. At first, the goldsmiths were very conservative and issued receipts exactly equal to the amount of gold stored in their vaults. However, some shrewd goldsmiths observed that net withdrawals in any period were only a fraction of all the gold "on reserve." This observation produced a powerful idea. Goldsmiths discovered that they could make loans for more gold than they actually held in their vaults. As a result, goldsmiths made extra profit from interest on these loans, and borrowers had more money for spending in their hands.

How a Single Bank Creates Money

The medieval goldsmiths were the first to practice fractional reserve banking. **Fractional reserve banking** is a system in which banks keep only a percentage of their deposits on reserve and lend out the remainder. In a 100 percent reserve banking system, banks would be unable to create money by making loans. However, holding less than 100 percent on reserve allows banks to make loans. And in turn, these loans create money in the economy.

Banker Bookkeeping

Consider the balance sheet of Typical Bank. A balance sheet gives the assets and liabilities of a bank at a point in time. Balance sheets are also called *T-accounts*. Balance Sheet 1 lists only major categories and omits details to keep things simple.

Figure 8-3

Balance Sheet 1

The Fed requires the bank to keep 10 percent of its checkable deposits in reserves. Holding $5 million in required reserves, the bank has zero excess reserves and $45 million in loans to earn profit.

TYPICAL BANK

Balance Sheet 1

Assets		Liabilities	
Required Reserves	$5 million	Checkable Deposits	$50 million
Excess Reserves	0		
Loans	45 million		
Total	$50 million	Total	$50 million

On the right side of the balance sheet are the bank's liabilities. *Liabilities* are the amounts the bank owes to others. In this example, the only liabilities are checkable deposits, or demand deposits. Note that checkable deposits are assets on the customers' personal balance sheets. But they are debt obligations of Typical Bank. If a depositor writes a check, the bank must pay this amount. Therefore, checkable deposits are liabilities to the bank.

On the left side of the balance sheet are Typical Bank's assets. Assets are amounts the bank owns. In the example, these assets consist of required reserves, excess reserves, and loans. **Required reserves** are the minimum balance of money that the Fed requires a bank to hold in cash or on deposit with the Fed. The Fed is the popular name for the **Federal Reserve System**. The Fed is the central banking system of the United States. The Fed will be discussed in more detail in Chapter 13.

The required reserve ratio (RRR) determines the minimum required reserves. The **required reserve ratio** is the percentage of deposits that the Fed requires a bank to hold in cash or on deposit with the Fed rather than being loaned. Here assume that the Fed's required reserve ratio is 10 percent. Thus, the bank must have required reserves of $5 million (10 percent of $50 million). This required reserve leaves Typical Bank with $45 million it may use to make loans that provide profit to the bank.

Typical Bank has zero excess reserves. **Excess reserves** are potential loan balances of reserves held on deposit with the Fed in excess of required reserves. Excess reserves play a starring role in the banking system's ability to change the money supply. The relationship between reserves accounts can be expressed as follows:

Total reserves = required reserves + excess reserves

or

Excess reserves = total reserves − required reserves

The final entry on the asset side of Typical Bank's balance sheet is loans. Loans are interest earning assets of the bank. Loans are bank assets because they represent outstanding credit payable to the bank. In a fractional reserve banking system, the bank uses balances not held in reserves to earn income. In this example, loan officers have written loans totaling $45 million. Note that Typical Bank's assets equal its liabilities. Any change on one side must be accompanied by an equal amount of change on the other side of the balance sheet.

Step 1 Accepting a New Deposit

Assume the required reserve ratio is 10 percent. One of Best National Bank's depositors, Brad Rich, takes $100,000 cash from under his mattress. Then he deposits it in his checking account. Balance Sheet 2 records this change by increasing the bank's checkable deposits by $100,000. Brad's deposit is a liability of the bank. This is because Brad could change his mind and withdraw his money. On the asset side, Brad's deposit increases assets. The bank has an extra $90,000 to lend after setting aside the required reserves. Balance Sheet 2 shows that the increase in total reserves is divided. It consists of required reserves of $10,000 (10 percent of the deposit) and excess reserves of $90,000 (90 percent of the deposit). Thus, the bank's assets and liabilities remain equal when Brad makes his deposit.

Here is an important point. Depositing coins or paper currency in a bank has no initial effect on the money supply (M1). Recall M1 includes currency in circulation. Therefore, the transfer of $100,000 in cash from the mattress to the bank creates no money because M1 already counts this amount. The money supply would not have increased had Brad Rich's initial $100,000 deposit been a check written on another bank. The increase in deposits to Best National Bank of $100,000 would decrease the deposits of the other bank by $100,000. Recall M1 also includes checkable deposits.

Best National Bank
Balance Sheet 2

Assets		Liabilities		Change in M1
Required Reserves	+$10,000	Brad Rich account	+$100,000	0
Excess Reserves	+90,000			
Total	$100,000	Total	$100,000	

Figure 8-4
Balance Sheet 2

Step 1: Brad Rich deposits $100,000 in cash, which increases checkable deposits. The Fed requires the bank to keep 10 percent of its new deposit in required reserves. So this account is credited with $10,000. The remaining 90 percent is excess reserves of $90,000. There is no effect on the money supply.

Step 2 Making a Loan

So far, M1 has not changed. As shown in Balance Sheet 2, Brad has taken $100,000 in currency and transferred it to a checkable deposit. Stated differently, the bank holds the same $100,000 for spending. Only the form has changed from cash to a checkable deposit. In step 2, the actual money creation process occurs. Best National Bank wants to make a profit from the new $90,000 excess reserves. It makes a profit by making loans and charging interest. Suppose that Connie Jones walks in, asking for a $90,000 loan. She wants to purchase equipment for her health spa. Connie has a fine credit record, so the bank accepts Connie's note (IOU) agreeing to repay the loan. Then the bank gives Connie a check for $90,000, which she deposits in her account with the bank. This increases the bank's liabilities by $90,000.

As shown in Balance Sheet 3, three entries on the assets side have changed. First, the loan to Connie Jones boosts the loans account to $90,000. Second, the bank must increase required reserves by $9,000. This is because of the $90,000 increase in checkable deposits on the liabilities side. Recall that required reserves are 10 percent of checkable deposits. Required reserves are now $19,000. Third, transferring $9,000 from excess reserves to required reserves reduces the bank's excess reserves from $90,000 to $81,000. Total reserves remain at $100,000 in both Balance Sheet 2 and Balance Sheet 3.

The entry on the liabilities side is the key of money creation. Checkable deposits have increased by $90,000 to $190,000. The reason is the bank issued Connie a check deposited in the bank. Thus, Best National Bank has performed money magic with this transaction. Look what happened to the $100,000 deposited by

Figure 8-5

Balance Sheet 3

Step 2: The bank loans Connie Jones $90,000 by crediting her checking account with this amount. A corresponding $90,000 balance is added to the loan account. The result is an increase in the money supply of $90,000.

BEST NATIONAL BANK
Balance Sheet 3

Assets		Liabilities		Change in M1
Required Reserves	$19,000	Brad Rich account	+$100,000	+$90,000
Excess Reserves	81,000	Connie Jones account	+$90,000	
Loans	+90,000			
Total	$190,000	Total	$190,000	

ETHICS *in Action!*

Making Loans That Won't Be Repaid

During the early years of the 21st century some financial institutions made home mortgage loans to people they knew would have difficulty repaying their debts. These transactions were called *sub-prime loans* because they involved greater risks of non-payment by borrowers than prime or the safest loans. You might wonder why a bank would make a loan that it thought stood a good chance of not being repaid. There are several possible answers. (1) Many subprime loans were made by employees who were paid according to the amount of funds they were able to lend regardless of the risk involved. (2) The borrowers often put some of their own money down which they would lose if they were unable to make their payments. The lender then got the property back through foreclosure as well as the amount paid by the borrower. (3) Many of these loans were sold to investors who stood to lose their funds if the borrowers were unable to make their payments. In this way banks passed on the risk to other people who often were not told how risky their investments were.

Eventually the inability of hundreds of thousands of subprime borrowers to meet their financial obligations contributed to the international financial meltdown that took place in 2008. Some banks such as HSBC, Citi, and Bank of America lost billions of dollars through subprime loans. A few, including Lehman Brothers failed, causing stockholders of these banks to lose all or most of their investments. Many people believe these financial difficulties were the result of greed and unethical behavior by banks and their employees.

Think Critically

1. What criteria should banks establish to determine who should or should not receive credit?

2. Do you believe that it is unethical for a bank to make a loan that it knows is not likely to be repaid? Should people who do not have much income be helped when they need to borrow funds? Explain your answer.

Brad Rich. It has generated a new $90,000 loan, which was added to checkable deposits. Therefore, the money supply increased by $90,000.

Take notice of the impact of these transactions on the money supply. In step 1, Brad's initial deposit did not change M1. But in step 2, M1 increased by $90,000 when Best National Bank created money by making the loan to Connie. Now Connie has more money in her checking account than she did before. And no one else has less. Connie can now use this money to buy goods and services.

Step 3 Clearing the Loan Check

Now Connie Jones can use her new money to purchase equipment for her spa. Suppose Connie buys it from Better Health Spa, and writes a check for $90,000 drawn on Best National Bank. The owner of Better Health Spa then deposits the check in the firm's account at Yazoo National Bank. Yazoo National will send the check to its Federal Reserve district bank for collection. Recall that each bank maintains required reserves either in cash in its own vault or at the Fed. The Fed clears the check by debiting the reserve account of Best National Bank. And the Fed also credits the reserve account of Yazoo National Bank. The Fed then returns the check to Best National Bank. This bank reduces Connie Jones's checking account by $90,000. As shown in Balance Sheet 4, Connie Jones's checking account falls to zero. And Best National Bank's liabilities are reduced by $90,000.

On the asset side of the balance sheet, required reserves decrease by $9,000, and excess reserves return to zero. Now Best National Bank has required reserves of $10,000 and an IOU for $90,000. Note that this check clearing process in step 3 has no effect on M1. The $90,000 increase in M1 created by Best National Bank's loan to Connie remains on deposit at Yazoo National Bank. It is in Better Health Spa's checking account.

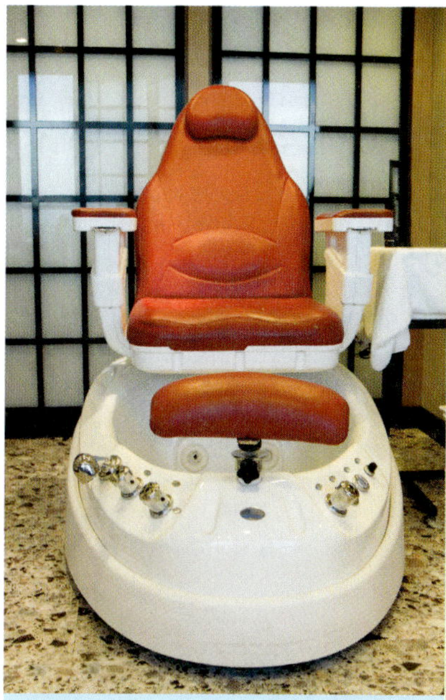

David Wetzel/Shutterstock.com

A pedicure chair is a necessary expense for any new health spa owner.

BEST NATIONAL BANK
Balance Sheet 4

Assets		Liabilities		Change in M1
Required Reserves	$10,000	Brad Rich account	$100,000	0
Excess Reserves	0	Connie Jones account	0	
Loans	90,000			
Total	$100,000	Total	$100,000	

Figure 8-6

Balance Sheet 4

Step 3: Connie Jones pays Better Health Spa with a $90,000 check drawn on Best National Bank. Better Health Spa deposits the check in Yazoo National Bank, which collects from Best National Bank. The result is a debit to Connie's account and her bank's reserves accounts.

CHECKPOINT

The key to banks creating money is that they make loans from their excess reserves. Do banks have to create loans with excess reserves? What reserves must banks not lend out?

LO 2-2 Multiplier Expansion of Money by the Banking System

The process of money creation (loans) does not stop at the doors of Best National Bank. There is a money multiplier process. Follow the effect on Yazoo National after Better Health Spa deposits $90,000 from Connie Jones. As shown in Balance Sheet 5, Yazoo National's checkable deposits increase by $90,000. Given a required reserve ratio of 10 percent, Yazoo National Bank must keep $9,000 in required reserves. The remaining $81,000 goes into excess reserves.

Figure 8-7

Balance Sheet 5

The required reserve ratio of 10 percent. Better Health Spa's deposit of $90,000 from Connie Jones creates $81,000 in additional excess reserves. The bank can lend these reserves, and create additional checkable deposits.

Yazoo National Bank

Balance Sheet 5

Assets		Liabilities	
Required Reserves	+$9,000	Better Health Spa account	+$90,000
Excess Reserves	+81,000		
Total	$ 90,000	Total	$90,000

Yazoo National's loan officer now has $81,000 in additional excess reserves to lend. This creates additional checkable deposits, excess reserves, and eventually loans in other banks. Figure 8-8 presents the expansion of the money supply created when Brad Rich makes his initial $100,000 deposit. Next, banks make loans that are deposited in other banks.

Figure 8-8

Expansion of the Money Supply

A $100,000 cash deposit in Best National Bank creates $900,000 in new deposits in other banks. Each round creates excess reserves. These are loaned to a customer who deposits the loan check in another bank in the next round.

Round	Bank	Increase in Checkable Deposits	Increase in Required Reserves	Increase in Excess Reserves
1	Best National Bank	$100,000	$10,000	$90,000
2	Yazoo National Bank	90,000	9,000	81,000
3	Bank A	81,000	8,100	72,900
4	Bank B	72,900	7,290	65,610
5	Bank C	65,610	6,561	59,049
6	Bank D	59,049	5,905	53,144
7	Bank E	53,144	5,314	47,830
.	.	.	.	.
.	.	.	.	.
.	.	.	.	.
Total all other banks		478,297	47,830	430,467
	Total increase	$1,000,000	$100,000	$900,000 (ΔM1)

In Figure 8-8, see the result of an initial deposit of $100,000 in Best National Bank. The banking system as a whole can eventually create a $900,000 increase in the money supply (ΔM1). The Greek symbol Δ (delta) means "change in." This is because Brad Rich's initial $100,000 deposit eventually creates total excess reserves of $900,000. This was created by new loans, and, in turn, new deposits in different banks. As this process continued, each bank accepts smaller and smaller increases in checkable deposits. The reason is that 10 percent of each deposit is held as required reserves. Note that the initial $100,000 was from cash already counted in M1. Therefore, it is not counted in the expansion of the money supply.

The Money Multiplier

Fortunately, you do not need to calculate all the individual bank transactions listed in Figure 8-8. You can derive the change in the money supply initiated by an initial deposit or withdrawal. Economists use the **money multiplier**, or deposit multiplier for this purpose. The money multiplier gives the maximum change in the money supply (checkable deposits) due to an initial change in the excess reserves held by banks. The money multiplier is equal to 1 divided by the required reserve ratio. Expressed as a formula:

$$\textbf{Money multiplier (MM)} = \frac{\mathbf{1}}{\textbf{required reserve ratio}} = \mathbf{1} \div \frac{\mathbf{1}}{\mathbf{10}} = \mathbf{10}$$

The actual change in the money supply is computed by the following formula:

Actual money supply change (ΔM1) = initial change in excess reserves (ΔER) × money multiplier (MM)

Using the Greek symbol Δ meaning "change in" and the data from Figure 8-8,

$$\mathbf{\Delta M1 = \Delta ER \times MM}$$

$$\$900{,}000 = \$90{,}000 \times 10$$

Figure 8-9 summarizes the money creation process described in this lesson.

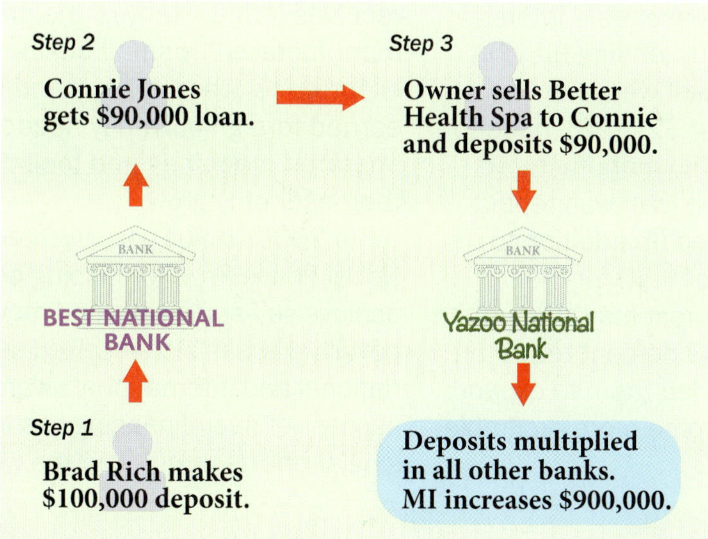

Figure 8-9
The Money Supply Creation Process

CHECKPOINT

The money multiplier formula is a theoretical model. What might happen to the money multiplier if during a financial crisis people lose confidence in the banking system and keep their cash on hand rather than depositing it in a bank?

PROFILE

Muhammad Yunus
Founder of Village Bank

(Brad Barket/PictureGroup) via AP IMAGES

Muhammad Yunus was born in Chittagong, Bangladesh. Yunus was awarded a Fulbright scholarship and received a Ph.D in economics from Vanderbilt University in 1969. Later he became head of the Economics Department at Chittagong University in Bangladesh. Yunus has served on several United Nations' advisory groups and on the board of directors of the United Nations Foundation, a public charity to address the world's most pressing problems.

Yunus developed the concept of *microcredit*. His idea was that if poor entrepreneurs with no collateral, especially women, were able to borrow money at reasonable rates, they would be able to pull themselves out of poverty. Traditional banks were not interested in making such small loans at reasonable interest rates. Yunus started by lending his own money to female basket weavers. One of his early loans was for $27 (US) made to a group of villagers who manufactured bamboo furniture. The loan was repaid and the owners earned (in addition to their wages) a profit of $.50 for their effort. Although this profit may seem quite small it was nearly a 2 percent return on their investment and led them to expand their business to become more profitable in later years.

In 1983, Yunus founded the Grameen Bank, which means, "village bank," to finance small businesses started by the poor. This bank also provided thousands of scholarships and student loans each year. These small business loans have helped Bangladesh as a nation as well as the individual business owners who received loans. Many of the products manufactured by small businesses are exported to other nations and have earned foreign currency needed to buy imported machines and tools that help their economy grow.

In 2006, Yunus was awarded the Nobel Peace Prize for helping people achieve self-sufficiency and move out of poverty. He has also received several other national and international awards. The success of microfinancing has inspired similar efforts throughout the world.

THINK CRITICALLY

Muhammad Yunus is an economist from one of the world's poorest nations. He stated "Poverty is not created by the poor." Explain this idea in terms of the banking system.

yienkeat/Shutterstock.com

8-2 Assessment

Key Concepts

LO 2-2 1. The __?__ multiplier is the maximum change in the money supply (checkable deposits) due to an initial change in the excess reserve banks hold. It is equal to 1 divided by the required reserve ratio.

LO 2-1 2. **TRUE OR FALSE** In a fractional reserve banking system, banks keep all their deposits on reserve.

LO 2-1 3. The minimum balance of reserves that the Fed requires a bank to hold on deposit with the Fed is called __?__ reserves.

LO 2-1 4. Potential loan balances of reserves held on deposit with the Fed in excess of required reserves are __?__ reserves.

Think About It

LO 2-2 5. Assume you deposit a $20 bill into a checking account, and your bank has a 10 percent reserve requirement. How much will the bank's excess reserves rise?

LO 2-2 6. Consider this statement: "Banks do not create money and influence the money supply." Do you agree or disagree? Explain.

LO 2-1 7. Where does a bank hold its required reserves? Assume the Fed has a 20 percent required reserve ratio. What amount of checkable deposits can be supported by $10 million in required reserves?

LO 2-2 8. Suppose you remove $1,000 from under your mattress and deposit it in First National Bank. Using a balance sheet, show the impact of your deposit on the bank's assets and liabilities. If the required reserve ratio is 10 percent, what is the maximum amount the bank can loan from this deposit?

LO 1-1 9. Describe the process through which banks create money.

LO 1-2 10. Explain and demonstrate how to calculate the money multiplier when the reserve requirement is 12.5 percent.

Make Academic Connections

LO 2-1 11. **LITERATURE** Relate Shakespeare's admonition "Neither a borrower nor a lender be" to the goldsmiths' evolutionary use of fractional reserve banking.

LO 2-2 12. **MATH** Suppose someone takes $100 from their piggy bank and deposits it in a checking account. If the required reserve ratio (RRR) is 10 percent, use the money multiplier formula to compute the maximum increase in the money supply throughout the banking system.

Teamwork

LO 2-2 13. Organize into three groups representing bankers, businesses, and consumers. Each group interviews relatives and asks them how lending practices of banks changed during the recent financial crisis and how it affected them. Each group reports their findings to the class.

Unit 4 Project: Making Sense of Money

MINTING OF COINS The United States Mint is responsible for making coins that are circulated in the United States. Visit the website and explore resources available to students. Read about the history of the mint (coins and medals) and prepare a flow chart of the steps taken from legislation to creation of a coin or medal.

yienkeat/Shutterstock.com, Chad Baker/Ryan McVay/Photodisc/Getty Images

Chapter 8

Summary

8-1 WHAT MAKES MONEY *MONEY*?

1. Money is anything people accept as payment for the purchase of goods or services. Money serves as a medium of exchange (something that people are willing to accept as payment for a good or service). Money serves as a unit of account (which is a measure of value). Money is also a store of value (able to hold its value over time).
2. Money must also be portable and divisible. People must be able to carry it around with them, and when they buy things, it must be in units that can be divided for purposes of making change. Commodity money serves as money when material from which it is made has market value. Precious metals (gold, silver, platinum, and others) have market value as commodities. Fiat money has value because the government has declared this to be true.
3. Our money supply is divided into two components: M1 (currency and checkable deposits), and M2 (M1 plus savings deposits and small time deposits).

8-2 HOW BANKS CREATE MONEY

4. Bank transactions expand (create) or contract (reduce) the money supply. Without minting coins or printing new currency, banks are able to create money. The creation of paper money began with goldsmiths, who gave receipts for gold that was stored in their vaults.
5. Today banks create money with a process called fractional reserve banking. That means the bank keeps on reserve only a portion of its deposits and is able to lend out the remainder to borrowers. This is the process of creating money.
6. The Federal Reserve System (central bank) requires banks to keep part of their deposits on hand or deposited in the Fed (the reserve requirement). If they are required to keep on hand 10% of their money, they can then lend out 90% of their deposits. Excess reserves are amounts held in reserve in excess of required reserves. Banks have at least three assets on their books: required reserves, excess reserves, and loans to customers.
7. When loans are made to customers, the money supply is increased by the amount of the loan. Banks make loans in order to make money (interest earnings). As the money from one loan is deposited into another account, more excess reserves are created. This is the multiplier expansion of money in the banking system. The money multiplier is the maximum ratio of change in the money supply that can result from an initial deposit, which causes a change in the excess reserves held by banks.

Chapter 8

Assessment

Vocabulary Review

Match each statement with the term that best defines it.

1. Anything that people accept as payment for goods and services
2. The primary function of money to be widely accepted in exchange for goods and services
3. The function of money to provide a common measurement of value for goods and services
4. The function of money to hold value over time
5. Money that has market value based on the material from which it is made
6. Money that is accepted by law, and not because of its tangible value
7. The total money in financial institutions that can be withdrawn by writing a check
8. An account with guaranteed interest for a period of time
9. A banking system in which banks keep only a percentage of their deposits on reserve and lend out the remainder
10. The minimum balance of reserves that the Fed requires a bank to hold on deposit with the Fed
11. The central banking system of the United States
12. The percentage of deposits that the Fed requires a bank to hold on deposit with the Fed or in cash rather than being loaned
13. Potential loan balances of reserves held on deposit with the Fed in excess of required reserves
14. The maximum change in the money supply (checkable deposits) due to an initial change in the excess reserves banks hold. It is equal to 1 divided by the required reserve ratio (RRR)

Vocabulary

a. checkable deposits
b. commodity money
c. excess reserves
d. Federal Reserve System
e. fiat money
f. fractional reserve banking
g. medium of exchange
h. money
i. money multiplier
j. required reserves
k. required reserve ratio (RRR)
l. store of value
m. time deposit
n. unit of account

Review Your Knowledge

LO 1-1 15. Anything can be money if it acts as a
   a. unit of account
   b. store of value
   c. medium of exchange
   d. all of the above must be correct

LO 1-1 16. Which of the following is *not* a store of value?
   a. dollar bills
   b. credit card
   c. coins
   d. gold

LO 1-1 **17.** A barter economy is one in which
   a. money serves as a medium of exchange
   b. only precious metals are accepted as money
   c. goods are traded directly for other goods
   d. paper money is backed by gold

LO 1-1 **18.** Comparing how many dollars it takes to attend college each year to annual earnings on a job represents the use of money as a
   a. medium of exchange
   b. unit of account
   c. store of value
   d. store of coincidence

LO 1-1 **19.** Fiat money is money
   a. accepted by law regardless of its tangible value
   b. not included as part of the M1 money supply
   c. backed by gold or silver held on reserve by the government
   d. such as coins that are made from metal

LO 1-2 **20.** The M1 money supply is defined to be the sum of currency and
   a. checkable deposits
   b. Treasury bonds
   c. savings accounts
   d. large time deposit

LO 2-2 **21.** The money multiplier equals
   a. 1 ÷ excess reserves
   b. excess reserves ÷ loans
   c. 1 ÷ actual reserves
   d. 1 ÷ required reserve ratio (RRR)

LO 1-1 **22.** The use of a dollar bill to buy a concert ticket represents the function of money as a
   a. medium of exchange
   b. unit of account
   c. store of value
   d. all of the above

LO 2-1 **23.** The required reserves of a bank are
   a. held in cash or as deposits with the Federal Reserve System
   b. equal to its loans
   c. equal to its checkable deposits
   d. none of the above

LO 2-1 **24.** Which of the following is responsible for controlling the money supply in the United States?
   a. U.S. Congress
   b. Federal Reserve System
   c. U.S. Treasury
   d. Council of Economic Advisors

LO 2-1 **25.** An individual bank can lend out at most its
   a. fractional reserves
   b. legal reserves
   c. checkable deposits
   d. excess reserves

LO 2-1 **26.** The amount of checkable deposits that banks hold is
   a. the fractional reserve requirement
   b. the excess reserve requirement
   c. the discount rate
   d. part of M1

Digging Deeper with Economics e-Collection

The Federal Reserve (the Fed) changes reserve requirements for banks in order to speed up or slow down the economy. The reserve requirement determines how much money a bank must keep on hand and how much money the bank can use for loans. Access the Gale Economics e-Collection at **www.cengage.com/school/economics/personalfinance**. Examine the reserve requirement over the past twenty years. Choose a range of years, such as 2007-2009, and explain why the Fed raised or lowered the reserve requirement. Describe what was going on in the economy at that time.

Think About It

LO 1-1 **27.** You are willing to accept cash today because you know you can spend it tomorrow. Consider what would happen if prices were rising so fast your money did not hold its value. For example, a dollar today would buy a loaf of bread. Consider what would happen if you expected the price of that same loaf of bread would be $1.50 tomorrow. How would the value of your money change?

LO 1-1 **28.** Money is no longer backed by gold—or any other commodity. When you accept currency (printed money), you are taking it on faith. What would it be like if only real gold or silver or some other commodity were accepted? Would that help or hurt the ability to buy and sell goods for consumers?

LO 1-1 **29.** Many consumers prefer debit cards and the use of credit cards is declining (following the Great Recession). Why do people prefer debit cards?

LO 1-2 **30.** A person who has a certificate of deposit of $100,000 or more has a jumbo account. They are offered higher interest rates and more account privileges, such as free accounts, free safe deposit boxes, and credit cards with low rates. Why?

Make Academic Connections

LO 1-2 **31. MATH** Marty has the following cash and savings: Currency in her pocket, $200; Checking account balance, $1,500; Savings account balance, $5,000; Certificate of deposit, $10,000. How much of this money would be counted in M1? M2?

LO 1-1 **32. HISTORY** After President Lincoln was assassinated and buried, a group of counterfeiters conspired to steal his body from the tomb and hold it ransom until members of their gang were released from prison. Research this historical event—what happened, how the Secret Service came into being (its original purpose), and how the U.S. government guards against counterfeiting today. Present an oral report to the class and include a visual display of your findings. (Abraham Lincoln Presidential Library website http://www.alplm.org)

LO 1-1 **33. ETHICS** Shady companies place ads on television, in newspapers, and on the Internet to buy your old jewelry, gold, precious metals, and gems. They offer to buy it from you at "top" prices. The consumer is expected to send in the jewelry in a special envelope. It will then be appraised and a check returned to the consumer. Can consumers rely on the offers as being fair deals? What can consumers do to protect themselves?

LO 2-2 **34. COMMUNICATIONS** A person you know has just said to you that "the only way that money is created is when the government prints more money." Write a one-page essay explaining how money is created in the banking system. Include a diagram to explain how money deposited in one account can lead to the money multiplier in the banking system.

Extend Your Learning

LO 2-2 **35.** Suppose Marcus Jones deposits $1,000 that was under his mattress in his checking account.

Assets		Liabilities	
Required Reserves	______	Checkable Deposits	______
Excess Reserves	______		
Loans	______		
Total	______	Total	______

a. If the required reserve ratio (RRR) is 20 percent, what is the effect on the required reserves?

b. What is the value of the money multiplier?

c. If each bank in the economy loans their excess reserves to the maximum, what is the effect on the money supply (M1)?

StockLib/iStockphoto.com

chapter 9

Financial Institutions and Markets

9-1 Individual Checking and Savings

9-2 Business Banking and Capital Markets

9-3 Labor Movement and Markets

yienkeat/Shutterstock.com

MARKETS *in Action!*

What Happens When Banks Fail?

In 2009, more than 100 banks failed, after 25 had already failed in 2008. During tough economic times, banks can fail for many reasons. One reason is because the bank made bad loans. Another reason is under-capitalization, which means the bank failed to meet minimum government requirements for stockholders' equity. The Federal Deposit Insurance Corporation (FDIC) is an agency of the federal government. When you have an account that is insured by the FDIC, you know that your deposits are protected up to a maximum amount that was $250,000 in 2012.

The FDIC maintains a *troubled* bank list and can step in to take action to protect a bank's depositors. Bank examiners visit banks to make sure the banks are meeting regulatory requirements. Banks are given ratings and when those ratings fall below acceptable levels, action by the FDIC begins. A bank is given a 90-day period to work on and improve the low rating. During that time, the FDIC gathers information about the bank's assets, deposits, and overall financial condition.

When a bank makes the troubled list, there are solutions depending on the reasons for trouble.

- If the bank's capital level is low, plans can be made to restore that to an acceptable level.
- If the bank has a bad group of loans, plans can be made to diversify the loans.
- The bank may need to change procedures or policies.
- The bank may need to hire new loan officers or makes changes to its board of directors so that the board becomes more active.

As the end of the 90 days draws near, if the bank is not improving significantly, the FDIC sets up procedures that allow other banks to bid for the acquisition of the troubled bank's assets, deposits, or both. The FDIC oversees the process of closure, including the transfer of assets to another bank or banks. It assures depositors that their accounts are safe. In most cases, the failing bank is replaced by the purchasing bank and the transition is both seamless and painless for the bank's depositors.

Many banks, both small and large, failed in 2008 and 2009.

Johnny Grieg/iStockphoto.com

Think Critically

1. Why do businesses fail during times when the economy is poor? What can business owners do during good economic times to prevent this failure?
2. As a bank depositor, why should you deposit your money with a bank that has FDIC insurance? Are there accounts (savings and checking) where you can deposit your money, but have no such insurance? Why might you choose an account without insurance?

yienkeat/Shutterstock.com

9-1 Individual Checking and Savings

Learning Objectives

LO 1-1 **Explain** how individuals use checking accounts, including the costs and benefits.

LO 1-2 **Describe** the purpose and types of savings plans, and interest earnings on savings.

LO 1-3 **Evaluate** the risks, costs, and benefits of maintaining accounts and using services of financial institutions.

Vocabulary

financial institution, p. 251
checking account, p. 251
reconciliation, p. 252
savings account, p. 253
interest, p. 253
compound interest, pp. 254
debit card, p. 256
service fee, p. 257

© Aleksandar Vrzalski/iStockphoto.com

REAL-WORLD FOCUS

Elizabeth works part-time and gets a regular paycheck. Her employer electronically deposits her paycheck into her checking account each month. Because of this deposit, Liz is able to have a free checking account. She can also link her checking account to her savings account, which enables her to transfer money between accounts, do online banking, and maintain a balance to cover the transactions she makes. "I just don't know what I would do without my accounts," she told her friend. "I don't know how people are able to get by just using cash."

WORK AS A TEAM When is the right time to open a checking and savings account at a bank? What kind of fees and other costs can you expect? Is it worth it to you to have bank accounts? Why or why not?

Cupertino/Shutterstock.com

When making a payment on the phone using credit, you must have the card in your possession so you can provide the account number, expiration date, and the card security number.

DO YOU THINK there is a difference when you pay with a debit card versus a credit card?

yienkeat/Shutterstock.com

LO 1-1 Checking Accounts

Financial institutions are businesses that provide banking services to consumers and businesses. Commercial banks, savings banks, credit unions, savings and loans, and brokerage firms are all types of financial institutions. These businesses or institutions are frequently referred to as banks because you can deposit money into various types of accounts, such as checking and savings, and purchase certificates of deposit (CD).

A **checking account** is a demand deposit account where you can make withdrawals and deposit money. It provides a safe place to keep money. It is a *demand deposit* because account holders can quickly and easily access their money. Most banks allow and encourage online access. At a bank's website you can verify your balance, make payments from your account, transfer money among your accounts, or perform other actions, such as online bill payment. Checking accounts are a low-risk way to manage your income and pay your bills.

Writing Checks

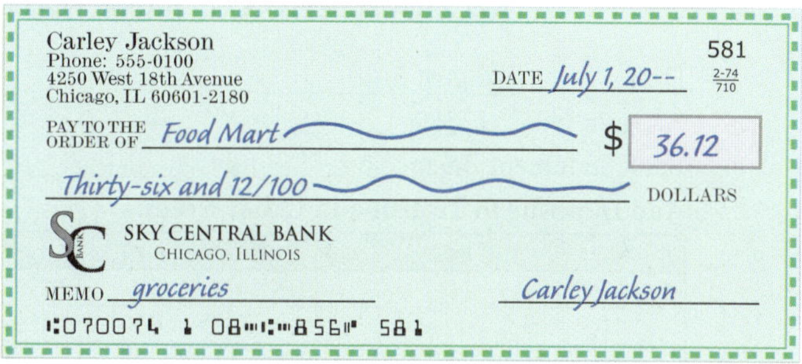
Carley Jackson
Phone: 555-0100
4250 West 18th Avenue
Chicago, IL 60601-2180
581
DATE July 1, 20--
2-74/710
PAY TO THE ORDER OF Food Mart $ 36.12
Thirty-six and 12/100 DOLLARS
SKY CENTRAL BANK
CHICAGO, ILLINOIS
MEMO groceries
Carley Jackson
⑆070074⑆ 08⑈856⑈ 581

Figure 9-1
Personal Check

A *check* is a written order to pay a stated amount to a designated person. Checks are an accepted form of payment for most bills and in many stores. A *cancelled check* is one that has been approved by the bank or financial institution and all of the involved accounts have been credited or debited. A cancelled check can serve as proof of payment. An account holder can get an image of a cancelled check from the bank or online.

Figure 9-1 shows a *personal check* that has been written to a local business by a consumer. To make a purchase by writing a personal check at a business, you generally will need to show identification.

To open a checking account, an initial deposit is needed, often as little as $50 or $100. A *bank signature form* is used to establish your identity as an account holder. Some checking accounts provide a free supply of checks. Others require you to order checks and pay a separate charge for them.

Making Deposits

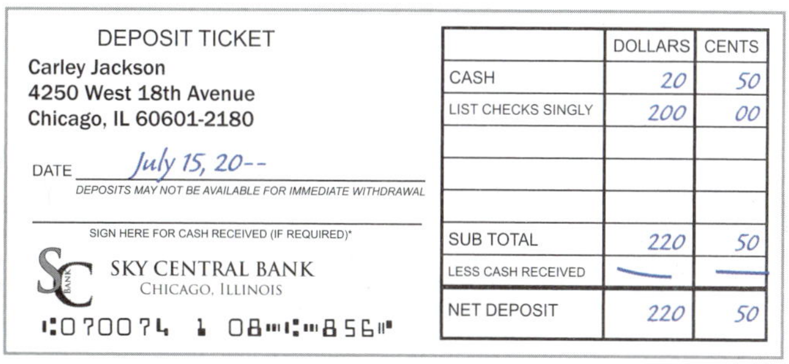
DEPOSIT TICKET
Carley Jackson
4250 West 18th Avenue
Chicago, IL 60601-2180
DATE July 15, 20--
DEPOSITS MAY NOT BE AVAILABLE FOR IMMEDIATE WITHDRAWAL
SIGN HERE FOR CASH RECEIVED (IF REQUIRED)
SKY CENTRAL BANK
CHICAGO, ILLINOIS
⑆070074⑆ 08⑈856⑈

	DOLLARS	CENTS
CASH	20	50
LIST CHECKS SINGLY	200	00
SUB TOTAL	220	50
LESS CASH RECEIVED	—	—
NET DEPOSIT	220	50

Figure 9-2
Deposit Ticket

You make deposits to your account using a *deposit ticket*. On the deposit ticket, you list cash and checks being deposited. You can make a deposit in person or at an ATM (Automated Teller Machine). Some accounts allow you to make deposits electronically, using your computer or smartphone. Most checking accounts also allow for automatic deposits of an employee's paycheck. Figure 9-2 shows a completed deposit ticket.

Reconciling an Account

Each month, you should verify that the amount in your checking account matches the bank's record of the amount in the account. This verification is the process of **reconciliation**. Whether a monthly paper statement or an online statement is received, it is important to verify deposits, withdrawals, and the balance in the account. Errors can result in overdraft fees. With *online banking* it is possible to check your balance daily and see up-to-the-minute changes in your account.

To reconcile an account, follow these steps as shown in Figure 9-3.

1. Enter the current (ending) balance as shown by the bank on the bank statement.
2. To this balance, add any deposits you have made, which are not yet showing on the statement. These are called *deposits in transit* and have not yet cleared your account, meaning the money has not been deposited into your account.

Figure 9-3
Reconciliation Form

RECONCILIATION OF BANK STATEMENT

Date August 3, 20--

Account No. 942869

Bank Statement Balance on July 31, 20-- $ 966.68 **1**

Add Deposits in Transit and Other Credits

Date	Amount
7/31/20--	220.50

Total Deposits in Transit/Credits $ 220.50

Subtotal $ 1,187.18 **2**

Deduct Outstanding Checks/Withdrawals

Check No.	Date	Amount
580	7/2/20--	20.00
581	7/29/20--	36.12
ATM	8/1/20--	40.00

Total Outstanding Checks/Withdrawals $ 96.12

Adjusted Bank Balance $ 1,091.06 **3**

Checkbook Register Balance on August 3, 20-- $ 1,096.06 **4**

Deduct Bank Charges

Description	Amount
Service charge, monthly fee	5.00

Total Bank Charges $ 5.00

Subtotal $ 1,091.06 **5**

Add Interest or Other Credits

Description	Amount

Total Credits $ 0.00

Adjusted Checkbook Register Balance $ 1,091.06 **6**

3. Now subtract any checks or other withdrawals that you have made that do not yet appear on the bank statement. These are known as *outstanding checks* or charges. The result is the adjusted bank balance.
4. Enter the current (ending) balance in your account as shown in your checkbook register.
5. To this balance, add any credits shown on your bank statement, such as interest earned on your account. The bank has already added these to your balance.
6. Now deduct any charges or debits the bank has taken from your account, such as monthly service fees, check fees, or other charges. The bank has already subtracted these from your account. The result is the adjusted checkbook balance. This amount should be the same as the adjusted bank balance (Step 3). If these amounts do not match, you must start over and examine each transaction until you find the error. Most errors are made by account holders. But occasionally, banks do make errors.

CHECKPOINT

Why is it important to reconcile your bank account?

LO 1-2 Savings Accounts

In addition to a checking account, you can have a savings account at a financial institution. A **savings account** is an account where you set aside money for future use. A savings account often has more restrictions than a checking account. For example, you may be limited in the number of withdrawals in a month. Like checking accounts, savings accounts are insured by the FDIC.

Savings accounts typically earn a low rate of interest. **Interest** is the earnings you receive on your balance in the account. When your savings account is linked to your checking account, you can move money back and forth between the accounts. This feature may help you avoid fees, such as overdraft charges or monthly service fees.

Money that can be set aside for longer periods of time can earn more interest. A *certificate of deposit* (CD) is an investment of a fixed sum at a fixed rate of interest for a fixed period of time. A three-year CD will earn a higher rate of interest than a six-month CD. The longer you can set aside money, the higher rate of return you will earn.

Benefits of Saving

Setting money aside helps you be prepared for emergencies and other unplanned events. It gives you flexibility so that you can make better buying decisions. For example, if you have savings, you can buy items at sale prices now rather than paying later or over time. Savings allow you to accumulate money for large purchases, such as a car or a house. Setting aside money today for use later is the first step toward financial security.

Akbudak Rimma/Shutterstock.com

Savings accounts are also used to hold money temporarily until you have enough to start investing. Money that isn't needed until sometime in the future can earn a higher rate of return. Money set aside grows over time because it earns interest. *Simple interest* is the amount of interest earned at a fixed rate of interest for a given period of time. Figure 9-4 shows how to compute simple interest.

Figure 9-4

Simple Interest

$$\textbf{Interest } (I) = \textbf{Principal } (P) \times \textbf{Rate } (R) \times \textbf{Time } (T)$$
$$= \$1{,}000 \times 6\% \text{ annual rate} \times 6 \text{ months}$$
$$= \$1{,}000 \times 0.06 \times \frac{6}{12}$$
$$= \$30$$

When interest is added to the original amount (principal), you will then be receiving interest on interest, or **compound interest**. When interest continues to accumulate on both principal and interest, your money grows at a more rapid rate.

Getting Started

A savings plan begins with setting aside money. That means you must spend less money than you make. By setting aside a small portion each month or pay period, you will see your money start to grow. As a new saver, you should start small, setting aside only money that you will leave in the bank. Then as you get raises and other increases in your cash flow, you can set aside more money rather than spending it. Over time you will see this money increase. Over a lifetime, savings will give you financial security and peace of mind. Consider these rules:

1. Set money aside from each paycheck.
2. As you get raises, earn, or receive more money, set aside a part of that money.
3. Always spend less than you make.
4. Once money is put into savings, do not withdraw it.
5. Look for ways to set aside money in accounts that pay higher interest rates.
6. Make sure your savings are insured so they will be safe from loss.

Some people use the emergency fund concept to get started saving. An *emergency fund* is money set aside to be used in case of an unexpected expense. Some people call this money their "put and take" account. When bills are paid, any excess can be deposited into the emergency fund account. When the emergency fund gets large and has more than would be needed, the excess can be deposited into a CD or long-term savings account that pays a higher rate of interest.

The important thing to remember is that you must spend less than you make. As money comes in, you must make a conscious effort to set part of it aside for the future. This action is called *systematic saving*, or setting money aside regularly as a planned action. The purpose is to provide for financial security. If you allow your spending to keep pace with your income, you will not be able to save. The sooner you can start setting aside money, the faster it will grow. Money set aside over a lifetime will provide you with a large reserve for your retirement years.

A couple uses online banking to check account balances and pay bills.

Risk Versus Return

A savings account is a safe way to set aside money for the future. Because the risk is low, the payback is also low. The rate of interest paid on safe investments is lower than the rate paid on higher-risk choices. Thus, for a six-month CD, your rate will be lower than if you set aside your money in a CD for three years. This trade-off occurs because you are taking less risk with the six-month CD. If interest rates rise, after six months you can re-invest at the higher rate. With a three-year CD you would have to wait longer to do this. The higher the risk, the higher return you require as an investor. When you take less risk, you should expect returns to be lower.

At many financial institutions you can also open an investment account. These accounts typically are not insured by the FDIC. There is no guaranteed rate of return. You could even lose part or all of your investment. Thus, your risk is higher. These accounts pay a higher market rate of return. That is, when the market for the investment rises, so does the account value.

CHECKPOINT

Why is it important to start saving early in your life?

ETHICS *in Action!*

Are Late Payments Ethical?

Most people have regular payments they must make. These could include rent, car payments, electric, gas, and water bills. If you have a credit card you are required to make at least a minimum payment every month. Failure to make payments on time can result in some sort of financial penalty. If you miss your credit card payment, for example, you might be required to pay an extra $30 and the interest rate you are charged could be increased. But some debts don't result in a penalty if you make them late.

Suppose you borrowed $500 from your friend and agreed to pay him $50 each month over the next ten months. There was no written agreement. Last month you spent more than you planned so you decided to deposit $50 in your savings account instead of paying your friend. This helped you meet your savings plan regardless of your extra spending but it made your friend angry. Although it is important to create a plan to save, a savings plan is in many ways a spending plan. It helps you live within your means, pay your debts, and still set some of your income aside for the future.

Think Critically

1. **Is it ethical for a person to intentionally miss making a payment on time? Why or why not?**
2. **Why is a savings plan really a plan for not spending? Why do many people have trouble following their saving plans?**

LO 1-3 Banking Services

In addition to checking and savings accounts, banks offer other products and services to customers. Services generally cost extra, although some are packaged with the account and do not involve additional fees. As times change, banks can raise their fees or begin to impose fees for services that had previously not been assessed a fee. You should consider the cost versus the benefit when choosing products and services from financial institutions:

Slavoljub Pantelic/Shutterstock.com

A customer must present a key to a bank employee, who also has a key, to access a safe deposit box.

SAFE DEPOSIT BOXES A *safe deposit box* is a secure container in the bank's vault. Customers can store important documents, such as deeds, stock certificates, and precious metals. Annual fees of $35 to $100 are charged based on the size of the container, but this fee may also be part of a package.

ACCOUNT SERVICES Account services generally cost a fee charged by the bank. As an account holder, you can request a stop payment. With a *stop payment*, the bank is instructed not to honor a check or electronic withdrawal you previously wrote or authorized. This order is usually good for six months.

Banks can provide cashier's checks for their customers. A *cashier's check* is a check that is debited from your checking account when it is written. The bank assumes the responsibility of paying the check.

Some banks also provide money orders. A *money order* is a type of check issued by the bank after a person has paid the bank an amount equal to the amount of the check plus a fee. Money orders, which are guaranteed for the amount of the check, are used to pay bills or make payments. People who do not have checking accounts often use money orders to send payments by mail.

Internet banking is offered by all financial institutions. *Internet banking* allows you 24-hour access to your accounts. You can check account balances, status of deposits and checks, and monitor your accounts. You can view and print statements, transfer money, and pay bills electronically.

BANK CARDS Financial institutions issue several types of cards, including *ATM cards* which allow you to deposit or withdraw money from your accounts using an ATM machine. A **debit card** is similar to an ATM card, except that it can also be used to make point-of-sale (POS) purchases at businesses. Most banks offer credit cards (Visa and MasterCard) to customers. These cards may charge lower interest rates and other fees than other sources that issue credit cards.

FINANCIAL ADVISING AND LOANS Many banks provide personal financial advising services. These advisors recommend financial products and investments. Banks also make loans to consumers based on the customer's ability to repay the loans. Your credit rating and status will determine your eligibility to borrow money.

Costs and Risks of Banking

Banks charge customers fees to cover costs of operations and to make a profit. Fees range from small to large amounts. Banks publish brochures that describe accounts, features, and the fees that go along with the services. Before you open an account, compare fees and services. In many cases, a credit union may offer you the most services for the least costs.

MONTHLY ACCOUNT FEES Many financial institutions charge a monthly **service fee** for maintaining a checking account. The fee may be $10 to $20, or more. Unless you maintain a minimum balance or have a special free account (such as for students or seniors), you will be charged this fee. Savings accounts can also be charged a monthly fee if they are below a set minimum balance.

NET Bookmark

Access www.cengage.com/school/economics/personalfinance and click on the link for Chapter 9. Visit the Federal Deposit Insurance Corporation (FDIC) website. Here you will find complete information about the role of the FDIC and services available to account holders, consumers, and others. Click on I Am A box and choose *Consumer.* Then, click on the I Want To box and choose *Prevent identity theft.* What can you do to avoid being an online victim?

www.cengage.com/school/economics/personalfinance

ATM AND DEBIT CARD FEES When you withdraw and deposit money to your accounts at an ATM owned by your bank, there is usually no charge. But if you use the ATM machine of another bank or business, there is often a fee of $2 or more per transaction. Debit card transactions result in fees paid by merchants to banks. You may be charged a processing fee by the merchant to cover this cost. Some banks also charge a monthly fee for a debit card.

NSF FEES When a check is written that has insufficient or non-sufficient funds (NSF) to cover the amount of the check, it is called a *bounced check.* Each bounced check is returned by the bank without paying the person to whom it was written. The person who wrote the check will be charged an NSF fee of $30 or more for writing a bad check. This NSF fee is also known as an *overdraft charge*, which is a fee imposed for exceeding the account balance. If you sign up for *overdraft protection,* you may be able to avoid or pay reduced NSF fees. There is a risk to this, however. In some cases, you can avoid having a dishonored transaction, but the cost can be high. For example, if you buy a coffee for $5 using an electronic transaction, but you have insufficient funds, the bank can cover that purchase, but charge you $35. That's a very expensive cup of coffee.

CHANGING ACCOUNTS AND FEES Banks routinely change their account structures and fees. With a 30-day written notice to the consumer, banks are able to start charging fees for services previously provided without charge. It is your responsibility to read such notices and do comparison shopping. When fees at your financial institution are rising and you can pay less elsewhere, it may be time to switch banks. You can consider credit unions and other options where services are similar, but fees and charges are less. When a bank fails and another takes it over, this action is likely to happen within the first year after the take-over. Bank customers should be prepared to accept the changes or switch to another bank. These are risks that all holders of bank accounts must be prepared to take.

CHECKPOINT

How does saving help the economy?

PROFILE

Mary Kay Ash
Mary Kay Cosmetics

AP Photo

Mary Kay Ash was an American businesswoman and founder of Mary Kay Cosmetics. Born in Harris County, Texas in 1918, Mary Kay attended Reagan High School in Houston, Texas and went on to graduate from the University of Texas.

Described as a "one-of-a-kind visionary," Mary Kay displayed a can-do spirit that was evident throughout her life. Mary Kay took on responsibilities as a child, taking care of her father during his illness. She worked hard and advanced in her career as a national training director. When she was treated unfairly, Mary Kay decided to take charge of her own life. (A male she had trained was promoted above her and at twice the pay.) Mary Kay's response in 1963 was revolutionary—not very many women were willing, or able to step out on their own—seeking and making opportunities that were hard to find in a workplace that was dominated by men.

Working for someone else gave Mary Kay the experience and knowledge she needed to start her own company. Mary Kay's attempt to write a book about her experiences with the "glass ceiling" led to her writing a business plan for the "ideal company." With her husband and 20-year-old son, Mary Kay started Mary Kay Cosmetics with an investment of $5,000. Her original store opened in 1963 in Dallas, Texas, where it grew rapidly and formed the basis of the large company it is today.

Being born in a modest family, Mary Kay had to save her money and work hard to achieve her goals. She also based her business on the Golden Rule. She designed a plan whereby people would be praised for their successes. Her company's marketing plan was designed to help women succeed and to praise them for the success they achieved. She is famous for her pink Cadillacs awarded to top sales people in her company. Mary Kay's slogan of "God first, family second, career third" expressed her viewpoint that workers must always keep their lives in balance.

At the time of her death in 2001, Mary Kay Cosmetics had over 800,000 representatives in 37 countries with total annual sales of more than $2 billion. By 2008, the company had more than 1.7 million consultants worldwide. Honored as one of the leading female entrepreneurs in American history, Mary Kay Ash is buried in Dallas, Texas.

THINK CRITICALLY

1. **What type of business is Mary Kay Cosmetics (how do they sell their products)?**
2. **How do business ethics contribute to the overall success of a company like Mary Kay Cosmetics?**

9-1 Assessment

Key Concepts

LO 1-1 1. Why do consumers have checking accounts?

LO 1-2 2. What is meant by systematic saving?

LO 1-3 3. What banking services are available at financial institutions?

LO 1-3 4. List three fees you can be charged for using banking services.

Think About It

LO 3-3 5. Why do consumers choose one bank over another? Some consumers choose banks (with higher fees) over credit unions (with lower costs). Why?

LO 3-3 6. Many businesses will not accept personal checks. They say too many personal checks have insufficient funds. Do you think paper checks will soon be unacceptable as a form of payment? Why or why not?

LO 1-2 7. Most banks allow electronic deposit of checks, either using an ATM or using a smart phone. With automatic deposits, electronic withdrawals, online bill payments, and other ways of using your account you never have to go into a bank. Do you think banks of the future will not need physical locations? Explain.

Make Academic Connections

LO 1-1 8. **TECHNOLOGY** With online banking, you can check your balance any time. You can verify deposits, checks written, and all transactions. Many people believe frequent checking of your balance is safer than reconciling their bank statement each month. Do you agree? Why or why not?

LO 1-2 9. **COMMUNICATION** Savings accounts are a safe form of investing, but interest rates may be low. Write a one-page paper, defending savings accounts as a way to provide for your future. Explain why it is important to set aside money in savings accounts whenever you can.

Teamwork

LO 1-2 10. Visit bankrate.com and use their online calculators. Compare how fast different lump sums and monthly savings amounts grow. Prepare a chart to display your findings.

LO 1-3 11. The use of debit cards has increased rapidly in recent years. Debit cards allow instant access to your account. But there are also dangers in using debit cards for purchases. Participate in a debate defending or attacking the use of debit cards for purchasing products.

Unit 4 Project: Making Sense of Money

BANKING SERVICES AND FEES Prepare a poster board display that includes brochures and data comparing banking services and fees in your local area. Based on data collected, rate the financial institutions from best to worst in terms of fees, types of accounts and other services available, interest rates on savings, and overall value to consumers.

9-2 Business Banking and Capital Markets

Learning Objectives	Vocabulary
LO 2-1 **Describe** business banking, services, and accounts.	**sweep account,** p. 261
LO 2-2 **Explain** how savings lead to capital formation in an economy.	**credit line,** p. 261
	relationship banking, p. 261
	production loan, p. 263
	capital market, p. 264
	commercial paper, p. 264

REAL-WORLD FOCUS

© Aleksandar Vrzalski/iStockphoto.com

Emily has a savings account at her local bank. She puts money into the account every paycheck. Her savings account earns interest, but very little. If Emily put a lump sum into a certificate of deposit (CD), she could double the interest rate paid. "I don't understand why one form of saving pays so much more than another form of saving," she told her friend. "I know they are lending out my money to businesses and others. So why is there a difference?"

WORK AS A TEAM When one person saves money, a bank can lend money to another person. Why do banks charge more interest for money loaned than they pay for money on deposit? When more people save more money, then banks are able to make more loans and bigger loans to businesses. Explain.

B. Richard Molony/Shutterstock.com

For a concrete company, their trucks are both a means of transportation and also the equipment used at the job site to mix and pour the cement.

DO YOU THINK when a concrete company borrows money to purchase a new fleet of trucks, the company uses a credit line or gets a production loan?

yienkeat/Shutterstock.com

LO 2-1 Business Banking

Businesses also use banking services. Many commercial banks specialize in business customer accounts. Some special services are offered to businesses.

Business Checking

Business accounts differ from consumer accounts. Business customers write checks to pay vendors, creditors, employees, government, and others. Business accounts must maintain balances sufficient to meet these ongoing expenses. Thus businesses often have accounts known as sweep accounts. A **sweep account** is one that is used to cover a minimum balance. When funds drop to a pre-set level, money is automatically moved from a separate account to the main business account. The separate, or sweep account, is a business investment account where higher rates of interest are paid and where the account receives deposits of loan funds and other types of financing.

Business Credit Lines

Businesses have a different fee schedule from consumers. Fees are based on services provided and balances maintained. For example, the business may have an agreement with the bank to provide ongoing financing for operations. A pre-arranged **credit line** allows the business to access funds as needed. Typically a business has peak seasons (where sales and revenues are high) and valley seasons (where sales and revenues are low). These businesses often need loans to get through the low points, and they are able to pay off the loans as they go through the high points.

nuno/iStockphoto.com

A successful business woman sits with her banker and signs a business loan application.

Relationship Banking

Businesses bring revenue to the bank when they process their sales transactions through the bank. For example, a business may accept credit and debit cards for purchases of merchandise. Each transaction is assessed a fee of 2 to 5 percent. The bank collects this fee at the point of sale or when transaction receipts are deposited with the bank. Based on the volume of fee revenue being generated, the business can negotiate lower rates and other business perks with the financial institution. The concept of having an ongoing group of services is known as **relationship banking**. An entire package of banking services involves assessing what a business has to offer to the bank and determining services and fees that can be offered to the business to attract and keep their business accounts.

Math CONNECTION

Sweep Account Transfers

Your company has a main business account from which expenses are paid. As the office manager, you keep the balance in this account at a minimum so that more of the company's money can be in a sweep account, where interest is paid on the balance. Your bank makes a daily transfer from the sweep account into the main business account to cover transactions that will be posted for the day and yet maintain the minimum balance. The main business account must have a balance of $1,000 to avoid a service fee. Transfers to the main business account are rounded up to thousands. Use the information given to find the daily balances of each account.

Main business account balance on Monday morning	$5,698.32
Sweep account balance on Monday morning	$156,449.78
Transactions to post Monday evening	$12,046.55
Transactions to post Tuesday evening	$4,356.12

SOLUTION

On Monday, how much should be transferred to maintain the minimum balance?

$12,046.55	Amount of Monday's transactions.
– 4,698.32	Current balance of $5,698.00 – $1,000
$ 7,348.23	$8,000 will be transferred.

The balances in each account after the transfer and after the transactions post are:

Sweep account after transfer	Main business account after transfer	Main business account after transactions posted
$156,449.78	**$5,698.32**	**$13,698.32**
–8,000.00	**+ 8,000.00**	**–12,046.55**
$148,449.78	**$13,698.32**	**$1,651.77**

On Tuesday, how much is needed for the transactions and minimum balance?

$4,356.12 – $651.77 = $3,704.35 $4,000 will be transferred.

The balances in each account after the transfer and after the transactions are:

Sweep account after transfer

$148,449.78 – $4,000.00 = $144,449.78

Main business account after transfer

$1,651.77 + $4,000.00 = $5,651.77

Main business account after transactions posted

$5,651.77 – $4,356.12 = $1,295.65

TRY IT

Find the balances in the accounts if transactions totaling $2,316.87 are posted on Wednesday.

Business Loans

When businesses borrow money, the loans are called production loans. With a **production loan**, the borrowed money will be used to buy something that will help repay the loan. When a consumer borrows money to buy something, it is called a *consumption loan.* A consumption loan is more risky because the loan is used to buy something, such as a car or a refrigerator, which will not be used to generate income. Because a production loan is less risky than a loan made to a consumer, interest rates are lower. Businesses generally pay lower rates to borrow money than consumers.

Business loans are usually pre-arranged with the financial institution, similar to lines of credit. The banking relationship is one of mutual benefit. As the business does well, the bank gets more revenue from processing transactions and managing accounts. Thus, they know and appreciate the financial needs of the business and are prepared to help them through difficult, but predictable, economic times. Businesses keep banks informed of their current and projected status and needs. This communication keeps the banking relationship strong and healthy.

Dmitry Kalinovsky/Shutterstock.com

A company that moves earth at a construction site might need a production loan to purchase a wheel loader excavator with a backhoe.

CHECKPOINT

How are consumer loans different from business loans?

Business Banking

Some banks specialize in business accounts and making loans to small businesses. Their services and fee schedules are different from consumer accounts. There are also different requirements for opening a business account.

Within the state and local economy, you may also find special services available to business customers. The purpose of these activities is to serve the needs of the local economy by stimulating business activity.

Investigate Your Local ECONOMY

Try it Out

Contact your local Chamber of Commerce, Better Business Bureau, or Toastmasters Club and ask what services they provide for local small business owners. Ask for brochures or other printed information available to the public.

LO 2-2 Savings and Capital Formation

Banks lend money to businesses from the bank's excess reserves. *Excess reserves* are created when customers deposit money that can then be used by the bank. For example, if there is a 20% reserve requirement, the bank can lend 80% of its deposits. So when one customer has savings of $100, that means the bank can create a loan for $80. As consumers and businesses save money, it is then made available for loans.

Businesses borrow money to make large purchases, such as capital equipment, buildings, factories, and other high-cost items. These purchases require large sums of money. When borrowing money from banks, the businesses pay interest. The interest rate charged to these commercial or business customers is higher than the rate of interest the bank pays to its customers who save money. The money that results from the difference between the two interest rates allows the bank to pay its expenses and earn a profit.

Brian K./Shutterstock.com

The owner of this apartment building most likely borrowed money to finance the construction of the building.

Capital Markets

Capital markets exist where businesses are able to go to finance operations as well as large purchases over long periods of time. Savings add to the capital markets by increasing the supply of money that is available for loans. Financial institutions represent a large segment of the capital market. They are able and willing to lend money to businesses because the risk is lower and the rates of return provide a solid revenue source. Businesses can also borrow large sums of money from other sources in the capital markets, including the sale of corporate bonds and the use of commercial paper.

Commercial paper involves one corporation borrowing from the excess cash of another corporation. Commercial paper is a form of short-term borrowing, often used until final financing can be arranged. In other words, corporations lend money to other corporations using capital markets as the intermediary. Money not currently being used for operations and not currently needed should be "working" for the company, by earning interest.

Tax Code Incentives

The Internal Revenue Service (IRS) Tax Code allows (and in some cases, requires) businesses to take advantage of business deductions and write-offs. Interest paid for loans to conduct business is tax deductible. Income earned by the company is reduced by the amount of interest paid. Thus, it is beneficial to businesses to borrow money to finance operations as well as capital purchases. One reason for these incentives is to encourage capital investments (purchase of equipment, machinery, and other tools of production) by businesses.

CHECKPOINT

How does saving money lead to capital formation?

Global View

Banking in Switzerland

Zurich, Switzerland is often referred to as the "banking capital of the world." Switzerland is a wealthy nation with a gross domestic product (GDP) higher than most European nations. The GDP represents a total dollar amount of all goods and services produced over a given time period. A high GDP in Switzerland indicates that its economy is good. The value of the Swiss franc (CHF) is relatively stable. An estimated one third of all money kept in accounts outside the U.S. is held in Swiss banks. These accounts are referred to as "offshore" funds.

All banks in Switzerland are regulated by the Swiss Financial Market Supervisory Authority (FINMA), which is an agency of the federal government. The country's unique tradition of bank "secrecy" dates back to the Middle Ages, although it first became an official law in 1934. The banking industry in Switzerland prospers because of their dedication to protecting the privacy of their account holders.

Switzerland's two largest banks are UBS and Credit Suisse. UBS was founded in June 1998, when the Union Bank of Switzerland (1862) merged with the Swiss Bank Corporation (1872). Headquartered in Zurich, UBS is Switzerland's largest bank. It has offices around the world (four in the U.S.). Credit Suisse is the second-largest Swiss bank. Based in Zurich, it was founded in 1856.

Norbert Derec/Shutterstock.com

The headquarters of Credit Suisse is located in Zurich, Switzerland.

Credit Suisse offers private banking (consumers), investment banking (businesses), and asset management services.

Swiss bank "secrecy" protects the privacy of bank clients. Under Swiss law, these rights are similar to confidentiality protections between doctors and patients or lawyers and their clients. The Swiss government views privacy as a basic human right that should be protected.

Think Critically

1. **Why do many wealthy persons who frequently travel internationally choose to keep their accounts in Swiss banks?**
2. **Why is privacy important to individuals and businesses when it concerns their money, loans, and bank accounts?**

9-2 Assessment

Key Concepts

LO 2-1 1. What is a sweep account?

LO 2-1 2. Why do businesses need lines of credit?

LO 2-1 3. How is a production loan different from a consumption loan?

LO 2-2 4. What tax incentive do businesses have with regard to interest paid on loans?

Think About It

LO 2-1 5. Business customers may have multiple accounts used for different purposes. They also have a greater amount of cash and a higher volume of activity in their accounts. Why is it so important that businesses manage account balances to avoid overdrafts?

LO 2-2 6. Many businesses make much of their annual profit during the holiday season each year. At other times their sales are lower and profits are smaller. How do these businesses use capital markets to borrow money during slow seasons?

7. Describe the meaning of commercial paper in terms of short-term borrowing.

8. Make of list of services that a bank might offer that would lead to relationship banking for customers.

Make Academic Connections

LO 2-1 9. **SOCIAL STUDIES** Businesses are able to negotiate lower fees for banking services than consumers because they have higher activity volume and generate fee revenue for banks. Is there any way that consumers can increase their negotiating power? Explain why negotiating skills are important in today's competitive society.

LO 2-2 10. **ACCOUNTING** Businesses must produce solid financial statements to secure loans from banks. What kind of information do you think the bank would like to see about a business to be assured that the loan can be repaid? Display a corporate financial statement and explain what information it contains.

LO 2-2 11. **ETHICS** The U.S. Tax Code has many "loopholes." Tax avoidance is a legal activity. Tax evasion is illegal. Businesses are allowed many deductions, such as interest paid on loans, which are not deductible for consumers. Is it ethical to "stretch" tax laws to expand deductions?

Teamwork

LO 2-2 12. Visit the Federal Reserve Bank's website (www.federalreserve.gov) and research information about how banks are regulated. Click on the link "about the Fed" and find out how the Federal Reserve controls banking activities, including interest rates and borrowing by the banks. Write a report and present it orally to the class.

LO 2-2 13. Visit the IRS website (www.irs.gov) and look for information about business tax deductions. Use key words to locate current tax years' allowable write-offs. Prepare a list of business deductions that can be claimed to reduce the tax liability of businesses.

9-3 Labor Movement and Markets

Learning Objectives	Vocabulary
LO 3-1 **Explain** the conditions that led to the need for labor unions in this country. **LO 3-2** **Describe** the formation of labor unions, laws passed, and the significance of the labor market in the free market system.	**work conditions,** p. 268 **labor union,** p. 269 **collective bargaining,** p. 269 **strike,** p. 269 **injunction,** p. 270 **closed shop,** p. 271 **union shop,** p. 271 **public employee union,** p. 272

© Aleksandar Vrzalski/iStockphoto.com

REAL-WORLD FOCUS

Matthew has a part-time job sorting and loading packages for a local delivery service. He has union dues withheld from his paycheck. When he first started the job, he had to pay a $200 initiation fee to the union. "Gee," says Matt, "I don't mind the monthly dues so much, but paying that up-front fee was tough. I didn't have any take-home pay left to spend."

WORK AS A TEAM Why does Matthew have to pay union dues when he works part-time? What is the purpose of an initiation fee? What kind of labor union do you think he has joined? Are there benefits to union membership?

In March 2011, people cheered for Jesse Jackson as they rallied in Madison, WI in support of collective bargaining rights.

DO YOU THINK collective bargaining is a process that seeks to only secure pay raises for workers? Explain your answer.

Suzanne Tucker/Shutterstock.com

yienkeat/Shutterstock.com

LO 3-1 The Need for Labor Rights

As America moved from an agricultural nation to an industrial nation in the late 1700s to the mid-1800s, there was high demand for labor. Citizens started working for employers and earning a paycheck. They worked in factories, in urban areas, and at jobs where they worked long, hard hours. Employers demanded that their workers put in ten or more hours a day. It was a new age and era. As such, there were no existing laws or guidelines. The workers accepted the pay and were grateful to have a job. Life as a laborer wasn't the great liberator many people thought it would be. To survive, many families had every member of the family working, which led to child labor in factories. Even the children were not treated well. They too were overworked and underpaid, and a long time passed before things started to change.

Work Life

Work conditions refers to the nature of the workplace and what is required for workers to succeed. Many factory and industrial jobs were unsafe. Workers were not provided adequate training, safety equipment, or clothing. They worked long hours, often without adequate breaks. They were at risk of injuries due to fatigue, their own lack of skills, and machinery that was often dangerous and poorly maintained. Because there were no laws protecting workers or their rights, workers often experienced serious injuries that could have been prevented. Some workers even died.

Child Labor

Children as young as six years old worked long hours for little pay. It was common for children to work 12 hours a day with only a one-hour break. It was common to see children working with and near large, heavy, and dangerous equipment. Many accidents occurred, injuring and even killing children. In 1833 activists in Great Britain were able to enact the Factory Act of 1833, which helped improve conditions for children. It wouldn't be until 1912 that activists in the U.S. were able to set up the Children's Bureau, which for the first time, made it the government's responsibility to monitor child labor.

ChipPix/Shutterstock.com

Young boys worked in this carpentry workshop in the 1800s before laws were made to monitor child labor.

Pay and Benefits

Hired workers were paid the going rate of pay. Employers paid a wage rate only high enough to attract workers. Few employers paid more than they had to. An exception was Henry Ford who opened the first automobile assembly line in Dearborn, Michigan in 1913. "I expect a full day's work for a full day's pay," said Mr. Ford, "and I pay my workers $5 a day, which is double that of my competitors, because I want to attract and keep the best workers." In fact, productivity did rise while employee training costs dropped. Workers were loyal to Ford and his competitive wage rates, and in Detroit, automotive workers were better paid than most working with factory jobs.

Most jobs offered few benefits, other than a few sick days and a few vacation days a year. Mostly sick days and vacation days were unpaid, but did allow workers some needed time away from the job. Health insurance coverage provided by employers wouldn't be common for another half a century.

CHECKPOINT

What was it like to work in a factory in the 1800s?

LO 3-2 The Labor Movement

Following the end of America's Civil War, it became apparent that workers needed protections in the workplace. In this time the first labor unions were formed. A **labor union** is a legal group that is formed to represent workers for the purpose of collective bargaining. **Collective bargaining** is the process of negotiating with employers on behalf of workers. Collective bargaining seeks to protect workers from unfair practices, as well as provide better pay and more favorable working conditions.

Suzanne Tucker/Shutterstock.com

Thousands of union workers gathered at the capitol building in Madison, WI on February 17, 2011 to protest a proposal that would eliminate collective bargaining rights.

Organized in 1869, the first major labor union in the U.S. was called the Knights of Labor. In less than two decades, the Knights of Labor grew to more than 800,000 members. Because anyone could join the union, from unskilled workers on farms to highly skilled workers in factories, it was difficult for the union's leader to control the organization. One of the first acts of some members of this union was to form a strike. A **strike** is a legal action of a union where members refuse to work until a labor agreement is reached. While the strike itself was legal, the Knights of Labor went too far. Members created a dangerous situation, known as the Chicago Haymarket Riot of 1886. As a result, the union lost favor with the public and with its own members. By 1917, the union had collapsed.

A New Focus: Unions and Laws

The American Federation of Labor (AFL) was formed in 1886. Headed by Samuel Gompers, this union focused on skilled workers seeking better pay and working conditions. It was known as a *craft union*, based on groups of workers in the same or similar crafts or trades. For example, plumbers, carpenters, and electricians were included in the membership. The AFL grew to more than 3 million members in the 1930s.

But it wasn't an easy road for labor unions. Courts often treated them as illegal entities. After all, there was no specific law that allowed unions to represent workers against their employers. It was common in the early 1900s for courts to issue injunctions against labor unions. An **injunction** is a court order requiring them to stop a certain activity. Most injunctions were issued to stop strikes and other organized activities by union members.

In 1932 the *Norris-LaGuardia Act* was passed by the U.S. Congress. This new law cut back on courts' ability to issue injunctions. It gave power to unions by reinforcing workers' rights to form unions and to bargain collectively for better pay and working conditions. In 1935, the *Wagner Act* was passed. This law required employers to act in good faith in collective bargaining. It also forced employers to

What Happens When a Union Calls a Strike?

maukun/Shutterstock.com

Some types of work require employees to belong to a union. This is because those employees will benefit from the union. They will receive wages and enjoy working conditions that are protected by collective bargaining by a labor union.

When a union calls a strike, it does so based on a vote of its members. Unions have the legal right to strike to gain better wages, benefits, or working conditions. However, there is a potential that employees could lose their jobs. The employer could hire permanent replacements. When the strike is over, the replacement workers may be entitled to keep the jobs.

If employees are striking due to an unfair labor practice, however, they are less likely to be replaced. They will be able to demand reinstatement when the strike is over. An *unfair labor practice* is defined as an action by an employer which is deemed unlawful, such as refusing to pay overtime for hours worked over a regular workweek.

Many collective bargaining agreements contain a provision that prohibits strikes. This provision is called a *no-strike clause*. If employees working under such an agreement entered into a strike, they could legally be fired.

In some cases, workers are not allowed to strike. Generally, this is because their jobs relate to public safety. For example, if firemen or police officers were to strike, the public would be left unprotected.

Think Critically

1. **Would you prefer to work for a company that has union membership as a requirement?**
2. **As a business owner, would you prefer to have your employees bargaining collectively (unionized)? Explain.**

accept labor unions that succeeded in organizing more than half the workers of a particular business as representatives of the workers, thus making collective bargaining a legal activity. The Wagner Act further set up a new administrative agency—the *National Labor Relations Board* (NLRB). This new agency was given the power to investigate unfair labor practices. As a result, union membership grew, as did the power of unions in the workplace.

The *Congress of Industrial Organizations* (CIO) was developed in 1938 by John L. Lewis. Lewis broke from the AFL to represent workers in major industries, such as steel and automobile manufacturing. The CIO was an *industrial union* (rather than a craft union) where all workers in a company and in similar companies, were organized regardless of craft or trade. These two unions (the AFL and the CIO) operated separately for many years. In 1955, the two merged into the AFL-CIO. Its first leader was George Meany.

tillsonburg/iStockphoto.com

Union workers on strike carry signs that declare they are on strike and fighting to end unfair labor practices.

The Pendulum Swings

As unions grew and wielded more power in the labor market, it soon became apparent that power can corrupt. Because workers were paying union dues that generated large sums of money for the union leaders, many corrupt practices evolved. Union leaders were accused of illegal activities. Union contracts would call for only employing workers who were members of the union. A **closed shop**, is a business that is required by union contract to hire only union members, meaning if individuals are not members of the union, they cannot be employed at that shop. A **union shop** is a business that requires employees to join a union after they are hired. The *Taft-Hartley Act* of 1947 was passed to monitor the activities and limit the power of unions. It made closed shops illegal although it did not outlaw union shops. Amending the Wagner Act, this law, also called the National Management Relations Act, limited the ability of unions to strike.

The *Landrum-Griffin Act* was passed in 1959 to control the corrupt practices of unions. Regular elections of officers became required. Former convicts were prohibited from holding office. Internal affairs of unions were brought to the public attention. For example, Jimmy Hoffa, who was head of the Teamsters Union, was accused (and convicted) of misappropriating pension funds (fraud), bribery, and jury tampering. The Teamsters union, made up of truck drivers and warehousemen, was one of the most powerful unions in the country. Hoffa's activities as president of the Teamsters from 1958 to 1972 included boycotts and strikes. Hoffa's 13-year prison sentence was commuted to time served (5 years) by President Nixon.

A **public employee union** is a union of employees who work for the city, county, state, or federal government. Beginning in the 1960s, these types of unions added vast numbers and power to the labor movement. Some public employee unions, such as police, fire, and air traffic controllers, hold positions vital to public safety. It is believed by many that these types of workers should not be allowed to strike. For example, in 1981 when nearly 12,000 members of the air traffic controllers walked off the job, President Reagan fired them and authorized airports to hire replacements.

The U.S. had entered into an era where many labor unions became too powerful and corrupt, in the opinion of some citizens. The 1990s and beyond witnessed a decline in membership in unions of all kinds, resulting in less union power in the workplace and labor market.

The Labor Market and the Economy

Today many workers benefit from the presence of unions in the economy, even though they themselves do not pay dues. Because of the presence of unions, many employers pay wages and benefits that are competitive. For example, a company may offer a compensation package that includes raises, bonuses, stock-option plans, and other perks for the purpose of keeping unions away.

There can be little doubt of the significance of labor unions in American history. They were needed to curb abusive practices of employers and to bargain for wages, benefits, and working conditions. Joining together gave workers the power they needed to gain *parity* in negotiations and to be able to earn competitive wages.

Robert J. Daveant/Shutterstock.com

In Columbus, OH demonstrators displayed their opposition to a senate bill that would stop collective bargaining for teachers, nurses, and fire fighters.

In a free market system, it is important for all members to have economic power in the marketplace. The labor market is no exception. Because more people are working in living wage jobs, they are able to buy more goods and services. This buying helps the economy grow and keeps other workers employed as businesses provide products for the market economy. Businesses benefit when consumers are able to buy their products and services. The *circular flow* is enhanced when businesses hire workers (resource markets) who are then able to buy goods and services (product markets).

Some argue that unions keep wages and benefits artificially high. In effect, businesses that are committed to union contracts have less flexibility in managing their businesses. When wages are too high, the business must charge higher prices. A higher price makes a product harder to sell and therefore a business loses both sales and profits. Others argue that labor unions continue to serve an important role in the economy by preventing employers from taking unfair advantage of workers. This may be particularly true of minority, female, and lower skill workers who lack the economic power to defend themselves in the labor market.

CHECKPOINT

Why were labor unions needed in the 1800s and beyond in this country?

9-3 Assessment

Key Concepts

LO 3-1 1. What was it like for workers in factories in the early to mid-1800s?

LO 3-1 2. What is the main purpose of a labor union?

LO 3-2 3. How is a craft union different from an industrial union?

LO 3-2 4. In the mid-1800s, employers were taking advantage of workers. By the mid-1900s, some labor unions were abusive to employers. What laws were passed to (a) give power to unions, and (b) take away power from unions?

Think About It

LO 3-1 5. What was wrong with working conditions in the factories that were transforming America from an agricultural to an industrial nation? How did these conditions affect children working in factories?

LO 3-1 6. Henry Ford was a pioneer of mass production of automobiles. He wanted an affordable car for every household. That meant prices had to be low enough that average people could afford a car. How could he keep prices low, while paying the highest wages of the day to his workers? What type of competition did he receive from new producers of cars?

Make Academic Connections

LO 3-2 7. **HISTORY** Why did President Reagan fire the air traffic controllers who went on strike in 1981? Write a paper describing what happened up to and following the strike.

LO 3-1 8. **SOCIAL STUDIES** What is the effect on a society when children work in factories to help support their families? Present an oral report explaining the consequences from the perspective of the child, the family unit, and society as a whole. Are there current-day examples?

Teamwork

LO 3-1 9. People who benefit from something but do not help pay for it, have been called "freeloaders." Explain how those who work for a company that is not unionized are able to benefit from those who are union members working for a competitor.

LO 3-2 10. As a group, do research on the life and disappearance of Jimmy Hoffa in 1975. What are the various theories about what happened to Mr. Hoffa and why? Present a report to the class explaining the events leading up to his disappearance.

LO 3-2 11. Form groups to debate the topic, "Are labor unions still needed in today's economy?" Students should address issues such as union involvement in politics, contributions of large sums of money to political campaigns by unions, and lobbying activities by unions on behalf of their members. They should also deal with situations in which unions are working to protect the exploitation of workers by employers.

Unit 4 Project: Making Sense of Money

UNIONS, WAGES, AND DUES Prepare an analysis of the economic impact of unions. Include public employee unions, trade unions, retail employee unions, and any other types of collective bargaining units in your state or local area. Display your findings and cite sources of information. Use the media of your choice.

Chapter 9 Summary

9-1 INDIVIDUAL CHECKING AND SAVINGS

1. Individual checking accounts are available from financial institutions. Customers can write checks, make deposits, and conduct online banking. It is important to reconcile a bank statement and account for all transactions during the month.
2. People maintain savings accounts to provide for future financial security. Systematic saving that starts at an early age will grow over time based on compound interest.
3. Bank services are plentiful and provide convenience, from overdraft protection to stop payment orders and safe deposit boxes. These services add value, but most cost extra fees. Money can be saved by bundling these services into a particular type of account.

9-2 BUSINESS BANKING AND ACCOUNTS

4. Businesses also maintain checking accounts with banks. Most businesses have several accounts. A sweep account allows businesses to keep most of their resources in a higher-interest account until the money is needed. It is then swept into the main checking account. Businesses have ongoing relationships with banks, who anticipate their needs for loans. Production loans are less risky than consumer loans, and thus require lower interest rates.
5. When individuals and businesses deposit money as savings in financial institutions, money is then available for banks to lend to others. This activity creates a supply of money in the capital market. It is a capital market because businesses can borrow money to purchase capital (long-term, expensive) equipment, machinery, and other assets.

9-3 LABOR MOVEMENT AND MARKETS

6. Harsh working conditions for laborers, including children, led to the need for the protection of labor rights in the 19th century. Workers typically worked 12 or more hours a day for little wages, often in unsafe conditions. Workers, including children, suffered accidents, injuries, and illnesses in the workplace and some workers even lost their lives.
7. Labor unions began in 1869, but didn't flourish until the early 1900s with the AFL, CIO, Teamsters, and then public employee unions. As workers gained rights, better working conditions, and better pay, some unions became corrupt. Laws were initially passed to protect workers' rights. Later, laws were passed to limit the power of unions.
8. Labor provides an important part of economic activity. Through living wage jobs, workers are able to buy goods and services produced by American businesses, thus allowing the economy to grow and prosper.

Chapter 9

Assessment

Vocabulary Review

Match each statement with the term that best defines it.

1. Negotiating with employers on behalf of employees
2. Due to this, money deposited in a bank account grows over time
3. A union made up of government workers
4. A process of covering minimum account needs by transferring in money from another account
5. Legal group formed to represent workers for collective bargaining
6. Place where businesses go to get financing for operations and for large purchases
7. Demand deposit where money is set aside for future use
8. An entire package or grouping of banking services
9. Verifying the amount in one's account matches the bank's record
10. Borrowing money by one corporation from excess cash of another corporation
11. A monthly charge assessed against checking accounts
12. Condition where the employer can only hire union workers
13. Nature of work and what is required for workers to succeed
14. Demand deposit account for immediate use by account holder
15. An act where employees refuse to work until agreement is reached
16. Interest that is paid on an original amount plus previously paid interest
17. Commercial banks, savings banks, credit unions, and others that provide deposit accounts
18. Loan made to a business customer
19. Pre-set loan amount that can be accessed when needed
20. Court order prohibiting or stopping an activity
21. Card issued by the bank that can be used for POS purchases and at an ATM
22. Condition where new workers must join a union after being hired

Vocabulary

a. capital markets
b. checking account
c. closed shop
d. collective bargaining
e. commercial paper
f. compounding
g. credit line
h. debit card
i. financial institution
j. injunction
k. interest
l. labor union
m. production loan
n. public employee union
o. reconciliation
p. relationship banking
q. savings account
r. service fee
s. strike
t. sweep account
u. union shop
v. work conditions

Review Your Knowledge

LO 1-1 **23.** Which is not a financial institution?
a. commercial bank
b. credit union
c. brokerage firm
d. government agency

LO 1-1 **24.** Which is needed to add money to an account manually?
a. check
b. deposit ticket
c. bank signature form
d. identification

LO 1-1 **25.** Checks that have not yet cleared your account are
a. cancelled checks
b. deposits in transit
c. outstanding checks
d. adjusted balance

LO 1-2 **26.** Which is a stash of money to be used for unexpected costs?
a. savings account
b. checking account
c. emergency fund
d. systematic saving

LO 1-3 **27.** Which is a check against a bank's funds?
a. cashier's check
b. money order
c. stop payment order
d. traveler's check

LO 1-3 **28.** Which allows you to make POS purchases?
a. ATM card
b. debit card
c. savings account
d. CD

LO 1-3 **29.** Which is also known as an NSF check?
a. stop payment
b. cashier's check
c. money order
d. bounced check

LO 2-1 **30.** Loans made to businesses are
a. production loans
b. risky loans
c. consumption loans
d. capital financing

LO 3-2 **31.** Which was the first major labor union in the U.S.?
a. Teamsters
b. AFL
c. CIO
d. Knights of Labor

LO 3-2 **32.** Which law monitors activities and limited power of unions?
a. Wagner Act
b. Taft-Hartley Act
c. Landrum-Griffin Act
d. Factory Act

Digging Deeper with Economics e-Collection

Personal income is measured in the United States by the Economics and Statistics Administration, a division of the U.S. Department of Commerce. As people save more, more money is available in the economy for investing. In 2011, the U.S. personal savings rate (as a percent of disposable personal income) was 5.3%. Access the Gale Economics e-Collection at **www.cengage.com/school/economics/personalfinance**. Examine the household savings rates of other countries. Prepare a comparison of savings rates in the United States and two other countries. Give reasons why savings rates are different for those countries. Explain what causes savings rates to increase and decrease over time.

Think About It

LO 1-2 **33.** As a consumer you have many options for checking and savings accounts. All banks are not created equal. Some have free checking accounts, while others do not. What will you do to ensure that you are receiving the most benefit from the bank where you have accounts?

LO 2-1 **34.** Business banking is usually based on a mutually beneficial relationship. Businesses receive the loans and services they need and banks earn money based on services provided. What steps do banks take to reduce their risks in making loans to businesses?

LO 3-2 **35.** Labor unions came into being in this country to protect workers' rights. Today labor unions are losing ground every year. Some people believe their time (of being needed) has passed and that unions today cause harm to the economy and businesses. Do you agree?

Make Academic Connections

LO 1-2 **36. MATH** Using Figure 9-4 as an example, compute interest earned on the following simple interest loans.

a. $1,500 at 6% for 60 days
b. $10,000 at 8% for 90 days
c. $5,000 at 7% for 180 days
d. $3,500 at 8.5% for 225 days

LO 1-2 **37. HISTORY** In 1929, the stock market crashed and the country began a period called the Great Depression. Many banks failed during this era. America saw "bank runs" and loss of consumer confidence in financial institutions. Do historical research about banks and bank failures after 1929. Present a report of your findings.

LO 3-2 **38. BUSINESS LAW** Every state has employment laws. Look up the Fair Labor Standards Act of 1938 (which established minimum wage at 25 cents an hour). Compare labor laws in your state to federal laws. Present a histogram explaining the labor laws in your state.

LO 1-2 **39. COMMUNICATION** Money set aside today will grow into a nice nest egg for the future. Write a two-page essay in which you outline your plans for saving money during your lifetime and what you hope to achieve as a result of taking this responsibility.

Extend Your Learning

LO 3-2 **40.** Choose a union that is strong in your state. Research the beginnings of that union and how it has affected jobs, income, and markets. Present your findings using PowerPoint slides.

LO 3-2 **41.** Do biographical research on the life and times of Henry Ford and how he treated workers in his factories in Michigan. Include his early treatment of workers (paying $5 per day when competitors paid half that rate) and his treatment of workers in his later years. Present an oral history using pictures and quotations.

AVAVA/iStockphoto.com

chapter 10

Consumer Credit and Debt

yienkeat/Shutterstock.com

MARKETS *in Action!*

Credit in America

Before the eighteenth century, the use of credit was very limited. Farmers and hunters negotiated with merchants who supplied goods on credit until the crop or labor was complete. The twentieth century brought greater demand for lending services. Individuals wanting to buy homes sought to borrow money for long-term debt. When the Federal Reserve and today's banking system was set up in 1913, it became easier for consumers to have accounts and to borrow money. Cash was the primary source of payments and deposits.

In the early 1900s, oil companies and department stores issued their own store accounts. These accounts were used for convenience, and as a way to create customer loyalty and improve customer service. The first bank card, *Charg-it*, was introduced in 1946 by John Biggins, a banker in Brooklyn. When used for a purchase, a request was forwarded to Biggins's bank. The bank paid the merchant and obtained payment from their customer. The bank card had been born.

The Diners Club charge card was next. This card allowed consumers to buy on credit, and pay off the balance when billed. In 1959, American Express introduced its charge card, and for the first time, the card was made of plastic. According to MasterCard, it was that same year (1959) when the revolving form of credit was offered. In 1966, the first general-purpose credit card, Visa, was established through Bank of America. The national credit card system was formed when credit-issuing banks joined together and formed both the MasterCard and Visa services. In 1987, American Express issued its first credit card that allowed customers to pay off their balances over time.

Between 1970 and 1990, buying on credit became a way of life. In the 1990s, record numbers of people declared bankruptcy. Millions of Americans became over-extended with credit. Many adopted a lifestyle dependent on the use of credit to make ends meet. To protect consumers from abusive practices by credit card issuers, the Credit CARD Act of 2009, effective in 2010, attempted to curb deceptive credit practices.

Following the Great Recession (2007-2009) use of credit diminished due to high interest rates, lowered credit limits, and the hard lessons learned from over-spending and carrying high credit balances.

Think Critically

1. Why is credit needed in an economy? Who benefits from the use of credit?
2. As a consumer, what rights and responsibilities do you have when using credit? Do you believe credit should be more (or less) tightly regulated by government? Why or why not?

10-1 Consumer Buying and Credit

Learning Objectives

LO 1-1 **Describe** the steps of preparing a good buying plan.

LO 1-2 **Discuss** the advantages and disadvantages of using credit.

LO 1-3 **Discuss** the responsibilities of using credit and the obligations of borrowing money.

Vocabulary

impulse buying, p. 281
buying plan, p. 281
spending limit, p. 281
criteria, p. 282
financing option, p. 283
comparison shopping, p. 283
late fee, p. 284
over-the-limit fee, p. 284

© Aleksandar Vrzalski/iStockphoto.com

REAL-WORLD FOCUS

Mayra plans to buy a used car during the summer break. She is working and needs regular and dependable transportation to get to work. "I would like to buy a new car," she told her father. "But I can't afford the payments. So I am going to buy something that fits into my budget. Do you think I can get a dependable used car for about $200 a month?"

WORK AS A TEAM Before you buy something that will commit future income for several years, you should consider many factors other than just the price. What else should Mayra think about before she makes a decision to buy a car? If she were going to be moving from home to a dormitory in a city far away in less than a year, how might that affect her decision?

SVLuma/Shutterstock.com

Driving a sports car is a dream shared by many teenagers and adults alike.

DO YOU THINK for an average American, an example of impulse buying is purchasing a new sports car?

yienkeat/Shutterstock.com

LO 1-1 Buying Plan

As a consumer, you should shop wisely to ensure that you are buying goods and services that will best meet your needs at the lowest possible cost. When you plan your purchases, you can avoid habits that result in wasting money, such as impulse buying. **Impulse buying** occurs when you buy something on the spot, without thinking about it. In most cases, you will later wish you hadn't wasted your money. Impulse purchases rarely meet your needs. They are spur-of-the-moment decisions, rather than carefully planned choices. A **buying plan** is an organized method for making good buying decisions. It will help you stretch your limited resources. It will also help prevent *buyer's remorse*, which is regret over a buying decision. When you make a major purchase or spend a large sum of money, a buying plan will help you do a thorough analysis before you buy.

The buying plan is shown in Figure 10-1. It is a five-step decision process that defines what it is you wish to achieve.

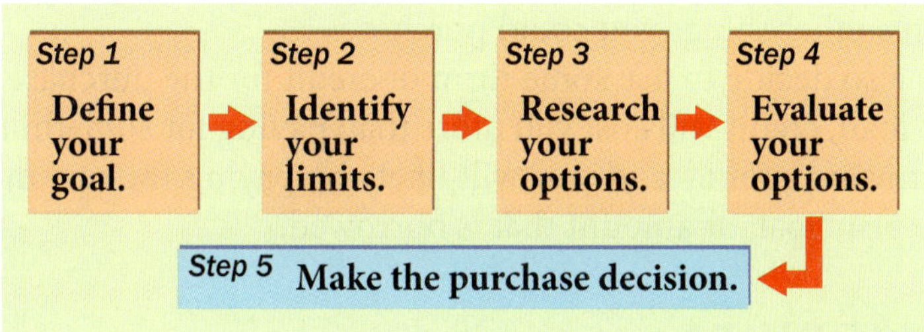

Figure 10-1 Buying Plan

Step 1 Define Your Goal

When you buy something, you are giving up one resource to acquire another. Before giving up a current resource, you should first decide what it is you want to achieve. By defining the need, want, or spending goal, you are able to visualize what you will get in exchange for what you give up. Defining your goal should take longer if you are making a large purchase. When you are giving up more of your resources, you should take more time to define your goal.

Step 2 Identify Your Limits

You may have limited time and you may have limited money. When your time is limited, you may need to make a choice that is less than optimal. Many people set spending limits. A **spending limit** is a pre-set amount that you will pay for an item. If you can't negotiate that price or a lower set price, then you will walk away. Setting a spending limit keeps you from an emotional purchase. Once you have weighed what it is worth to you, setting a spending limit will help you hold that line.

Step 3 Research Your Options

Most decisions have two or more possible choices. If you are thinking of buying a lawn mower, there are at least three options: buy a used machine, buy a new machine, or refurbish your old lawn mower. You might also consider the cost of hiring someone

Paying with a credit card is easy but it may not deter people from buying items on impulse.

else to mow the lawn, or you could replace the lawn with a rock garden. **Criteria** are standards or rules by which something is judged. For an item you want to buy, the criteria might be features, functions, and quality of the item. You should make a list of the options and criteria that are important to you.

Step 4 Evaluate Your Options

It's important to carefully consider the pros and cons of all your options. Careful assessment will help you reach the right choice. The right choice may involve not buying. Each option represents a choice you should evaluate in light of the other choices. How does it add value? Is it worth the cost?

Step 5 Make the Purchase Decision

Once you decide you will purchase an item, you must determine how you will pay for it. Using cash may be your best option. While you give up the cash, you receive the item and it is yours. Giving up the cash may be tough because the cash also represents other things you could purchase.

You may also decide to use some form of credit for the purchase. Unless you can get a 0% loan, credit will cost you more than paying for something with cash. You are borrowing money and you will likely be paying interest in addition to repaying the principal, or amount that is borrowed.

CHECKPOINT

What is the advantage of using a buying plan?

LO 1-2 Credit: Friend and Foe

As a consumer, you build *creditworthiness* in the way you handle your financial responsibilities. You should recognize that credit can lead to money problems.

Benefits of Credit

Andresr/Shutterstock.com

This couple paid for their hotel stay with credit. They will not pay the bill until after they have returned from their vacation.

Use of credit can be beneficial for consumers and for the economy. Consider these positive effects of using credit:

- **Credit increases your standard of living.** You are able to buy many things sooner that otherwise you would have to wait to buy.
- **Credit is convenient.** It allows you to pay in the future, often allowing you to spread the cost of purchases over time.
- **Credit is safer than carrying cash.** If your card is lost or stolen, you can get it replaced.
- **Credit gives you buying power.** With a credit card or account, you can get quicker action if there is a dispute. Because you haven't paid for the goods yet, the

merchant may be more willing to work with you until you are happy with your purchase.

- **Credit gives you records.** Your monthly statement provides a record of your spending and allows you to verify purchases and make returns.
- **Credit can pay you back.** With a credit card or account that pays *rewards*, points, or *rebates*, you can receive bonuses in the form of cash or increased spending power.
- **Using credit builds your *credit history*.** If you need to use credit in the future, the fact that you have successfully used credit in the past will help you get credit when you need it.
- **Credit increases your financing options.** A **financing option** is a way to pay for purchases. If you can use a credit card, open an account, or borrow from a credit union, you can finance your purchase without using cash.

NET Bookmark

Access www.cengage.com/school/economics/personalfinance and click on the link for Chapter 10. Visit the Federal Trade Commission's Bureau of Consumer Protection website, where you will find information for consumers about how to use credit. Click on the Consumer Information tab. Under Consumer Categories locate information useful to consumers as they use credit. What resources are available at this site? What steps can you take to guard against credit card fraud? Why is it important to report credit card losses and fraud immediately?

www.cengage.com/school/economics/personalfinance

Dangers of Credit

Using credit can also have pitfalls. If you don't use credit wisely, you may have trouble getting credit when you need it. Disadvantages of using credit include:

- **Credit can lead to overspending.** Because you are not parting with actual cash, you may feel that you aren't really spending your money. Thus with credit, people tend to spend more than if they use cash.
- **Credit can reduce comparison shopping.** The process of looking for the best value for the money spent is **comparison shopping**. When credit is used, people often buy where they have credit available, whether or not they are getting the best price.
- **Credit is expensive.** You will pay more for purchases unless you pay off your credit card bill each month. *Interest* charged on credit accounts and cards can cause the real cost of your purchase to be much higher.
- **Credit ties up future income.** Because you have committed to payments in the future, money used for payments cannot be used for other things, such as savings. This reduces your future spending and saving power.
- **Credit can be dangerous in tough economic times.** Banks and credit card companies can raise interest rates on new amounts charged, lower credit limits, charge fees, and increase minimum payments. If you lose your job, making credit card payments may be difficult.

CHECKPOINT

How can credit be dangerous to your financial future?

LO 1-3 Responsibilities of Credit

"There is no such thing as a free lunch." When you borrow money, it is not free. You pay *interest* for the privilege of borrowing money. Interest increases the cost of your purchases. As a user of credit, you have many responsibilities.

craig hill/Shutterstock.com

Paying a credit card bill by its due date means you avoid paying late fees.

Regular, On-Time Payments

As a *borrower*, you are required to make regular payments in a timely manner. You must make a payment on or before the day the payment is due, or you may be charged a late fee. A **late fee** can be a set amount, such as $35, or a percentage of the late amount. When you pay late, you are sending a signal to creditors, that you are not being responsible in your use of credit. You are a higher risk and if you can get credit in the future, you are likely to be charged higher interest rates.

Secure Payments

If you write a check or authorize an electronic withdrawal, it is your responsibility to be sure that the funds are available so the amount will be paid. You can make electronic payments through online banking. You may also pay electronically at the creditor's website. Entering correct account numbers and routing numbers ensure the transaction will be processed correctly and promptly.

Careful Use of Credit

Use credit carefully so you won't go over your credit limit. When you spend over your authorized credit limit, you incur an **over-the-limit fee**. This fee penalizes you for using excess credit. It signals creditors that you are not being responsible in your use of credit. This fee may be a flat amount of $40 or more. It may also result in increased interest rates and other actions.

Monitor Accounts

Keep receipts and match them to your credit statements each month. If there is an error, you should notify the creditor in writing to dispute a charge. Failure to act in a timely manner can cause you to lose your right to have a mistake corrected.

Notifications and Help

Inform the creditor if you have difficulty meeting your obligations. Do not skip payments or make them late. Call the creditor to explain any circumstances where you need to delay payments. If you lose your job or some other problem occurs, discuss options with your creditor immediately. Failure to do so can cause harm to your relationship with this and other creditors, both now and in the future. The creditor may be willing to negotiate a payment plan. You may be able to get payments and/or interest rates lowered.

CHECKPOINT

What are three obligations you have as a user of credit?

PROFILE

J. K. Rowling
Author

© AP Photo/Joel Ryan

World-famous author of the *Harry Potter* series of books, J.K. Rowling (Joanne Rowling) was not born rich or affluent. Born in England in 1965, Rowling has won many awards and has sold more than 400 million copies of her books, which have now been made into movies that have grossed hundreds of millions of dollars each.

Rowling is famous for her "rags to riches" story. She was poor and living on welfare benefits when she took a train ride that gave her the inspiration to write her books. As an author, Rowling was self-employed and managed her own writing schedule. Within five years, she would become one of the richest billionaires in the world. Today she is a notable philanthropist, supporting charities such as One Parent Families, the Multiple Sclerosis Society of Great Britain, and Comic Relief.

Her first *Harry Potter* book was written under the name "Joanne Rowling," but her publisher required that she use initials rather than her full name, since her target audience was young boys. She has no middle name, so she chose the letter K as her middle initial, taken from her paternal grandmother, Kathleen Rowling.

In 1990, Rowling started writing her first *Harry Potter* book. She completed the book in 1995 on an old manual typewriter and was still living on state welfare support. She was unable to get credit or borrow money, but managed to squeak by with help from her family. Her book was submitted to twelve publishing houses, all of which rejected the manuscript. A year later she was given a £1500 advance by Bloomsbury, a small publishing house in London, for the right to publish her first book. In June 1997, Bloomsbury published *Harry Potter and the Philosopher's Stone* initially printing only 1000 copies, of which 500 went to libraries. Today those copies have values from £16,000 to £25,000 each. In 1998, Scholastic, Inc. published the book in the U.S. under the title, *Harry Potter and the Sorcerer's Stone.* The rest is history.

THINK CRITICALLY

1. **Creativity and talent are often difficult to sell. It takes awhile for audiences to discover the product and buy it. Can you think of other ideas and products that were initially rejected, but later became very popular, making their inventors very rich?**
2. **When J.K. Rowling needed credit, she was unable to get it. She was poor until her writing became famous. Today, she gives money to help causes she finds important. Why do rich and famous people give money away?**

yienkeat/Shutterstock.com

10-1 Assessment

Key Concepts

LO 1-1 1. List the five steps of a buying plan.

LO 1-1 2. How does setting a spending limit improve your decision making?

LO 1-2 3. What are three benefits of using credit? three pitfalls?

LO 1-3 4. What are three responsibilities of using credit?

Think About It

LO 1-1 5. Have you ever experienced buyer's remorse? Describe what happened. What will you do differently to avoid this situation in the future?

LO 1-2 6. Spending can be for the wrong reason. For example, if you are sad or going through a difficult time, you may be tempted to buy something you don't really need or want. Explain how following a buying plan can help you avoid this type of purchase.

LO 1-2 7. Buying something includes the decision of how to pay for the purchase. Sometimes you can get a discount for paying cash. Sometimes using credit can cause a purchase to cost considerably more. Explain how using credit causes a higher cost.

Make Academic Connections

LO 1-1 8. **RESEARCH** Determining minimum acceptable criteria for a purchase will help you narrow down your choices. Many people do this part of their buying plan by researching on the Internet. Pick something you would like to buy. Gather information about it by researching at least three websites. Prepare a summary of your findings and include your website references.

LO 1-2 9. **COMMUNICATION** Research online about the Credit CARD Act of 2009. Prepare an oral report that discusses the features of the law that are beneficial to consumers. Based on your research, explain why the law was passed and what its intent was for protecting consumers. Do you think the law has been effective in accomplishing this purpose? Why or why not?

LO 1-3 10. **CONSUMER ECONOMICS** Consumers can maximize resources with careful spending habits. Visit a store and list unit prices for ten products in various sizes. Circle the quantities and prices that are the best buys. How might the use of credit get in the way of good comparison shopping?

Teamwork

LO 1-2, 1-3 11. As a group, discuss the advantages and disadvantages of using credit. Prepare a report that cites cases where members of your group (or their families) benefited from the use of credit. In the same report, cite cases where consumers were hurt economically because they used credit. Explain how better responsibility in using credit might lead to a different outcome.

Unit 5 Project: Making Sense of Money

MAKING PURCHASE DECISIONS Prepare a step-by-step decision model that you will use when faced with a need to purchase a large-ticket item and use credit over several years (tying up income into the future). Include an overview that describes steps along the way. Use Excel or Word tables to present your model.

10-2 Consumer Loans and Credit Scores

Learning Objectives

LO 2-1 **List and describe** the types of loans and sources of credit available to consumers.

LO 2-2 **Explain** the contents of a credit report and how to improve your credit score.

Vocabulary

installment loan, p. 288
promissory note, p. 288
co-signer, p. 289
line of credit, p. 289
revolving credit, p. 290
credit bureaus, p. 291
credit report, p. 291
credit score, p. 292

© Aleksandar Vrzalski/ iStockphoto.com

REAL-WORLD FOCUS

Erin plans to start college next year. She is saving her money and will go to a community college for her first two years to pay lower tuition costs. "The less I have to borrow in terms of financial aid, the less I will have to pay back," she told her friend Ally. "When you take out student loans you have to pay them back, plus interest. And even if you go bankrupt, you will still have to pay back your student loans."

WORK AS A TEAM Why is it important to plan for how you will pay for the cost of your college education? Besides borrowing money from financial aid, how else can you finance your college education?

For many young adults, their first experience of applying for a loan from a commercial lender is when they seek money to attend a college or trade school.

DO YOU THINK all student loans require a co-signer?

yienkeat/Shutterstock.com

zimmytws/Shutterstock.com

2-1 Loans and Sources of Credit

Consumers who are creditworthy are able to borrow money. *Credit* is the ability to borrow money and pay it back later. Those who borrow money are *debtors*. *Creditors* are lenders willing to make loans because they are confident that the debtor will be able to repay the debt.

Jaimie Duplass/Shutterstock.com

A loan officer indicates where the borrower needs to sign the forms for his consumer loan.

Consumer Loans

Banks and other companies loan money to consumers. A *consumer loan* is a direct loan of cash made to a consumer at a set interest rate for a specific period of time. For example, a consumer might borrow $1,000 at 8% interest for one year. When the consumer makes regular monthly payments for a set period of time, the consumer has an **installment loan**. Each payment made is part principal and part interest. The final payment makes the loan paid in full. Another type of loan is a *single-payment loan,* which is repaid on a set date in the future. With this type of loan, the entire principal plus interest is paid off at the same time. A single-payment loan gives you use of the full amount borrowed for the entire time of the loan.

Consumers are also able to borrow money to purchase goods and services. Most loans involving large sums of money, such as to buy a house or a car, involve some form of collateral. Recall from Chapter 6, that *collateral* is something of value that can be repossessed if the borrower fails to pay the loan as agreed. These types of loans are also called *secured debt* because the collateral serves as security for payment of the loan.

Some loans are financed directly with the seller. Others are financed through a bank, credit union, or other financial institution. Student loans are a form of installment debt. The money will be repaid after graduation.

Whether you take out a consumer loan, buy goods and services on a payment plan, or take out a student loan, you will have to sign a loan agreement. The agreement requires the borrower to sign a **promissory note**, which is a legal contract that requires the borrower to make principal payments plus *interest.*

Figure 10-2 is a promissory note signed by a consumer for the purpose of buying a car. A promissory note is a *negotiable instrument.* This means it can be sold or assigned to another person or company for collection.

Figure 10-2

Promissory Note

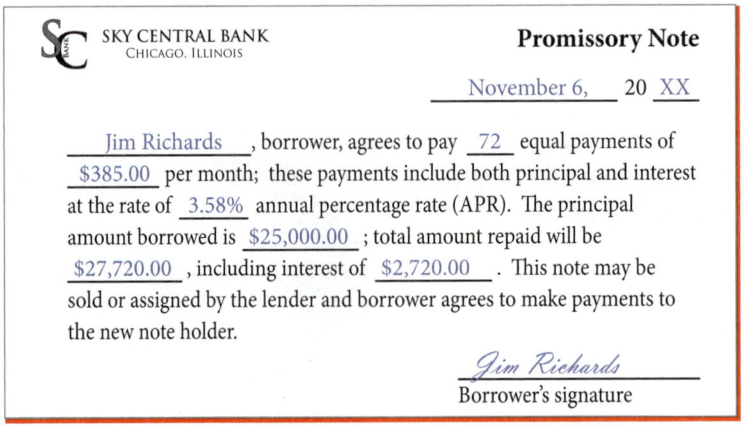

SKY CENTRAL BANK
CHICAGO, ILLINOIS

Promissory Note

November 6, 20 XX

Jim Richards, borrower, agrees to pay 72 equal payments of $385.00 per month; these payments include both principal and interest at the rate of 3.58% annual percentage rate (APR). The principal amount borrowed is $25,000.00; total amount repaid will be $27,720.00, including interest of $2,720.00. This note may be sold or assigned by the lender and borrower agrees to make payments to the new note holder.

Jim Richards
Borrower's signature

Payday Loans

Investigate Your Local ECONOMY

In your local area you will find check-cashing businesses that advertise no bank account is needed. *Payday loan* businesses offer money to people who are expecting regular paychecks, but need money before their payday. The loan is intended as a bridge loan or a short-term obligation used to get a person through an emergency financial need. The fees for cashing checks and obtaining payday loans are very high. Some states cap those fees and interest rates because they are excessive and prey on those who can least afford to pay them.

Many people believe that payday loans are a trap. They often lead to ongoing payday loans when the worker is unable to get caught up and have enough money to meet regular expenses. The ongoing cycle of payday loans results in less take-home pay and a lowered standard of living.

Try it Out

Visit check-cashing or payday loan businesses in your local area and pick up brochures with information about their services. Prepare a chart displaying the results and explain the fees and other charges.

When a consumer's creditworthiness is not good enough to borrow money, the lender may require a co-signer. A **co-signer** is a person who also signs the loan agreement and agrees to pay the loan if the borrower is unable to do so. The co-signer is responsible for the full amount of the debt, as well as the monthly payments. Often, young people who have not established credit are required to have parents act as co-signers for loans to be able to borrow money.

A personal **line of credit** is a preapproved loan amount that a borrower can access as needed. The consumer fills out a loan application and is approved to borrow up to a set amount. That amount is available for use as needed. Setting up a line of credit at a financial institution is a good way to know how much you can borrow before you begin the process of buying a good or service.

Student Loans

Needing help to pay for post-secondary education is a fact of life for most students. Many types of loans are available. A *federal student loan* is money given by the government based on the FAFSA, Free Application for Federal Student Aid. *Subsidized Federal Stafford Loans* are need-based government-secured loans with low interest rates, deferred payments, and flexible repayment plans. *Unsubsidized Federal Stafford Loans* are not need-based loans and unlike subsidized loans accrue interest from the day the loan is given. Another type of loan students may seek is a *Federal Perkins Loan*. These loans are for those that have the greatest need and meet rigid eligibility requirements. Banks and credit unions also offer student loans that are not tied to government monies. The common aspect of any type of student loan is repayment does not have to start until the student has stopped going to school, and most offer a six-month deferment option.

Global View

Banco do Brasil (The Bank of Brazil)

The Bank of Brazil, founded in 1808, is the oldest active bank in Brazil, and one of the oldest financial institutions in the world. The bank is controlled by the Brazilian government. Its stock is traded at the Sao Paulo Stock Exchange and its management follows standard international banking practices.

Interest rates on loans vary to a great extent in Brazil. The Banco do Brasil is known for having high interest rates. *The Economist* "Survey of International Banking" (2006) reported that the average Brazilian interest rate on credit cards was an astounding 222%. As of June 1999, the standard interest rate in Brazil was 8.5% per month (102% per year).

Think Critically

1. **Why do banks charge high interest rates on their credit cards?**
2. **What would it be like to pay more than 100% interest on borrowed money? How might your spending habits be affected?**

Sources of Credit

A common type of credit available to consumers is service credit. *Service credit* is the ability to receive services and pay for them later. If you use electricity, water, sewer, cable, and utilities, you are using service credit. You may also receive service credit from doctors, dentists, and others. Some companies that offer service credit require you to pay a deposit before beginning your service, especially if you are a new customer. After a good payment record, the deposit is often refunded to you.

A *credit card* is a plastic card linked to a credit account that can be used to make purchases. Using a credit card is a form of consumer loan or debt. Credit cards are available from banks and other financial companies. With *general-purpose credit cards*, you can make purchases at retail, service, and other businesses around the world. You can also borrow money at ATM machines using a credit card.

Credit cards are a form of revolving credit. With **revolving credit**, you can charge to the account, make payments, and keep using the account until you reach your maximum limit or you close the account. Your account may have an ongoing balance. A minimum monthly payment is required to remain in good standing. If you make only the minimum payment, you will pay considerable *interest* on the outstanding balance. To avoid paying interest, pay off your balance in full each month. To reduce the amount of interest you pay, make a payment for more than the minimum amount. Credit cards often have annual fees and other costs, such as a fee for withdrawing cash, a *cash advance*, using the card.

A *store account* is a specific-purpose credit card. Unlike a general-purpose credit card, you can only use this credit card at that one store or business that issued the card. Store accounts can be revolving credit or they can be installment credit. Credit card and store accounts are referred to as *unsecured debt*, when specific assets cannot be claimed if the debt isn't paid.

A *charge card* is a form of credit where you pay the balance in full each month. A charge card represents short-term borrowing. Because there is no interest or service fee charged to the user, these cards often require a large annual fee. Examples of charge cards are traditional American Express and Diners Club cards. Many consumers who use charge cards want them for convenience and safety and not for the purpose of borrowing money.

CHECKPOINT

How is installment credit different from revolving credit?

LO 2-2 Credit Records, Reports, and Scores

Every person who uses credit creates a credit history. Your *credit history* helps determine your creditworthiness which allows lenders to decide whether to extend credit to you. The credit industry is large and thriving. **Credit bureaus** are businesses that gather, store, and sell credit information about consumers to their business members. There are three national credit bureaus that maintain files and supply credit information, ratings, and scores:

- TransUnion (www.transunion.com)
- Experian (www.experian.com)
- Equifax (www.equifax.com)

Fotoline/Shutterstock.com

A bill that is not paid by its due date is considered *past due*.

Credit bureaus enter data into your credit record based on your social security number. Local and regional credit bureaus access these computer networks and make the information widely accessible.

Credit Reports

A **credit report** is a statement of your credit history issued by a credit bureau. It is a complete record of your borrowing and repayment performance. It states how many accounts you have open, current balances of those accounts, and current payments being made. It states how much unused credit you have. *Unused credit* is the difference between your credit limit and your credit balance on each account. The credit report lists any closed accounts and adverse conditions. If you make a late payment, the creditor reports that to the credit bureau. If you get an over-the-limit charge, that also is reported.

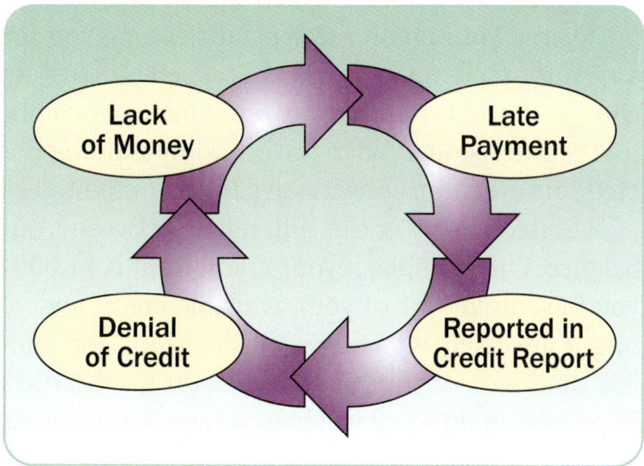

© Cengage Learning 2013

Figure 10-3

Circular-flow Model of Problems Caused by Mismanaging Credit

The credit report lists all your current debts and payment records as long as there is a balance. Information about closed accounts is kept for three years, except foreclosures, bankruptcies, or repossessions. These records are kept for ten years. Most financial advisors recommend consumers check their credit report once a year to verify that it is accurate.

You have the right to see your credit report, although there may be a fee. If you are denied credit, you have 30 days to request a free report. You can challenge information you believe is inaccurate. The error must be corrected if you can prove it is wrong. You must write a letter explaining the error and providing evidence. Even if the credit bureau decides the information is correct, it must keep a copy of your letter and issue it along with the credit report.

Credit Scores

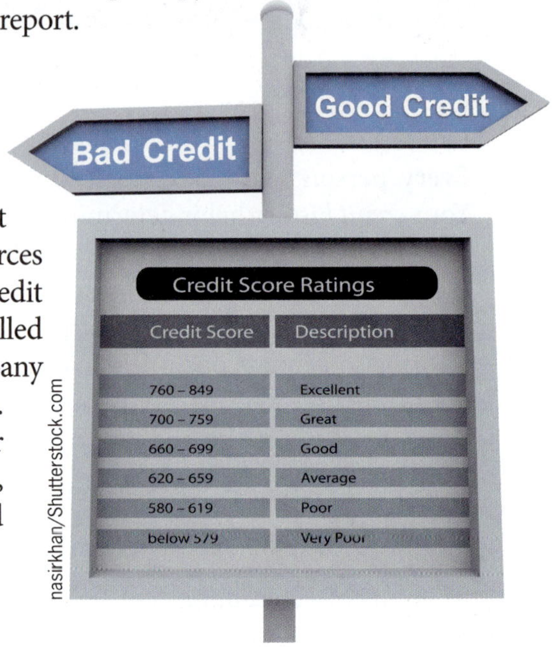

nasirkhan/Shutterstock.com

Your **credit score** is a numeric rating that is compiled on a point system by the credit bureaus. You may have a different score at each bureau, depending on sources of information reported to them. Most credit scores are based on a system of ratings called *FICO* for Fair Isaac Corporation, the company that originally designed the rating system. As your credit information changes, your score will reflect the changes. FICO scores, which range from 350 to 850, are calculated on five categories:

1. Payment history (35%)
2. Amounts owed (30%)
3. Length of credit history (15%)
4. New credit from recently opened accounts (10%)
5. Types of credit used (10%)

HadK/Shutterstock.com

Excellent FICO scores are in the 760–850 or higher range. A very good score is in the 700s and is often considered the minimum score for obtaining credit for long-term debt, such as a mortgage. An average score is in the 600s. A score below 500 means that a person either has a poor credit record or has not used credit long enough to have a higher score.

Even if your credit score is satisfactory, you may be turned down for credit if a creditor feels you are risky because you have too much credit, you don't have enough unused credit, or any other factor or combination of factors they consider for their decisions. When the economy is doing poorly and people are losing jobs, creditors are more conservative in their credit decisions. The reason is risk.

Unused credit is the difference between your credit limit and your credit balance. For example, if your credit limit is $1,000 and your balance is $750, then you have used 75% of your available credit and your unused credit is 25%. This might adversely affect a credit decision. You should try to keep your balances less than 50% of your available credit in order to improve your credit score. An improved credit score will help you get lower interest rates and better credit offers.

FreeSoulProduction/Shutterstock.com

Math CONNECTION

Percent of Unused Credit

The guidelines for improving credit scores suggest keeping balances owed on accounts less than 50% of the available credit. To check an account against the guidelines, you simply make an estimated comparison of your unused credit to 50%. Divide the credit limit in half and compare that amount to the balance on the account.

An account with a credit limit of $1,800 has a current balance of $975. Is the balance less than 50% of the available credit on the account? Does this account meet the guidelines?

SOLUTION

1,800 ÷ 2 = 900	Dividing by 2 is the same as taking one-half of a number.
900 < 975	Compare half of the limit to the balance.

This account has less than 50% unused credit. It does not meet the guidelines.

TRY IT

Determine if each account meets the guidelines. Write yes or no.

1. credit limit $5,000, a balance of $2,275
2. credit limit $500, a balance of $325
3. credit limit $8,400, a balance of $4,155

The more risk creditors take, the more careful they become in granting of or increasing of credit lines. You can become a lower-risk borrower by improving your credit score. To improve your credit score, you can do the following.

- Pay your debts promptly—on or before the due date.
- Pay more than the minimum payment.
- Reduce your outstanding credit (compared to credit available).
- Don't apply for more than one new account or card at a time. New credit lowers your overall score.
- Keep a good mix of credit. Too much revolving credit, such as credit cards, will lower your overall score.
- Check your credit report often to be sure it is accurate.
- Manage your credit wisely—keep balances paid down, avoid interest where possible, pay off cards with higher interest rates, and switch to lower-interest rate cards when possible.

CHECKPOINT

Why is it important to be a low-risk borrower?

10-2 Assessment

Key Concepts

LO 2-1 1. What is an installment loan?

LO 2-1 2. What is the purpose of a promissory note?

LO 2-1 3. What is the purpose of requiring a co-signer?

LO 2-1 4. What is revolving credit?

LO 2-2 5. What is contained in a credit report?

Think About It

LO 2-1 6. You may be able to get a better interest rate if you open a store account to buy a large item, such as a refrigerator, rather than use your credit card. Why might this be true?

LO 2-2 7. Why is it a good idea to check your credit report at least once a year?

LO 2-1 8. Some types of service credit, such as doctors and dentists, require payment when services are rendered. Others allow patients to pay just the co-payment when they have insurance. Why do these businesses require payment up front rather than billing their patients?

Make Academic Connections

LO 2-1 9. **CONSUMER ECONOMICS** Use of credit allows consumers to purchase more goods and services without waiting until they save the money. Describe and analyze purchases made by a typical family in a month. How many involve the use of credit? Is this good or bad? Write a one-page paper, citing at least one source of information.

LO 2-1 10. **MATH** Using the formula I = PRT (Interest = Principal × Rate × Time), how much interest would you pay if you borrowed $5,000 at 12% interest for 90 days? (Remember time is a fraction: 90/360.)

LO 2-2 11. **ETHICS** Many people believe that credit bureaus have too much power and that they freely gather and use information about consumers without their knowledge or consent. Based on this information, whether it is accurate or not, decisions are made that affect consumers. Do you believe this type of service is in the best interest of consumers, businesses, and the general public? Participate in a debate on this issue.

Teamwork

LO 2-2 12. Do Internet research about credit protection services that are available to consumers. Describe what type of protection is offered—what do consumers get and what is the cost of this service? Does this service have value for most consumers? Why or why not?

Unit 5 Project: Making Sense of Money

AVOIDING CREDIT PROBLEMS Prepare a three-page report discussing recent trends in the use of credit in America, why people get into trouble with credit, leading causes of bankruptcy, and what consumers can do to avoid credit problems. Cite at least three sources of information. Present your report orally, using PowerPoint or some type of visual display to support your findings.

yienkeat/Shutterstock.com, Chad Baker/Ryan McVay/Photodisc/Getty Images

10-3 Consumer Debt and Bankruptcy

Learning Objectives

LO 3-1 **List and explain** ways to reduce debt and avoid the high costs of credit.

LO 3-2 **Evaluate** the costs and benefits of declaring personal bankruptcy.

Vocabulary

billing cycle, p. 296
grace period, p. 296
debt load, p. 296
equity stripping, p. 297
discharge, p. 298
automatic stay, p. 299
bankruptcy exemption, p. 299

© Aleksandar Vrzalski/ iStockphoto.com

REAL-WORLD FOCUS

Ian has a full-time job and has established a good credit record. He had an emergency medical condition last year, and his insurance paid 80% of the cost. His 20% co-pay has left him with a considerable debt and high monthly payments. "I'm really feeling the pressure of making these monthly payments," he told his credit counselor. "Is there anything I can do to get out of these payments?"

WORK AS A TEAM Ian's unexpected medical bills have left him short of cash for anything but basic necessities. What are some things he can do to deal with the problem? Is declaring bankruptcy his first and best choice?

In the first quarter of 2011, Borders filed for bankruptcy and had a *going out of business sale* to liquidate inventory and generate cash to pay off some of their debt.

DO YOU THINK **Borders filed for Chapter 11 or Chapter 13 bankruptcy?**

Jose Antonio Perez/Shutterstock.com

yienkeat/Shutterstock.com

LO 3-1 Managing Credit and Debt

When you begin using credit, plan to use it wisely. Go slowly. Do not use too much credit at first. It's important to establish your creditworthiness so that it will be there when you need it. There are several important ways you can manage credit to maximize the benefit while minimizing the cost.

Time Is Everything

The **billing cycle** is the time period when the account is closed to prepare your monthly statement. For example, if you have a closing date of the 5th of each month, what you purchase on the 6th won't be billed until the following month. Timing your purchases can expand your ability to minimize the interest on the balance.

If you are paying on an account that has an ongoing balance, the sooner you pay your bill, the less interest you will pay.

Knowing your grace period helps you manage payments. The **grace period** is the amount of time you have to pay your credit card bill without being charged interest on new purchases. Most credit cards allow at least 20 days from the bill's closing date. The longer the grace period, the more time you have to pay before interest is charged.

Blend Images/Jupiter Images

Using electronic transfers is a common way to make credit payments on time.

Analyze Credit Offers

When you receive credit offers, analyze them carefully. You may receive them by U.S. Mail, by email, in advertisements, at stores, and elsewhere. Consider carefully the interest rate, the annual fee, transaction fees, cash advance fees, late fees, over-the-limit fees, any penalties, and rewards programs offered. For example, some credit card companies charge a fee for cancellation of a credit card prior to a one- or three-year period of time, raise the interest rate, or impose other charges to discourage people from shopping for the best rates.

Manage Your Debt Load

A **debt load** is a person's outstanding debt obligations at any point in time. Whether or not your debt load is acceptable depends on your ability to make regular payments, your ability to pay off debt quickly if necessary, and your level of comfort with the amount of debt you owe.

The 20/10 rule states that installment debt (other than a house payment) should not exceed 20% of yearly take-home pay and that credit card (revolving debt) payments should be no more than 10% of your monthly take-home pay. Because debt represents future income that cannot be spent, it's important that your debt be at a reasonable level. For each dollar of debt, you should have significant cash or savings. Thus, you don't have to worry if some economic downturn occurs. For example, if you lose your job, you should not be in danger of immediately losing your house and car.

When making small purchases, it's a good idea to use cash. Charging your lunch and other daily expenses can add up quickly. If you can't pay the balance in full each month, you will then be paying interest on things that are long gone.

When you use cash, you may be likely to spend it more carefully because you actually see the money leaving your pocket.

When you are feeling uncomfortable with the amount of debt you have, there are several things you can do to reduce and eliminate credit card debt. Set up a *debt repayment plan.* List your accounts and their balances, minimum payments, and interest rates. Put them in order of priority so you will pay off high-interest balances first.

Consumer credit counseling services are available. These nonprofit organizations help consumers negotiate lower interest rates so they can pay off their debts. They also help consumers avoid credit and debt problems in the future.

If you have collateral (property), you may be able to get a *debt consolidation loan.* This is a loan that pays off all the individual smaller amounts. The interest rate of the overall loan is usually much lower and the single payment is often considerably less than combined payment amounts.

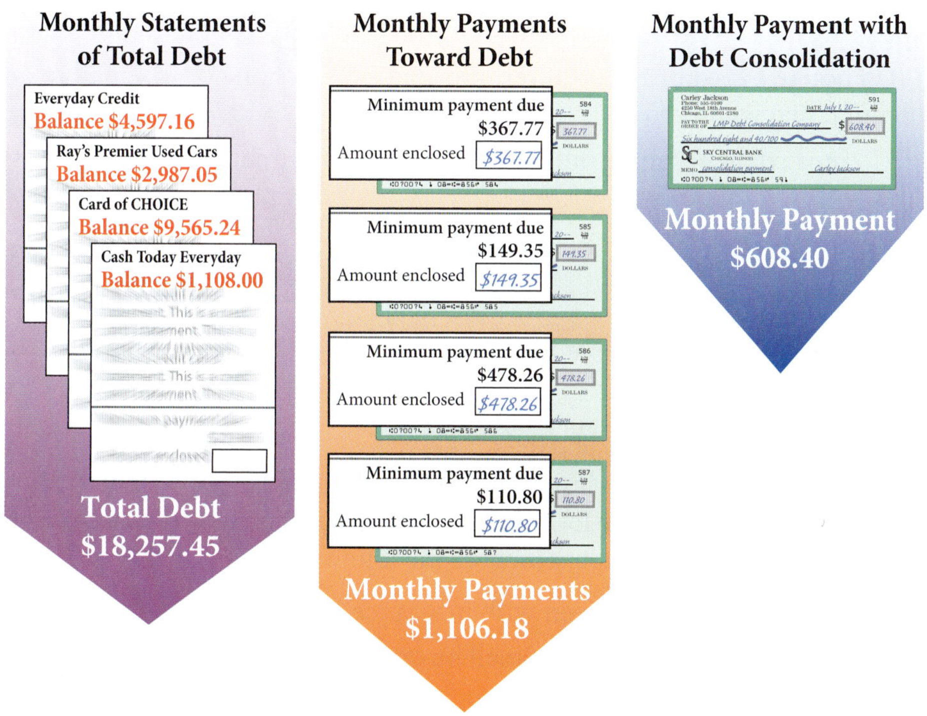

Figure 10-4
Benefit of Debt Consolidation

Avoid Unethical Loan Practices

When you are desperate you may fall prey to loan scams. **Equity stripping** is the unethical practice of extending a loan to a distressed homeowner who cannot afford the loan payments. As a result the lender soon repossesses the home. Homeowners should build equity, not cash it out as soon as it grows.

An *advance-fee loan* is a loan with a large upfront fee. This fee greatly reduces the amount that is borrowed. The debtor pays back the original loan amount, although he or she received much less cash. The effective interest rate on this type of loan is very high.

Other such scams pop up from time to time. Beware of offers that sound too good to be true. Quick and easy cash comes with a high price.

Prevent Credit Card Fraud

Credit card fraud is a serious crime. If you are a victim, notify the creditor immediately. Take these steps to avoid credit card fraud:

- Carry only the cards you need.
- Keep a list of account numbers and phone numbers to call so you can quickly report a card lost or stolen.
- Verify purchases and account balances.
- Shred receipts and statements.
- Do not loan credit cards to friends. Always know where your cards are.
- Close inactive accounts because they are often targeted by thieves.
- Have mail delivered to a post office box or secure mailbox.
- Mail payments from a secure mailbox or post office. Use online payments that are secure.
- Use only secure websites and buy online only from reputable companies.
- Do not give credit card or other information by phone or by email to anyone contacting you.
- Monitor credit accounts online often, verifying purchases and payments.

CHECKPOINT

Why is it important to assess your debt load?

LO 3-2 Bankruptcy as the Choice of Last Resort

Bankruptcy is a legal procedure to relieve a person of excessive debt. Bankruptcy is granted by a federal district court. Common reasons why debtors cannot pay their bills and seek bankruptcy include the following:

- Excessive medical bills (even with insurance coverage)
- Small business failure (Many small businesses fail each year.)
- Overspending and unwise use of credit
- Loss of employment and being overextended
- Having no savings or emergency fund when unexpected large losses occur
- Extreme economic downswings over long periods of time causing depletion of economic resources

One purpose of bankruptcy law is to give a debtor a fresh start when bills are so high that they could never be repaid. A second purpose is to ensure fair treatment for creditors. Bankruptcy laws exist to help in hopeless situations. Three common types of bankruptcy are Chapter 7, Chapter 11, and Chapter 13.

1. **Chapter 7 bankruptcy** This is also called straight bankruptcy, or liquidation bankruptcy. With this type of bankruptcy, the debtor forfeits assets in exchange for discharge of debts. A **discharge** is a court order that pardons the debtor from having to pay previous debt obligations. The debtor's assets are sold

ETHICS *in Action!*

What Is Bankruptcy Fraud?

When debtors try to hide assets so they cannot be used to pay off debts, this action is *bankruptcy fraud*, a serious crime. For example, if you put your valuables into storage or hide money in offshore bank accounts, this is considered an intentional act to hide assets. When people purposely run up debt with the intention of declaring bankruptcy, they can be accused of defrauding their creditors. In bankruptcy law, revolving or credit card debt must be at least three years old to be discharged without a repayment plan. One way people try to hide assets is by transferring ownership to another person. If discovered, the debtor can be denied bankruptcy protection. Bankruptcy laws are intended as a shield, to help consumers in hopeless situations.

Think Critically

1. **Do you think there are people who abuse bankruptcy law? Why would they take such an action?**
2. **Do you think bankruptcy laws are a good thing to have, or should they be abolished? Why or why not?**

(liquidated) and the money is used to repay as much debt as possible. Then all remaining debts (with some exceptions) are discharged.

2. **Chapter 11 bankruptcy** This is known as business reorganization. Businesses filing bankruptcy have the opportunity to retain assets and remain in operation after a plan for reorganization is filed and approved by the court.
3. **Chapter 13 bankruptcy** Also known as *individual debt adjustment*, this plan calls for individuals to enter a repayment plan. It is designed for debtors who have a source of income. Rather than liquidate assets, debtors follow a court-ordered plan to repay as much debt as reasonable over a three- to five-year period. Then remaining balances are discharged, again with exceptions.

Benefits of Bankruptcy

Sometimes bankruptcy is the best choice. For people who have reached their last resort, bankruptcy has several significant benefits:

- As soon as you file for bankruptcy protection, the debtor has an **automatic stay**, which means no further action may be taken by creditors, including collection of debts.
- Most debts are erased, leaving you a clean slate to start over fresh.
- Those who declare bankruptcy are allowed to keep some of their property (it is not subject to claims of creditors). A **bankruptcy exemption** is property that the debtor does not have to forfeit to pay creditors. For example, there is a homestead exemption that allows the debtor to keep roughly $22,000 worth of equity in a home. If the debtor has this amount or less of equity in his or her home, it does not have to be sold off to pay creditors. Each state has a bankruptcy exemption schedule. It is updated regularly to keep pace with inflation.

How Many Times Can You Go Bankrupt?

Popularly known as "The Donald," Donald Trump is also known for the phrase, "You're fired." Donald Trump is a businessman, entrepreneur, socialite, author, and television personality. Trump formed his first business in 1971. His business grew into hotel renovations, the airline industry, and even the casino business. By 1989, Trump was unable to make his loan payments. He financed his third casino, the $1 billion Taj Mahal, with high-interest junk bonds. The increasing debt brought Trump to business bankruptcy and on the brink of personal bankruptcy. He filed Chapter 11 bankruptcy in 1991 and again in 1992.

In the late 1990's, his financial situation improved and he completed the Trump Tower, and other projects. By 1998 his company was nearly $3 billion in debt. He filed for Chapter 11 again in November of 2004.

maukun/Shutterstock.com

Emerging from restructuring, Trump started building the Trump International Hotel and Towers of Honolulu and Chicago. The financial crisis of 2008 caught Trump in a bad situation. He was unable to pay a $45 million loan to Deutsche Bank. In February of 2009, once again Trump filed for Chapter 11 bankruptcy protection.

Think Critically

1. **What is the purpose of Chapter 11 bankruptcy? Does it allow the business to continue operations?**
2. **What can you learn from entrepreneurs like Donald Trump who never give up?**

Costs of Bankruptcy

Bankruptcy also has serious disadvantages:

- Bankruptcy damages your credit rating. It stays in your credit file for ten years; you cannot declare bankruptcy again for six years.
- Businesses are reluctant to do business with you unless you pay cash upfront.
- Creditors charge higher rates because you are a high-risk borrower.
- Bankruptcy may make it difficult for you to get credit, buy a home, get life insurance, and sometimes, get a job.
- Some types of debt are not discharged by bankruptcy, such as student loans, child support, spousal support, and government liens. These debts continue.
- Secured debt (such as mortgages on a house) will remain even if you claim the home as exempt.

Declaring bankruptcy should be considered only in extreme circumstances. It's a good idea to get legal advice to be sure bankruptcy is your best choice. In some cases, you can restructure debt and avoid bankruptcy.

CHECKPOINT

When is bankruptcy a debtor's best choice of action?

10-3 Assessment

Key Concepts

LO 3-1 1. How is timing important in managing your credit?

LO 3-1 2. List ways to reduce debt and lower interest paid on accounts.

LO 3-1 3. How can you help prevent credit card fraud?

LO 3-2 4. What are the three types of bankruptcy?

LO 3-2 5. What are the benefits of declaring bankruptcy? What are the costs?

Think About It

LO 3-1 6. When you buy things, are you willing to save your money so you can buy with cash? Or would you prefer to charge it and pay for it later? Explain.

LO 3-2 7. Every year, people from all socio-economic backgrounds get into trouble with credit. What advice would you give to people who (a) have too much credit available, (b) use credit for small purchases and don't pay off the balance each month, and (c) feel uncomfortable or stressed with the amount of debt they currently have?

LO 3-1 8. Having a credit card or account is a privilege, not a right. Explain ways that credit card holders can (a) use their accounts wisely, and (b) help protect themselves from fraud.

9. Describe how you can use the grace period for your credit card account to plan purchases and save money on interest.

10. Write about a fictitious person and a situation in which debt consolidation would be a good choice for dealing with his or her debt problems.

Make Academic Connections

LO 3-2 11. **HISTORY** Comprehensive bankruptcy laws were first passed in 1898; recent legislation (early 2000s) modified those laws to make it tougher for debtors to declare bankruptcy. Write a historical report on bankruptcy in the U.S. since the early 1900s—how and why has it changed? Why were new laws passed?

LO 3-2 12. **SOCIAL STUDIES** Many people declare bankruptcy each year due to high medical bills. Even with insurance, the co-payments can cost tens of thousands of dollars, and more. What can consumers do to help protect themselves from these types of enormous bills? Explain.

LO 3-2 13. **COMMUNICATIONS** Most financial experts believe that bankruptcy should be a person's choice of last resort. Write a paper explaining the advantages and disadvantages of bankruptcy, including when it is a good choice and when it should be avoided. Include two references to defend your answer.

Teamwork

LO 3-1 14. As a group, prepare a poster that compares the benefits and costs of using credit. Illustrate the responsibilities of using credit—to other consumers, to creditors, and to society as a whole.

LO 3-2 15. From newspaper classified ads, cut or download and print bankruptcy notices from your local area. Pick three such notices and prepare a slide presentation or written report listing the assets, the debts, and the net amount of bankruptcy protection being sought.

yienkeat/Shutterstock.com, Chad Baker/Ryan McVay/Photodisc/Getty Images

Chapter 10

Summary

10-1 CONSUMER BUYING AND CREDIT

1. A buying plan is an organized method to analyze purchase needs and how to best meet them. It helps consumers avoid impulse buying and its resulting buyer's remorse. Steps include defining goals, setting limits, researching options, evaluating options, and the purchase decision.
2. Using credit has many benefits, including more current purchasing power and a higher standard of living, convenience, and good records. Credit also has dangers because it often leads to reduced comparison shopping, overspending, higher cost, and tying up future income.
3. Using credit requires responsible behavior such as paying on time, making sure your payment is honored, avoiding fees and charges for improper use of credit, and getting help if you cannot make payments.

10-2 CONSUMER LOANS AND CREDIT SCORES

4. Consumer loans include installment (secured) loans, lines of credit, revolving (unsecured) credit, store accounts, and charge cards.
5. Each person who uses credit has a credit file. Credit bureaus gather, store, and sell credit information about consumers to their business members in the form of a credit report. The credit report contains information about a person's open accounts, current balances, and payments. It also lists any new applications for credit, unused credit, and any negative information such as late payments. A person's FICO score is based on payment history, amounts owed, length of credit history, new credit, and types of credit used.

10-3 CONSUMER DEBT AND BANKRUPTCY

6. Consumers must learn to use credit wisely, taking advantage of its benefits and minimizing the cost. Techniques include using your billing cycle to time purchases and payments, carefully analyzing credit offers, managing your debt load, avoiding hazardous loan practices, and taking precautions to prevent credit card fraud. A debt load consists of credit and debt obligations at a point in time; an unacceptable debt load occurs when a consumer is unable to make regular payments, when they cannot pay off debt quickly, and when they are uncomfortable and stressed with the level of debt.
7. Bankruptcy should be a debtor's choice of last resort. Bankruptcies are designed to give debtors a fresh start (when there is no other way to get back on their feet) and to protect creditors to ensure fair treatment. Bankruptcy discharges most debts, but some remain (such as student loans, child support, and certain liens). Bankruptcy does serious damage to one's credit rating and costs of credit in the future.

Chapter 10

Assessment

Vocabulary Review

Match each statement with the term that best defines it.

1. A person's outstanding debt at any point in time
2. Property a debtor does not have to forfeit in bankruptcy
3. Debt that has payments which include principal and interest
4. Pre-set amount that you will pay for an item
5. An organized method for making good purchasing decisions
6. Making a loan against equity in a home knowing it cannot be paid
7. A person who is obligated for the debt of another person
8. Penalty for spending more than the authorized maximum amount
9. Standards or rules by which something can be judged
10. A condition where no further action can be taken against you
11. Pre-approved loan amount that can be accessed as needed
12. Time period when an account is "closed" to prepare a bill
13. A statement of credit history prepared by a credit bureau
14. A legal document agreeing to payments plus interest
15. Process of looking for best value for money spent
16. A numeric rating on a point system of your creditworthiness
17. Ongoing account with charges and payments
18. A business that gathers, stores, and sells credit information
19. When a purchase is made without thinking about it
20. A way to pay for your purchases using credit
21. Court order that pardons a debtor from paying a previous debt
22. Charge for making a late payment

Vocabulary

a. automatic stay
b. bankruptcy exemption
c. billing cycle
d. buying plan
e. comparison shopping
f. co-signer
g. credit bureau
h. credit report
i. credit score
j. criteria
k. debt load
l. discharge
m. equity stripping
n. financing option
o. impulse buying
p. installment loan
q. late fee
r. line of credit
s. over-the-limit fee
t. promissory note
u. revolving credit
v. spending limit

Review Your Knowledge

LO 1-1 **23.** A buying plan is designed to prevent
a. credit purchases
b. impulse buying
c. all forms of buying
d. emergency buying

LO 1-1 **24.** The third step in a buying plan is
a. identify your limits
b. evaluate your options
c. research your options
d. define your goal

LO 1-2 **25.** Which of these is not a true statement about credit?
a. credit increases current spending power
b. credit is safer than carrying cash
c. credit is convenient
d. credit is less expensive than paying cash

LO 1-2 **26.** Money charged for the use of borrowed money is
a. interest
b. principal
c. income
d. debt

LO 2-1 **27.** A person who loans money to another person is a
a. debtor
b. borrower
c. creditor
d. contractor

LO 2-1 **28.** Property used as security for a loan is
a. a promissory note
b. collateral
c. an installment loan
d. a negotiable instrument

LO 2-1 **29.** A credit card is which type of debt?
a. installment loan
b. revolving credit
c. service credit
d. consumer loan

LO 2-1 **30.** Which of these is specific-purpose credit?
a. Visa
b. MasterCard
c. store account
d. revolving credit

LO 2-1 **31.** Which of these does not charge interest to the consumer?
a. credit card
b. store account
c. general-purpose card
d. charge card

LO 2-1 **32.** Which type of loan requires that you have collateral?
a. unsecured loan
b. debt consolidation loan
c. credit card
d. charge card

LO 3-2 **33.** Which of these forms of bankruptcy is also known as reorganization?
a. Chapter 11 bankruptcy
b. Chapter 7 bankruptcy
c. Chapter 13 bankruptcy
d. straight bankruptcy

LO 3-2 **34.** Which of these is not a true statement about bankruptcy?
a. It remains on your credit for ten years.
b. It discharges most types of debt.
c. It may be your best choice with insurmountable debt.
d. It damages credit for only a short time.

Digging Deeper with Economics e-Collection

A credit report contains a lot of information about an individual consumer. The information is gathered from public sources as well as from businesses who supply data regularly. Businesses, landlords, insurance companies, potential employers, and others can access your credit file. As a consumer, it is your responsibility to be sure information contained in your credit file is accurate. Access the Gale Economics e-Collection at **www.cengage.com/school/economics/personalfinance**. Locate a sample credit report. Prepare a visual display of the contents of a credit report.

Think About It

LO 1-3 **35.** Credit is a privilege, not a right. As a consumer, you have many responsibilities as you use credit in your lifetime. How will you use credit wisely to take advantage of its opportunities, but minimize its cost?

LO 2-2 **36.** Your credit score and report contain your credit history and will be judged by others to assess your ability to manage credit. What are some strategies you can use to ensure your credit score is as high as possible?

Make Academic Connections

LO 3-1 **37.** **MATH** With the yearly take-home pay listed below, compute the maximum installment debt and the monthly credit card payments (assuming yearly pay is divided by 12) that each person can make according to the 20/10 rule.

a. \$25,000 yearly take-home pay
b. \$50,000 yearly take-home pay
c. \$10,000 yearly take-home pay

LO 3-1 **38.** **SOCIAL STUDIES** Money is the primary cause of divorce in this country. In a research-based report, prepare an analysis of how money interferes with successful relationships. Include the use of credit and debt in this country and its impact on relationships.

LO 3-1 **39.** **BUSINESS LAW** Look up the Credit CARD Act of 2009, and prepare a poster or diagram that lists protections for cardholders, such as eliminating double-cycle billing, due-date gimmicks, and misleading terms as provided in this "Credit Cardholders' Bill of Rights."

LO 1-2 **40.** **COMMUNICATION** Credit should not be used to buy things you cannot afford. Write a two-page essay in which you outline your philosophy about the use of credit and how it has affected society, spending habits of individuals, and overall costs of using credit.

Extend Your Learning

LO 1-1 **41.** In groups, pick several large retail companies. Individual members of the group should be assigned a company to research and prepare a report about its history from its beginning to current times. They should visit the company's website and read articles written about the company. Find out what type of credit they accept and how that has evolved over time. Each group should prepare an oral report that summarizes their findings to share with the class.

LO 1-2 **42.** Interview three adults who have used credit for ten years or longer. Ask them about their opinions of credit and the impact it has made in their lives. Ask them if they intend to change anything about their future use of credit. Ask how the economy has affected them and their use of credit. Finally, prepare a summary of your findings and make it into a slide presentation or a written report.

UNIT 5 Measure Economic Performance

Unit 5 explains how economic activity is measured in a free market economy and discusses challenges to the economic system. In Chapter 11, you will study gross domestic product (GDP), the most widely used measure of economic activity. You will learn what GDP counts and what it does not count. You will be introduced to the circular flow model and learn how it works in the free marketplace. You will learn how GDP is computed and used to measure production. You will study the difference between real and nominal GDP and what these measures mean to you and your quality of life. In Chapter 12, you examine major challenges to economic performance. You will find that unemployment affects businesses, individuals, and the economy in many ways. You will also study inflation and how it reduces your purchasing power and affects your lifestyle.

UNIT 5 Project

Economic Indicators

Project Objectives

PARTNERSHIP FOR 21ST CENTURY SKILLS

- Analyze how economic growth, stability, and full employment are measured.
- Use standard grammar, spelling, sentence structure, and punctuation.
- Transfer information from one medium to another including written to visual and statistical to written or visual using computer software as appropriate.
- Create written, oral, and visual presentations of social studies information.
- Evaluate economic data using charts, tables, graphs, and maps.

chapter 11

Gross Domestic Product, p. 320

Prepare a chart of GDP for the past eight quarters; graph the data as a trend line. Based on the data gathered, summarize whether the economy is growing or slowing.

Business Cycles, p. 331

Based on information from the National Bureau of Economic Research prepare an analysis of business cycles through the history of the U.S.

chapter 12

Unemployment Rate, p. 347

Prepare a report detailing the current unemployment rate for your state and the national rate; explain how the unemployment rate is changing and why.

Inflation in the U.S., p. 357

Prepare a display board that lists the positive features of the Consumer Price Index (CPI) and the shortcomings of that same tool as a measurement device.

Project Wrap-up

Create a poster, website, oral report, slide presentation, or video that explains measures of economic activity, including GDP, the business cycle, the unemployment rate, inflation, and taxes. Include current rates and a graph of rates over time. Save a copy of all final work completed to be a part of your economics portfolio.

Dean Mitchell/Shutterstock.com

yienkeat/Shutterstock.com

Katrina Brown/Shutterstock.com

chapter 11

Gross Domestic Product and Economic Growth

11-1 Gross Domestic Product

11-2 Business Cycles and Economic Growth

yienkeat/Shutterstock.com

MARKETS *in Action!*

Michael Dell
Founder of Dell, Inc

In May of 1984, Dell Computer Corporation opened its doors in Austin, Texas. As a business start-up, the company began with a handful of employees and one energetic entrepreneur named Michael Dell. A few people took orders and a few others filled them. The manufacturing staff consisted of three guys assembling the electronic parts. Their initial startup funding was $1,000.

Michael Dell was born in 1965 in Houston, Texas. An entrepreneur at a very early age, Dell bought his first calculator at age seven and began programming (a teletype machine) in junior high school. At age 15, he bought his first computer, took it apart, and learned how it worked.

While a pre-med student at the University of Texas, Dell had his own side business where he upgraded and repaired computers in his residential hall room. He applied for and received a vendor license to bid on contracts for the State of Texas, and was able to win bids because his overhead was so low. In January of 1984, Dell had the brilliant idea of selling PCs directly to consumers rather than working through the conventional manufacturer-to-retailer chain. It was an idea that would prove enormously profitable to his rapidly growing enterprise.

In 1992, Dell became the youngest CEO to have his company ranked in *Fortune* magazine's top 500 corporations. He was just 27. In 1996, Dell began selling computers over the Internet. Within a short few years, Dell was earning more than $1 million a day from its online sales. Over the next ten years, Dell's world market share increased dramatically, giving his company nearly one third of total computer sales of desktops, notebooks, and servers.

Before the economic downturn of 2008, Dell employed more than 90,000 people. Although this number fell to just over 70,000 workers by 2011, Dell was still one of the largest employers in the computer industry. Dell defined the three C's of e-commerce as content, commerce and community, articulating his strategy for offering a superior online customer experience.

In 2004, Michael Dell stepped down as CEO of Dell, Inc., but remained chairman of the Board. Dell is renowned as an American business magnate and one of the richest people in the world, with a net worth of more than $14 billion in 2010. He was named "Entrepreneur of the Year" by *Inc.* magazine (at age 24), "Top CEO in American Business" in *Worth* magazine, and "CEO of the Year" from *Financial World* magazine. He currently serves on the Foundation Board of the World Economic Forum.

Dell, an international company, has laptop computers on display at the Electronics and Automobile Show in Yangon, Myanmar.

AP Photo/Khin Maung Win

Think Critically

1. Michael Dell had a natural instinct for business. How did he put together his innovative ideas to meet demand in the new Internet marketplace?
2. What value did Dell Computers add to the product markets and resource markets in the circular-flow model?

yienkeat/Shutterstock.com

11-1 Gross Domestic Product

Learning Objectives

LO 1-1 Define GDP and what is included and not included.

LO 1-2 Analyze how the circular flow model represents economic activity.

LO 1-3 Understand how GDP is computed.

Vocabulary

gross domestic product (GDP), p. 311
transfer payment, p. 311
final goods, p. 312
intermediate goods, p. 312
circular-flow model, p. 313
nominal GDP, p. 316
real GDP, p. 318
GDP per capita, p. 318

REAL-WORLD FOCUS

Jenny works at the local produce market. She also buys all of her family's fresh fruits and vegetables at the market. She appreciates the quality of the goods when she shops for organic foods. "You are one of my best customers," her employer commented. "I could never fire you because I'd be afraid you might take your business elsewhere. Without you, I wouldn't sell enough fruits to stay in business."

WORK AS A TEAM Explain how Jenny and her employer are simultaneously meeting each other's needs.

Today circuit boards that contain computer chips are installed in all types of household items, from a refrigerator to a remote control.

DO YOU THINK computer chips are a final good or an intermediate good? Why?

LO 1-1 What Is Gross Domestic Product?

The most widely reported measure of a nation's economic performance is gross domestic product. **Gross domestic product (GDP)** is the market value of all final goods and services produced annually in a country. Why is GDP important? GDP tells a country how well its economy is doing. An advantage of GDP is that it avoids the "apples and oranges" problem. Suppose an economy produces ten apples one year and ten oranges the next. Can you say that the value of output has changed? To answer this question, price tags must be added to evaluate the monetary value of apples and oranges. GDP measures value using dollars, rather than counting the number of cars, toothbrushes, and tanks produced.

GDP Counts Only New Production

Government accountants calculating GDP carefully exclude the following types of transactions.

Secondhand Transactions GDP includes only transactions that involve newly produced goods or services. It does not include the sale of a used car or the sale of a home constructed some years ago. Such transactions are merely exchanges of previously produced goods and not current production of new goods. Used items were counted in GDP in the year when they were newly produced.

Transfer Payments GDP does not count transfer payments. A **transfer payment** is a government payment to persons not in exchange for goods or services produced. Welfare, Social Security, veterans' benefits, and unemployment benefits are transfer payments. These transactions are considered nonproductive. The reason is because these payments are not for any current output. Transfer payments are made to people who are entitled to them. The reason could be because of being poor or reaching a certain age.

Stock Market Transactions Stocks and bonds represent only the exchange of certificates of ownership (stocks) or indebtedness (bonds). Stocks and bonds are not new production of goods and services. Therefore, stock and bond sales are not counted in GDP.

Nonmarket Activities GDP counts only market transactions. It excludes certain unpaid activities, such as homemaker production, child rearing, and do-it-yourself home repairs. If you take your dirty clothes to the laundry, GDP increases by the amount of the cleaning bill paid. GDP ignores the value of laundering these same clothes if you wash them yourself. Nonmarket activities are excluded from GDP because it would be difficult to place a dollar value on services that people provide for themselves.

The Underground Economy Illegal gambling, stolen cars, illegal guns, and illegal drugs are goods and services that meet the requirements for GDP. They are final goods with a value determined in markets. But GDP does not include unreported criminal activities

ftwitty/iStockphoto.com

The amounts paid by customers of a laundry service are counted in the GDP.

because no record is made of the transactions. GDP also ignores the value of production that is paid off the books. If you paint your neighbor's porch for $500 and fail to report this income on your tax return (even though you are legally required to do so), it will not be included as part of GDP.

GDP Counts Only Final Goods

GDP counts only **final goods**, which are goods and services sold to the final user. Including all goods and services produced would inflate GDP by double counting. This is counting items more than once. To count only final goods and avoid overstating GDP, be careful not to include intermediate goods. **Intermediate goods** are goods and services used as inputs for the production of final goods. Intermediate goods are not produced for consumption by the ultimate user.

Suppose a wholesale distributor sells glass to an automaker. This transaction is not included in GDP. The glass is an intermediate good used in the production of cars. When a customer buys a new car from the car dealer, the value of the glass is included in the car's selling price. The car's value is a final good counted in GDP. Consider another example. A wholesale distributor sells glass to a hardware store. GDP does not include this transaction because the hardware store is not the final user. When a customer buys the glass from the hardware store to repair a broken window, the final purchase price of the glass is added to GDP.

CHECKPOINT

Name five goods or services that are not included in GDP.

Education and State Gross Domestic Product

Investigate Your Local ECONOMY

Every state in the United States is different. They produce different products and have different services specific to their localities. Although students can live anywhere when they leave home, more than half of all high school and college graduates stay in their home state when they join the workforce. For this reason and others, schools want to increase high school and college graduation rates. Research the *Statistical Abstract of the United States*. Under Education, find the five states with the highest and lowest percentage of high school graduates. Also find this statistic for your state if it is not among these states.

Try it Out

In the *Statistical Abstract of the United States*, under Income, Expenditures, Poverty, & Wealth, find state gross domestic product. Is there a correlation between a state's GDP and the percent of high school graduates? How may these data be affected by a state's population?

LO 1-2 Circular-Flow Model

GDP is like an enormous puzzle with many pieces to fit together. How can you fit all these puzzle pieces together? One way is to use a macroeconomic model called the circular flow model. The **circular-flow model** shows the exchange of money, products, and resources between businesses, households, and government. Figure 11-1 shows the circular flow for a basic free market system.

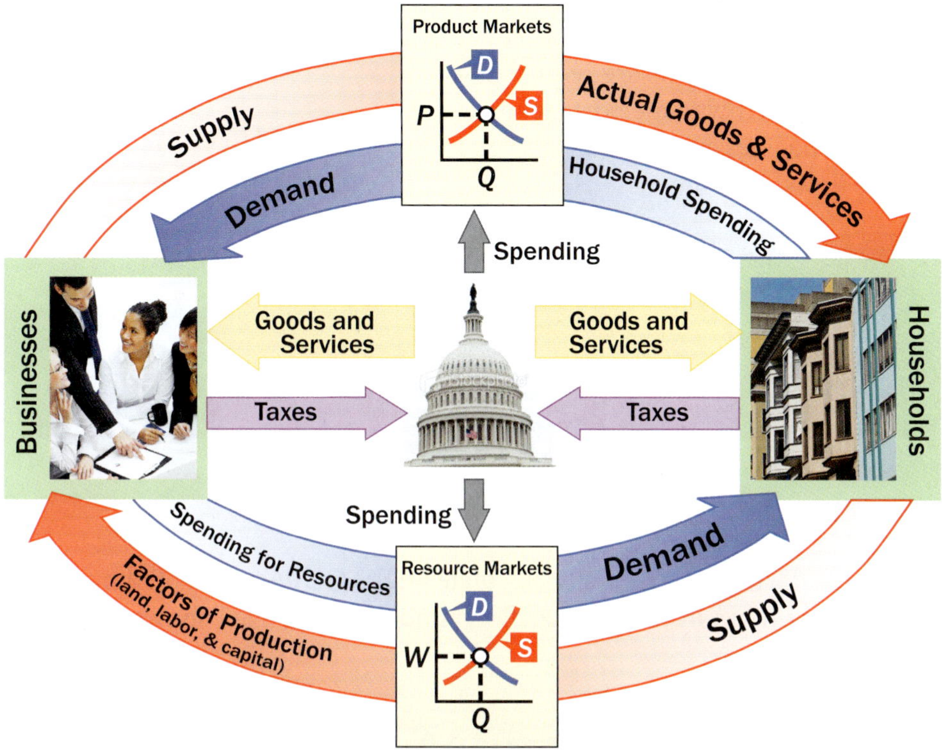

Art © Cengage Learning 2013; left photo: Yuri Arcurs/Shutterstock.com; right photo: Rick S/Shutterstock.com

Figure 11-1

Circular-Flow Model for a Free Market System

The circular-flow model shows transactions between businesses, households, and government. Households buy goods and services from businesses in product markets. In the resource markets in the lower loop, resources are sold to businesses. The government collects taxes and spends money in the product and resource markets.

The upper half of the model represents *product markets.* Here households exchange money for goods and services produced by firms. The red supply arrow in the top loop represents all goods and services produced and sold to consumers. The blue demand arrow in the top loop shows consumption spending from households flowing to businesses. Notice that the box labeled product markets contains a supply and demand graph. This means the forces of supply and demand in individual markets determine the price and quantity of each product exchanged.

The bottom half of the circular flow model consists of the *resource markets.* In this market, firms demand natural resources, labor, capital, and entrepreneurship. These resources are used to produce the goods and services sold in the product markets. The red supply arrow in the bottom loop represents this flow of resources from households to firms. The blue demand arrow is the flow of money payments to households for these resources. These payments are the source of income for households. Also, in resource markets, market supply and demand determine the prices of resources.

The government is represented in the middle of the circular-flow model. There are two blue arrows showing flows of spending to the product and resource markets. In the product markets, the government purchases computers, military equipment, and other products from businesses. In the resource market, the government spends money to pay the salaries of government employees, such as teachers, police, and firefighters. The government also purchases land for military bases or new schools. The government also provides goods and services to businesses and households shown by the two red arrows. To finance government spending, businesses and households are required to pay taxes. The blue arrows labeled taxes between government, businesses, and households illustrate these flows of money.

Salaries of police officers are part of the resource market and paid by government funds.

CHECKPOINT

Suppose taxes increase. Use the arrows in the circular flow model to explain the effect.

LO 1-3 How Is GDP Computed?

How does the government actually calculate GDP? GDP is computed by adding all the spending flows in the circular flow model. Figure 11-2 shows 2010 GDP divided into its four sectors.

Figure 11-2
GDP Formula

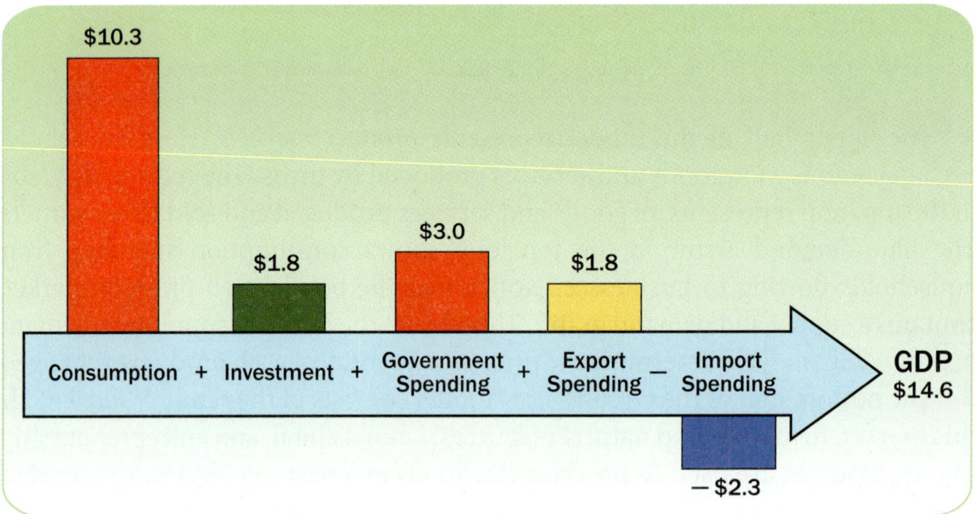

GDP is expressed mathematically in trillions of dollars as

$$GDP = C + I + G + (X - M)$$

For 2010 $\$14.6 = \$10.3 + \$1.8 + \$3.0 + (\$1.8 - \$2.3)$

Consumption (C) is spending by households. Investment (I) is spending by businesses. Government spending (G) is spending by all levels of government. Net exports ($X - M$) is net spending for foreign trade.

Consumption (*C*)

The largest component of GDP (71 percent) in 2010 was $10.3 trillion for consumption (*C*). Consumption spending is total spending by households for durable goods, nondurable goods, and services. Durable goods include items such as automobiles and appliances because these items last longer than three years. Food, clothing, soap, and gasoline are examples of nondurables. Nondurable items are considered used up or consumed in less than three years. Spending for services is larger than either durables or nondurables. Services include recreation, medical treatment, and education. Because spending for services is larger than spending for either durables or nondurables, the U.S. economy is often referred to as a service economy.

Services, such as medical care, are part of consumption spending.

Investment (*I*)

In 2010, $1.8 trillion was spent by businesses for investment. Investment here does not mean stocks or bonds. Investment (*I*) includes capital assets that are expected to earn profits in the future. Investment consists of spending for newly produced capital goods, such as plants, equipment, tools, and computers. It also includes spending for products that are produced and held in inventory.

Government Spending (*G*)

Government spending (*G*) includes purchases by government at the federal, state, and local levels. For example, the government spends for police and education. Also the government spends for defense, schools, highways, bridges, and government buildings. In 2010, government spending totaled $3.0 trillion.

Net Exports (*X* – *M*)

The last GDP account is net exports, expressed in the formula (*X* – *M*). Exports (*X*) are spending by foreigners for U.S. domestically produced goods. Imports (*M*) are the dollar amounts of U.S. purchases of Japanese automobiles, French wine, clothes from China, and other goods produced abroad. The positive sign (+*X*) means that money flows into the United States from foreigners to pay for exports. The negative sign (–*M*) indicates dollars are flowing out of the United States to pay for imports. In 2010, export spending was $1.8 trillion and import spending was –$2.3 trillion. Net exports were therefore –$0.5 trillion. A negative sign for net exports means the United States is spending more dollars to purchase foreign products than it is receiving from abroad for U.S. goods. The effect of a negative net exports figure is to reduce U.S. GDP. Stated another way, higher exports (*X*) relative to imports (*M*) increases GDP.

GDP in Other Countries

Figure 11-3 compares GDP for selected countries in 2010. The United States had the world's highest GDP and China has the second largest GDP. U.S. GDP, for example, was about two and a half times the size of China's GDP.

Figure 11-3

International Comparison of GDPs, 2010

This figure shows GDPs in 2010 for selected countries. The United States had the world's highest GDP. U.S. GDP, for example, is about two and a half times the size of Japan's and China's GDP.

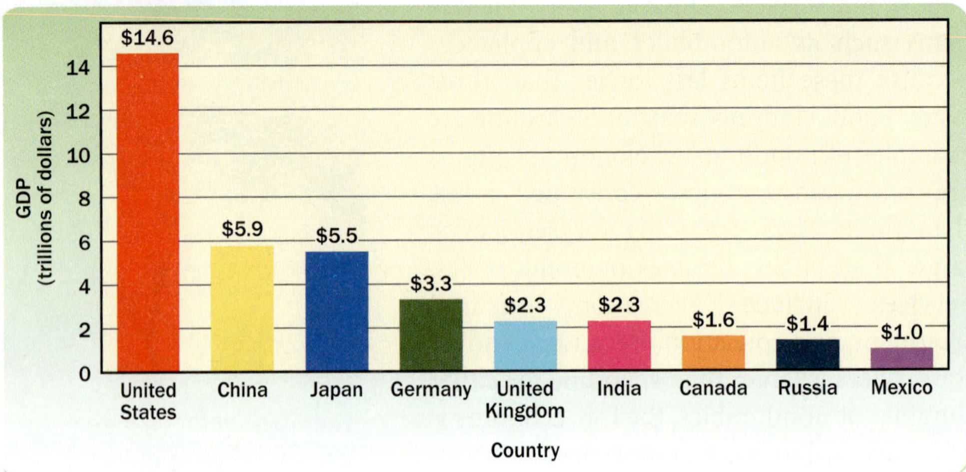

Nominal GDP, Real GDP, and GDP Per Capita

So far, GDP has been expressed as nominal GDP. **Nominal GDP** is GDP measured in current prices. Nominal GDP grows in three possible ways: First, output rises and prices remain unchanged. Second, prices rise and output is constant. Third, in the typical case, both output and prices rise. The problem is how to adjust GDP for only changes in output and not changes in prices. This adjusted GDP allows meaningful comparisons over time when prices are changing.

Changing prices can have a huge impact on how you compare dollar figures of output. Suppose a newspaper headline reports that a recent film entitled *The History of Economic Thought* is the biggest box-office sales movie of all time. You ask, how could this be? What about *Gone with the Wind*? Reading the article reveals that this claim is based on the nominal measure of gross box-office receipts. This gives a recent movie with higher ticket prices an advantage over a movie released in 1939 when the average ticket price was about $1. A better measure of popularity is to compare real box office receipts by multiplying the actual number of tickets sold for each movie by a base year movie price.

Assume that 25 million tickets at $1 were sold in 1939 for *Gone with the Wind.* And in 2010, 25 million tickets were sold for $6 to see *The History of Economic Thought.* You might say sales of the economics movie were six times those of *Gone with the Wind.* However, the reason is only because the price of a ticket rose from $1 to $6. To adjust for the rise in ticket price and accurately measure growth in ticket sales (output), a base year price must be selected. Choose the 2010 base year price of $6 and multiply this price by ticket sales in both 1939 and 2010. Now the real sales are the same. There was no actual growth in the value of ticket sales between the two years after adjusting for the change in ticket prices over time. The same principle applies to measuring GDP growth over time.

Global View

Hong Kong: A Leaping Pacific Rim Tiger of Free Enterprise

The Pacific Rim economies are called The Four Tigers of East Asia. They are Hong Kong, Singapore, South Korea, and Taiwan. Hong Kong is a great success story. When Adam Smith published his famous book, *The Wealth of Nations*, in 1776, Hong Kong was little more than a small island void of natural resources. Today, Hong Kong is a bustling model of free enterprise. This is in spite of the fact that seven million inhabitants are crowded into only about 400 square miles. In fact, Hong Kong has one of the highest population densities in the world.

What is the reason for Hong Kong's success? Following the doctrine of Adam Smith, this "miracle economy" is a model of free enterprise. Hong Kong has one of the lowest tax rates in the world. It also has almost no legal restrictions on business. Hong Kong has become the largest banking center in the Pacific region after Tokyo. International trade is also largely unrestricted. Hong Kong depends largely on trade through its magnificent harbor for its economic success. Hong Kong is known as a safe-haven warehouse and trading center. Here there is little or no interference from the government.

Hong Kong has proven what industrious people and entrepreneurs working hard on a crowded island can do. With minimum regulations and open trade, they improved their living standard without natural resources. Nevertheless, Hong Kong faces economic and political uncertainty. In 1997, the United Kingdom transferred Hong Kong to the People's Republic of China. Will China allow Hong Kong to continue to follow Adam Smith's free market philosophy? It is anyone's guess. So far China has not tampered with Hong Kong's free market economy. And its economic freedom ranking remains higher than any country in the world.

okasana.perkins/Shutterstock.com

Think Critically

Visit the Frazer Institute website and click on Economic Freedom of the World Reports. Research the latest report and find the latest ranking of economic freedom for Hong Kong and other countries. What relationship do you find between quality-of-life variables and ranking in economic freedom?

Measuring the difference between changes in output and changes in the price level involves the difference between nominal GDP and real GDP. **Real GDP** is GDP adjusted for changes in prices over time. The government currently uses 2005 prices as the base year. Figure 11-4 compares actual nominal and real GDP figures for selected years. Note that nominal GDP has risen more sharply than the real GDP. This increase is the result of rising prices included in the nominal figures.

Figure 11-4

Nominal GDP and Real GDP for Selected Years

Year	(1) Nominal GDP (trillions of dollars)	(2) Real GDP (trillions of 2005 dollars)
1970	$1.0	$4.3
1980	2.8	5.8
1990	5.8	8.0
2000	10.0	11.2
2005	12.6	12.6
2010	14.6	13.2

GDP per Capita and Quality of Life

GDP per capita is GDP divided by the total population. It can be argued that GDP per capita only measures income and not the quality of life. Figure 11-5 presents other selected variables that measure the quality of life. These variables are life expectancy at birth, infant mortality rate, literacy rate, per capita energy consumption, and economic freedom ranking. Take a close look at the statistics in Figure 11-5. These data reflect the dimensions of poverty in many countries. A person born in Japan has a life expectancy that is much longer than someone born in Mozambique. And the infant mortality rate is dramatically higher in Mozambique.

How good is GDP per capita as an indicator of the quality of life? Figure 11-5 shows that lower GDP per capita is highly correlated with lower quality of life.

Figure 11-5

Quality-of-Life Indicators for Selected Countries, 2010

Country	(1) GDP per Capita	(2) Life Expectancy at Birth (years)	(3) Infant Mortality Rate[1]	(4) Literacy Rate[2]	(5) Per Capita Energy Consumption[3]	(6) Economic Freedom Rank[4]
United States	$47,284	79	7%	99%	7,075	6
Japan	42,820	83	2	99	3,713	24
Mexico	9,566	75	15	93	1,646	69
China	4,382	73	17	94	1,598	82
India	1,265	64	50	63	545	87
Bangladesh	638	67	41	56	175	113
Mozambique	458	48	96	55	416	121

[1]Per 1,000 live births. [2]Percentage age 15 and over who can read and write. [3]Kilograms of oil equivalent. [4]The Fraser Institute.

Note that GDP per capita and other quality-of-life indicators are generally related to the ranking in economic freedom. Countries with greater economic freedom generally have higher standards of living, and vice versa.

CHECKPOINT

Assume country Alpha experiences a 3 percent growth rate in GDP for ten years and country Beta experiences a 6 percent growth rate in GDP for ten years. At the end of five years, which of the following is the best prediction for the standard of living? (1) Alpha's residents are better off. (2) Beta's residents are better off. (3) Which country's residents are better off cannot be determined from the given information? Explain your answer.

ETHICS *in Action!*

The Underground Economy: Working Off the Books

Imagine that you started a business last summer cutting lawns and doing garden work for people who live in your neighborhood. Your business was successful and you often worked more than forty hours a week. At the end of the summer you added up your earnings and found they totaled $3,245.50. Although you knew you were legally required to, you filed no federal or state income tax return at the end of the year. You figured that most of your income would not have been taxed and the part that would have been was so small that it would not be important to the government. What you did is referred to as "working off the books." It is against the law if you earn $400 or more in unreported income. At a minimum you should have paid Social Security taxes on your earnings. If your parents claim you as a deduction on their income tax returns, you should also have paid income tax on part of your earnings. These taxes would probably have totaled between $500 and $700. You might have thought that this was a pretty hefty part of your earnings to pay to the government. If you did, you would not have been alone. Some experts believe that as much as 15 percent of earned income goes unreported and therefore untaxed.

You may wonder how important working off the books is to the government. The answer is, "No one knows for sure," because there are no data reported to the government about this income. Estimates, however, have placed the annual value of lost tax revenue well into the hundreds of billions of dollars. Some experts believe that the government loses as much as $300 to $500 billion each year in taxes that are not paid on unreported income. Many people consider working off the books to be unethical as well as illegal.

Think Critically

1. **Do you believe that failing to report or pay taxes on income is unethical? Explain your answer.**
2. **Why is it reasonable to believe that the largest share of unreported income is earned by workers who are in the United States illegally?**

11-1 Assessment

Key Concepts

LO 1-2 1. Gross domestic product (GDP) adjusted for changes in prices over time is __?__ GDP.

LO 1-1 2. **TRUE OR FALSE** Goods and services sold as inputs for other goods and services are final goods.

LO 1-1 3. A __?__ payment is paid by the government to persons not in exchange for goods and services produced.

LO 1-2 4. **TRUE OR FALSE** A circular-flow model shows the exchange of money, products, and resources between businesses and households.

LO 1-1 5. Goods and services used as inputs for the production of final goods are __?__ goods.

LO 1-2 6. **TRUE OR FALSE** Nominal GDP is gross domestic product measured in current prices.

LO 1-1 7. Gross domestic product (GDP) is the market value of all __?__ goods and services produced annually in a country.

Think About It

LO 1-1 8. Classify each of the following as final or intermediate goods or services.

a. haircut from a hair salon
b. new automobile
c. oil filter installed in a new automobile
d. crude oil

LO 1-1 9. Explain why a new forklift sold for use in a warehouse is a final good even though it is fixed investment (capital) used to produce other goods. Is there a double counting problem if this sale is added to GDP?

LO 1-3 10. Explain how net exports affect the U.S. economy. Describe both positive and negative impacts on GDP. Why do national income accountants use net exports to compute GDP, rather than adding exports to the other expenditure components of GDP?

Make Academic Connections

LO 1-1 11. **MATH** A small economy produced the following final goods and services during a given month: 3 million pounds of food, 50,000 shirts, 20 houses, 50,000 hours of medical services, 1 automobile plant, and 2 tanks. Calculate the value of this output at the following market prices:

$1 per pound of food	$20 per shirt
$50,000 per house	$20 per hour of medical services
$1 million per automobile plant	$500,000 per tank

Teamwork

LO 1-1 12. Work in five groups. One group explains the circular-flow model. The other four groups prepare presentations on the four components of GDP—consumption, investment, government spending, and net exports.

Unit 5 Project: Economic Indicators

GROSS DOMESTIC PRODUCT Prepare a chart of GDP for the past eight quarters. Graph the data as trend line. Based on the data gathered, summarize whether the economy is growing or slowing. Compare real and nominal GDP and use this to estimate the current rate of inflation. Cite your source(s) of information.

yienkeat/Shutterstock.com, Chad Baker/Ryan McVay/Photodisc/Getty Images

11-2 Business Cycles and Economic Growth

Learning Objectives	Vocabulary
LO 2-1 **Explain** the four phases of the business cycle and business cycle indicators.	**business cycle,** p. 322
LO 2-2 **Analyze** the causes of business cycles.	**peak,** p. 322
	recession, p. 322
	trough, p. 323
	expansion, p. 325
	economic growth, p. 326
	leading indicators, p. 327
	coincident indicators, p. 327
	lagging indicators, p. 328

© Aleksandar Vrzalski/ iStockphoto.com

REAL-WORLD FOCUS

Antonio works for an auto body repair shop in an urban industrial park. "Business is really slow lately," his co-worker complained. "People aren't getting their cars fixed like they used to. It's this recession. Some people say things are getting better, but I don't see it. If things were getting better, we would have more customers."

WORK AS A TEAM Why do people cut back on spending during an economic recession? Explain what happens during this part of the business cycle. Who gets hurt?

mdd/Shutterstock.com

During trading hours, a stock board shows the current trading prices and other related information to the stocks displayed on the board.

DO YOU THINK stock market prices are a coincident, lagging, or leading indicator?

yienkeat/Shutterstock.com

LO 2-1 The Business Cycle Roller Coaster

The business cycle is often compared to a roller coaster that climbs to the peak and then drops sharply before climbing to another peak.

The headline in the morning newspaper reads "The Economy Is in Deep Recession." Later in the day, a radio announcer begins the news by saying, "The unemployment rate rose for the tenth consecutive month." On television, the evening news broadcasts an interview with several economists who predict that the slump will last for another year. Next, a presidential candidate appears on the screen and says, "It's time for change." And the media are abuzz with speculation on the political implications. The growth rate of the economy is headline catching news. Indeed, this measure of macroeconomics is important because it affects your future. When real GDP rises and the economy "booms," jobs are more plentiful. A fall in real GDP means a "bust." The economy forces some firms into bankruptcy and workers lose their jobs. Losing a job or not being able to find one when you want to is a painful experience not easily forgotten.

A central concern of macroeconomics is the upswings and downswings of the economy called the business cycle. The **business cycle** consists of alternating periods of economic growth and contraction. Business cycles always exist in market economies. A free market system is driven by ever-changing forces of supply and demand. A key measure of cycles is the rise and fall in real GDP. This mirrors changes in employment and other key measures of the macro economy. Recall from the previous lesson that real GDP is adjusted for changes in prices.

The Four Phases of the Business Cycle

Figure 11-6 illustrates a theoretical business cycle. A business cycle is divided into four phases. They include the *peak*, *recession*, *trough*, and *expansion*. The business cycle looks like a roller coaster. It begins at a peak, drops to a bottom, climbs steeply, and then reaches another peak. Forecasters cannot precisely predict the phases of a cycle. However, the economy is always operating along one of these phases.

Two peaks are illustrated in Figure 11-6 on the next page. At a **peak**, real GDP reaches its maximum. As explained in Lesson 2-3, the economy is operating near its production possibilities curve. A peak is a temporary high point. A macro setback called a *recession* or *contraction* follows each peak. A **recession** is a downturn in the business cycle during which real GDP declines. Business profits fall, unemployment rises, and production capacity is underutilized.

NET Bookmark

Access www.cengage.com/school/economics/personalfinance and click on the link for Chapter 11. Visit Global Business Cycle Indicators. Click on the Conference Board Leading Economic Index (LEI) for U.S. and select Download a PDF of the press release with a graph and summary table. Based on this graph, what is your forecast for the economy?

www.cengage.com/school/economics/personalfinance

A general rule is that a recession is six months in which there is a decline in real GDP. This means the economy is functioning inside its production possibilities curve.

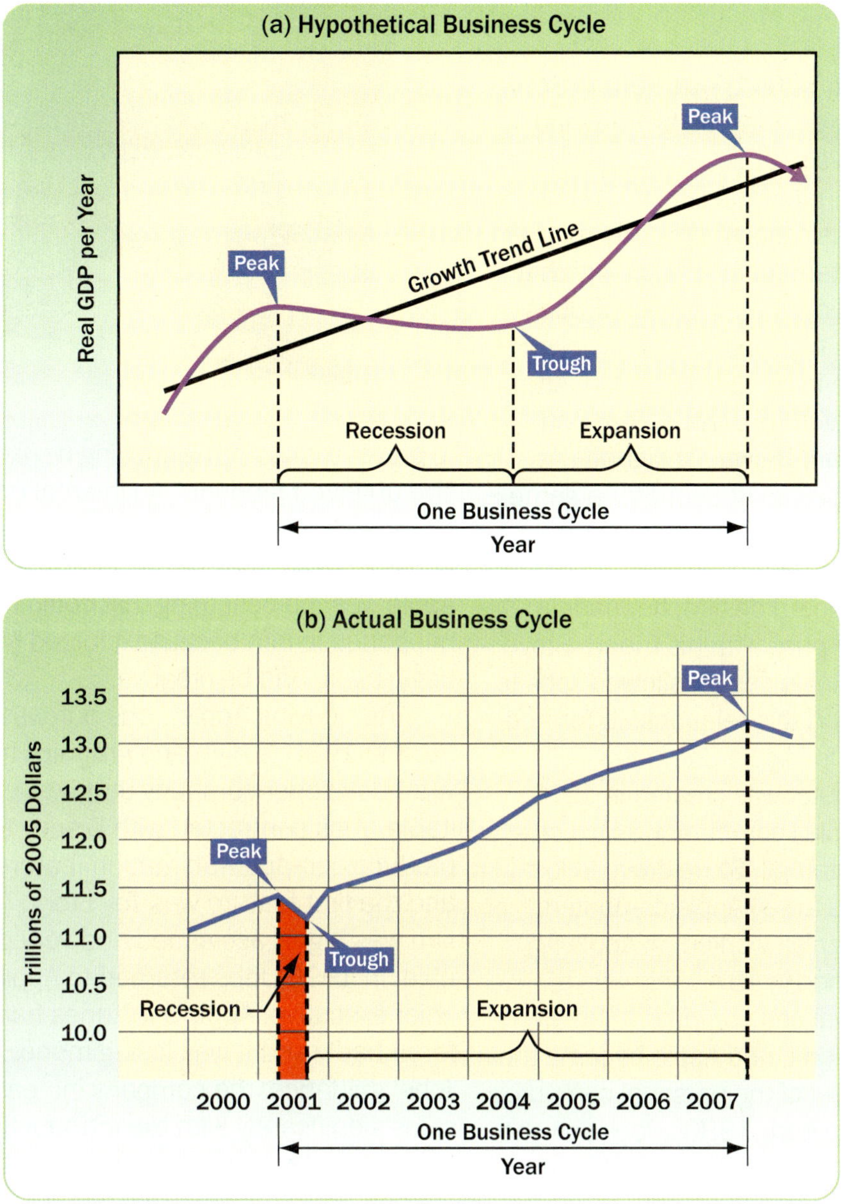

Figure 11-6

Hypothetical and Actual Business Cycles

Part (a) illustrates a hypothetical business cycle consisting of four phases: peak, recession, trough, and expansion. These fluctuations of real GDP can be measured by a growth trend line, which shows that over time real GDP has trended upward.

Part (b) illustrates actual ups and downs of the business cycle. After a recession in 2001, an upswing continued until another recession began in 2007.

What is the difference between a recession and a depression? According to the old saying, "A recession is when your neighbor loses his or her job. A depression is when you also lose your job!" This is close to the true distinction between these two concepts. No recession has approached the prolonged severity of the Great Depression from 1929 to 1933. The term *depression* is primarily a historical reference to this extremely deep and long recession. The Great Depression is discussed further in Unit 6.

The **trough** is where real GDP reaches its lowest level after falling during a recession. At the trough, unemployment and idle productive capacity are at their highest levels relative to recent years. The length of time between the peak and the trough is the duration of the recession. Since the end of World War II, recessions in the United States have averaged 11 months.

PROFILE

Steve Jobs
Apple

Featureflash/Shutterstock.com

Steve Jobs (1955-2011) was born in San Francisco and was adopted by Paul and Clara Jobs. Steve's father was a machinist for a company that made lasers, and he taught Steve basic electronics. His mother was an accountant for one of the first high-tech firms in Silicon Valley. In 1972, Jobs graduated from high school and enrolled at Reed College in Portland, Oregon. After only one semester, he dropped out and took a job at Atari. He was assigned the task of creating a circuit board for a game, with the promise of a prize for successful completion. Since Jobs had little knowledge of circuit board design, he made a deal to split the prize with his friend, Steve Wozniak. Wozniak's design allowed Jobs to win the prize, and this relationship formed the foundation for Apple Computer.

Apple Computer was created in 1976, and the first Apple I computer was assembled in Steve's garage. Steve drove to local computer stores to sell Apple computers. Meanwhile, Wozniak worked on Apple II, which was finished in 1977. This was a much more advanced computer than anything on the market, and Apple became the worldwide symbol of the personal computer revolution. In the early 1980s, Jobs saw the commercial potential for Xerox PARC mouse-driven graphics, which led to the creation of the Macintosh computer. Macintosh became the first commercially successful computer using a mouse. While Jobs was persuasive and charismatic, others wanted to prevent Jobs from launching new expensive untested products. An internal power struggle developed, and Jobs resigned from Apple in 1985. Jobs said later that quitting Apple was the best thing that could have happened to him because it forced him to begin again and be creative.

After leaving Apple, Jobs purchased Pixar in 1986, a high-end graphics hardware developer company that was unprofitable. Jobs contracted with Disney to produce computer-animation feature films, and the first feature was *Toy Story*. This film was highly acclaimed and very profitable. In 1996, Jobs returned to Apple as its chief executive. Apple's fortunes had suffered badly and it was losing money. Under Jobs' guidance, the company increased sales significantly with the introduction of new products with improved digital applications, appealing designs, and powerful branding. In 2001, iPod and iTunes were introduced followed by iPhone (2007) and iPad (2010). These products changed the world of personal computers.

THINK CRITICALLY

A famous economist, Joseph Schumpeter (1883-1950), developed the theory of "creative destruction" to explain the business cycle: The innovations of entrepreneurs cause old innovation, ideas, technologies, and skills to become obsolete (destroyed). This process causes variations in economic growth. Give two examples other than Apple in U.S. history that illustrate Schumpeter's theory of creative destruction.

yienkeat/Shutterstock.com

As shown in Figure 11-7, the last recession, called the Great Recession, lasted 18 months from December 2007 to June 2009. The percentage decline in real GDP was –4.1 percent, and the national unemployment rate hit a high of 9.7 percent. The Great Recession is the longest recession since the Great Depression, which lasted 43 months.

Recession Dates	Duration (months)	Percentage Decline in Real GDP (percent)	Peak Unemployment Rate (percent)
Nov 1948 – Oct 1949	11	−1.7	7.9
Jul 1953 – May 1954	10	−2.7	5.9
Aug 1957 – Apr 1958	8	−1.2	7.4
Apr 1960 – Feb 1961	10	−1.6	6.9
Dec 1969 – Nov 1970	11	−0.6	5.9
Nov 1973 – Mar 1975	16	−3.1	8.6
Jan 1980 – Jul 1980	6	−2.2	7.8
Jul 1981 – Nov 1982	16	−2.9	10.8
July 1990 – Mar 1991	8	−1.3	6.8
Mar 2001 – Nov 2001	8	−0.3	5.6
Dec 2007 – Jun 2009	18	−4.1	9.7
Average	**11**	**−2.0**	**7.6**

Figure 11-7
Severity of Post World War II Recessions

The trough is both bad news and good news. It is the bottom of the "valley" of the downturn. The foot of the "hill" of improving economic conditions is called an *expansion* or *recovery*. An **expansion** is an upturn in the business cycle during which real GDP rises. During expansion, profits generally improve, real GDP increases, and employment rises. Figure 11-6(b) illustrates an actual business cycle by plotting the movement of real GDP in the United States from 2000 to 2007. The economy's initial peak, recession, and trough occurred in 2001.

The GDP, business cycles, and leading indicators are commonplace among evening news stories.

A strong expansion phase lasted until a second peak in 2007. The longest expansion in U.S. history occurred over ten years from 1991 to 2001.

Economic Growth

In Lesson 2-3, recall that an outward shift of the production possibilities curve illustrated economic growth. Increases in resources, technological advances, and productivity are key reasons for economic growth. Now the discussion of economic growth is expanded. **Economic growth** is defined by economists as an increase in a nation's real GDP during an expansion.

STEVECOLEccs/iStockphoto.com

Economists are often invited to sit as panel members when news media are reporting on economic growth or decline.

The growth trend line in Figure 11-6(a) illustrates that over time real GDP tends to rise. This general, long term upward trend in real GDP persists in spite of the peaks, recessions, troughs, and recoveries. As shown by the dashed line in Figure 11-8, since 1930, real GDP in the United States has grown at an average annual rate of 3.5 percent. This annual change may seem small. However, about 3 percent annual growth will lead to a doubling of real GDP in only 24 years. A challenging policy goal is to maintain or increase the growth rate.

Figure 11-8

Business Cycles in the United States, 1929–2010

Real GDP has increased at an average annual growth rate of 3.5 percent since 1930. Following the Great Recession of 2007, the annual growth rate was a negative 2.6 percent in 2009 before rising to 2.9 percent in 2010.

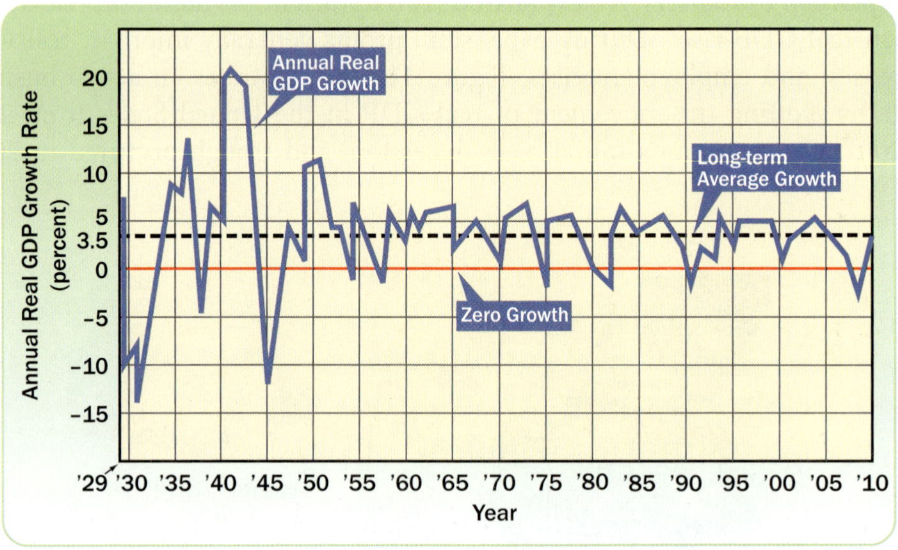

Closer examination of Figure 11-8 reveals the growth path of the U.S. economy. Over time it is not a smooth, rising trend. Instead it is a series of year-to-year changes in real GDP. Following the Great Recession beginning in 2007, the growth rate was a −2.6 percent in 2009 (negative growth) before rising to the below average rate of 2.9 percent in 2010.

Real GDP Growth Rates in Other Countries

Figure 11-9 presents real GDP growth rates for selected countries in 2010. China and India had the largest rates of growth at 10.3 percent. The United States and other countries throughout the world had lower growth rates.

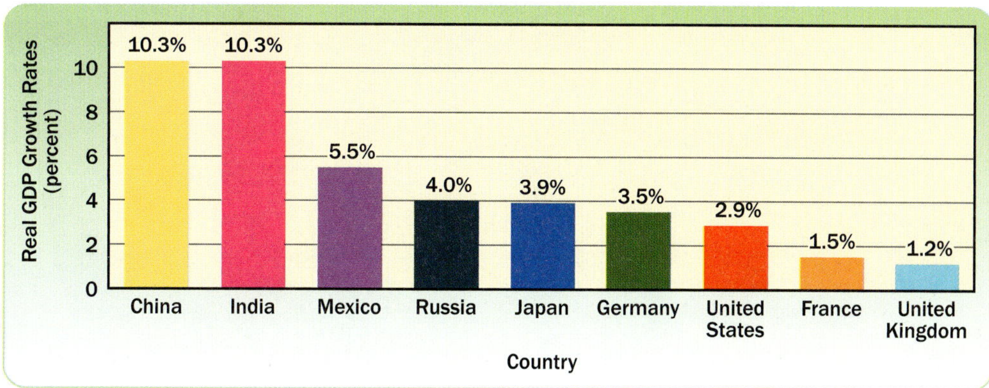

Figure 11-9

An International Comparison of GDP Growth Rates, 2010

The figure shows that China and India had the largest rates of growth of 10.3 percent, respectively. In contrast, the United States and other Western industrialized countries had lower growth rates.

Business Cycle Indicators

The media often report several other macro variables that measure business activity. The government's chief forecasting gauge for business cycles is the index of leading indicators. **Leading indicators** are key variables that change before real GDP changes. This index captures the headlines when there is concern over swings in the economy. The first set of ten variables in Figure 11-10 is used to forecast the business cycle months in advance.

Leading indicators	
Average workweek	New building permits
Unemployment claims	Stock prices
New consumer goods orders	Money supply
Delayed deliveries	Interest rates
New orders for plant and equipment	Consumer expectations
Coincident indicators	**Lagging indicators**
Nonagricultural payrolls	Unemployment rate
Personal income	Duration of unemployment
Industrial production	Labor cost
Manufacturing sales	Consumer prices
	Commercial and industrial loans
	Consumer credit to personal income ratio
	Best consumer loan rates

Figure 11-10

Business Cycle Indicators

The second data series of variables listed are four coincident indicators. **Coincident indicators** are key variables that change at the same time that real GDP changes. For example, as industrial production rises or falls, real GDP rises or falls.

The variables in the third group listed are lagging indicators. **Lagging indicators** are seven variables that change after real GDP changes. For example, the duration of unemployment is a lagging indicator. As real GDP increases, this variable does not fall until months after the beginning of the expansion.

CHECKPOINT

Suppose the economy is in a recession. A television reporter interviews Terrence Carter, a local car dealer, to find his thoughts about the economy recovering. Carter reports in the third quarter of this year more cars were sold than in the second quarter, but sales in these two quarters were far below the first quarter. His observations are consistent with which phases of the business cycle?

LO 2-2 What Causes the Business Cycle?

The uneven historical pattern of economic growth for the U.S. economy gives rise to the following question. What causes business cycles? The theory generally accepted by economists is that changes in total spending cause variations in real GDP.

Recall from the previous lesson that GDP consists of spending by households, businesses, government, and foreign buyers. Expressed as follows:

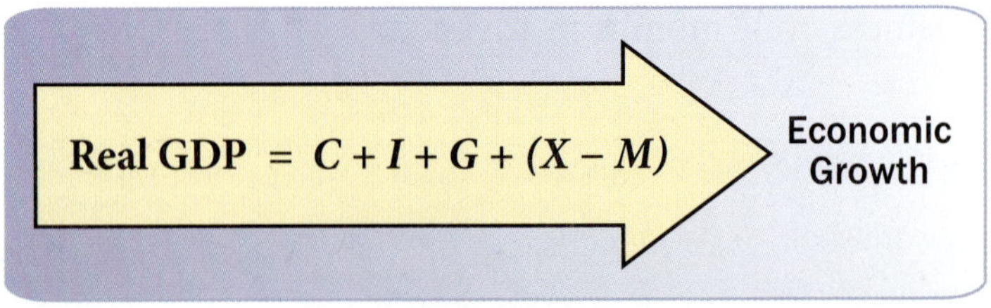

When consumers are optimistic about the economy, increased consumer spending contributes to economic growth.

Math CONNECTION

Changes in Trade and GDP

When foreigners purchase more or less U.S. exports (*X*) or U.S. consumers, businesses, and government spend more or less on imports (*X*), the value of the net exports (*X* – *M*) component of GDP changes the value of GDP, assuming all other components of GDP (*C* + *I* + *G*) remain unchanged. Given the formula GDP = *C* + *I* + *G* + (*X* – *M*), assume that *C*, *I*, and *G* do not change. Determine the net change in GDP that will result in the following situations.

Month	Value of Exports (*X*) (in billions of dollars)	Value of Imports (*M*) (in billions of dollars)
August	Decrease $50	Increase $30
September	Decrease $15	Decrease $6
October	Increase $2	Decrease $17

SOLUTION

August **Net change in GDP = –$50 – (+$30) = –$80 billion**
September **Net change in GDP = –$15 – (–$6) = –$9 billion**
October **Net change in GDP = +$2 – (–$17) = +$19 billion**

TRY IT

Determine the GDP for each month.

	Month	Value of Exports (*X*) (in billions of dollars)	Value of Imports (*M*) (in billions of dollars)
1.	November	Increase $11	Decrease $14
2.	December	Increase $7	Increase $18

Why do changes in total spending cause the level of GDP to rise during an expansion? Suppose consumers are optimistic about the economic future. If consumer spending (*C*) increases, then businesses find it profitable to increase investment (*I*) in plants and equipment. When firms become more productive, they use more land, labor, and capital. Such increased spending leads to economic growth in output, employment, and incomes. Economic growth may also result from an expansion of government spending (*G*) or from increases in foreign spending for exports (*X*) versus spending for imports (*M*).

A recession is the result of declines in sectors of real GDP. Now assume consumers become pessimistic about their economic futures. If consumer spending (*C*) decreases, then business profits fall, and they decrease investment (*I*) in plants and equipment. Business becomes less productive and uses fewer resources. A decline in economic growth may also be caused by a reduction in government spending (G) or from a decrease in foreign spending for exports (X) relative to spending for imports (M).

CHECKPOINT

Suppose an economy is in recession. How could low interest rates boost real GDP and create an expansion?

Does a Stock Market Crash Cause Recession?

The stock market soared during the "Roaring 20s." Lavish spending was in style as people enjoyed their new wealth. Then, on October 29, 1929, Black Tuesday, the stock market crashed. During the Great Depression, banks failed, businesses closed their doors, real GDP plummeted, and unemployment soared.

The impact of a stock market crash on the economy was seen again in 2001. The National Association for Business Economics (NABE) was holding its annual meeting in the World Trade Center on September 11, 2001. Just the day before a panel of NABE economists predicted slow growth for the economy. But no recession was forecasted. That forecast became obsolete the moment the first plane hit the World Trade Center in New York City. Analysts changed their forecasts and predicted a recession. The reason was that they expected the stock market would dive as profits fell. And it did fall. The stock market suffered its worst one-week loss since the Great Depression.

Stock market plunges are widely reported headline news. One result of these plunges is that many Americans feel poorer because of the threat to their life's savings. In only a few hours, stock losses reduce the wealth that people are counting on to pay for homes, automobiles, college tuition, or retirement. Although not all U.S. households own stock, everyone fears a steep downhill ride on the Wall Street roller coaster. If a stock market crash leads to a recession, it would cause layoffs and cuts in profit-sharing and pension funds. Businesses fear families will postpone buying major consumer items because they need their cash during bad economic times ahead. Lower spending causes prices and profits to fall. Falling sales and anxiety about a recession may lead many businesses to postpone modernization plans. Rather than buying new factories and equipment, businesses continue with used plants and machinery. This means lower investment spending, employment, output, and income for the overall economy.

In early October 2008, stocks fell to their lowest since the 2001 terrorist attacks. The longest recession since the Great Depression officially began in December of 2007 and ended in June 2009.

Think Critically

1. **What kind of business-cycle indicator are downward plunges in stock prices?**
2. **Relate a fall in stock prices to the business cycle. Your answer should include changes in the formula for GDP.**

11-2 Assessment

Key Concepts

LO 2-1 1. Key variables that change after real GDP changes are __?__ indicators.

LO 2-1 2. **TRUE OR FALSE** A recession is a downturn in the business cycle during which real GDP declines.

LO 2-1 3. The phase of the business cycle in which real GDP reaches its lowest point after falling during a recession is a __?__.

LO 2-1 4. **TRUE OR FALSE** Coincident indicators are key variables that change randomly as real GDP changes.

LO 2-1 5. An increase in a nation's real GDP during an expansion is economic __?__.

LO 2-1 6. **TRUE OR FALSE** Leading indicators are key variables that change before real GDP changes.

LO 2-1 7. The phase of the business cycle in which real GDP reaches its maximum after rising during a recovery is a __?__.

LO 2-1 8. **TRUE OR FALSE** The business cycle consists of alternating periods of economic growth and contractions measured by changes in real GDP.

Think About It

LO 2-1 9. Real GDP figures for ten quarters are shown in the table. Plot these data points, and identify the four phases of the business cycle.

Quarter	Real GDP (billions of dollars)
1	$400
2	500
4	200
5	300
6	500
7	800
8	900
9	1,000
10	500

Make Academic Connections

LO 2-2 10. **HISTORY** The Great Depression of the 1930s was the deepest and most well-known economic downturn in recent U.S. history. There have been many other recessions. Years in which these recessions occurred include 1837, 1873, 1893, and 1907. Investigate one of these events. What was the cause of the recession? What happened to employment and real GDP?

Teamwork

LO 2-1 11. Work in six groups. Three groups select different countries with high GDP per capita. The other three groups select countries with low GDP per capita. Each group constructs a chart with data they believe measures quality of life. After each group reports its findings to the class, prepare a master chart by GDP per capita. What principle can the class draw from the chart?

Unit 5 Project: Economic Indicators

BUSINESS CYCLES Based on information from the National Bureau of Economic Research, prepare an analysis of business cycles through the history of the U.S. Compute the longest period of contraction, the longest period of expansion, and the times between troughs and peaks. Based on your data analysis, infer the current position in the business cycle and project when you think things will change, and why.

Chapter 11

Summary

11-1 GROSS DOMESTIC PRODUCT

1. GDP is the market value of all final goods and services produced annually in a country. It counts only new production. It does not count secondhand transactions, transfer payments, stock market transactions, nonmarket activities, or the underground economy. GDP counts only final (not intermediate) goods.
2. The circular-flow model shows the exchange of money, products, and resources between business and households, with government in the middle, also spending and collecting taxes.
3. GDP is computed using the formula $C + I + G + (X - M)$, where C is spending by consumers, I is investment by business, and G is government spending. Net exports is exports X minus imports M. Nominal GDP is not adjusted for inflation and is measured in current prices. Real GDP is adjusted for changes in price over time. GDP per capita is GDP divided by the total population. It is a direct correlation with quality of life (higher GDP per capita means a higher quality of life).

11-2 BUSINESS CYCLES AND ECONOMIC GROWTH

4. The business cycle is an ongoing pattern of upswings and downswings in economic activity. There are four phases to the business cycle: peak, recession, trough, and expansion. The peak represents output near the production possibilities curve. It is a temporary high point. The recession occurs when GDP declines and the economy is contracting. The trough is the bottom or lowest level after a recession. Expansion or economic recovery is when GDP is rising once again and the economy is expanding.
5. There are leading, coincident, and lagging indicators. Leading indicators happen before GDP changes. Coincident indicators happen at the same time. Lagging indicators happen after GDP changes. These indicators help you understand what is happening in the economy and what is likely to happen next.
6. The business cycle is caused by changes in total spending which affect GDP, causing it to rise and fall. When consumers are optimistic and thus their spending increases, this increase leads to business investments and hiring of more people. This growth leads to more income and thus more spending (an economic upswing). Growth may also be caused by greater government spending or an increase of exports versus imports. Likewise, when consumers are pessimistic, they decrease spending which causes business profits to fall, decreasing their investments and laying off people. Economic growth can also decline because of decreased government spending or a rise in imports versus exports.

Chapter 11 Assessment

Vocabulary Review

Match each statement with the term that best defines it.

1. A model that shows the exchange of money, products, and resources between businesses, households, and government
2. Key variables that change at the same time that real GDP changes
3. Gross domestic product (GDP) measured in current prices
4. Key variables that change after real GDP changes
5. Alternating periods of economic growth and contraction measured by changes in real GDP
6. An upturn in the business cycle during which real GDP rises
7. The phase of the business cycle in which real GDP reaches its lowest point after falling during a recession
8. Gross domestic product (GDP) adjusted for changes in prices over times
9. Key variables that change before real GDP changes
10. A downturn in the business cycle during which real GDP declines
11. Goods and services used as inputs for the production of final goods
12. The market value of all final goods and services produced annually in a country
13. The phase of the business cycle in which real GDP reaches its maximum after rising during a recovery
14. A government payment to a person not in exchange for goods or services produced
15. An increase in a nation's real GDP during an expansion
16. Goods and services sold to the final user
17. Gross domestic product (GDP) divided by the total population

Vocabulary

a. business cycle
b. circular flow model
c. coincident indicators
d. economic growth
e. expansion
f. final goods
g. GDP per capita
h. gross domestic product
i. intermediate goods
j. lagging indicators
k. leading indicators
l. nominal GDP
m. peak
n. real GDP
o. recession
p. transfer payment
q. trough

Review Your Knowledge

LO 1-1 18. Government payments to people not in exchange for goods and services currently produced are
a. transfer payments
b. government purchases
c. consumption expenditures
d. investment expenditures

LO 2-1 19. Economic growth is measured by the annual percentage increase in a nation's level of
a. nominal GDP
b. real GDP
c. real GDP deflator
d. economic indicators

LO 1-1 **20.** Gross domestic product (GDP) is defined as
   a. the market value of all final goods and services produced in a nation
   b. incomes received by all of a nation's households
   c. the quantity of each good and service produced by U.S. residents
   d. none of the above

LO 1-2 **21.** Nominal gross domestic product is based on
   a. existing prices at which final goods and services are actually sold
   b. prices of final goods and services adjusted for inflation
   c. prices at which intermediate goods are sold
   d. none of the above

LO 1-2 **22.** The circular-flow model
   a. money flows from the firms to the households through the product market
   b. money flows from the households to the firms through the product market
   c. money flows from the households to the firms through the resource market
   d. resources flow to the households from the firms through the product market

LO 2-1 **23.** Economists use the phrase business cycle when referring to fluctuations in
   a. real GDP
   b. the chain price index
   c. the consumer price index
   d. the general level of prices

LO 1-1 **24.** All final goods and services that make up GDP can be expressed as
   a. $GDP = C + I - G + (X + M)$
   b. $GDP = C + I + G + (X + M)$
   c. $GDP = C + I + G + (X - M)$
   d. $GDP = C + I + (X - M)$

LO 2-1 **25.** The government's chief forecasting gauge for business cycles is the
   a. unemployment rate
   b. real GDP
   c. personal income index
   d. index of leading indicators

LO 1-1 **26.** Which of the following would not be included in GDP?
   a. Purchase of new lawnmower
   b. Purchase of silver cup previously sold new in 1950
   c. Purchase of ticket to latest movie
   d. All of the above would be counted in GDP

LO 1-2 **27.** Real GDP means GDP
   a. valued at prices in a base year
   b. that does not change from year to year
   c. corrected for changes in quality
   d. valued at prices at which goods are actually sold

LO 2-1 **28.** The point real GDP reaches a maximum during a business cycle is the
   a. peak
   b. recession
   c. expansion
   d. trough

LO 2-1 **29.** What stage of the business cycle immediately follows the trough?
   a. peak
   b. expansion
   c. recession
   d. depression

Digging Deeper with Economics e-Collection

There appears to be a direct connection between consumer confidence and consumer spending. When consumers are feeling optimistic about their futures, their jobs, and the economy in general, they tend to spend more. Access the Gale Economics e-Collection at **www.cengage.com/school/economics/personalfinance.** Consider consumer confidence reports and trends. Based on the latest report, how do you expect overall consumer spending to change within the next six months? Cite information about previous examples in your analysis.

Think About It

LO 1-1 **30.** The output of a nation is based on GDP. If a large amount of underground activity is going on, then that measure is less accurate. Do you think there's a big impact (understating GDP) from "underground" activity in the U.S.? Explain.

LO 1-3 **31.** When exports exceed imports, GDP increases. This contributes to economic growth. Do you believe it's important to support the economy of the U.S. with your purchases? Why or why not?

LO 2-1 **32.** An economic recession is often plagued by unemployment. What are negative effects of unemployment besides reduced income?

LO 2-2 **33.** Consumer spending is often cited as the cause for fluctuations in GDP and thus business cycles. Explain.

Make Academic Connections

LO 1-1 **34.** **SOCIAL STUDIES** Many people believe that GDP is an indicator of economic well-being in a country. Others believe it only measures output, not the quality of the output. In other words, just because a nation is producing more, doesn't mean that what it is producing will lead to increased quality of life. Write a one-page essay defending or rejecting this theory.

LO 1-2 **35.** **HISTORY** Pick a period of economic expansion or a period of economic contraction (recession) in this country. Explain the length of the economic period and give data about the GDP and other economic indicators.

LO 2-1 **36.** **RESEARCH** Visit the Bureau of Labor Statistics (BLS) online at www.bls.gov. Click on a news article about unemployment in the United States. Prepare a graph to display your findings about the rates of unemployment and the current business cycle.

LO 2-2 **37.** **INTERNATIONAL STUDIES** Pick a foreign country that exports goods to the United States. Do online research to find that country's GDP. Explain how exports affect their overall business cycle.

Extend Your Learning

LO 1-2 **38.** Assume you are given this data for country Alpha and country Beta.

a. Based on the GDP per capita data given, in which country would you prefer to live?

b. Now assume you are given this additional quality-of-life data. In which country would you prefer to reside?

Country	GDP per Capita
Alpha	$25,000
Beta	15,000

Country	Life Expectancy at Birth (years)	Daily per Capita Calorie Supply	Per Capita Energy Consumption*
Alpha	65	2,500	3,000
Beta	70	3,000	4,000

*Kilograms of oil equivalent

yienkeat/Shutterstock.com

JustASC/Shutterstock.com

chapter 12

Challenges to the Free Market System

12-1 Unemployment

12-2 Inflation

yienkeat/Shutterstock.com

MARKETS *in Action!*

Oprah Winfrey
Media Entrepreneur

Oprah Winfrey was born into poverty in rural Mississippi in 1954. She was raised by her grandmother while her mother moved north to seek employment. Winfrey's grandmother taught Oprah to read at the early age of three, and she recited Bible verses in local churches. During these early years, the community viewed her as a gifted child. Winfrey was sent at age 6 to live with her mother in Milwaukee. Her mother was a maid and the family struggled to survive. These were unhappy years for Oprah, but her life changed dramatically when she moved to live with her father in Nashville.

Oprah's father was a strict disciplinarian, and she credits him with saving her life. He provided a secure home life, and required Oprah to read a book each week and write a book report. In this new structured environment, Oprah excelled. In high school, she became an honor student and won prizes for oratory and dramatic readings. In her senior year, she was employed part time at a local radio station to read the news.

At age 17, Oprah won the Miss Black Tennessee beauty pageant and won a full scholarship to Tennessee State University where she majored in speech communications and performing arts. Also, she was offered a job reporting and anchoring the evening news at a local TV station. After graduating in 1976, Winfrey joined a television station in Baltimore as a co-anchor and news reporter. Here, she co-hosted her first talk show, *People Are Talking*, and found a job that was perfectly suited to her outgoing and intelligent personality.

In 1984 Oprah was hired to host an unsuccessful half-hour morning TV program in Chicago. In less than a year, she turned *AM Chicago* into the hottest show in town. In 1985, the format was expanded to an hour, and the show was renamed *The Oprah Winfrey Show.* A year later, the show was broadcast nationally, and it quickly became the number one talk show in national syndication. In 2011, Oprah retired from her famous talk show and is devoting her time to her many other interests.

Oprah created her own film and television production company, Harpo Productions. In 1996, she began her on-air book club titled "Oprah Book Club." Oprah is also co-founder of Oxygen media, which is a cable channel presenting programming primarily for women. In 2000, she founded *O, The Oprah Magazine.* Winfrey also created Oprah.com and OWN (Oprah Winfrey Network). Oprah has been ranked as the richest African-American in history. Oprah has shared her success by contributing to her own Family for Better Lives Foundation.

yienkeat/Shutterstock.com

Think Critically

1. It is said that the free market system allows people in poverty to rise to prosperity. Do you agree?
2. How has Oprah's entrepreneurship created jobs in the economy?

12-1 Unemployment

Learning Objectives

LO 1-1 **Explain** how economists measure unemployment.

LO 1-2 **Identify** the different types and impact of unemployment.

Vocabulary

unemployment rate, p. 339
discouraged worker, p. 340
underemployed, p. 340
frictional unemployment, p. 342
seasonal unemployment, p. 342
structural unemployment, p. 342
outsourcing, p. 343
cyclical unemployment, p. 344
full employment, p. 344

© Aleksandar Vrzalski/iStockphoto.com

REAL-WORLD FOCUS

Dustin currently works two part-time jobs in order to pay his bills and help out with family expenses. "My dad lost his job 15 months ago," he told his advisor. "His unemployment benefits have run out. He has been looking for a skilled labor position without any luck. When the plant replaced workers with machines, my dad's skills became obsolete."

WORK AS A TEAM What can Dustin's father do to get another job? Is he likely to find a job that pays as well as his former position? What can you do to protect yourself from this type of crisis?

Lloyd Paulson/Shutterstock.com

In some parts of the country, winter months provide employment opportunities for people willing to work on the roads during inclement weather.

DO YOU THINK people who work only during certain seasons of the year can get unemployment benefits in your state?

yienkeat/Shutterstock.com

LO 1-1 Measuring Unemployment

Each month the Bureau of Labor Statistics (BLS) conducts a survey of a random sample of 60,000 households in the United States. Each person 16 years of age or older is asked whether he or she is employed or unemployed. Suppose the person is not employed. The next question is whether he or she has looked for work in the last month. If so, the person is said to be unemployed. Based on its survey data, the BLS publishes the unemployment rate monthly. The **unemployment rate** is the percentage of the civilian labor force that is actively seeking work but is not employed. Who is actually counted as an unemployed worker, and which people belong to the civilian labor force? Many people without jobs are not classified as unemployed and are not counted as part of the labor force. Babies, full-time students, and retired persons are not counted as unemployed. Individuals who are ill or severely disabled are not considered to be unemployed. And there are other groups that are not counted.

When unemployment statistics are released each month, journalists report these percentages and how the economy is impacted.

Examine Figure 12-1. The *civilian labor force* is the number of people aged 16 years and over who are either employed or officially designated as unemployed. This excludes groups listed in the "persons not in labor force" category.

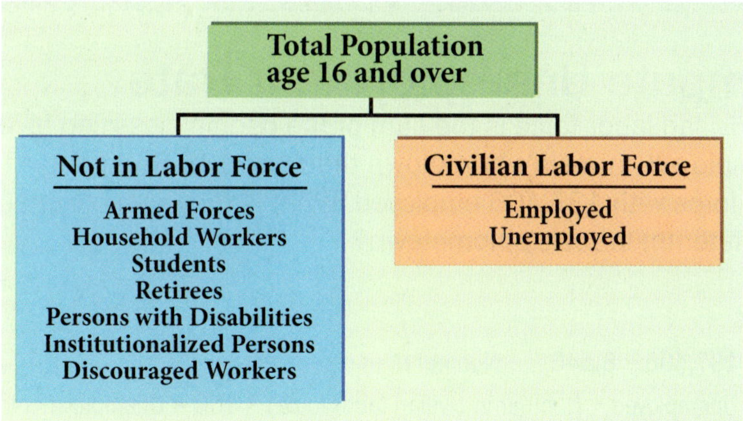

Figure 12-1
Population, Employment, and Unemployment, 2010

	Number of Persons (millions)
Total civilian population age 16 and over	237.8
Not in labor force	–83.9
Civilian labor force	153.9
Employed	139.1
Unemployed	14.8
Civilian unemployment rate	9.6%

erwin_ps/iStockphoto.com

Many people are underemployed because they work at jobs below their skill levels.

The unemployment rate, for example, does not count discouraged workers. **Discouraged workers** are persons who want to work, but have given up looking for work. The BLS includes discouraged workers in the "not in labor force" category. Many people believe that during a recession, the unemployment rate underestimates the problem of people who lack work by not counting discouraged workers.

The unemployment rate also does not include workers who are underemployed. **Underemployed** persons work at jobs below their skill levels, or work part-time when they want to work full-time. For example, a college graduate takes a job not requiring his or her level of skills. Or suppose an employer cuts an employee's hours of work from 40 to 20 per week. Such losses of work potential are greater during a recession, but are not reflected in the government's unemployment rate.

Based on survey data, the BLS computes the civilian unemployment rate, using the following formula.

$$\textbf{Unemployment rate} = \frac{\textbf{unemployed}}{\textbf{civilian labor force}} \times \textbf{100}$$

In 2010, the unemployment rate was

$$9.6\% = \frac{14.8 \text{ million persons}}{153.9 \text{ million persons}} \times 100$$

FreeSoulProduction/Shutterstock.com

Math CONNECTION

Compute Unemployment Rate

The civilian labor force is the sum of the people classified as employed and unemployed. In Josie's hometown there are 146,252 people in the civilian labor force with 137,406 employed. What is the unemployment rate (to the nearest tenth) in Josie's hometown?

SOLUTION

146,252 − 137,406 = 8,846   Number of unemployed

(Number of unemployed ÷ Number in civilian labor force) × 100 = Unemployment rate

(8,846 ÷ 146,252) × 100 = 6.0

The unemployment rate is 6.0%.

TRY IT

Find each unemployment rate to the nearest tenth.

1. Number of employed: 68,220; Number of unemployed: 12,865
2. Number in civilian labor force: 111,760; Number of employed: 102,042
3. Number of unemployed: 9,504; Number in civilian labor force: 201,688

Figure 12-2 charts a historical record of the U.S. unemployment rate since 1929. Note that the highest unemployment rate reached was 25 percent in 1933 during the Great Depression. At the other extreme, the lowest unemployment rate was 1.2 percent in 1944. Following the Great Recession, the unemployment rate reached 9.6 percent in 2010. This was the highest annual rate since 1983.

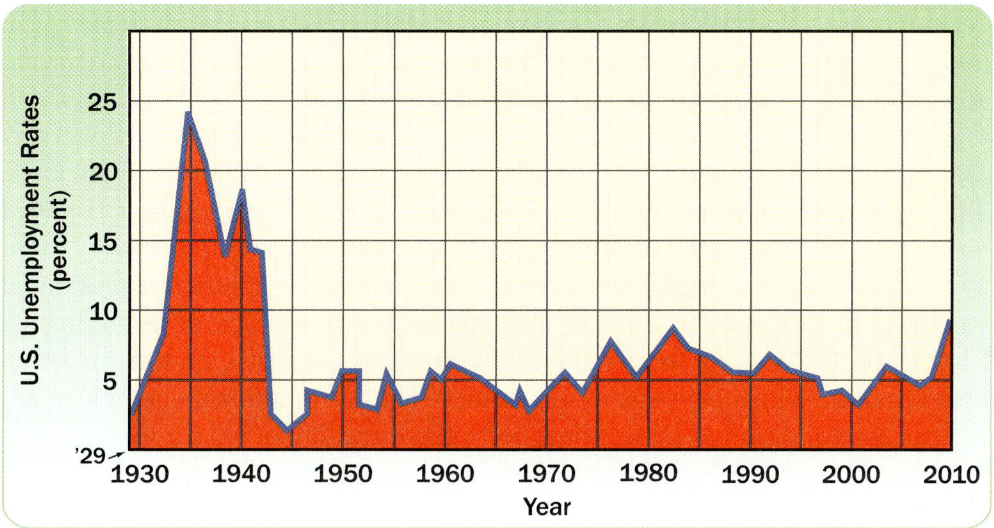

Figure 12-2

U.S. Unemployment Rate, 1929–2010

This figure shows fluctuations in the civilian unemployment rate since 1929. The unemployment rate reached a high point of 25 percent in 1933 during the Great Depression.

Unemployment in Other Countries

Figure 12-3 shows unemployment rates for selected countries in 2010. South Africa, Greece, and France had unemployment rates higher than the United States. The U.S. unemployment rate was 9.6 percent, while Japan and China had the lowest rates.

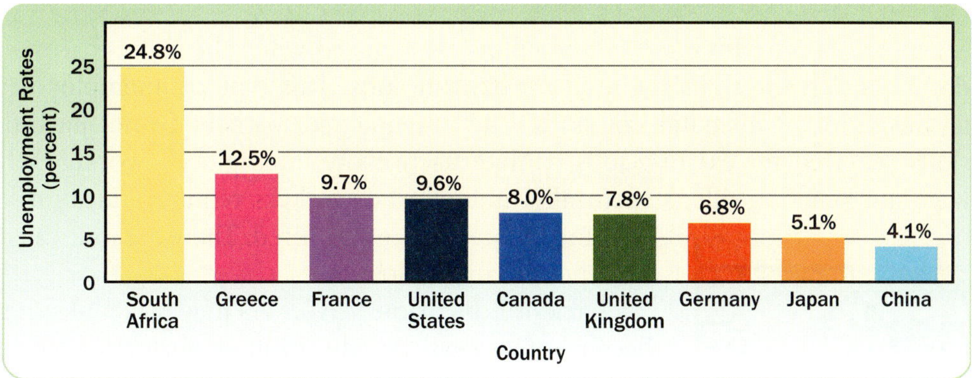

Figure 12-3

Unemployment Rates for Selected Nations, 2010

In 2010, many major industrialized nations had lower unemployment rates than the U.S., while a few had higher rates.

CHECKPOINT

Suppose the civilian population over age 16 is 120 million people and the number of these people not in the labor force is 40 million. There are 10 million unemployed people. What is the unemployment rate?

LO 1-2 Types of Unemployment

Economists have classified unemployment in four categories according to its cause. These are *frictional, seasonal, structural,* and *cyclical.*

Frictional Unemployment

For some unemployed workers, the absence of a job is only temporary. At any given time, some people with marketable skills are fired. Others voluntarily quit jobs to accept or look for new ones. There are always young people who leave school and search for their first jobs. Jobs requiring the skills of these unemployed workers are available. These unemployed workers are therefore considered "between jobs." This type of unemployment is called frictional unemployment, and it is not of great concern. **Frictional unemployment** is temporary unemployment caused by the time required for workers to move from one job to another or find initial employment. Examples are workers first entering the labor force, or reentering the labor force. The cause of frictional unemployment is the transition time to match a job applicant with a job vacancy. Economists consider frictional unemployment as a normal condition of an economy permitting freedom of job choice.

Seasonal Unemployment

Other workers are "seasonally unemployed." **Seasonal unemployment** is unemployment caused by changes in the seasons. For example, ski resort workers will be employed in the winter, but not in the summer. Certain crops are harvested "in season." A construction worker may be laid off in cold weather. In each case after a period of time, these workers will be employed again. This type of unemployment always exists.

Structural Unemployment

Structural unemployment is unemployment caused when the skills of workers do not match the skills required for existing jobs. This type of unemployment is caused by a "mismatch" of skills. The unemployed workers do not have the skills required for existing jobs. Unlike frictionally unemployed workers who have marketable skills, structurally unemployed workers require education or training before they can be hired. There are four causes of structural unemployment.

Lack of Education Workers may face joblessness because they lack the education to perform available jobs. This type of structural unemployment particularly affects teenagers. People who drop out of school lack the skills to be employed. Jobs exist that require computer skills, for example, but these people must be educated to be hired.

Changes in Consumer Demand The consuming public may decide to increase the demand for computer products and decrease the demand for Chevrolet Corvettes. This shift in demand would cause U.S. auto workers to lose their jobs making Corvettes in Bowling Green, Kentucky. This means they become structurally

NET Bookmark

Access www.cengage.com/school/economics/personalfinance and click on the link for Chapter 12. Visit the Bureau of Labor Statistics state unemployment. What states have the highest unemployment rate? Compare your state's unemployment rate with the rate for the nation as a whole. What might account for the difference?

www.cengage.com/school/economics/personalfinance

unemployed. To regain employment, these unemployed auto workers must retrain. They must find job openings in other industries. For example, workers could be trained for manufacturing IBM computer printers in North Carolina.

Technological Advances Implementation of the latest technology may also cause structural unemployment. The U.S. textile industry can fight less expensive foreign textile imports by installing modern machinery. This new capital may replace textile workers. But these unemployed textile workers do not wish to move where jobs are available. The costs of moving and family ties are understandable reasons for reluctance to move. Instead of moving, the workers become structurally unemployed until they are retrained for other jobs.

Globalization U.S. companies sometimes use outsourcing of U.S. jobs to India, China, and other countries. **Outsourcing** is the practice of a company having its work done by another company in another country. As a result, U.S. workers can lose their jobs and require retraining for other jobs. The same effect can happen when a U.S. company moves an assembly line to another country.

There will always be some mismatching between skills and jobs. Therefore, economists consider a certain level of structural unemployment inevitable.

What Kind of Unemployment Do Robot Musicians Cause?

You're the ECONOMIST

Modern machines can effectively duplicate string sections, drummers, and even horn sections, so the jobs available to live musicians are growing fewer by the day. It is not the first time that technology has cost musicians their jobs. Talking pictures ended vaudeville. Then recorded music replaced live music in radio station studios. Each time musicians lost jobs.

The threat to musicians' jobs continues. The Toyota Motor Corp. unveiled its instrument-playing humanoid robots at the 2005 World Exposition. The robots played drums and horn instruments, such as trumpets and tubas. And in 2008, a humanoid robot walked on the stage, said, "Hello, everyone." It lifted the baton, and conducted the Detroit Symphony Orchestra.

Now there is a Robot Hall of Fame at Carnegie Mellon University. The robots fall into two categories—robots from science and robots from science fiction. A panel of experts, each serving a two-year term, chooses robots in each category to be inducted into the Hall of Fame. Envelope please! The first winners were: The Unimate, the first industrial robot; the Sojourner robot from NASA's Mars Pathfinder mission; R2D2, the "droid" from the *Star Wars* films; and HAL-9000, the rogue computer from the film *2001: A Space Odyssey*.

Think Critically

1. **Are the musicians experiencing frictional, structural, or cyclical unemployment? Explain.**
2. **What solution would you propose for the musicians mentioned above?**

Cyclical Unemployment

Cyclical unemployment is directly attributable to the lack of jobs caused by the business cycle. **Cyclical unemployment** is unemployment caused by the lack of jobs during a recession. When real GDP falls, companies close, jobs disappear, and workers scramble for fewer available jobs. This situation is similar to the game of musical chairs. There are not enough chairs (jobs) for the number of players (workers) in the game.

The Great Depression is a dramatic example of cyclical unemployment. There was a sudden decline in consumption, investment, government spending, and net exports. As a result of this striking fall in real GDP, the unemployment rate rose to about 25 percent (see Figure 12-2). The Great Recession beginning in 2007 is another example of cyclical unemployment. Falling home prices and a plunge in stock prices caused households to cut back on consumption spending. This effect combined with a fall in business investment spending. The result was a negative growth rate and sharp rise in the unemployment rate to a high of 9.7 percent at the end of the recession in 2009. A focus of macroeconomic policy is to moderate cyclical unemployment. Figure 12-4 gives a summary of the types of unemployment and examples.

Figure 12-4

Types of Unemployment

Types of Unemployment	Definition	Examples
Frictional unemployment	Temporary unemployment caused by the time required for workers to move from one job to another.	Jane left her job last month as a nurse and is looking for a nursing job at another hospital.
Seasonal unemployment	Unemployment caused by changes in the seasons.	George is a ski instructor during the winter. In the summer he is unemployed.
Structural unemployment	Unemployment caused when the skills of workers do not match the skills required for existing jobs.	Martin lost his job at the textile plant. A new factory has opened to make computer printers. After a period of training, Martin will be able to be employed.
Cyclical unemployment	Unemployment caused by the lack of jobs during a recession.	Sally lost her job because sales of the product she makes fell during a recession. When the economy recovers she will be rehired.

The Goal of Full Employment

When an economy is working below full employment, frictional, seasonal, structural, and cyclical unemployment are present. When the economy is at full employment, it does not mean zero percent unemployment. Full employment occurs when an economy operates at an unemployment rate equal to the sum of the frictional, seasonal, and structural unemployment rates. **Full employment** is the rate of unemployment that exists without cyclical unemployment.

Unfortunately, economists cannot state with certainty what unemployment rate is the full employment rate. Full employment is difficult to define. Moreover, it changes over time. Currently, the consensus among economists is the rate is close to 5 percent. However, some economists argue the rate is closer to 7 percent.

The Impact of Unemployment

Various labor market groups share the impact of unemployment unequally. Figure 12-5 presents the unemployment rates experienced by selected demographic groups. In 2010, the overall unemployment rate was 9.6 percent, but there is an unequal burden by gender, race, age, and education. First, the unemployment rate for males was greater than for females. Second, the unemployment rate for African-Americans was higher than for whites and Hispanics. Third, teenagers experienced a high unemployment rate. They are new entrants to the workforce who have little employment experience, high quit rates, and little job mobility. Race is a strong factor. The unemployment rate for African-American teenagers was greater than for white teenagers. Finally, comparison of the unemployment rates in 2010 by education reveals the importance of education as an insurance policy against unemployment. Firms are much less likely to lay off a higher-skilled worker with a college education.

Demographic Group	Unemployment Rate (percent)
Overall	9.6%
Gender	
Male	10.5
Female	8.6
Race	
White	8.7
Hispanic	12.5
African American	16.0
Teenagers (16–19 years old)	
All	25.9
White	23.2
Hispanics	32.2
African American	43.0
Education (25 years and over)	
Less than high school diploma	14.9
High school graduates	10.3
Bachelor's degree and higher	4.7

Figure 12-5
Civilian Unemployment Rates by Selected Demographic Groups, 2010

CHECKPOINT

Did the invention of the wheel cause frictional, seasonal, structural, or cyclical unemployment?

PROFILE

Bill Gates
Founder, Microsoft

EdStock/iStockphoto.com

Born William Henry "Bill" Gates III, Bill Gates is a business magnate, author, chairman of Microsoft, and philanthropist. He is a well-known entrepreneur of the personal computer revolution.

His family was in the upper middle class when Gates was born in Seattle, Washington in 1955, Gates attended private school where he took an interest in programming. He wrote his first computer program in the language BASIC. At age 17, Gates and his high school friend Paul Allen formed their first business venture. Gates and Allen worked together to start up Microsoft, Inc.

Graduating from high school in 1973, Gates scored 1590 out of 1600 on the SAT, and enrolled at Harvard in the fall of that year. While at Harvard he met Steve Ballmer, who later took over for Gates as CEO of Microsoft.

During Microsoft's early years, all the employees had broad responsibility for the company's business. Gates oversaw business details. He also worked writing computer code. When IBM developed its first personal computer, it was Bill Gates who developed the MS-DOS that made the system a success. The sales and success of the IBM PCs made Bill Gates a major player in the computer industry. It was a few short years later (1985) that Microsoft launched its first version of Windows. Gates is credited for reinventing both himself and the computer industry. In doing so, he made himself the richest man in America.

In 2006, Gates transitioned out of his role of CEO in order to dedicate more time to philanthropy. Gates works full time running the Bill and Melinda Gates Foundation, which was founded in 2000.

In becoming a philanthropist, Gates studied the work of Andrew Carnegie and John D. Rockefeller. His charitable foundation focus is modeled after the Rockefeller Foundation—resolving global problems that are ignored by governments and other organizations. As of 2007, Gates's Foundation had given more than $28 billion to charitable causes.

Gates has received many awards and honors for work around the world in the areas of health and education. He has authored two books: *The Road Ahead* (1995) and *Business @ the Speed of Thought* (1999).

THINK CRITICALLY

1. **Job creation is a cure for the challenge of unemployment. Microsoft over the years has created countless jobs. Bill Gates used his intelligence and his perseverance to carve out a career for himself in a field he loved: computer programming. How can you turn a passion into a full-time, lifetime job?**
2. **What types of workers may have become structurally unemployed because of Microsoft's success?**

yienkeat/Shutterstock.com

12-1 Assessment

Key Concepts

LO 1-2 1. __?__ occurs when there is no cyclical unemployment.

LO 1-1 2. **TRUE OR FALSE** The unemployment rate is the percentage of the civilian labor force that is unemployed.

LO 1-2 3. Temporary unemployment caused by the time required for workers to move from one job to another is __?__.

LO 1-1 4. **TRUE OR FALSE** A part-time worker is not considered underemployed.

LO 1-2 5. Unemployment caused when the skills of workers do not match the skills required for existing jobs is __?__ unemployment.

LO 1-1 6. **TRUE OR FALSE** A discouraged worker is a person who is frustrated with their job.

LO 1-2 7. Unemployment caused by the lack of jobs during a recession is __?__ unemployment.

Think About It

LO 1-1 8. In a given year, there are 10 million unemployed workers and 120 million employed workers in an economy. Excluding members of the armed forces and persons in institutions, and assuming these figures include only civilian workers, calculate the civilian unemployment rate.

LO 1-1 9. How has the official unemployment rate been criticized for overestimating and underestimating unemployment?

LO 1-2 10. How does structural unemployment differ from cyclical unemployment?

LO 1-1 11. How does the government measure unemployment and employment?

LO 1-2 12. What are the four classifications of unemployment?

LO 1-2 13. Name several ways unemployment impacts individuals and society in general?

Make Academic Connections

LO 1-2 14. **ENGLISH** Read *The Grapes of Wrath* by John Steinbeck or a summary of this novel. This book describes what it was like for people to live through the Great Depression of the 1930s. Describe why these conditions led the government to create many of the programs that aid people in poverty today.

LO 1-2 15. **HISTORY** Search the Internet for the Great Depression and find sources of information. Write a paper presenting a story of what it was, how long it lasted, how it affected people, and what President Franklin Roosevelt did to aid in ending the Great Depression and get people back to work.

Teamwork

LO 1-2 16. Work in four groups. As a group choose one type of unemployment. Write and perform a skit that demonstrates this type of unemployment.

Unit 5 Project: Economic Indicators

UNEMPLOYMENT RATE The *Monthly Labor Review* is published by the U.S. Department of Commerce. Access this resource and prepare a report detailing the current unemployment rate for your state and the national rate. Explain how the unemployment rate is changing and why.

yienkeat/Shutterstock.com, Chad Baker/Ryan McVay/Photodisc/Getty Images

12-2 Inflation

Learning Objectives

LO 2-1 **Explain** the impact of inflation, how it is measured, and how it affects consumer lifestyles and decision making.

LO 2-2 **Define** the patterns of inflation in a market economy.

LO 2-3 **Describe** the causes and effects of inflation in a market economy.

Vocabulary

inflation, p. 349
disinflation, p. 351
deflation, p. 352
hyperinflation, p. 352
demand-pull inflation, p. 354
cost-push inflation, p. 354
real-cost inflation, p. 355

© Aleksandar Vrzalski/ iStockphoto.com

REAL-WORLD FOCUS

Jorge recently purchased a car. He had budgeted for the monthly payments, insurance, maintenance, and gasoline. "Lately, the price of gas has increased dramatically," Jorge told his friend. "I have to cut something else out of my budget to pay for the increased cost, or I have to drive less. I refuse to charge it to my credit card and pay interest on gasoline purchases."

WORK AS A TEAM What can you do when prices increase without warning on products you use a lot in your daily life? Are there ways you can adjust for these changes over the long run?

gnohz/Shutterstock.com

Apartment complexes and hotels have expenses for chemicals used to keep their swimming pools clean and sanitary.

DO YOU THINK managers of apartments and hotels that know about deinflation can save money on pool chemicals?

yienkeat/Shutterstock.com

LO 2-1 Impact of Inflation

Everone is affected by the prices paid for products purchased in the marketplace. **Inflation** is the increase in general price level for goods and services. When prices rise faster than income, buyers lose purchasing power. In other words, the money workers earn will buy less as prices rise. Rising price levels affect both consumers and producers in a market economy. As the value of the dollar goes down, it buys less. As inflation goes up, the value of the dollar goes down.

Many workers receive annual *cost-of-living adjustments (COLAs)* which are pay increases from employers that are intended to offset the effects of inflation. The COLA does not provide more spending power. It keeps purchasing power equal to the rising costs of living. On top of COLA, workers may also receive merit raises and bonuses. These increases in income provide additional purchasing power for consumers.

Businesses are also affected when their costs are rising. To maintain the same levels of profit, businesses must raise prices. Profits are needed so the business can grow, invest in new technology, and remain competitive in the marketplace. Raising prices to meet the impact of inflation does not give the business more spending power. It merely maintains the current level of business profits.

aldomurillo/iStockphoto.com

Measuring Inflation

Inflation is measured by the U.S. government. The measurement tool most often used is the *Consumer Price Index (CPI)*. The CPI uses a list of goods and services (called a market basket) that are commonly bought by consumers. The index measures changes in price from a base year or starting point in time compared to the current time. For example, if the price of an item was \$1.00 in the base year, and it is now \$1.12, that is a 12 percent increase in price since the base year. If the increase happened in just one year and it happened to all goods on the list, the inflation rate for that year would be 12 percent. The formula for computing the annual rate of inflation is

$$\textbf{Rate of Inflation} = \frac{\textbf{Change in CPI from the previous year}}{\textbf{CPI from last year}} \times \textbf{100}$$

The CPI is computed by the Bureau of Labor Statistics and can be viewed at www.bls.gov/cpi.

Inflation and Decision Making

When prices are rising rapidly and the nation is experiencing inflation, good consumer decision-making skills are critical. Consumers should recognize when inflation is causing their spending power to diminish and be prepared to take action. To preserve spending power, decisions should take rising price levels into account.

AlexRaths/iStockphoto.com

Individuals who live on a fixed income are those impacted the most by inflation.

Who benefits from inflation? To answer this question you should be aware that increased rates of inflation are generally associated with higher interest rates. Those who are in a position to profit from rising prices are often those who are not dependent on credit. Businesses in a solid financial position and able to fund growth internally (rather than borrowing) will benefit. Businesses that have money to lend (creditors) will benefit. Consumers who have savings or are able to save money will earn higher rates of interest for their deposits.

Who gets hurt from inflation? Those on fixed incomes who must cut back or consume less are hurt. Those who depend on credit will pay higher interest rates and get less for the money they borrow. Consumers whose income or investment earnings do not go up as fast as the rate of inflation will lose purchasing power and wealth.

Consumers must be able to respond to changing conditions in the economy. Assume that you are currently earning 2.5 percent on your savings. Because of rising inflation, your credit card company has raised its interest rate to 18 percent. Is it wise to carry a credit card balance of $1,000 (paying 18 percent) when you have a savings account that has a balance of $1,000 (earning 2.5 percent)? The rational choice may be to pay off your credit-card debt with your savings and save the 15.5 percent difference in interest rates.

Investors should consider choices that will keep the value of their investments in pace with inflation as well. That often means taking more risk. Without taking the risk, you may be losing significant purchasing power. For example, assume you have an investment in a bond fund that is paying an annual rate of 3.3 percent. If the annual rate of inflation is 6.5 percent, your investment has less purchasing power at the end of the year compared to its value at the beginning of the year. Thus, you should consider moving your money to an investment that will earn at least 6.5 percent and allow you to break even. Even better would be a choice that would bring more than 6.5 percent although this would require you to accept a higher level of risk.

Consumers must understand inflation and actions they can take to reduce its impact. Those who have liquid resources (cash) can generally lend money to others at high interest rates to offset the effects of high inflation. An inflationary period is a good time to pay off high-interest debt and be prepared to make choices that will bring sufficient payback to counter the effects of inflation.

When businesses perceive that rising prices will affect them directly, they often take measures to reduce the impact. For example, assume oil prices are rising rapidly and this trend seems to be out of control. If a business relies heavily on oil, then it is likely to buy a futures contract in oil. A futures contract locks in a specific price at a future date that will not change even if oil prices go up. They might also buy stocks in oil companies. Then if those stock prices rise, they will offset the cost of oil. A *hedge* against inflation is a defensive move.

CHECKPOINT

How does inflation affect a person's income and lifestyle?

LO 2-2 Patterns of Inflation

Inflation is the measure of changes in price over time. Whether business activity is slow or robust makes a difference in how producers respond. Inflation affects pricing as well as purchasing decisions.

Disinflation

When prices are rising but the rate of increase is slowing, the economy is in a period of **disinflation**. Some products and services do not increase in price as fast as others. Often this happens when demand for a product is not the same throughout the year. For example, in the spring and summer, the price of swimsuits may be rising. In the fall and winter, however, if the price is rising, it is likely to be doing so at a much slower rate.

Taking advantage of disinflation requires planning. Consumers can stock up, or purchase items ahead of time. They can look for less expensive options. Avoiding high seasonal prices will help to control their spending.

Price Increases

When there are severe weather conditions that affect crops, prices of those products will rise significantly in stores. Seasonal price changes also occur when products are in short supply. Consider products your family purchases on a regular basis. How are the prices changing over time for these products? To what can you attribute the changes of price?

Investigate Your Local ECONOMY

Try it Out

Visit three local grocery stores. Compare prices on several types of items, including fresh produce, frozen foods, canned food (such as tuna fish or cat food), and bulk foods. How are prices changing? How do prices vary among stores? Why do you think they are different from one store to the next in the local area?

franckreporter/iStockphoto.com

In the late 1970s, the United States experienced double-digit inflation.

Hyperinflation

When prices are rising so rapidly that they are out of control, there is **hyperinflation**. In the United States, there have been periods of double-digit inflation. Inflation reached over 10 percent in the late 1970s. However, hyperinflation rates are much higher than this. Although there is no set rule, many economists consider inflation rates of 50 percent or higher to be hyperinflation. For example, Germany's monthly inflation rates reached over 300 percent in the years following World War I.

The effects of hyperinflation can be devastating. With rapidly rising prices, consumers are forced to spend their money as fast as they can. They do this because they fear that prices will be even higher if they wait. This spending frenzy leads to even more inflation. Soon people are unable to buy the goods they need to live comfortably.

While the United States has not experienced hyperinflation (other than rapidly increasing oil prices over a short period of time), it is an event that could happen in the future.

Deflation

When the general level of prices is decreasing, the economy is experiencing a period of **deflation**. It is the opposite of inflation. Prices are going down because demand is sluggish. Deflation occurs when consumer spending is declining due to real or perceived fear, pessimism, or reduced income. In many cases, deflation

Global View

Hyperinflation in Russia

The nature of hyperinflation in Russia in the 1990s was due to the expansion of the money supply by the central bank of Russia. At the same time, price controls were maintained. Removing price controls would have created a temporary price increase. Holding price controls in place created a shortage and contributed to the creation of a *black market* (underground economy). Those who could not buy enough at the controlled price had to go to the black market and pay a higher price.

When the money supply expanded in excess of real growth in the economy, the result was inflation. In the case of Russia, the economy was contracting. As the price level continued to rise, bigger loans were needed. Inflation briefly reached a level of 5,000 percent a year. According to the International Monetary Fund (IMF), inflation of consumer prices in Russia between 1993 and 2004 totaled 874 percent. This hyperinflation was brought under relative control by 2004 at 10.9 percent. This change happened when a new person was selected to head the central bank who reduced the flow of new money into the Russian economy. The effects of hyperinflation were impoverishment of those on fixed incomes and destruction of the value of savings.

Think Critically

1. **How do artificially low prices lead to shortages?**
2. **How are people on fixed incomes hurt by inflation?**

occurs during economic declines when unemployment is rising and people are feeling insecure.

Some products go down in price over time even when the market as a whole is not experiencing a period of deflation. For example, a computer that uses a new, faster processor may sell at a high price when first introduced to the market. A year later, the same computer may sell for hundreds of dollars less. The price is lower because the computer is no longer the newest, fastest one available.

Oleksiy Mark/Shutterstock.com

To adjust the deflated prices, producers will seek new innovations that are attractive to consumers. For example, new electronic devices that display the latest technology will be in demand, regardless of price. Even during the Great Recession (2007–2009), people continued to buy newer, better cell phone technology, regardless of price.

CHECKPOINT

How is disinflation different from inflation?

LO 2-3 Inflation Causes and Effects

Inflation can result from many different factors in the economy. Consumers may want to buy more goods or services than are available, driving up prices. Producers may have to pay more for resources needed to make products, and thus may need to raise prices. Both situations can lead to inflation.

Demand-Pull Inflation

The most common form of inflation is called demand-pull inflation. **Demand-pull inflation** results in higher prices because consumers want to buy more goods and services than producers are willing or able to supply. Consumers are driving up prices because they are spending money as soon as it is received. Often they are also buying more with the use of credit, tying up future income. This spending causes businesses to scramble to meet the demand for goods. Because products are selling so quickly, businesses are able to raise prices to balance supply with demand and make bigger profits. This type of inflation is often described as "too many dollars chasing too few goods."

Cost-Push Inflation

Cost-push inflation occurs when producers raise prices because their costs to create products are rising. For example, when wages go up, the cost of producing a product goes up. Producers raise prices to cover the increased costs. If they do not raise prices, profits will shrink.

The cost of labor represents a significant expense to many businesses. When wage rates continue to rise without an increase in output, the result is called a *wage-price spiral*. Increased wages lead to higher production costs, which lead to higher prices, which lead to higher wages, and so on.

AISPIX/Shutterstock.com

Three factory workers discuss productivity that lowers cost-push inflation.

ETHICS *in Action!*

What Is Price Gouging?

As their costs are truly rising, businesses need to raise prices to maintain the same level of profitability. When prices are raised to take advantage of temporary conditions, the result is windfall (enormous) profits. This practice is called *price gouging* because it takes advantage of a real (or perceived) crisis where consumers are unable to avoid the increased prices.

For example, when Hurricane Katrina was predicted to hit the Gulf cities in Louisiana, residents were advised to evacuate as quickly as possible. In light of the critical need by consumers, some gas station owners in the area raised their prices to double or triple the regular price, thus taking advantage of fleeing citizens who desperately needed the gas. Price gouging is unethical and is often investigated by the Justice Department to determine whether the action is legal.

Think Critically

1. **How can consumers help protect themselves from price gouging?**
2. **Why is price gouging considered unethical? Aren't businesses entitled to set prices that meet demand?**

Cost-push inflation is affected by productivity. *Productivity* is a measure of the efficiency with which goods and services are made. It compares total output (quantity of goods or services produced) to total inputs (resources used, such as land, labor, or capital). When input costs, such as wages or the cost of new equipment, are offset by higher output, productivity rises. Higher productivity lowers the cost of each unit produced. Lower costs enable the producer to maintain the same price levels. In this case, a price increase is not needed. The producer is able to maintain profits due to increased efficiency.

Real-Cost Inflation

As resources become scarce or more difficult to get, prices rise in the form of **real-cost inflation**. For example, when the nation's supply of natural gas becomes depleted, then companies have to dig deeper to get it. This raises their real costs of production. Over time, resources in high demand may shrink in supply. With a growing population's ever-increasing demands, this may happen with many resources. To avoid this type of inflation, societies must find alternate resources or products or change their habits to reduce the need for the resource. Real-cost inflation can result from a combination of demand-pull and cost-push happening at the same time.

Inflation Affects Employment

Economists believe there is a direct relationship between inflation and employment. When rising prices are the result of increased demand, there is demand-pull inflation. Consumers are spending more and producers are making more profits. In an effort to keep up with demand, businesses hire more workers, reducing unemployment. Unfortunately, the opposite is also true. When prices are falling because of reduced demand, businesses are making less money. Employees

Jeff Wilber/Shutterstock.com

are laid off in order to reduce costs. When prices increase because of growing costs of production there is cost-push inflation. In this situation employers lay off workers because sales have declined. The relationship between change in employment and prices is called the *inflation/employment tradeoff.*

Inflation Affects Spending, Saving, and Investing

Some workers receive annual pay raises or adjustments to their pay level according to labor contracts. Employees who do not receive raises that are large enough to keep pace with inflation lose purchasing power.

Retirees who are drawing a fixed monthly pension also lose purchasing power when prices are rising. In such cases, consumers have two choices: they can buy less, or they can dip into savings or borrow money to continue buying the same products and services. Either way, it takes more money to maintain the same standard of living.

Inflation also affects the amount of money consumers are able to save. In times of rising prices, consumers have less money left over at the end of the month. When people are able to save less, they also have less money to invest. Yet inflationary times are the best times for investing. Money that is invested is likely to bring a rate of return that is equal to or greater than the rate of inflation, whereas money in savings accounts usually is not growing as fast as the rate of inflation. A fixed-rate savings account or a certificate of deposit (CD) will lose value when the rate of inflation is greater than the rate being paid on the account or the CD.

Figure 12-6 shows the inflation rates for the U.S. as measured by the CPI-U (Consumer Price Index for Urban Dwellers) for twenty years. It shows that the U.S. has experienced relatively low inflation rates, especially when compared to the inflation rates of other countries.

Figure 12-6

Inflation Measured by CPI-U, 1991–2010

Year	Inflation Rate	Year	Inflation Rate
1991	3.1%	2001	1.6%
1992	2.9%	2002	2.4%
1993	2.7%	2003	1.9%
1994	2.7%	2004	3.3%
1995	2.5%	2005	3.4%
1996	3.3%	2006	2.5%
1997	1.7%	2007	4.1%
1998	1.6%	2008	0.1%
1999	2.7%	2009	2.7%
2000	3.4%	2010	1.5%

CHECKPOINT

What is the most common form of inflation?

12-2 Assessment

Key Concepts

LO 2-1 1. How is inflation measured?

LO 2-1 2. How are consumers hurt by inflation?

LO 2-3 3. How is demand-pull inflation different from cost-push inflation?

LO 2-3 4. How does inflation affect saving?

Think About It

LO 2-1 5. As you get started saving and investing, you must also be concerned with the inflation rate, both now and in the future. Why?

LO 2-2 6. The U.S. has not experienced hyperinflation. Is it possible for that to happen? What might it look like for consumers in that event?

LO 2-3 7. When demand-pull inflation and cost-push inflation occur at the same time, what type of inflation often results?

LO 2-3 8. Explain how rising prices and falling prices affect employment rates. In what state are prices currently and how is employment being affected?

Make Academic Connections

LO 2-1 9. **RESEARCH** Visit the CPI-U online at the Bureau of Labor Statistics website. Search through the tables that show a market basket of goods and services. Are there items you have purchased recently that are not on the list?

LO 2-1 10. **MATH** The price of tires in the current year is $81. The price of tires in the base year was $77. How much inflation has taken place in the price since the base year?

LO 2-2 11. **COMMUNICATION** Consumers may create inflation when they buy without careful shopping and price comparisons. Write a paper describing how consumers can help control prices with careful shopping.

LO 2-3 12. **ECONOMICS** Productivity is an important concept for measuring real output in a nation's economy. Visit government websites (such as the Bureau of Labor Statistics). Prepare a report on productivity in the United States.

Teamwork

LO 2-1 13. New inventions and discoveries are in high demand. Even in recessionary times, people will pay for devices, gadgets, tools, and media that enhance their lives. Prepare an analysis on new products and services that have emerged in the last year or two. Explain what needs are being met and how the price reflects consumer demand.

LO 2-1 14. Due to tough economic times, workers may be required to take a pay freeze for a year or longer. In the meantime, inflation is increasing. What does this mean to consumers whose pay is frozen?

LO 2-2 15. Not everyone gets hurt by inflation. In fact some businesses and consumers benefit by rising prices and interest rates. Explain.

Unit 5 Project: Economic Indicators

INFLATION IN THE U.S. The Consumer Price Index (CPI) measures inflation based on a market basket of goods and services. Prepare a display board that lists the positive features of the CPI and the shortcomings of that same tool as a measurement device.

Chapter 12 Summary

12-1 UNEMPLOYMENT

1. The nation's unemployment rate is published by the Bureau of Labor Statistics which conducts a survey to determine who is not employed but is looking for work. Children, students, retired persons, people in the military and housewives are not in the civilian labor force. Discouraged workers (who have given up looking for work) are also not counted.
2. Underemployed workers are over-qualified for their jobs and are not counted as unemployed. People working part-time are also not counted. The civilian labor force consists of people who are age 16 and older who are employed or are actively looking for work.
3. There are four types of unemployment. Frictional unemployment is caused by the time required to move from one job to another. Seasonal unemployment changes with the seasons; typically, there is no work in the "off season." Structural unemployment exists when skills of workers are mismatched with skills needed by employers. Cyclical unemployment is caused by fluctuations in the business cycle.
4. The goal of full employment is to minimize unemployment to include only frictional, seasonal, and structural unemployment, or about 5 percent. Unemployment has a significant impact on demographic groups, some more seriously than others.

12-2 INFLATION

5. Inflation affects both consumers and businesses. Rising prices cause the value of the dollar to decrease and thus purchasing power is reduced. Workers who receive COLAs are better able to keep pace with inflation; businesses that raise prices to meet inflation are not increasing profits.
6. Inflation is measured by the Consumer Price Index (CPI), computed by the Bureau of Labor Statistics. It is based on the price of a market basket of goods and services compared to the price of that same group of goods in a base year. Decisions made by consumers and businesses can reduce the impact of inflation on prices, profits, and quality of life.
7. Disinflation occurs when prices are increasing but at a falling rate. Hyperinflation is rapid, out-of-control price increases. Deflation occurs when prices are dropping.
8. Demand-pull inflation is caused by consumers spending too much money too quickly, creating excess demand. Cost-push inflation is created by rising costs to producers, such as wages. Real-cost inflation occurs when real costs of obtaining resources go up.
9. Inflation affects employment. More people are hired when there is demand-pull inflation, while workers will be laid off when there is cost-push inflation. Inflation also affects spending, saving, and investing.

Chapter 12

Assessment

Vocabulary Review

Match each statement with the term that best defines it.

1. Employment rate that exists without cyclical unemployment
2. Percentage of the civilian labor force that is unemployed
3. Unemployment caused by lack of jobs during a recession
4. Prices increasing at a slower rate
5. Unemployment caused by a mismatch of worker skills to existing jobs
6. Inflation caused by scarce and diminishing resources
7. General decreasing of price levels
8. Persons working at jobs below their skill level
9. Rising prices due to increased cost of production
10. Unemployment caused by changes in the seasons
11. Higher prices caused by consumer over-spending
12. Practice of hiring workers in another country
13. Persons who want to work but who have given up looking for work
14. Increase in general price level for goods and services
15. Temporary unemployment caused by the time required for workers to move from one job to another
16. Rapidly rising prices that are out of control

Vocabulary

a. cost-push inflation
b. cyclical unemployment
c. deflation
d. demand-pull inflation
e. discouraged worker
f. disinflation
g. frictional unemployment
h. full employment
i. hyperinflation
j. inflation
k. outsourcing
l. real-cost inflation
m. seasonal unemployment
n. structural unemployment
o. underemployed
p. unemployment rate

Review Your Knowledge

LO 1-2 17. Structural unemployment is unemployment caused by
   a. temporary changes in jobs
   b. discrimination
   c. the time required to match employers and workers
   d. a mismatch between worker skills and employer requirements

LO 2-2 18. Which is a **true** statement about hyperinflation?
   a. The U.S. experiences it regularly
   b. The U.S. has experienced it once or twice
   c. The U.S. is not likely to ever experience it
   d. The U.S. has not experienced it to date

LO 1-1 19. Which one of the following would *not* be considered a part of the labor force?
a. A steel worker who was laid off last week and is seeking work
b. A steel worker who was laid off last year and is no longer seeking work
c. A student who also works part-time
d. A retired college professor paid to teach a summer course

LO 1-1 20. A person who has given up searching for work is
a. frictionally unemployed
b. structurally unemployed
c. a discouraged worker
d. unemployed

LO 1-2 21. Sally lost her job when her company went out of business because of a recession. This is an example of
a. frictional unemployment
b. structural unemployment
c. cyclical unemployment
d. technological unemployment

LO 2-1 22. Which of these is the measure of the nation's inflation rate?
a. COLA
b. CPI
c. disinflation
d. deflation

LO 2-1 23. Who benefits from a period of high inflation?
a. retired persons
b. businesses who must borrow money
c. creditors who have money to lend
d. consumers

LO 2-1 24. Which is a long-term strategy?
a. buy less of a product with rising prices
b. find a new energy source
c. use your credit card for purchases
d. hire more people as prices rise

LO 2-2 25. Which is a general decrease in prices?
a. deflation
b. disinflation
c. hyperinflation
d. real-cost inflation

LO 2-3 26. Which creates a wage-price spiral?
a. demand-pull inflation
b. cost-push inflation
c. real-cost inflation
d. hyperinflation

LO 2-3 27. Which is generally caused by consumer spending?
a. demand-pull inflation
b. cost-push inflation
c. real-cost inflation
d. hyperinflation

LO 2-3 28. Which is *most* likely to keep up with rising inflation?
a. savings accounts
b. CDs
c. investments
d. retirement pensions

LO 2-1 29. Who gets hurt the *most* from rising prices?
a. businesses
b. creditors
c. people on fixed incomes
d. people with large investments

LO 2-1 30. Workers lose their purchasing power when
a. prices rise the same as their pay
b. prices rise slower than their pay
c. prices rise faster than their pay
d. they receive an annual COLA

LO 2-1 31. Taking actions to offset price increases is
a. hedging
b. borrowing
c. using credit
d. COLA

LO 2-2 32. Which usually happens during a recession?
a. real-cost inflation
b. disinflation
c. deflation
d. hyperinflation

Digging Deeper with Economics e-Collection

The Bureau of Labor Statistics publishes the Consumer Price Index (CPI) monthly. Information is compiled based on goods and services typically purchased by consumers. Access the Gale Economics e-Collection at **www.cengage.com/school/economics/personalfinance** to view CPI data. Take a look at the CPI over time and prepare a graph that shows changes in prices for a particular product or service (such as gasoline or haircuts) over a ten-year period of time. What can you conclude about demand for the product or service? How do price increases affect households and individual consumers?

Think About It

LO 1-1 **33.** The unemployment rate measures people who are in the labor force but are not working. It excludes a lot of people, including those providing domestic help, students, and discouraged workers. Do you think the published rate reflects an accurate number?

LO 1-2 **34.** Frictional unemployment is said to be a "good type of unemployment" because it allows people to change jobs (freedom of choice). Do you agree? Explain.

LO 2-1 **35.** Inflation hurts some people and businesses more than others. What can you do to lessen the impact of rising prices?

Make Academic Connections

LO 2-1 **36.** **MATH** Assuming this year's market basket of goods and services was at 106.8 and last year was the base year, what was the rate of inflation over the past year?

LO 2-3 **37.** **ETHICS** Assume you own a store in an area where a snow storm has been forecast. Based on the forecast, you buy additional snow shovels and supplies. When you realize other stores have not anticipated a shortage, you raise your prices by 50 to 100%. Are you acting ethically or are you price gouging? Explain.

LO 1-1 **38.** **SOCIAL STUDIES** Unemployment can have serious social impact, not just for those who are unemployed, but for their families as well. Describe possible outcomes associated with lack of employment.

LO 2-2 **39.** **HISTORY** Do research about the hyperinflation that occurred in Germany following World War I (1919 to 1923). Explain what happened in the economy to cause the problems of food shortages and other negative consequences. Write a paper and prepare an oral presentation of your findings.

Extend Your Learning

LO 1-1 **40.** Copy the diagram. Describe several specific examples of unemployed workers who would illustrate each type of unemployment. Do not use the same examples that appeared in this chapter.

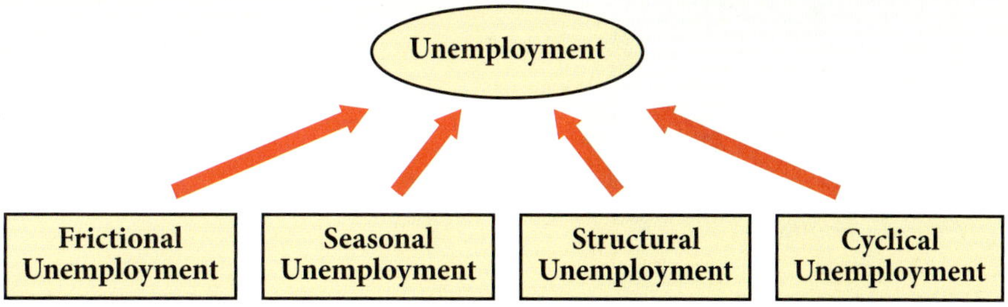

UNIT 6

Government in the Macro Economy

This unit begins with Chapter 13 that presents in Lesson 1 the theoretical aggregate demand and aggregate supply model to help you understand federal government taxing and spending policies. Here the focus is the debate between Keynesian and classical economic theories. Lesson 2 explains actual measures of government spending and taxation patterns. The chapter concludes with a discussion of the hotly debated topics of federal deficits and the national debt. Chapter 14 discusses the interesting topic of money. This chapter explains how the Federal Reserve and the banking system influence the supply of money in circulation in the economy and how this affects real GDP, prices, and employment.

UNIT 6 Project

The Role of Government

Project Objectives

PARTNERSHIP FOR 21ST CENTURY SKILLS

- Use economic-related terminology correctly.
- Use standard grammar, spelling, sentence structure, and punctuation.
- Transfer information from one medium to another including written to visual and statistical to written or visual using computer software as appropriate.
- Create written, oral, and visual presentations of social studies information.
- Evaluate economic data using charts, tables, graphs, and maps.

chapter 13

Governmental Units, p. 372

Obtain an organizational chart of your city, county, or state government. Research actions taken by the governmental unit you have chosen.

The National Debt, p. 389

Participate in a debate regarding the national debt. One team should support the usefulness of the debt. The other team should explain the consequences of massive debt.

chapter 14

History of the Fed, p. 405

Prepare a historical report on the Federal Reserve System—when it was created, why it was created, its role throughout the previous century, and its role today.

Monetary Policy, p. 415

List the functions of monetary policy (what the Fed does) on a one-page brochure. Explain the impact of those actions on the economy (such as expansionary or contractionary).

Project Wrap-up

Create a slide presentation, brochure, or video that compares and contrasts fiscal policy versus monetary policy. Include examples of how each works and how they have been used by the Fed, the President, and Congress in U.S. history. Save a copy of all final work completed to be a part of your economics portfolio.

Jaimie Duplass/Shutterstock.com

yienkeat/Shutterstock.comc

22655624729/Shutterstock.com

chapter 13

Government Spending and Taxing

yienkeat/Shutterstock.com

MARKETS *in Action!*

Maya MacGuineas
President, Committee for a Responsible Federal Budget

The Committee for a Responsible Federal Budget (CFRB) describes itself as a bipartisan, non-profit organization that is dedicated to educating the public about financial policy issues in the United States. Members of the committee are experts in budgeting and fiscal management. This committee is not a part of government, but is outside of government, and acts as a watchdog group to try to assure that sound fiscal policy is followed.

As a part of the New America Foundation, the CFRB seeks to make new voices and new ideas heard in budget debates. It sponsors a wide variety of research, writings, conferences, and other events to discuss important current fiscal issues. A current project is the U.S. Budget Watch, a project funded by Pew Charitable Trusts.

Maya MacGuineas is the current president of CFRB. She is also the Director of the Fiscal Policy Program at the New America Foundation. She was born in 1968 in Washington, D.C. and graduated from Northwestern University with a bachelor's degree in economics and psychology. She also earned a master's degree in public policy from the John F. Kennedy School of Government, Harvard University.

MacGuineas has published articles in various financial magazines, and is often cited by broadcast news and by the national press as an expert in the area of fiscal policy and budgetary issues, such as health care reform debate and Social Security.

As President of the CFRB, Maya MacGuineas "oversees the Foundation's efforts to bring accountability to the budget process, address the challenges presented by the nation's underfunded entitlements programs, and propose comprehensive tax reforms to improve both the efficiency and the equity of the tax code." MacGuineas regularly appears before U.S. Congress to testify on economic issues. She advises the administration and publishes articles. As a political independent, she has advised candidates for political office from both parties. She is dedicated to making a difference in the nation's approach to fiscal responsibility.

Courtesy of New America Foundation, www.Newamerica.net

Think Critically

1. What is the overall purpose of the CRFB?
2. Why is the federal budget important to you as a citizen?

yienkeat/Shutterstock.com

13-1 Fiscal Policy

Learning Objectives

LO 1-1 Explain expansionary and contractionary fiscal policy.

LO 1-2 Understand the difference between classical and Keynesian economics.

Vocabulary

fiscal policy, p. 367
expansionary fiscal policy, p. 367
contractionary fiscal policy, p. 367
aggregate demand curve, p. 367
aggregate supply curve, p. 367
macroeconomic equilibrium, p. 367
classical economics, p. 369
Keynesian economics, p. 369
Laffer curve, p. 371

© Aleksandar Vrzalski/iStockphoto.com

REAL-WORLD FOCUS

Kate just finished watching the evening news with her parents. "The president is talking about fiscal policy," she said. "He wants to increase tax rates to pay off government debts. It seems to me if you raise tax rates, you will actually take more money from consumers and thus slow down the economy. Is that a good thing to do while we are in a recession?"

WORK AS A TEAM How does fiscal policy help speed up or slow down the economy? According to the Laffer curve, what might be the actual result of raising tax rates?

jordi espel/Shutterstock.com

Lawmakers in Washington, D.C. debate about fiscal policies that will stabilize prices and lead to economic growth.

DO YOU THINK Congress is currently trying to increase or decrease government spending or increase or decrease government taxes?

yienkeat/Shutterstock.com

LO 1-1 Two Types of Fiscal Policy

The government uses fiscal policy to try to achieve full employment, stable prices, and economic growth. **Fiscal policy** is the use of federal government spending and taxes to achieve these economic goals. Fiscal policy decisions are among the most important decisions the federal government makes. There are two basic policies used depending on the condition of the economy. During a recession the government may use expansionary fiscal policy. **Expansionary fiscal policy** uses an increase in federal government spending or a reduction in taxes to increase real GDP. When the economy is suffering from inflation, the government can use contractionary fiscal policy. **Contractionary fiscal policy** employs a decrease in federal government spending or an increase in taxes to decrease real GDP. Figure 13-1 summarizes the two types of fiscal policy.

Expansionary fiscal policy	Contractionary fiscal policy
Increase government spending	Decrease government spending
Decrease taxes	Increase taxes

Figure 13-1
Two Types of Fiscal Policies

The Aggregate Demand/Aggregate Supply Model

In Chapter 4, the intersection of demand and supply curves sets the equilibrium price in a market. This was microeconomic analysis for an individual market, like wheat or athletic shoes. Now a macroeconomic model will be developed using a demand side and a supply side. The aggregate demand side is represented by the aggregate demand curve in Figure 13-2. The **aggregate demand curve** (AD) shows real gross domestic product that will be purchased at different price levels. The supply side is represented by the aggregate supply curve. The **aggregate supply curve** (AS) shows real gross domestic product that will be produced at different price levels.

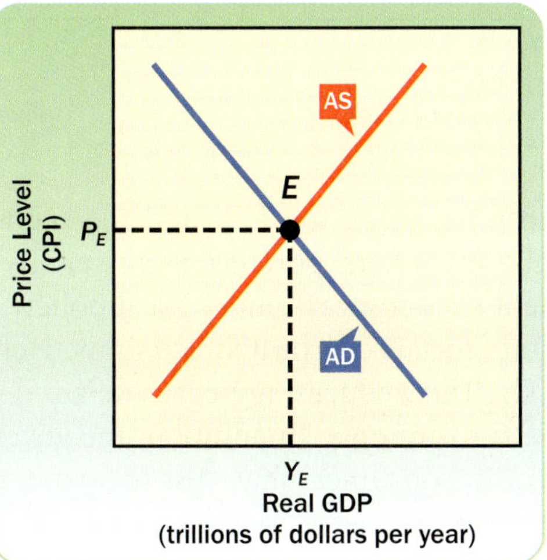

Figure 13-2
Aggregate Demand and Aggregate Supply
Macroequilibrium at point *E* in an economy results from the forces of aggregate demand (AD) and aggregate supply (AS).

Macroeconomic equilibrium is at point *E*. **Macroeconomic equilibrium** is the price level where the aggregate demand curve intersects the aggregate supply curve. Point E corresponds to P_E and Y_E. P_E is the price level measured by the CPI (Consumer Price Index) explained in the previous chapter. Y_E is the amount of real GDP. If the price level is above P_E, the real GDP supplied is greater than real GDP purchased. As a result, the surplus of unsold products forces businesses to lower their prices. Over time, the price level falls to P_E and macro equilibrium is restored. At a price level below P_E, real GDP demanded exceeds real GDP supplied. The shortage disappears as consumers bid up the prices of goods and services. Businesses respond by producing more until equilibrium returns at P_E.

The AD/AS model can be used to demonstrate expansionary and contractionary fiscal policy. In Figure 13-3(a) suppose the economy is in recession at E_1. To encourage growth and reduce unemployment, the federal government can increase spending. Recall that government spending (G) is a component of real GDP, which is aggregate demand (AD). Cutting taxes also works like government spending. When taxes are lower, consumers have more to spend. This increases the consumer spending (C) sector of real GDP (aggregate demand, AD). Either increasing government spending and/or cutting taxes shifts AD_1 rightward to AD_2. Equilibrium changes from point E_1 to point E_2. This increase in aggregate demand has two effects. Real GDP increases from Y_1 to Y_2. As a result, employment (not shown in the figure) rises. Also, the prices of goods and services measured by the CPI rise from P_1 to P_2.

Figure 13-3

Impact of Fiscal Policy

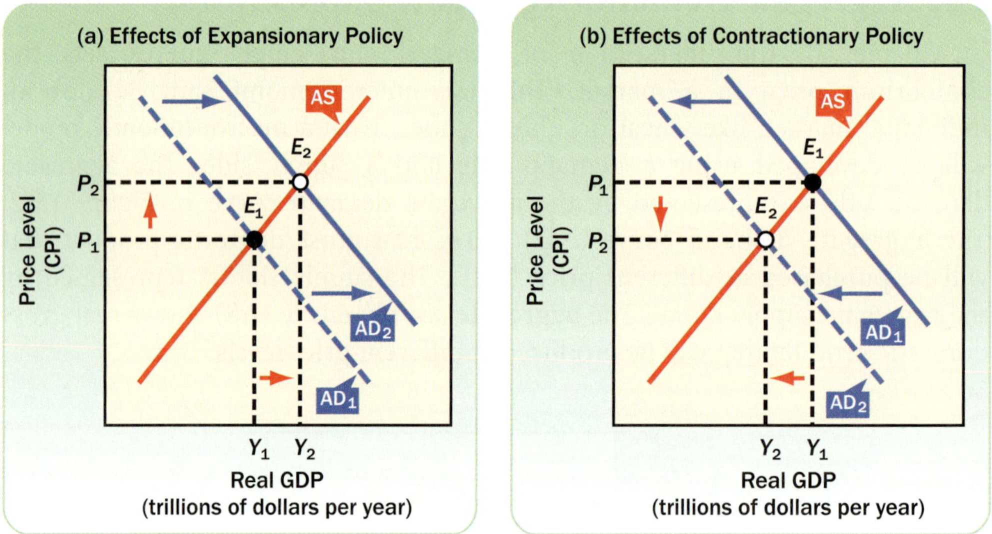

Now assume prices are rising too fast, and the economy is at E_1 in Figure 13-3(b). Inflation cuts consumers' purchasing power. To achieve price stability, the federal government uses contractionary fiscal policy. The goal in this case is to slow the growth rate for an overheated economy. Here the government can decrease spending (G). This reduces aggregate demand (AD) because there is less total spending in the economy. In addition, the government could increase taxes. Higher taxes mean consumers have less to spend, and aggregate demand (AD) decreases. The result in Figure 13-3(b) is that AD_1 shifts leftward to AD_2. Equilibrium changes from point E_1 to point E_2 and the price level falls from P_1 to P_2. Lower inflation, however, comes with a cost. Real GDP decreases from Y_1 to Y_2 and this means fewer jobs.

CHECKPOINT

What fiscal policy would be used in a recession? Explain the goal. Assume that the economy has an inflation problem. What fiscal policy would be used? Explain.

LO 1-2 Classical versus Keynesian Economics

The use of fiscal policy to regulate the economy is controversial. The dominant school of economic thought before the Great Depression in 1929 was classical economics. **Classical economics** is the theory that free markets will restore full employment in a recession without government intervention. This theory was introduced by Adam Smith in *The Wealth of Nations*. His theory was followed by most eighteenth- and nineteenth-century economists. Classical theory assumes that in the long run free markets will bring about full-employment equilibrium.

The classical view that the economy was self-regulating was challenged by the Great Depression. How long would it take for markets to return to full employment equilibrium? In short, how much time is the "long run"? Is it two years, five years, or how long? This question set the stage for a famous economist to explain that the answer could be "never." John Maynard Keynes (pronounced Canes) explained with the famous comment: "In the long run we are all dead."

Keynes developed a new theory of economics. It argued that an economy could remain in a downturn indefinitely unless the federal government takes action. Keynes wrote *The General Theory of Employment, Interest, and Money*, called simply *The General Theory* (1936). Keynes provided a new economic model to get an economy out of a crisis like the Great Depression. He suggested that a prolonged downturn in the economy causes people and businesses to be frightened and reduce their spending. The solution is that government must make up for the loss in spending by consumers and businesses by spending more or taxing less. This idea is the basis of what is today called Keynesian economics. **Keynesian economics** is the theory that the federal government should increase or decrease aggregate demand to achieve economic goals. Keynesian economics is also called *demand-side economics*. As shown in Figure 13-3(b) Keynesian economics can also be used to fight inflation.

After his election in 1932, Franklin D. Roosevelt used expansionary fiscal policies to try to restore the economy. His New Deal paid people to build highways, parks, dams, schools, and plant trees. The objective was to create jobs using public works projects. Using fiscal policy to influence the economy has been an important idea since the Keynesian revolution of the 1930s. In 2001, the United States experienced a recession. During the next two years, President George W. Bush proposed and signed into law tax cuts to stimulate the economy. In 2008, Americans received a $170 billion tax-rebate stimulus package. This was followed by another $787 billion federal spending stimulus package enacted during the President Obama administration in 2009.

As in the past, disagreement between classical economics and Keynesian economics continues. There are economists on both sides. Some economists argue for using government taxing and spending to correct the economy. Other economists believe that free markets will self-regulate the economy.

A PROFILE

John Maynard Keynes
Father of Modern Economics

AP Photo

In *The General Theory of Employment, Interest, and Money*, Keynes wrote:

> The ideas of economists and political philosophers, both when they are right and when they are wrong, are more powerful than is commonly understood. Indeed the world is ruled by little else. Practical men, who believe themselves to be quite exempt from any intellectual influences, are usually the slaves of some defunct economist. Madmen in authority, who hear voices in the air, are distilling their frenzy from some academic scribbler of a few years back.

Keynes (1883–1946) is regarded as the father of modern macroeconomics. He was the son of an eminent English economist, John Neville Keynes. Keynes was educated at Eton and Cambridge in mathematics and probability theory. Ultimately, he selected economics and accepted a teaching position at Cambridge. Keynes was a many-faceted man. He was an honored and supremely successful member of the British academic, financial, and political communities. Keynes served as a trustee of King's College and increased its endowment over ten fold.

Keynes is best remembered for *The General Theory*, published in 1936. This work attacked the classical theory that suggested capitalism would self correct from a severe recession. Keynes based his model on the belief that increasing aggregate demand will achieve full employment. Moreover, his bold policy prescription was for the federal government to raise its spending and/or reduce taxes during a recession. The goal is to increase the economy's aggregate demand curve and put the unemployed back to work.

THINK CRITICALLY

Price Level, Real GDP, and Unemployment Rate, 1933–1941

Year	CPI	Real GDP (billions of 2000 dollars)	Unemployment Rate (percent)
1933	13.0	$ 635	24.9
1939	13.9	951	17.2
1940	14.0	1,034	14.6
1941	14.7	1,211	9.9

Was Keynes correct? Based on the above data, use the aggregate demand and aggregate supply model to explain Keynes's theory that increases in aggregate demand propel an economy toward full employment.

The Laffer Curve

An interesting question is whether tax cuts can increase tax revenues. The surprising answer is maybe yes or maybe no. The **Laffer curve**, attributed to economist Arthur Laffer, shows the relationship between tax rates and total tax revenues. As shown in Figure 13-4, the hypothetical Laffer curve shows the federal tax rate on the horizontal axis. Total tax revenue is on the vertical axis. The idea is that the federal tax rate affects the incentive for people to work, save, invest, and produce. This in turn influences tax revenue. As the tax rate climbs, Laffer argues that the erosion of incentives shrinks total tax collections.

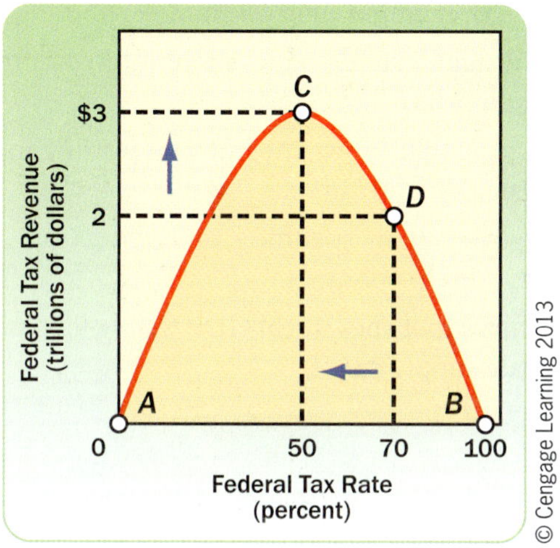

Figure 13-4

The Laffer Curve

The Laffer curve shows the theoretical relationship between changes in the federal tax rate and tax revenues. Both high and low tax rates yield the same revenues. At some tax rate between the extreme of 0 and 100 percent, the maximum revenue is collected.

Suppose the federal government sets the federal income tax rate at zero (point *A*). At a zero income tax rate, people have the maximum incentive to work, and earn income. But there is zero tax revenue. Now assume the federal government sets the income tax rate at the opposite extreme of 100 percent (point *B*). Now people have no reason to work, take business risks, produce, and earn income. People seek ways to reduce their tax liabilities by not reporting income or by not working at all. As a result, no tax revenue is collected.

Congress sets the federal income tax rate between zero and 100 percent. Figure 13-4 assumes that the income tax rate is related to tax revenue as shown. The maximum tax revenue of $3 trillion is collected at a tax rate of 50 percent (point *C*). Now assume that the federal income tax rate is 70 percent at point *D*. The result would be tax revenue of $2 trillion. Reducing the federal income tax rate from 70 percent to 50 percent therefore leads to an increase in tax revenue from $2 trillion to $3 trillion. At 50 percent people, would increase their work effort, saving, and investment. They would reduce their attempts to avoid paying taxes. Thus, Laffer argued that a cut in federal income tax rates would unleash economic activity and boost tax revenues. The Laffer curve remains controversial. There is considerable uncertainty about the shape of the Laffer curve. It may be that tax revenue is maximum at some tax rate higher or lower than 50 percent. Note that below the 50 percent tax rate, rate increases do increase total revenue.

CHECKPOINT

Assume an economy is in recession. Briefly explain the Keynesian versus classical prescription for recovery.

13-1 Assessment

Key Concepts

LO 1-2 1. The theory that the role of the federal government is to increase or decrease aggregate demand to achieve economic goals is __?__ economics.

LO 1-1 2. The use of federal government spending and taxes to achieve economic goals is __?__ policy.

LO 1-2 3. **TRUE OR FALSE** Classical economics is the theory that free markets will restore full employment without government intervention.

LO 1-2 4. The price level where the aggregate demand curve intersects the aggregate supply curve occurs at __?__ equilibrium.

LO 1-1 5. **TRUE OR FALSE** The curve that shows the index of leading indicators at different price levels is the aggregate demand curve.

LO 1-1 6. An increase in federal government spending or a reduction in taxes to increase aggregate demand is __?__ fiscal policy.

LO 1-1 7. **TRUE OR FALSE** The curve that shows real GDP that will be produced at different price levels is the aggregate supply curve.

Think About It

LO 1-1 8. In which direction would each of the following changes in conditions cause the aggregate demand curve to shift? Explain your answers.
   a. Consumers expect an economic downturn.
   b. A new U.S. president is elected, and the profit expectations of business executives rise. As a result investment spending increases.
   c. The federal government increases spending for highways, bridges, and schools.
   d. The United States increases exports of wheat and other crops.

9. The aggregate demand and aggregate supply curves intersect at a CPI level of 100. Explain the effect a shift in the aggregate supply curve to the left would have on the CPI.

Making Academic Connections

LO 1-2 10. **HISTORY** When Keynes first asserted that the government could stabilize the economy by adjusting its spending and taxing, his ideas were met with doubt. Events during World War II, however, caused most people to change their minds. Investigate government spending that took place during World War II and explain how it supports Keynes's ideas.

Teamwork

LO 1-2 11. Work in three groups. One group explains how President Roosevelt's New Deal programs reflected Keynesian economics. The second group explains how Keynesian economics was applied to the Great Recession of 2007. The third group explains how classical economics would treat the Great Depression and the Great Recession.

Unit 6 Project: The Role of Government

GOVERNMENTAL UNITS Obtain an organizational chart of your city, county, or state government. Research actions taken by the governmental unit you have chosen and explain how they affect you, your neighbors, and/or other citizens of your local area or state. Be sure to include monetary obligations that were created and who will benefit from the actions taken.

yienkeat/Shutterstock.com, Chad Baker/Ryan McVay/Photodisc/Getty Images

13-2 Government Budgets and Types of Taxes

Learning Objectives

LO 2-1 Identify the categories of government spending and taxing at the national, state, and local levels.

LO 2-2 Understand progressive, regressive, and proportional types of taxation.

Vocabulary

sales tax, p. 375
property tax, p. 375
tax base, p. 377
progressive tax, p. 378
regressive tax, p. 378
proportional tax, p. 379

© Aleksandar Vrzalski/ iStockphoto.com

REAL-WORLD FOCUS

After just receiving his cell phone bill, Charles was upset. "When I signed up for my annual plan, they told me it was 'before taxes,'" he told his friend. "I didn't realize that meant sales tax in addition to the 911 charge and the local, state, and federal excise taxes. My bill is almost 10% higher because of these taxes. What is the purpose of these taxes?"

WORK AS A TEAM What is the rate of sales tax in your state? For a cell phone bill, what are the total taxes and fees that are added on to the basic charge each month? How much are taxes as a percentage of the cell phone basic service?

If you live in a state that collects sales tax, you must pay that tax at the time you purchase the car.

DO YOU THINK the amount of sales tax can be included in the amount borrowed by the purchaser?

mangostock/Shutterstock.com

yienkeat/Shutterstock.com

LO2-1 Government Spending and Taxing Categories

How big is government spending in the United States? Figure 13-5 shows federal, state, and local governments as a percentage of GDP since 1929. Total government spending skyrocketed during World War II. Since 1950, total government spending grew to about one third of GDP beginning in 1975. Then total spending increased sharply in 2010 following the Great Recession to a record 38 percent of GDP.

Figure 13-5

Government Spending as a Percentage of GDP in the United States, 1929–2010

The graph shows the federal, state, and local government spending as a percentage of GDP since 1929. Spending rose dramatically during World War II. Total government spending increased sharply following the Great Recession to a record 38 percent of GDP.

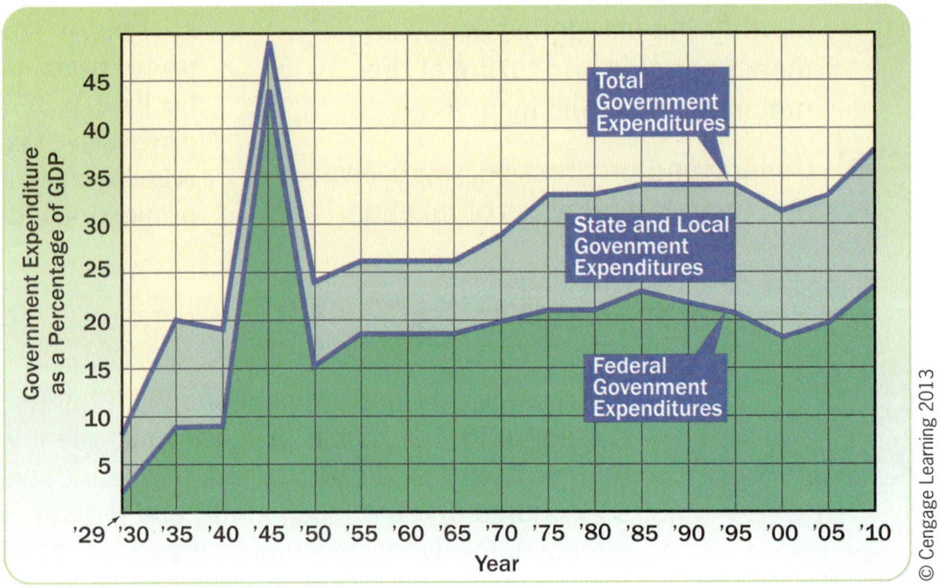

Government Spending Patterns

Figure 13-6(a) shows program categories for federal government spending for 2010. The largest category in the federal budget is income security. *Income security* means *transfer* or *entitlement* payments that provide income to the elderly or disadvantaged. Programs include Social Security, Medicare, unemployment compensation, welfare, retirement, and disability benefits. The second largest category of spending is *national defense*. Federal spending for *education and health* is in third place. *Interest on the federal debt* is in fourth place.

Figure 13-6

Federal, State, and Local Government Spending Budgets

Income security is the largest category of federal spending. National defense is the second largest. Income security and national defense combined account for almost 71 percent of federal spending in 2010. The largest spending for state and local government is for education.

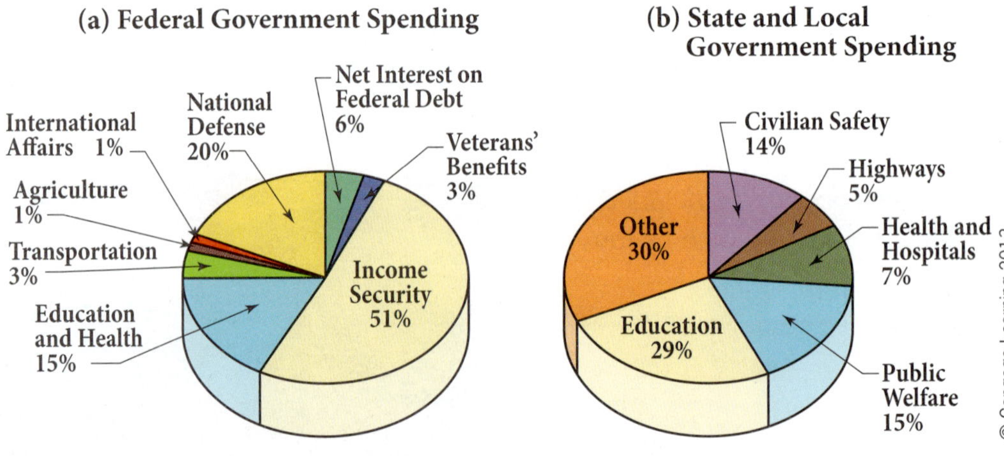

Figure 13-6(b) shows the combined spending of all state and local governments. By far the largest priority in state and local government budgets is education. Public welfare was second and civilian safety (fire, police, and corrections) was third. Health and hospitals was fourth and highways were in fifth place. The Other category includes spending for administration, utilities, unemployment compensation, and interest on debt.

Financing Government Budgets

Where does the government obtain the funds to finance its spending? Figure 13-7 tells the story. In Figure 13-7(a), the largest revenue source for the federal government in 2010 was individual income taxes. The Sixteenth Amendment to the Constitution, ratified in 1913, gives the government the authority to impose an income tax. The second largest category is social insurance taxes. This category includes taxes paid for Social Security, workers' compensation, and unemployment insurance. The third greatest revenue source was corporate income taxes. Excise taxes contributed 3 percent of total tax receipts. An *excise tax* is a tax on the purchase of a specific good or service that is paid by the producer or retailer. This tax generally becomes part of the price paid by consumers. Each time people buy gasoline, for example, state and federal excise taxes are part of the price.

NET Bookmark

Tax freedom day is the day of the year when taxpayers have earned enough money to pay the average tax burden for the year. For 2011, that day was April 12 for the entire country. You work more than three full months to pay for taxes. Do you consider that a fair tax burden? Why? Access www.cengage.com/school/economics/personalfinance and click on the link for Chapter 13. Visit the website of The Tax Foundation. Click on Tax Freedom Day. What day of the year is tax freedom day for your state?

www.cengage.com/school/economics/personalfinance

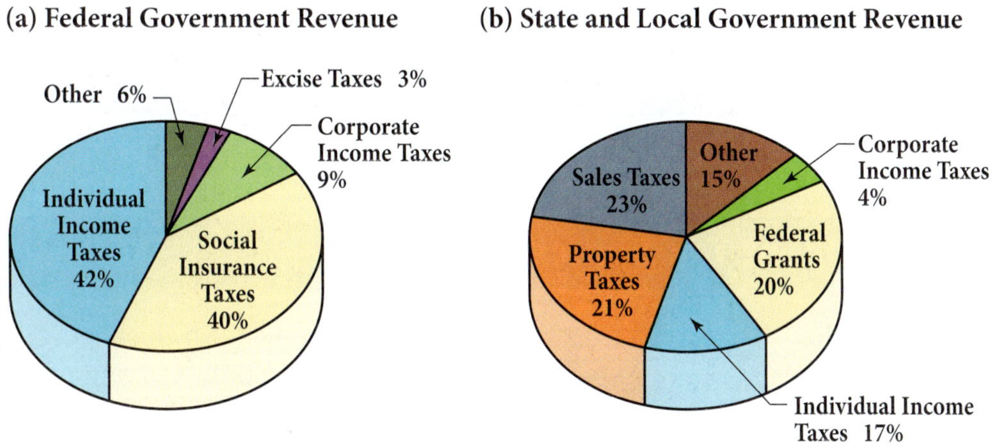

Figure 13-7

Federal, State, and Local Government Tax Revenues, 2010

In 2010, the largest source of revenue for the federal government was individual income taxes, and the second largest source was social insurance taxes. State and local government revenues were collected primarily from sales taxes, property taxes, and federal grants.

Figure 13-7(b) shows the combined tax revenues for state and local governments for comparison with federal tax sources. There is quite a difference between the sources of receipts. Instead of individual income taxes, the two largest sources of receipts were sales taxes and property taxes. A **sales tax** is a tax on the value of the sale of a good or service. A **property tax** is a tax on the value of assets. Property taxes are collected on the market value of homes, land, buildings, automobiles, and furniture. Corporate income taxes contributed a small percentage of tax receipts. Death taxes, gift taxes, and motor vehicle licenses are in the other category. It should be remembered that much government spending is supported by borrowing rather than by current tax receipts. This borrowing does not appear on these graphs.

Another way to study the burden of taxation in the United States is to observe changes over time. Figure 13-8 charts the growth of taxes as a percentage of GDP in the United States since 1929. Total government taxes climbed to its highest level of 34 percent in 2000. Then the level of taxation fell to 29 percent in 2010.

Figure 13-8

Growth of Taxes as a Percentage of GDP in the United States, 1929–2010

The graph shows the growth in federal, state, and local government taxes as a percentage of GDP since 1929. Total government taxes climbed to their highest level of 34 percent in 2000 before falling to 29 percent in 2010.

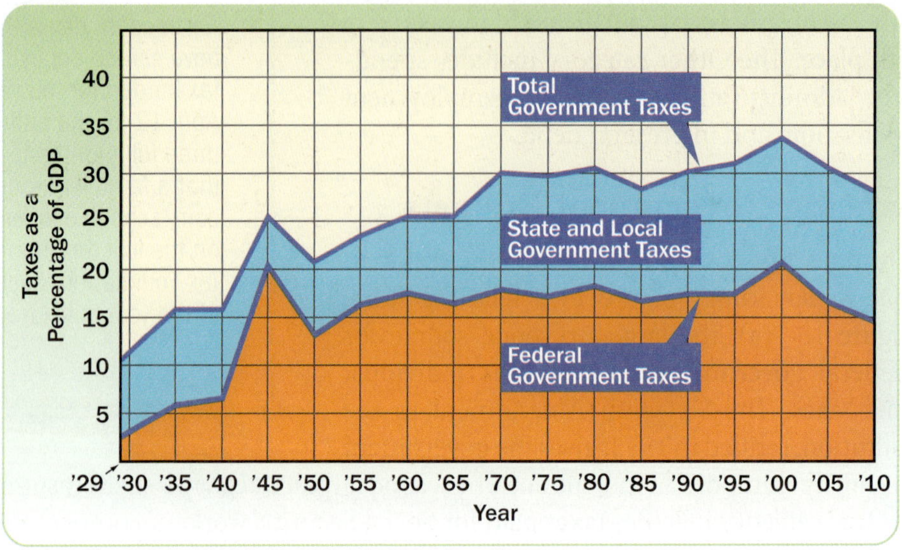

CHECKPOINT

Transfer or entitlement programs make up the Income security major category of federal government spending. Social insurance taxes to finance these programs are the second largest category of federal government tax revenues. What are these transfer or entitlement programs?

State and Local Government Tax Sources

Investigate Your Local ECONOMY

State and local governments need to collect taxes to generate revenues. These revenues are used to pay for government employees and services that assist or protect citizens. States provide services that are commonly provided by all states (such as police protection and auto licensing) and some provide services that may be unique to that state. Some local governments provide services that are only provided in the locality, while other services paid for by local governments are also provided and paid for by state governments.

Try it Out

Does your state have a state income tax? If so, what is the tax rate schedule? If not, how does your state collect its revenues? What is the property tax rate for your local government? How is a property tax bill computed?

FreeSoulProduction/Shutterstock.com

Math CONNECTION

State and Federal Excise Taxes on Gasoline

The federal government imposes an excise tax of 18.4 cents on each gallon of gasoline sold to consumers. State governments also impose an excise tax on gasoline. Some states also charge additional taxes on each gallon. In the state of Texas, 38.4 cents of the price paid per gallon is the total of federal and states taxes. How much of that tax amount goes to the state?

SOLUTION

The federal excise tax is 18.4 cents per gallon.

38.4¢ − 18.4¢ = 20.0¢ Total amount of tax − federal amount = state amount

The state of Texas receives 20 cents in taxes from each gallon of gasoline sold.

TRY IT

Find the amount of tax each state receives per gallon of gasoline.

1. California consumers pay a total of 67.5 cents in taxes per gallon.
2. Florida consumers pay a total of 52.9 cents in taxes per gallon.
3. Wyoming consumers pay a total of 32.4 cents in taxes per gallon.

LO 2-2 The Art of Taxation

Jean Baptiste Colbert, finance minister to King Louis XIV of France, once said the following: "The art of taxation consists of so plucking the goose as to obtain the largest amount of feathers while promoting the smallest amount of hissing." Each year, Congress debates various ways of raising revenue without causing too much "hissing." The task is difficult because each type of tax has a different characteristic.

AP Photo/Cliff Owen

In 2011, President Obama proposed the American Jobs Act to stimulate the economy.

Progressive, Regressive, and Proportional Taxes

Governments raise revenues from various taxes, such as income taxes, sales taxes, excise taxes, and property taxes. Economists classify each of these taxes into three types of taxation: progressive, regressive, and proportional. These three concepts describe the relationship between changes in tax rates and changes in income. Income is the tax base because people pay taxes out of income. A **tax base** is the form of wealth

kali9/iStockphoto.com

Families pay sales taxes on retail items they purchase.

that is subject to taxes. In addition to income, other examples of tax bases include land, buildings, automobiles, or furniture.

Progressive Taxes Individual and corporate income taxes are progressive taxes. A **progressive tax** charges a higher percentage as income rises. This type of tax follows the concept that those who have higher incomes can afford to pay higher tax rates. Figure 13-9 illustrates the progressive nature of the federal income tax for a single person filing a 2010 tax return. As the amount of taxable income rises, the tax rate rises. There are six ranges of income, or tax brackets. Each bracket applies a higher tax rate. For example, a single person with a taxable income between $8,355 and $34,000 paid 15 percent. The highest rate of 35 percent was paid by persons with a taxable income above $373,650. The tax rate schedules change over time to reflect changes in the federal tax code.

Figure 13-9

Federal Tax Progressive Tax Brackets Versus a Flat Tax

There are six "stair step" federal tax rates or tax brackets. In contrast to this progressive tax, a flat tax charges a single rate of 20 percent.

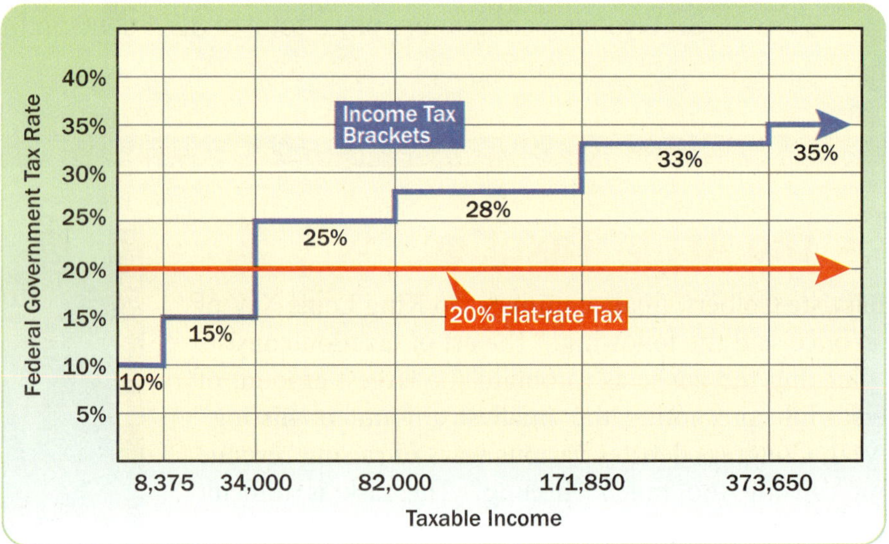

Regressive Taxes Sales, excise, and property taxes are regressive taxes. A **regressive tax** charges a lower percentage of income as income rises. Suppose Kanya, who is earning $10,000 a year, pays a tax of $5,000. Ramone, who earns $100,000 a year, pays $10,000 in taxes. Although Ramone pays twice the absolute amount, this is regressive taxation. This is because richer Ramone pays a tax rate of 10 percent and poorer Kanya suffers a 50 percent tax bite. Such a tax violates the ability-to-pay principle of taxation.

Assume that there is a 5 percent sales tax on all purchases. Also assume that the Garcia family earned $80,000 during the last year and the Jefferson family earned $20,000. The Garcias, with an $80,000 income, can afford to spend $40,000 on groceries and clothes and save the rest. The Jeffersons, with a $20,000 income, must spend their entire income to feed and clothe the family.

Each family pays a 5 percent sales tax. The lower income Jeffersons pay sales taxes of $1,000 (0.05 × $20,000). This $1,000 sales tax is 5 percent of their income ($1,000/$20,000). The higher income Garcias pay sales taxes of $2,000 (0.05 × $40,000). The richer Garcias family pays twice the amount of sales tax to the tax collector. But this $2,000 sales tax is only 2.5 percent of their income ($2,000/$80,000). The sales tax is regressive because the sales tax rate is higher for the lower income Jeffersons.

woodsy/Shutterstock.com

Property taxes are also considered to be regressive for two reasons. In most cases property taxes are a higher percentage of income for poor families than rich families. The reason is that the poor spend a much greater proportion of their income for housing. Also, property taxes paid by landlords are reflected in the rents tenants pay. Most renters have relatively low incomes and therefore are in effect paying a larger share of their income for taxes than more affluent property owners.

Proportional Taxes One proposal to simplify the federal progressive income tax is to use a proportional tax, also called a *flat tax*. A **proportional tax** charges the same percentage of income, regardless of the size of income. One way to reform the federal tax system would be to eliminate all deductions, exemptions, and loopholes. Then simply apply the same tax rate, say, 20 percent of income to everyone. Such a reform is illustrated by the flat line in Figure 13-9. This might avoid some of the "hissing" from taxpayers. Taxpayers would no longer require accountants to file their tax returns. A 20 percent tax would collect $20,000 from Ms. "Rich," who earns $100,000 a year. It would collect $2,000 from Mr. "Poor," who is earning $10,000 a year. Both taxpayers pay the same 20 percent of their incomes. There is no perfect example of a flat tax in the United States.

Figure 13-10 gives a summary of the three types of taxes with examples.

Type of Tax	Definition	Example
Progressive	The tax rate rises as income rises.	Federal income taxes
Regressive	The tax rate falls as income rises.	Sales tax, excise tax and property tax
Proportional	The tax rate remains the same as income rises.	Flat tax

Figure 13-10
Types of Taxes and Examples

CHECKPOINT

Individual income tax is the top source of tax revenue for the federal government. Excise taxes are a small percentage. However, sales taxes and property taxes are a much larger source of tax revenue for state and local governments. Individual income taxes are a smaller percentage. Relate this to the overall impact of progressive versus regressive taxation.

Global View

Is It Time for the Flat Tax?

It is a remarkable development that former communist countries of Eastern Europe have led the way in the flat tax revolution. In 1994, Estonia was the first to adopt a 25 percent rate flat tax a few years after the collapse of the Soviet Union. Latvia followed with a 25 percent rate and Lithuania chose a 33 percent rate. These "Baltic Tigers" have become role models for the region. In 2001, Russia learned from it neighbors and adopted a 13 percent flat tax. Serbia, Ukraine, Romania, and Georgia later joined the bandwagon with a flat tax rate of 13 percent. In 2011, Hungary introduced a flat tax of 16 percent.

BackyardProduction/iStockphoto.com

The capital of Estonia is Tallinn, which is famous for its heritage, town walls, and cobbled streets. Estonia adopted a 25 percent flat tax in 1994.

The objective of these countries is to increase tax revenues because of the Laffer curve theory that lower tax rates lead to high total tax revenues. Also, in a global economy, jobs and capital move from high-tax nations to low-tax nations.

The flat tax is a controversial reform that is often debated in the United States. Such a tax would tax income above a given amount at a fixed percent with no deductions. The flat-tax plan creates serious political problems. Eliminating deductions would face strong opposition from the public. For example, eliminating the mortgage interest deduction and exemptions for health care and charity would be a difficult political battle. And there is the fairness question. People at the lower end of the current system could face a tax increase. But upper-income people would get the biggest tax break. The counterargument is that under the current tax system many millionaires pay nothing. This is because they shelter their incomes. Under a flat-tax scheme, they would not be able to take deductions and credits.

Think Critically

Should the United States follow other countries and adopt the flat tax and is a flat tax fair?

13-2 Assessment

Key Concepts

LO 2-2 1. A tax that charges the same percentage of income, regardless of the size of income is a __?__ tax.

LO 2-1 2. **TRUE OR FALSE** An excise tax is a general tax on all retail sales.

LO 2-1 3. A tax on the value of the sale of a good or services is a __?__ tax.

LO 2-2 4. **TRUE OR FALSE** A regressive tax is a tax that charges a lower percentage of income as income rises.

LO 2-1 5. A tax on the value of assets is a __?__ tax.

LO 2-2 6. **TRUE OR FALSE** A tax base is the form of wealth that is subject to taxes.

LO 2-2 7. A tax that charges a higher percentage of income as income rises is a __?__ tax.

Think About It

LO 2-1 8. Identify the major differences between federal government spending and spending by state and local governments.

LO 2-1 9. What are the greatest categories for taxing and spending for federal, state, and local governments?

LO 2-2 10. What is the definition of progressive, regressive, and proportional taxes? Give an example of each.

Make Academic Connections

LO 2-2 11. **MATH** Complete the following table, which describes the sales tax paid by individuals at various income levels. Indicate whether the tax is progressive, proportional, or regressive.

Income	Total Spending	Sales Tax Paid	Sales Tax Paid as a Percentage of Income
$ 1,000	$ 1,000	$ 100	__?__
5,000	3,500	350	__?__
10,000	6,000	600	__?__
100,000	40,000	4,000	__?__

Teamwork

LO 2-2 12. Work in groups. Research the types and rates of taxes levied on consumers in your state. Prepare a chart to display the types of taxes, which government agency is in charge of collecting them, who must pay these taxes, and the rate of the tax. Explain to the class what each tax represents and why it is being levied.

yienkeat/Shutterstock.com, Chad Baker/Ryan McVay/Photodisc/Getty Images

13-3 Budget Deficits and the National Debt

Learning Objectives

LO 3-1 **Explain** the federal budget process and how federal budget deficits are financed.

LO 3-2 **Analyze** the impact of fiscal policy decisions on the national debt.

Vocabulary

budget deficit, p. 384
budget surplus, p. 384
balanced budget, p. 384
treasury bill (T bill), p. 385
treasury note, p. 385
treasury bond, p. 385
national debt, p. 386

REAL-WORLD FOCUS

Lenitia was reading the business section of the local newspaper. "I see that we are going to have a national budget deficit this year," she told her mom. "Is that the same as my spending more money than I received and not balancing my personal budget? Why should I care about the national budget?"

WORK AS A TEAM Who prepares the budget of the Unites States? What is a national deficit and how does it affect you as a consumer?

This is a photograph of the original National Debt Clock in New York City on March 13, 1989. The national debt today is more than $15,000,000,000,000.

DO YOU THINK **the national debt increases by more than one million dollars every minute?**

LO 3-1 The Federal Budget Balancing Act

The annual "battle of the budget" on Capitol Hill involves important decisions. How much does the government plan to spend? Where will the money come from to finance spending? The following is a brief look at the federal budgetary process.

UrsaHoggle/iStockphoto.com

The president begins the budget process by submitting the federal budget in January each year.

Step 1 The President Submits the Budget

The president must submit the budget to Congress on or before the first Monday in February of each year. This unveiling of the administration's budget is always big news. Does the president recommend that less money be spent for defense and more for education? Is there an increase in the Social Security spending or the income tax? And how large is the nation's debt?

Step 2 Budget Resolution

After the president submits the budget, Congress takes the lead. The president's budget is the starting point for congressional consideration. The Congressional Budget Office (CBO) advises Congress on the budget. Budget committee hearings are held in both the House of Representatives and the Senate. After debate, in May Congress approves an overall budget outline called the *budget resolution*. This budget sets target levels for spending and tax revenue.

Step 3 Budget Passed

Throughout the summer, Congress and the president debate the budget. Meanwhile congressional committees prepare specific spending and tax law bills. The budget resolution guides the spending and revenue decisions of these committees. Congress then passes and the president signs the spending and revenue bills. With the president's signature, the federal government has its actual budget for spending and tax collection. The budgetary process is summarized in Figure 13-11.

Figure 13-11

Major Steps in the Federal Budgetary Process

First, is the president sends the budget to Congress. Second, Congress passes targets for spending and taxes. Third, Congress passes the budget. The president signs it.

Federal Budget Deficits and Surpluses

Over the years, the federal government budget has always been unbalanced, running either a deficit or a surplus. A **budget deficit** occurs when government spending exceeds tax revenues. A **budget surplus** occurs when tax revenues exceed government spending. A **balanced budget** is a budget in which government spending equals tax revenues. As shown in Figure 13-12, between 1998 and 2001 budget surpluses existed. Deficits returned after the 2001 recession. Following the Great Recession of 2007, deficits reached record highs. In 2009, a record-breaking federal budget deficit was about $1.4 trillion.

Figure 13-12

U.S. Federal Budget Surpluses and Deficits, 1998–2010

During 1998 through 2001, the federal budget was in surplus each year. After the recession of 2001, these surpluses disappeared and deficits appeared.

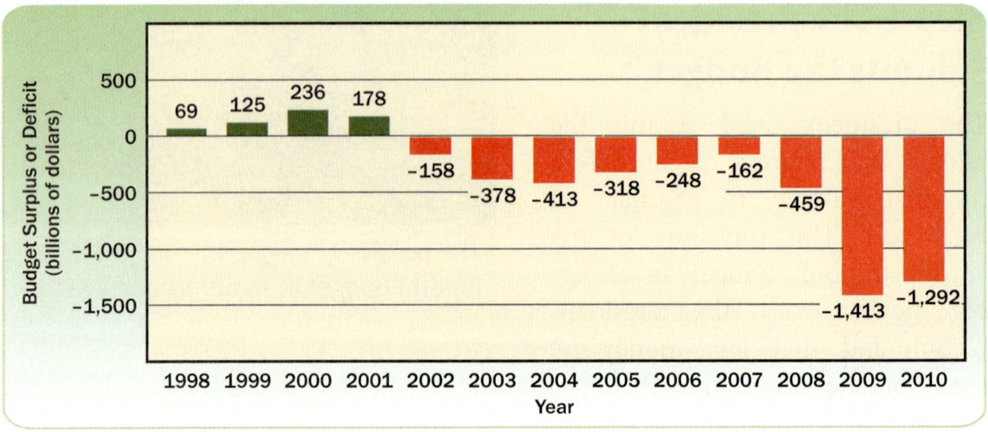

Figure 13-13 shows the federal budget deficit or surplus as a percentage of GDP. Following the 1990–1991 recession the deficit again reached close to 5 percent of GDP. In 2000, a budget surplus peaked at 2.4 percent. Following the latest recession, the federal deficit in 2010 soared to a record high of 10 percent of GDP. During the Great Depression, federal deficits were unimpressive by today's standards. As a share of GDP, Roosevelt's New Deal budget deficits peaked at 5.9 percent of GDP in 1934.

Figure 13-13

Deficits and Surpluses as a Percentage of GDP, 1990–2010

In 1992, the federal deficit as a percentage of GDP was about 5 percent. In 2000, the budget surplus reached a peak of 2.4 percent. Then the federal budget deficit soared to a historic high of 10 percent of GDP in 2009.

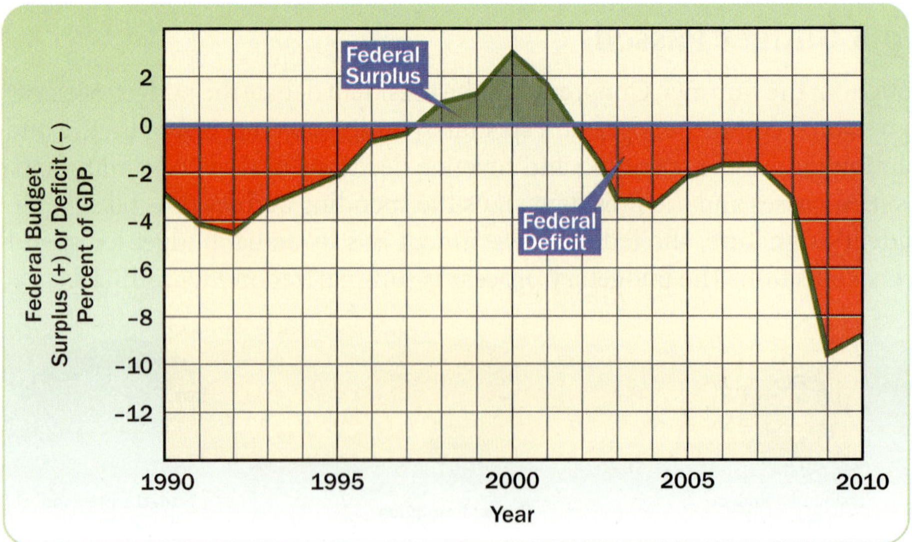

Financing Budget Deficits

ohdub/iStockphoto.com

The Federal Reserve Building is located in Washington, D.C.

What happens when the government spends more than it collects in taxes? The answer is the U.S. Treasury borrows by selling Treasury bills (T bills), notes, and bonds. A **treasury bill (T bill)** is a security that the federal government repays in one year or less. A **treasury note** is a security that the federal government repays between one to ten years. A **treasury bond** is a security that the federal government repays between twenty to thirty years. These government securities are IOUs of the federal government. They are considered a safe haven for idle funds and are purchased by the Federal Reserve, government agencies, private banks, corporations, individual U.S. citizens, and foreigners. If you own a U.S. government savings bond, for example, you have loaned your funds to the federal government.

ETHICS *in Action!*

Asking for Unneeded Benefits

In 2010 the federal government allocated almost $2.2 trillion to pay for programs that provided payments or services to individual Americans. This amount was just over 62 percent of all federal government spending for that year. Although much of this spending was used appropriately some of it was not. It was estimated, for example, that as much as 20 percent of the $430 billion allocated to Medicare paid for unnecessary services or services that were never provided.

For example, payments were made for electric scooters used by elderly people. The actual retail cost of these scooters is in the range of $2,000 to $3,000. Medicaid was often billed as much as $5,000 or more for these devices. There is reason to believe that many people who were provided with these scooters did not really need them. They were told by suppliers that they could get them free from the government. The suppliers, of course, earned a good profit for each scooter they supplied. This practice was often not illegal but many people believe it was unethical.

Think Critically

1. **Would you accept a medical device you did not need if you didn't personally pay for it?**
2. **How do practices like this contribute to the national debt?**

Figure 13-14 shows who owns the securities that the U.S. Treasury has issued. In 2010, foreigners owned 32 percent of the total national debt. The largest foreign holder of the debt was China with 8 percent of the total national debt. Japan was the second largest holder with 6 percent. Forty percent was held by federal, state, and local governments. Federal agencies such as the U.S. Treasury, the Social Security Administration, and the Federal Reserve hold U.S. securities. The private sector, consisting of individuals, banks, corporations, and insurance companies, held 28 percent of the national debt.

Figure 13-14

Ownership of U.S. Treasury Securities, 2010

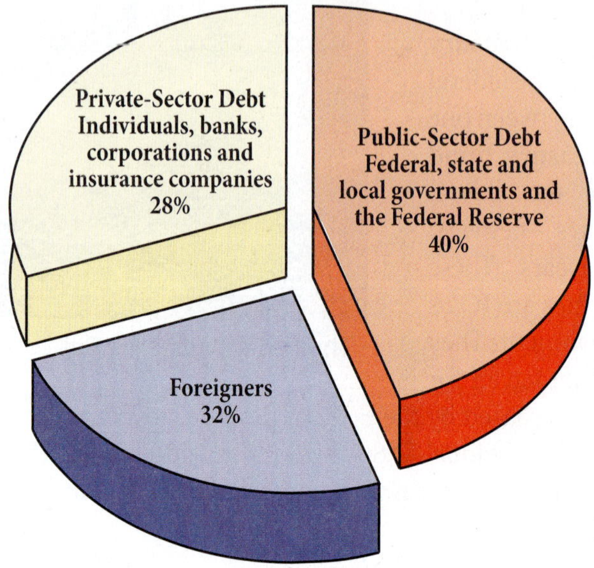

CHECKPOINT

Suppose you are a Keynesian economist. What are positive effects of government deficit spending on the economy?

LO 3-2 The National Debt

The stock of U.S. Treasury T-bills, notes, and bonds outstanding is the national debt. The **national debt** is the total amount owed by the federal government to owners of government securities. You may have seen national debt clocks that display the amount of money owed by the federal government. The national debt is the accumulation of federal deficits over time. As shown in Figure 13-15(a), the national debt crossed \$1 trillion in 1982. After 14 years, the debt rose by \$4 trillion to reach the \$5 trillion mark in 1996. Fourteen years later, the national debt had grown by \$8 trillion to over \$13 trillion in 2010.

What are some major causes of the rising national debt? In wartime, the government must increase military spending sharply and escalate the national debt. Recessions also cause the debt to rise rapidly. The reason is lower tax collections and greater spending for unemployment compensation and welfare.

Debt must be judged relative to the debtor's ability to repay the principal and interest on the debt. Figure 13-15(b) shows the national debt as a percentage of GDP. It is lower today than at the end of World War II. In 1945, national debt was about 120 percent of GDP, and by 1980 the ratio of debt to GDP had fallen to 33 percent. This means the debt grew considerably slower than GDP between 1945 and 1980. Since 1980, however, the trend has reversed. The debt has grown faster than GDP. Between 1980 and 2010, the national debt grew from 33 percent to 93 percent of GDP.

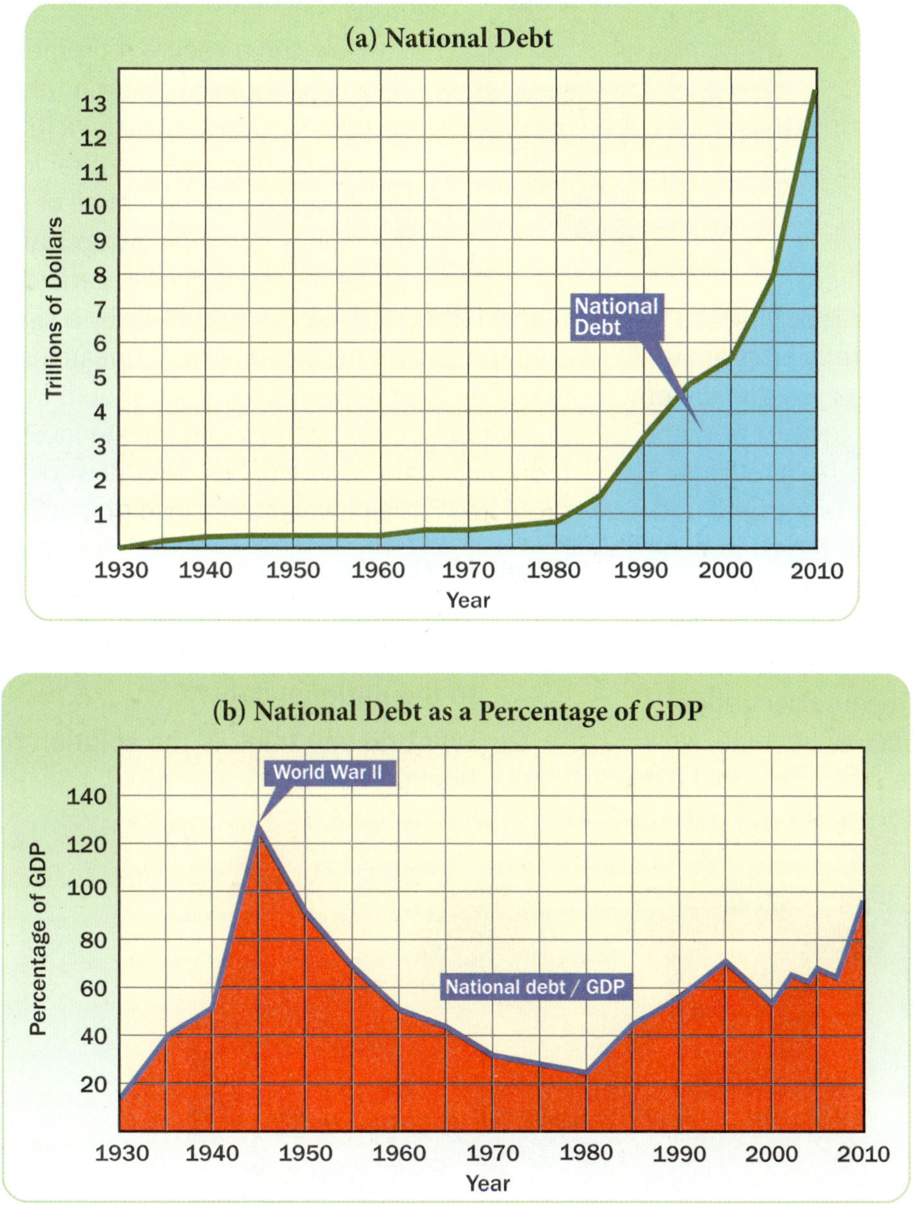

Figure 13-15

National Debt, 1930-2010

In Part (a), you see that the federal debt has skyrocketed since 1980.
In Part (b), the national debt as a percentage of GDP has declined since the end of World War II, when it reached a peak of about 120 percent. After 1980, the federal debt as a percentage of GDP increased, and has risen sharply to a historic high of about 93 percent.

CHECKPOINT

What makes the national debt grow? What would reduce or eliminate growth in the national debt?

Social Security: Past, Present, and Future

President Franklin D. Roosevelt signed the Social Security Act in 1935. This was a bedrock of the New Deal program to help Americans suffering from the Great Depression. On December 1, 1936 the first Social Security card was drawn from a stack of applications. The recipient was John D. Sweeney, Jr. He was the son of a wealthy factory owner and had grown up in a 15-room home staffed with servants. Unfortunately, Mr. Sweeney died at the age of 61 without ever receiving any benefits from the Social Security program.

You're the ECONOMIST

Social Security is a "pay as you go" system. Social Security taxes paid by today's workers are used to pay benefits to today's retirees. Prior to 2010, the Social Security Trust Fund collected more revenues than it paid in benefits. A misconception is that the surpluses were deposited in a vault, or special account. This is not what happened. The balance was invested in interest-bearing U.S. Treasury securities. After 2010 revenues fell below benefits. Now the system will cash in its securities from the trust fund to make up the difference. In 2037, it is estimated that the trust fund will be depleted. The problem is life expectancy is rising. Also, there is a large number of "baby boomers" born between 1945 and 1964 who are retiring.

How can a secure retirement program be established for future generations? One idea is to increase the retirement age. Another idea is to allow people to invest all or some of the money into their own private stock market account. Stocks generally outperform U.S. Treasury securities by a significant margin. There are important questions for this plan. First, how much money should workers divert from Social Security into private investment accounts? Second, how should workers be protected if their investments lose money?

Think Critically

1. **Why would the Social Security trust fund cashing in its securities contribute to the national debt?**
2. **What do you think is the solution for Social Security?**

Monkey Business Images/Shutterstock.com

Many baby boomers are considering their options as they move to retirement.

13-3 Assessment

Key Concepts

LO 3-2 1. The total amount owed by the federal government to owners of government securities is the __?__ debt.

LO 3-1 2. **TRUE OR FALSE** A balanced budget is a budget in which government spending equals tax revenues.

LO 3-1 3. A Treasury __?__ is a security that the federal government repays in a year or less.

LO 3-1 4. **TRUE OR FALSE** A budget deficit is a budget in which government spending exceeds tax revenues.

LO 3-1 5. A Treasury __?__ is a security that the federal government repays between twenty to thirty years.

Think About It

LO 3-2 6. Suppose you are the economic policy adviser to the president and are asked what should be done to eliminate a federal deficit. What would you recommend?

LO 3-2 7. Explain the relationship between budget deficits and the national debt.

LO 3-2 8. Explain this statement: "The national debt is like taking money out of your left pocket and putting it into your right pocket."

LO 3-1 9. How are federal budget deficits financed?

LO 3-2 10. How are fiscal policy decisions related to the national debt?

Make Academic Connections

LO 3-2 11. **MATH** Suppose the federal government has no national debt and spends $100 billion, while raising only $50 billion in taxes.

a. What amount of government bonds will the U.S. Treasury issue to finance the deficit?

b. Next year, assume tax revenues remain at $50 billion. The government pays 10 percent interest. Add the debt servicing interest payment to the government's $100 billion expenditure for goods and services the second year.

c. For the second year, compute the deficit, the amount of new debt issued, and the new national debt.

Teamwork

LO 3-1 12. Work in five groups. As a group choose one of the following time periods: 1940s, 1970s, 1980s, 1990s, or 2000–present. Research causes of increasing federal government deficits or budget surpluses during the period. Decide if you would have taken different actions than those taken by the federal government.

Unit 6 Project: The Role of Government

THE NATIONAL DEBT Participate in a debate regarding the national debt. One team should support the usefulness of the debt as stimulating the economy and providing for societal needs, and as a percentage of GDP over time and compared to other nations. The other team should explain the consequences of massive debt and the effect on future generations. Document all sources of information and opinion.

yienkeat/Shutterstock.com, Chad Baker/Ryan McVay/Photodisc/Getty Images

Chapter 13

Summary

13-1 FISCAL POLICY

1. There are two types of fiscal policy: expansionary and contractionary. Fiscal policy is the use of government spending and taxes to speed up (expansion) or slow down (contraction) the economy.
2. Aggregate (total) demand in an economy is represented by the aggregate demand curve; total supply is represented by the aggregate supply curve. Macroeconomic equilibrium is the price level where the aggregate demand curve intersects the aggregate supply curve.
3. Classical economic theory suggests that the market will regulate itself without government manipulation (fiscal policy). Keynesian economics is the theory that the federal government should speed up or slow down the economy to promote economic stability. This enhances full employment or discourages inflation.
4. The Laffer curve explains that higher tax rates can lead to lower collection of tax revenues. According to this theory, there is a tax rate that when reached will result in maximum tax collections that will decline if rates are raised further.

13-2 GOVERNMENT BUDGETS AND TYPES OF TAXES

5. Government spending at the state and federal levels is a significant part of the economy, providing for education, welfare, and safety. To finance government spending, taxes are levied.
6. There are three types of taxes: progressive, regressive, and proportional. Progressive taxes (income tax) charge a higher percent of income as income rises. Regressive taxes (sales tax) charge a lower percentage of income as income rises. Proportional taxes charge a flat tax rate, regardless of income. There are no perfect examples of proportional taxes in the United States.

13-3 BUDGET DEFICITS AND THE NATIONAL DEBT

7. The annual budget process begins with the president submitting the proposed budget. Congress then conducts hearings to reach a budget resolution. The budget is debated until disputes are resolved and the budget is passed and signed by the president.
8. A budget deficit occurs when government spending exceeds tax collections. A budget surplus occurs when tax revenues exceed government spending. A balanced budget occurs when government spending equals revenues.
9. Government deficits are financed with debt, which includes treasury bills, notes, and bonds. The national debt is the total amount owed by the federal government to owners of government securities (debt).

Chapter 13

Assessment

Vocabulary Review

Match each statement with the term that best defines it.

1. A security that the government repays between one and ten years
2. The use of federal government spending and taxes to achieve economic goals
3. A budget in which government spending exceeds government tax revenues
4. A tax that charges a lower percentage of income as income rises
5. A tax on the value of the sale of a good or service
6. The curve that shows real GDP produced at different price levels
7. The form of wealth that is subject to taxes
8. The total amount owed by the federal government to owners of government securities
9. A graph showing the relationship between tax rate cuts and total tax revenue
10. A security that the government repays between twenty to thirty years
11. A decrease in federal government spending or an increase in taxes to decrease real GDP
12. A tax on the value of assets
13. An increase in federal government spending or a reduction in taxes to increase real GDP
14. A budget in which government spending equals tax revenues
15. The curve that shows real gross domestic product that will be purchased at different price levels
16. The theory that the role of the federal government is to increase or decrease aggregate demand to achieve economic goals
17. A security that the government repays in one year or less
18. The price level where the aggregate demand and aggregate supply curves intersect
19. A budget in which government tax revenues exceed government spending
20. A tax that charges the same percentage of income, regardless of the income
21. The theory free markets restore full employment without government intervention
22. A tax that charges a higher percentage of income as income rises

Vocabulary

a. aggregate demand curve
b. aggregate supply curve
c. balanced budget
d. budget deficit
e. budget surplus
f. classical economics
g. contractionary fiscal policy
h. expansionary fiscal policy
i. fiscal policy
j. Keynesian economics
k. Laffer curve
l. macroeconomic equilibrium
m. national debt
n. progressive tax
o. property tax
p. proportional tax
q. regressive tax
r. sales tax
s. tax base
t. Treasury bill (T bill)
u. Treasury bond
v. Treasury note

Review Your Knowledge

LO 1-1 **23.** A government spending and taxation policy to achieve macroeconomic goals is
a. countercyclical policy
b. fiscal policy
c. monetary policy
d. a balanced budget
e. presidential discretion

LO 1-1 **24.** The government is pursuing an expansionary policy if it
a. decreases its spending and increases its tax revenues
b. increases its spending or increases its tax revenues
c. decreases its spending or reduces its tax revenues
d. increases its spending and/or reduces its tax revenues

LO 1-1 **25.** Contractionary fiscal policy is deliberate government action to influence aggregate demand and the level of real GDP through
a. expanding and contracting the money supply
b. encouraging business to expand or contract investment
c. regulating net exports
d. decreasing government spending or increasing taxes

LO 1-2 **26.** The Laffer curve is a graph of the relationship between tax rates and
a. real GDP
b. total tax revenues
c. government spending
d. inflation

LO 2-2 **27.** When the tax structure is progressive, as incomes increase, the tax rate
a. declines
b. remains the same
c. increases
d. is proportional

LO 2-2 **28.** A tax is regressive if it collects a
a. larger amount as income rises
b. constant amount as income rises
c. smaller fraction of income as income falls
d. smaller fraction of income as income rises

LO 2-2 **29.** A tax that is structured so that all people pay the same percentage of their income in taxes is a(an)
a. flat tax
b. regressive tax
c. progressive tax
d. excise tax

LO 3-1 **30.** When the federal government is running a budget deficit
a. government tax revenues exceed government spending
b. government spending exceeds government tax revenues
c. the economy must be in an economic recession
d. the size of the national debt will decline

LO 3-1 **31.** If the federal government were to run a budget deficit, this would
a. increase the size of the national debt
b. reduce the size of the national debt
c. leave the size of the national debt unchanged
d. increase the national debt only if the government also expands the supply of money

LO 3-2 **32.** To finance a federal budget deficit, the U.S. Treasury borrows by selling
a. Treasury bills
b. Treasury notes
c. Treasury bonds
d. All of the above

LO 3-2 **33.** What is the difference between the federal budget deficit and the national debt?
a. The budget deficit is the amount by which government spending exceeds tax revenues in a year, while the national debt is the sum of all past budget deficits
b. The budget deficit is the cumulative effect of all prior national debts
c. The national debt includes all outstanding bonds, while the budget deficit excludes bonds held by government agencies
d. There is no difference between the budget deficit and the national debt

Digging Deeper with Economics e-Collection

As personal income taxes rise, consumers have less money to spend for personal choices. Government has increased money to spend. Reducing tax rates is a technique used to stimulate the economy. Raising tax rates has the opposite effect — it reduces consumer spending. Access the Gale Economics e-Collection at **www.cengage.com/school/economics/personalfinance**. View marginal income tax rates over time. Based on current tax rates (and any proposed changes), make an assessment as to future tax collections and the effect on the economy as a whole (economic growth).

Think About It

LO 1-1 **34.** Classical economics is the theory that the market will correct itself to reach full-employment equilibrium. This was prevalent until the Great Depression. Why did economic thinking begin to change at that point?

LO 3-2 **35.** The national debt, as a percentage of GDP, has increased in most years since 1980. What does this measurement mean? Why should you be concerned?

Make Academic Connections

LO 1-2 **36. SOCIAL STUDIES** Inflation lowers spending power. But combating inflation often means taking action to "slow down" the economy. When the economy slows down, the result is fewer jobs. Prepare a flow chart illustrating this concept.

LO 2-1 **37. MATH** John owns real estate with assessed value of $200,000. He is charged property tax at the rate of $13 per thousand dollars of assessed value. Last year he earned $74,000 in taxable income and is in the 28% federal income tax bracket and the 7% state income tax bracket. He also bought $22,000 worth of goods subject to the sales tax of 8%. How much property, income, and sales tax did John pay last year?

LO 3-2 **38. COMMUNICATIONS** Many people believe the national debt is a giant problem that future generations will have to pay high taxes to resolve. Others believe the debt is needed so that the economy can be stimulated and get people back to work paying taxes. Research about the present and future consequences of the debt and what it would be like to pay it down or off—who would benefit? Who would suffer?

Extend Your Learning

LO 1-2 **39.** Complete the following causation chain diagram on a separate piece of paper.

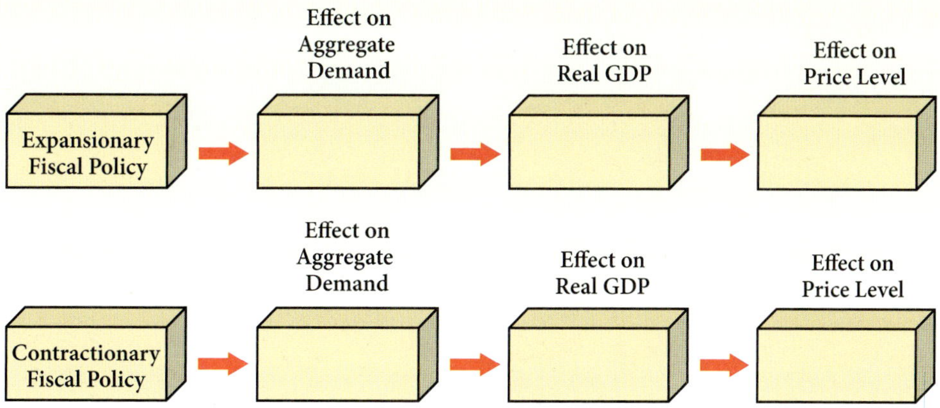

yienkeat/Shutterstock.com

orgnmaster/iStockphoto.com

chapter 14

Federal Reserve and Monetary Policy

14-1 Federal Reserve System

14-2 Monetary Policy

yienkeat/Shutterstock.com

MARKETS *in Action!*

Ben S. Bernanke
Chairman, Board of Governors of the Federal Reserve System

In 2005, Ben Bernanke was appointed to be the 14th Chairman of the Board of Governors of the Federal Reserve System by President George W. Bush. Born December 13, 1953 in North Augusta, South Carolina, his father was a pharmacist and his mother was a school teacher. In high school he was a high achiever. He taught himself calculus, edited the school newspaper, and was class valedictorian. He achieved the highest SAT score in the state the year he graduated, scoring 1590 out of a possible 1600.

Bernanke attended Harvard University and graduated with a BA in economics (1975). He also earned a PhD in economics from MIT (1979). He taught at Stanford University from 1979 to 1985 and later became a tenured professor at Princeton University. In 2002 he was appointed to the Federal Reserve's Board of Governors and became its chairman in 2005. He was reappointed to this post by President Obama in 2009.

As chair of the Federal Reserve Board, Bernanke affects all Americans' lives in many important ways. Along with other members of the Board, he sets monetary policy. He leads the Board to make decisions that change interest rates, adjust the money supply, implement open market operations, and other actions. The goal of the Fed's Board of Governors is to stabilize the economy and encourage economic growth that is accompanied by low inflation.

Bernanke believes in the need for financial responsibility. He understands how inflation erodes purchasing power and why it is the duty of individuals as well as the government to be financially responsible and to take steps to protect our economy from inflation. In his role as Chairman of the Board of Governors, Bernanke leads the Fed to lower interest rates when the economy is slowing. These lower rates encourage spending and economic growth because it makes money easier to borrow. When the economy is moving too fast, he leads the Fed to raise interest rates to discourage borrowing and spending that could cause inflation.

Bernanke's actions (whether lowering or raising interest rates, or just making comments about the economy) can have an immediate and dramatic effect on the stock market and investments in the U.S. When he makes public statements, the stock market often rises (or falls) in response. This affects all Americans even those who do not personally own stock because the value of stocks is an important factor that helps determine how much people and businesses are willing to spend or invest. And spending and investment have much to do with the number of jobs that exist in our economy.

Ben Bernanke speaks at the National Press Club.

Albert H. Teich/Shutterstock.com

Think Critically

1. Explain how Bernanke, as the Chair of the Federal Reserve System's Board of Governors, can affect your life.
2. How might your family be affected if the Fed took actions that increased interest rates by 2 percent or more?

14-1 Federal Reserve System

Learning Objectives

LO 1-1 **Understand** the structure of the Federal Reserve System.

LO 1-2 **Explain** the functions of the Federal Reserve System.

Vocabulary

Federal Reserve Districts, p. 397
Board of Governors of the Federal Reserve System, p. 398
Federal Open Market Committee (FOMC), p. 399
Federal Advisory Council (FAC), p. 399
check clearing, p. 400
Federal Deposit Insurance Corporation (FDIC), p. 401
Consumer Financial Protection Bureau (CFPB), p. 403

© Aleksandar Vrzalski/iStockphoto.com

REAL-WORLD FOCUS

As a student and part-time worker, Keisha must carefully manage her income and expenses. "I wrote a check just yesterday and it has already been processed out of my account," she complained. "I also deposited a check yesterday. The bank put a temporary hold on it, so that amount is not available for me to spend. It seems that checks I write leave my account a lot faster than the deposits I make are made available for use."

WORK AS A TEAM Why would the bank place a temporary hold on a check deposited to an account? Why do some checks (both those written and those deposited) clear an account faster than others?

Ben Haslam/Haslam Photography/Shutterstock.com

The Salt Lake City office of CIT bank displayed the FDIC logo. In November 2009, CIT Bank's parent, CIT Group, Inc, filed Chapter 11 Bankruptcy.

DO YOU THINK the customers of CIT Bank lost all their deposited funds when the bankruptcy was filed?

yienkeat/Shutterstock.com

LO 1-1 Structure of the Federal Reserve System

Who controls the money supply in the United States? As defined in Lesson 8-3, the answer is the Federal Reserve System, popularly called the "Fed." The Fed is the central bank for the nation. It provides banking services to commercial banks, other financial institutions, and the federal government. The Fed regulates, supervises, and is responsible for policies concerning money. Congress and the president consult with the Fed.

Other major nations have central banks. Examples are the Bank of England, the Bank of Japan, and the European Central Bank. The movement to establish a central banking system in the United States gained strength from The Panic of 1907. In that year, stock prices fell, many businesses and banks failed, and millions of depositors lost their savings. To prevent financial panic, the government wanted to establish more centralized control over banks. This desire for more safety in banking led to the Federal Reserve Act of 1913. The Federal Reserve is an independent agency of the federal government. Congress is responsible for overseeing the Fed. Although the Fed enjoys independent status, its independence could be revoked by an act of Congress.

The Fed's Organizational Chart

The Federal Reserve System consists of 12 Federal Reserve districts. **Federal Reserve Districts** are the 12 banking districts which are served by a Federal Reserve district bank. Each Federal Reserve bank acts as a central bank for the private banks in its region. The United States is the only nation in the world to have 12 separate regional banks instead of a single central bank. In addition, 25 Federal Reserve branch banks are located throughout the country. The map in Figure 14-1 shows the 12 Federal Reserve districts.

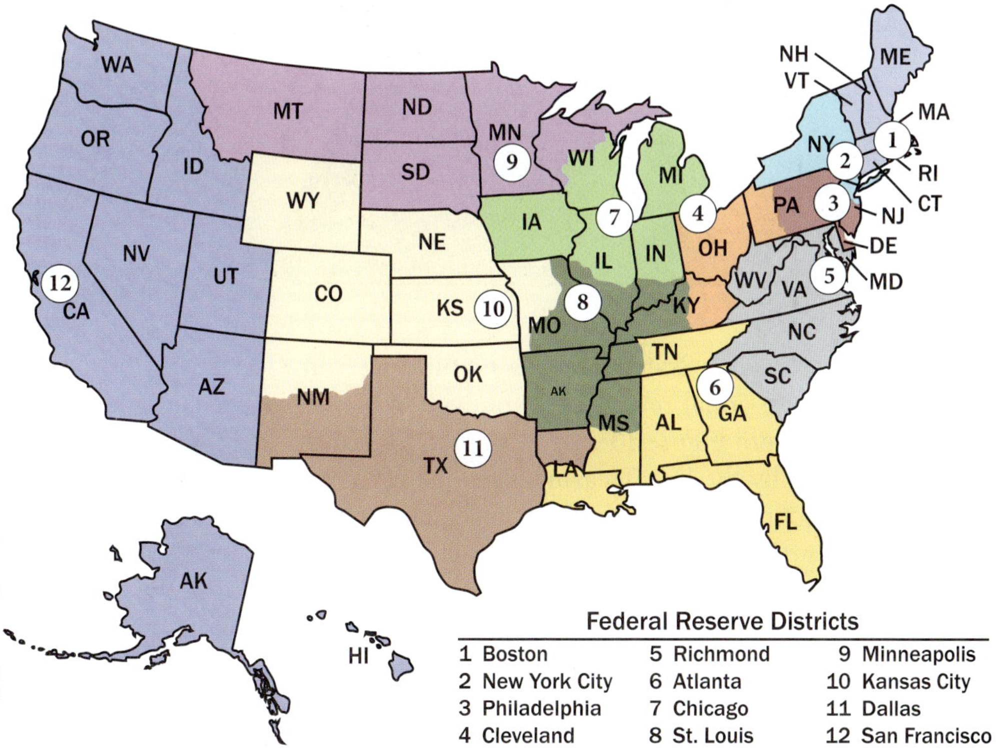

Figure 14-1
The 12 Federal Reserve Districts

In fact, the Fed's structure is the result of a compromise between opposing sides. One side favored a single central bank. Another viewpoint distrusted concentration of financial power in the hands of a few. Although each district enjoyed a degree of independence when the Federal Reserve System was first created, since 1935 they have been directed by the central authority of the Fed's Board of Governors located in Washington, D.C.

The organizational chart of the Fed in Figure 14-2 shows the Board of Governors, located in Washington, D.C., at the top of the chart. The **Board of Governors of the Federal Reserve System** is the seven-member board that supervises the banking system of the United States. Board members are appointed by the president and confirmed by the U.S. Senate. They serve for one nonrenewable 14-year term. Their responsibility is to supervise and control the money supply and the banking system of the United States. A 14-year term for Fed governors insulates the Fed from politics. These terms are staggered so one term expires every two years. Staggering terms prevents a president from stacking the board with members favoring the incumbent party's political interests. A president usually makes two appointments in a one-term presidency and four appointments in a two-term presidency. The president designates one member of the Board of Governors to serve as chairman for a four-year term. The chairman is the principal spokesperson for the Fed and has considerable power over policy decisions. It is often argued that the Fed's chairman is the most powerful individual in the United States next to the president. The current chairman is Ben Bernanke, who was appointed by President George W. Bush.

Figure 14-2

Organization of the Federal Reserve System

The Federal Open Market Committee (FOMC) and the Federal Advisory Council (FAC) assist the Federal Reserve System's Board of Governors. The 12 regional Federal Reserve district banks implement policies affecting the money supply.

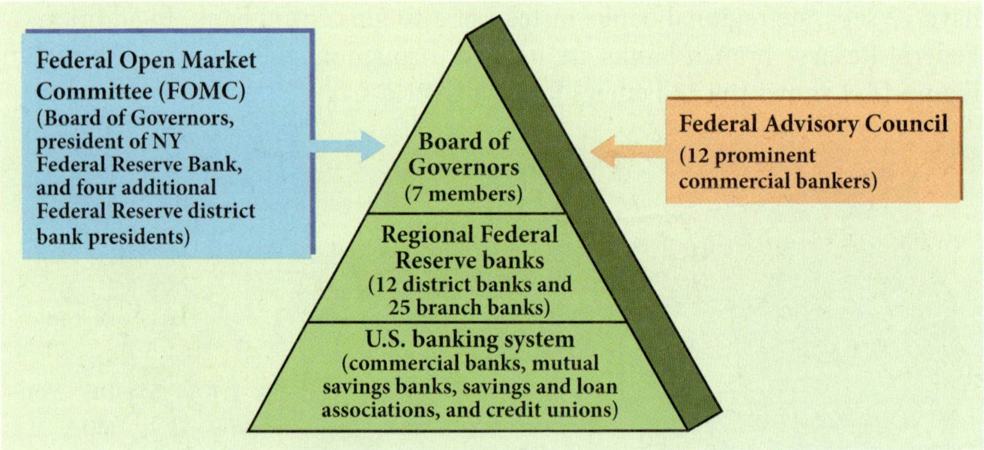

The Federal Reserve System receives no funding from Congress. This removes the fear of congressional review of its budget. Where does the Fed get funds to operate? Recall from Figure 13-14 in Chapter 13 that the Fed holds government securities issued by the U.S. Treasury. The Fed earns interest income from these government securities. Also, the Fed makes loans to banks that pay the Fed a relatively low rate of interest. The Fed returns most of the profits it earns to the Treasury. This makes it motivated to adopt policies to promote the economy's well being, rather than earning a profit. The Board of Governors does not take orders from the president or legislators. Thus, the Board of Governors is the independent, self-supporting authority of the Federal Reserve System.

The Federal Reserve System

The law that created the Federal Reserve System divided the country into 12 banking districts that are identified by a number from 1 to 12. Each district has a Federal Reserve Bank that is located in one of the Federal Reserve Cities: Boston, New York, Philadelphia, Cleveland, Richmond, Atlanta, Chicago, St. Louis, Minneapolis, Kansas City, Dallas, and San Francisco. Within these districts, there are branch banks that serve the district. Twenty-five branch banks are spread across the country with most districts having two or more branch banks. District 7 (the Great Lakes region) and District 9 (northern central and mid-western states bordering Canada) each have only one branch bank.

Investigate Your Local ECONOMY

Research the closest Federal Reserve district bank or Federal Reserve branch bank.

Try it Out

Define the area served, and find out the main duties performed by the federal reserve district bank. Is there anything unique about the bank in your area?

On the left side of the organizational chart in Figure 14-2 is the very important **Federal Open Market Committee (FOMC)**, which directs the buying and selling of U.S. government securities by the Fed. The FOMC consists of the seven members of the Board of Governors and the president of the New York Federal Reserve Bank. Also, the presidents of four other Federal Reserve district banks are members. The FOMC meets to discuss trends in inflation, unemployment, growth rates, and other macro data. FOMC members express their opinions on various monetary policies. Then they vote on issues and publish policy statements known as *FOMC directives*. A directive might require the Fed to stimulate or restrain the money supply (M1) to influence the economy.

On the right side of the chart is the **Federal Advisory Council (FAC)**. This council is a 12-member board of bankers selected from each Federal Reserve District to advise on business and financial issues. Each of the 12 Federal Reserve district banks selects one member each year. The council meets periodically to advise the Board of Governors.

At the bottom of the organizational chart is the remainder of the Federal Reserve System. This consists of about 3,000 member banks of the approximately 7,500 commercial banks in the United States. These 3,000 Fed member banks represent less than half of U.S. banks. However, they have about 70 percent of all U.S. bank deposits. A sure sign of Fed membership is the word National in a bank's name. The U.S. comptroller of the currency charters national banks that are required to be Fed members. Banks that do not have National in their title can also be Fed members. States can also charter banks, and these state banks have the option of joining the Federal Reserve. Less than 20 percent of state banks choose to join the Fed. Figure 14-3 shows the top 10 U.S. banks based on their assets. Nonmember depository institutions are not official members of the Fed team. They are, however, influenced by and depend on the Fed for a variety of services. The top 10 banks in the United States in 2010 included Bank of America, JPMorgan Chase, and Wells Fargo.

Figure 14-3

Top 10 Banks in the United States, 2010

The top 10 banks in the United States included Bank of America, JPMorgan Chase, and Wells Fargo.

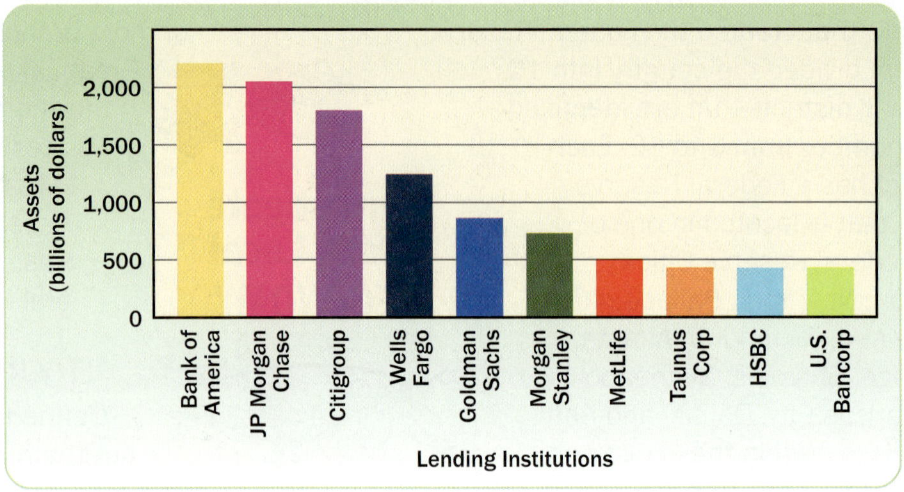

CHECKPOINT

How is the Federal Reserve System different from a government agency?

LO 1-2 What a Federal Reserve Bank Does

The typical bank customer never enters the doors of a Federal Reserve district bank. The Fed does not offer the public checking accounts, savings accounts, or any of the services provided by banks. Instead, the Federal Reserve serves as a "banker's bank." Following are brief descriptions of some of the principal functions of the Federal Reserve.

Controlling the Money Supply

The primary role of the Fed is to control the nation's money supply. The Fed has three policy tools it can use to change the stock of money in the banking system, and therefore in the economy. Changes in the money supply affect real GDP, employment, and the price level. These three policy tools are discussed in the next lesson.

Clearing Checks

Check clearing is an important function. **Check clearing** is a Federal Reserve service that collects funds from a check writer's bank and transfers them to the recipient's bank. Suppose you live in Oregon and have a checking account with a bank in that state. While on vacation in California, you purchase tickets to Disneyland with a check for $200. Disneyland accepts your check and then deposits it in its business checking account in a California bank. This bank must collect payment for your check. It does so by sending an electronic copy of your check to the Federal Reserve bank in San Francisco. From there, the electronic copy of your check is sent to your bank in Oregon, which subtracts the $200 from your personal checking account. The funds are credited to the bank in California. A copy of your check is returned to you, or it can be viewed online. At one time this process was done manually with the checks actually being transported from bank to bank through the Federal Reserve System. It is now done almost entirely electronically. The electronic clearinghouse process is much speedier than depending on the movement of a check between commercial banks. Figure 14-4 summarizes the check clearing process using electronic funds transfer (EFT).

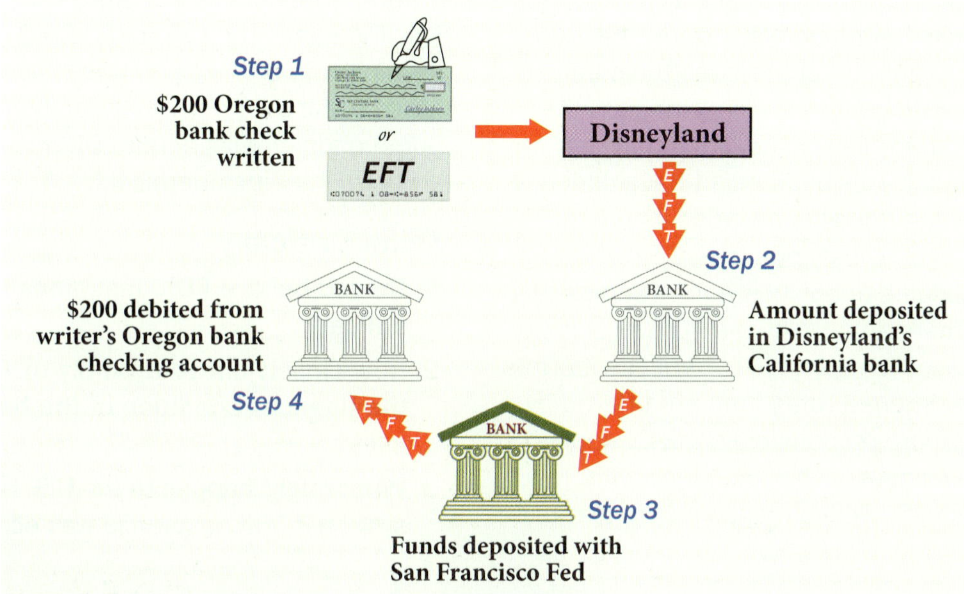

Figure 14-4
Check Clearing Path

Supervising and Regulating Banks

The Fed examines banks' books, approves bank mergers, and works with the **Federal Deposit Insurance Corporation (FDIC)**. The FDIC is a government agency that insures customer deposits up to a predetermined limit if a bank fails. Congress created the FDIC in 1933 in response to the huge number of bank failures during the Great Depression. At that time, the insurance limit was $25,000. With a safety net, people are less likely to panic and withdraw their funds during economic uncertainty. If a bank fails, this agency of the government stands ready to pay depositors. Banks that are members of the Fed are required to be members of the FDIC. State agencies supervise state chartered banks that are not members of either the Federal Reserve System or the FDIC. In response to bank failures in 2008, the FDIC raised coverage of bank deposits from $100,000 to $250,000 per customer.

Maintaining and Circulating Currency

Recall that the M1 money supply consists of currency (coins and Federal Reserve notes) and checkable deposits. Note that the Fed does *not* print currency. It maintains and circulates money. All Federal Reserve notes are printed at the U.S. Bureau of Engraving and Printing facilities in Washington, D.C., and Fort Worth, Texas. The Treasury mints and issues all coins. Coins are made at U.S. mints

ETHICS *in Action!*

Is the FDIC Ethical?

There is an argument that it is a mistake for the FDIC to guarantee deposits in banks. The argument is that this insurance encourages savers to make deposits in irresponsible banks because the government guarantees the safety of their deposits. Imagine Bank XYZ has made many ill-advised loans that may not be repaid. This bank might have difficulty attracting deposits because its mistakes have been widely publicized. However, because its deposits are insured to some maximum amount by the FDIC, this is not the case. To maintain its deposits it offers higher interest rates than are offered by other more responsible banks. People and businesses may decide to withdraw funds from well-managed banks to make deposits in Bank XYZ because they know that they cannot lose their deposits up to the maximum insured amount. Thus, funds flow from more responsible banks to those that are irresponsible and are likely to fail. This increases the risk to the FDIC and the possibility that this government agency will have to bail out poorly-managed banks. Some people believe that FDIC insurance borders on being unethical.

Think Critically

1. **Do you believe FDIC insurance is unethical?**
2. **How closely did your family examine the financial condition of the bank it uses?**
3. **What might happen to the U.S. banking system if FDIC insurance was eliminated?**

located in Philadelphia and Denver. The bureau and the mints ship new notes and coins to the Federal Reserve banks for circulation. Much of this money is printed or minted simply to replace worn out bills and coins. Another use of new currency is to meet public demand. Suppose it is the holiday season and banks need more paper money and coins to meet their customers' shopping needs. The Federal Reserve must be ready to ship extra cash by armored trucks from its large vaults.

ollo/iStockphoto.com

Armored trucks are used to transport currency to banks and retailers.

Protecting Consumers

Since 1968, the Federal Reserve has played a role in protecting consumers. Perhaps the most important is the *Equal Credit Opportunity Act*. This act prohibits discrimination based on race, color, gender, marital status, religion, or national origin in the extension of credit. It also gives married women the right to establish credit histories in their own names. The Federal Reserve receives and tries to resolve consumer complaints against banks.

In 2010, the **Consumer Financial Protection Bureau** (CFPB) was established. This is an independent bureau within the Federal Reserve that helps consumers make financial decisions. The goal of the CFPB is to promote fairness and make mortgages, credit cards, and other consumer financial services understandable. The objective is to let consumers see clearly the costs and features of loans. As a result, consumers are less likely to be surprised by hidden fees or sign loans they cannot afford.

Maintaining Federal Government Checking Accounts and Gold

The U.S. Treasury has the Fed handle its checking account. From this account, the federal government pays for its expenses. Examples include federal employees' salaries, Social Security, tax refunds, veterans' benefits, defense, and highways. It is interesting to note that the New York Federal Reserve District Bank holds one of the oldest forms of money, gold. This gold belongs mainly to foreign governments and is one of the largest accumulations of this precious metal in the world. Viewing a Federal Reserve bank's vault is not something that most tourists typically have on their list of things to do. But it is a strongly recommended tour.

The gold vault at the New York Federal Reserve Bank is nearly half the length of a football field. It is filled with steel and concrete walls several yards thick. Most cells contain the gold of only one nation. Only a few bank employees know the identities of the owners. When trade occurs between two countries, payment between the parties can be made by transferring gold bars from one cell to another. The Fed and the monetary system of the Yapese have a similarity. Recall from the Global View in Lesson 8-1 that in Yap large stone wheels are not moved, rather they just change ownership.

luismmolina/iStockphoto.com

Each gold bar weighs 1,000 grams, which is the same as 1 kilogram.

Lender of Last Resort

The Fed acts as the lender of last resort to prevent a banking crisis. For example, after the terrorist attacks in 2001, the Fed issued billions in loans to banks throughout the United States. And in 2008 several large banks collapsed and others were on the verge. The Fed lent banks enough so that they could meet required reserve balances as well as their obligations to depositors. Recall the discussion of required reserves from Lesson 8-2.

CHECKPOINT

It is often said that the Federal Reserve prints money. Is this correct?

Global View

Birth of the Euro

In 1958, several European nations formed a Common Market to eliminate trade restrictions among member countries. The Common Market called for gradual removal of tariffs and import quotas on goods traded among member nations. Later the name was changed to the European Economic Community (EEC), and it is now called the European Union (EU). This organization established a common system of tariffs for imports from nonmember nations.

In 1999, 11 European countries, joined later by Greece and other nations, followed the United States as an example. They united in the European Economic and Monetary Union (EMU). In the United States, 50 states are linked with a common currency. The Federal Reserve serves as the central bank by conducting monetary policy for the nation. Among the states, trade, labor, and investment enjoy freedom of movement. In 2002, the EMU members replaced their national currencies with a single currency, the euro. The objective was to remove exchange rate fluctuations that impede cross-border transactions. This is why the U.S. Congress created a national currency in 1863 to replace state and private bank currencies.

The EU faces many unanswered questions. Unlike the states of the United States, the EU's member nations do not share a common language or government. This makes maintaining common macro policies difficult, and in recent years several members have experienced financial crises. Coordinating monetary policy among EU nations is also difficult. Although the EU has established the European Central Bank headquartered in Frankfurt, Germany with sole authority over the supply of euros, the central banks of member nations still function. Only time will tell whether EU nations will perform better with a single currency than with separate national currencies. Currently, the United Kingdom, Denmark, and Sweden still use their own currencies.

European Union (EU) Members

Austria	Finland	Latvia	Romania
Belgium	France	Lithuania	Slovakia
Bulgaria	Germany	Luxembourg	Slovenia
Cyprus	Greece	Malta	Spain
Czech Republic	Hungary	Netherlands	Sweden
Denmark	Ireland	Poland	United Kingdom
Estonia	Italy	Portugal	

Think Critically

Why might having central banks of member European Union nations still functioning be a problem?

14-1 Assessment

Key Concepts

LO 1-2 1. A Federal Reserve service that collects funds from a check writer's bank and transfers them to the recipient's bank is __?__.

LO 1-2 2. **TRUE OR FALSE** The Consumer Financial Protection Bureau (CFPB) is an independent bureau within the Federal Reserve that helps consumers make financial decisions.

LO 1-2 3. __?__ is the government agency that insures customer deposits up to a limit if a bank fails.

LO 1-1 4. **TRUE OR FALSE** The Federal Advisory Council (FAC) is a 12-member board of business executives selected from each Federal Reserve District to advise on business and financial issues.

LO 1-1 5. The twelve banking districts served by a Federal Reserve district bank are __?__.

LO 1-1 6. **TRUE OR FALSE** The Board of Governors of the Federal Reserve System is the seven-member board that supervises the banking system of the United States.

LO 1-2 7. The Federal Reserve Committee that directs the buying and selling of U.S. government securities is __?__.

Think About It

LO 1-1 8. What is the major purpose of the Federal Reserve System? What is the major responsibility of the Board of Governors and the Federal Open Market Committee?

LO 1-2 9. Which banks must be insured by the FDIC? Which banks can choose not to be insured by the FDIC?

10. Describe the structure of the Federal Reserve System.

LO 1-2 11. What are the primary functions of the Federal Reserve System?

Make Academic Connections

LO 1-2 12. **CONSUMERISM** Visit the Consumer Financial Protection Bureau (CFPB) at www.consumerfinance.gov/. Click on Protecting You. Select an article from Real Stories and read it. Based on this story, create a presentation using visual aids to present the advice that you found most useful.

LO 1-2 13. **HISTORY** The savings and loan crisis of the 1980s and early 1990s was one of the worst U.S. financial crises since the Great Depression. Research this crisis and explain its connection to the Monetary Control Act of 1980.

Teamwork

LO 1-1 14. Work in five groups. As a group research one of the following: Federal Reserve District Bank, Board of Governors of the Federal Reserve System, Federal Open Market Committee (FOMC), Federal Advisory Council (FAC), and the gold vault at the New York Federal Reserve Bank. Report your group's findings to the class.

Unit 6 Project: The Role of Government

HISTORY OF THE FED Prepare a historical report on the Federal Reserve System—when it was created, why it was created, its role throughout the previous century, and its role today. You may want to include a time line or a chart to illustrate the major historical events.

14-2 Monetary Policy

Learning Objectives

LO 2-1 **Analyze** the three basic tools used to implement U.S. monetary policy.

LO 2-2 **Explain** how monetary policy affects the economy.

Vocabulary

monetary policy, p. 407
expansionary monetary policy, p. 407
contractionary monetary policy, p. 407
open market operations, p. 408
discount rate, p. 409
federal funds rate, p. 409

© Aleksandar Vrzalski/ iStockphoto.com

REAL-WORLD FOCUS

Trinh attends high school, works on weekends, and participates in many after-school activities. His parents gave him permission to buy his own car as long as he could make the payments. "I applied for a car loan," he told his friend, "but I decided not to buy a car because the best interest rate I can get is not acceptable. Without a lower rate, my car payments would be too high."

WORK AS A TEAM How do interest rates affect a person's spending? If a person pays for their purchases in cash, are they concerned about interest rates? Why or why not?

Stephen VanHorn/Shutterstock.com

Being approved for a residential loan depends not only on your economic situation, but also on the economic state of the country.

DO YOU THINK it is easier to get credit when the Federal Reserve is using an expansionary monetary policy or a contractionary monetary policy?

yienkeat/Shutterstock.com

LO2-1 How the Fed Changes the Money Supply

Recall from Lesson 13-1 that fiscal policy can be used to achieve economic goals. The goals include full employment, stable prices, and economic growth. Here you will learn how monetary policy can be used for the same purpose. **Monetary policy** is the Federal Reserve's use of changes in the money supply to achieve economic goals. Using monetary policy, the Fed can limit or expand deposit creation by the banks. This action in turn changes the money supply (M1).

There are two basic policies the Federal Reserve uses depending on the condition of the economy. During a recession, the Fed may use expansionary monetary policy, also called an easy-money policy. **Expansionary monetary policy** uses an increase in the money supply to increase real GDP. When the economy is suffering from inflation, the Fed can use contractionary monetary policy, also called a tight-money policy. **Contractionary monetary policy** uses a decrease in the money supply to decrease real GDP.

Skyhobo/iStockphoto.com

The headquarters for the United States Federal Reserve is located in Washington, D.C.

Expansionary Monetary Policy

Suppose the economy is in recession. The objective is to increase real GDP and reduce unemployment. The Fed's goal is to increase the money in circulation and make credit more available by lowering interest rates. With more money and credit, consumers and business will increase consumption spending (*C*) and investment spending (*I*). Lower interest rates make it easier for consumers to make purchases. At lower interest rates, businesses can more easily afford to invest in new plants and equipment. Increased spending causes aggregate demand to increase. As a result, real GDP increases and firms hire more workers.

Contractionary Monetary Policy

Now assume that the economy is suffering from rising prices. Aggregate demand is too high, and the problem is inflation. The objective is to decrease real GDP. For this cure, the Fed decreases the money in circulation and makes credit less available by raising interest rates. Having less money and credit, consumers and businesses decrease consumption spending (*C*) and investment spending (*I*). Higher interest rates make it harder for consumers to buy goods and services. High interest rates cause businesses to borrow less money to finance plants and equipment. The result is decreased total spending (aggregate demand) in the economy. Real GDP declines and the price level falls.

In Lesson 8-2, you learned how bank transactions of Brad Rich and Connie Jones worked through the banking system and increased M1. Here you will learn how the Fed can expand or contract the money supply and change interest rates. Imagine the Fed has three "levers" to pull. Each time it pulls a lever, the money supply is affected. The following is a discussion of the three levers (or tools) used by the Fed to achieve its goals.

© dbimages/Alamy

The Federal Reserve Bank of New York, located in lower Manhattan, is built in neo-Renaissance style. The Federal Open Market (FOMC) conducts its business here.

Open Market Operations

Open market operations are the most important tool used by the Fed to regulate the money supply. This is the most-used monetary policy tool. **Open market operations** is the buying and selling of government securities to affect the money supply. Recall from the previous lesson that the Federal Open Market Committee (FOMC) conducts open market operations. Open market operations begin on a typical day at the trading desk located at the Federal Reserve Bank of New York. The manager of the trading desk starts the day by studying estimates of reserves in the banking system. If excess reserves are low, few banks have funds to lend. High excess reserves mean many banks can make loans. After collecting this information, the manager looks at the directive from the FOMC. Then the manager has traders in the trading room call dealers who trade in government securities for price quotations. The open market operation has two alternative objectives: purchase or sell U.S. government securities, such as Treasury bills and bonds. Remember the U.S. government issues securities to finance federal government deficits.

Open Market Purchases During a recession, the Fed uses expansionary policy and buys government securities. For example, the Fed purchases a $10,000 Treasury bond from a bank. The Fed accepts the security and makes a $10,000 payment to the reserve balance of the selling bank. When banks have additional reserves, they can make new loans and the money supply increases. Almost like magic, "out of thin air," the Fed created money in circulation. Consumers and businesses have more money to spend and aggregate demand increases. The result is greater real GDP and employment.

Open Market Sales In times of inflation, the Fed uses contractionary monetary policy and sells government securities. Now the Fed sells a $10,000 Treasury bond to a bank. The bank accepts the security and pays the Fed by reducing its reserves by $10,000. When banks have less reserves, they have less money available for loans. In this case, the money supply decreases. Again like magic, money disappeared "into thin air." Consumers and businesses have less money to spend and aggregate demand falls. As a result, real GDP declines and the inflation rate drops.

Changing the Discount Rate

The banking system depends on excess reserves acquired from new checkable deposits. Recall that Brad Rich took $100,000 cash from under his mattress and deposited it into Best National Bank. Then the bank covered its required reserves by taking $10,000 from this $100,000 deposit. Actually, the Fed itself provides another option for banks to obtain reserves through its *discount window*. This is a department within each of the Federal Reserve district banks and not an actual window. Best National Bank can borrow $10,000 reserves from the Fed and pay the discount rate. The **discount rate** is the interest rate the Fed charges on loans of reserves to banks. Changes in the discount rate often signal the Fed's monetary policy direction.

In times of recession, the Fed can choose to lower the discount rate. A lower rate encourages banks to borrow funds from the Fed and offer loans to the public at lower interest rates and still earn profits. Lower interest rates encourage consumers and businesses to spend and aggregate demand increases.

In inflationary times, the Fed can decide to raise the discount rate. A higher rate means it costs banks more to borrow from the Fed. To maintain their profits, banks will increase the interest rate on loans to their customers. Higher interest rates discourage consumer and business spending and aggregate demand decreases.

There is an important interest rate set by private banks that needs to be explained. Banks wanting to expand their reserves in order to seek profitable loan opportunities can also turn to the *federal funds market*. The federal funds market is a private market in which banks lend reserves to each other for less than 24 hours. The word *federal* does not mean it is a government market. It simply means this is an economy wide or national market. In this market, a bank short of reserves can borrow some reserves from another bank. Using the interbank loan market, Best National Bank can borrow reserves from Yazoo National and pay the federal funds rate. The **federal funds rate** is the interest rate one bank charges another for overnight loans of reserves. Reserves borrowed in the federal funds market have no effect on the money supply. This is because such borrowing simply moves reserves from one bank to another. In practice, the Fed keeps the discount rate close to the federal funds rate. Also, the federal funds rate is a key barometer of Fed policy reported in the media.

NET Bookmark

Access www.cengage.com/school/economics/personalfinance and click on the link for Chapter 14. Visit Economagic.com website. Select the Federal Funds Rate and record this rate for the past 20 quarters. Next scroll down to Bank Prime Loan, which indicates the prime interest rate (the interest rates banks charge their most credit-worthy customers) and record the prime rate over the last 20 quarters. What is the gap between the federal funds rate and the prime rate? Explain this gap. Is there a relationship between the change in the prime lending rate and the federal funds rate? Explain.

www.cengage.com/school/economics/personalfinance

PROFILE

Milton Friedman
Free Market Economist

AP Photo/Pool/Peter Knopp

Milton Friedman graduated from and spent most of his career teaching at the University of Chicago. Here he helped create free-market ideas called the "Chicago School of Economics." In 1976 Friedman received the Nobel Prize in economics. He explained that monetary policy has a strong impact on the economy. Friedman and Anna Schwartz, in their book *A Monetary History of the United States*, argued that the Great Depression was caused by the decline in the money supply. What should the Fed have done? Friedman and Schwartz argued that the Fed should have used open market operations to increase the money supply. Instead the Fed decreased the money supply. Thus, they concluded that the Fed was to blame for not pursuing an expansionary policy. This would have reduced the severity and duration of the contraction.

Friedman built his career on challenging almost every major economics doctrine. His critical belief was the economy works best when the government leaves it alone. Friedman's most popular books were *Capitalism and Freedom* (1962) and *Free to Choose* (1980). These books advocate free market solutions, such as school vouchers, income tax reform, and repeal of government regulations.

Concerning monetary policy, Friedman humorously once proposed replacing the Fed with an intelligent horse. Each New Year's Day, the horse would stand in front of Fed headquarters to answer monetary policy questions. Reporters would ask, "What is going to happen to the money supply this year?" The horse would tap its hoof four times, and the next day headlines would read "Fed to Once Again Increase the Money Supply Four Percent." Friedman favored a fixed rule for the Fed. The horse is a sarcastic way of rejecting Keynesian activist monetary policies of changing the money supply that in his opinion destabilize the economy. Instead, he believed the Fed should set a fixed growth rate for the money supply. He even argued that the Board of Governors of the Federal Reserve System should announce the growth rate for the money supply each year and must resign if the target is missed.

THINK CRITICALLY

By decreasing the money supply, what kind of monetary policy was the Fed following during the Great Depression?

yienkeat/Shutterstock.com

Changing the Reserve Requirement

The Fed can set reserve requirements by law for all banks. However, this is the least-used monetary policy tool. Recall that the *required reserve ratio* (RRR) is the percentage of deposits that the Fed requires a bank to hold on deposit with the Fed or in cash rather than being loaned. By changing the required reserve ratio, the Fed can change banks' excess reserves and therefore banks' lending abilities. This is potentially a powerful policy tool.

Suppose a bank has checkable deposits of $20 million and required reserves ratio is 10 percent. The bank would be required to keep $2 million on reserve with the Fed (0.10 × $20 million = $2 million). The bank now has $18 million to lend. If recession is the problem, the Fed will follow an easy-money policy. The Fed's board wants to make loans easier to obtain. If the required reserve ratio is lowered, banks must keep less in required reserves. This means they have more excess reserves to lend. More money in circulation boosts aggregate demand and economic recovery.

Now assume the Fed's concern is inflation. Following contractionary monetary policy, the Fed's target is to tighten credit. To make loans harder to obtain, the Fed can increase the required reserve ratio. When banks must keep more in required reserves, they have less excess reserves to lend. Less money supply decreases total spending. As a result of a decrease in aggregate demand, the price level falls.

Figure 14-5 presents a summary of the impact of monetary policy tools.

Monetary Policy	Monetary Policy Action	Mechanism	Change in the Money Supply
Expansionary	Open market operations purchase	Reserves increase	Increases
Contractionary	Open market operations sale	Reserves decrease	Decreases
Expansionary	Discount rate decreases	Borrowing reserves becomes cheaper	Increases
Contractionary	Discount rate increases	Borrowing reserves becomes costlier	Decreases
Expansionary	Required reserve ratio decreases	Money multiplier increases	Increases
Contractionary	Required reserve ratio increases	Money multiplier decreases	Decreases

Figure 14-5
Effect of Monetary Policy Tools on the Money Supply

CHECKPOINT

What authority does the president or members of Congress have over monetary policy?

FreeSoulProduction/Shutterstock.com

Math CONNECTION

Changes in Reserve Requirements

The amount of money the Federal Reserve requires a bank to keep on reserve can be calculated using the following formula.

Checkable deposits × Percent required = Required reserve

The MP National Bank has $45 million on deposit. Federal Reserve has changed the requirement from 10% to 12%. What is the change to the amount of money that must be on kept on reserve? Is more money or less money required?

SOLUTION

$45,000,000 × 0.10 = $4,500,000	Required reserve at 10%
$45,000,000 × 0.12 = $5,400,000	Required reserve at 12%
5,400,000 – 4,500,000 = 900,000	Additional amount on reserve

An additional $900,000 is required to be kept on reserve.

TRY IT

Find the difference in the amount of money of the required reserve.

	Checkable Deposits	Original Percent Required	Percent Required after Change	Difference in Amount of Required Reserve (more or less)
1.	$68 million	15%	10%	__?__
2.	$36 million	10%	15%	__?__
3.	$110 million	8%	11.5%	__?__

Denis Pepin/Shutterstock.com

LO 2-2 Monetary Policy Using the AD/AS Model

The AD/AS model was introduced in Lesson 13-1 to illustrate fiscal policy. Here this model is used to demonstrate expansionary and contractionary monetary policy. In Figure 14-6(a) suppose the economy is in recession at E_1. To encourage growth and reduce unemployment, the Fed can increase the money supply and decrease interest rates. Lower interest rates encourage consumers to borrow and spend more (*C*) and businesses to increase their investment spending (*I*). The result is a rightward shift from AD_1 to AD_2. Equilibrium changes from point E_1 to point E_2. This increase in aggregate demand causes two effects. The first effect is real GDP increases from Y_1 to Y_2 and employment rises. The second is the prices of goods and services measured by the CPI rise from P_1 to P_2.

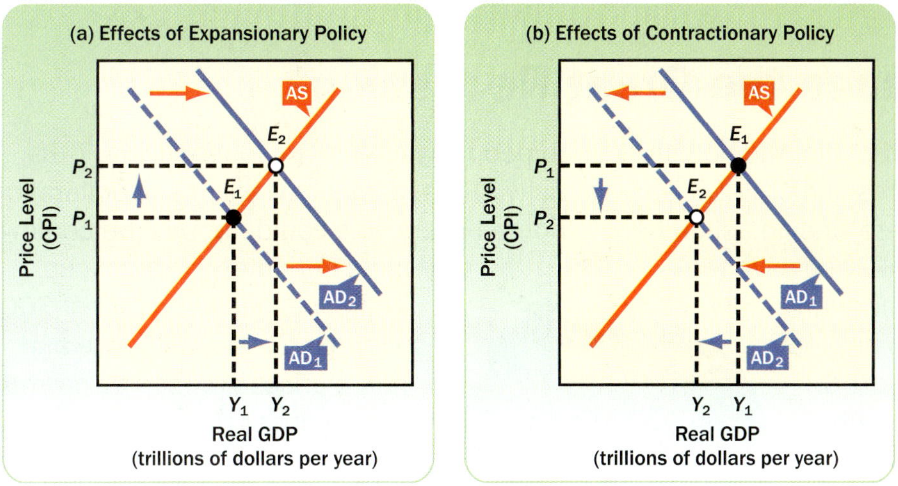

Figure 14-6

Impact of Monetary Policy

In Part (a), begin at equilibrium E_1 and assume the Fed follows expansionary monetary policy. An increase in the money supply and decrease in interest rates causes the aggregate demand curve AD_1 to increase to AD_2. At E_2, prices rise from P_1 to P_2, real GDP increases from Y_1 to Y_2, and employment increases.

In Part (b), start at equilibrium E_1 and assume the Fed conducts contractionary monetary policy. A decrease in the money supply and higher interest rates shifts the aggregate demand curve leftward from AD_1 to AD_2. The result at E_2 is the price level falls from P_1 to P_2, real GDP falls from Y_1 to Y_2, and employment falls.

Now assume prices are rising too fast, and the economy is at E_1, as shown in Figure 14-6(b). To achieve price stability, the Fed uses contractionary monetary policy. The goal in this case is to slow the growth rate for an "overheated" economy. The Fed can decrease the money supply and increase interest rates. This reduces aggregate demand (AD) because there is less total spending in the economy. The result is that AD_1 shifts leftward to AD_2. Equilibrium changes from point E_1 to point E_2. As a result, the price level falls from P_1 to P_2. Lower inflation, however, comes with a cost. Real GDP decreases from Y_1 to Y_2 and there are fewer jobs.

During the Great Recession in 2007, the Fed followed expansionary monetary policy. It used open market purchases to sharply increase the money supply. The Fed also decreased interest rates by pushing the federal funds rate to a historic low near zero percent. Moreover, the Fed reduced its reserve requirement. It also dramatically expanded its scope in response to the loss in confidence among lenders and panic sweeping financial markets that resulted in the flow of credit falling sharply. Using Depression-era emergency powers, the Fed took the radical step of becoming a "lender of last resort." It was the source of short-term loans for a wide range of institutions other than banks. For example, the Fed provided funds to bail out Fannie Mae (the Federal National Mortgage Association) and Freddie Mac (the Federal Home Mortgage Corporation). These agencies backed about half of the nation's mortgage loans. And the Fed provided loans for AIG, the huge insurance firm, because it was judged to be too large to fail.

When the Fed cuts interest rates, stock brokers react.

CHECKPOINT

If there is a recession or a problem with inflation, should fiscal policy and monetary policy be used?

Did the Fed Cause the Great Recession?

The story of the worst collapse of the housing market and the Great Recession of 2007 is filled with villains. And there was no action hero to sweep down from the sky and save the day. It was an Alice in Wonderland story with plenty of blame to go around: homeowners who bought a Trojan horse, rampant speculation, predatory lenders, slick Wall Street operators, greedy CEOs, lax regulators, political pressure, and debatable Fed policy.

The stage was set for the housing crisis by the Fed's response to the recession of 2001. The annual change in the money supply jumped sharply upward from –3.1 percent in 2000 to an 8.7 percent increase in 2001. And, as shown in the figure, the Fed decreased interest rates sharply after 2001. Then the Fed kept them historically low in order to boost aggregate demand and prevent another recession.

Next in 2004, Alan Greenspan, former Federal Reserve Chairman, addressed the Credit Union Association and said, "American consumers might benefit if lenders provided greater mortgage product alternatives to the traditional fixed rate mortgage." And adjustable rate mortgages (ARMs) became the loan of choice for subprime borrowers with poor credit scores. Mailboxes were stuffed with offers to borrow 100 percent or more of a home's value with zero money down. Television shows advertised that anyone could make it rich in real estate. Housing became a speculative game. Payments and "teaser" interest rates were held artificially low for the first few years of the loan. Then they would jump sharply upward. Forget worrying about not affording the home. Your income would not be checked following a "no document" lending practice. Some loans were made to people who were no longer living. Thus, using risky ARMs, banks lent billions of dollars to home buyers who could not pay the bank when the payments and interest rates rose.

Beginning in the summer of 2005, subprime foreclosures rose and home prices dropped as payments rose under these ARMs. Once the value of homes fell below the loan value, people could not refinance to get lower payments. When people walked away from their mortgages, Wall Street and foreign investors were stuck with bad loans to write off. As a result, lenders greatly tightened their lending standards to avoid further risky loans. This credit crunch made home financing difficult to obtain. The most serious financial crisis since the Great Depression led to the Great Recession of 2007.

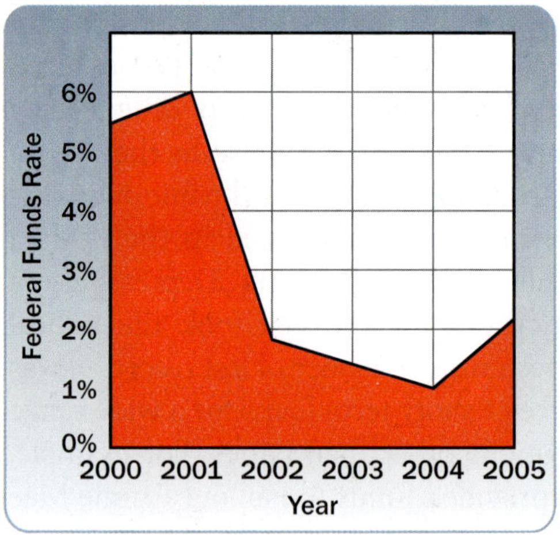

Think Critically

1. **Argue in support of the Fed's monetary policy between the 2001 recession and the Great Recession (2007–2009).**
2. **Criticize the Fed's monetary policy between the recession of 2001 and the Great Recession (2007–2009).**

14-2 Assessment

Key Concepts

LO 2-1 1. The interest rate one bank charges another for overnight loans of reserves is the __?__ rate.

LO 2-1 2. **TRUE OR FALSE** The Federal Reserve's use of changes in the money supply to achieve economic goals is called monetary policy.

LO 2-1 3. The buying and selling of government securities by the Federal Reserve System to affect the money supply is __?__ operations.

LO 2-1 4. **TRUE OR FALSE** Expansionary monetary policy is when the Federal Reserve decreases taxes to increase real GDP.

LO 2-1 5. The interest rate that the Federal Reserve System charges on loans of reserve to banks is the __?__ rate.

LO 2-1 6. **TRUE OR FALSE** Contractionary monetary policy occurs when the Federal Reserve decreases the money supply to decrease real GDP.

Think About It

LO 2-1 7. Why might business cycles make monetary policy difficult? Give an example of how a monetary policy might be badly timed.

LO 2-1 8. Briefly describe the effect on the money supply of the following monetary policies.
   a. The Fed purchases $20 million worth of U.S. Treasury bonds.
   b. The Fed increases the discount rate.
   c. The Fed decreases the discount rate.
   d. The Fed sells $40 million worth of U.S. Treasury bills.
   e. The Fed decreases the required reserve ratio.

LO 2-1 9. Identify and explain how each of the three basic tools of monetary policy could be used to adjust the money supply.

LO 2-2 10. Describe how an increase or decrease in the money supply would impact the economy.

Make Academic Connections

LO 2-1 11. **HISTORY** Research the change in the money supply during the Great Depression and compare it to the policy during the Great Recession.

Teamwork

LO 2-1 12. Work in four groups. As a group research one of the following monetary policy tools: open market operations, discount rate, or the reserve requirement. Another option for research is the federal funds rate. Present your group's report to the class on how the Federal Reserve System influenced the monetary policy tools during the Great Recession (2007–2009).

Unit 6 Project: The Role of Government

MONETARY POLICY List the functions of monetary policy (what the Fed does) in a one-page brochure. Explain the impact of those actions on the economy (such as expansionary or contractionary). Include a photo of the current Chairman of the Federal Reserve System and give a brief biography.

yienkeat/Shutterstock.com, Chad Baker/Ryan McVay/Photodisc/Getty Images

Chapter 14 Summary

14-1 FEDERAL RESERVE SYSTEM

1. The Federal Reserve System, known as "the Fed," controls the money supply in the United States. The Fed is the central bank. It provides services to banks as well as the government. It also regulates and supervises banks, and forms monetary policy.
2. The Federal Reserve System consists of 12 districts; each district reserve bank serves as central bank for its region. An additional 25 Federal Reserve branch banks are located throughout the country. At the head of the Fed is the Board of Governors, a seven-member group that supervises the banking system in the United States. They control the money supply which affects consumers directly. The Fed receives no funding from Congress, but is an independent, self-supporting entity.
3. The Fed's Open Market Committee sets goals for the Fed's purchase and sale of U.S. government securities. The buying and selling of securities serve to expand or contract the money supply and therefore the economy. This is done to control inflation (slow down the economy) or to fight unemployment (speed up the economy).
4. The Fed controls the money supply including currency and coins as well as checkable deposits. It also serves as a clearinghouse for checks written against banks around the country. The Fed supervises and regulates banks. The Fed helps to protect consumers as it makes and enforces policies in financial, credit, and mortgage markets. The Fed maintains government checking accounts and holds the nation's gold supply. When there is a need, the Fed loans money to banks.

14-2 MONETARY POLICY

5. Monetary policy is the Fed's actions to expand or contract the economy. To expand the economy, the Fed increases the money supply. With more money in circulation, credit becomes more available as the interest rate drops. This causes an increase in aggregate (total) demand. To contract the economy it does the opposite.
6. Open market operations is the primary tool used by the Fed to regulate the money supply. When the Fed buys government securities, it is an expansionary policy. More money is available to banks who can loan more money to businesses and consumers. Open market sales contract the economy because banks have less money to loan.
7. Changing the discount rate can expand or contract money supply and the economy. When the discount rate is lowered, banks are encouraged to borrow from the Fed so they can make loans at lower rates. This serves to increase spending.
8. The Fed can change the reserve requirement, or the share of deposits banks are required to keep on reserve (rather than be available to be loaned). As this requirement is raised, the economy will contract because less money is available for borrowing and spending.
9. Monetary policy affects aggregate demand and aggregate supply. By increasing money supply and decreasing interest rates, the Fed encourages consumer and business spending. By decreasing money supply and increasing interest rates, the Fed is able to slow the economy by reducing spending.

Chapter 14 Assessment

Vocabulary Review

Match each statement with the term that best defines it.

1. The government agency that insures customer deposits up to a limit if a bank fails
2. The seven-member board that supervises the banking system of the United States
3. The interest rate one bank charges another for overnight loans of reserves
4. A 12-member board of bankers selected from each Federal Reserve District to advise on business and financial issues
5. The interest rate the Fed charges on loans of reserves to banks
6. The Federal Reserve increases the money supply to increase real GDP
7. The twelve banking districts which are served by a Federal Reserve district bank
8. The Federal Reserve decreases the money supply to decrease real GDP
9. The buying and selling of government securities by the Federal Reserve System to affect the money supply
10. A Federal Reserve service that collects funds from a check writer's bank and transfers them to the recipient's bank
11. An independent bureau within the Federal Reserve that helps consumers make financial decisions
12. The Federal Reserve committee that directs the buying and selling of U.S. government securities
13. The Federal Reserve's use of changes in the money supply to achieve economic goals

Vocabulary

a. Board of Governors of the Federal Reserve System
b. Consumer Financial Protection Bureau (CFPB)
c. check clearing
d. contractionary monetary policy
e. discount rate
f. expansionary monetary policy
g. Federal Advisory council (FAC)
h. Federal Deposit Insurance Corporation (FDIC)
i. federal funds rate
j. Federal Open Market Committee (FOMC)
k. Federal Reserve Districts
l. monetary policy
m. open market operations

Review Your Knowledge

LO 1-1 **14.** Which of the following is *not* part of the Federal Reserve System?
   a. Council of Economic Advisors
   b. Board of Governors
   c. Federal Open Market Committee
   d. 12 Federal Reserve District Banks
   e. Federal Advisory Council

LO 1-1 **15.** The Fed's principal decision-making body, which directs buying and selling U.S. government securities, is the
   a. Federal Deposit Insurance Corporation
   b. District Board of Governors
   c. Federal Open Market Committee
   d. Reserve Requirement Regulation Conference

LO 1-2 **16.** Which of the following is *not* a function of the Federal Reserve System?
   a. To control the money supply
   b. To print new money
   c. To supervise and regulate banks
   d. To aid in the check clearing process
   e. To maintain and circulate currency

LO 1-2 **17.** The major protection against sudden mass attempt to withdraw cash from banks is the
   a. Federal Reserve
   b. Consumer Protection Act
   c. deposit insurance provided by the FDIC
   d. gold and silver backing the dollar

LO 2-2 **18.** The term *open market operations* refers to the
   a. loan-making activities of commercial banks.
   b. effect of expansionary monetary policy on interest rates.
   c. operation of competitive markets in the banking industry as the result of deregulation.
   d. buying and selling of government securities by the Federal Reserve.

LO 2-1 **19.** Which of the following is in charge of the buying and selling of government securities by the Fed?
   a. The President
   b. The Federal Open Market Committee
   c. The Congress
   d. None of the above

LO 2-1 **20.** If there is a recession, the Fed would most likely
   a. increase bank reserves by raising the discount rate
   b. increase bank reserves by buying government securities
   c. decrease bank reserves by raising the discount rate
   d. decrease bank reserves by selling government securities
   e. decrease bank reserves by lowering the legal reserve requirement

LO 2-1 **21.** The discount rate is the interest rate charged by
   a. major banks to their best customers
   b. banks for overnight loans to other banks
   c. the Fed on loans of reserves to banks
   d. banks for business loans of less than 24 hours

LO 2-1 **22.** The federal funds rate is the interest rate charged by
   a. banks for loans to other banks
   b. the Fed for overnight loans
   c. the Fed for borrowed reserves
   d. the federal government on loans to member banks

LO 2-1 **23.** Which of the following would cause the money supply in the United States to expand?
   a. a decrease in reserve requirements
   b. an increase in the discount rate
   c. the sale of U.S. government bonds by a Federal Reserve bank
   d. an increase in the world supply of gold

Digging Deeper with Economics e-Collection

When the Fed raises or lowers the discount rate, this is a part of monetary policy. It has an immediate impact on the economy, including individual consumers. For example, when the discount rate rises, so do credit card rates, mortgage loan rates, and bank loan rates. Access the Gale Economics e-Collection at **www.cengage.com/school/economics/personalfinance**. Research the changes in discount rates over the past twenty years. For each change, what was the Fed's reason for raising or lowering the rate? In what year was the rate changed multiple times, and why? In other years, the rate wasn't changed at all. Explain why.

Think About It

LO 2-1 **24.** Federal Reserve Banks do not serve consumers directly (you cannot open an account). But consumers may benefit because of actions taken by the Fed. Explain one specific example of how consumers have benefited from actions of the Fed.

LO 2-1 **25.** The Fed receives no funding from the U.S. Congress, but its profits are returned to the U.S. Treasury. Explain how this contributes to the Fed's ability to maintain its independence from the U.S. Congress and the political system.

LO 2-2 **26.** Increasing the money supply can lead to an increase in real GDP and reduce the unemployment rate. This type of monetary policy has an almost immediate effect on the economy while fiscal policy with the same objective (increasing GDP) can take much longer. Why is this the case?

LO 2-2 **27.** Sometimes the economy is growing too fast and interest rates are rising rapidly. How can an economy grow "too fast"? Isn't economic growth the objective of monetary and fiscal policy?

Make Academic Connections

LO 1-1 **28. HISTORY** Fort Knox, Kentucky, is a place where many people believe the United States stores gold. Research so that you can explain the significance and historical context of Fort Knox.

LO 1-2 **29. TECHNOLOGY** The Federal Reserve Bank of Chicago publishes a website that contains links of interest to consumers. Visit the site at http://www.chicagofed.org and click on publications, events, or education. Describe the resources available to you (as a consumer) through this site.

LO 2-2 **30. COMMUNICATIONS** Explain how consumers can benefit when the Fed initiates contractionary and expansionary monetary policy. Give specific examples such as consumers who save money or consumers who must borrow money.

Extend Your Learning

LO 2-2 **31.** Copy and complete the tree map with the correct monetary policy tool required to achieve the indicated effect.

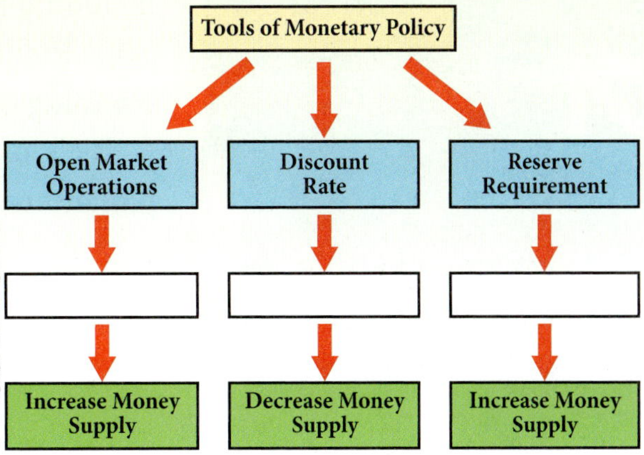

UNIT 7

Global Trade and Investing

Chapter 15 is devoted to global topics. This chapter explains the importance of free trade and exchange rates. Here you will find a feature on the history of the gold standard. In Chapter 16 you will evaluate renting versus buying, including the costs and the benefits and the steps involved in home ownership. You will also explore leasing versus buying a car. The use of credit, types of loans, and obligations of debt are covered, along with risk management and the need for insurance. Finally, you will discover the costs and benefits of buying and disposing of property, along with restrictions on the use of property. In Chapter 17 you will learn about investing. Stocks and bonds are long-term choices, some of which are more high-risk than others. Both of these choices are a part of most people's retirement plans. You will look at other investment options, including risks and rewards, from metals and gems to futures. The unit ends with retirement planning concepts, options, and risks, along with a look at the costs and benefits of philanthropy.

UNIT 7 Project

Building a Global Future

Project Objectives

PARTNERSHIP FOR 21ST CENTURY SKILLS

- Explain a point of view on an economic issue.
- Use standard grammar, spelling, sentence structure, and punctuation.
- Transfer information from one medium to another including written to visual and statistical to written or visual using computer software as appropriate.
- Create written, oral, and visual presentations of social studies information.
- Analyze economic information by sequencing, categorizing, identifying cause-and-effect relationships, comparing, contrasting, finding the main idea, summarizing, making generalizations and predictions, and drawing inferences and conclusions.

chapter 15

International Trade, p. 430

The U.S. Bureau of Economic Analysis presents economic accounts and information about international trade. Visit this website.

Free Trade, p. 438

Prepare a chart that lists the advantages and disadvantages of free trade.

chapter 16

Renting vs. Buying, p. 466

Prepare a chart comparing and contrasting the pro's and con's of renting and buying/leasing (a home or a car).

Risk Management, p. 474

Risk management is more than buying insurance. Prepare a visual display or presentation that depicts the various steps you would go through.

chapter 17

The Stock Market, p. 492

Choose five stocks from the NYSE and/or the NASDAQ. Track their progress for two weeks.

Philanthropy, p. 513

Assume you have $1 million to donate to charities. Determine how much you would give to each organization.

Project Wrap-up

Create an advertisement, brochure, newsletter, or flyer that describes how to invest in the stock market, the bond market, mutual funds, and other investments. Explain the risks and benefits of investment. Save a copy of all work to include in your portfolio. Prepare a cover page and table of contents for your portfolio. Include a brief description of each unit's work. Describe the major highlights of this course.

Odua Images/Shutterstock.com

yienkeat/Shutterstock.com

donvictorio@o2.pl/Shutterstock.com

chapter 15

International Trade

15-1 Why Nations Trade

15-2 Barriers to Free Trade

15-3 Measures of Trade

yienkeat/Shutterstock.com

MARKETS *in Action!*

Bono
Irish Rock Star

According to *Time* magazine, the rock star Bono is also Africa's biggest advocate. U2's singer believes that pop stars have an important role in the world and that role isn't just delivering music.

At a recent meeting of the World Economic Forum, Bono worked with Bill Gates (Microsoft) to discuss the importance of taking action now to help save a continent. According to Bono and others, helping Africa save itself is in fact in America's best interests.

Bono is the founder and spokesperson for DATA, a non-profit, debt-relief advocacy group whose mission is to bring true financial aid to African nations. These industries and people can do little to compete in world markets without the help of some form of protection. Africa needs more than gifts of money and free products. According to Bono, African businesses need to be protected from other countries as well as corrupt African governments that cripple their ability to be productive world citizens. This means, among other things, that African businesses need to have infant industry protection from more advanced businesses in developed nations.

Bono believes that Africa has a great future. According to *The Observer* (February 20, 2011), the continent stands on the brink of becoming an economic powerhouse. There's great potential because there's entrepreneurial talent, vast resources, and untapped opportunity.

Bono and others believe that many U.S. companies are taking massive quantities of resources (from minerals to diamonds) out of Africa. He argues that this flow needs to be disclosed, both what is leaving and how much is being paid to African governments that are enriched. It's more than a job for the U.S. It's more than providing money. It's about protection: protection that would give African businesses and workers a chance to become competitive over time. According to Bono, Africa's citizens should benefit from their continent's resources as much as, if not more than, those who take these resources and resell them for enormous gains.

U2 performs a concert in the Amsterdam Arena in Amsterdam, Netherlands.

J van der Wolf/Shutterstock.com

Think Critically

1. What types of economic conditions currently exist in many African nations?
2. How can protecting resources help Africa develop its own industries and become independent exporting countries?
3. How can helping Africa become self-sustaining be beneficial to America both now and in the future?

yienkeat/Shutterstock.com

15-1 Why Nations Trade

Learning Objectives

LO 1-1 **Understand** why nations specialize in trade.

LO 1-2 **Explain** the concepts of comparative advantage and absolute advantage.

Vocabulary

export, p. 425
import, p. 425
absolute advantage, p. 426
comparative advantage, p. 426

© Aleksandar Vrzalski/iStockphoto.com

REAL-WORLD FOCUS

"My uncle just bought a new car," Jonathon told his friend. "He said it was sold by an American car company, but that 80% of the parts came from Japan and the car was assembled in Mexico. So my question is, 'Is this car an import?'"

WORK AS A TEAM When you buy a product, do you check the label to see where it was made or where its parts came from? Why do some countries make and sell products while other countries import them?

Keysurfing/Shutterstock.com

Countries that grow pineapple include Brazil, the Philippines, Thailand, and the United States (in Hawaii).

DO YOU THINK the United States exports more pineapple than it imports?

yienkeat/Shutterstock.com

LO 1-1 Why Nations Trade

Just imagine your life without world trade. For openers, you could not eat bananas from Honduras or chocolate from Nigerian cocoa beans. Nor could you sip Colombian coffee, or Indian tea. Also forget about driving a Japanese motorcycle or automobile. In addition, you could not buy Italian shoes, most televisions, and personal computers. The list goes on and on, so the point is clear. World trade is important because it gives consumers more power by expanding their choices. Today, the speed of transportation and communication means producers must compete on a global basis.

simmax/Shutterstock.com

Why doesn't the United States become self-sufficient and grow its own bananas?

The United States leads the world in imports while also being one of the top exporters in the world. Figure 15-1 reveals which regions are major trading partners with the United States (exports plus imports). An **export** is a good produced in one country and sold to another country. An **import** is a good produced in one country and purchased by another country. Thus, all exports of one nation are also imports of other nations. Leading the list of nations the United States trades with is Canada, the largest trading partner, followed by China, Mexico, and Japan. Leading U.S. exports are chemicals, machinery, agricultural products, computers, and automobiles. Major imports include petroleum, cars, trucks, clothing, and electronics. Why does a nation bother to trade with the rest of the world? Does it seem strange for the United States to import goods it could produce for itself? Indeed, why doesn't the United States become self-sufficient? To accomplish this the U.S. would need to grow all its own food, including bananas, sugar, and coffee. Should the U.S. make all its own cars, and prohibit sales of all foreign goods?

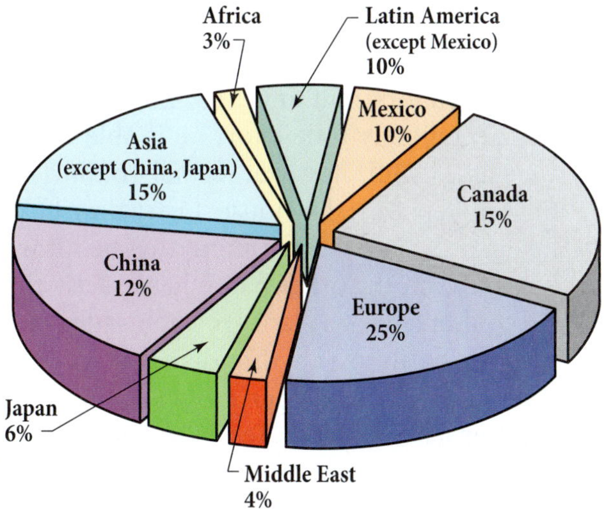

© Cengage Learning 2013

Figure 15-1

U.S. Trading Partners, 2010

In 2010, Canada, China, Mexico, and Japan accounted for 43 percent of U.S. trade (exports plus imports).

CHECKPOINT

What nations are major trading partners of the United States?

Imports and Exports

Businesses of all sizes can import and export goods. Some businesses import goods that are used in manufacturing, while others import goods to sell directly in the retail market. Other businesses export goods they manufactured, which may be sold directly to consumers in another country or may be used in foreign manufacturing. Import and export business is important to local economies.

Investigate Your Local ECONOMY

Try it Out

Research and find an example of a good or service produced in your local economy that is exported and a good or service that is imported. Investigate the producer to find what countries are involved in the trade.

LO 1-2 Absolute and Comparative Advantage

How can a country benefit by specializing in the production of more wheat than it needs and exporting the surplus? At the same time, why would this country produce no steel that it needs creating a shortage that must be filled by importing steel? The answer to why nations trade can be found in the theories of absolute and comparative advantage. **Absolute advantage** is the ability of a country to produce more of a good using the same or fewer resources as another country. **Comparative advantage** is the ability of a country to produce a good at a lower opportunity cost than another country.

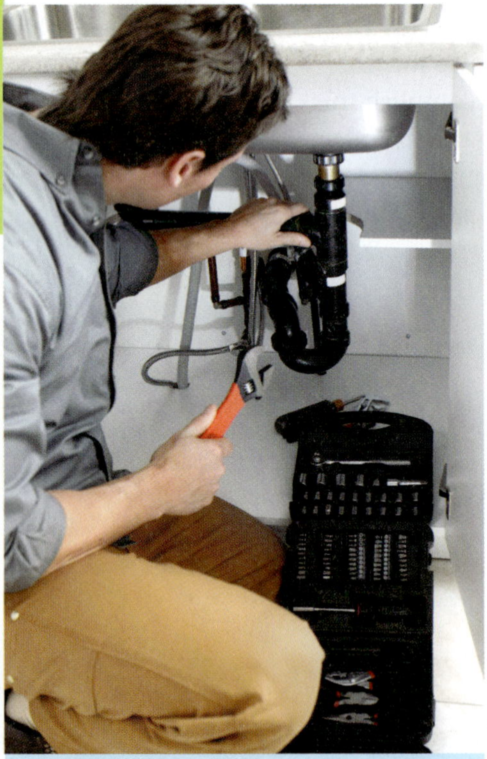
Kurhan/Shutterstock.com

Having a leaky sink fixed in trade for fresh vegetables is an example of trading goods and services that benefits both parties involved.

Perhaps a simple example will clarify the difference between absolute advantage and comparative advantage. Imagine two neighbors, Bill and Ted. Bill is a really good gardener. With seemingly little effort he is able to grow prize-winning vegetables. Bill, however, is "all thumbs" when it comes to making repairs to his house. Every time he picks up a hammer he ends up with a sore thumb that he hit when he missed the nail. Ted, on the other hand, has exactly the opposite talents. He couldn't make a plant grow if his life depended on it, but he is able to fix almost anything as good as new and in record time. Both Bill and Ted have an *absolute advantage*. Bill is absolutely a better gardener and Ted is absolutely a better handy man. Bill therefore should spend his time growing vegetables and Ted should spend his time fixing broken things. Then, by trading the goods or services they produce best, both Bill and Ted will be better off. They will be using their resources (time and effort) in the most productive ways. What is true of Bill and Ted is also true of countries. According to the theory of absolute advantage countries should specialize in producing the products they make more efficiently than other countries and trade with other nations for products that they do not make as well.

What would happen if Bill were more efficient at both gardening and fixing things? Would there be any reason for Bill and Ted specializing and trading their production? According to the theory of *comparative advantage* the answer is a definite "yes!" Imagine that Bill is very efficient at gardening and also good at home repair. Ted is an awful gardener but is a pretty good handy man, although he is not quite as good as Bill. Bill should specialize in gardening and Ted should spend his time making home repairs because this is the most productive use of their time and effort.

Ivonne Wierink/Shutterstock.com

This backyard garden will produce more lettuce than one family needs. There will be a surplus that can be traded.

Based on comparative advantage, specialization and trade between Bill and Ted can be viewed from an opportunity costs perspective. When Ted specializes in making repairs he gives up almost no production of vegetables so his *opportunity cost* of using his time to make repairs is very low. Bill does give up production of making repairs when he specializes in growing vegetables. But by specializing and trading he is able to increase the total amount of vegetables and home repairs he is able to enjoy. All Bill has to do is trade some of his surplus of vegetables to Ted who makes necessary repairs to both of their homes. As a result, Ted and Bill's specialization and trade increases their total production and benefits them both.

International Trade and Comparative Advantage

Consider an example that demonstrates the importance of comparative advantage in international trade. Imagine a world in which there are only two nations, Zuba and Econa. These countries are *self-sufficient* and produce only two products, steel and wheat. They do not trade. Each nation uses its resources to produce steel and wheat for its own consumption alone. As shown in Figure 15-2, Zuba manufactures 20 tons of steel using a portion of its resources and grows 60 bushels of wheat from the other portion. Econa is unable to produce either steel or wheat as efficiently as Zuba. Using part of its resources, it only produces 10 tons of steel and 30 bushels of wheat from the other part. Since Zuba has an absolute advantage in production of both products, does Zuba benefit from trade? The answer is "*Yes!*" based on comparative advantage.

To determine specialization, each country must consider its production possibilities. Suppose Econa's production possibilities are either to shift all its resources to produce 40 tons of steel or use 100 percent of its resources to produce 40 bushels of wheat. This means the opportunity cost of producing

40 tons of steel is 40 bushels of wheat or 1 bushel of wheat sacrificed for each ton of steel produced. Conversely, to produce 40 bushels of wheat would result in an opportunity cost of 40 tons of steel not produced or 1 ton of steel given up for each bushel of wheat.

Now assume Zuba's production possibilties are to use all its resources to produce 50 tons of steel or 100 bushels of wheat. If Zuba specializes in wheat, the opportunity cost of producing one bushel of wheat is ½ ton of steel. Zuba has a comparative advantage in wheat because Econa's opportunity cost is higher at 1 ton of steel per bushel of wheat. Consequently, Zuba will specialize in 100 bushels of wheat production.

What is the opportunity cost if Zuba specializes in steel and produces 50 tons of steel? The opportunity cost is 100 bushels of wheat or 2 bushels of wheat per ton of steel. In this case, Econa has the comparative advantage with a lower opportunity cost of 1 bushel of wheat per ton of steel. Econa therefore specializes in 40 tons of steel production.

Figure 15-2 summarizes the benefits of trade based on comparative advantage. Compare being self-sufficient to specialization with trade. Assume Econa trades 20 of its 40 tons of steel produced to Zuba for 30 bushels of its 100 bushels of wheat produced. Total production of steel increases from 30 to 40 tons and wheat rises from 90 to 100 bushels. Zuba has 10 bushels more wheat to consume, and Econa also benefits. Econa ends up with 10 more tons of steel to consume.

Figure 15-2

The Benefits of Trade

Without trade Zuba and Econa can be self-sufficient and produce a total of 30 tons of steel and 90 bushels of wheat. If Zuba specializes, it can produce either 50 tons of steel or 100 tons of wheat. If Econa specializes, it can produce either 40 tons of steel or 40 tons of wheat. Based on specialization and trade, both countries benefit because total production of steel and wheat increase.

	Steel Production (tons per day)	Wheat Production (bushels per day)
Self-Sufficient		
Zuba	20	60
Econa	10	30
Total Production	30	90
Specialization without Trade		
Zuba	50 – all resources	0 – no resources
	0 – no resources	✓100 – all resources
Econa	✓40 – all resources	0 – no resources
	0 – no resources	40 – all resources
Specialization with Trade		
Zuba	20 – import from Econa	70 – of 100 produced
Econa	20 – of 40 produced	30 – import from Zuba
Total Production	40	100

✓Specialization choice based on comparative advantage.

CHECKPOINT

How are nations able to increase the quantity of goods and services from which they may choose by following the theories of absolute and comparative advantage?

PROFILE

David Ricardo
British Economist

© Classic Image/Alamy

David Ricardo (1772–1823) was born in London, England and was the third of 17 children of a Jewish family. His father was a successful stockholder, and Ricardo joined him at the age of 14. At age 21, he became a Unitarian and married a Quaker. His father disowned him, and his mother never spoke to him again. Without family support, he started his own stockbroker business dealing with government securities and became quite successful. During the Battle of Waterloo, for example, he speculated against a French victory and invested heavenly in British securities. At age 42, he retired with a huge fortune and became a country gentleman on a large estate. In 1819, Ricardo was elected to the House of Commons where he served until his death. He supported a tax on capital to pay off the national debt, currency reform, removal of trade barriers protecting British wheat, and military reform.

While on vacation, Ricardo became interested in economics in 1799 after a chance reading of Adam Smith's *The Wealth of Nations.* Ten years later his first writings on economics were published. Ricardo became one of the most influential of the classical economists who followed Adam Smith. His work in economics laid the foundation for many developments in the field of economics. Those who favor and those who oppose free enterprise often draw on Ricardo's theories. Ricardo's approach was to formulate a simple abstract model used for public policy conclusions. He had a rare ability to solve complex economic problems without any of the sophisticated mathematical tools used today.

Ricardo's major work was *Principles of Political Economy and Taxation* published in 1817. This work developed the principle of comparative advantage. This theory is the cornerstone of free trade. Ricardo opposed Britain's protectionist Corn Laws, which restricted imports of wheat. Instead Ricardo argued for free trade based on comparative costs, today called "comparative advantage." He used an example that if Portugal makes two products more efficiently than England, then both Portugal and England would benefit from specialization and trade. This idea is today the main basis for most economists' belief in free trade.

THINK CRITICALLY

Does the theory of comparative advantage apply to individuals as well as nations? Explain.

yienkeat/Shutterstock.com

15-1 Assessment

Key Concepts

LO 1-1 1. A good produced in country A and purchased by country B is an __?__ to country A.

LO 1-2 2. **TRUE OR FALSE** Absolute advantage is the ability of a country to produce more of a good using the same or fewer resources than another country.

LO 1-2 3. The ability of a country to produce a good at a lower opportunity cost than another country is an example of __?__.

LO 1-1 4. A good produced in country A and sold to country B is an __?__ to country B.

Think About It

LO 1-2 5. Consider this statement: "The principles of specialization and trade according to comparative advantage among nations also apply to states in the United States." Do you agree or disagree? Explain.

LO 1-2 6. Bill can paint either two walls or one window frame in one hour. In the same time, Frank can paint either three walls or two window frames. To minimize the time spent painting, who should specialize in painting walls, and who should specialize in painting window frames?

LO 1-2 7. How do nations that specialize and trade benefit?

LO 1-2 8. Define and provide an example for each of the theories of absolute and comparative advantage.

Make Academic Connections

LO 1-2 9. **MATH** The countries of Alpha and Beta produce diamonds and pearls. The table shows two possible production possibilities in tons per year. Using the data in the table, answer the following questions.

Production Possibilities	Alpha		Beta	
	Diamonds	Pearls	Diamonds	Pearls
A	150	0	90	0
B	100	25	60	60

a. What is the opportunity cost of diamonds for each country?
b. In which good does Alpha have a comparative advantage?

Teamwork

LO 1-1 10. Work in five groups. Identify five goods that are imported to the United States. Consider an advantage to the United States from each traded item. Present the list of goods and advantages to the class.

Unit 7 Project: Building a Global Future

INTERNATIONAL TRADE The U.S. Bureau of Economic Analysis presents economic accounts and information about international trade, including balance of payments, trade in goods and services, international investing, and other related data. Visit this website. Read the information about the current position of U.S. international trade. Prepare charts or diagrams to explain balance of payments, the U.S. trade deficit, and how international trade has changed over time.

yienkeat/Shutterstock.com, Chad Baker/Ryan McVay/Photodisc/Getty Images

15-2 Barriers to Free Trade

Learning Objectives

LO 2-1 Identify different types of trade barriers.

LO 2-2 Understand arguments for and against protectionism.

Vocabulary

free trade, p. 432
protectionism, p. 432
embargo, p. 432
tariff, p. 432
World Trade Organization (WTO), p. 433
quota, p. 434

© Aleksandar Vrzalski/ iStockphoto.com

REAL-WORLD FOCUS

Erica works part-time at an import/export store in the inner city. "The goods we import from other countries are often very unique and unavailable anywhere else in the world. They are also very expensive and supplies are low," she told her friend. "Many customers would buy more if they could afford to."

WORK AS A TEAM Why do nations seek to prevent the import of goods from other nations? How are consumers and businesses affected by these limits? What are the long-term effects of these actions?

It is common to find duty-free shopping at international airports. Many tourists believe that they can save money by shopping duty free.

DO YOU THINK duty-free shopping means that you do not pay taxes or tariffs on the items purchased?

Brendan Howard/Shutterstock.com

yienkeat/Shutterstock.com

LO 2-1 Free Trade Versus Protectionism

In theory, global trade should be based on comparative advantage and free trade. **Free trade** is the flow of goods between countries without restrictions or special taxes. In practice, despite the advice of economists, every nation protects its own domestic producers to some degree from foreign competition. Behind these barriers to trade are special interest groups whose jobs and incomes are threatened. They clamor to the government for protectionism. **Protectionism** is the government's use of trade barriers to protect domestic producers. The following is a discussion of trade barriers.

EvrenKalinbacak/Shutterstock.com

Most goods imported and exported around the world travel on container ships.

Embargo

Embargoes are the strongest limit on trade. An **embargo** is a law that bars trade with another country. For example, the United States and other nations in the world imposed an arms embargo on Iraq in response to its invasion of Kuwait in 1990. The United States also maintains embargoes against Iran, Cuba, and North Korea.

Tariff

Tariffs are the most popular and visible measures used to discourage trade. A **tariff** is a tax on an import. Tariffs are also called *customs duties*. Suppose the United States imposes a tariff of 2.9 percent on autos. If a foreign car costs \$40,000, the amount of the tariff equals \$1,160 (\$40,000 × 0.029), and the U.S. price, including the tariff, is \$41,160. The current U.S. tariff code specifies tariffs on nearly 70 percent of U.S. imports. The average U.S. tariff is less than 5 percent, but individual tariffs vary widely. Tariffs are imposed to reduce imports by raising import prices and to generate revenues for the U.S. Treasury. Figure 15-3 shows the trend of the average tariff rate since 1930.

Figure 15-3

The United States Average Tariff Rate, 1930–2010

Under the Smoot-Hawley Act of 1930, the average tariff rate peaked at 20 percent. Since the GATT in 1947 and other trade agreements, tariffs have declined to less than 5 percent.

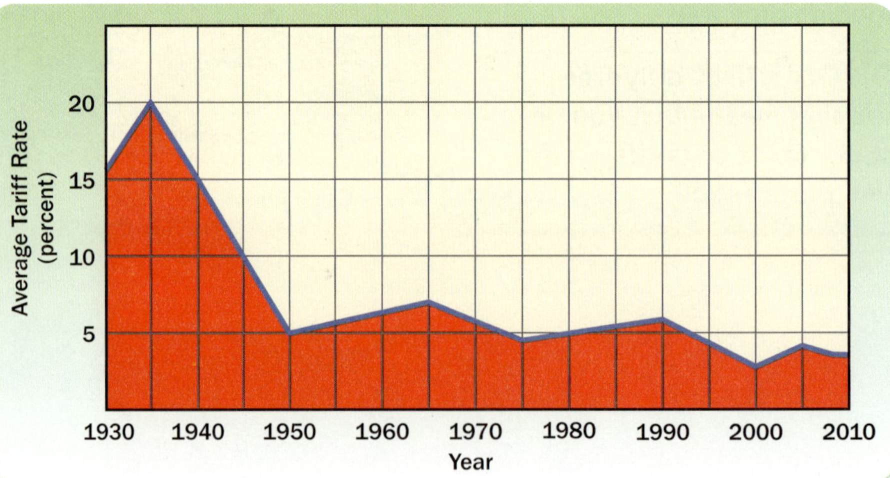

FreeSoulProduction/Shutterstock.com

Math CONNECTION

Tariffs

Tariff rates are usually a percentage of the declared value of an item. A tariff tax is similar to a sales tax, but tariff rates are different for all products. The rates are not even consistent for one type of item. For example, tariff rates on imported shoes vary from zero percent to 67 percent of the declared values. Herman owns a shoe store that sells all types of shoes. The most popular imported athletic shoe sold in his store has a declared value of $12. He has to pay a tariff of 37% on each pair of these shoes. What is the cost to Herman for the $12 athletic shoes?

SOLUTION

The total price of the shoes is 100% of the cost of the shoe plus 37% of the cost for the tariff tax. To find the price of the shoes including the tariff tax, multiply by 1.37.

$12 × 1.37 = $16.44   100% + 37% = 137% or 1.37

Herman has to pay $16.44 for the pair of shoes that has a value of $12.

TRY IT

Find the price Herman must pay for each pair of shoes, including the tariff tax.

1. Canvas gym shoes with a declared value of $3, a tariff rate of 67%
2. Leather flats with a declared value of $20, a tariff rate of 5%
3. Hiking boots with a declared value of $54, a tariff rate of 11%

mary416/Shutterstock.com

The headquarters for the World Trade Organization is in Geneva.

During the worldwide depression of the 1930s, when one nation raised its tariffs to protect its industries, other nations retaliated by raising their tariffs. Under the Smoot-Hawley tariffs of the 1930s, the average tariff in the United States reached a peak of 20 percent. Durable imports, which were one-third of imports, were subject to an extreme tariff rate of 60 percent. In 1947, most of the world's industrialized nations agreed to end the tariff wars by signing the *General Agreement on Tariffs and Trade* (GATT). Since then, GATT nations have met periodically to negotiate lower tariff rates. GATT agreements have significantly reduced tariffs over the years among member nations. In 1995, the Geneva-based **World Trade Organization (WTO)** was created to enforce rulings on global trade disputes. The WTO has 150 members and a standing appellate body to make final decisions regarding disputes between WTO members.

Quota

Another way to limit foreign competition is to impose a quota. A **quota** is a limit on the quantity of a good that can be imported in a given time period. For example, the United States may allow 10 million tons of sugar to be imported over a one year period. Once this quantity is reached, no more sugar can be imported for the year. About 12 percent of U.S. imports are subject to import quotas. Examples include import quotas on sugar, dairy products, textiles, steel, and even ice cream. Quotas can limit imports from all foreign suppliers or from specific countries. Critics argue that, like other barriers to trade, quotas invite nations to retaliate with their own measures to restrict trade. And consumers are harmed by higher prices because of the lack of competition from lower-priced imports.

CHECKPOINT

What advantage might a government gain from using a tariff rather than a quota to restrict imports?

LO 2-2 Arguments For and Against Protection

Free trade provides consumers with lower prices and larger quantities of goods from which to choose. Removing import barriers might save each family a few hundred dollars a year. The problem, however, is that imports could cost some workers their jobs and thousands of dollars per year from lost income. Thus, it is not surprising that, in spite of the greater total benefits from free trade to consumers, trade barriers exist. The reason is primarily because workers and owners from import competing firms have more at stake than consumers or are better able to influence the government to create trade barriers than the public at large. So these special interest groups lobby Washington for protection. The following are some of the most popular arguments for protection. These arguments have strong political or emotional appeal, but weak support from economists.

Lissandra/Shutterstock.com

Many special interest lobby groups spend a great deal of time in Washington, D.C. trying to influence senators and representatives.

Infant Industry Argument

As the name suggests, the *infant industry argument* is that a new domestic industry needs protection because it is not yet ready to compete with older, more established foreign competitors. An infant industry is in a formative stage. It must bear high start up costs to train an entire workforce, develop new technology, and establish marketing channels. Economists ask where one draws the arbitrary line between an "infant" and a "grown-up" industry. Once protection is granted, the new industry may lack the incentive to become competitive. Once an industry is given protection, it is difficult politically to take it away.

ETHICS in Action!

Is It Better to Vacation in America?

For many years it was against the law for Americans to take vacations in Cuba. There was, in effect, an embargo on American travel to that communist island nation. This travel restriction was designed to place economic pressure on the government of Cuba because it followed many policies that the U.S. government disapproved of. Although travel to Cuba was illegal for Americans, it was not difficult to accomplish. All you had to do was to travel first to a country, such as Canada, that did not have a similar travel ban, and leave for Cuba from there. In this way thousands of Americans visited Cuba every year even when it was against the law. The money they spent in Cuba helped the Cuban government gather U.S. dollars that it could use to buy needed imports from other nations although it could not legally purchase goods or services from businesses in the United States.

AYakovlev/iStockphoto.com

Havana, Cuba is one location that Americans may want to visit.

In 2011, the Obama administration eased travel restrictions on Cuba. It became possible for Americans to visit Cuba by leaving from the United States from a limited number of cities and on specific approved airlines. Although it became legal for Americans to visit Cuba some people believe it is unethical. They argue that the dollars Americans spend in Cuba help extend the life of a communist government that the Cuban people and the world would be better off without.

Think Critically

1. **Do you believe that travel to Cuba is unethical even though it is legal? Explain your answer.**
2. **Many Americans who have relatives living in Cuba send them regular gifts of money and products to make their lives easier. Do you believe Americans should be allowed to do this? Explain your answer.**

National Security Argument

Another common argument is that defense-related industries must be protected to ensure national security. By protecting critical defense industries, a nation will not be dependent on foreign countries for the essential defense related goods it needs in wartime. The *national defense argument* has been used to protect a long list of industries. These include petrochemicals, munitions, steel, and rubber. This argument gained validity during the War of 1812. Great Britain, the main trading partner of the United States, became an enemy that blockaded the U.S. coast. Today, this argument makes less sense for the United States. The government stockpiles missiles, sophisticated electronics, petroleum, and most goods needed in wartime. Food production is a similar argument. Some argue that because food typically takes one year to grow, a certain percentage of food consumed in the U.S. should be produced in the U.S. for national security reasons.

Protecting Jobs Argument

The *protecting jobs argument* suggests that restricting imports increases domestic jobs in protected industries. According to this protectionist argument, the sale of an imported good comes at the expense of a domestically produced good. Lower domestic output therefore leads to higher domestic unemployment than would otherwise be the case.

It is true that protectionism can increase output and save jobs in some industries at home. This argument ignores the higher prices paid by consumers because protectionism reduces competition between domestic goods and imported goods. In addition, there are employment reduction effects to consider. For example, suppose a strict quota is imposed on imported steel. Reduced foreign competition allows U.S. steelmakers to charge higher prices for their steel. As a result, prices rise and sales fall for cars and other products using steel. The result is that production and employment fall in these industries. Thus, the import quota on steel may save jobs in the steel industry. But this is achieved at the expense of other jobs that are lost in steel consuming industries.

Cheap Foreign Labor Argument

Another often heard popular claim is the *cheap labor argument*. It goes something like this: "How can the United States compete with such unfair competition? Labor costs $20 an hour in the United States, and firms in many developing countries pay only $1 an hour. Without protection against outsourcing jobs, U.S. wages will be driven down, and the standard of living will fall."

A major flaw in this argument is that it neglects the reason for the difference in the wage rates between countries. The reason is the difference in productivity. A U.S. worker has more education, training, capital, and access to advanced technology. Therefore, U.S. workers produce more output per hour than workers in many other countries. It follows that U.S. workers will earn higher wages without a competitive disadvantage. Suppose textile workers in the United States are paid $10 per hour. If a U.S. worker takes 1 hour to produce a rug, the labor cost per rug is $10. Now suppose a worker in India

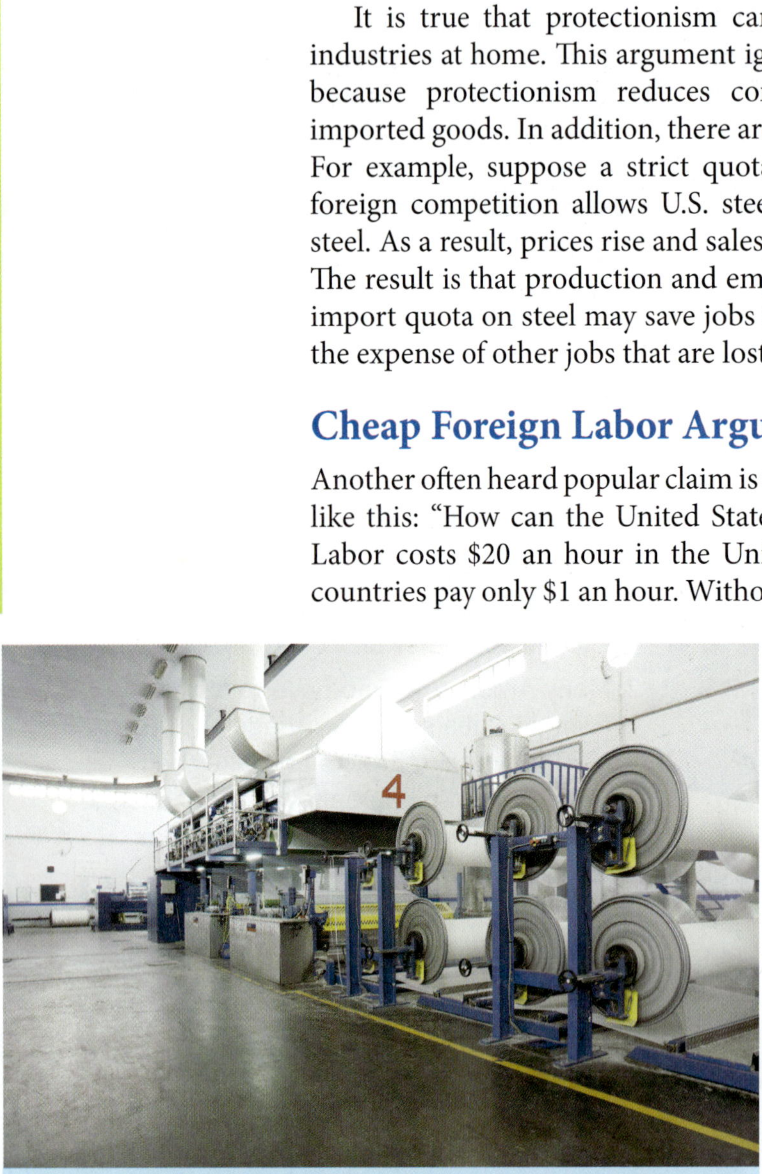

Rehan Qureshi/Shutterstock.com

In the United States, yarn sizing machines are used in textile weaving mills. Such capital increases output per hour and worker earnings.

earns $1 per hour, but requires 20 hours to produce a rug on a handloom. In this case, the labor cost per rug is $20. Although the wage rate is 10 times higher in the United States, U.S. productivity is 20 times higher. This is because a U.S. worker can produce 20 rugs in 20 hours, while the worker in India produces only 1 rug in the same amount of time.

CHECKPOINT

It can be argued that protectionism saves domestic jobs, but at what cost?

Global View

World Trade Slips on Banana Peel

Growing bananas for European markets was a multibillion-dollar bright spot for Latin America's struggling economies. In fact, about half of this region's banana exports traditionally were sold to Europe. Then, in 1993, the European Union (EU) adopted a package of quotas and tariffs aimed at cutting Europe's banana imports from Latin America. The purpose of these restrictions was to give trade preference to 66 banana-growing former colonies of European nations in Africa, the Caribbean, and the Pacific. Ignored was the fact that growers in Latin America grow higher-quality bananas at half the cost of EU-favored growers. This is a result of their low labor costs and flat tropical land near port cities.

In 1999, the World Trade Organization (WTO) ruled that the EU was discriminating in favor of European companies importing the fruit. The WTO imposed $191.4 million per year in punitive tariffs on European goods. This was the first time in the four years the WTO had been in existence that such retaliation had been approved. When the EU failed to comply with the WTO findings, the United States enforced its WTO rights by imposing increased duties on EU imports. The effect of the sanctions was to double the wholesale prices of these imports.

In 2001, it appeared that the banana dispute might be resolved. The EU agreed to increase market access for U.S. banana distributors. American companies, including Chiquita Brands International and Dole Food Company, grow most of their bananas in Latin America. The United States lifted its retaliatory duties on EU products. But the banana story just kept "slipping along." European Union anti-fraud officials say that illegal banana trafficking was proving more lucrative than ever. Italian banana importers used false licenses to pay greatly reduced customs duties on non-quota fruit. The fraud netted smugglers hundreds of millions of euros over a two-year period. The banana war continued in 2008 when a WTO dispute panel ruled for the third time that the EU tariff/quota banana regime was unfair.

Think Critically

Make an argument in favor of the European import restrictions. Make an argument against this plan.

15-2 Assessment

Key Concepts

LO 2-1 1. The government's use of trade barriers to protect domestic production is __?__.

LO 2-1 2. **TRUE OR FALSE** Free trade is the flow of goods between countries without restrictions or special taxes.

LO 2-1 3. The worldwide organization that enforces rulings on global trade disputes is the __?__.

LO 2-1 4. A limit on the quantity of a good that can be imported in a given period is a __?__.

LO 2-1 5. An __?__ is a law that bars trade with another country.

LO 2-1 6. **TRUE OR FALSE** A tariff is a tax on an export.

LO 2-2 7. The __?__ industry argument is that new domestic industries need protection. The reason is because such industries are not yet ready to compete.

LO 2-2 8. **TRUE OR FALSE** The protecting jobs argument is that the sale of an imported good comes at the expense of a domestically produced good.

LO 2-2 9. The __?__ argument is that a nation must not be dependent on foreign countries for essential defense-related goods it needs in wartime.

LO 2-2 10. **TRUE OR FALSE** The cheap labor argument is that the United States cannot compete against unfair low-wage competition.

Think About It

LO 2-1 11. Suppose the United States passed a law stating there would no purchasing of imports from any country that imposed any trade restrictions on U.S. exports. Who would benefit and who would lose from such retaliation?

LO 2-1 12. Consider question 11 in terms of the law's impact on domestic producers that export goods. Does this policy adversely affect domestic producers that export goods?

LO 2-2 13. Consider this statement: "Unrestricted foreign trade costs domestic jobs." Do you agree or disagree? Explain.

LO 2-1 14. Describe each of the three major types of trade barriers.

LO 2-2 15. Explain each of the four major arguments in favor of trade protectionism. What effect does protectionism have on the prices consumers must pay and the product choices they are able to make?

Make Academic Connections

LO 2-1 16. **HISTORY** Research tariff policy in the United States before and after the Civil War. Explain the position of the South and North on tariffs.

Teamwork

LO 2-2 17. Work in four groups. In your group, discuss the pros and cons of one of the protectionist arguments: infant industry, national security, protecting jobs, and cheap foreign labor. Report on the group's discussion.

Unit 7 Project: Building a Global Future

FREE TRADE Prepare a chart that lists the advantages and disadvantages of free trade. Include trade barriers such as tariffs and quotas, and explain their effect on trade. Use color, graphics, and clip art, pictures, or artwork to display your findings.

15-3 Measures of Trade

Learning Objectives

LO 3-1 **Understand** exchange rates and abandonment of the gold standard.

LO 3-2 **Explain** the effect of changes in the value of the U.S. dollar on balance of trade.

Vocabulary

exchange rate, p. 440
fixed exchange rate system, p. 440
flexible exchange rate system, p. 440
depreciation of currency, p. 442
appreciation of currency, p. 442
balance of trade, p. 443
trade surplus, p. 443
trade deficit, p. 443

© Aleksandar Vrzalski/iStockphoto.com

REAL-WORLD FOCUS

"When our family vacationed in Canada last year," Tricia explained, "we were shocked at the exchange rate. Our dollars weren't worth as much as the Canadian dollars and we had to spend a lot more for our trip than we had planned to spend. Just a few years ago when we visited Canada, it was a lot different. What happened?"

WORK AS A TEAM What causes the value of one country's currency to change over time? How is one country's currency affected by what happens in another country?

June Marie Sobrito/Shutterstock.com

Tourists visiting New York City from other countries can use the currency exchange booth at Grand Central Station to get American dollars for their country's currency.

DO YOU THINK it is easy to exchange currency in every city in the United States or just in major cities?

yienkeat/Shutterstock.com

LO 3-1 Exchange Rates

Each transaction in global trade requires an exchange of one country's currency for that of another. Suppose you buy a Japanese car made in Japan, say, a Mazda. Mazda wants to be paid in yen and not dollars. So dollars must be traded for yen. Or the Pink Panther Airline Company in France purchases an airplane from Boeing in the United States. Pink Panther has euros to pay the bill, but Boeing wants dollars. Consequently, euros must be exchanged for dollars.

The critical question for everyone involved in world trade is, "What is the exchange rate?" The **exchange rate** is the number of units of one nation's currency that equals one unit of another nation's currency. For example, assume 1.81 dollars can be exchanged for 1 British pound. This means the exchange rate is 1.81 dollars = 1 pound. Alternatively, the exchange rate can be expressed as a reciprocal. Dividing 1 British pound by 1.81 dollars gives 0.552 pounds per dollar. Suppose you are visiting England and want to buy a T shirt with a price tag of 10 pounds. Knowing the exchange rate tells you the T shirt costs $18.10 (10 pounds × $1.81/pound). For most of the years between World War II and 1971, currency exchange rates were pegged or *fixed*. A **fixed exchange rate system** is a system in which exchange rates are held constant by a country's government. Exchange rates were based primarily on gold. For example, the German mark was fixed at about 25 cents. The dollar was worth 1/35 of an ounce of gold, and 4 German marks were worth 1/35 of an ounce of gold. Therefore, 1 dollar equaled 4 marks, or 25 cents equaled 1 mark. In 1971, Western nations agreed to stop fixing their exchange rates and they abandoned the gold standard. This meant that countries would allow their currencies to *float*. A **flexible exchange rate system** is a system in which exchange rates are determined by the forces of supply and demand. Most major currencies use the flexible exchange rate system. Figure 15-4 illustrates that these rates can fluctuate widely. For example, in 1980, 1 dollar was worth about 230 Japanese yen. After gyrating up and down over the years, the exchange rate hit a postwar low of 93 yen per dollar in 2010.

NET Bookmark

Access www.cengage.com/school/economics/personalfinance and click on the link for Chapter 15. Visit the Universal Currency Converter. How much is the U.S. dollar currently worth in terms of the euro? How much is the U.S. dollar currently worth in terms of the Japanese yen?

www.cengage.com/school/economics/personalfinance

Figure 15-4

Changes in the Yen per Dollar Exchange Rate, 1980–2010

Today, most economies are on a system of flexible exchange rates. As the demand and supply curves for currencies change, exchange rates change.

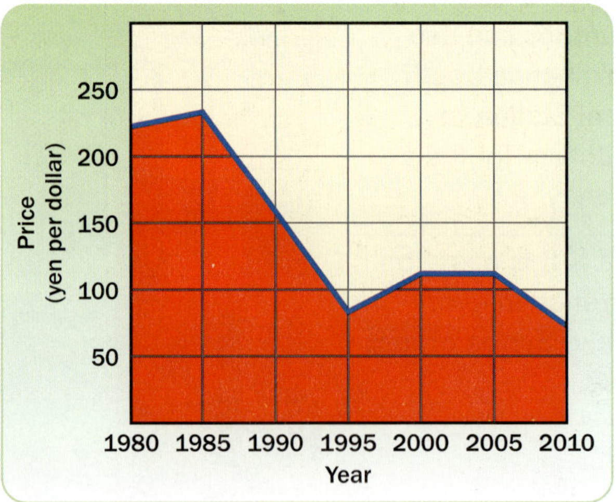

Return to the Yellow Brick Road?

Like Dorothy, in *The Wonderful Wizard of Oz*, some people believe nations should follow a yellow brick road when it comes to setting international exchange rates. Others argue that, like what Dorothy found, there is nothing magic in Oz or in the yellow (golden) bricks.

The United States adopted the gold standard in 1873. Until the 1930s, most industrial countries were on the gold standard. The gold standard worked fairly well as a fixed exchange rate system so long as nations did not face sudden or severe swings in flows from their stocks of gold. The Great Depression marked the beginning of the end of the gold standard. In 1933, President Franklin D. Roosevelt took the United States off the gold standard. He ordered all gold coins to be returned to the government, melted down, and not circulated. Although individuals could not cash in dollars for gold after 1933, foreign governments could. As long as U.S. prices were relatively low there was no reason for these governments to trade their dollars for gold. They would just spend them for American products they wanted to buy. Over time, this situation would change.

In 1944 near the end of World War II, the finance ministers of Western nations met at Bretton Woods, New Hampshire to establish a new international monetary system. Under this system, nations were expected to maintain fixed exchange rates for their currencies within a narrow range. In the 1960s and early 1970s, the Bretton Woods system became strained as prices in the United States rose relative to those in other countries. This caused U.S. exports to become more expensive and U.S. imports to become less expensive. The result was an increase in the supply of dollars abroad. U.S. monetary authorities worried that foreign central banks would demand gold for their dollars. If so, the U.S. gold stock could not cover the number of dollars held by other nations. There was a chance that there would be a run on U.S. gold that could destroy international trade.

Something had to give, and it did. In August 1971, President Richard Nixon announced that the United States would no longer sell gold at $35 an ounce. By 1973, the gold standard was dead, and most nations were letting the forces of supply and demand determine exchange rates.

Today, some people advocate returning to the gold standard. These gold buffs do not trust the government to control the money supply without the discipline of a gold standard. They argue that if governments have the freedom to print money, political pressures will cause them to increase the money supply too much causing high rates of inflation.

One argument against the gold standard is that no one can control the supply of gold. Big gold discoveries could cause inflation and have done so in the past. On the other hand, slow growth in the stock of mined gold could lead to slow economic growth and a loss of jobs. Governments therefore are unlikely to return to the gold standard. This would mean turning monetary policy over to uncontrollable swings in the supply of gold.

Think Critically

Do you believe the United States should return to the gold standard? Explain.

A Weak Versus Strong Currency

Exchange rates between most major currencies are flexible. Instead of being pegged to gold, their value is determined by the laws of supply and demand. Consequently, shifts in supply and demand create a weaker or a stronger dollar. Suppose the exchange rate between dollars and euros is $1 for €0.90. Later the exchange rate changes the $1 for €0.60. The dollars is weaker. It buys fewer euros. A weak currency depreciates. **Depreciation of currency** is a decrease in the value of a currency relative to other currencies. Conversely, a strong currency appreciates. **Appreciation of currency** is an increase in the value of a currency relative to other currencies. Exchange rates do not fluctuate with total freedom. Governments often buy and sell currencies to prevent wide swings in exchange rates.

The strength or weakness of any nation's currency has a profound impact on its economy. A "weak" dollar is a "mixed blessing." Ironically, a weak dollar makes U.S. producers happy. Foreigners pay less of their currency for dollars making U.S. products appear less costly to foreign buyers. As export sales rise, jobs are created in the United States. On the other hand, a weak dollar makes foreign producers and domestic consumers unhappy. The reason is because the prices of Japanese cars, French wine, and Italian shoes are higher. As U.S. imports fall, jobs are lost in foreign countries.

Now assume the exchange rate between dollars and euros changes from $1 for €0.60 to $1 for €0.90. The dollar is stronger. It buys more euros. A "strong" dollar is also a "mixed blessing." A strong dollar makes major trading partners happy. U.S. buyers pay fewer dollars for foreign currency, which means the prices of Japanese cars, French wine, and Italian shoes are lower. A strong dollar, contrary to the implication of the term, makes U.S. producers unhappy. Their exports are more expensive and related jobs decline. Conversely, a strong dollar makes foreign producers happy because the prices of their goods and services are lower to U.S. consumers. This causes U.S. imports to rise.

Figure 15-5

Effects of a Strong or Weak Dollar on U.S. Trade

A strong dollar leads to a decrease in exports and an increase in imports. A weak dollar leads to an increase in exports and a decrease in imports.

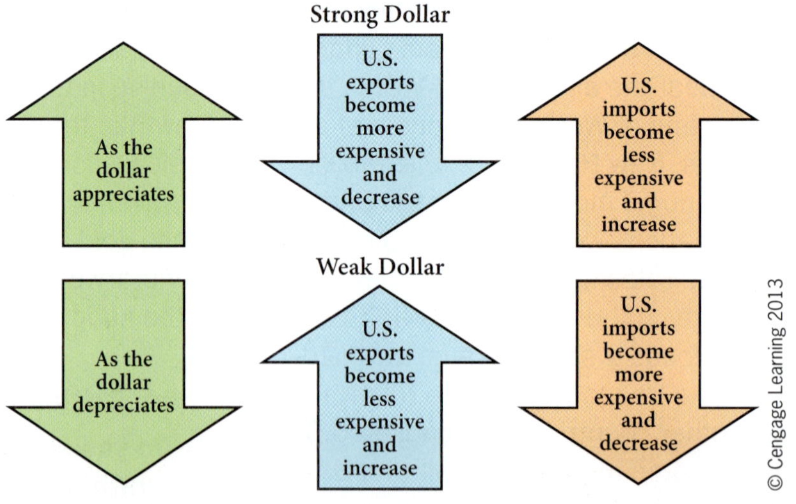

CHECKPOINT

Suppose the exchange rate is $1 for €0.90. Explain how this exchange rate can be expressed two ways.

LO 3-2 The Balance of Trade

Figure 15-6 charts the annual balance of trade for the United States from 1975 through 2010. **Balance of trade** is the value of a nation's imports subtracted from the value of its exports. Observe that the United States experienced a trade surplus in 1975. A **trade surplus** arises when the value of a country's exports is greater than the value of its imports. This is called a *favorable balance of trade.* Since 1975, however, sizable trade deficits have occurred. A **trade deficit** occurs when the value of a nation's imports is greater than the value of its exports. These trade deficits have attracted much attention.

Between 2005 and 2008, the U.S. trade deficits reached record breaking levels of about $700 billion due in part to the rising price of oil imports. During this period, the price per barrel grew steadily until reaching a peak in 2008, and the U.S. trade deficit with OPEC countries doubled while our trade deficit with China tripled. After 2008, oil import prices plunged sharply from a high of $134 per barrel in 2008 to $82 per barrel in 2010 and U.S. trade deficits with OPEC countries fell while U.S. trade deficits with China remained constant. These factors contributed to the fall in the U.S. balance of trade in 2010.

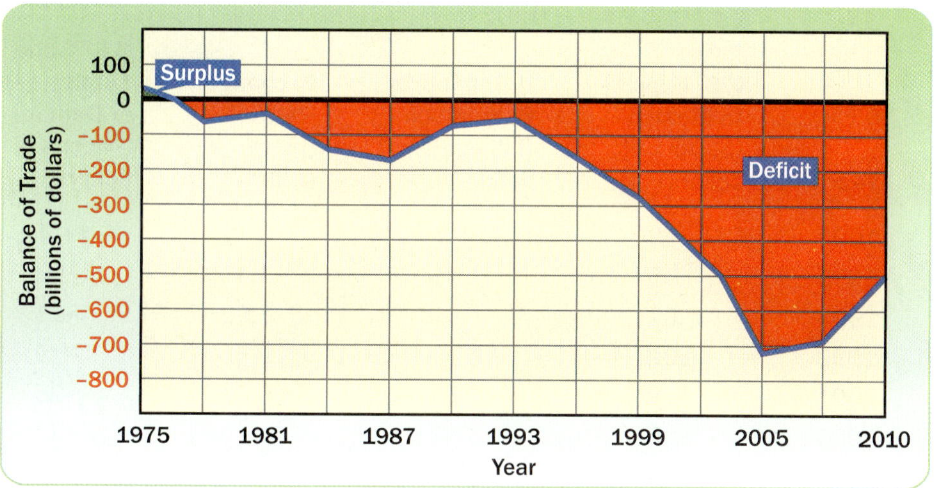

Figure 15-6

U.S. Balance of Trade, 1975–2010

Since 1975, the United States has experienced trade deficits, in which the value of goods imports has exceeded the value of goods exports. The deficits continued to grow until reaching an all-time high of over $800 billion in 2008.

Figure 15-7 shows that the United States has its largest trade deficits with China, Mexico, Japan, and Germany respectively.

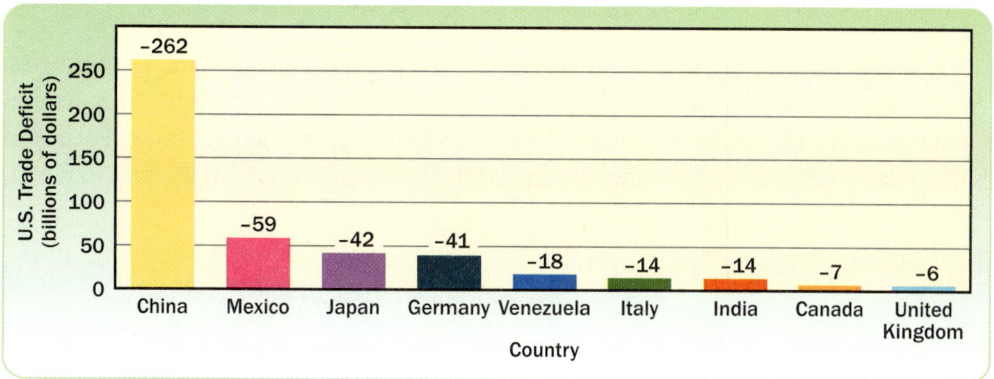

Figure 15-7

U.S. Balance of Trade with Selected Countries, 2010

The United States has its greatest trade deficits with China, Mexico, Japan, and Germany.

The Effect of Changes in the Value of the Dollar

Here is an illustration of the impact of a free trade agreement and the effect of a strong dollar. In 1993, Congress approved the North American Free Trade Agreement (NAFTA). NAFTA is an agreement between the United States, Canada, and Mexico. In January 1994, NAFTA began a gradual phase out of tariffs and other trade barriers. Figure 15-7 provides trade data for the United States and Mexico for the years surrounding NAFTA. As Figure 15-8 shows, both exports and imports of goods increased sharply after NAFTA. On the other hand, a small U.S. trade surplus of $4 billion with Mexico in 1993 turned into a huge trade deficit of $60 billion in 2010.

Before blaming this trade deficit entirely on NAFTA, you must note that the exchange rate rose from 3.12 to 12.62 pesos per dollar. Since 1995, the peso was devalued. The stronger dollar has put the price of U.S. goods out of reach for many Mexican consumers. This is one reason U.S. exports to Mexico have been lower than they would have been otherwise. At the same time, Mexican goods became less expensive for U.S. consumers, so U.S. imports from Mexico have risen.

Figure 15-8
U.S. Trade Balances with Mexico, 1993–2010

Year	U.S. Exports to Mexico (billions of dollars)	U.S. Imports from Mexico (billions of dollars)	Exchange Rate (pesos per dollar)	U.S. Trade Surplus (+) or Deficit (−) (billions of dollars)
1993	$ 52	$ 48	3.12	$+ 4
1995	55	71	6.45	−16
1997	82	97	7.92	−15
1999	101	120	9.55	−19
2001	118	143	9.34	−25
2003	115	152	10.79	−37
2005	143	188	10.89	−45
2008	178	236	11.14	−58
2010	187	247	12.62	−60

In 2011, the United States had free trade agreements (FTAs) with 17 countries: Australia, Bahrain, Canada, Chile, Costa Rica, Dominican Republic, El Salvador, Guatemala, Honduras, Israel, Jordan, Mexico, Morocco, Nicaragua, Oman, Peru, and Singapore. Free trade agreements were pending with Columbia, Korea, and Panama.

CHECKPOINT

What happens to a nation's balance of trade if the nation's currency appreciates?

15-3 Assessment

Key Concepts

LO 3-2 1. An unfavorable balance of trade that occurs when the value of a nation's imports is greater than the value of its exports is a trade __?__.

LO 3-1 2. **TRUE OR FALSE** A fixed exchange rate system is one in which exchange rates are held constant by a country's government.

LO 3-2 3. A favorable balance of trade that occurs when the value of a nation's exports is greater than the value of its imports is a trade __?__.

LO 3-2 4. **TRUE OR FALSE** Balance of trade is the value of a nation's exports subtracted from its imports.

LO 3-1 5. Depreciation of currency is a(n) __?__ in the price (value) of one currency relative to another.

LO 3-1 6. **TRUE OR FALSE** A flexible exchange rate system is one in which exchange rates are determined by the forces of supply and demand.

LO 3-1 7. Appreciation of currency is a(n) __?__ in the price (value) of one currency relative to another.

LO 3-1 8. **TRUE OR FALSE** The exchange rate is the number of units of one nation's currency that equals one unit of another nation's currency.

Think About It

LO 3-1 9. Research changes in the exchange rate of the dollar relative to other currencies. Make a chart for the past five years for the exchange rates of the dollar compared to the euro, British pound, Japanese yen, and Mexican peso.

LO 3-1 10. Research the Big Mac Index published by *The Economist* as a simple way to measure the actual purchase of a single good to the overall market exchange rate listed on foreign exchanges. Big Mac was chosen because it is sold around the world. Comparing the Big Mac Index to market exchange rates allows you to compare exchange rates between different currencies. Suppose the Big Mac cost an average of $3.75 in the United States and €3.00 euros.

   a. What is the exchange rate for Big Macs?
   b. Suppose the actual exchange rate is 1.50. Is the purchasing power of the euro undervalued or overvalued? By what percentage?
   c. Now suppose the actual exchange rate of the dollar against the euro weakened. What would be the effect on U.S. trade with the EU?

LO 3-1 11. Explain how fixed exchange rates worked and why they were abandoned in 1971.

LO 3-2 12. How would a depreciation in the value of the U.S. dollar impact the balance of trade?

Make Academic Connections

LO 3-2 13. **HISTORY** Fort Knox is famous for storing the gold supply of the United States. Research and write a brief paper on the history of Fort Knox Bullion Depository. Why was the Fort Knox Bullion Depository built? Is all of the U.S. gold supply stored at Fort Knox?

Teamwork

LO 3-2 14. Work in groups to research the issue of U.S. trade with China. Develop a description of the problem and possible solutions.

Chapter 15 Summary

15-1 WHY NATIONS TRADE

1. Trade means that each nation does not have to produce everything it needs. Instead, countries export items that they have an absolute or comparative advantage over others. This allows those countries that can produce products the most efficiently to do so, while importing those they cannot efficiently produce.
2. Specialization allows countries to produce those things that use the fewest resources for the highest output. Net consumption after trade allows countries that trade to maximize the use of their resources while minimizing their opportunity costs.
3. Comparatively speaking, all nations are better off when they produce (and export) those things they make most efficiently. This allows them to import other things they cannot produce efficiently.

15-2 BARRIERS TO FREE TRADE

4. Nations impose restrictions to free trade in order to protect their domestic producers. Embargoes bar trade with another country; tariffs increase the cost of imports which discourages trade; and quotas limit the quantity that can be imported. These measures can lead to retaliation by other nations as they impose embargoes, tariffs, and quota limits as well.
5. Protectionism is the act of preventing or limiting imports from other countries. This is done to protect infant (new) industries, to protect national security, and to protect domestic jobs. Some people believe that goods that use cheap foreign labor undermine the standard of living in the U.S. All of these arguments may reap short-term benefits but often have long-term consequences, including inefficient use of worldwide resources.

15-3 MEASURES OF TRADE

6. Exchange rates are used to translate one nation's currency into that of another country. Exchange rates are no longer held constant, nor are they based on the price of gold. Flexible exchange rates allow the value of currencies to fluctuate over time according to demand and supply.
7. Countries with falling exchange rates can export more goods because the price of their products to foreign nations is going down. However, their currency is worth less in world markets and will buy less as well. A decrease in the value of a currency is called depreciation. When the value of currency rises, it is called appreciation.
8. A "strong" U.S. dollar (exchange rate) is a mixed blessing. The dollar will buy more in world markets but the U.S. is able to export less because the price of those exports to foreigners is higher, thus reducing the quantity demanded. This will also cause imports in the U.S. to rise.

Chapter 15

Assessment

Vocabulary Review

Match each statement with the term that best defines it.

1. The government's use of trade barriers to protect domestic producers
2. An unfavorable balance of trade that occurs when the value of a nation's imports is greater than the value of its exports
3. A good produced in one country and sold to another country
4. A system in which exchange rates are held constant by a country's government
5. A worldwide organization that enforces rulings on global trade disputes
6. The ability of a country to produce more of a good using the same or fewer resources than another country
7. A fall in the price (value) of one currency relative to another
8. The number of units of one nation's currency that equals one unit of another nation's currency
9. The flow of goods between countries without restrictions or special taxes
10. The value of a nation's imports subtracted from its exports
11. A tax on an import
12. A rise in the price (value) of one currency relative to another
13. A favorable balance of trade that occurs when the value of a nation's exports is greater than the value of its imports
14. A limit on the quantity of a good that can be imported in a given time period
15. A good produced in one country and purchased by another country
16. A law that bars trade with another country
17. The ability of a country to produce a good at a lower opportunity cost than another country
18. A system in which exchange rates are determined by the forces of supply and demand. Also called a floating rate

Vocabulary

a. absolute advantage
b. appreciation of currency
c. balance of trade
d. comparative advantage
e. depreciation of currency
f. embargo
g. exchange rate
h. export
i. fixed exchange rate
j. flexible exchange rate
k. free trade
l. import
m. protectionism
n. quota
o. tariff
p. trade deficit
q. trade surplus
r. World Trade Organization (WTO)

Review Your Knowledge

LO 1-1 **19.** Specialization and trade allow an economy to expand its
   a. production possibilities
   b. consumption possibilities
   c. technological advantage
   d. absolute advantage

LO 1-2 **20.** A country has an absolute advantage in the production of a good when
   a. its opportunity cost of producing the good is lower than another country
   b. it can produce the good using fewer resources than another country
   c. it specializes in the production of the good
   d. all of the above

LO 1-2 **21.** The theory of comparative advantage suggests that nations should produce a good if they
   a. have the lowest opportunity cost
   b. have the lowest wages
   c. have the most resources
   d. can produce more of the good than any other nation

LO 2-1 **22.** In the years following the completion of NAFTA in 1993, trade between the United States, Canada, and Mexico
   a. remained essentially unchanged
   b. grew rapidly
   c. fell slowly
   d. fell rapidly

LO 3-2 **23.** A favorable balance of trade occurs when the value of a nation's
   a. exports are greater than the value of imports
   b. imports are greater than the value of exports
   c. international trade is an increasing share of total output
   d. currency is appreciating

LO 2-1 **24.** A limit on the quantity of a good that may be imported in a given time period is
   a. an embargo
   b. a tariff
   c. a quota
   d. dumping

LO 1-1 **25.** Which is *not* an argument in favor of protectionism?
   a. To protect an "infant" industry
   b. To protect domestic jobs
   c. To preserve national security
   d. To reduce prices paid by domestic consumers

LO 3-1 **26.** A fixed or pegged exchange rate is determined by
   a. forces of supply and demand
   b. a nation's government
   c. the World Bank
   d. the North American Free Trade Agreement

LO 3-1 **27.** Flexible, or floating, exchange rates are determined by the
   a. World Bank
   b. forces of supply and demand for a currency
   c. price of gold
   d. Federal Reserve

LO 3-1 **28.** If the dollar appreciates
   a. imports to the United States become more expensive for foreigners
   b. exports from the United States become more expensive for foreigners
   c. imports become more expensive for U.S. citizens
   d. exports from the United States become cheaper
   e. the dollar will exchange for fewer units of a foreign currency

LO 2-1 **29.** A tax levied on imported goods is a(n)
   a. flat tax
   b. quota
   c. foreign profits tax
   d. tariff

Digging Deeper with Economics e-Collection

The U.S. has maintained a trade deficit for most of the past 40 years. This is a net drain on the economy as the country buys more goods from foreign countries than they buy from us. Access the Gale Economics e-Collection at www.cengage.com/school/economics/personalfinance. View the trade deficit/surplus data for the United States. Participate in a debate on the good and the bad point of trade deficits. Explore these questions:

Why do U.S. citizens buy so many foreign goods?

How can the United States improve its deficit/surplus position?

Why should citizens of the United States be concerned with a trade deficit?

Think About It

LO 1-1 **30.** Self-sufficiency allows nations to be independent and not have to rely on imports from other countries to meet their needs. Why do countries like the U.S. avoid trying to be self-sufficient?

LO 2-2 **31.** With embargoes and quotas, products do not flow freely from those who produce them to those who demand them. This can create a "black market" for the goods. Explain how this result is not a good outcome.

LO 3-2 **32.** A trade deficit means a country is importing a greater value of products than it is exporting. Why are leaders, businesses, and others concerned about the large and growing trade deficit in the U.S.?

Make Academic Connections

LO 1-2 **33.** **COMMUNICATIONS** Individual consumers also benefit from comparative and absolute advantage. For example, people work to earn money at jobs. They do not try to grow and raise everything they eat. Explain how consumers realize a consumption gain from this individual form of "trade."

LO 2-1 **34.** **SOCIAL STUDIES** Many workers lost their jobs when producers in America moved their production facilities to Mexico or Canada after NAFTA was agreed to. Explain the social impact of the loss of jobs that are now obsolete, thus creating the need to learn new skills, often as a worker reaches middle age and must start over in a new career.

LO 3-1 **35.** **TECHNOLOGY** If you travel to a foreign country, you will likely need a credit card that has a chip in it that allows for easy access to accounts and instant currency translation. Explain how technology has enhanced travel as well as access to foreign markets to buy and sell goods and services around the globe.

Extend Your Learning

LO 2-2 **36.** The trend has been for nations to negotiate trade agreements that reduce trade barriers. One idea is titled the Free Trade Area of the Americas (FTAA) that would span the Western Hemisphere except Cuba. What are some arguments in favor of and against having such a free-trade area?

Andy Dean Photography/Shutterstock.com

chapter 16

Build Assets and Wealth

16-1 Rent or Own a Home

16-2 Lease or Buy a Car

16-3 Risk Management and Insurance

16-4 Purchase, Use, and Dispose of Property

yienkeat/Shutterstock.com

MARKETS *in Action!*

What Caused the Housing Crash?

In 2007, the housing market was severely hurt when the economy slowed down and many people were unable to make their mortgage payments. In years leading up to 2007, many loans were made with zero down payments. That is, people could buy homes without having any cash upfront. In addition, many loans were made to risky buyers. It was an era of *liar loans*. With a liar loan, a prospective buyer could state any amount of income (to qualify for a mortgage loan) on the loan application. The buyers did not have to prove their income matched the amount stated on the application. These loans were approved and sold into the real estate investment markets.

People were buying real estate with the intent of flipping it. They expected to buy property, fix it up (or not), and then sell it within a year or two. They expected to make profits due to inflation and rapidly rising home prices. But when the real estate market crashed, they were unable to sell these houses.

Going into the recession, many people were upside down in their mortgages. This phrase means they owed more on their mortgages than the new (deflated) prices of the homes. With recession comes unemployment. Having lost their jobs, many people were unable to make their house payments. Some people simply walked away from their mortgages and their homes. The properties were *foreclosed* (taken back by the lenders) and this action led to a massive number of distressed properties listed for sale. As a result, the resale values of all homes plummeted due to the drastically increased supply of homes for sale.

Otherwise known as the *housing bubble*, when prices are rising too fast, people cannot afford to buy. When creative ways of financing home purchases included practices such as selling to unqualified buyers, the results were disastrous. Many loan brokers and banks went out of business as a result of making these bad loans. Banks lost billions of dollars on loans that were in default.

Real estate has been a solid investment for many decades. But real estate values go up and down, and when resale values go down, owners must be able to wait for the market to come back. When they cannot make payments, or they cannot wait for values to rise again before selling, the result is a real estate market glutted with sellers and falling prices.

Andy Dean Photography/Shutterstock.com

Think Critically

1. Why is it important for home buyers to have verifiable sources of income when buying a home?
2. Why is it important for home buyers to put down a sizeable down payment when they purchase real estate?
3. What can you do to make sure your decision to buy a piece of real estate is a good choice?

yienkeat/Shutterstock.com

16-1 Rent or Own a Home

Learning Objectives

LO 1-1 **Evaluate** the costs and benefits of renting a residence.

LO 1-2 **Analyze** the advantages and disadvantages of buying a home rather than renting.

LO 1-3 **Assess** the steps and financial aspects of transitioning from renting to owning.

Vocabulary

rental agreement, p. 454
tax shelter, p. 455
foreclosure, p. 455
down payment, p. 456
mortgage, p. 457
closing costs, p. 457

© Aleksandar Vrzalski/ iStockphoto.com

REAL-WORLD FOCUS

Larry is leaving home to go to college in the fall. This summer he is planning his move. He will gather what he needs for his dorm room. "I need to bring enough supplies for a term," he told his dad, "but not so much that it won't fit into the limited space I will have available. My roommate and I will share some things too, such as a DVD player and sound system.

WORK AS A TEAM When moving out on your own, what items do you need to take with you? What kinds of things get in the way and are not useful? Explain the steps you will take when preparing to move for the first time.

Olivier Le Queinec/Shutterstock.com

Homes being sold have to be inspected to verify the home meets minimum standards.

DO YOU THINK **the person buying the home or selling the home pays for the inspection? Why?**

yienkeat/Shutterstock.com

LO 1-1 Renting a Residence

As a young adult, there are many choices when you first move away from your parents' home. If you go to a residential college, you can choose on-campus housing. Other students prefer a shared apartment, duplex, condominium, or multiplex living, or even a house.

On-Campus Living

On-campus housing has several advantages, including closeness to classes and campus activities, libraries, and other resources. As an on-campus student, at some colleges you have several choices.

A *dormitory* is an on-campus building that contains rooms rented to students. These rooms are furnished. All you need to bring are your personal belongings. With your residential plan, you purchase meals, called *room and board.* Typically, you share the dorm room with another person. A housing cooperative, or *co-op*, is a similar arrangement on campus. In co-ops, the costs are often lower because you agree to have added responsibilities, such as sharing in the cooking, cleaning, and maintenance of the building.

Another option is a *sorority* (for women) or a *fraternity* (for men). These are social groups who share housing.

Lori Howard/Shutterstock.com

An on-campus dormitory can house several hundred students in one building.

Off-Campus Housing

Some residential colleges and universities do not allow younger students to live off campus. Commuter campuses do not provide on-campus housing. When you live off campus, you have several choices.

An *apartment* is a single living facility among many similar units. An *apartment complex* is a large group of units, often as many as a hundred or more. A *studio apartment* is the least expensive. It is one large room that serves as kitchen, living room, and bedroom. Larger apartments have separate living areas, kitchens, and bedrooms.

A *townhouse* has living space on two or more levels. Typically, living and dining space is on one level and bedrooms are upstairs or downstairs.

A *duplex* is a building that has two separate living units, and often a garage or carport in between. With only one close neighbor, these units often have private laundry facilities and a similar layout to a single family house. A *multiplex* is a building with multiple units, such as a *fourplex* or an *eightplex*. These units are connected, and sometimes share common facilities such as a kitchen and laundry.

A *condominium*, or condo, is an individual unit of any size that has an owner. The owner of a condo may rent it. The renter has the same rights and responsibilities as the condo owner. The advantage of living in a condo is having all the amenities of home ownership without many of the responsibilities (such as mowing the lawn or caring for a yard).

You can also *rent a house*. Rent varies, depending on the size and features. You are paying for neighborhood living, garage space, more privacy, and other comforts of being in a single family residence. Rented houses are typically investments for the owners. Owners of rental properties may choose to sell them at any time. If an owner puts the property on the market, the renter must make it available for viewing by potential buyers on short notice.

Advantages of Renting

Renting gives you flexibility. As long as you give proper notice and abide by the agreement signed between you and the owner, you can move out when your conditions change or you want to live somewhere else. You have the use of a living space for a relatively small amount of money. You can enjoy it without the costs or responsibilities of maintaining it. If a pipe breaks or the roof leaks, the repair is made by the *landlord* (owner).

Many rental properties come with nice amenities. Tenants can enjoy pools, spas, exercise rooms, and tennis courts on the premises. Most rental units also have laundry, mail, and other services at low or no additional cost. Rental units are often at convenient locations. You can use public transportation and reach shopping and other services quickly.

ivylingpy/Shutterstock.com

Many apartment complexes include amenities such as an outdoor swimming pool.

Disadvantages of Renting

As a *tenant* (renter), your monthly rent is not tax-deductible. Rent paid is a cost that has no future benefit. Tenants must obey the rules of the facility, including quiet times, use of pool or exercise equipment, use of laundry facilities, and so on. You may hear noise from neighbors.

You must give written notice before you move out of rental property and, if you signed a lease, you must honor the rules and guidelines in that lease. A **rental agreement** is a written agreement that specifies rights and duties of both the landlord and the tenant. Tenants can be *evicted* (forced to move out) if they do not obey the terms of the written agreement.

Most rental properties are *unfurnished*. Most major appliances (stove and refrigerator) are supplied, but you must bring small appliances, such as a toaster. You also need a dining room table and chairs, living room furniture, lamps and tables, bedroom furniture, and linens.

Renting often involves *deposits* which are refundable sums of money that assure you meet the terms of the rental agreement. A *security deposit* ensures the landlord that rent payments will be made or cost of damage you cause will be paid. A *pet deposit* ensures that cost of damage by your cat or dog is covered. You may also be charged *fees*, such as a *cleaning fee* so that your apartment is clean when you move in or out.

You also may have to pay for utilities, including heat, water, garbage, and sewer. These costs are in addition to rent. Many renters find that storage space is limited, and may need to rent additional storage space. Parking spaces may cost extra, especially when the space is covered or reserved.

CHECKPOINT

What are advantages of renting?

LO 1-2 Buying a House

When you are ready to stay in a geographic area for a while, it may be time to become a homeowner. A single family residence is the typical choice for people buying homes. Sometimes buying a condominium is a good choice.

Advantages of Owning a Home

One of the greatest advantages of ownership is the tax savings benefit. Because property taxes and interest on home loans are tax deductible (thus reducing your income tax liability), home ownership is a **tax shelter**.

As you make payments, you are building equity. *Equity* is the value of property you own, or the difference between what you owe for your home loan and the amount for which you could sell the property. The values of most homes appreciate, or increase in market value, over time. When you sell your home, there may be a *capital gains tax* on the increase. You can avoid this tax if you trade up to another home or if you don't exceed the maximum gain ($250,000 for single individual and $500,000 for married couples).

Owning your own home offers privacy, more space, and more personal freedom. Owning real estate positively affects your credit score and creditworthiness. Owning a house can give a sense of stability and belonging in the community.

Disadvantages of Home Ownership

As a homeowner, you are responsible for maintaining your property including repairs both inside and outside. Before choosing to buy, you must be prepared to invest the time and money to keep your home in good condition. What you do affects your property value, as well as the values of properties around you.

Ongoing maintenance includes painting, mowing, weeding, and fixing things that break or wear out. As a homeowner, you not only incur the costs, but also the responsibility for doing the tasks or paying someone to do them.

As a homeowner, you must obey government regulations such as zoning laws and ordinances. You are legally responsible for what happens on your property, and thus you need liability insurance to cover possible risks.

Because most homes are larger than rental units, utility bills are usually higher. The homeowner must pay for all utilities, which include water, sewer, storm drain assessments, lighting fees, gas, electricity, and other costs.

Although the value of most homes increases over time this is not always true. It is possible for the value to decline causing owners to lose money if they need to sell.

Real estate owners pay property taxes. *Property taxes* are taxes assessed against the owners of real property. If you don't pay your property taxes, your home can be foreclosed and sold to pay the delinquent taxes. **Foreclosure** is a process of taking away private property to pay for debts levied against it. When property is foreclosed, the owner loses his or her rights of ownership and must move out so it can be sold by the creditor or governmental unit.

CHECKPOINT

What is the main advantage of home ownership?

LO 1-3 From Renting to Owning

Many people seek home ownership as they become settled and want to start families or put down roots. There are many steps to take and financial costs to consider when making this transition.

Steps of Buying

When buying real estate, you can search for properties for sale on the Internet. Many homeowners are seeking to sell their properties "for sale by owner." When you find a property you are interested in buying, you should arrange to visually inspect it. You may find it easier to locate and arrange viewings of properties by using the services of a *real estate agent*.

Real estate agents charge a fee for their services called a *sales commission*. This commission is a percent of the sales price of the home. The seller generally pays this fee and it is included in the sales price. You can also engage the services of a real estate agent under a buyer's agent agreement, where the real estate sales person represents you rather than the seller. Either way, when a real estate sales agent is involved, the commission cost increases the cost of purchase. Whether you use a real estate agent or not, you should hire an attorney to represent your interests. Without proper advice, you can end up with costly expenses that could have been avoided.

It is a good idea for buyers to get pre-approved for a real estate loan. With a good credit record, solid income, and employment history, buyers apply for a mortgage loan up to a maximum amount. As a qualified buyer, this amount establishes a maximum value of property that can be purchased.

Once you have found property you wish to buy, you prepare an offer, called an *earnest money offer*, in which the buyer offers a price and terms to the seller. If the seller accepts the offer, then the process of buying the home begins. When the seller makes a *counteroffer*, the process continues until there is an agreement or until the offer is rejected.

Home inspection is the process of making sure the property meets minimum standards of livability. An inspector comes to the property to check the roof, walls, floors, appliances, plumbing, and electrical systems. Any deficiencies are reported and the buyer and seller agree as to disposition. In case of serious damage, such as *dry rot* or the presence of pests such as carpenter ants, the seller generally pays the cost of repairs. A *preliminary title report* is also ordered from a title insurance company. This report discloses any liens against the property or against the seller. The seller may need to take action to clear the title for sale. In many cases, negotiation is required between the buyer and seller to resolve any disputes, repairs, conditions, or liabilities.

Costs of Buying

Mortgage lenders usually require that a home buyer pay a certain amount of money toward the purchase price. A **down payment** is usually between 10% and 20% of the purchase price. For example, if you buy a home that costs $200,000, you need a down payment of $20,000 to $40,000. This money is your initial equity in the home, and assures lenders that you are serious. It also reduces risk to the lender if you are unable to make payments and the property is foreclosed on and sold at a loss.

A **mortgage** is a long-term debt obligation. A mortgage involves making payments over a long period of time. Mortgages can be *conventional* (financed through a commercial bank or mortgage broker) or a government-sponsored loan, such as an FHA loan. An *FHA loan* (Federal Housing Administration) is guaranteed by mortgage insurance premiums paid on the loan. It is administered through a government agency and has special fees and requirements. Often first-time home buyer programs are available to help people get started as a homeowner. Mortgages can be for any number of years, but are usually for 15 years or 30 years.

Your mortgage payment includes both principal and interest. With smaller down payments, the borrower must also pay money into a *reserve or escrow account*. Money in that account is used to pay property taxes, mortgage insurance premiums, and other costs. If there is no reserve account, property owners must pay property taxes directly when due. Property taxes are often assessed yearly and paid semi-annually.

NET Bookmark

Access www.cengage.com/school/economics/personalfinance and click on the link for Chapter 16. When buying or selling homes, most people work with a real estate agent. Visit the National Association of Realtors website. Here you will find information about real estate, how to locate properties for sale, and important things for homeowners to know about. You can also find housing and economic statistics. What is the most current indices for Pending Home Sales and Existing Home Sales? How do these numbers compare to the previous month?

www.cengage.com/school/economics/personalfinance

Closing costs, or settlement costs, are expenses incurred in transferring ownership from the buyer to the seller. Closing costs generally add three to five percent to the purchase price. Buyers' closing costs typically include:

- Title insurance (for the buyer and for the mortgage company)
- Prorated interest (from the loan origination to the date of the first payment)
- Prorated taxes (from the time of the assessment to when the buyer becomes responsible for the property tax)
- Escrow fees (costs for the escrow closing agent)
- Recording fees (to record the mortgage, trust deed, and other documents)
- Credit report (on the buyer)
- Loan origination fee (fee to the mortgage lender for issuing a loan) or loan assumption fee (fee for assuming a previous mortgage)

Costs of Moving

Moving into a new home can be expensive and time consuming. *Moving costs* include the time and money spent in packing, loading, transporting, unloading, and unpacking. Professional movers charge according to the amount of personal property packed and the distance from the existing residence to the new residence. You can save money by doing your own packing. You can save more money by renting a truck or trailer and doing your own loading, driving, and unloading. If you are moving across town, renting may be cheaper if you can return the vehicle to the place where you rented it. One-way rental fees are usually a flat rate plus mileage, gasoline, and a security deposit.

Math CONNECTION

Calculating Prorated Interest

When you get a mortgage loan to buy a house, the closing is a meeting between you and the lender where all the legal documents are signed. The date of this meeting is the first day you will pay interest for borrowing the money. At closing, you learn on what day of each month your payment is due. Interest on mortgage loans is paid in arrears, which means each monthly payment includes the amount of interest due for the previous month's loan. The interest on the days between the date of closing and the date of your first payment is *prorated interest*. The prorated interest is paid at closing. Katrina closes on her mortgage loan on July 23 and her first payment is due September 1. The daily amount of interest due is $23.17. How much prorated interest does she have to pay at closing?

SOLUTION

When Katrina makes her first payment on September 1, the payment amount will include interest for the days in August. She also has to pay for July 23 to July 31 at the closing.

31 – 23 + 1 = 9	Subtract the date of closing from the last date of the month. Add 1 to include the day of the closing.
$23.17 × 9 = $208.53	Multiply the daily amount by the number of days.

Katrina pays $208.53 at closing in prorated interest.

TRY IT

Find the amount of prorated interest due for each loan.

1. Closing: March 26, First payment: May 1, Daily interest: $18.79
2. Closing: Oct 2, First payment: Dec 1, Daily interest: $26.44
3. Closing: June 18, First payment: August 1, Daily interest: $16.08

When you move into a new residence, you may be required to pay an initial deposit to secure services such as gas and electric. You may also be charged a fee for *installation charges*, such as land line (telephone), cable TV, and Internet. You may be able to save some money if you can bundle these services. *Bundling* is combining services into one package. For example, you could combine telephone, cable TV, and Internet service into a package from one company that would cost less than if you used three different companies.

CHECKPOINT

What are some costs of moving?

PROFILE

Ted Turner

Businessman and Real Estate Mogul

Albert H. Teich/Shutterstock.com

Robert Edward (Ted) Turner was born in Cincinnati, Ohio in 1938. He attended Brown University and was active in debating and majored in economics. He began sailing when he was nine and went on to compete in the Olympic trials in 1964. In 1977, he defended the America's Cup for the U.S. as skipper of the *Courageous*.

Ted Turner started his business career at age 24, inheriting his father's business after his father's death. The business was worth approximately $1 million when Turner took over in 1963. Today it is worth more than $2 billion. His acumen for business is well established. Turner is best known as founder of the cable television network CNN, the first 24-hour cable news channel (1980). His modern "all news, all the time" format was the result of his vow upon launching the network, where he said, "We won't be signing off until the world ends."

Throughout his life, Ted Turner has devoted his assets to a blend of environmentalism and capitalism. He owns more land than almost any other American. He has the largest herd of bison in the world. His ranch in New Mexico of 920 square miles is the largest privately owned contiguous tract of land in the U.S.

As a businessman, he has also successfully ventured into sports team ownership (the Atlanta Braves), environmental initiatives, billboard advertisement (Turner Outdoor Advertising), and restaurant ownership (Ted's Montana Grill) in Bozeman, Montana, just to mention a few. He didn't always win, but he did always keep trying. Economic downturns hurt Turner and his investments significantly. But he didn't give up or complain. He learned from his mistakes and he kept looking for new entrepreneurial challenges. In 1991, Ted Turner was named *Time* magazine's Man of the Year.

In his long and exciting career, Ted Turner took many risks, but grew his business ventures into well-known enterprises. At the same time, he has cared deeply about the environment and social issues of the times.

THINK CRITICALLY

1. Ted Turner was highly successful in the field of managing assets. He blended risks with fulfilling his passions. How can a person grow $1 million to $2 billion in a lifetime?
2. Why did Mr. Turner purchase so much real estate? Can you name reasons why people invest in real estate, especially large tracts of land?

yienkeat/Shutterstock.com

16-1 Assessment

Key Concepts

LO 1-1 1. What are your choices of on-campus living?

LO 1-1 2. What are reasons why you would choose to rent an apartment?

LO 1-1 3. What are some disadvantages of renting?

LO 1-2 4. What are several reasons why people buy homes?

LO 1-2 5. What are some disadvantages of home ownership?

LO 1-3 6. What steps are involved in moving?

Think About It

LO 1-1 7. Living on campus is very different from commuting to school. Do you live near a community college where you would be commuting? Why would you choose this for your first two years of college?

LO 1-1 8. As a tenant, you have the right to occupy a rented space. You also have responsibilities to other tenants, as well as to your landlord. What kinds of obligations do you and other tenants have in an apartment community?

LO 1-3 9. Deposits are refundable. Fees are not. Suppose you paid a security deposit (rather than fee) of $500 when you moved into an apartment. What would you need to do to be sure you get back your deposit when you move out?

LO 1-3 10. Describe the costs of moving from a rental unit to your own home.

Make Academic Connections

LO 1-2 11. **RESEARCH** Look in your local newspaper, local sales brochures, pamphlets and flyers, and online real estate listings. Find a description of your ideal home. Prepare a report describing the home, its cost, and the features.

LO 1-3 12. **ECONOMICS** The real estate market—including sales as well as new housing starts—is a leading economic indicator. If the real estate market is doing well, the economy is doing well. Research online about the real estate market in the U.S., including new housing starts. Prepare a two-page report. Include a graph or chart that shows recent trends.

LO 1-1 13. **BUSINESS LAW** A rental agreement is often a standard contract. Go online and look up the basic clauses (provisions) of a rental agreement. Prepare a visual display to list all of the major contents of a rental agreement.

Teamwork

LO 1-3 14. As a group, contact a local real estate sales agent or office. Make an appointment and ask questions about the home buying process and costs. Prepare a timeline that illustrates the steps and time required. Prepare a group presentation to share with the class about the average home price and closing costs in your local area.

Chad Baker/Ryan McVay/Photodisc/Getty Images

16-2 Lease or Buy a Car

Learning Objectives

LO 2-1 **Analyze** the reasons for and costs of leasing a car.

LO 2-2 **Describe** the process of buying a car, including financing the purchase and responsibilities of car loan debt.

Vocabulary

car lease, p. 462
mileage allowance, p. 462
business expense, p. 463
factory warranty, p. 463
preapproval, p. 464
extended warranty, p. 464

REAL-WORLD FOCUS

© Aleksandar Vrzalski/iStockphoto.com

Jeff has a part-time job and is able to buy a used car. He has saved money for the purchase and will get a small loan for the balance. "I need flexibility so that if I lose my job, I won't lose my car," he told his friend. "I like the idea of a used car rather than a new one. It will save me a lot of money that I just don't have right now."

WORK AS A TEAM What kinds of costs can Jeff expect to incur when buying a used car? How are those costs different from buying a new car? What can he do to ensure that the used car doesn't need major repairs?

Some people commute more than 50 miles to work, so they put at least 100 miles on their cars each workday.

DO YOU THINK a person who drives a lot of miles to and from work should have concerns about leasing a car?

Stephen Finn/Shutterstock.com

yienkeat/Shutterstock.com

LO 2-1 To Buy or Not to Buy

Consider the well-known phrase: "Buy assets that appreciate, rent assets that depreciate." A car is a *depreciating* asset. That means it is going down in value over time. According to some financial advisors, why would you want to own something that is losing its value? Other advisors say that leasing is just another form of buying. Before you can decide which method is best for you, consider the reasons for and the costs of leasing versus buying a car.

Monkey Business Images/Shutterstock.com

People who lease a car usually start a new lease for a new vehicle every two to three years.

Leasing Pro's and Con's

A **car lease** is a contract where you agree to take possession of a vehicle for a set period of time and make regular lease payments. Typically, you make a relatively small *down payment*. As *lessee,* you are obligated to take good care of the car, maintain its interior and exterior, get regular maintenance (oil changes), and present the car for warranty work. Any major repairs are the responsibility of the *lessor* (owner) of the car, typically a leasing company.

The lessee agrees to an annual **mileage allowance**, such as 10,000 miles. If you exceed this amount, you will be charged a set amount for each additional mile driven. Some car leases provide that the lessee *prepay* miles. That is, you can buy additional miles upfront for a reduced rate. For example, your penalty rate may be 50 cents per mile, but you could buy up to 2,000 additional miles for 25 cents per mile. You would pay $500, and save a penalty of $500 (2,000 miles × $0.50 per mile).

The lease period is usually two or three years. When you turn in the car, you may pick out another car and renew your lease. If you do this, typically you do

Car Dealerships

Investigate Your Local ECONOMY

In your local area there are *car dealerships*, which are businesses that sell new and used cars. These businesses also provide maintenance and repair services for your vehicle. If your vehicle needs warranty work, or there is a safety recall, you will return the vehicle to the dealership to have that work done at no cost to you.

Make a list of local car dealerships. Include the type of vehicles sold at each business, and other services provided. Get a price list, if possible, of services offered and their prices, such as 15,000-mile bundled services. Explain what is covered, such as tire rotation, brakes check, and checking fluid levels. Prepare an estimate of what it costs to keep a car in good running condition.

Try it Out

As a group, prepare a comparison of dealership costs and regular repair shops in your local area. Report your findings using charts and visual displays. Do all repair shops charge the same fees for the same services?

not have to make an additional down payment. Most car leases do not provide a *bargain purchase option*. You can buy the car at the end of the lease, but the price may be high. The leasing company makes money by reselling the vehicle at its current market value. With low mileage and excellent condition, a good profit is likely.

For self-employed entrepreneurs and business owners, the vehicle lease is a business expense. A **business expense** is a cost that is tax deductible and reduces income that is subject to tax. For the business owner, the entire cost of the lease is tax deductible when it is used for business purposes. It makes sense to lease a vehicle rather than buy it when (a) you need a new car every two or three years, and (b) the leasing costs are a *tax shelter* for the lessee.

An advantage of leasing is that you never have to pay off a vehicle. Consider that you will trade it in for another one within a few years. Car payments typically last five to seven years to pay off a new vehicle purchase.

On the other hand, you do not own the vehicle and you must honor the terms of the lease agreement. Violating the terms can be very expensive. Vehicle leasing is available only to qualified buyers.

Buying a Car

Buying a car begins with an assessment of your needs. Consider what you need to do with the car to help you determine what kind of vehicle you need. Fuel efficiency may be a concern. A gas-powered vehicle can be expensive to run with the rising and unpredictable cost of gasoline. An electric, hybrid, or alternate energy source car may be a better choice, depending on your driving habits. There are also economic incentives to consider when buying this type of car, such as a tax credit or buying credit. With a *tax credit*, the buyer receives an immediate reduction in income tax. This credit was recently set at $7,500. If you can't use the entire tax credit one year, you can carry forward the unused portion.

Some families need a vehicle that can haul many people or large amounts of gear. For example, if your family goes camping, your needs are different from those of a person who uses the vehicle for commuting to work.

Your ability to pay for the car is also important to consider. How much can you afford for a monthly car payment? Most car loans today are for five to seven years so that the monthly payment is more affordable.

Buying a used car may be an option. When you buy a new car, it loses its value rapidly. The vehicle begins to *depreciate*, or go down in value, as soon as it is driven off the dealer's lot. Buying a used car can be more complicated. Often there is no factory warranty remaining on the vehicle. A **factory warranty** is a guarantee that if something goes wrong, the cost of repairs is covered by the manufacturer. A typical factory warranty covers buyers for the first 36,000 miles or three years, whichever comes first. It does not cover the cost of routine maintenance and repair, such as oil changes. But if something major goes wrong, it is repaired by the manufacturer at no cost to you.

CHECKPOINT

When is leasing a car, rather than buying, a good idea?

LO 2-2 The Car Buying Process

Because a car purchase is for a large amount over a long period of time, considerable thought and effort should go into the buying process.

Steps in Buying

When you have decided that buying is your best choice, follow some simple steps to make the process go more smoothly and to minimize your costs.

Dana E. Fry/Shutterstock.com

Many used car dealers display an asking price so that potential buyers can shop without interacting with a salesperson until ready to make an offer.

1. **Do considerable research.** Research both online and in person, to decide what type of vehicle meets your needs. Explain that you are at the beginning of your car buying process and you are gathering information. Take your time. Don't be in a hurry when shopping for a car. It is a big purchase and it deserves time.
2. **Get pre-qualified.** Find out how much you are qualified to borrow for a car loan. Your bank or credit union gives you a **preapproval** for a set amount of a vehicle loan. This way, you can separate the financing from the purchasing of the vehicle. It allows you to compare the total costs of buying. For example, if the car dealership offers you a financing plan, you can compare the interest rate and payment amounts to your preapproved loan and choose the one that works best for you.
3. **Check its history.** When buying a used car, get a history of the car. The *vehicle identification number* for each car is unique. It can be used to trace the vehicle through Carfax. A report may cost $25 or more. It is also a good idea to have your mechanic inspect a used car to be sure it doesn't need major repairs before you buy it.
4. **Test drive the car.** Make sure it has the features you want and that they are working properly. Compare features and values in the NADA (National Automobile Dealers Association) Guides. For used cars, check the *Kelley Blue Book* to make sure the asking price is fair and reasonable.
5. **Check insurance rates.** Cars are rated according to costs of making repairs and other statistics, such as theft rates of popular vehicles. Make sure you can afford the insurance premiums.
6. **Make an offer.** Be prepared to walk away if you cannot get a reasonable price. Your offer should represent a fair price for the vehicle, considering its value to you. Be prepared to *negotiate*. Set your spending limit and stick to it. If you have poor negotiation skills, you might consider using a car buying service. Your local credit union or even membership in a wholesale club might have *a car buying service*. With this type of plan, the negotiations are done for you.
7. **Avoid dealer add-ons.** After you have agreed to a price, the dealer may try to increase the purchase price. Dealer add-ons are high-priced, high-profit dealer services that add little or no value. For example, dealer preparation should be done without extra charge. An **extended warranty** covers your car beyond the factory

warranty period, often for 100,000 miles or more. You are merely paying upfront for repairs that may or may not be needed. You certainly don't want to pay interest on future repair bills by adding these contracts to the price of your vehicle.

Financing Your Purchase

The best way to buy a car is with cash. You will have maximum negotiating power. You won't have to pay interest. Unfortunately, many people have to finance at least a portion of the money needed to purchase the car. You can save by continuing to make payments after your car is paid for—just put the money into your own savings account. When you get ready to buy your next car, perhaps you will have enough money saved to avoid a car loan.

Banks, credit unions, and other financial institutions offer vehicle loans for 36-, 48-, 60-, and even 72-month periods. Shorter time periods cost you less interest, but your monthly payments are higher. A lower interest rate will also lower your total cost. It's a good idea to shop as diligently for the car loan as you do for the car itself.

You may be able to get financing through car dealerships. A *sales finance company* is a business that loans money to consumers at the point of sale. GMAC (General Motors Acceptance Corporation) is an example of a sales finance company. On certain makes and models, you may be offered 0% financing terms and/or rebates. When available, these loans may be your best choice. If a rebate is offered, however, it may be better to take it and finance your loan through an alternative lender. Always do the math to find your best deal. Read the offer carefully. There may be conditions. For example, if you make a late payment, your 0% rate may suddenly become very high.

Debt Responsibilities

Your car loan is a debt obligation. You are borrowing money for several years. With a vehicle, your car is likely to be going down in value faster than your loan amount. Nevertheless, you are responsible to make your monthly car payments as agreed.

Your credit rating benefits from responsible debt repayment. It suffers if you aren't responsible. Failure to make payments can lead to repossession of your car. *Repossession* is taking away your car. The lender resells it to recover the cost of the loan. If you have difficulty making your loan payments, you should contact the lender immediately and work out payment arrangements.

Before incurring a long-term debt obligation, you should be sure you can afford the payments. Prepare a budget to determine whether you have adequate income. Make sure the car payment won't crowd out other expenses. If it does, you should look for a less expensive vehicle that requires a smaller loan. Taking debt obligations seriously is an important part of being a responsible adult and borrower. Your ability to get a future car loan, and the interest rate you will pay, depend on it. Risky borrowers pay higher interest rates than those who meet their debt obligations.

CHECKPOINT

Why should you get preapproved for a car loan?

16-2 Assessment

Key Concepts

LO 2-1 1. When is leasing a car a good idea?

LO 2-2 2. What is the purpose of getting loan preapproval?

LO 2-2 3. Why are negotiation skills important when buying a car?

LO 2-2 4. What can happen if you don't make your car payments?

Think About It

LO 2-1 5. People who feel the need to drive a new car every two years often find it to their advantage to lease rather than buy a car. Why?

LO 2-2 6. What type of vehicle is ideal for the types of driving and uses that your family has today? How will that be different (or the same) for the first car you purchase?

LO 2-2 7. The *invoice price* is what car dealers pay for a car from the manufacturer. The sticker price represents retail prices, not costs. Consumers can find the invoice price online. How does knowing the invoice price help you prepare for negotiations?

Make Academic Connections

LO 2-1 8. **COMMUNICATIONS** Write a one-page paper describing the car of your dreams, its features, its cost (including payments), and why you want to own that vehicle.

LO 2-2 10. **TECHNOLOGY** List three or four technological advances in vehicles in the past three to five years. Explain how they have improved safety, efficiency, and/or comfort for the owner/driver.

Teamwork

LO 2-1 11. Do online research about speed limits and traffic laws in three other countries. Write a report comparing those laws to similar laws in your state. How are they different? How do auto accident rates compare among the three countries and your state?

LO 2-2 12. Visit the *Kelley Blue Book* website and look up the trade-in value of your or your family's car. Now look in ads of cars for sale and compare the prices. Explain why the numbers are different.

LO 2-2 13. Find out the costs of vehicle registration, title, driver's license fees, and vehicle emission tests in your city or county. You can get this information from your state's Bureau of Motor Vehicles, either in person or online. Prepare a visual display listing the costs of owning a car.

Unit 7 Project: Building a Global Future

RENTING VS. BUYING Prepare a chart comparing and contrasting the pro's and con's of renting and buying/leasing (a home or a car). Interview two experts in your local area to get first-hand knowledge. Use a hypothetical situation, comparing the bottom line for choosing renting over buying and for choosing buying over renting. Cite at least one dependable online source.

Chad Baker/Ryan McVay/Photodisc/Getty Images

16-3 Risk Management and Insurance

Learning Objectives

LO 3-1 **Explain** the process of identifying risks and strategies to protect income and assets.

LO 3-2 **Evaluate** the costs and benefits of buying insurance.

Vocabulary

risk, p. 468
risk management, p. 468
self-insuring, p. 469
deductible, p. 470
co-pay, p. 470
multi-line discount, p. 472

© Aleksandar Vrzalski/ iStockphoto.com

REAL-WORLD FOCUS

Curtis just got his car insurance bill and he is not happy. "They raised my premiums by more than 20%," he told another agent. "I'm ready to switch. I have a good driving record, I get good grades, and I drive an older car. I need to find a rate that fits my budget."

WORK AS A TEAM How can Curtis reduce his insurance costs without putting himself at greater risk if something should occur where he needs to use his insurance?

SVLuma/Shutterstock.com

A serious injury, such as a broken leg, may result in an impairment that prevents the injured person from working.

DO YOU THINK a person benefits more from health insurance or disability insurance when he or she suffers from a serious injury?

yienkeat/Shutterstock.com

Monkey Business Images/Shutterstock.com

Many people ski without having an injury, while others experience unfortunate accidents.

LO 3-1 Consumer Risks

Risk is the chance of injury, damage, or economic loss. Driving a car and snow skiing are behaviors that involve risk. Accidents can cause personal injury as well as damage to property. There are many types of risk. Some risks are avoidable and have a small chance of happening. Other risks are unpredictable and unavoidable. Some risks can lead to small losses, while other risks can have serious consequences. The likelihood of a risk actually turning into a loss is called *probability.*

Measuring Risks

Consumers face *personal risks* (losing something of value to you) as well as *financial risks* (losing money). For example, if you break your leg, you risk not being able to participate in activities you enjoy until the leg heals. You may also face the financial risk of paying for the costs of setting the broken bones and possible surgery. Financial risks are serious when your income and assets are threatened. If you drive a car without insurance, or without adequate insurance coverage, you are taking a risk that you may owe money in the thousands of dollars to cover property damage or the costs of injuries others suffer as a result of an accident you cause.

Risk management is the process of assessing risks and planning actions to reduce and avoid the losses that could occur. The first step in risk management is to identify your risks and what you could lose (both personal risks and financial risks). Then you assess the probability of events occurring that could cause the loss. When the risk is high and the potential loss is also high, action is definitely needed. Figure 16-1 is an assessment of risks and a prioritization based on the possible consequences.

Figure 16-1
Risk Assessment

Description of Risk	Probability	Seriousness Rating*	Consequences
Losing my job	Medium	10	Missing payments; Lower credit score
Getting in car accident	Unknown	10	Personal injury; Lawsuit; Payment of claim
Injury from snowboarding	Medium	5	Missed work; Medical bills; Pain
Having bike stolen	Low	2	Need to buy new bike

* 1 is low, 5 is medium, 10 is high

Risk Strategies

Once risks are assessed, you must decide what you can do to protect yourself. When a risk is serious, you want to take some type of action to protect yourself from the losses that could occur. There are four risk strategies to manage risks.

1. **Reduce Risk** The process of *risk reduction* involves finding ways to lower your chance of incurring a loss. You can accomplish this by changing actions and events. For example, you can take skiing lessons or choose the least

hazardous slopes to reduce your risk. You could reduce your risk of financial loss by having health insurance to pay for injuries you might suffer.

2. **Avoid Risk** If the risk of personal and financial loss is both serious and has a high probability of occurring, you might want to avoid the risk. With *risk avoidance*, you stop the behavior to avoid the risk. You might choose cross-country skiing over downhill skiing, for example.
3. **Transfer Risk** When you face substantial loss that you cannot reduce or avoid, transferring risk is a good idea. *Risk transfer* (or risk shifting) occurs when you buy insurance. This transfer shifts the risk of financial loss to an insurance company.
4. **Assume Risk** When the risk of personal and financial loss is low and not serious, you may wish to assume the risk yourself. *Risk assumption* is a strategy in which you are prepared to accept the consequences of risk. One type of risk assumption is self-insuring. With **self-insuring**, you set aside money to be used in the event of injury or loss. If a loss does occur, money is taken from the money set aside to pay for the loss.

CHECKPOINT

What are four risk strategies?

LO 3-2 Buying Insurance

Insurance protects you from the losses that occur for which you are responsible. Some insurance protects against property damage (home and car) and the liabilities associated with property. Three types of insurance protect you and your family from losses due to illness, injury, or death: health insurance, disability insurance, and life insurance.

Denise Kappa/Shutterstock.com

Hurricane winds cause severe wind damage to homes and widespread power outages.

Property Insurance

If you own a home, a *homeowner's policy* protects you from losses to your property if there is a fire, break-in, weather damage, or other occurrence. It can also shield you from liability for injuries that are suffered by others while they are on your property.

As a renter, you also need insurance. A *renter's policy* protects the contents of your apartment or rented residence. If there is a fire, water damage, or other event, your personal belongings are covered. The renter's policy also shields you from liability for injuries to your guests.

Motor Vehicle Insurance

In all states, liability coverage is required on the vehicle you drive. *Liability coverage* protects others from injuries caused by an accident that is your fault. You may also want (or be required to have) *full coverage* on your vehicle. If you owe money on the vehicle, the creditor will require full coverage. This coverage protects the lender should the car be damaged or stolen. The proceeds of the insurance would pay off or repair the car so that the creditor does not suffer financial loss.

Full coverage includes collision, comprehensive, personal injury protection, and uninsured/underinsured coverage. *Collision coverage* protects you if your vehicle is damaged or destroyed by colliding with another vehicle or object, when the accident is your fault. Without this coverage, the cost of the repairs to your car would not be covered if the accident was your fault.

Comprehensive coverage protects you from damages to your car for acts other than collision. Examples of this type of damage are rock chips, dents caused in parking lots, theft, hail, vandalism, and broken windshields.

Personal injury protection is coverage for the medical costs of the passengers of a vehicle that is in an accident. It pays for the medical, hospital, and funeral costs of the insured and all others in the vehicle at the time of the accident. *Uninsured coverage* protects you from damages caused by a person who collides with you and has no car insurance. Likewise, *underinsured coverage* protects you from damages caused by a person who does not have adequate insurance to cover the damages he or she caused.

Health Insurance

Health insurance plans are available through employers (group plans) or you may be able to buy an individual policy. Three basic types of health insurance plans are available.

A *fee-for-service plan* allows patients to choose doctors and other providers for medical services. Typically, the policy has a **deductible**, which is the amount of money you have to pay before insurance begins to pay for services. The insurance also pays a set percentage of medical costs. For example, the insured may have a $250 deductible and pay 20% of all costs after the deductible is met. So, for the first bill of the year, a medical bill of $1,000, the patient would pay $250 plus $200 (20% of $1,000). After the deductible is met, then medical expenses are covered at a straight 80%.

A *preferred provider organization (PPO)* is a network of independent health care providers (doctors, hospitals, clinics, and labs) that work together to provide health services. Patients choose providers from a list. Typically, patients pay a co-pay at time of the service. A **co-pay** is the amount you pay each time you incur a medical service. For example, when you visit the doctor, you pay $25, and the PPO coverage pays the balance of the bill. Generally, there is no deductible.

A *health maintenance organization (HMO)* is health coverage that provides prepaid medical care for its members. HMOs typically have their own facilities—hospitals, medical offices, clinics, and labs—and offer a full range of services. Patients choose a *primary care physician*, who refers the patient to a specialist if and when one is needed. HMOs emphasize preventive care and wellness. Typically, you have a co-pay when accessing services and the HMO plan would pay the rest.

All types of health insurance coverage involve health insurance premiums to cover the cost of the insurance. The insurance company collects premiums from a large group of insured people, and then pays claims as they arise from those in the group. They hope to collect more in premiums than they pay out in claims.

Basic health care insurance protects you from costs involved in seeing a physician and having lab work done. *Major medical coverage* insurance protects you from the costs of very serious injuries or illness, such as an accident, illness, surgery, and hospitalization that can cost hundreds of thousands of dollars. Many people have both basic health care coverage and major medical coverage.

Disability Insurance

Disability insurance is a form of protection from loss of income. It replaces a portion of normal income earnings when the insured is unable to work due to a non work-related injury or illness. If a person is injured or becomes ill because of work conditions, workers' compensation coverage provides benefits. Both short-term disability (usually three to six months) and long-term disability (two or more years) coverage are available.

Life Insurance

Life insurance provides income protection. Families who depend on the income of the wage earner(s) are *beneficiaries*. Life insurance can be either temporary or permanent. Temporary life insurance provides a death benefit only. Permanent life insurance provides a death benefit and builds cash value.

Term life insurance is a temporary insurance policy that provides death benefits for a period of time, such as 20 years. It is considered "pure insurance" because you aren't paying for anything but insurance. Typically, parents have term insurance until their children reach adulthood. Then the insurance expires.

Whole life is a form of permanent insurance. The insured pays premiums for a lifetime. Whenever the insured dies, the life insurance benefits are paid to the beneficiaries. This type of policy builds cash value. You can borrow against the cash value, but if you don't pay it back, it reduces death benefits. There may be better ways of investing your money.

Other types of permanent insurance also are sold. Some have varying premiums, while others have fixed premiums, or a lump-sum premium. All of these forms of permanent life insurance also contain savings type of investments. The premiums are much higher than for term insurance.

Cost of Insurance

Insurance protects you from large and unpredictable losses. Buying insurance is a logical way to manage those risks. You can also maximize the value of your insurance while minimizing the cost.

Higher deductibles lower your premiums. In cases where risk is lower, you may think it is worth it to pay less in insurance premiums. For example, having a \$250 deductible for comprehensive coverage rather than a \$50 deductible can save you 10% or more on your car insurance.

To lower overall health care costs, you can set up a *flexible spending account (FSA)* with your employer, if your employer has such a plan. Money is set aside pre-tax, and can be used to pay deductibles, co-pays, and other medical costs not paid by insurance. Money withheld but not spent by year-end is forfeited. People with an FSA need to estimate medical expenses carefully to avoid having a balance, which is lost, at the end of the year.

ETHICS *in Action!*

What Is Insurance Fraud?

Filing a false claim to collect insurance proceeds is *insurance fraud*, which is a crime. For example, if a car is broken into and the policy holder reports items missing at higher than actual values, the policy holder is committing insurance fraud. Claiming property that did not exist is another way that people file false claims.

Another form of insurance fraud is when people purposely hide assets, claiming they were stolen. When people file false insurance claims, the cost of insurance rises for all consumers. Insurance companies must raise premiums on all policies to make up for the fraud losses.

Insurance companies can be unethical too. When a company denies legitimate claims, it is cheating people out of what they rightly deserve. When companies raise premiums without considering risk factors, just to add more money to the bottom line, this action is also unethical.

Think Critically

1. **Insurance is a method of the pooling resources of many to cover losses of a few. How does fraud disrupt that balance?**
2. **Both consumers and insurance companies can act unethically with claims. Does one simply balance out the other, making them both okay?**

If you have a high deductible on your health insurance policy, you can set up a *health spending account (HSA)*. This type of pre-tax account can be used for your deductible as well as other costs not paid by insurance, and the unused amount carries forward each year.

The frequency of when you pay premiums can affect your cost for insurance. For example, if you pay your insurance semi-annually rather than monthly, you may be able to save 10% or more.

If you have more than one policy with an insurance company, known as *stacking*, it usually results in the policy holder getting a **multi-line discount**. Many people have a homeowner's policy and a vehicle policy with the same insurance company. The total cost of stacked policies is less than if you carried the policies with separate insurance companies.

Insurance companies also set premiums based on risk. If you lower risk, you can qualify for *discounts*. Smoke detectors and security alarms can lower homeowner's and renter's premium costs. Buying theft protection devices, having a good driving record, and getting good grades can lower your car insurance premiums.

You should compare premiums and coverage at least every three years and be prepared to switch. As a teenage driver, you can save money by being added on to your parents' insurance policy, rather than taking out an individual policy.

CHECKPOINT

When is it a good idea to buy insurance?

16-3 Assessment

Key Concepts

LO 3-1 1. How are personal risks different from financial risks?

LO 3-1 2. Which risk strategy involves buying insurance?

LO 3-1 3. How can you reduce risks of personal injury?

LO 3-1 4. How can you avoid risks of financial loss?

Think About It

LO 3-2 5. Financial responsibility laws in all states require drivers to carry at least some minimum amount of liability insurance. Why?

LO 3-2 6. Why are insurance policies purchased from online sources less expensive than policies purchased from an agent you deal with in person? What do you give up in order to get lower premium costs?

LO 3-2 7. Why is it important to find a way to manage the rising costs of health care? (Consider health care spending as a percentage of GDP.)

LO 3-2 8. How much life insurance do you need at this point in your life? How will that change over time?

Make Academic Connections

LO 3-2 9. **MATH** Josh has health insurance that covers 80% of covered costs after a $150 deductible. He received a statement of covered costs for $1150. How much does Josh owe?

LO 3-1 10. **HISTORY** Write a two-page report about a natural disaster and its impact on the economy where the disaster occurred. Examples: Thailand (Sumatra) Tsunami of 2004, or Hurricane Katrina (Louisiana) in 2005.

LO 3-2 11. **GOVERNMENT** In 2010, the U.S. passed a comprehensive health care reform package. Research the current status of that legislation and its probable impact on you. Discuss the problems, benefits, and controversies associated with health care reform.

Teamwork

LO 3-2 12. Conduct online research about no-fault insurance laws. List states that have no-fault provisions. Present an oral report and explain what happens when there is an accident in a state with no-fault insurance laws.

LO 3-2 13. Many states have high-risk insurance pools, making it possible for people with poor driving records to purchase car insurance at relatively high rates. Prepare a chart of states that have high-risk pools and explain how the pools work in a particular state. Compare that to the high-risk pool laws (or lack thereof) in your state.

Unit 7 Project: Building a Global Future

RISK MANAGEMENT Risk management is more than buying insurance. Prepare a visual display or presentation that depicts various steps you would use to manage your risk and four possible courses of action. Include ways to minimize the cost of insurance when the best option is to shift the risk.

Chad Baker/Ryan McVay/Photodisc/Getty Images

16-4 Purchase, Use, and Dispose of Property

Learning Objectives

LO 4-1 **Explain** the costs and benefits of buying, using, and selling property.

LO 4-2 **Evaluate** the restrictions government places on the use of property by individuals and businesses.

Vocabulary

wealth, p. 475
cash flow, p. 475
listing agreement, p. 476
easement, p. 476
title report, p. 476
lien, p. 476

© Aleksandar Vrzalski/iStockphoto.com

REAL-WORLD FOCUS

Jasmine's parents own a piece of beach property in a nearby coastal town. Every summer they spend a week camping out at the property. "My dad is considering building a house on the property," she told her aunt. "He thinks maybe he will retire and live there someday. It's a nice place to visit, but I don't think I'd like to live there."

WORK AS A TEAM Why do people buy vacant plots of land, other than for their retirement? What kind of property would you like to own, and what would be your proposed use of that property?

Susan Leggett/Shutterstock.com

The sidewalks in this neighborhood are on portions of the homeowners' land that have an easement.

DO YOU THINK the homeowners pay for the sidewalks in front of their homes?

yienkeat/Shutterstock.com

LO 4-1 Own Property

When you buy property, you are purchasing an *asset*, or item of value that will change in value over time. **Wealth** is an accumulation of assets, including bank accounts, real estate, securities, and other investments. As you buy property and other assets, you must consider the costs as well as the benefits of the purchase, use, and disposal of the items of value.

Purchase Process

Most assets purchased as long-term investments involve much time and preparation. You may be considering buying rental property or vacant land. To be sure you are paying a fair price for real estate, you should get it appraised. An *appraisal* is a comparison of features, size, location, and other similar properties to determine a fair price. An appraiser gathers the information and gives you a projected *market value* of the property. An appraiser charges a fee for the appraisal.

The appraisal for income property (rentals) includes analysis of the income potential and costs, as measured by past revenues, vacancy rates, and projected market conditions. Market value of business property (property that will generate income) considers the cash flow. Determining your likely cash flow is important. A **cash flow** is the net amount you receive over and above the costs you have to pay. A *negative cash flow* means your costs are greater than your revenues. Past records of previous owners can provide good information. Comparisons of similar properties in the same geographic area are also useful.

RTimages/Shutterstock.com

Personal property refers to assets that are not permanently attached to land. Personal property such as cars, computers, furniture, and fixtures can easily be moved without causing damage to real property (buildings, land). Buying or leasing personal property is less complicated. The price is usually much lower. Personal property generally does not last as long, either. A computer may have a useful life of one to five years, while a building lasts for 30 years or longer. Personal property is usually financed with short-term loans, similar to car loans or leases. Businesses also purchase other long-term assets, such as buildings, factories, natural resources, and equipment. *Commercial property* refers to assets a business uses to generate income. This type of property includes buying existing businesses, franchises, licenses, patents, and copyrights. These assets represent future cash flows to the business.

Use of Property

Private property ownership is important in a free market economy. Individuals can own personal property, land, buildings, and other forms of real property. Owners have free access to their property and free enjoyment of the property. Owners can make improvements to the property, or use the property for any legal purpose. Owners are responsible for maintaining both real and personal property. Vehicles that are not properly serviced do not last as long. Real property must also be maintained.

Owners of real property must pay property taxes. *Property taxes* are assessed against owners based on the value of the property. Property may be required to have a septic tank, street lighting, and other improvements. Owners must pay for the installation of such features, and must pay annual assessments to keep them properly serviced.

Disposal of Property

Property can be sold in the open market. Personal and business property can be sold for its remaining book value. *Book value* is what remains after allowable depreciation expense has been written off. Real estate can be sold by its owner, or by using the services of a real estate agent. Sales commissions are charged by real estate agents. A **listing agreement** is a legal contract that describes the property being sold, the price being asked, and the sales commission. If an owner decides to sell without using a real estate agent, it is a good idea to get legal advice to be sure that personal interests are protected.

When property is sold, it is subject to taxes. Some state laws assess a *transfer tax* or fee against the seller of the property. Other states charge a sales tax for real estate transfers. Typically such taxes and fees are withheld from the seller's proceeds at the closing of the sale of the property.

CHECKPOINT

Why is an appraisal needed before buying real estate?

LO 4-2 Restrictions on Property

Private property can have restrictions on its use. For example, an **easement** represents the legal right of another entity to have limited use of property. A *utility easement* allows the use of property, usually below the surface, for placement of electric, cable, and other lines. Owners must obey local laws related to requirements for sidewalks, sewer, storm drains, and other areas of the property.

Property owners must also obey *CCRs* (covenants, conditions, and restrictions) that are formed when a subdivision, commercial tract, or property lot is created, plotted, or modified. A list of CCRs is included on a title report. A **title report** is created by a title insurance company. It is a record of ownership (title) and all legal restrictions on a property. The title report includes any debt or other liens attached to the property. A **lien** is a legal obligation that must be paid before a clear title to property can be passed to a new owner. For example, if property taxes are unpaid, the money owed accumulates as a lien. A title report also reveals existing limitations. For example, a housing subdivision may require that owners build a certain type of fence or use a certain type of building material. A commercial lot may require a minimum number of parking spaces for a business building to be constructed on the site.

Real property is also subject to local *zoning laws* and ordinances. Zoning laws restrict the type of construction as well as the purpose of a lot or other real property. For example, when land is zoned residential, it cannot be developed for commercial (business) activity. Local ordinances or laws can set requirements

Global View

Life in Dubai

Incorporated in 1833, the modern emirate of Dubai was created after gaining independence from the United Kingdom in 1971. Dubai, together with four other emirates, formed the United Arab Emirates. In 1966, when oil was discovered in Dubai, the new oil economy led to the massive influx of foreign workers. Today, Dubai is a global city and a business hub.

Although originally built on an oil economy, today's model of business is similar to that of Western countries. Its main revenues are from tourism, real estate, and financial services. In the new century Dubai gained world attention with its innovative and large construction projects and sporting events. Like the housing bubble in the United States, the Recession of 2008 and 2009 caused a deterioration of property values in Dubai as well.

Dubai emirate is a flat and sandy desert that gives way to mountains along its border with Oman. The desert surrounding the city of Dubai supports grasses and palm trees. Natural parks include exotic birds, fish, and mammal life. Dubai, with a population of over 2.2 million people, boasts an international airport, metro rail lines, and commercial ports. You can buy any type of real estate, from houses to condos, or flats, both in urban and suburban areas of the city.

Think Critically

1. **What do you think it would it be like to live in a foreign country?**
2. **What economic advantages are offered by a global city such as Dubai?**

such as height regulations, set-back regulations, sanitation rules, and other local restrictions on uses of the property.

Sometimes the rights of the many outweigh the rights of the few. When private property is needed for public purposes (such as building a freeway or urban renewal) private property can be taken away from owners. The process called *eminent domain* is the legal surrender of private property for public use. It requires fair compensation of owners for property that is taken.

In addition to government restrictions, groups of owners may band together and set additional restrictions and conditions. A *homeowners' association* is a group of owners in a subdivision or other geographic location. The group meets, elects officers, and represents the owners when dealing with local government units as well as governing owners in the group. Property owners may have to pay dues or other fees to the association. Business owners can also belong to an industrial park or other business development area. As such, they must also obey the requirements which may include how the property is accessed, the type of activity conducted, and how customers are served.

CHECKPOINT

Why would a prospective buyer of property want to see a title report?

Property Management

You're the ENTREPRENEUR

Owning real estate as an investment can have many advantages. Whether you own a rental home, duplex, or apartment complex, you have business deductions that give you a *tax shelter*. At the same time you are collecting rent from your tenants, you are also paying off the underlying mortgage. When that mortgage is paid off, the net cash flows provide the owner with monthly income.

As the property owner, you must decide how you will manage the rental unit(s). Some owners live at the property in an apartment or separate building. As a *residential owner*, you deal directly with the tenants. Duties include selecting tenants, collecting rent payments, arranging for repairs, and doing the daily tasks to make sure the property is properly maintained.

Some apartment unit owners choose to pay another person(s) to live at the property and do these functions. The *apartment manager* acts on behalf of the owner to select renters, collect rent payments, and coordinate repairs and maintenance. An apartment manager provides an accounting of these activities to the owner on a regular basis.

Some owners have multiple units of property, which may include houses, duplexes, and other buildings. They may hire a *property management company.* This type of off-site management business interviews prospective tenants and makes sure they are capable of making rent payments. They also inspect the property, arrange for repairs and maintenance, and make regular reports to the owners. The advantage of this type of service is that the property owner does not have to live nearby or be concerned with the day-to-day care of the property.

Whenever you hire someone else to manage your property, you pay them a fee. Apartment managers are usually paid a monthly fee and receive reduced or free rent in a unit at the property. A property management company usually receives a percentage of the rent collected. For example, if you charge $800 a month rent for the unit, the property management company's monthly fee may be $120 (15%) a month per unit, or more. You sign an agreement with the property management company that specifies duties and the fee charged.

Think Critically

1. **Do you think that owning real estate as an investment is a good way to provide for your future financial security? Why or why not?**
2. **If you were a property owner, which form of management would you choose: residential ownership, an apartment manager, or hiring a property management company? Why?**

16-4 Assessment

Key Concepts

LO 4-1 1. What is meant by market value of property?

LO 4-1 2. What is property tax and who pays it?

LO 4-2 3. What is a CCR and where is it found?

LO 4-2 4. What happens when a government exercises its right of eminent domain over property?

Think About It

LO 4-1 5. The process of buying property begins with determining what the property is worth. Why do buyers need to know market value?

LO 4-1 6. How is personal property different from real property?

LO 4-1 7. Why is it important for owners of property to keep it maintained and serviced as needed?

LO 4-2 8. When owners don't pay property taxes or other debts, the amounts owed can become liens against real property. What does that mean to the owner?

Make Academic Connections

LO 4-1 9. **MATH** If you bought property for a purchase price of $180,000, with a down payment of 15%, how much cash would you need for the down payment?

LO 4-1 10. **RESEARCH** Do online research about property values in your geographic area. Prepare a graph or chart that lists average home values compared to national averages over a two- or three-year period.

LO 4-2 11. **COMMUNICATIONS** You plan to invest in real estate as a landlord. Prepare an oral report describing the type of property you would purchase, how much rent you would charge, and rules you would require your tenants to obey. Explain how you set the monthly rental price.

LO 4-2 12. **SOCIAL STUDIES** Assume you and all of your neighbors belong to a neighborhood association. The association has elected its officers. A meeting has been called to discuss the feasibility of requiring all homeowners to paint their homes at least once every five years. Discuss the implications (good and bad) of such a decision.

Teamwork

LO 4-2 13. As a group, do research in your local area about commercial (business) property for sale. Find out local occupancy rates (how much property is not being rented) and prices per square foot. Prepare a report explaining the current situation and its costs.

LO 4-2 14. Visit a title insurance company or its website. Investigate title reports and title searches. Bring information and handouts to the class. Explain what is contained in title reports and how title information is found. Prepare a visual display of the contents of a title report.

Chapter 16 Summary

16-1 RENT OR OWN A HOME

1. When you first leave home, you will have many choices. You may go to college and live on campus or choose an apartment or other housing off campus. Renting gives you flexibility and convenience. But it can also be noisy or crowded, you must obey the rules of the property, and you pay fees and deposits.
2. Buying a house has many advantages, such as privacy and rights of ownership. Home ownership also provides a tax shelter because interest and property taxes are deductible for income tax purposes. Homeowners must maintain their property and make payments as agreed.
3. Moving and buying property takes time and costs money. The buying process can take months and there are many steps, including inspection to make sure the property is sound. A down payment is required along with a mortgage, which is a long-term debt obligation.

16-2 LEASE OR BUY A CAR

4. Leasing a car is advantageous for those who can deduct the expense and for those who need a new car every two or three years. Buying a car involves debt. Car loans often take 5 to 7 years to pay off.
5. The car buying process involves doing considerable research, getting pre-qualified, checking a car's history, test driving, checking insurance rates, negotiations and making an offer, and avoiding added costs.

16-3 RISK MANAGEMENT AND INSURANCE

6. Consumers face personal and financial risks. Risks can be reduced, avoided, transferred, and assumed. Transferring risk is buying insurance to protect against financial losses.
7. Property insurance covers homes, cars, and other forms of physical property. Health, disability, and life insurance cover costs from illness, injury, or death. Insurance premiums depend on risk. You can lower your premiums when you lower risk to the insurance company or assume more risk yourself.

16-4 PURCHASE, USE, AND DISPOSE OF PROPERTY

8. Wealth is ownership of assets such as property. The purchase of assets such as real estate involves a lengthy process. An appraisal gives you a good idea of the market value of property. Both real and personal property involve a buying process to analyze future benefits.
9. Private property allows free access, privacy, and many positive features. Owners are also responsible to maintain the property and pay any fees or assessments. This property can be sold in the open market based on its value.
10. Government restrictions on use and taxes are imposed on owners of property. Easements, zoning laws, ordinances, and public rights of eminent domain are examples of the types of government restrictions.

Chapter 16

Assessment

Vocabulary Review

Match each statement with the term that best defines it.

1. Process of taking away private property to pay debt
2. Tax savings that results from allowable deductions
3. Contract for using a vehicle for a set period of time
4. Contract describing property being sold
5. Contract that specifies rights and duties of landlord and tenant
6. Amount you pay before insurance starts paying benefits
7. Long-term debt used to purchase real property
8. Getting a loan amount approved in advance
9. Amount you pay each time you use a service
10. Preset maximum amount of mileage per year
11. Percentage of the price of a home that is paid at closing
12. Setting aside money to pay for a financial loss
13. A cost that reduces taxable income
14. Having two types of insurance policies to reduce premiums
15. Expenses incurred in transferring ownership
16. The chance of injury, damage, or economic loss
17. Record of ownership and legal restrictions on property
18. Net amount received after expenses are paid
19. Accumulation of assets over time that increase in value
20. Legal right to limited use of another person's property
21. Legal obligation that must be paid to clear title
22. Manufacturer's assurance against defects in a product
23. Assessing risks and planning actions to manage them
24. Coverage beyond manufacturer's assurance

Vocabulary

a. business expense
b. car lease
c. cash flow
d. closing costs
e. co-pay
f. deductible
g. down payment
h. easement
i. extended warranty
j. factory warranty
k. foreclosure
l. lien
m. listing agreement
n. mileage allowance
o. mortgage
p. multi-line discount
q. preapproval
r. rental agreement
s. risk
t. risk management
u. self-insuring
v. tax shelter
w. title report
x. wealth

Review Your Knowledge

LO 1-1 25. Which is a living space on two levels?
a. condominium
b. studio apartment
c. townhouse
d. multiplex

LO 1-2 26. Increased value gained from home ownership is called
a. equity
b. tax shelter
c. capital loss
d. business deduction

LO 1-2 27. If you don't pay property taxes, your property can be subject to
a. inspection
b. foreclosure
c. forfeiting deposits
d. contractor liens

LO 1-3 28. Buying a house begins with an offer, called a(n)
a. preapproval
b. earnest money
c. counteroffer
d. home inspection

LO 1-3 29. Which is not a closing cost?
a. title insurance
b. prorated interest
c. escrow fees
d. moving costs

LO 2-1 30. The owner of a vehicle being leased is the
a. lessee
b. lessor
c. mortgagor
d. tax advisor

LO 2-2 31. Which is the first step in the car buying process?
a. get preapproval
b. check the car's history
c. do considerable research
d. test drive the car

LO 3-1 32. Which strategy will lower your risk of loss?
a. risk avoidance
b. risk transfer
c. risk reduction
d. risk assumption

LO 3-2 33. Which coverage protects you if your car's windshield is broken?
a. liability
b. collision
c. comprehensive
d. uninsured motorist

LO 4-1 34. Which takes into consideration cash flows on property?
a. market value
b. personal property
c. property taxes
d. listing agreement

LO 4-2 35. Which is a process that allows the government to take property for public use?
a. foreclosure
b. eminent domain
c. repossession
d. easement

Digging Deeper with Economics e-Collection

The U.S. housing market is often cited as a leading economic indicator. When the market does poorly, the economy is going into decline. It is often cited also in terms of recovery. When the housing market does well, the economy starts to grow. Access the Gale Economics e-Collection at **www.cengage.com/school/economics/personalfinance**. View the history of the U.S. housing market since 1950, as measured by new housing construction. Prepare a chart relating the housing market to the GDP for a ten-year period.

Think About It

LO 1-1 36. Many people moving into apartments choose to split living expenses with a roommate to lower the costs of living on their own. What are some things to consider when doing this?

LO 2-1 37. Besides car payments, there are many other expenses in owning a vehicle. If you used your car as part of your job (deliveries), how much would you need to pay your costs?

LO 3-1 38. Losing your job is a serious risk. What can you (the employee) do to lower this risk?

Make Academic Connections

LO 4-1 39. **MATH** Property taxes are assessed on value. Assume that the tax rate is $13 per thousand dollars of assessed value. Compute property tax owed on properties with these assessed values:

a. $150,000
b. $300,000
c. $110,900
d. $450,000

LO 1-1 40. **ETHICS** By law, landlords must return deposits paid by tenants. Some landlords charge tenants for damage they didn't do. How can tenants protect themselves from pre-existing damage (it was there when they moved in)?

LO 3-1 41. **SOCIAL STUDIES** Taking risks can lead to serious injury or even death. Why do people engage in highly risky activities such as mountain climbing and sky diving? What do they do to reduce their risk of injury and death? Why do they (you) consider the risk worth taking?

LO 4-2 42. **COMMUNICATIONS** Government restrictions on the use of private property are part of local and state laws. Many of them are to provide for the common good. Pick a restriction (such as a zoning law or ordinance preventing burning garbage in the city limits) and explain why it is needed and how it benefits society as a whole.

Extend Your Learning

LO 2-1 43. Do research from *Consumer Reports*, either the actual magazine or at their website, concerning automobile safety. Compare safety ratings, car crash tests, safety features, and other items you find in your research. Present your findings, ranking vehicles according to the analyses and articles you find. Show your data.

LO 2-2 44. Discuss the car buying process with three adults who have purchased vehicles in the last three years. Ask them how they chose their vehicle, steps they took in buying, and the negotiations that were needed. Prepare a written report of your findings.

LO 3-2 45. Go online and get insurance quotes from three companies using the same vehicle information. Keep coverage the same (using full coverage) and compare the quotes you receive.

monkeybusinessimages/iStockphoto.com

chapter 17

Invest for the Future

yienkeat/Shutterstock.com

MARKETS *in Action!*

What Are Bulls and Bears?

Stocks are bought and sold at a *stock exchange.* The New York Stock Exchange (NYSE) is located on Wall Street in New York City. Over time Wall Street has come to mean a geographic location that includes the downtown Manhattan financial district. Offices of several other major stock exchanges are also located in the financial district, including the NASDAQ, AMEX, NYMEX, and NYBOT.

The words "bull" and "bear" are used to describe the ups and downs of the stock markets. According to Investopedia.com, *bull* and *bear* are used to describe the way the animals attack their opponents. A bull thrusts its horns up into the air while a bear swipes its paws down. These actions are metaphors for the movement of a market. Bull markets are characterized by optimism, investor confidence, and expectations that strong business results are coming. Bear markets are characterized by pessimism, where investors are nervous and expect weak business results in the future.

In a bull market, prices of stocks are steadily and consistently rising. That does not mean that prices go up every day and that there are no days when prices are lower. Nor does it mean that all stock prices are rising. In a bull market the overall trend of stock market prices is in an upward direction. Investors in a bull market hope to make money by buying stocks when they are at their lowest prices and selling when they are at their highest prices.

In a bear market, prices of stocks are steadily and consistently falling. Again, it does not mean that prices are falling every day and that there are no days when prices are rising. Nor does it mean that all stock prices are falling. In a bear market, the overall trend of stock market prices is a downward direction. In a bear market, many investors hold their stocks and hope to buy more stock when the price is at the lowest.

The longest-lived bull market in U.S. history began in 1991 and ended in 2000. Others occurred in the 1920s, 1950s, late 1960s, and the mid-2000s. They all ended in recessions. The Great Depression is the most well-known bear market. Others occurred in 1973–74, 1981–82, 2000–02, and 2007–09. In 2010–11, the stock market made gains on some days, but losses on other days were greater.

On the trading floor at the NYSE on Wall Street, there is continuous action of traders making transactions on behalf of investors.

EdStock/iStockphoto.com

Think Critically

1. How can you recognize a bull market? Bear market?
2. Why is it important for investors to be familiar with the stock market and know if prices in general are rising or falling?

yienkeat/Shutterstock.com

17-1 Invest in Stocks

Learning Objectives

LO 1-1 **Explain** the concept of direct investing in stocks, including examples of how to reduce risk.

LO 1-2 **Describe** the concept of indirect investing and the risks, rewards, and economic impact of investing.

Vocabulary

equity financing, p. 487
portfolio, p. 488
diversification, p. 488
mutual fund, p. 489
asset allocation, p. 489

© Aleksandar Vrzalski/ iStockphoto.com

REAL-WORLD FOCUS

Neil has managed to keep his bills (payments) low so he can set aside a regular amount of money each month for investing. He recently opened a brokerage account and has begun the process of making indirect investments. "I prefer to put my initial investments into a fairly safe choice," Neil told his financial advisor. "Later, when I have a solid base, I'll think more about direct investing and other riskier options."

WORK AS A TEAM If you were able to set aside a regular amount each month, what would be your first investment choice? Explain how risk and expected return might influence your choice.

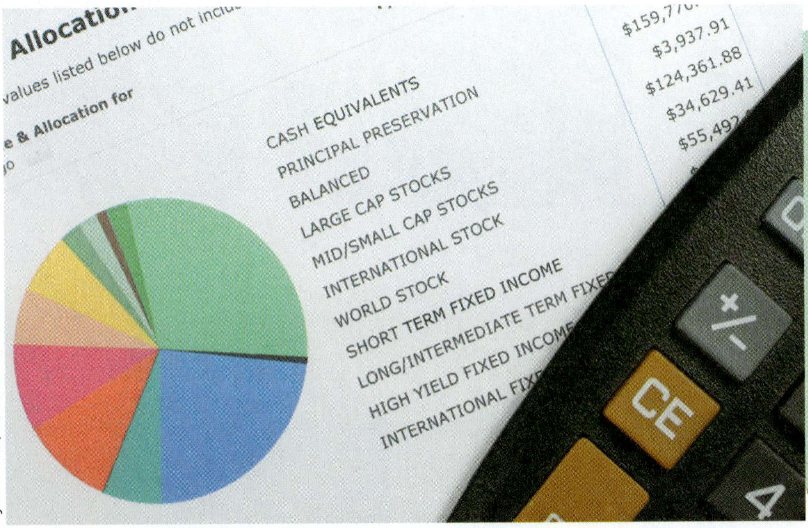

Ryan R Fox/Shutterstock.com

An investor's ideal portfolio depends on personal preferences, personal data, and long-term goals. A portfolio should be diversified and change as the investor's situation changes.

DO YOU THINK **a portfolio can be too diversified or modified too often?**

yienkeat/Shutterstock.com

LO 1-1 Direct Investing

For consumers, saving and investing are closely related. Setting aside money (savings) provides funds that can be used for investing. As investments grow, *wealth* can be accumulated. Saving and investing provide financial security. The first purpose of saving should be to have a reserve you can count on. An *emergency fund* is an amount of money available for unplanned expenses. Ideally, when an emergency situation arises, you should be able to use cash from savings rather than borrow. If you set aside $10,000 for an emergency fund, and then used the rest of your savings for permanent investing, you would less likely to have to sell an investment when an emergency arose.

For investing, you might choose to buy common stock in publicly-held corporations. The purchase of stocks from individual companies is *direct investing*. For the corporation, this is a form of equity financing. **Equity financing** is the sale of corporate stock to generate cash. The stockholders have shares of stock, and are owners of the corporation. The corporation receives funds when the stock is first sold. When you buy stock from a current owner the corporation does not receive more funds.

As an investor, you face several types of risk. With more risk comes the possibility of greater rewards. You must also be willing to accept that the value of your investment (principal amount) may actually decrease. *Investment risk* is the potential for change in value of your investment. To offset this risk, you look for choices that will, on average, go up more than they go down. The goal is to increase the value of your investment over time.

Investment Risks

There are four important types of investment risk when investing directly in the stocks of individual companies.

INFLATION RISK When prices are rising rapidly in the economy, your investment may lose value. *Inflation risk* is the chance that the rate of inflation will grow faster than the rate of return on your investment. For example, assume you purchase a stock at $50 a share, and by the end of the year it has risen 10 percent in value, and now it is worth $55. That sounds like a nice return. But if the annual rate of inflation is greater than 10 percent, then your investment is worth less today than it was at the beginning of the year.

INDUSTRY RISK Industry risk is the chance that factors affecting an industry as a whole will negatively affect the value of an investment. For example, you invest in a company in the oil business. When oil prices and profits are rising, your stock investment gains in value. When alternate sources of energy are developed, stocks in the oil industry may lose value. Industry risk occurs in all sectors, from pharmaceuticals to agricultural products.

POLITICAL RISK This type of risk is probably the most unpredictable, both in terms of when it might happen and also in terms of how serious the effects might be. Political risk is the chance that some political event, such as a new law or policy, a war, a natural disaster, or an election, could disrupt business and cause unpredictability. For example, a political uprising in a country on the other side of the world can affect individual stock prices.

STOCK RISK When you purchase shares of stock in a corporation, you become a stockholder. As a stockholder, you risk losing part or all of your investment, depending on how well the company is able to generate profits over time. *Stock risk* is the chance that activities or events that affect an individual company change the value of an investment in that company.

NET Bookmark

Access www.cengage.com/school/economics/personalfinance and click on the link for Chapter 17. The FINRA (Financial Industry Regulatory Authority) is the self-regulatory agency for stockbrokers in the United States. It sets rules for brokers and helps investors recover losses when their stock funds have not been properly managed. What are the four categories into which most common claims fall?

www.cengage.com/school/economics/personalfinance

Reduce Investment Risk

Rather than buying many shares of just one type of stock, you can lower your risk by buying fewer shares of many different types of stocks. In other words, buy stocks in several different industries. A group of different types of investments is called a **portfolio**. Stocks are an important part of a typical portfolio because they provide the potential for long-term growth, even though prices may vary in the short term.

To reduce the overall risk of your portfolio of investments, you should diversify. **Diversification** is the process of selecting different types of investments with different levels of risk. For example, to offset the high risk of direct investing in stocks, you might also choose to have some low-risk investments, some real estate, and other choices. Then, if an event that results in a loss in one of your investment choices, the others can keep your entire portfolio from crashing.

You can reduce overall investment risk by *investment tracking*. This process involves tracking stock performance over time. If you are satisfied with trends over five or ten years, you can elect to buy that stock. Once you buy a stock, you continue to track its progress. When the performance over time isn't as good as you can find in other investments, it's time to sell.

Market timing involves buying and selling stocks based on what the market is expected to do. The goal is to buy low, sell high. When stock prices are low, such as immediately following a stock split, you buy. The most common stock split is 2:1. For every share of stock, an investor now has two. The number of shares issued will double, while the value is cut in half. So if you had 100 shares worth $50 per share ($5,000), you would now have 200 shares worth $25 per share ($5,000). When stock prices are higher, such as a period of strong growth, it can be a good time to sell unless you are convinced that the stock's value will continue to grow in the future.

Finally, *dollar-cost averaging* is a technique where you invest the same amount of money on a regular basis, such as monthly, regardless of the market. Over time, the dollar cost per share will be comparable to the average price of the stock.

CHECKPOINT

What are four types of investment risk?

LO 1-2 Indirect Investing

You can lower your investment risk by choosing to invest indirectly. *Indirect investing* is purchasing mutual funds, joining investment clubs, and other choices instead of owning individual stocks.

Mutual Funds

A **mutual fund** is a professionally managed group of investments. The fund holds a portfolio that may consist of stocks, bonds, or other investments from gold to commodities, based on a stated set of objectives. For example, an income fund specializes in buying investments that pay a steady rate of return. A growth fund specializes in buying investments that are expected to grow over time. Figure 17-1 is a list of many of the mutual fund types.

Figure 17-1

Mutual Fund Types

Mutual Fund Type	Description
Balanced Fund	A diversified portfolio that includes some low-risk, some medium-risk, and some high-risk stocks. Goal: balance between income and growth, lowering overall risk while maintaining a solid growth. Medium risk.
Bond Fund	Investment in corporate bonds or government bonds to minimize risk and receive a steady return. Low risk in most cases.
Global Fund	Investment in international companies, new industries in foreign countries, and companies in the world marketplace. High risk.
Growth Fund	Investment in new and small companies expected to grow over long run and large companies that are expanding. High risk.
Income Fund	Invest in bonds and stocks that produce steady and reliable income (dividends and interest) that are passed along to investors. Low risk.
Index Fund	Diversified investment in securities to match a market index with the goal of having returns similar to the index. Medium risk.
Money Market Fund	Invest in short-term securities that have a return that goes up and down with current interest rates and current economic conditions. Low risk.
New Venture Fund	Investment in new and emerging businesses and industries. High risk.
Precious Metal Fund	Invest in companies that are associated with precious metals such as gold, silver, and platinum. High risk.
Stock Fund	Stock portfolio that can specialize in a certain type of stocks, such as blue chips, technology, medical, and so on. Risk depends on sector of investment.

With mutual funds, you can manage your investment goals and your risk. **Asset allocation** is the process of choosing a combination of funds that can be found in different mutual funds. For example, you may choose an allocation that is 25 percent bond fund, 20 percent growth fund, 40 percent income fund, and

15 percent global fund. You can change those percentages with notification to the mutual fund company.

Investment Clubs

You may wish to join a group of people who share your same financial goals. This group pools its resources and makes investments. *Investment clubs* usually form a legal business entity, such as a partnership. It is a form of indirect investing when a diversified group of stocks, bonds, mutual funds, and other investment choices are made. Even if the club purchases stocks directly from companies, the individual investor would still be lowering his or her risk. The club owns the stocks and divides the profits (or losses) among its members. Better Investing is an organization that helps people form investment clubs.

Other Forms of Indirect Investing

You can also invest your money indirectly through retirement accounts. For example, you can open an IRA (individual retirement account) that uses money its members provide to invest in stocks or bonds. Your account represents your share of the investments made by the funds in selected companies.

Annuities may be purchased through life insurance companies. Your money pays a fixed return and the underlying investment supports the payments you will receive in the future. You are not buying stocks or bonds directly. The insurance company buys the stocks or bonds and manages the accounts.

Risk, Reward, and Economic Impact

All forms of investing come with some risk. While risk cannot be avoided, it can be reduced. You will take less risk if you are an astute investor and take the time to learn about markets and investment opportunities. Knowledge is power; the more you know, the better prepared you will be to make good decisions. If you are unwilling or unable to put the time and energy into managing your own investments, you can lower your risk by hiring experts. Indirect investing involves using experts. When you invest with a mutual fund you are relying on the expertise of professionals who manage funds.

When individuals and businesses invest in stocks of corporations, they are supporting economic growth. Corporations use the money initially invested by stockholders to buy equipment, buildings, factories, and other capital goods. They also hire workers and are able to generate profits. *Dividends,* which are a share of the profits generated by the company, are a reward or payback to those who invest in stocks. As an investor, you hope to be able to sell your stock at a price higher than you paid for it so that you can make a capital gain.

Investing in stocks of publicly traded companies leads to greater output of goods and services, and greater exchange within the product and resource markets. When investing is robust, the economy is likely to grow because resources are available to meet new wants and needs. Investors provide money that can be used for expansion, innovation, and growth.

CHECKPOINT

How does indirect investing reduce your risk?

PROFILE

Mark Cuban
American Entrepreneur

Helga Esteb/Shutterstock.com

Born in 1958, Mark Cuban is owner of the National Basketball Association's Dallas Mavericks. He also owns Landmark Theaters, Magnolia Pictures, and is chairman of the HDTV cable network HDNet. HDNet is a men's interest television channel available only in HD format on cable and satellite television. He also is a part-time "shark" investor (a wealthy investor who judges new ideas on the Shark Tank television series).

Cuban first stepped into the world of business at the age of 12 when he sold garbage bags to pay for an expensive pair of basketball shoes. He held a variety of jobs while attending school, including bartender, dancing instructor, and party promoter. He paid for college with his entrepreneurial activities, such as collecting and selling stamps.

Graduating from Indiana University in 1981 with a bachelor's degree in business administration, Cuban moved to Dallas, Texas. There he started a company, MicroSolutions. In 1990 Cuban sold his company to CompuServe for a net of $2 million after taxes. Having an avid interest in basketball and webcast, Cuban went on to invest in Broadcast.com. This company grew and by 1999 it was worth over $5.9 billion. It was sold to Yahoo! later that year.

In January of 2004, Cuban bought a majority interest in the Dallas Mavericks for $280 million (from H. Ross Perot). Unlike many owners who sit in skyboxes, Cuban sits with the crowd and enjoys the game with the fans.

Through the years, Cuban has invested money wisely, hoping to avoid the risk of a market failure. In 2011 he was listed as #459 on Forbes's "World's Richest People" list, amassing a personal wealth of $2.5 billion. Cuban continues to make investments directly in companies, in joint ventures, and in start-up technology businesses.

Cuban's love of sports has led him to continued interest in team ownership, including baseball, hockey, and wrestling entertainment. Claiming inspiration from Ayn Rand's *The Fountainhead*, Cuban said, "It was incredibly motivating to me. It encouraged me to think as an individual, take risks to reach my goals, and responsibility for my successes and failures."

THINK CRITICALLY

1. **Mark Cuban took risks as he moved through his entrepreneurial career. Yet he sought to minimize the risks where possible. Why?**
2. **Cuban's life has not been without controversy. He has been involved in a number of lawsuits, both filed by him and against him. He maintains a personal weblog and takes an active role in politics. Why do many successful businessmen like Cuban participate so visually in world affairs? What do they have to gain?**

yienkeat/Shutterstock.com

17-1 Assessment

Key Concepts

LO 1-1 1. What is meant by direct investing?

LO 1-1 2. How can you reduce the risk of direct investing?

LO 1-2 3. What is meant by indirect investing?

LO 1-2 4. What is the purpose of an investment club?

LO 1-2 5. How are risk and reward related?

Think About It

LO 1-1 6. Having an emergency fund helps you take care of unplanned events and expenses. How much money should you have set aside?

LO 1-1 7. When you put your money into a savings account and receive 0.5 percent interest, are you staying ahead of inflation? What kinds of investments should you make to be able to earn a greater return than inflation?

LO 1-2 8. Indirect investing is less risky than direct investing. What else can you do to lower your overall risk?

Make Academic Connections

LO 1-2 9. **HISTORY** Look up the Stock Market Crash of 1929. Prepare a report explaining what led up to the crash, who was affected, how much money was lost, and the impact on the economy.

LO 1-2 10. **SOCIAL STUDIES** Taking risks is necessary in order to grow your wealth. Many people are not comfortable with high levels of risk. Prepare an oral report describing the various kinds of investment risks and how people are affected when risks turn into losses.

LO 1-1 11. **TECHNOLOGY** Today you can follow stocks and other investments online, including daily stock transactions and stock market reports. Follow the news reports and stock markets from the U.S. and world markets for a week. Prepare a graph that illustrates how the various stock exchanges went up or down during the week you followed.

Teamwork

LO 1-1 12. As a group, pick a well-known stock, a well-known mutual fund, and one other lesser-known stock or mutual fund. Find out all you can about these investment alternatives at websites, from news articles, and other sources. Compare the risks you would take in investing in each of them and prepare a comparative analysis.

Unit 7 Project: Building a Global Future

THE STOCK MARKET Choose five stocks from the NYSE and/or the NASDAQ. Using an Excel worksheet, keep track of the progress of those stocks for two weeks. Assume you begin with a purchase of $10,000 divided among the stock choices. Compute your gains/losses at the end of two weeks.

yienkeat/Shutterstock.com, Chad Baker/Ryan McVay/Photodisc/Getty Images

17-2 Invest in Bonds

Learning Objectives

LO 2-1 **Describe** types of corporate bond investments, including risks, rewards, and economic impact.

LO 2-2 **Describe** types of government and tax-free bonds, including risks, rewards, and economic impact.

Vocabulary

debt financing, p. 494
corporate bonds, p. 494
municipal bond, p. 497
savings bond, p. 498
agency bond, p. 499
risk-free investment, p. 499

REAL-WORLD FOCUS

Yueer has just one form of investing—her employer's retirement plan. She contributes 5 percent of her gross pay which is invested in the company's common stock. "I think it's time for me to start setting aside money in a separate account," she told her mother. "The company stock is risky, so I think I should start out with bonds to offset that. I'm thinking about municipal bonds."

WORK AS A TEAM What kind of risk is associated with investment in government bonds? Why is it important to have low-risk choices in your initial portfolio of investments?

© Aleksandar Vrzalski/iStockphoto.com

All people who travel on a toll road must pay the per-axle fee each time they pass through the collection sites. Many states build a toll road with the thought that those who use the road should pay for the road.

DO YOU THINK funds used to build a new toll road are generated from corporate bonds, municipal bonds, or agency bonds?

jcpjr/Shutterstock.com

yienkeat/Shutterstock.com

LO 2-1 Investing in Corporate Bonds

Corporations rely on two forms of investing—stocks and bonds. While stocks represent equity or ownership in a company, bonds represent debt to the company. **Debt financing** is borrowing by a corporation. It includes short-term debt, such as notes payable, as well as long-term debt, such as bonds and mortgages. For many large corporations, bonds are a major way to raise large sums of cash to pay for expansion, new technology, innovation, and long-term growth and survival.

Corporate bonds are long-term debt obligations of publicly-held corporations. These bonds are generally issued in multiples of $1,000 and pay a fixed interest rate each year. They also repay the *face value* (principal) or amount that is borrowed at maturity. *Maturity* is a point in the future when the full amount of principal and interest must be repaid. For example, a $1,000, ten-year, 5 percent bond has a face value of $1,000 and pays annual interest at a fixed rate of 5 percent ($50). At the end of ten years, the face value of $1,000 is repaid.

AVAVA/Shutterstock.com

For many large corporations, a team of financial experts determine if debt financing is necessary and the amount they want to raise by selling corporate bonds.

Bonds are considered a fairly safe investment choice because they pay a fixed rate of interest. Large, publicly-held corporations are able to issue bonds after they go through an approval process to make sure they are able to repay the debt. Investors in bonds are taking less risk and thus the return is also lower. Lower risk generally means lower return.

Bonds are rated by bond rating services such as Moody's and Standard & Poor's. These ratings are based on the financial condition of the company, and range from AAA (superior) to D (likely to default).

Types of Bonds

A *debenture* is a corporate bond that is based on the general creditworthiness of the company. The company does not pledge any specific asset to assure repayment of the loan. Thus, a debenture is often called unsecured debt. The investor has made a fairly low-risk investment choice because corporations use the borrowed money to buy assets which will generate cash to pay off the debt. Most publicly-traded corporate bonds are debentures.

A *secured bond*, often called a mortgage bond, is backed by specific assets, which serve as security to assure repayment of the debt. If the corporation does not repay the debt as agreed, the bondholder (or mortgagor) can claim the property used as security for the debt. The assets most often used for security are real estate, a building, or equipment.

A *serial bond* repays principal and interest during the term of the bond. For example, suppose a corporation issues a ten-year, $10 million, 5 percent bond. The annual interest is $500,000 ($10,000,000 × 5%). Each year the corporation pays interest and 1/10 of the principal or $1 million. Thus at the end of each year (for ten years), the corporation pays $1.5 million to its bondholders.

FreeSoulProduction/Shutterstock.com

Math CONNECTION

Exchange a Convertible Bond for Shares

In an ideal situation, the holder of a convertible bond (discussed on the following page) will be able to decide when to convert the bond to shares of stock. The time to make the conversion is when the common stock is worth more than the amount paid for the convertible bond.

Malcolm purchased a \$1,200 corporate bond which is convertible to 80 shares of common stock in the corporation. Malcolm watches how the corporation performs in the stock market daily. At what price per share should Malcolm exercise his right to convert the bond to shares? Will he make or lose money if he converts when the shares are valued at \$16.18? How much money will you make or lose?

SOLUTION

1,200 ÷ 80 = \$15 Divide investment by the number of shares received in conversion.

Malcolm should make the conversion when a share of stock is trading for more than \$15.

\$16.18 × 80 = \$1,294.40 Multiply the price per share by the number of shares.

\$1,294.40 − \$1,200 = \$94.40 Subtract amount of investment from the value of shares.

Malcolm will make \$94.40.

TRY IT

Determine if each bond could be converted at the listed price per share to make money. Name the amount made if the bond is converted.

1. \$5,000 corporate bond convertible to 120 shares; price per share: \$42
2. \$7,500 corporate bond convertible to 200 shares; price per share: \$37
3. \$1,500 corporate bond convertible to 20 shares; price per share: \$90
4. \$1,000 corporate bond convertible to 25 shares; price per share: \$40

A *term bond* is one that pays interest only during the term of the bond. For example, suppose a corporation issues a ten-year, \$10 million, 5 percent bond. Each year it pays \$500,000 interest. At the end of the tenth year, it also repays the principal amount of the bond, \$10 million.

A *zero-coupon bond* is a bond sold at a deep discount. It has no annual interest payments. They are typically sold at 50 percent or more below face value. As the bond ages, it increases in value. Bondholders may make money by selling the bonds before maturity at a price higher than they paid for them.

A *junk bond* is a form of debt from companies that don't have an investment grade rating. In other words, they are unable to borrow money selling typical bonds. A typical junk bond might offer an annual interest rate of 25 percent. Junk bonds are known as *high-yield debt* and can be very risky. The investor should be aware it is possible the corporation issuing junk bonds could fail. Investors should recognize that while interest rates are higher on these bonds, they represent proportionately higher risk.

Global View

The Canadian Bond Market

Within the Canadian bond market, investors can buy both government and corporate bonds. Among the bond markets in Canada, the corporate bond market is the most thriving.

The Canadian bond market is generally characterized as a safe investment that has relatively low levels of risk. In 2011 the risk was low because of Canada's low annual inflation rates, giving the nation economic stability and predictability. Bond investment in Canada has led to improved corporate performances. Large corporations have benefited the most from the influx of cash from individual investors. This allows them a source of debt financing that is stable (at fixed interest rates) rather than borrowing from commercial banks and making more risky investments in the U.S. and elsewhere.

In 2011 Canada's junk bond market was set to boom as buyers sought higher interest rate returns. The global high-yield (junk bond) market is currently worth around $1 trillion. The Canadian share of that market is very small.

Think Critically

1. **Why would U.S. citizens choose to invest in Canadian bonds?**
2. **What economic advantage is available in Canada that is not apparent in other countries, including the United States?**

Features of Bonds

A *convertible bond* can be exchanged for shares of stock at a preset date or within a preset period of time. For example, assume you purchase a $1,000 corporate bond which is convertible to 50 shares of common stock. You should convert the bond to stock if the common stock is worth $20 or more per share. Assuming the common stock was selling for $22 a share, you would then get 50 shares of stock worth $1,100 for your bond that cost you $1,000.

A *callable bond* is a bond where the issuer (corporation) has the right to pay off (call back) a bond at a preset date or within a preset period of time. For example, a ten-year, $1,000, 5 percent bond issued in 2010 might be callable in or after the year 2015. If interest rates have fallen (below 5 percent), the corporation might wish to buy back the bond. When the corporation exercises its right to call a bond, it usually pays a preset amount above face value of the bond. For example, the $1,000 bond may be called for $1,020.

A *participating bond* is one that has a fixed rate of return, but it also shares in profits of the corporation. After common stockholders have received their dividends, the board of directors may also have more profits that can be shared with these bondholders. Participating bonds usually sell for a higher price than other bonds because of this attractive feature which allows for the possibility of greater returns.

Sometimes bond features increase the selling price of a bond. For example, a participating bond is attractive to investors because the potential return is greater while the risk does not rise. Other bond features may decrease the selling price (market value) of a bond. For example, a callable bond may force an investor to give up a bond that was a solid rate of return.

Earnings on Bonds

All corporate bonds are issued with a stated face value, maturity date, and fixed interest rate. Earnings are computed at simple interest rates. For example, a $1,000, 5 percent, ten-year term bond would pay annual interest of $50 ($1,000 × 0.05 = $50). This is computed using the simple interest formula of Interest = Principal × Rate × Time. If the bond pays semi-annual interest the bondholder receives $25 twice each year.

The interest rate on the bond is fixed. However, the *market price* (what you could sell the bond for before its maturity date) is not fixed. Assume the $1,000 bond sold in 2010 at a fixed rate of 5 percent. In the year 2011, interest rates dropped. Because your bond pays a higher rate than the current market rate, the value of your bond has increased. If, however, market rates have risen, your fixed-rate, 5 percent bond is worth less.

CHECKPOINT

How do bondholders make money on their investments?

LO 2-2 Investing in Government Bonds

In addition to loaning money to corporations, you can also loan money to the government by purchasing various types of government bonds. Government bonds are issued by the federal, as well as state and local, governments. There are four types of government bonds—municipal, savings, treasury, and agency bonds.

Municipal Bonds

A bond issued by state and local governments is called a **municipal bond**. The minimum investment is usually $5,000, although brokers often ask more than this amount as an initial investment. Often called "munis," municipal bonds can be backed by specific projects or by the general taxing ability of a governmental unit. Municipal bonds generally pay a lower interest rate than corporate bonds. However, interest is often exempt from federal income tax, and state and local taxes as well. As shown in Figure 17-2, a municipal bond may actually generate more net income (after tax) than a corporate bond.

	Corporate Bond	Municipal Bond
Face value (principal)	$10,000	$10,000
Fixed interest rate	5%	4%
Annual interest earnings	$500	$400
Tax on earnings (30% rate)	$150	0
Net interest earnings after tax	$350	$400

Figure 17-2
Comparison of Corporate and Municipal Bonds

A *revenue bond* is a municipal bond issued to raise money for a public-works project. The revenue (income) generated by the project is used to pay the interest and principal at maturity. Major projects financed by revenue bonds include airports, hospitals, toll roads, and public housing facilities.

A *general-obligation bond* is a municipal bond that is backed by the power of the issuing state or local government to levy taxes which will pay back the debt. For example, school districts issue bonds to build new classrooms. The city may issue a bond to build a new public service building. The general-obligation bond is repaid with the government's general revenue sources, such as property taxes, fees, fines, tuition, and other sources of income.

Savings Bonds

You can buy U.S. savings bonds from banks, through payroll deduction plans, or online from Treasury Direct. A **savings bond** is a long-term loan to the U.S. government. You can buy up to $5,000 worth of savings bonds a year.

A *Series EE bond* is sold at one half its face value. This is a *discount bond*. For example, you can buy a $1000 bond for $500. It grows due to compounding of interest until it reaches its face value. Interest rates on bonds issued after 2005 are fixed. The bond continues to compound interest for a total of 30 years. EE bonds can be purchased in maturity (face) values of $50 to $10,000. When EE bonds are purchased for education purposes, interest on these bonds is not taxable for most people. Otherwise, interest earnings are subject to federal income tax.

WalterGalloway/iStockphoto.com

An *I bond* is also a savings bond, but it is sold at face value. It has a fixed interest rate, but that rate also increases with general price increases, or inflation. This type of savings bond helps to protect the investor from the risk of losing purchasing power through inflation. Like EE bonds, I bonds gain value with the long-term compounding of interest. Effective January 2012, all bond transactions become electronic (no paper copies will be issued).

Treasury Securities

U.S. treasury securities include treasury notes, bills, and bonds. These loan obligations of the federal government are kept electronically and the investor receives a regular statement of account. A *treasury bill (T-bill)* is a short-term security sold in terms ranging from 4 to 52 weeks. T-bills are sold at a discount from face value. For example, you might pay $950 for a $1000 bond.

A *treasury note (T-note)* is a medium-term security, ranging from two to ten years, at a fixed rate of interest determined when the note is sold. The minimum purchase amount is $100.

A *treasury bond* is a long-term security, with a maturity date of 30 years. Having a fixed rate, they pay interest every six months until maturity. Interest rates are usually higher than T-bills or T-notes because of the longer term. The minimum purchase amount is $100. Investors often choose treasuries because earnings are not taxable by state and local governments.

Agency Bonds

Federal agencies also issue debt securities. Federal agencies include the Federal Home Loan Mortgage Corporation (Freddie Mac), the Federal National Mortgage Association (FNMA), the Federal Housing Administration (FHA), and the Student Loan Marketing Association (Sallie Mae). An **agency bond** is a loan of money to a government agency. Government agencies use the money to provide low-cost financing to certain groups of people, such as first-time home buyers or students attending college. Although agency bonds are typically considered *risk-free*, they offer a slightly higher interest rate than securities issued by the treasury. In 2008, the federal government took over the administration of the Fannie Mae and Freddie Mac lending programs. This action lends further stability and protection against risk.

Agency bonds can be bought directly through banks or from brokers. Typically they are also exempt from state and local taxes, but not federal income taxes.

CEFutcher/iStockphoto.com

The majority of students attending college have student loans, many of which are agency bonds.

Risk, Reward, and Economic Impact

Investing in U.S. government securities is generally said to be risk-free. A **risk-free investment** is one without the inherent risk of default. For purposes of risk management, this is the safest form of investing possible. Many individuals as well as investment groups, retirement funds, and other large investors keep a certain level of risk-free investment choices in their portfolios. This practice serves to offset the high-risk choices that could lead to large losses. Of course, one should also expect that lower risk is generally associated with lower rewards. Those rewards are enhanced, however, when the income is tax-free and thus serves as a method of investing without incurring tax liabilities on the earnings. For those in higher income brackets, this form of investing can be very attractive.

When individuals and businesses loan money to the government, they are in effect supporting government spending. Because the government (whether federal, state, or local) has money to spend, economic activity is increased. Contractors are hired to build buildings. Employees are hired to staff them. The result leads to economic growth, although it is often within the government sector. As government grows in size, it also requires more resources and ongoing funding to maintain the buildings and other programs that are established as a result of loaning money to the government.

CHECKPOINT

Why are government bonds a lower-risk investment than corporate bonds?

17-2 Assessment

Key Concepts

LO 2-1 1. What is meant by debt financing?

LO 2-1 2. What are six types of corporate bonds?

LO 2-2 3. What is the major advantage of municipal bonds over corporate bonds?

LO 2-2 4. List three U.S. treasury securities.

Think About It

LO 2-1 5. Most corporate bonds pay fixed rates of interest and make annual payments of interest to investors. What type of a person would invest in bonds?

LO 2-1 6. Younger investors might prefer a convertible bond or a participating bond rather than a callable bond. Why?

LO 2-2 7. Many people buy U.S. savings bonds (EE) to finance their children's education. Why would they choose EE bonds over stocks?

LO 2-2 8. U.S. government bonds are said to be risk-free. How does this benefit investors? What is the downside? How does the purchase of government bonds impact the economy? Explain.

Make Academic Connections

LO 2-1 9. **RESEARCH** *The Wall Street Journal* publishes a list of bond transactions (printed and online). Prepare a chart reporting the results of following five corporate bond listings for one week.

LO 2-1 10. **MATH** Lenita invested in a $10,000, ten-year, 4 percent corporate bond. How much interest does she earn in one year? How much interest will she earn over the life of the bond?

LO 2-2 11. **TECHNOLOGY** Investors are able to buy bonds online. They can also purchase them through financial institutions. Explain how technology enables investors to make better choices and lower risk.

Teamwork

LO 2-1 12. Choose a corporate bond listed on the New York Stock Exchange. Use Moody's Industrial Manuals available at public libraries, or Moody's online to answer the following questions.

a. What is Moody's rating for the bond?
b. What is the purpose of the bond?
c. Does the bond have a call provision?
d. Is this an unsecured bond (debenture) or secured bond?
e. Based on the information your group found, make a conclusion about whether this is a good investment. Why or why not?

LO 2-2 13. Visit the website of the U.S. Treasury. Read a link, such as "Find Out How Treasury Auctions Work" or "Get More Information about EE Savings Bonds." Prepare a report of your findings.

LO 2-2 14. Explain why junk bonds are the most risky form of bond investments. Give a report on an example of a particular junk bond, tracking its market value over time. Explain the risks and rewards of this type of investment.

yienkeat/Shutterstock.com, Chad Baker/Ryan McVay/Photodisc/Getty Images

17-3 Other Investing Options

Learning Objectives

LO 3-1 Describe real estate investment choices, including their unique features and requirements.

LO 3-2 Evaluate other investing options you might consider.

Vocabulary

illiquid investment, p. 502
rental property, p. 502
precious metals, p. 503
collectibles, p. 504
futures, p. 505
option, p. 505

© Aleksandar Vrzalski/iStockphoto.com

REAL-WORLD FOCUS

Kasey owns more than two dozen Barbie dolls. Last year she went to a garage sale and bought several very old dolls. "My collection brings me pleasure," Kasey told her friend. "I'm not trying to make a profit. Some day they may be worth money. Right now, I'm simply enjoying my collection."

WORK AS A TEAM Should people buy things for their potential future value or should they buy things that bring them pleasure? What types of things that exist today do you think will be worth money in the future?

A duplex is a single structure designed to house two tenants. The building usually has two separate entrances so each tenant has access to only half of the dwelling.

DO YOU THINK the owner of a duplex who lives in half of the structure and rents the other half collects enough rent from the tenant to make each monthly mortgage payment?

Susan Law Cain/Shutterstock.com

yienkeat/Shutterstock.com

LO 3-1 Investing in Real Estate

In addition to owning your own home, you may also consider real estate a good long-term investment. Over the long run, real estate values have kept pace with or exceeded the annual rate of inflation. However, real estate is often described as an illiquid investment. An **illiquid investment** is an investment that can be difficult to sell in the short run. You may not be able to sell it quickly without taking a substantial loss or a reduced price. Some real estate investments are considered *speculative*, and while they can be very profitable if the right things happen, they can also result in significant or total loss of value. Most investors buying speculative properties are unable to get bank financing because of the risk involved.

Vacant Land

Vacant land, or unimproved property, is often considered a speculative investment. You are hoping that at some time in the future the land will increase in value. Perhaps the city will grow and the property will then bring a big price for development.

Some people buy vacant land or a vacant lot for purposes of retirement planning. They hope to build on the property at a later time when they are able to afford it or when they are ready to move there.

Rental Properties

Landlords are owners of property that is rented to others. **Rental property** may be a single-family house, a duplex, triplex, apartment building, or condominium—anything where you collect rent and allow another person to occupy your property. Purchasing rental property often requires a large down payment of cash. Once the property's income-producing potential is documented, however, the owner may be able to secure very favorable financing. As the property is being rented, the underlying mortgage or other financing is being paid down or off. Once the property is free-and-clear, the ongoing rental payments provide a regular monthly income. In addition, rental property is *depreciated*, which means you are writing down a portion of the value each year. This property provides a *tax shelter* for those in higher income groups.

Skyhobo/iStockphoto.com

Many homes purchased as vacation or retirement homes are beachfront property.

Some people purchase second homes to be used for vacations or for their retirement years. Often these properties are rented out to generate income during the times they are not being used by the owners. In some cases the absent owner lives a considerable distance away from the property and must hire professional management to collect the rents and maintain the property. This lowers the profits for the owner. It also lowers profits when properties are vacant. It may be hard to find a qualified tenant. Sometimes tenants do not pay rent as agreed. Sometimes tenants cause damage to the property and deposits collected may not cover the damage. Also it is the owner's responsibility to maintain the property in a habitable condition.

Indirect Real Estate Investing

Some people do not wish to be responsible for the land and improvements. With indirect investing, they are able to own real estate and enjoy its tax and other advantages without actually doing the work or having as much risk.

A *real estate syndicate* (a form of limited partnership) is a group of investors who pool their money to buy real estate. This limited-purpose group owns property and shares profits with its investors. Most real estate syndicates own several types of properties to lower overall risk. Properties are managed by professionals to maximize the return for investors and to relieve them of the need to manage the property themselves.

A *real estate investment trust (REIT)* is similar to a mutual fund. It is a corporation that pools the money of many investors. It uses money to buy real estate, and like a mutual fund, the REIT makes all the buy-and-sell decisions. You can buy and sell REIT shares at will. REITs are traded on stock exchanges and over-the-counter markets.

A *participation certificate* is an investment in a pool of mortgages that were purchased by a government agency such as Fannie Mae or Freddie Mac. You can invest directly or you can invest through a mutual fund that buys participation certificates as part of its portfolio.

CHECKPOINT

What are three ways to invest in real estate besides owning a home?

LO 3-2 Other Investments

Almost anything can prove to be a good (or bad) investment choice over time. Some will bring income. Others will appreciate in value. In many cases, these choices depend on your personal values and tastes.

Metals, Gems, and Collectibles

Investments in this group are usually considered speculative. You are betting that the value will increase over time. Like real estate, these investments can also be very illiquid. They can be difficult to sell in a hurry and usually do not provide current income. Market prices may vary greatly over time.

Gold, silver, and platinum are examples of precious metals. **Precious metals** are tangible metals that have known values around the world. You can buy precious metals as coins, medallions, jewelry, and bullion. You can also buy stocks and mutual funds that specialize in businesses that own, process, mine, store, or otherwise trade in precious

BrianAJackson/iStockphoto.com

Gold bullion can be in the form of a bar or a coin. The value of the bullion is based purely on its precious metal content.

Collectibles

When you search, you can find all types of things offered to buy, sell, and exchange. There are sections in newspapers and websites that specialize in listing such items with the intention of bringing a seller and a buyer together. These listings often represent items people have collected over time. Sometimes you find these items at swap meets or collectible shows that attract a certain type of "investor." Review the collectibles sections in your local newspaper ads and on the Internet. Do you have anything you could sell within this media?

Investigate Your Local ECONOMY

Try it Out

As a group, make a list of items you find for sale that interest you, that are unique, and that you find ridiculous. Prepare a chart with pictures and asking prices to share with the class.

metals. Prices for these and other metals are listed in the financial sections of newspapers and online.

Gems are natural, precious stones such as diamonds, rubies, sapphires, and emeralds. Their prices are usually high and subject to change. Both precious metals and gems have their greatest retail value as jewelry. However, when you buy at retail prices, you are paying markups of 50 to 500 percent or higher. Prices must increase greatly in world markets before you can recover your cost or make a profit reselling jewelry. The gems market is small and unpredictable. The risk is high for the owner who does not know values and have the inside track to find buyers who will pay market value.

Collections of valuable or rare items, such as antiques, art, baseball cards, stamps, and comic books, are called **collectibles**. They are valuable because they are old, antique, rare, unusual, irreplaceable, no longer produced, or of historic importance. Coins are the most commonly collected items. Silver coins are often worth more than 20 times their face value.

Andrey Khrolenok/Shutterstock.com

Financial Instruments

For those who are willing and able to make some risky but potentially profitable investments, there are some very lucrative choices.

Futures are contracts to buy and sell commodities or stocks for a specified price on a specified date in the future. *Commodities* include farm products, such as wheat, corn, or cattle. Commodities also include metals such as gold or silver. Crude oil is also a commodity. Commodity prices are volatile because supply and demand are disrupted by all kinds of mostly unpredictable situations, from political upheaval to the weather. When you buy a future you are controlling the price you will pay in the future. Unfortunately, if market prices have dropped along the way, you will be paying more than if you had not purchased the contract.

An **option** is the right (but not the obligation) to buy or sell a commodity or stock for a specified price within a specified period of time. A *call option* is the right to buy shares of stock at a set price before an expiration date. A *put option* is the right to sell stock at a fixed price before an expiration date. A person who expects a stock price to rise will purchase a call option. A person who expects a stock price to fall may purchase a put option (to safeguard against the risk). Options are risky and not for inexperienced investors.

Futures and options can generate large, but unpredictable profits (or losses). Only those with money they can afford to lose should play this type of risky game.

CHECKPOINT

Why are precious metals, gems, and collectibles risky choices?

ETHICS *in Action!*

What Is Churning?

When a financial advisor's interests conflict with those of the investor, it becomes an ethical problem. *Churning* is the act of engaging in securities transactions for the purpose of generating sales commissions rather than for the benefit of the customer.

When brokers and other advisors make a profit from transactions, they must be cautious to ensure that they are not purposely creating revenue for themselves without providing benefits for investors. The SEC regulates the financial markets and takes decisive action when this type of activity is disclosed. Following an investigation, the licensee may be disciplined or the securities license may be revoked.

Think Critically

1. **How can investors protect themselves from churning?**
2. **You must be able to trust your financial advisor with private and sensitive information. Why is this necessary?**

17-3 Assessment

Key Concepts

LO 3-1 1. Why is real estate considered an illiquid investment?

LO 3-1 2. How does rental property provide a tax shelter?

LO 3-2 3. What is the highest retail value for metals and gems?

LO 3-2 4. Give three examples of commodities.

Think About It

LO 3-1 5. Why might you consider buying a vacant lot today when you have no plan to build on it soon?

LO 3-1 6. What are some of the risks of owning rental property?

LO 3-1 7. Is it possible for real estate values to drop? How can you protect yourself (lower your risk) from this possibility?

LO 3-2 8. Why are metals and gems considered to be illiquid?

LO 3-2 9. Do you have a collection of some type that might grow in value over time? Did you buy it for its future investment value?

LO 3-1 10. Describe real estate investment choices, including their unique features and requirements.

LO 3-2 11. Evaluate other investing options you might consider.

Make Academic Connections

LO 3-2 12. **INTERNATIONAL STUDIES** Gold is a world commodity. Do online research about the international price of gold over the last ten years. Prepare a line graph and explain the fluctuations over time.

LO 3-2 13. **SOCIAL STUDIES** People often collect items that later become very valuable. Estate sales, inheritances, and random findings can become something rare and expensive. Prepare a report about people's collections—what they collect and what need is being met. Interview a person with a collection and ask how it evolved.

LO 3-1 14. **BUSINESS LAW** Landlord-tenant laws exist in every state. Look up landlord tenant laws in your state. Describe responsibilities of property owners to the community, neighboring properties, and tenants.

Teamwork

LO 3-1 15. Conduct online research about vacant land, vacant lots, and commercial property in your local area. Prepare a chart that shows the size, location, and asking price for the property.

LO 3-1 16. Some people have cabins at the beach. Others have cabins in the mountains. Look in real estate brochures or research online about second home properties in your area or in a recreation area near you. Describe properties that are available for purchase, their features, and their prices.

LO 3-2 17. Visit a local coin shop, card store, or antiques dealer. Ask the owner if you may take pictures of goods offered for sale to prepare a chart of collectibles that are available in your area. Prepare an analysis of what is available, who the likely purchaser would be, and your estimates of the future resale values.

17-4 Retirement Planning and Philanthropy

Learning Objectives

LO 4-1 **Explain** the concept of setting aside money in individual and employer-provided retirement accounts.

LO 4-2 **Evaluate** the provisions needed for retirement, estate planning, and philanthropy.

Vocabulary

traditional IRA, p. 508
Roth IRA, p. 508
SEP IRA, p. 508
401(k) plan, p. 509
403(b) plan, p. 509
estate, p. 510
health care directive, p. 512
philanthropy, p. 512

© Aleksandar Vrzalski/iStockphoto.com

REAL-WORLD FOCUS

Josef just began his first job as a part-time server. He is living at home and his parents provide for his living expenses. "I am able to save most of what I make," Josef told his dad. "I think I'd like to open a Roth IRA so I can set my money aside for the long term. Since the income on a Roth IRA is never taxable, it will grow rapidly over the years."

WORK AS A TEAM Do you think Josef's reasoning is sound? What might be the pitfalls in setting aside money permanently into a Roth IRA? What are the advantages?

Doctors and other health care professionals take an oath to use all measures possible, including the best medical technology available, to save a patient's life.

DO YOU THINK an individual's health care directive outweighs a doctor's decision to take extreme measures to save a person's life?

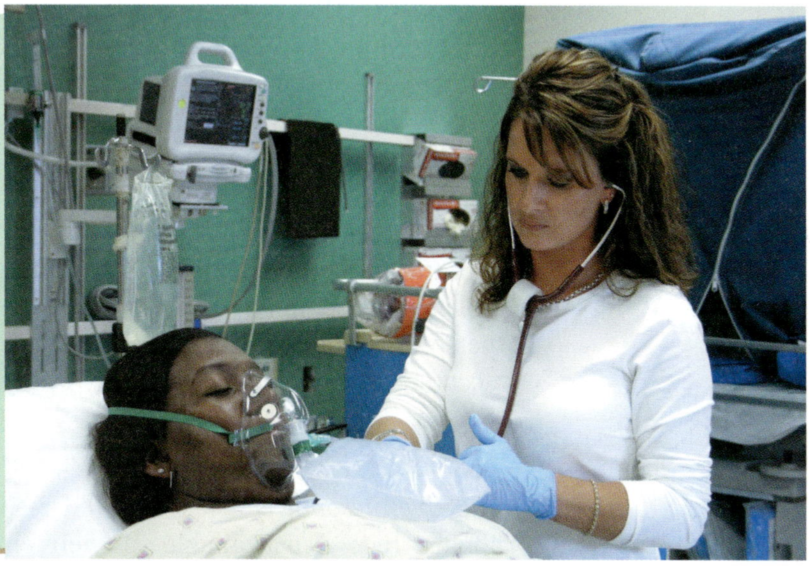

Andrew Gentry/Shutterstock.com

yienkeat/Shutterstock.com

LO 4-1 Retirement Plans

A retirement plan is a good way to save for your future. You can open a retirement account as an individual or often through your employer. Money deposited today can be withdrawn at retirement without penalty. You may manage the account by choosing your own investments and objectives or your account may be professionally managed. Earnings remain in the retirement account, allowing it to grow even faster. A major advantage of many individual and employer-sponsored plans is that they are *tax-deferred*, which means you won't pay taxes on them or their earnings until the money is withdrawn. Ideally, you will be in a lower tax bracket when you withdraw the money.

IRA Accounts

An *IRA (individual retirement account)* allows you to put money into an account during your working years and withdraw it later. IRAs can be set up at banks, brokerage firms, insurance companies, and other financial institutions. You are responsible for managing the account. Individual retirement accounts are not insured unless you put the account into a financial institution that has FDIC insurance on its deposits and accounts. For most IRA accounts, the investor wants a greater return, and thus the risk is higher. Many IRA accounts are invested in stocks, mutual funds, and other portfolio assets that are not insured. As a long-term investment, the payback over time can be substantial.

The amount you can put into an IRA account is limited. This amount changes periodically. You can begin withdrawing money at age 59½ or later. Money withdrawn before age 59½ is subject to regular tax rates plus a 10 percent early withdrawal penalty. At age 70½, you must begin withdrawing money from your account. When you withdraw money from most of these accounts, it is subject to income taxes.

A **traditional IRA** is an individual retirement account that allows individuals to contribute pre-tax income to an account that grows *tax-deferred*. You will not pay taxes on contributions to the account or its earnings until the money is withdrawn. Money you contribute to an IRA is deducted from gross income, which lowers your current year's taxable income and income tax liability.

A **Roth IRA** is an individual retirement account for which contributions are taxed but earnings are never taxed. In other words, you don't deduct the contribution from your taxable income. But all income earned in this IRA is *tax-free*. When you retire, money you withdraw is not taxable.

A **SEP IRA** is a tax-deferred retirement plan for small business owners and their employees. SEP stands for Simplified Employee Pension plan. It is similar to a traditional IRA, except that the amount of money you can set aside is a percent of your annual income. The maximum contribution is determined by either a dollar amount or a percent of income, whichever is greater. A self-employed person may have a SEP IRA for themselves and they may also set up SEP IRA accounts for their employees.

Keogh Accounts

A *Keogh account* is a tax-deferred retirement plan for self-employed professionals. It is also available to their employees. Similar to a SEP, it is more complex to establish. Keogh accounts are used for high-income professionals, such as doctors, lawyers, and accountants. Up to $195,000 a year can be put into a Keogh account.

Annuities

An *annuity* is a contract purchased from an insurance company. It guarantees a series of regular monthly payments for a set period of time. To buy an annuity, you make monthly payments into the account for a number of years (such as 20). You can also invest a lump sum. At the end of the set number of years, you start receiving monthly payments. Annuities can be tax-deferred. These investments are not insured by the FDIC.

Employer-Sponsored Plans

Some employers provide some type of retirement plan for their employees, as a part of the employee compensation package. Some of these plans allow you to set aside pre-tax money and defer taxes until the money is withdrawn. These types of plans add considerable value to your retirement portfolio.

A *defined-benefit plan* is an employer-sponsored retirement plan. At retirement employees are guaranteed a monthly benefit based on their earnings amount (not the amount of money paid in). These accounts are often funded entirely by employers. With these plans employees become *vested* (have ownership rights) after a certain number of years of service. This type of pension plan is offered by fewer companies now than in the past.

A *defined-contribution* plan is an employer-sponsored retirement plan in which an employee will receive a retirement benefit based on how much was deposited in the account and how well the account performed over the years. There is no set amount guaranteed as a monthly benefit. Usually, employees pay a percentage of their salaries into these accounts each month. When they retire, the account starts paying them monthly benefits.

401(K) PLANS One type of defined-contribution plan is the 401(k). A **401(k) plan** is a tax-deferred retirement plan funded by employees of profit-seeking businesses. Employees set aside pre-tax dollars through payroll deduction. Employer contributions are optional. Employees can choose investments (asset allocation) based on their willingness to take risks. These accounts and their earnings are not taxed until the money is withdrawn.

403(B) PLANS Another type of defined-contribution plan is the 403(b). A **403(b) plan** is a tax-deferred retirement plan funded by employees of government and nonprofit organizations. Teachers, school staff, nurses, doctors, and ministers are examples of people who qualify for a 403(b) plan. Money is set aside through pre-taxed payroll deductions. These amounts are sometimes paid by employers, employees, or shared by both. Like 401(k) accounts, employees chose their investments and the account is not taxed until money is withdrawn.

CHECKPOINT

What is a major advantage to setting aside money in a retirement account?

LO 4-2 Retirement and Estate Planning

Most people plan to work for a number of years and then at some point leave full-time work and enjoy retirement. *Retirement* should be a period of time when you are not working but are able to meet expenses through savings, investments, and other income. Sources of retirement income include employer-sponsored plans, individual retirement plans, Social Security benefits, savings, and investments. Some expenses, such as those related to working and often the mortgage on your home, are eliminated at retirement. Other costs such as groceries and utilities tend to stay the same. The costs of medical care and prescriptions may rise significantly.

Yuri Arcurs/iStockphoto.com

For many couples, planning for retirement starts early because the money invested for a longer period of time provides more financial security in their retirement years.

Retirement and estate planning should start when you begin your first career. Think about the things you'd like to do and the lifestyle you would like to have. Then consider how much income you will need to support your choices. Many people, especially the elderly, require long-term medical care at some time during their lives. Retirement planning should include ways to pay for long-term care if it is needed. When you consider your future needs at retirement, it should be a call to start saving and investing as soon as you can. The longer your money is set aside, the more it will grow.

Estate Planning

An **estate** is all that a person owns (assets) less debt owed, at the time of that person's death. Assets may include bank accounts, investments, property, and other items of value. Money that is not used for living expenses, travel, and leisure activities add to the value of your estate. Life insurance proceeds are also part of your estate unless a specific beneficiary is named. *Estate planning* is the process of preparing a plan for transferring property during your lifetime and after your death.

Estate planning often involves preparing a will. A *will* is a document that passes title or property after a person dies. For property held in joint names, a will is not needed. If you have property in your name only, then a will lets you decide where that property goes at the time of your death. If you die without a will, your property will be distributed according to the laws of the state in which you live. This may or may not be how you would want your property divided at death. Most states require that you be the age or majority (18 in most states) to draw a valid will. There are several types of wills:

- A *simple will* is a document that distributes your property to adult *heirs*, or people who will inherit from you. You name an *executor* who will represent you in administering your will. *Probate* is the process of gathering estate assets, paying final expenses, and distributing the rest to your heirs.

- A *holographic will* is a handwritten document that declares your wishes. It is valid in many states. To be sure you are making a valid will, you should check the laws in your state. You can purchase a *will kit* that guides you through the appropriate steps and language to use in the document.
- A *trust will* is a document that distributes property to heirs, some or all of which may be minors. This is a complex document which requires the services of an attorney. *Guardianships* are set up for children along with a *trustee* to protect the estate's assets.

Giving Back to Society

Every year wealthy people give massive amounts of money to various causes. The largest individual bequest was a $37 billion gift from Warren Buffett to the Bill and Melinda Gates Foundation. While massive dollar donations grab media attention, there are many other forms of charity.

maukun/Shutterstock.com

- *Giving circles* are groups of individuals who become friends and pool their charitable donations. Together they decide how to use the money to benefit the causes they care about.
- *Volunteerism* is a form of philanthropy where people provide service to others. Many volunteers are needed to serve food in shelters and provide services for those who cannot pay for them.
- *Charitable organizations* exist to support worthy causes. These organizations seek donations of both time and money. Most such organizations receive the bulk of their funding from individuals who give less than $100 each.

Everyone has the opportunity to give something back. Many non-wealthy people also donate substantial amounts of time, effort, and personal resources to charitable causes. When you give of your time, you are in fact giving the most valuable thing you have. Time is something that cannot be stored or regained once it is gone. It is in limited supply for everyone.

How do you know which charity is the right one to which you should donate your time, money, talent, or assets? You are right to suspect that there are scams pretending to collect money for charities and provide nothing of value. The American Institute of Philanthropy (AIP) is a watchdog group that keeps track of, rates, and publishes reports on more than 500 charitable organizations. You can learn about any legitimate charity—what it does and does not do. You can learn how the charity is run and what percentage of your donation is used for the purposes you specify. The AIP also provides tips for giving wisely, instructions for how to give online, and answers to your questions.

Think Critically

1. **What is your favorite charitable organization? Why?**
2. **What is your greatest gift (talent)? How could you use that gift to help others?**
3. **If you had money to spare, far beyond your needs and wants, how would you choose to use it?**

Many people design and sign a **health care directive**. This important document serves to protect your interests. Also called a "living will," it describes your wishes at the end of life. It specifies the type of effort you want taken in the event you would not recover from an injury or illness. You designate a person to act as your representative. When there is no such document prepared for you, health care workers preserve life and do not terminate life support, even if you cannot recover. A health care directive states preferences for organ donation and other critical personal preferences. Without a directive, your relatives make those decisions for you.

In addition to leaving possessions to heirs, many people designate a portion of their estate for philanthropic causes. They make allowances for donations to their favorite charities and universities. They may request that money go toward establishing a *foundation.* A foundation is a fund or organization established and maintained for the purpose of supporting an institution or a cause. Foundations usually seek to help others, achieve a social objective, and enrich the community. They support specific activities such as education, research, veterans' benefits, or cultural literacy.

Charitable Giving

Philanthropy is a form of charitable giving that supports some type of societal purpose over an extended period of time. *Philanthropists* want to leave the world a better place than they found it. Often they want to give back from the wealth they have gained. Some people give time; others give money. The cost is tax-deductible when gifts are given to 501(c)3 nonprofit organizations. These organizations in turn provide goods and services to people who are less fortunate and provide funding for many worthwhile causes.

Philanthropy is the primary source of funding for the fine arts, the performing arts, and most religious and humanitarian causes. It also supports private (and some public) schools and universities. Many cultural institutions would not exist without the generosity of philanthropists.

Andrew Carnegie (1835–1919) was a Scottish-American industrialist and a world-renowned philanthropist. Born in Scotland, he emigrated to the U.S. as a child. His first job was as a factory worker in a bobbin factory. He worked hard and consistently. Carnegie built his wealth in the steel industry. Carnegie believed in using his fortune for others and doing more than making money. He spent his last years as a philanthropist. From 1901 forward, he devoted himself to worthy projects. Carnegie is often regarded as the second-richest man in history (after John D. Rockefeller). Among his efforts was the establishment of public libraries across the U.S. The Andrew Carnegie Dictum (his view of the purpose of life) was as follows:

- To spend the first third of one's life getting all the education one can
- To spend the next third making all the money one can
- To spend the last third giving it all away to worthwhile causes

CHECKPOINT

What is the purpose of estate planning?

17-4 Assessment

Key Concepts

LO 4-1 1. What is meant by "tax deferred"?

LO 4-1 2. List three types of IRA accounts.

LO 4-2 3. What is the purpose of a will?

LO 4-2 4. Why is philanthropy important in America?

Think About It

LO 4-1 5. For young people who do not need tax deductions, a Roth IRA offers a significant advantage—earnings are tax-free. Why is this important?

LO 4-1 6. Why are companies abandoning pension plans paid by the employer in favor of 401(k) plans?

LO 4-2 7. Retirement and estate planning should begin early in life. Why?

LO 4-2 8. A holographic will can be broken fairly easily when potential heirs are excluded. Why would anyone challenge a will?

LO 4-1 9. Explain the concept of setting aside money in individual and employer-provided retirement accounts.

Make Academic Connections

LO 4-2 10. **TECHNOLOGY** Find an online future value calculator. Estimate how much you would have at retirement if you set aside equal monthly payments for 20, 30, and 40 years. Assume an 8 percent rate of return. Prepare a chart to report your results.

LO 4-2 11. **RESEARCH** Do online research about physician's directives, living wills, and other forms of health care directions. Prepare one for yourself. Include donor instructions.

LO 4-1 12. **COMMUNICATIONS** Look the ERISA law (a federal law to protect retirement accounts and pensions). Write a paper explaining what protections exist for employees whose retirement accounts are managed and controlled by their employers.

Teamwork

LO 4-2 13. As a group, search the Internet to find biographies of three successful entrepreneurs. How did they earn their wealth? Do they participate in or sponsor any foundations or charitable organizations? Have they published books or articles to share their success strategies? Explain how each person contributed to society, their ethics, and their legacy.

LO 4-2 14. Make a list of local nonprofit, community service organizations. Briefly describe what each group does and how they contribute to society.

Unit 7 Project: Building a Global Future

PHILANTHROPY Assume you have a lump sum of money ($1 million) that you plan to divide among three to five charitable organizations. Research the organizations of your choice and explain how much you would give to each one, the causes you would be promoting, and how your money would be used. Visit websites and cite your sources of information.

Chapter 17

Summary

17-1 INVEST IN STOCKS

1. Direct investing involves buying individual stocks from corporations. Corporations sell stocks as their equity financing; stockholders are owners of the company and share in its profits through dividends.
2. Direct investing involves inflation risk, industry risk, political risk, and stock risk. Investing directly may have relatively high risk but also potentially high rewards.
3. Indirect investing can be achieved by investing in mutual funds, joining investment clubs, and using retirement accounts. Indirect investing offers diversification which lowers your overall risk of investing.

17-2 INVEST IN BONDS

4. Corporate bonds are a form of long-term debt financing for corporations. Bondholders are loaning money to the corporation. Bonds most often are issued in multiples of $1,000, carry a fixed interest rate, and pay regular interest payments. The face value (principal) is also repaid.
5. Corporate bonds can be convertible, callable, or participating. Corporations issue debentures, secured bonds, serial bonds, term bonds, zero-coupon bonds, and junk bonds. Bonds are rated from high (AAA) to likely to default (D).
6. Government bonds include municipal, savings, treasury, and agency bonds. They are issued or sold by the federal, as well as state and local, governments. Treasury securities include bills, notes, and bonds. Most government bonds are considered safe and risk-free.

17-3 OTHER INVESTING OPTIONS

7. Real estate investing includes vacant land, rental properties, and indirect investments (syndicates, REITs, and participation certificates).
8. Other investments include metals, gems, and collectibles, all of which are very risky and highly volatile. Financial instruments are also risky and include futures and options.

17-4 RETIREMENT PLANNING AND PHILANTHROPY

9. Private retirement plans include IRA accounts (traditional, Roth and SEP), Keogh accounts, and annuities. These accounts offer tax shelter advantages or tax-deferred or tax-free status.
10. The most common employer-sponsored plans are the 401(k) for profit-seeking companies and the 403(b) for nonprofit and government workers. All are tax-deferred.
11. Retirement and estate planning should begin when you are young so you can accumulate enough resources for a comfortable lifestyle when you retire. An estate is what you will leave behind for your heirs; you should have a will and a health care directive. Charitable giving and philanthropy are important parts of giving back and leaving the world a better place.

Chapter 17

Assessment

Vocabulary Review

Match each statement with the term that best defines it. Some terms may not be used.

1. A group of investment choices
2. Retirement plan for employees of profit-seeking businesses
3. Assets and other items of value owned at time of death
4. Retirement account whose earnings are tax-free
5. Process of choosing combination of funds
6. A long-term debt (loan) to a federal government agency
7. Right to buy or sell a commodity at a specified price
8. Collections of rare or valuable items
9. An investment that can be difficult to sell in the short run
10. An individual retirement account that is tax-deferred
11. Loan of money to a government agency
12. Professionally managed group of investments
13. Sale of corporate stock to generate large sums of cash
14. Bond issued by state and local governments
15. Retirement plan provided for employees of government units
16. Real estate used to generate income from a tenant
17. Retirement account for small business owners
18. An investment without risk of default
19. Long-term debt obligations of publicly-held corporations
20. Charitable giving to support a worthy cause over time
21. Selection of various types of investments to reduce risk
22. Long-term debt (loan) to the federal government
23. Contracts to buy and sell commodities on a specified date in the future

Vocabulary

a. agency bond
b. asset allocation
c. collectibles
d. corporate bonds
e. debt financing
f. diversification
g. equity financing
h. estate
i. 401(k) plan
j. 403(b) plan
k. futures
l. health care directive
m. illiquid investment
n. municipal bond
o. mutual fund
p. option
q. philanthropy
r. portfolio
s. precious metals
t. rental property
u. risk-free investment
v. Roth IRA
w. savings bond
x. SEP IRA
y. traditional IRA

Review Your Knowledge

LO 1-1 **24.** Holding stock in individual corporations is which type of investing?
a. debt financing
b. equity financing
c. direct investing
d. indirect investing

LO 1-1 **25.** Investment risk that rising prices will exceed a stock's rate of return.
a. industry risk
b. inflation risk
c. stock risk
d. political risk

LO 1-2 **26.** Purchasing a mutual fund is which of these types of investing?
a. direct
b. indirect
c. risk-free
d. high-risk

LO 1-2 **27.** The payback to the owners of corporate stock is called
a. dividends
b. interest
c. profits
d. wages

LO 2-1 **28.** Which of these bonds pays interest only during the term of the bond?
a. serial bond
b. zero-coupon bond
c. term bond
d. junk bond

LO 2-1 **29.** Which of these is a desirable feature of a bond for the investor?
a. callable
b. unsecured
c. convertible
d. non-participating

LO 2-2 **30.** Which of these is sold at a discount?
a. EE bond
b. I bond
c. revenue bond
d. general obligation bond

LO 3-1 **31.** Which of these is considered speculative?
a. rental property
b. vacant land
c. REITs
d. certificate of participation

LO 4-1 **32.** Which of these is tax-deferred?
a. traditional IRA
b. Roth IRA
c. savings account
d. stock dividends

LO 4-2 **33.** Which of these types of retirement plans is being phased out?
a. defined-contribution plans
b. 401(k) plans
c. defined-benefit plans
d. 403(b) plans

LO 3-2 **34.** Which of these is the most common collectible?
a. gold
b. stamp collections
c. baseball cards
d. coins

Digging Deeper with Economics e-Collection

Gold is an international commodity. When other forms of investing seem shaky, investors turn to gold. Access the Gale Economics e-Collection at **www.cengage.com/school/economics/personalfinance**. Research the current price of gold and the prices of gold since 1965. Research prices of other precious metals, such as platinum or silver. Compare the price of gold with prices for the other precious metals. Prepare trend lines that show these prices over time. Compare these trends to parts of the business cycle in the United States or another measure of economic activity, such as the unemployment rate.

Think About It

LO 1-1 **35.** Investments are more risky than savings because they are not insured. Why do people choose investments, such as stock, where they can lose value?

LO 3-1 **36.** Illiquidity can be a very undesirable trait of investment choices. Why is it important to be able to sell an investment quickly?

LO 4-1 **37.** A retirement plan should contain a combination of tax-free, tax-deferred, and other choices that balance risk with reward. Why should an investor not have only tax-deferred investments?

Make Academic Connections

LO 2-2 **38. MATH** Which of these would bring you the greatest net return on your investment—a corporate bond yielding 8 percent or a municipal bond yielding 7 percent, assuming you are in a 25 percent tax bracket?

LO 3-2 **39. ETHICS** Pawn shops loan money to individuals who possess items such as precious metals and gems. The loan is usually 10 percent of the retail value of the property. If the borrower cannot repay the loan in the specified time period, it is forfeited. The pawn broker then resells the property at a much higher price. Is this an ethical practice? Why or why not?

LO 4-2 **40. SOCIAL STUDIES** Philanthropy is considered a very noble thing to do. Many wealthy people choose to donate large sums of money to organizations that provide goods and services to those less fortunate. Pick a charitable organization and describe the types of services it provides for individuals and communities, and explain the value of their service to society.

LO 1-1 **41. TECHNOLOGY** Computer technology makes it possible for all people to learn about investment choices, risks, returns, and investment strategies. Research the Internet to find the various types of advice available to consumers from private investment advisors, from government sponsored sites, and from citizen watchdog groups. Prepare a report of your findings.

Extend Your Learning

LO 2-1 **42.** Mutual funds are often considered a good starting investment for new and young investors. Follow the progress of three different mutual funds offered by firms such as Vanguard, Fidelity, or Magellan, using the Internet or your newspaper for a period of two weeks. Prepare a chart to illustrate your findings.

LO 4-2 **43.** Retirement and estate planning is a field where many professionals make a career of advising. Some charge fees for their services. Others make money from the sale of investment choices. Research the advisors and experts advertising in your paper and online. Write a paper briefly evaluating each source.

LO 1-2 **44.** Do research on mutual fund companies, listing all the different types of funds they offer. Download information about mutual funds, their prices, and other information available. Based on your research, rank the top three companies based on how long they have been in business, size of invested assets, cost of account maintenance fees, performance over the last ten years, and other criteria you are able to discover.

Glossary

A

Absolute advantage The ability of a country to produce more of a good using the same or fewer resources as another country p. 426

Agency bond A loan of money to a government agency p. 499

Aggregate demand curve (AD) The curve that shows real GDP (gross domestic product) that will be purchased at different price levels p. 367

Aggregate supply curve (AS) The curve that shows real GDP (gross domestic product) that will be produced at different price levels p. 367

Appreciation of currency A rise in the price (value) of one currency relative to another p. 442

Asset allocation The process of choosing a combination of funds that can be found in different mutual funds p. 489

Assumption Something that is accepted as being true p. 37

Automatic stay An action taken when a person files for bankruptcy protection that means no further action may be taken by creditors, including collection of debts p. 299

B

Balance of trade The value of a nation's imports subtracted from the value of its exports p. 443

Balanced budget A budget in which government spending equals tax revenues p. 384

Bankruptcy exemption Property that the debtor does not have to forfeit to pay creditors p. 299

Barrier to entry An obstacle that makes it difficult for a new firm to enter a market p. 131

Barter The process of exchanging one product for another p. 157

Billing cycle The time period each month when an account is closed to prepare your monthly statement p. 296

Board of Governors of the Federal Reserve System The seven-member board that supervises the banking system of the United States p. 398

Branding Gives recognition that leads to customer loyalty p. 159

Budget deficit A budget in which government spending exceeds government tax revenues p. 384

Budget surplus A budget in which government tax revenues exceed government spending p. 384

Business cycle The alternating periods of economic growth and contraction measured by changes in real gross domestic product (GDP) p. 322

Business expense A cost that is tax deductible and reduces income that is subject to tax p. 462

Business license A document issued by a local government unit that allows business activities within a certain geographic area p. 164

Business plan A written document that lists all the things a business owner will do to ensure business success p. 202

Business tax deduction A write-off that allows business owners a favored tax status p. 163

Buying plan An organized method for making good buying decisions that should help you stretch your limited resources p. 281

C

C corporation A corporation that is organized to sell stock to the general public p. 178

Capital Human-made goods that are used to produce other goods and services p. 9

Capital In the business sense, money, credit, and other financial resources p. 210

Capital market Markets that exist where businesses are able to finance operations as well as large purchases over long periods of time p. 264

Capitalism An economic system based on private ownership of resources and markets. Also called the free market system p. 25

Car lease A contract where you agree to take possession of a vehicle for a set period of time and make regular lease payments p. 462

Cartel A group of firms that formally agree to reduce competition by coordinating the price and the output of a product p. 145

Cash flow The net amount received after expenses are paid p. 475

Change in demand An increase (rightward shift) or a decrease (leftward shift) in the demand curve. The shift is caused by a change in a demand shifter factor p. 73

Change in quantity demanded A movement between points along a stationary demand curve because of a change in price p. 73

Change in quantity supplied A movement between points along a stationary supply curve because of a change in price p. 100

Change in supply An increase (rightward shift) or a decrease (leftward shift) in the quantity supplied at each possible price. The shift is caused by a change in a supply shifter factor p. 100

Check clearing A Federal Reserve service that collects funds from a check writer's bank and transfers them to the recipient's bank p. 400

Checkable deposits The total money in financial institutions that can be withdrawn by writing a check p. 230

Checking account A demand deposit account where consumers can make withdrawals and deposit money p. 251

Circular-flow model A model that shows the exchange of money, products, and resources between businesses, households, and government p. 313

Classical economics The theory that free markets will restore full employment without government intervention p. 369

Closed shop A business that is required by union contract to hire only union members p. 271

Closing costs Settlement costs or expenses incurred in transferring ownership from the buyer to the seller p. 457

Coincident indicators Key variables that change at the same time that real GDP (gross domestic product) changes p. 327

Collateral Assets that have value and can be sold for cash p. 165

Collectibles Valuable or rare items, such as antiques, art, baseball cards, stamps, and comic books p. 504

Collective bargaining The process of negotiating with employers on behalf of workers; seeks to protect workers from unfair practices, as well as provide better pay and more favorable working conditions p. 269

Command economy An economic system that answers the *What*, *How*, and *For Whom* questions by a dictator or central authority p. 25

Commercial paper One corporation borrowing from the excess cash of another corporation; a form of short-term borrowing often used until final financing can be arranged p. 264

Commodity money Money that has market value based on the material from which it is made p. 228

Common stock A class of stock in a corporation that carries the biggest risk p. 180

Communism A classless economic system in which all resources are owned by the workers. There is no government and people share production according to their needs. In Marx's view, this is the highest form of socialism toward which the revolution should strive p. 26

Comparative advantage The ability of a country to produce a good at a lower opportunity cost than another country p. 426

Comparison shopping The process of looking for the best value for the money spent p. 283

Complement Goods that consumers purchase together with another good p. 77

Compound interest Interest that continues to accumulate on both principal and interest causing money in an account to grow at a more rapid rate p. 254

Consumer Financial Protection Bureau (CFPB) An independent bureau within the Federal Reserve that helps consumers make financial decisions p. 403

Consumer sovereignty The freedom of consumers to buy, or not to buy, at prices set in competitive markets p. 15

Contractionary fiscal policy A decrease in federal government spending or an increase in taxes to decrease real GDP p. 367

Contractionary monetary policy Uses a decrease in the money supply to decrease real GDP (gross domestic product) p. 407

Co-pay The amount you are required by your insurance provider to pay each time you incur a medical service p. 470

Corporate bond Long-term debt obligation of publicly-held corporations p. 494

Co-signer A person who also signs the loan agreement and agrees to pay the loan if the borrower is unable to do so p. 289

Cost-benefit analysis An analysis comparing the additional rewards and costs of an action to determine if the benefits outweigh the costs p. 48

Cost-push inflation A period when producers raise prices because their costs to create products are rising p. 354

Cover letter A short letter included with a business plan p. 206

Credit bureaus Businesses that gather, store, and sell credit information about consumers to their business members p. 291

Credit line A pre-arranged plan that allows a business to access funds from a lender as needed p. 261

Credit report A complete record of a consumer's credit history that includes the consumer's borrowing and repayment performance p. 291

Credit score A numeric rating that is compiled on a point system by the credit bureaus to describe a consumer as a good or bad credit risk p. 292

Criteria Standards or rules by which something is judged p. 282

Cyclical unemployment Unemployment caused by the lack of jobs during a recession p. 344

D

Debit card A card similar to an ATM card used to make point-of-sale (POS) purchases at businesses; the amount of the purchase is deducted from your account when the purchase is made p. 256

Debt financing A type of funding where a profit-seeking, public corporation sells corporate bonds so that it can use borrowed money over a term of 10 to 30 years p. 194

Debt load A person's outstanding debt obligations at any point in time p. 296

Deductible The amount of money a policy owner has to pay before insurance to pay for services p. 470

Deflation A period when the general level of prices is decreasing p. 352

Demand The relationship between the price and the quantity demanded for a good or service, when other variables are held constant p. 67

Demand curve The line connecting the possible price and quantity purchased responses of consumers p. 68

Demand schedule A table that lists the quantity of a good or service consumers purchase at various possible prices p. 67

Demand-pull inflation A period that results in higher prices because consumers want to buy more goods and services than producers are willing or able to supply p. 354

Depreciation of currency A fall in the price (value) of one currency relative to another p. 442

Deregulation The removal of government restrictions or controls on a market p. 120

Direct relationship A positive relationship between two variables p. 38

Discharge A court order that pardons a debtor from having to pay previous debt obligations p. 298

Discount rate The interest rate the Fed charges on loans of reserves to banks p. 409

Discouraged worker A person who wants to work, but has given up looking for work p. 340

Disequilibrium A market price at which the quantity demanded does not equal the quantity supplied. At a disequilibrium price, either a surplus or shortage exists p. 109

Disinflation A period when prices are rising but the rate of increase is slowing p. 351

Diversification The process of selecting different types of investments with different levels of risk p. 488

Dividends Part of the profits earned by a company that is returned to owners p. 178

Down payment A certain amount of money paid by a person purchasing a home that is required by the mortgage lender to be applied toward the purchase price p. 456

E

Easement The legal right of another entity to have limited use of property p. 476

Economic growth An outward shift of the production possibilities curve, which allows an economy to produce greater levels of output p. 55

Economic growth An increase in a nation's real GDP (gross domestic product) p. 326

Economic system The methods used to answer the *What, How,* and *For Whom* questions p. 23

Economics The study of how society chooses to use its scarce resources for the production of goods and services to satisfy unlimited wants p. 10

Efficiency An economy produces the maximum output with given resources and technology p. 52

Elastic demand The percentage change in quantity demanded is greater than the percentage change in price. Therefore, the elasticity of demand is greater than 1 p. 82

Elasticity of demand The ratio of the percentage change in the quantity demanded of a product to a percentage change in its price p. 82

Embargo A law that bars trade with another country p. 432

Entrepreneur A leader who seeks to make profits by combining resources to produce new goods and services p. 8

Equilibrium A market price at which the quantity demanded equals the quantity supplied. At the equilibrium price, there is no surplus or shortage p. 110

Equity financing A type of funding where a company sells stocks to be able to raise large sums of cash p. 192

Equity stripping The unethical practice of extending a loan to a distressed homeowner who cannot afford the loan payments p. 297

Estate All that a person owns (assets) less debt owed at the time of that person's death p. 510

Excess reserves Potential loan balances of reserves held on deposit with the Fed in excess of required reserves p. 236

Exchange rate The number of units of one nation's currency that equals one unit of another nation's currency p. 440

Excise tax A tax paid by the seller on the production or sale of a good or service p. 102

Executive summary A page long summary of an entire business plan p. 207

Expansion An upturn in the business cycle during which real GDP rises p. 325

Expansionary fiscal policy An increase in federal government spending or a reduction in taxes to increase real GDP p. 367

Expansionary monetary policy Uses an increase in the money supply to increase real GDP (gross domestic product) p. 407

Export A good produced in one country and sold to another country p. 425

Extended warranty A warranty that covers your car beyond the factory warranty period; same as paying upfront for repairs that may or may not be needed p. 464

F

Factory warranty A guarantee that if something goes wrong with an item purchased, the cost of repairs is covered by the manufacturer p. 463

Federal Advisory Council (FAC) A 12-member board of bankers selected from each Federal Reserve District to advise on business and financial issues p. 399

Federal Deposit Insurance Corporation (FDIC) A government agency that insures customer deposits up to a predetermined limit if a bank fails p. 401

Federal funds rate The interest rate one bank charges another for overnight loans of reserves p. 409

Federal Open Market Committee (FOMC) A committee that directs the buying and selling of U.S. government securities by the Fed p. 399

Federal Reserve Districts The 12 banking districts which are served by a Federal Reserve district bank p. 397

Federal Reserve System The central banking system of the United States p. 236

Fiat money Money accepted by law, and not because of its tangible value p. 228

Final goods Goods and services sold to the final user p. 312

Financial institution Businesses that provide banking services to consumers and businesses p. 251

Financing The money needed to get a business going and help it keep operating p. 202

Financing option A way to pay for purchases without using cash, such as a credit card, opening an account, or borrowing from a credit union p. 283

Fiscal policy The use of federal government spending and taxes to achieve economic goals p. 367

Fixed exchange rate system A system in which exchange rates are held constant by a country's government p. 440

Flexible exchange rate system A system in which exchange rates are determined by the forces of supply and demand. Also called a floating rate p. 440

For Whom question An economy to decide which people receive the goods and services produced p. 19

Foreclosure A process of taking away private property to pay for debts levied against it p. 455

401(k) plan A tax-deferred retirement plan funded by employees of profit-seeking businesses where employees set aside pre-tax dollars through payroll deduction and employer contributions are optional p. 509

403(b) plan A tax-deferred retirement plan funded by employees of government and nonprofit organizations p. 509

Fractional reserve banking A system in which banks keep only a percentage of their deposits on reserve and lend out the remainder of the deposits p. 235

Franchise A legal contract that gives you the right to sell another company's product or service in a geographic area p. 197

Free market The freedom of consumers and businesses to buy and sell products with a minimum of government restrictions. Also known as free enterprise. p. 7

Free trade The flow of goods between countries without restrictions or special taxes p. 432

Frictional unemployment Temporary unemployment caused by the time required for workers to move from one job to another or find initial employment p. 342

Full employment The rate of unemployment that exists without cyclical unemployment p. 344

Futures Contracts to buy and sell commodities or stocks for a specified price on a specified date in the future p. 505

G

GDP (gross domestic product) per capita GDP divided by the total population p. 318

General partnership A business with partners that manage the company and share in the profits (or losses) from the business p. 171

Grace period The amount of time you have to pay your credit card bill without being charged interest on new purchases p. 296

Gross domestic product (GDP) The market value of all final goods and services produced annually in a country p. 311

H

Health care directive A document, also called a living will, that describes a person's wishes at the end of life with regards to type of effort taken to save one's life in the event of an injury or illness p. 512

How question An economy to decide which combination of technology and resources to use for producing goods and services p. 19

Hyperinflation A period when prices are rising so rapidly that they are out of control p. 352

I

Illiquid investment An investment that can be difficult to sell in the short run without taking a substantial loss or a reduced price p. 502

Import A good produced in one country and purchased by another country p. 425

Impulse buying Occurs when you buy something on the spot, without thinking about it p. 281

Individual demand curve The demand curve for a single consumer p. 69

Individual supply curve The supply curve for a single seller p. 96

Industrialization The process of making large quantities of goods and services in factories p. 157

Inelastic demand The percentage change in quantity demanded is less than the percentage change in price. Therefore, the elasticity of demand is less than 1 p. 83

Inferior good Any good with a demand curve that shifts leftward (decreases) when consumers' incomes increase p. 76

Inflation The increase in general price levels for goods and services p. 349

Injunction A court order usually issued to union members that requires the stoppage of a certain activity p. 270

Installment loan A loan that requires the consumer to make regular monthly payments for a set period of time p. 288

Interest The earnings received on the balance in an account p. 253

Intermediate goods Goods and services used as inputs for the production of final goods p. 312

Inventory An accumulated amount of the product that the company provides for sale p. 210

Inverse relationship A negative relationship between two variables p. 40

Invisible hand A phrase that expresses the belief that the best interests of a society are served by markets guided by self-interest p. 25

K

Keynesian economics The theory, first advanced by John Maynard Keynes, that the role of the federal government is to increase or decrease aggregate demand to achieve economic goals p. 369

L

Labor The mental and physical capacity of workers to produce goods and services p. 8

Labor union A legal group formed to represent workers for the purpose of collective bargaining p. 269

Laffer curve A graph that shows the relationship between tax rates and total tax revenues p. 371

Lagging indicators Key variables that change after real GDP (gross domestic product) changes p. 328

Land Any natural resource provided by nature and used in the production process p. 8

Late fee A set amount of money or a percentage of the late amount p. 284

Law of demand A law that states there is an inverse relationship between the price of a good or service and the quantity buyers purchase p. 67

Law of increasing opportunity cost A law that states that the opportunity cost increases as production of an output expands p. 54

Law of supply A law that states there is a direct relationship between the price of a good and the quantity sellers offer for sale p. 95

Leading indicators Key variables that change before real GDP (gross domestic product) changes p. 327

Lien A legal obligation that must be paid before there is a clear title to property p. 476

Lifestyle business A business with employees that do specific tasks p. 192

Limited liability Means business owners will be held liable for debts or obligations of the company only to the extent of their financial investment in the company p. 174

Limited Liability Company (LLC) A form of business ownership that creates a sole proprietorship without unlimited liability; not a corporation, nor a partnership; formed by filing an "articles of organization" with a state p. 166

Limited Liability Partnership (LLP) An ownership plan that allows general partnerships to provided limited financial liability for general partners p. 175

Limited partnership A business where there is at least one general partner and at least one limited partner p. 174

Line of credit A preapproved loan amount that a borrower can access as needed p. 289

Listing agreement A contract that describes the property being sold, the price asked, and the sales commission p. 476

M

Macroeconomic equilibrium The price level where the aggregate demand curve intersects the aggregate supply curve p. 367

Macroeconomics The branch of economics that studies decision making for the economy as a whole, rather than individual parts p. 10

Marginal analysis A decision about how much more or less to do p. 48

Marginal benefit The extra gain from an additional unit of change p. 48

Marginal cost The extra cost from an additional unit of change p. 48

Market Any place or method used by buyers and sellers to exchange goods and services p. 10

Market demand curve The sum of all the individual demand curves in a market p. 69

Market economy An economic system that answers the *What, How*, and *For Whom* questions based on voluntary exchange in markets p. 23

Market research A study to find out what consumers will buy and what price they are willing to pay p. 195

Market structure The key characteristics of a market, including the number of firms, the similarity of products they sell, and how easy or difficult it is for new firms to enter the market p. 131

Market supply curve The sum of all the individual supply curves in a market p. 96

Mechanization The use of tools and machines that makes it possible to make more, better, and cheaper products p. 158

Medium of exchange Anything widely accepted in trade for goods or services p. 225

Microeconomics The branch of economics that studies decision making by individuals, families, or businesses p. 10

Mileage allowance An annual mileage allowance agreed to by the lessee; If this mileage is exceeded, the lessee is charged a set amount for each additional mile driven p. 462

Minimum wage A legally established lowest hourly wage rate that can be paid to workers p. 118

Mixed economy An economic system that answers the *What, How,* and *For Whom* questions through a mixture of traditional, command, and market systems p. 27

Model A simplification of reality used to understand the relationship between variables p. 37

Monetary policy The Federal Reserve's use of changes in the money supply to achieve economic goals p. 407

Money Anything that people accept as payment for goods and services p. 225

Money multiplier The maximum change in the money supply (checkable deposits) due to an initial change in the excess reserves held by banks. Money multiplier is equal to 1 divided by the required reserve ratio p. 241

Monopolistic competition A market structure characterized by many small sellers, a differentiated product, and easy market entry p. 140

Monopoly A market structure in which a single seller sells a unique product and entry into the market is impossible p. 133

Mortgage A long-term debt obligation to purchase a home that involves making payments over a long period of time p. 457

Multi-line discount A discount given for having more than one policy with an insurance company p. 473

Municipal bond A bond issued by state and local governments p. 497

Mutual fund A professionally managed group of investments. The fund holds a portfolio that consists of stocks, bonds, and other investments from gold to commodities and based on a stated set of objectives p. 488

N

National debt The total amount owed by the federal government to owners of government securities p. 386

Nationalization The act of transforming a private enterprise into a government enterprise p. 27

Natural monopoly A market in which the average cost of production is lowest when only one firm supplies a good or service p. 136

Net benefit The difference between the marginal benefit and the marginal cost of an option p. 48

Nominal GDP (gross domestic product) GDP measured in current prices p. 316

Normal good Any good with a demand curve that shifts rightward (increases) when consumers' incomes increase p. 76

Normative economics An analysis based on value judgments p. 42

O

Oligopoly A market structure characterized by a few large sellers, either identical or differentiated product, and difficult market entry p. 143

Open market operations The buying and selling of government securities to affect the money supply p. 408

Operations The day-to-day management of a business and its resources p. 205

Opportunity cost The best option sacrificed for a chosen option p. 46

Option The right (but not the obligation) to buy or sell a commodity or stock for a specified price within a specified period of time p. 505

Outsourcing The practice of a company having its work done by another company in another country p. 343

Over-the-limit fee A fee charged that is a penalty for spending more than the authorized credit amount p. 284

P

Partnership Two or more people who form a business together as co-owners p. 171

Partnership agreement An agreement that clearly states what each partner of a business has agreed to p. 171

Peak The phase of the business cycle in which real GDP reaches its maximum after rising during a recovery p. 322

Perfect competition A market structure in which a large number of small firms sell identical products, and entry into the market is easy p. 131

Philanthropy A form of charitable giving that supports some type of societal purpose over an extended period of time p. 512

Portfolio A group of different types of investments p. 488

Positive economics An analysis based on facts or statements that can be proven either true or false p. 42

Preapproval Advanced approval for a set amount of a vehicle loan given by a bank or credit union p. 464

Precious metals Tangible metals that have known values around the world p. 503

Preferred stock A class of stock in a corporation that typically has a guaranteed annual dividend p. 181

Price ceiling A legally established highest price a seller can charge for a good or service p. 117

Price floor A legally established lowest price a seller can charge for a good or service p. 118

Price maker A seller that does not consider competition when setting its price p. 137

Price taker A seller that has no control over the price of the product it sells. The seller can sell all its output at the equilibrium prices, but none at other prices p. 132

Price war Occurs when businesses keep lowering prices in order to sell goods p. 211

Private property rights The rights of individuals and groups to own businesses and resources p. 14

Pro forma statements Estimated or budgeted results that tell a story of what will happen if funding and market conditions work to a business's favor p. 205

Product differentiation A process of creating differences between similar goods and services p. 141

Production loan A loan made to a businesses that will be used to buy something that will help repay the loan p. 263

Production Possibilities Curve (PCC) A curve that shows the maximum possible output for an economy p. 52

Productivity The value of outputs compared to the cost of inputs p. 159

Progressive tax A type of tax that charges a higher percentage as income rises which follows the concept that those who have higher incomes can afford to pay higher tax rates p. 378

Promissory note A legal document agreeing to repay the principal plus interest p. 288

Property tax A tax on the value of assets p. 375

Proportional tax A type of tax that charges the same percentage of income regardless of the size of income p. 379

Protectionism The government's use of trade barriers to protect domestic producers p. 432

Public employee union A union of employees who work for a city, county, state, or federal government p. 272

Purpose statement A statement that tells the reader in a paragraph or two the exact purpose of a business plan p. 207

Q

Quantity demanded The amount of goods and services purchased at a given price p. 67

Quantity supplied The amount of goods or services sellers offer for sale at a given price p. 95

Quota A limit on the quantity of a good that can be imported in a given time period p. 434

R

Real GDP (gross domestic product) GDP adjusted for changes in prices over time p. 318

Real-cost inflation A period when resources become scarce or more difficult to get causing prices to rise p. 355

Recession The downturn in the business cycle during which real GDP (gross domestic product) declines. Also called a contraction p. 322

Reconciliation The process verifying that the amount in your checking account matches the bank's record of the amount in the account p. 252

Regressive tax A type of tax that charges a lower percentage of income as income rises p. 378

Regulation Government rules or laws designed to control business behavior p. 119

Relationship banking An ongoing group of services provided by a banking service that involves assessing what a business has to offer to the bank and determining services and fees that can be offered to the business; used to attract and keep a bank's business accounts p. 261

Rent control A price ceiling placed by government in some metropolitan areas in the United States p. 117

Rental agreement A written agreement that specifies rights and duties of both the landlord and the tenant p. 454

Rental property Property owned by someone who collects rent and allows another person to occupy the property which can be a single-family house, a duplex, triplex, apartment building, or condominium p. 502

Required Reserve Ratio (RRR) The percentage of deposits the Fed requires a bank to hold in cash or on deposit with the Fed rather than being loaned p. 236

Required reserves The minimum balance of money that the Fed requires a bank to hold in cash or on deposit with the Fed p. 236

Resources The basic categories of inputs used to produce goods and services. The three categories are land, labor, and capital. Also called factors of production p. 8

Revolving credit An account you can keep using until you reach your maximum limit while you make regular payments to pay down the balance p. 290

Risk The chance of injury, damage, or economic loss p. 467

Risk management The process of assessing the risks faced and planning actions to reduce and avoid the losses that could occur p. 467

Risk-free investment An investment without the inherent risk of default and is considered the safest form of investing p. 499

Roth IRA (Individual Retirement Account) An individual retirement account for which contributions are taxed but earnings are never taxed p. 508

Royalties Regular payments to the franchise owner, usually based on a percentage of profits p. 197

S

S corporation A small business entity that is created under state laws p. 179

Sales tax A tax on the value of the sale of a good or service p. 375

Savings account An account where you set aside money for future use p. 253

Savings bond A long-term loan to the U.S. government p. 498

Scarcity The condition in which human wants are forever greater than the available supply of time, goods, and resources p. 7

Seasonal unemployment Unemployment caused by changes in the seasons p. 342

Self-insuring Setting aside money to be used in the event of injury or loss p. 469

Self-interest The focus of buyers and sellers on their own personal benefit p. 16

SEP IRA (Individual Retirement Account) A tax-deferred retirement plan for small business owners and their employees; SEP stands for Simplified Employee Pension plan p. 508

Service fee An amount of money charged for maintaining a checking account p. 257

Shortage A market price at which the quantity supplied is less than the quantity demanded. Shortages occur only at prices *below* the equilibrium price p. 109

Side business A business that is part-time and owners do something they enjoy and are good at to bring in added income p. 191

Socialism An economic system based on government ownership of resources and centralized decision making p. 26

Sole proprietorship A business owned and managed by a single person p. 163

Specialization Occurs where workers are doing just a few tasks and learning to do them well p. 157

Spending limit A pre-set amount that you will pay for an item p. 281

Standard of living The level of economic well-being of people p. 17

Startup business A company that starts small but has every intention of growing into a large corporation; a company that will grow until it reaches full maturity p. 192

Stockholders Individuals who buy shares of stock to become part owners in a corporation p. 180

Stock-out What happens when you make or buy too few goods to sell p. 211

Store of value The ability of money to hold value over time p. 226

Strike A legal action of a union where members refuse to work until a labor agreement is reached p. 269

Structural unemployment Unemployment caused when the skills of workers do not match the skills required for existing jobs p. 342

Subsidy A payment from the government to support a business p. 102

Substitute Goods that compete for consumer purchases p. 77

Supply The relationship between the price and quantity supplied for a good or service, when other variables are held constant p. 95

Supply curve The line connecting the possible prices and quantity supplied responses of sellers p. 95

Supply schedule A table that lists the quantity of a good or service sellers offer for sale at possible prices p. 95

Surplus A market price at which the quantity supplied is greater than the quantity demanded. Surpluses occur only at prices *above* the equilibrium price p. 108

Sweep account An account used to cover a minimum balance p. 261

T

Tariff A tax on an import p. 432

Tax base The form of wealth that is subject to taxes p. 377

Tax shelter Home ownership as a tax savings benefit because property taxes and interest on home loans are tax deductible which results in reducing a person's income tax liability p. 455

Technology The body of knowledge applied to how goods and services are produced p. 52

Time deposit An account with guaranteed interest for a period of time p. 231

Title report A record of ownership and all legal restrictions on a property p. 476

Total revenue The total dollars a firm earns from the sale of a good or service. It is equal to the price multiplied by the quantity demanded p. 82

Trade deficit An unfavorable balance of trade that occurs when the value of a nation's imports is greater than the value of its exports p. 443

Trade surplus A favorable balance of trade that occurs when the value of a nation's exports is greater than the value of its imports p. 443

Trade-off All the options given up when a decision is made p. 46

Traditional economy An economic system that answers the *What, How,* and *For Whom* questions the way they have been answered for generations p. 23

Traditional IRA (Individual Retirement Account) An individual retirement account that allows individuals to contribute pre-tax income to an account that grows tax-deferred p. 508

Transfer payment A government payment to persons not in exchange for goods or services produced p. 311

Treasury bill (T bill) A security that the federal government repays in one year or less p. 385

Treasury bond A security that the federal government repays between twenty to thirty years p. 385

Treasury note A security that the federal government repays between one to ten years p. 385

Trough The phase of the business cycle in which real GDP reaches its lowest point after falling during a recession p. 323

U

Underemployed Persons work at jobs below their skill levels, or work part-time when they want to work full-time p. 340

Underutilization An economy that fails to fully use its resources. The result is producing less than maximum output. All points inside a production possibilities curve are inefficient p. 53

Unemployment rate The percentage of the civilian labor force that is actively seeking work but is not employed p. 339

Unexpected growth Occurs when a business grows too fast p. 210

Union shop A business that requires employees to join a union after they are hired p. 271

Unit of account The function of money to provide a common measurement of value for goods and services p. 226

Unitary elastic demand The percentage change in quantity demanded is equal to the percentage change in price. Therefore, the elasticity of demand is equal to 1 p. 84

Unlimited liability Means as a proprietor your assets (even your car and your home) are at risk p. 165

Unplanned investment The money and resources used that generate excess inventory that results in inventory build-up p. 211

V

Voluntary exchange Buyers and sellers decide what to buy and sell with a minimum of government intervention p. 16

W

Wealth An accumulation of assets, including bank accounts, real estate, and other investments p. 475

What question An economy to decide the mix and quantity of goods and services that it will produce p. 18

Work conditions The nature of the workplace and what is required for workers to succeed p. 268

World Trade Organization (WTO) A worldwide organization that enforces rulings on global trade disputes p. 433

Spanish Glossary

A

Absolute advantage ***ventaja absoluta*** La habilidad de un país de producir más de un bien utilizando los mismos o menos recursos que otro país. p. 426

Agency bond ***bono de agencia*** Un préstamo de dinero a una agencia del gobierno. p. 499

Aggregate demand curve (AD) ***curva de demanda total*** La curva que muestra el PIB (Producto Interno Bruto) real que será comprado a diferentes niveles de precio. p. 367

Aggregate supply curve (AS) ***curva de oferta total*** La curva que muestra el PIB (Producto Interno Bruto) real que será producido a diferentes niveles de precio. p. 367

Appreciation of currency ***aumento en valor de moneda*** Un aumento en el precio (valor) de una moneda relativa con otra. p. 442

Asset allocation ***asignación de activos*** El proceso de elegir una combinación de fondos que pueden ser encontrados en diferentes fondos mutuos. p. 489

Assumption ***asumir*** Algo que se acepta ser verdad. p. 37

Automatic stay ***suspensión automática*** Una acción tomada cuando una persona solicita protección por bancarrota que significa que ya ninguna acción puede ser tomada por parte de los acreedores, incluyendo la recuperación de deudas. p. 299

B

Balance of trade ***balance comercial*** El valor de las importaciones de una nación restada del valor de sus exportaciones. p. 443

Balanced budget ***presupuesto equilibrado*** Un presupuesto en el cual los gastos del gobierno son igual a los ingresos fiscales. p. 384

Bankruptcy exemption ***exención de bancarrota*** La propiedad que no tiene que renunciar un deudor para pagarle a los acreedores. p. 299

Barrier to entry ***barreras de entrada*** Un obstáculo que hace difícil que una nueva empresa entre al mercado. p. 131

Barter ***trueque*** El proceso de intercambiar un producto por otro. p. 157

Billing cycle ***ciclo de cobranza*** El período de tiempo cada mes cuando una cuenta se cierra para preparar su estado de cuenta mensual. p. 296

Board of Governors of the Federal Reserve System ***Consejo de Gobernadores del Sistema de la Reserva Federal*** El consejo de siete miembros que supervisan el sistema bancario de los Estados Unidos. p. 398

Branding ***marca*** Da reconocimiento que lleva a la lealtad del cliente. p. 159

Budget deficit ***déficit del presupuesto*** Un presupuesto en el cual los gastos del gobierno exceden los ingresos fiscales. p. 384

Budget surplus ***excedente del presupuesto*** Un presupuesto en el cual los ingresos fiscales exceden los gastos del gobierno. p. 384

Business cycle ***ciclo de negocios*** Los períodos alternativos de crecimiento y contracción de la economía medido por los cambios en el Producto Interno Bruto (PIB) real. p. 322

Business expense ***gastos de negocio*** Un costo que es deducible de impuestos y reduce el ingreso que está sujeto a impuestos. p. 462

Business license ***licencia comercial*** Un documento emitido por una unidad del gobierno local que permite actividades de negocio dentro de cierta área geográfica. p. 164

Business plan ***plan de negocios*** Un documento por escrito que enumera todas las cosas que el dueño de un negocio hará para asegurar el éxito del negocio. p. 202

Business tax deduction ***deducción de impuestos por gastos del negocio*** Un descuento que le permite a los dueños de negocios un estado fiscal favorable. p. 163

Buying plan ***plan de compras*** Un método organizado de tomar buenas decisiones de compra que debería ayudarle a que rindan sus recursos limitados. p. 281

C

C corporation ***corporación C*** Una corporación es organizada para vender acciones al público en general. p. 178

Capital ***capital*** Bienes hechos por humanos que son usados para producir otros bienes y servicios. En el sentido de negocios, el capital se define como dinero, crédito, y otros recursos económicos. p. 9; p. 210

Capital market ***mercado de capital*** Los mercados que existen en donde los negocios pueden tanto financiar sus operaciones como hacer compras grandes sobre largos plazos de tiempo. p. 264

Capitalism ***capitalismo*** Un sistema económico basado en los mercados y recursos de propiedad privada. También llamado el sistema de empresa libre. p. 25

Car lease ***contrato de arrendamiento de carro*** Un contrato en donde usted acuerda tomar posesión de un vehículo por un período de tiempo fijo y hacer pagos de arrendamiento regularmente. p. 462

Cartel ***cartel*** Un grupo de empresas que formalmente acuerdan de reducir la competencia al coordinar el precio y la producción de un producto. p. 145

Cash flow ***flujo de dinero*** La cantidad neta recibida después de que los gastos son pagados. p. 475

Change in demand ***cambio en demanda*** Un aumento (desplazamiento hacia la derecha) o reducción (desplazamiento hacia la izquierda) en la curva de demanda. El desplazamiento es causado por un cambio en un factor de demanda. p. 73

Change in quantity demanded ***cambio en cantidad demandada*** Un movimiento entre puntos a lo largo de una curva de demanda fija debido a un cambio en precio. p. 73

Change in quantity supplied ***cambio en cantidad ofrecida*** Un movimiento entre puntos a lo largo de una curva de oferta fija debido a un cambio en precio. p. 100

Change in supply ***cambio en oferta*** Un aumento (desplazamiento hacia la derecha) o una reducción (desplazamiento hacia la izquierda) en la cantidad ofrecida a cada precio posible. El desplazamiento es causado por un cambio en un factor de oferta. p. 100

Check clearing ***compensación de cheques*** Un servicio de la Reserva Federal que recolecta fondos de los bancos de los que escriben cheques y los transfiere al banco del beneficiario. p. 400

Checkable deposits ***depósitos verificables*** El dinero total en una institución financiera que puede ser retirado al escribir un cheque. p. 230

Checking account ***cuenta de cheques*** Una cuenta de depósitos a la vista de la cual los consumidores pueden retirar y depositar dinero. p. 251

Circular-flow model ***modelo de flujo-circular*** Un modelo que muestra el intercambio de dinero, productos, y recursos entre los negocios, los hogares, y el gobierno. p. 313

Classical economics ***economía clásica*** La teoría de que los mercados libres restaurarán el empleo completo sin la intervención del gobierno. p. 369

Closed shop ***negocio agremiado*** Un negocio que según su contrato con el sindicato, se le requiere contratar solamente a miembros de sindicatos. p. 271

Closing costs ***costos del cierre*** Los costos de cierre o los gastos incurridos de un comprador al vendedor en la transferencia de titularidad. p. 457

Coincident indicators ***indicadores coincidentes*** Los variables claves que cambian al mismo tiempo que el PIB (Producto Interno Bruto) real cambia. p. 327

Collateral ***colateral o garantía*** Los activos que tienen valor y pueden ser vendidos por efectivo. p. 165

Collectibles ***coleccionables*** Artículos valiosos o raros, tal como las antigüedades, arte, tarjetas de béisbol, estampillas, y revistas de caricaturas. p. 504

Collective bargaining ***negociación colectiva*** El proceso de negociar con los empleadores por parte de los trabajadores; busca proteger a los trabajadores de las prácticas injustas, así como también proveer mejor paga y mejores condiciones de trabajo. p. 269

Command economy ***economía planificada*** Un sistema económico que responde a las preguntas de *¿Qué?, ¿Cómo?,* y *¿Para quién?* Por un dictador u autoridad central. p. 25

Commercial paper ***documento comercial*** Una corporación tomando prestado del exceso de efectivo de otra corporación; una forma de pedir prestado a corto plazo frecuentemente usado hasta que la financiación final se pueda arreglar. p. 264

Commodity money ***dinero de producto básico*** Dinero que tiene valor de mercado basado en el material del cual fue hecho. p. 228

Common stock ***acción común*** Una clase de acción de una corporación que lleva el mayor riesgo. p. 180

Communism ***comunismo*** Un sistema económico sin clases sociales dentro del cual los trabajadores son dueños de todos los recursos. No hay gobierno, y las personas comparten la producción de acuerdo a sus necesidades. En la perspectiva de Marx, este es la forma más alta de socialismo hacia el cual debería de aspirar la revolución. p. 26

Comparative advantage ***ventaja comparativa*** La habilidad de un país de producir un bien a un costo de oportunidad más bajo que otro país. p. 426

Comparison shopping ***comparación de compras*** El proceso de buscar el mejor valor por el dinero gastado. p. 283

Complement ***complemento*** Los bienes que los consumidores compran junto con otro bien. p. 77

Compound interest ***interés compuesto*** El interés que sigue acumulándose tanto sobre el capital principal como del interés causando que el dinero en una cuenta crezca a un índice más rápido. pp. 254

Consumer Financial Protection Bureau (CFPB) ***Agencia de Protección Financiera al Consumidor (CFPB)*** Una agencia independiente dentro de la Reserva Federal que le ayuda al consumidor a tomar decisiones financieras. p. 403

Consumer sovereignty ***soberanía del consumidor*** La libertad del consumidor de comprar o no comprar a los precios fijados en los mercados competitivos. p. 15

Contractionary fiscal policy ***política fiscal restrictiva*** Una reducción en los gastos del gobierno o un aumento en los impuestos para reducir el PIB (Producto Interno Bruto) real. p. 367

Contractionary monetary policy ***política monetaria restrictiva*** Usa una reducción en el abastecimiento de dinero para reducir el PIB (Producto Interno Bruto) real. p. 407

Co-pay ***copago*** Según el requerimiento de su proveedor de seguro, la cantidad que usted debe pagar cada vez que recibe un servicio médico. p. 470

Corporate bond ***bono corporativo*** La obligación de deuda a largo plazo de las corporaciones que cotizan en la bolsa. p. 494

Co-signer ***cosignatario*** Una persona que también firma el acuerdo del préstamo y acuerda en pagar el préstamo si el prestamista falla en hacerlo. p. 289

Cost-benefit analysis ***análisis costo-beneficio*** Un análisis comparando los beneficios o costos adicionales de una acción para determinar si los beneficios superan los costos. p. 48

Cost-push inflation ***inflación de costos*** Un período durante el cual los productores aumentan los precios porque sus costos de producción están aumentando. p. 354

Cover letter ***carta de presentación*** Una carta incluida con un plan de negocio. p. 206

Credit bureaus ***agencias de crédito*** Negocios que juntan, almacenan, y venden información crediticia sobre los consumidores a sus miembros de negocio. p. 291

Credit line ***línea de crédito*** Un plan de previo acuerdo con un prestatario que le permite a un negocio tener acceso a fondos según sea necesario. p. 261

Credit report ***reporte de crédito*** Un archivo completo del historial de crédito de un consumidor que incluye el desempeño del consumidor de pedir prestado y de reembolso. p. 291

Credit score ***calificación de crédito*** Una clasificación numérica que se acumula de un sistema de puntos por parte de las agencias de crédito para clasificar a los consumidores como un buen o mal riesgo de crédito. p. 292

Criteria ***criterio*** Estándares o reglas por las cuales se juzga algo. p. 282

Cyclical unemployment ***desempleo cíclico*** El desempleo causado por la falta de empleos durante una recesión. p. 344

D

Debit card ***tarjeta de débito*** Una tarjeta similar a una tarjeta de cajero automático que se usa para hacer compras en el punto de venta (POS) en un negocio; la cantidad de la compra es deducida de su cuenta al hacerse la compra. p. 256

Debt financing ***financiamiento de deudas*** Un tipo de financiación en la cual una corporación pública que busca ganancias vende bonos corporativos para que pueda usar dinero prestado a lo largo de un plazo de 10 a 30 años. p. 194

Debt load ***deuda total*** Las deudas pendientes de una persona en cualquier momento. p. 296

Deductible ***deducible*** La cantidad de dinero que un asegurado tiene que pagar antes de que la compañía de seguros pague por servicios. p. 470

Deflation ***deflación*** Un período cuando el nivel general de precios está disminuyendo. p. 352

Demand ***demanda*** La relación entre el precio y la cantidad demandada por un bien o servicio, cuando otros variables se mantienen constantes. p. 67

Demand curve ***curva de demanda*** La línea que une el posible precio y cantidad comprada de las respuestas del consumidor. p. 68

Demand schedule ***tabla de demanda*** Una tabla que muestra la cantidad de un bien o servicio que los consumidores compran a varios posibles precios. p. 67

Demand-pull inflation ***inflación de demanda*** Un período que resulta en precios más altos debido a que los consumidores quieren comprar más bienes y servicios de los que los productores están dispuestos o capaces de ofrecer. p. 354

Depreciation of currency ***depreciación de moneda*** Una reducción en el precio (valor) de una moneda en relación con otra. p. 442

Deregulation ***desregulación*** La eliminación de las restricciones o control del gobierno sobre un mercado. p. 120

Direct relationship ***relación directa*** Una relación positiva entre dos variables. p. 38

Discharge ***descargo*** Una orden de la corte que perdona a un deudor de tener que pagar deudas anteriores. p. 298

Discount rate ***tasa de descuento*** La tasa de interés que el Sistema de la Reserva Federal (Fed) le cobra a los bancos por préstamos de las reservas. p. 409

Discouraged worker ***trabajador desanimado*** Persona que quiere trabajar, pero se ha dado por vencida en buscar empleo. p. 340

Disequilibrium ***desequilibrio*** Un precio de mercado al cual la cantidad demandada no es igual a la cantidad ofrecida. A un precio de desequilibrio, existe un excedente o una escasez. p. 109

Disinflation ***desinflación*** Un período en el cual los precios están aumentando pero la velocidad del aumento está disminuyendo. p. 351

Diversification ***diversificación*** El proceso de elegir diferentes tipos de inversiones con diferentes niveles de riesgo. p. 488

Dividends ***dividendos*** Parte de las ganancias que genera una compañía y que se les regresa a los dueños. p. 178

Down payment ***enganche*** Una cierta cantidad de dinero pagado por una persona que compra una vivienda, la cual es requerida por el prestamista hipotecario para ser aplicado hacia el precio de compra. p. 456

E

Easement ***servidumbre*** El derecho legal de que otra entidad tenga uso limitado de propiedad. p. 476

Economic growth ***crecimiento económico*** Un desplazamiento hacia afuera de la curva de posibilidades de producción, la cual permite que una economía produzca niveles más altos de producción. También definido como un aumento en el PIB (Producto Interno Bruto) real de una nación. p. 55; p. 326

Economic system ***sistema económico*** Los métodos usados para responder a las preguntas del *¿Qué?, ¿Cómo?,* y *¿Para quién?* p. 23

Economics ***Economía*** El estudio de cómo la sociedad elige utilizar sus escasos recursos para la producción de bienes y servicio para satisfacer los deseos ilimitados. p. 10

Efficiency ***eficiencia*** Una economía produce la producción máxima con los recursos y tecnología determinada. p. 52

Elastic demand ***demanda elástica*** El cambio en porcentaje en cantidad demandada es mayor que el porcentaje de cambio en precio. De modo que la elasticidad de demanda es mayor que 1. p. 82

Elasticity of demand ***elasticidad de demanda*** El índice del porcentaje de cambio en la cantidad demandada de un producto a un porcentaje de cambio en su precio. p. 82

Embargo ***embargo*** Una ley que prohíbe el comercio con otro país. p. 432

Entrepreneur ***empresario*** Un líder quien busca sacar ganancias al combinar recursos para producir nuevos bienes y servicios. p. 8

Equilibrium ***equilibrio*** Un precio de mercado al cual la cantidad demandada es igual a la cantidad ofrecida. Al precio de equilibrio, no hay excedente ni escasez. p. 110

Equity financing ***financiamiento de capital*** Tipo de financiamiento en donde una compañía vende acciones para poder recaudar grandes cantidades de efectivo. p. 192

Equity stripping ***disminución del valor líquido*** La práctica inmoral de extender un préstamo a un propietario de casa angustiado, quien no puede pagar el préstamo. p. 297

Estate ***patrimonio*** Todo lo que es propiedad de una persona (activos) menos las deudas al tiempo del fallecimiento de esa persona. p. 510

Excess reserves ***reservas en exceso*** Los posibles balances de préstamos de reservas que están en depósito con el Fed en exceso de las reservas requeridas. p. 236

Exchange rate ***tasa de cambio*** El número de unidades de la moneda de una nación que es igual a una unidad de moneda de otra nación. p. 440

Excise tax ***impuesto sobre consumos específicos*** Un impuesto en la producción o venta de bienes y servicios. p. 102

Executive summary ***resumen ejecutivo*** Un resumen del plan de negocios completo. p. 207

Expansion ***crecimiento*** Una mejora en el ciclo de negocios durante el cual el PIB real aumenta. p. 325

Expansionary fiscal policy ***política fiscal expansiva*** Un aumento en los gastos del gobierno federal o una reducción en los impuestos para aumentar el PIB (Producto Interno Bruto) real. p. 367

Expansionary monetary policy ***política monetaria expansiva*** Utiliza un aumento en el abastecimiento de dinero para aumentar el PIB (Producto Interno Bruto) real. p. 407

Export ***exportación*** Un bien producido en un país y vendido a otro país. p. 425

Extended warranty ***garantía extendida*** Una garantía que cubre su carro más allá del período de la garantía de fábrica; lo mismo que pagar de antemano por reparaciones que puedan o no ser necesarias. p. 464

F

Factory warranty ***garantía de fábrica*** Una garantía de que si algo falla con un artículo comprado, el costo de reparación está cubierto por el fabricante. p. 463

Federal Advisory Council (FAC) ***Comité de Asesoría Federal (FAC)*** Un comité de 12 banqueros seleccionados de cada Distrito de la Reserva Federal para asesorar sobre los temas de finanzas y negocios. p. 399

Federal Deposit Insurance Corporation (FDIC) ***Corporación Federal de Seguros de los Depósitos Bancarios (FDIC)*** Una agencia del gobierno que asegura los depósitos de clientes hasta un límite predeterminado si un banco fracasa. p. 401

Federal funds rate ***tasa de fondos federales*** El interés que un banco le cobra a otro banco por los préstamos de reservas de un día para otro. p. 409

Federal Open Market Committee (FOMC) ***Comité Federal de Mercado Abierto (FOMC)*** Un comité que dirige la compra y venta de valores del gobierno de los Estados Unidos por parte de los Distritos de la Reserva Federal del Fed. p. 399

Federal Reserve Districts ***Distritos de la Reserva Federal*** Los 12 distritos bancarios que son atendidos por un banco de distrito de la Reserva Federal. p. 397

Federal Reserve System ***Sistema de la Reserva Federal*** El sistema bancario central de los Estados Unidos. p. 236

Fiat money ***dinero fiduciario*** El dinero aceptado por ley, y no por su valor tangible. p. 228

Final goods ***bienes terminados*** Los bienes y servicios vendidos al usuario final. p. 312

Financial institution ***institución financiera*** Negocios que proveen servicios bancarios a consumidores y negocios. p. 251

Financing ***financiamiento*** El dinero necesario para empezar un negocio y mantenerlo funcionando. p. 202

Financing option ***opción de financiamiento*** Un modo de pagar por las compras sin usar efectivo, tal como tarjetas de crédito, abrir una cuenta, o pedir prestado de una cooperativa de crédito. p. 283

Fiscal policy ***política fiscal*** El uso de gastos del gobierno e impuestos para alcanzar las metas económicas. p. 367

Fixed exchange rate system ***sistema de tasa de cambio fijo*** Un sistema en el cual las tasas de cambio se mantienen constantes por el gobierno de un país. p. 440

Flexible exchange rate system ***sistema de tasa de cambio flexible*** Un sistema en el cual las tasas de cambio se determinan por las fuerzas de la oferta y demanda. También llamado tasa variable. p. 440

For Whom question ***pregunta ¿Para quién?*** Una economía a decidir que personas reciben los bienes y servicios producidos. p. 19

Foreclosure ***ejecución hipotecario*** Un proceso de quitar propiedad privada para pagar las deudas en su contra. p. 455

401(k) plan ***plan 401(k)*** Un plan de retiro de impuestos diferidos que es financiado por empleados de empresas que operan con fin de ganancias en donde los empleados apartan dólares antes del impuesto por medio de deducciones de nómina y la contribución por parte del empleador es opcional. p. 509

403(b) plan ***plan 403(b)*** Un plan de retiro de impuestos diferidos que es financiado por los empleados del gobierno y de las organizaciones sin fines de lucro. p. 509

Fractional reserve banking ***banca de reserva fraccional*** Un sistema en el cual los bancos retienen solamente un porcentaje de sus depósitos en reserva y prestan el resto de los depósitos. p. 235

Franchise ***franquicia*** Un contrato legal que le da el derecho de vender el producto o servicio de otra compañía en una área geográfica. p. 197

Free market ***mercado libre*** La libertad del consumidor y negocios de comprar o vender productos con un mínimo de restricciones del gobierno. También conocido como empresa libre. p. 7

Free trade ***libre comercio*** El flujo de bienes entre países sin restricciones ni impuestos especiales. p. 432

Frictional unemployment ***desempleo fraccional*** El desempleo temporal causado por el tiempo requerido para que trabajadores se muevan de un empleo a otro o encuentran empleo inicial. p. 342

Full employment ***empleo completo*** El índice de desempleo que existe sin un desempleo cíclico. p. 344

Futures ***contratos de futuros*** Contratos para la compra y venta de producto básico u acciones a un precio específico a una fecha específica en el futuro. p. 505

G

GDP (gross domestic product) per cápita ***PIB (Producto Interno Bruto) por cápita*** El PIB dividido por la población total. p. 318

General partnership ***sociedad general*** Un negocio con socios que administran la compañía y comparten las ganancias (o pérdidas) del negocio. p. 171

Grace period ***período de gracia*** El plazo de tiempo que tiene para pagar su factura de tarjeta de crédito sin que se le cobren intereses por las nuevas compras. p. 296

Gross domestic product (GDP) ***Producto Interno Bruto (PIB)*** El valor de mercado de todos los bienes y servicios terminados anualmente en un país. p. 311

H

Health care directive ***directiva de cuidado médico*** Un documento también conocido como "testamento vital" la cual describe los deseos de una persona al final de su vida en cuestión de los esfuerzos tomados para salvarle la vida en caso de lesión o enfermedad. p. 512

How question ***pregunta ¿Cómo?*** Una economía a decidir que combinación de tecnología y recursos utilizar para producir bienes y servicios. p. 19

Hyperinflation ***hiperinflación*** Un período en el cual los precios aumentan tan rápido, que están fuera de control. p. 352

I

Illiquid investment ***inversión ilíquida*** Una inversión que puede ser difícil de vender a corto plazo sin correr el riesgo de sufrir una pérdida considerable o un precio reducido. p. 502

Import ***importación*** Un bien producido en un país y comprado en otro país. p. 425

Impulse buying ***compra impulsiva*** Ocurre cuando compra algo en el momento, sin pensarlo. p. 281

Individual demand curve ***curva de demanda individual*** La curva de demanda de un sólo consumidor. p. 69

Individual supply curve ***curva de oferta individual*** La curva de oferta de un sólo vendedor. p. 96

Industrialization ***industrialización*** El proceso de hacer grandes cantidades de bienes y servicios en fábricas. p. 157

Inelastic demand ***demanda inelástica*** El cambio en porcentaje de la cantidad demandada es menor al cambio en porcentaje del cambio en precio. De modo que la elasticidad de demanda es menos que 1. p. 83

Inferior good ***bien inferior*** Cualquier bien con una curva de demanda que se desplaza hacia la izquierda (disminuye) cuando los ingresos del consumidor aumentan. p. 76

Inflation ***inflación*** El aumento en el nivel de precio general de bienes y servicios. p. 349

Injunction ***medida cautelar*** Una orden de la corte generalmente otorgado a los miembros del sindicato, la cual requiere que ciertas actividades se paren. p. 270

Installment loan ***préstamo a plazos*** Un préstamo que requiere que el consumidor haga pagos mensuales regularmente por un plazo fijo de tiempo. p. 288

Interest ***interés*** Las ganancias recibidas sobre el balance en una cuenta. p. 253

Intermediate goods ***bienes intermedios*** Bienes y servicios utilizados como aportaciones para la producción de bienes terminados. p. 312

Inventory ***inventario*** Una cantidad acumulada del producto que la compañía provee para la venta. p. 210

Inverse relationship ***relación inversa*** Una relación negativa entre dos variables. p. 40

Invisible hand ***mano invisible*** Una frase que expresa la creencia de que los mejores intereses de una sociedad que son servidos por los mercados guiados por el interés propio. p. 25

K

Keynesian economics ***economía Keynesiana*** La teoría, primero desarrollada por John Maynard Keynes, que el papel del gobierno federal es de aumentar o reducir la demanda total para lograr las metas económicas. p. 369

L

Labor ***labor*** La capacidad mental y física de los trabajadores de producir bienes y servicios. p. 8

Labor union ***sindicato laboral*** Un grupo legalmente formado para representar a los trabajadores con el propósito de la negociación colectiva. p. 269

Laffer curve ***curva de Laffer*** Una gráfica que muestra la relación entre las tarifas de impuestos y los ingresos fiscales totales. p. 371

Lagging indicators ***indicadores retrasados*** Variables claves que cambian después de que cambie el PIB (Producto Interno Bruto) real. p. 328

Land ***terrestre*** Cualquier recurso natural proveído por la naturaleza y utilizado en el proceso de producción. p. 8

Late fee ***recargo*** Una cantidad fija de dinero o un porcentaje de la cantidad retrasada. p. 284

Law of demand ***ley de la demanda*** Una ley que estipula que hay una relación inversa entre el precio de un bien o servicio y la cantidad que compra el consumidor. p. 67

Law of increasing opportunity cost ***ley del costo de oportunidad creciente*** Una ley que estipula que el costo de oportunidad aumenta al paso que el volumen de la producción aumenta. p. 54

Law of supply ***ley de la oferta*** Una ley que estipula que hay una relación directa entre el precio de un bien y la cantidad que los vendedores ofrecen a la venta. p. 95

Leading indicators ***indicadores principales*** Variables claves que cambian antes de que cambie el PIB (Producto Interno Bruto) real. p. 327

Lien ***gravamen*** Una obligación legal que debe ser pagada antes de que haya una titularidad clara de propiedad. p. 476

Lifestyle business ***empresa de estilos de vida*** Un negocio con empleados que se dedican a labores específicas. p. 192

Limited liability ***responsabilidad limitada*** Quiere decir que los dueños de negocios serán responsables por las deudas u obligaciones de la compañía solamente hasta el grado de su inversión financiera en la compañía. p. 174

Limited Liability Company (LLC) ***compañía de responsabilidad limitada*** Una forma de propiedad de negocio que crea una empresa de propietario único sin la responsabilidad ilimitada; no una corporación, ni una sociedad; se forma al solicitar una "acta constitutiva" con el estado. p. 166

Limited Liability Partnership (LLP) ***sociedad de responsabilidad limitada*** Un plan de propiedad empresarial que permite que las sociedades generales provean responsabilidad limitada a los socios generales. p. 175

Limited partnership ***sociedad limitada*** Un negocio en el cual hay al menos un socio general y al menos un socio limitado. p. 174

Line of credit ***línea de crédito*** Una cantidad de préstamo pre aprobada al cual un prestamista puede tener acceso según sea necesario. p. 289

Listing agreement ***acuerdo o convenio de venta*** Un contrato legal que describe la propiedad siendo vendida, el precio solicitado, y la comisión de la venta. p. 476

M

Macroeconomic equilibrium ***equilibrio macroeconómico*** El nivel de precio en donde la curva de demanda total se cruza con la curva de oferta total. p. 367

Macroeconomics ***macroeconomía*** La división de la economía que estudia la toma de decisiones para la economía total, en vez de por partes individuales. p. 10

Marginal analysis ***análisis marginal*** Una decisión sobre cuanto más o cuanto menos hacer. p. 48

Marginal benefit ***beneficio marginal*** El beneficio adicional de una unidad adicional de cambio. p. 48

Marginal cost ***costo marginal*** El costo adicional de una unidad adicional de cambio. p. 48

Market ***mercado*** Cualquier lugar o método utilizado por los compradores y vendedores para intercambiar bienes y servicios. p. 10

Market demand curve ***curva de demanda del mercado*** La suma de todas las curvas de demanda individuales en un mercado. p. 69

Market economy ***economía de mercado*** Un sistema económico que responde a las preguntas de *¿Qué?, ¿Cómo?,* y *¿Para quién?* basado en intercambio voluntario en los mercados. p. 23

Market research ***investigación de mercados*** Un estudio para descubrir qué comprarán y qué precio están dispuestos a pagar los consumidores. p. 195

Market structure ***estructura de mercado*** Las características claves de un mercado, incluyendo el número de empresas, la similitud de los productos que venden, y que tan fácil o difícil es para las empresas nuevas de entrar al mercado. p. 131

Market supply curve ***curva de oferta del mercado*** La suma de todas las curvas de oferta individuales en un mercado. p. 96

Mechanization ***mecanización*** El uso de herramientas y máquinas que hace posible fabricar más productos, mejores y baratos. p. 158

Medium of exchange ***medio de intercambio*** Cualquier cosa ampliamente aceptada a cambio de bienes y servicios. p. 225

Microeconomics ***microeconomía*** La división de la economía que estudia la toma de decisiones de los individuos, las familias, y los negocios. p. 10

Mileage allowance ***limitación de millas*** Un límite de millas anual acordado por el arrendatario; si el límite de millas se excede, se le cobra al arrendatario una cantidad fija por cada milla adicional que maneje. p. 462

Minimum wage ***salario mínimo*** La cantidad mínima por hora establecida legalmente que se le puede pagar a los trabajadores. p. 118

Mixed economy ***economía mixta*** Un sistema económico que responde a las preguntas de *¿Qué?, ¿Cómo?,* y *¿Para quién?* mediante una mezcla de sistemas tradicionales, planificadas, y de mercado. p. 27

Model ***modelo*** Una simplificación de la realidad utilizada para entender la relación entre variables. p. 37

Monetary policy ***política monetaria*** El uso de cambios en el abastecimiento de dinero por parte de la Reserva Federal para logras metas económicas. p. 407

Money ***dinero*** Cualquier cosa que las personas acepten como pago por bienes y servicios. p. 225

Money multiplier ***multiplicador monetario*** El cambio máximo en el abastecimiento de dinero (depósitos verificables) debido a un cambio inicial en los excedentes de reservas mantenidos por los bancos. El multiplicador monetario es igual a 1 dividido por la proporción de reserva requerida. p. 241

Monopolistic competition ***competencia monopolística*** Una estructura de mercado caracterizada por varios vendedores pequeños, un producto diferenciado, y facilidad de entrada al mercado. p. 140

Monopoly ***monopolio*** Una estructura de mercado en la cual un vendedor singular vende un producto único y la entrada al mercado es imposible. p. 133

Mortgage ***hipoteca*** Una obligación de deuda a largo plazo para comprar una vivienda, la cual implica hacer pagos sobre un largo plazo de tiempo. p. 457

Multi-line discount ***descuento por líneas múltiples*** Un descuento dado por tener más de una póliza con una compañía de seguros. p. 473

Municipal bond ***bono municipal*** Un bono emitido por los gobiernos estatales y locales. p. 497

Mutual fund ***fondo mutuo*** Un grupo de inversiones profesionalmente administrado. El fondo mantiene una cartera de inversiones que consiste de acciones, bonos, y otras inversiones desde el oro hasta los productos básicos, y está basado en un conjunto de actividades fijas. p. 488

N

National debt ***deuda pública*** La cantidad total que debe el gobierno federal a los dueños de los valores gubernamentales. p. 386

Nationalization ***estatización*** El acto de transformar una empresa privada a una empresa del gobierno. p. 27

Natural monopoly ***monopolio natural*** Un mercado en el cual el costo promedio de producción es el más bajo cuando solamente una empresa ofrece el bien o servicio. p. 136

Net benefit ***beneficio neto*** La diferencia entre el beneficio marginal y el costo marginal de una opción. p. 48

Nominal GDP (gross domestic product) ***PIB (Producto Interno Bruto) nominal*** EL PIB medido en precios actuales. p. 316

Normal good ***bien nominal*** Cualquier bien con una curva de demanda que se desplaza hacia la derecha (aumenta) cuando los ingresos de los consumidores aumentan. p. 76

Normative economics ***economía normativa*** Un análisis basado en juicios de valor. p. 42

O

Oligopoly ***oligopolio*** Una estructura de mercado caracterizado por algunos vendedores mayores, ya sea productos idénticos o diferenciados, y dificultad de entrada al mercado. p. 143

Open market operations ***operaciones del mercado abierto*** El comprar y vender valores gubernamentales para afectar el abastecimiento de dinero. p. 408

Operations ***operaciones*** La administración del día a día de un negocio y sus recursos. p. 205

Opportunity cost ***costo de oportunidad*** La mejor opción sacrificada por la opción elegida. p. 46

Option ***opción*** El derecho (pero no la obligación) de comprar o vender un producto básico o una acción a un precio específico dentro de un período de tiempo específico. p. 505

Outsourcing ***externalización*** La práctica de que una compañía realice el trabajo de otra compañía en otro país. p. 343

Over-the-limit fee ***cargo por sobregiro*** Un cargo que es una multa por gastar más de la cantidad de crédito autorizado. p. 284

P

Partnership ***sociedad*** Dos o más personas quienes forman un negocio juntos como copropietarios. p. 171

Partnership agreement ***acuerdo de sociedad*** Un acuerdo que estipula claramente a lo que ha acordado cada socio de un negocio. p. 171

Peak ***auge*** La etapa del ciclo de negocios en el cual el PIB (Producto Interno Bruto) real alcanza su máximo después de crecer durante una recuperación. p. 322

Perfect competition ***competencia pura y perfecta*** Una estructura de mercado en la cual un gran número de pequeñas empresas venden productos idénticos y la entrada al mercado es fácil. p. 131

Philanthropy ***filantropía*** Una forma de donaciones a caritativas que apoya algún tipo de propósito social sobre un plazo de tiempo extendido. p. 512

Portfolio ***cartera de inversiones*** Un grupo de diferentes tipos de inversiones. p. 488

Positive economics ***economía positiva*** Un análisis basado en hechos o declaraciones que pueden ser comprobadas de ser verdaderas o falsas. p. 42

Preapproval ***pre-aprobación*** Previa aprobación de una cantidad fija de un préstamo para automóvil otorgado por un banco o cooperativa de crédito. p. 464

Precious metals ***metales preciosos*** Metales tangibles que tienen valores conocidos por todo el mundo. p. 503

Preferred stock ***acciones preferenciales*** Una clase de acciones en una corporación que típicamente tienen un dividendo anual garantizado. p. 181

Price ceiling ***precio máximo*** El precio más alto legalmente establecido que un vendedor puede cobrar por un bien o servicio. p. 117

Price floor ***precio mínimo*** El precio más bajo legalmente establecido que un vendedor puede cobrar por un bien o servicio. p. 118

Price maker ***fijador de precios*** Un vendedor que no considera la competencia al establecer su precio. p. 137

Price taker ***agente económico*** Un vendedor que no tiene control sobre el precio de los productos que vende. El vendedor puede vender toda su producción al precio de equilibrio, pero ninguno a otros precios. p. 132

Price war ***guerra de precios*** Ocurre cuando los negocios continúan bajando los precios para poder vender los bienes. p. 211

Private property rights ***derechos de propiedad privada*** Los derechos de los individuos y grupos de tener un negocio y recursos. p. 14

Pro forma statements ***informe pro forma*** Los resultados estimados o presupuestados que cuentan una historia de que pasará si el financiamiento y las condiciones del mercado están a favor del negocio. p. 205

Product differentiation ***diferenciación de producto*** Un proceso de crear diferencias entre bienes y productos similares. p. 141

Production loan ***préstamo productivo*** Un préstamo hecho a un negocio que será utilizado para comprar algo que ayudará a pagar el préstamo. p. 263

Production Possibilities Curve (PCC) ***curva de posibilidades de producción*** Una curva que muestra la producción máxima posible para una economía. p. 52

Productivity ***productividad*** El valor de la producción comparado con los costos de las aportaciones. p. 159

Progressive tax ***impuesto progresivo*** Un tipo de impuesto que cobra un porcentaje más alto mientras que los ingresos aumenten, el cual sigue el concepto de que aquellos con un ingreso mayor pueden pagar un impuesto más alto. p. 378

Promissory note ***pagare*** Un documento legal acordando en pagar el capital más el interés. p. 288

Property tax ***impuestos de propiedad*** Un impuesto sobre el valor de los activos. p. 375

Proportional tax ***impuesto proporcional*** Un tipo de impuesto que cobra el mismo porcentaje sobre los ingresos, sin importar la cantidad de los ingresos. p. 379

Protectionism ***proteccionismo*** El uso de barreras por parte del gobierno para proteger a los productores domésticos. p. 432

Public employee union ***sindicato de trabajadores públicos*** Un sindicato de empleados quienes trabajan para el municipio, condado, estado, o gobierno federal. p. 272

Purpose statement ***declaración de intenciones*** Una declaración que le dice al lector en uno o dos párrafos los propósitos exactos de un plan de negocios. p. 207

Q

Quantity demanded ***cantidad en demanda*** La cantidad de bienes y servicios comprados a un precio determinado. p. 67

Quantity supplied ***cantidad ofrecida*** La cantidad de bienes y servicios que los vendedores ofrecen a un precio determinado. p. 95

Quota ***límite*** Un límite a la cantidad de un bien que puede ser importado en un período determinado. p. 434

R

Real GDP (gross domestic product) ***PIB (Producto Interno Bruto) real*** El PIB ajustado debido a los cambios con el tiempo. p. 318

Real-cost inflation ***inflación de costos reales*** Un período cuando los recursos se vuelven escasos o más difíciles de conseguir causando que los precios aumenten. p. 355

Recession ***recesión*** La etapa decreciente del ciclo de negocios durante el cual el PIB (Producto Interno Bruto) real disminuye. También llamado contracción. p. 322

Reconciliation ***reconciliación*** El proceso de verificar que la cantidad en su cuenta de cheques es igual a la cantidad registrada en su cuenta, según el banco. p. 252

Regressive tax ***impuesto regresivo*** Un tipo de impuesto que cobra un porcentaje más bajo sobre los ingresos mientras que los ingresos aumentan. p. 378

Regulation ***regulación*** Las reglas o leyes del gobierno diseñados para controlar el comportamiento de los negocios. p. 119

Relationship banking ***relación bancaria*** Un grupo de servicios continuos proveídos por un servicio bancario que implica evaluar lo que un negocio puede ofrecerle al banco y determinar los servicios y cargos que se le puede ofrecer al negocio; utilizado para atraer y retener las cuentas comerciales de un banco. p. 261

Rent control ***control de arrendamiento de vivienda*** Un precio máximo establecido por los gobiernos en algunos lugares metropolitanos de los Estados Unidos. p. 117

Rental agreement ***acuerdo de arrendamiento*** Un acuerdo por escrito que especifica los derechos y deberes de tanto el arrendador como el arrendatario. p. 454

Rental property ***propiedad de arrendamiento*** Propiedad en la cual el dueño cobra renta y permite que otra persona ocupe la propiedad, la cual puede ser una unidad sencilla, un dúplex, de tres unidades, un edificio de departamentos, o un condominio. p. 502

Required Reserve Ratio (RRR) ***proporción de reserva requerida*** El porcentaje de depósitos que el Fed requiere que un banco mantenga en efectivo o depositado con el Fed en vez de que sea prestado. p. 236

Required reserves ***reservas requeridas*** La cantidad mínima de dinero que el Fed requiere que un banco mantenga en efectivo o depositado con el Fed. p. 236

Resources ***recursos*** Las categorías básicas de aportaciones utilizadas para producir bienes y servicios. Hay tres categorías, tierra, laboral, y capital. También llamados factores de producción. p. 8

Revolving credit ***crédito renovable*** Una cuenta que puede seguir utilizando hasta que llegue su límite máximo mientras que haga pagos regulares para reducir el saldo. p. 290

Risk ***riesgo*** La probabilidad de lesión, daño, o pérdida económica. p. 467

Risk management ***administración de riesgos*** El proceso de evaluar el riesgo enfrentado y planificar las acciones para reducir o evitar la pérdida que pueda ocurrir. p. 467

Risk-free investment ***inversión libre de riesgo*** Una inversión sin el riesgo inherente de incumplimiento y es considerado la forma más segura de invertir. p. 499

Roth IRA (Individual Retirement Account) ***IRA (Cuenta Individual de Jubilación) tipo Roth*** Una cuenta individual de jubilación en la cual se impone un impuesto sobre las contribuciones pero no a las ganancias. p. 508

Royalties ***regalías*** Pagos regulares al dueño de la franquicia, generalmente basado en un porcentaje de las ganancias. p. 197

S

S corporation ***corporación S*** Una pequeña empresa que es creada bajo leyes estatales. p. 179

Sales tax ***IVA*** Un impuesto sobre el valor de la venta de un bien o servicio. p. 375

Savings account ***cuenta de ahorros*** Una cuenta en donde guarda dinero para uso en el futuro. p. 253

Savings bond ***bono de ahorros*** Un préstamo de largo plazo al gobierno de los Estados Unidos. p. 498

Scarcity ***escasez*** La condición en la cual los deseos humanos siempre son mayores que la oferta disponible de tiempo, bienes, y recursos. p. 7

Seasonal unemployment ***desempleo por temporada*** El desempleo causado por los cambios en las temporadas. p. 342

Self-insuring ***seguro propio*** El guardar dinero para ser utilizado en caso de una lesión o pérdida. p. 469

Self-interest ***interés propio*** El enfoque de los compradores y vendedores de sus propios beneficios personales. p. 16

SEP IRA (Individual Retirement Account) ***IRA (Cuenta Individual de Jubilación) tipo SEP*** Un plan de retiro de impuestos diferidos para los dueños y empleados se las pequeñas empresas; SEP significa Pensiones Simplificadas para Empleados. p. 508

Service fee ***cargo de servicio*** Una cantidad de dinero cobrado por la administración de una cuenta de cheques. p. 257

Shortage ***déficit*** Un precio de mercado al cual la cantidad ofrecida es menos que la cantidad en demanda. Un déficit ocurre solamente a precios por debajo del precio de equilibrio. p. 109

Side business ***negocio secundario*** Un negocio que es de tiempo parcial para generar un ingreso adicional y en la cual sus dueños hacen lo que disfrutan y de lo cual son buenos. p. 191

Socialism ***socialismo*** Un sistema económico basado en que el gobierno es propietario de todos los recursos y la toma de decisiones está centralizada. p. 26

Sole proprietorship ***empresa de propietario único*** Un negocio de la que es dueño y administra una sola persona. p. 163

Specialization ***especialización*** Ocurre cuando los trabajadores están haciendo solamente algunas de las labores y aprendiendo a hacerlas bien. p. 157

Spending limit ***límite de gasto*** Una cantidad predeterminada que pagara por un artículo. p. 281

Standard of living ***nivel de vida*** El nivel del bienestar económico de las personas. p. 17

Startup business ***negocio de arranque*** Una compañía que comienza pequeña pero con toda la intención de crecer a ser una corporación grande; una compañía que crecerá hasta llegar a su madurez completa. p. 192

Stockholders ***accionistas*** Individuos que compran acciones para hacerse dueños parciales de una corporación. p. 180

Stock-out ***desabastecimiento*** Lo que pasa cuando produce o compra muy pocos bienes para vender. p. 211

Store of value ***valor conservado*** La habilidad del dinero de conservar su valor al paso del tiempo. p. 226

Strike ***huelga*** Una acción legal de un sindicato en la cual los trabajadores reúsan trabajar hasta que se llegue a un acuerdo laboral. p. 269

Structural unemployment ***desempleo estructurado*** El desempleo que ocurre cuando las habilidades de los trabajadores no igualan a las habilidades requeridas en los empleos existentes. p. 342

Subsidy ***subsidiario*** El pago por parte del gobierno para apoyar un negocio. p. 102

Substitute ***sustituto*** Los bienes que compiten por las compras del consumidor. p. 77

Supply ***oferta*** La relación entre el precio y la cantidad ofrecida por un bien o servicio, cuando los otros variables se mantienen constantes. p. 95

Supply curve ***curva de la oferta*** La línea que une los posibles precios y las cantidades ofrecidas de las respuestas del consumidor. p. 95

Supply schedule ***tabla de oferta*** Una tabla que muestra las cantidades de un bien o servicio que los vendedores ofrecen a la venta a posibles precios. p. 95

Surplus ***excedente*** Un precio de mercado en el cual la cantidad ofrecida es mayor a la cantidad demandada. Un excedente ocurre solamente a precios sobre el precio de equilibrio. p. 108

Sweep account ***cuenta continua*** Una cuenta utilizad para cubrir un saldo mínimo. p. 261

T

Tariff ***arancel*** Un impuesto sobre una importación. p. 432

Tax base ***base de impuesto*** La forma de riqueza que está sujeto a impuestos. p. 377

Tax shelter ***refugio tributario*** El ser dueño de un hogar es un beneficio de impuestos porque los impuestos de propiedad y el interés de la hipoteca son deducibles de impuestos, lo cual resulta en reducir la responsabilidad tributaria sobre los ingresos de una persona. p. 455

Technology ***tecnología*** La base de conocimientos que se aplica a cómo son producidos los bienes y servicios. p. 52

Time deposit ***depósito plazo fijo*** Una cuenta que garantiza intereses por un período de tiempo. p. 231

Title report ***informe de titulo de propiedad*** Un registro de titularidad y toda restricción legal sobre una propiedad. p. 476

Total revenue ***ingreso total*** El total de dólares que una empresa gana de las ventas de un bien o servicio. Es igual al precio multiplicado por la cantidad demandada. p. 82

Trade deficit ***déficit de comercio*** Un balance no favorable de comercio que ocurre cuando el valor de las importaciones de una nación es mayor que el valor de sus exportaciones. p. 443

Trade surplus ***exceso de comercio*** Un balance favorable que ocurre cuando el valor de las exportaciones de una nación es mayor al valor de sus importaciones. p. 443

Trade-off ***intercambio*** Renunciar a todas las opciones cuando una decisión sea tomada. p. 46

Traditional economy ***economía tradicional*** Un sistema económico que responde a las preguntas de *¿Qué?, ¿Cómo?,* y *¿Para quién?* de igual modo que se han respondido por generaciones. p. 23

Traditional IRA (Individual Retirement Account) ***IRA (Cuenta Individual de Jubilación) tradicional*** Una cuenta de retiro individual que le permite a los individuos a contribuir ingresos antes de los impuestos a una cuenta que crece diferido de impuestos. p. 508

Transfer payment ***transferencia de pago*** Un pago del gobierno a las personas y que no es a cambio de bienes y servicios producidos. p. 311

Treasury bill (T bill) ***Letras de la Tesorería (T-bill)*** Un valor que el gobierno federal reembolsa en un año o menos. p. 385

Treasury bond ***bono de tesorería*** Un valor que el gobierno reembolsa entre veinte y treinta años. p. 385

Treasury note ***nota de tesorería*** Un valor que el gobierno reembolsa entre uno y diez años. p. 385

Trough ***punto mínimo*** La fase del ciclo de negocios en la cual el PIB (Producto Interno Bruto) real llega a su punto más bajo después de caer durante una recesión. p. 323

U

Underemployed ***subempleo*** Las personas trabajan en empleos que están por debajo de sus habilidades, o trabajan de tiempo parcial cuando quieren trabajar de tiempo completo. p. 340

Underutilization ***subutilización*** Una economía que fracasa en utilizar plenamente sus recursos. El resultado es producir menos producción. Todos los puntos dentro de la curva de posibilidades de producción son ineficientes. p. 53

Unemployment rate ***desempleo*** El porcentaje de la fuerza laboral civil que está activamente buscando empleo pero no está empleada. p. 339

Unexpected growth ***crecimiento inesperado*** Ocurre cuando un negocio crece demasiado rápido. p. 210

Union shop ***negocio con afiliación al sindicato*** Un negocio que requiere que sus empleados se afilien a un sindicato después de que sean contratados. p. 271

Unit of account ***unidad de cuenta*** La función del dinero de proveer una medida común de valor por bienes y servicios. p. 226

Unitary elastic demand ***elasticidad de demanda unitaria*** El porcentaje de cambio en la cantidad demandada es igual al porcentaje de cambio en el precio. De modo que la elasticidad de demanda es igual a 1. p. 84

Unlimited liability ***responsabilidad ilimitada*** Quiere decir que como propietario, sus activos (también su carro y su vivienda) están en riesgo. p. 165

Unplanned investment ***inversión no planificada*** El dinero y los recursos utilizados que generan un exceso en inventario, lo cual resulta en una acumulación de inventario. p. 211

V

Voluntary exchange ***intercambio voluntario*** Compradores y vendedores deciden que comprar y vender con una intervención mínima del gobierno. p. 16

W

Wealth ***patrimonio*** La acumulación de activos, incluyendo cuentas bancarias, bienes inmuebles, y otras inversiones. p. 475

What question ***pregunta ¿Qué?*** Una economía a decidir la mezcla y cantidad de bienes y servicios que va a producir. p. 18

Work conditions ***condiciones laborales*** La naturaleza del lugar de empleo y lo que es requerido para el éxito de los trabajadores. p. 268

World Trade Organization (WTO) ***Organización Mundial de Comercio (WTO)*** Una organización mundial que hace cumplir las decisiones en las disputas de comercio global. p. 433

Index

C

F

G

H

I

J

K

L

M

N

O

P

Q

R

S

W

Y

Z